황토빛이야기

The Color of WATER

KIM DONG HWA

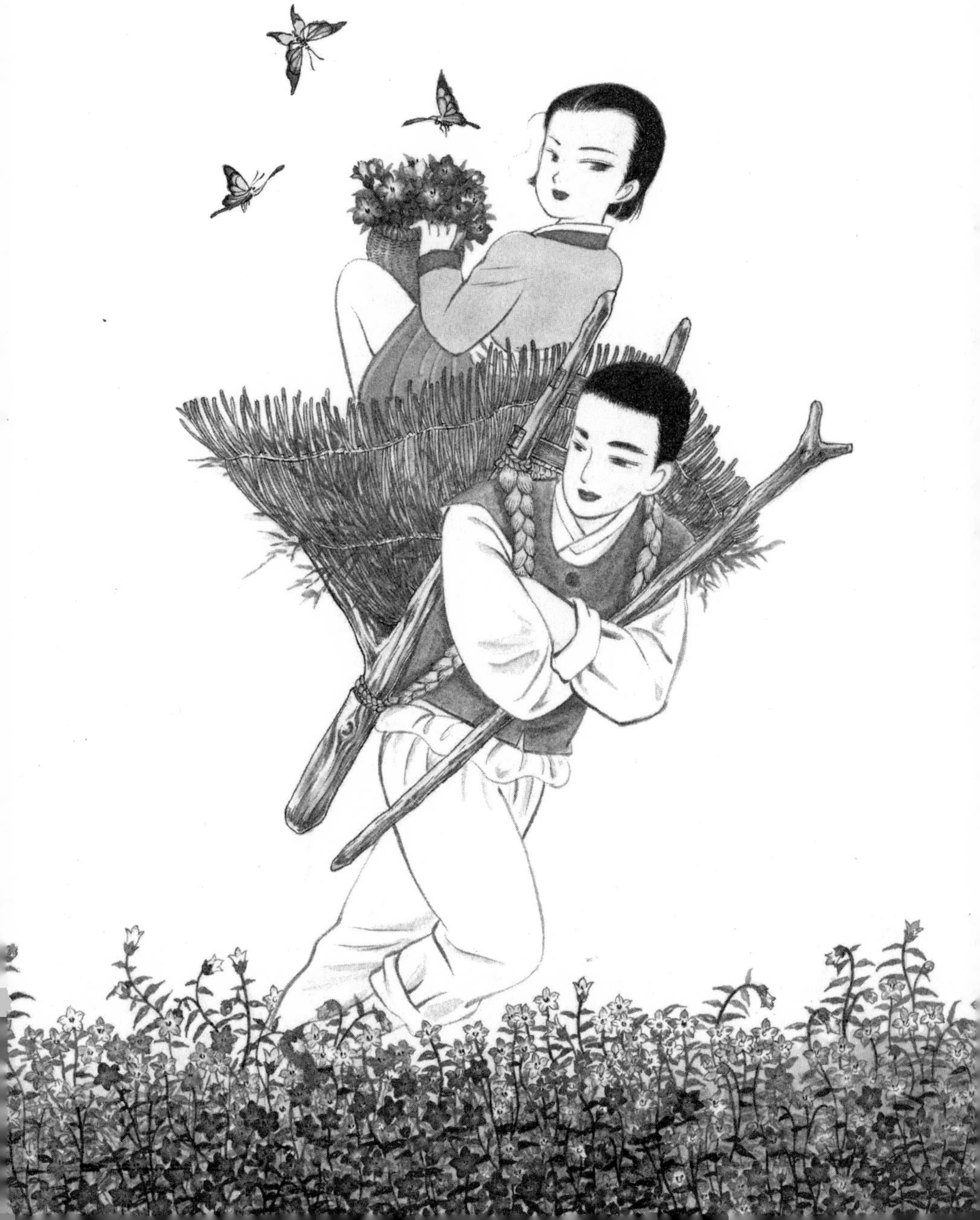

First Second

New York & London

The Story of Life on the Golden Fields Vol. 2 © 2003 by Kim Dong Hwa
All Rights Reserved
English translation copyright © 2009 by First Second

Published by First Second
First Second is an imprint of Roaring Brook Press,
a division of Holtzbrinck Publishing Holdings Limited Partnership
175 Fifth Avenue, New York, NY 10010

All rights reserved.

Distributed in Canada by H. B. Fenn and Company Ltd.
Distributed in the United Kingdom by Macmillan Children's Books,
a division of Pan Macmillan.

First published in Korea in 2003 by Kim Dong Hwa
English translation rights arranged with Kim Dong Hwa through Orange Agency
English edition © 2009 by First Second

Cataloging-in-Publication Data is on file at the Library of Congress.

ISBN: 978-1-59643-459-2

First Second books are available for special promotions and premiums.
For details, contact: Director of Special Markets, Holtzbrinck Publishers.

First American Edition June 2009
Printed in the United States of America
3 5 7 9 10 8 6 4 2

황토빛이야기

The Color of WATER

KIM DONG HWA

Translated from the Korean by Lauren Na

:01

First Second

New York & London

My beloved has arrived, but rather than greeting him,
All I can do is bite the corner of my apron with a blank expression—
What an awkward woman am I.

My heart has longed for him as hugely and openly as a full moon
But instead I narrow my eyes, and my glance to him
Is sharp and narrow as the crescent moon.

But then, I'm not the only one who behaves this way.
My mother and my mother's mother were as silly and stumbling as I am
when they were girls...

Still, the love from my heart is overflowing,
As bright and crimson as the heated metal in a blacksmith's forge.

Deeply etched on my mother's face are wrinkles as fine as the
strands on a spider's web. As I remove these threads, one at a time,
I see her transform into a blushing sixteen-year-old girl.

Now, open for you to read, is the tale of this clumsy sixteen-year-
old girl. From an era where time stood still, her story is revealed in
bits and pieces, a tale that slowly escapes from the past.

Little gems from my mother's life at sixteen...

Ochre-colored earth stories...

From the West Bridge—
Kim Dong Hwa

CONTENTS

Little gems from my mother's life at sixteen...

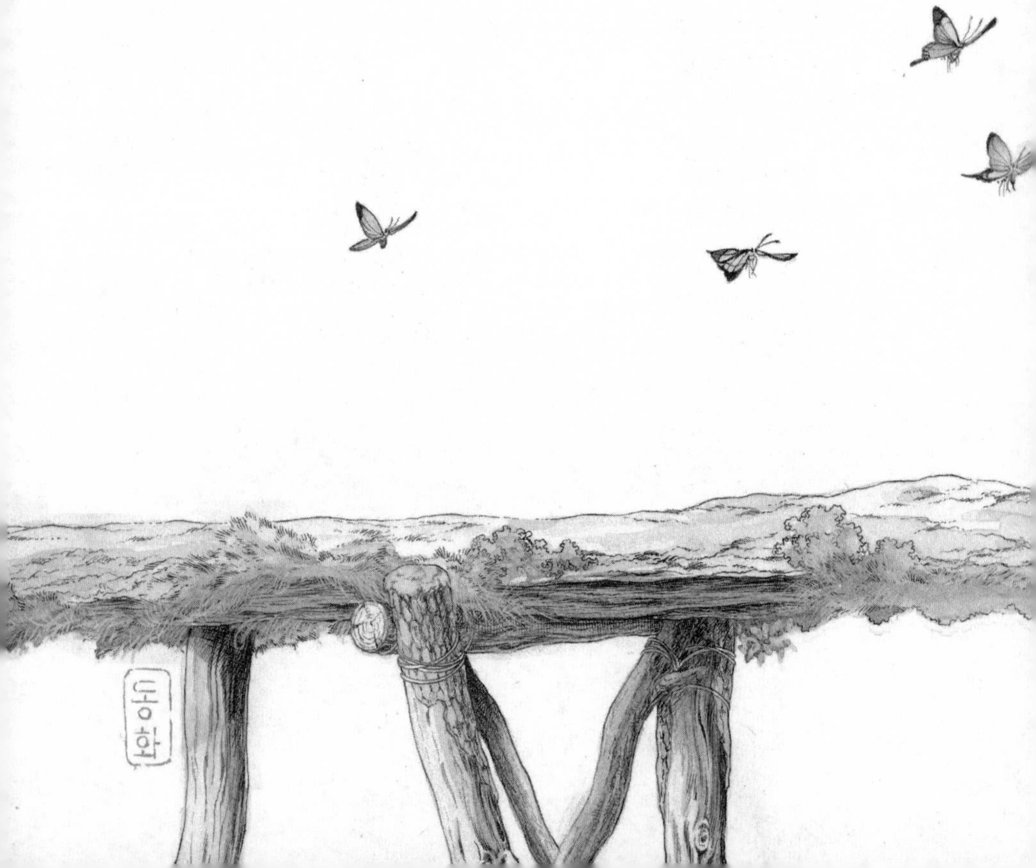

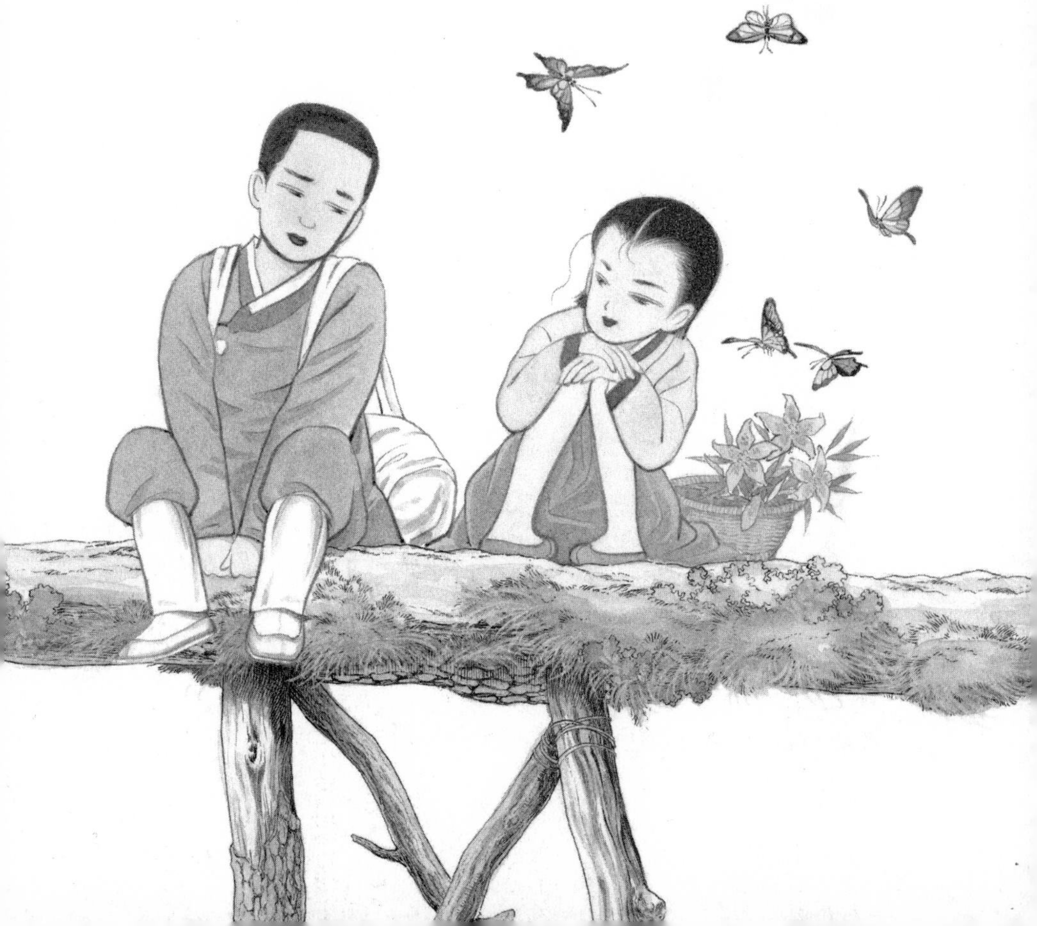

Chapter One

MARCH WINDS AND APRIL SHOWERS BRING MAY FLOWERS

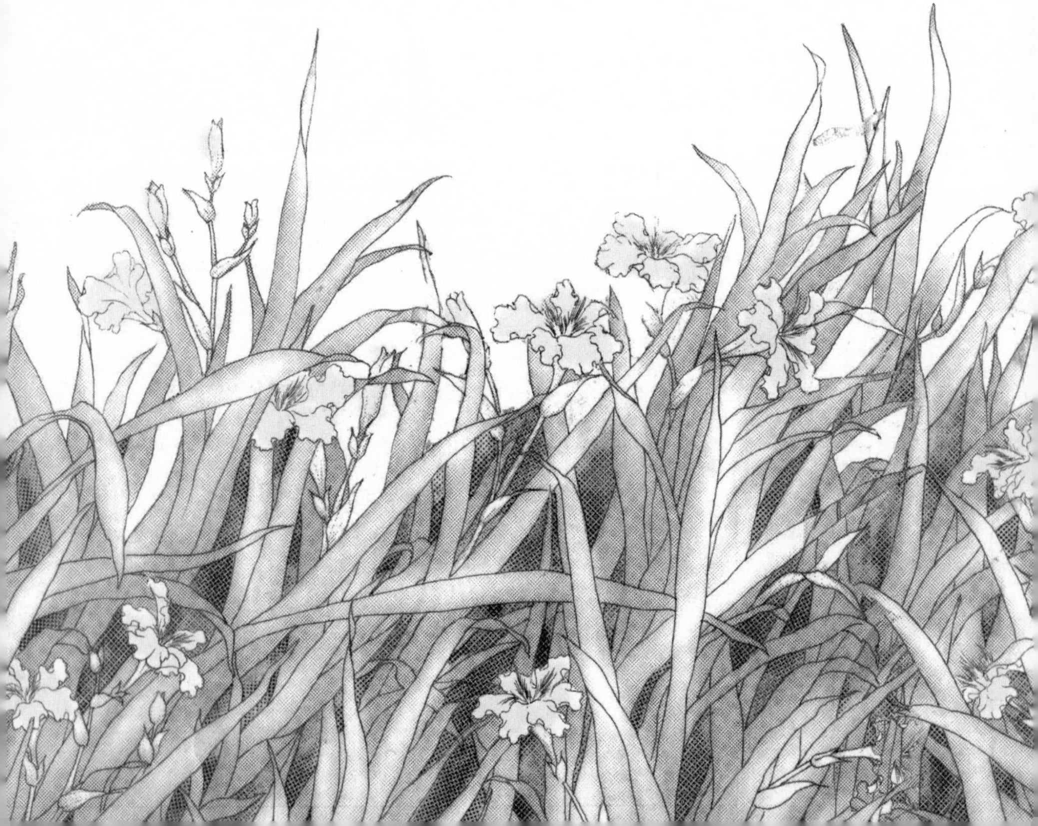

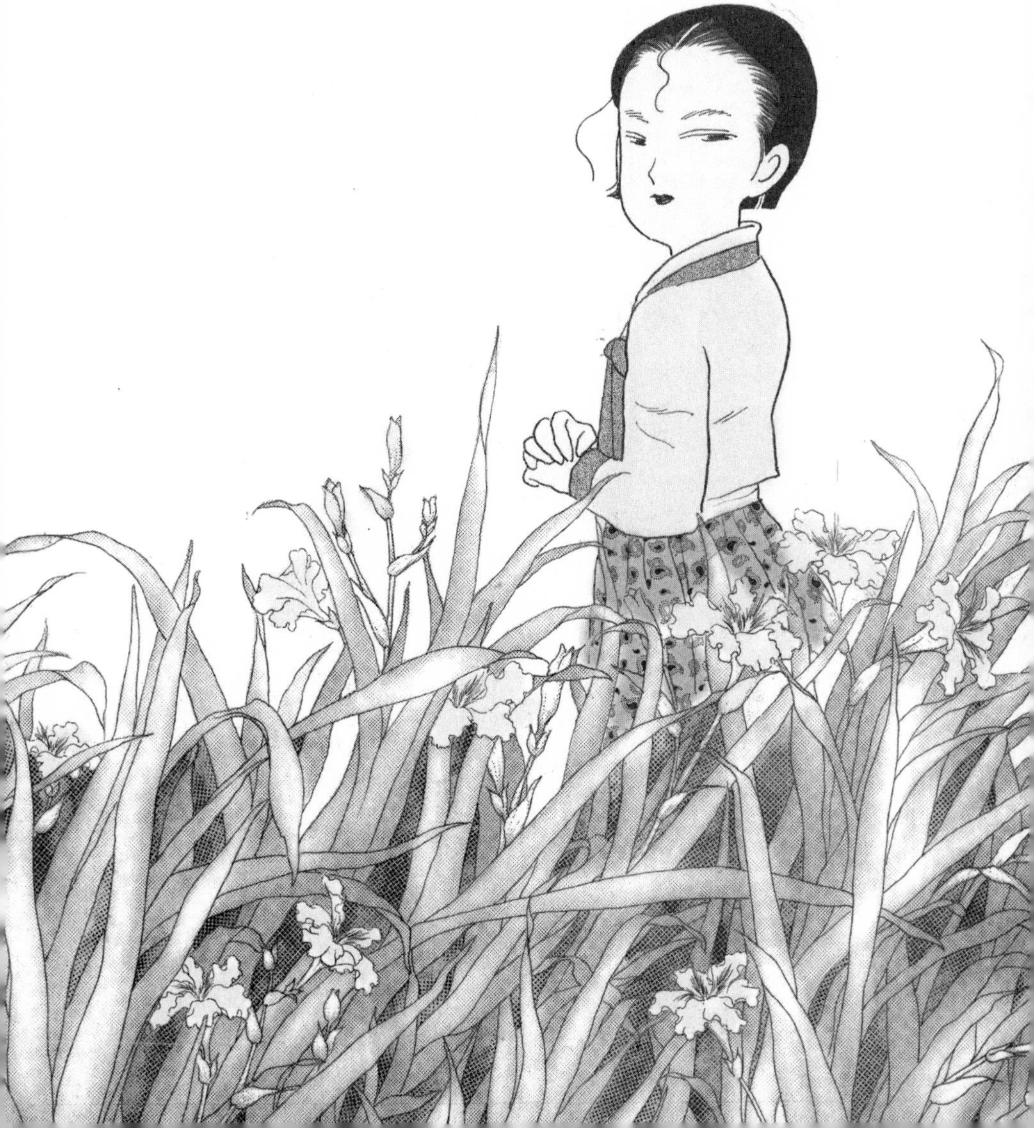

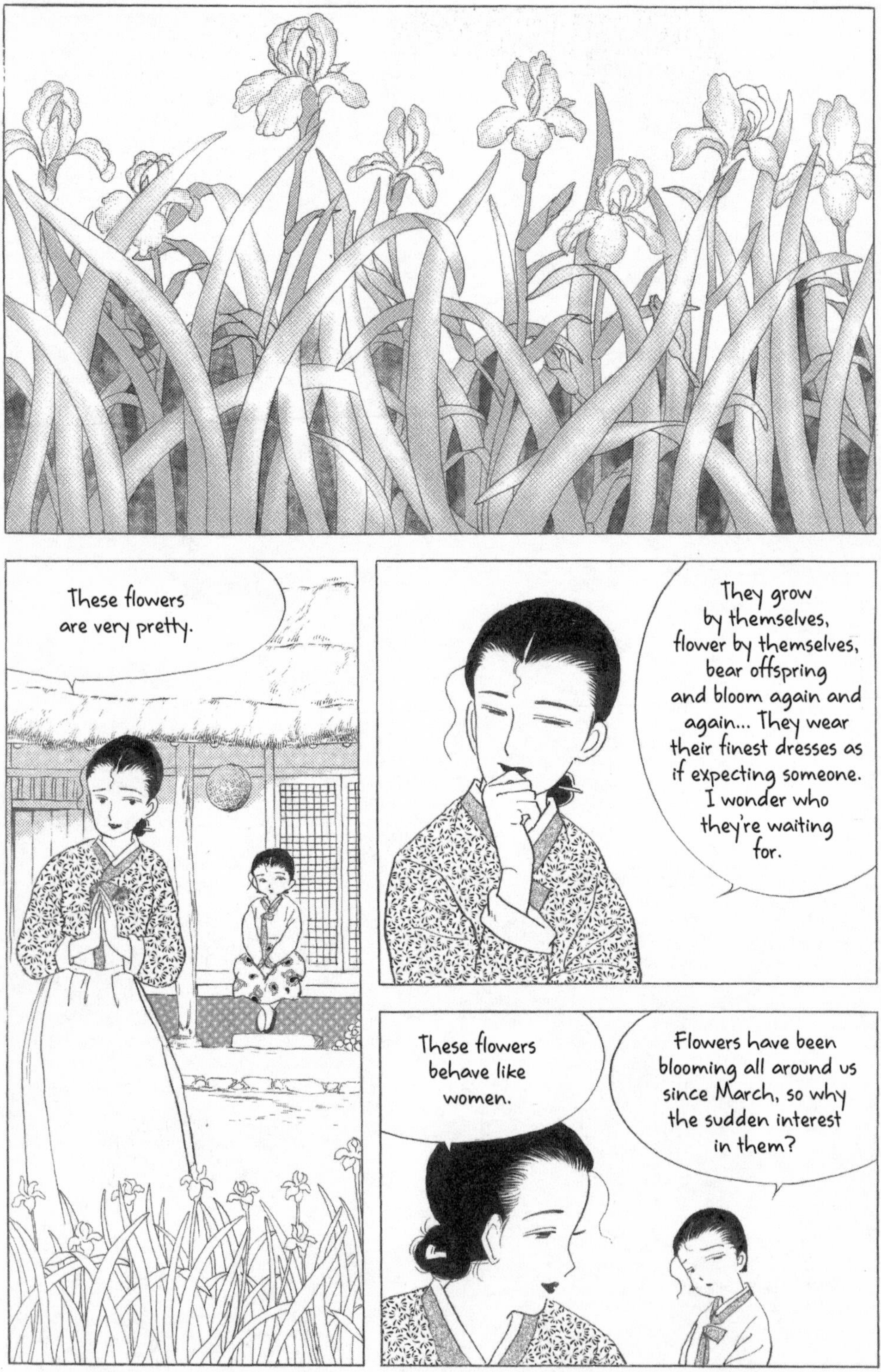
These flowers are very pretty.
They grow by themselves, flower by themselves, bear offspring and bloom again and again... They wear their finest dresses as if expecting someone. I wonder who they're waiting for.
These flowers behave like women.
Flowers have been blooming all around us since March, so why the sudden interest in them?

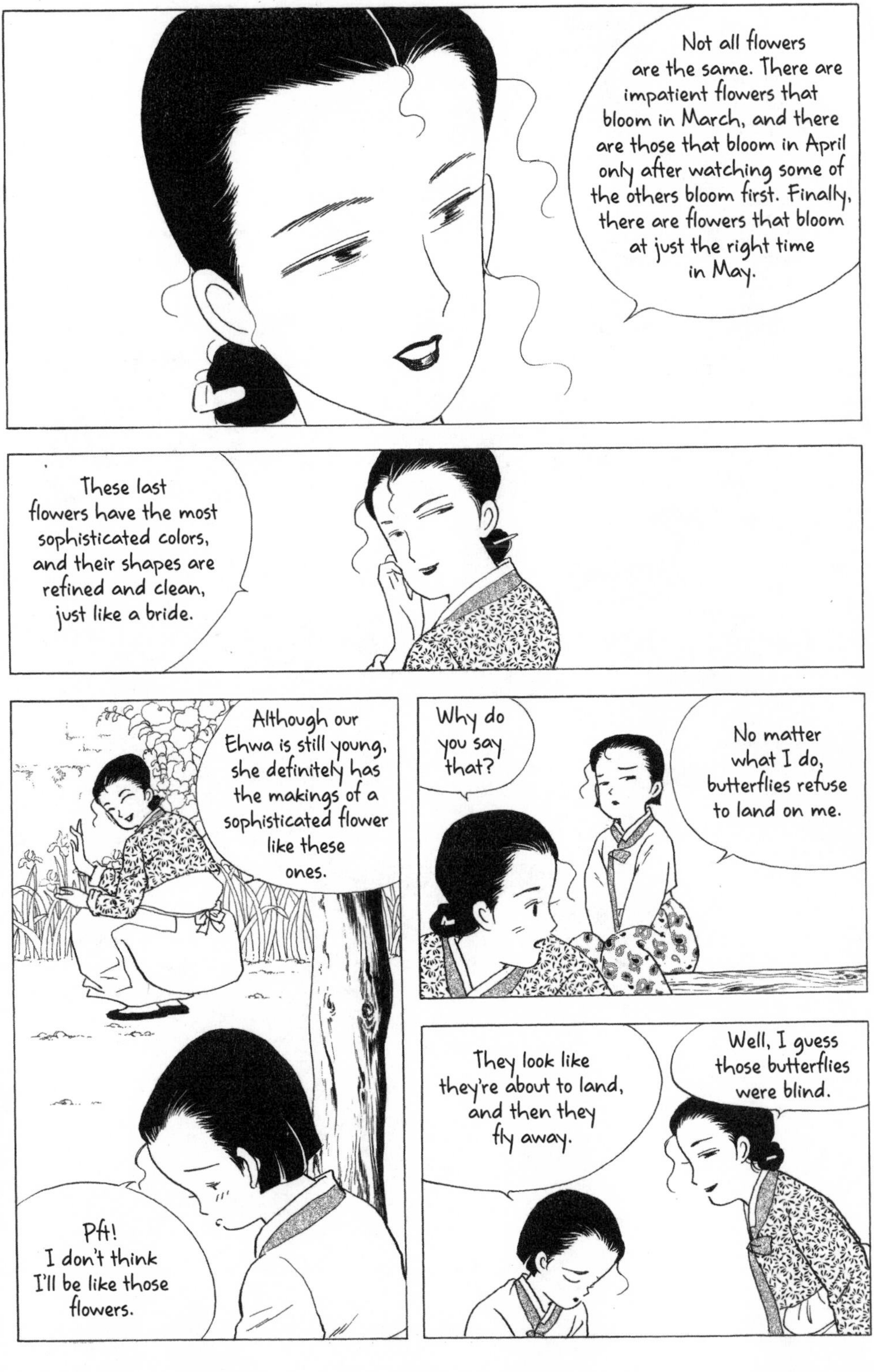
Not all flowers are the same. There are impatient flowers that bloom in March, and there are those that bloom in April only after watching some of the others bloom first. Finally, there are flowers that bloom at just the right time in May.
These last flowers have the most sophisticated colors, and their shapes are refined and clean, just like a bride.
Although our Ehwa is still young, she definitely has the makings of a sophisticated flower like these ones.
Pft! I don't think I'll be like those flowers.
Why do you say that?
No matter what I do, butterflies refuse to land on me.
They look like they're about to land, and then they fly away.
Well, I guess those butterflies were blind.

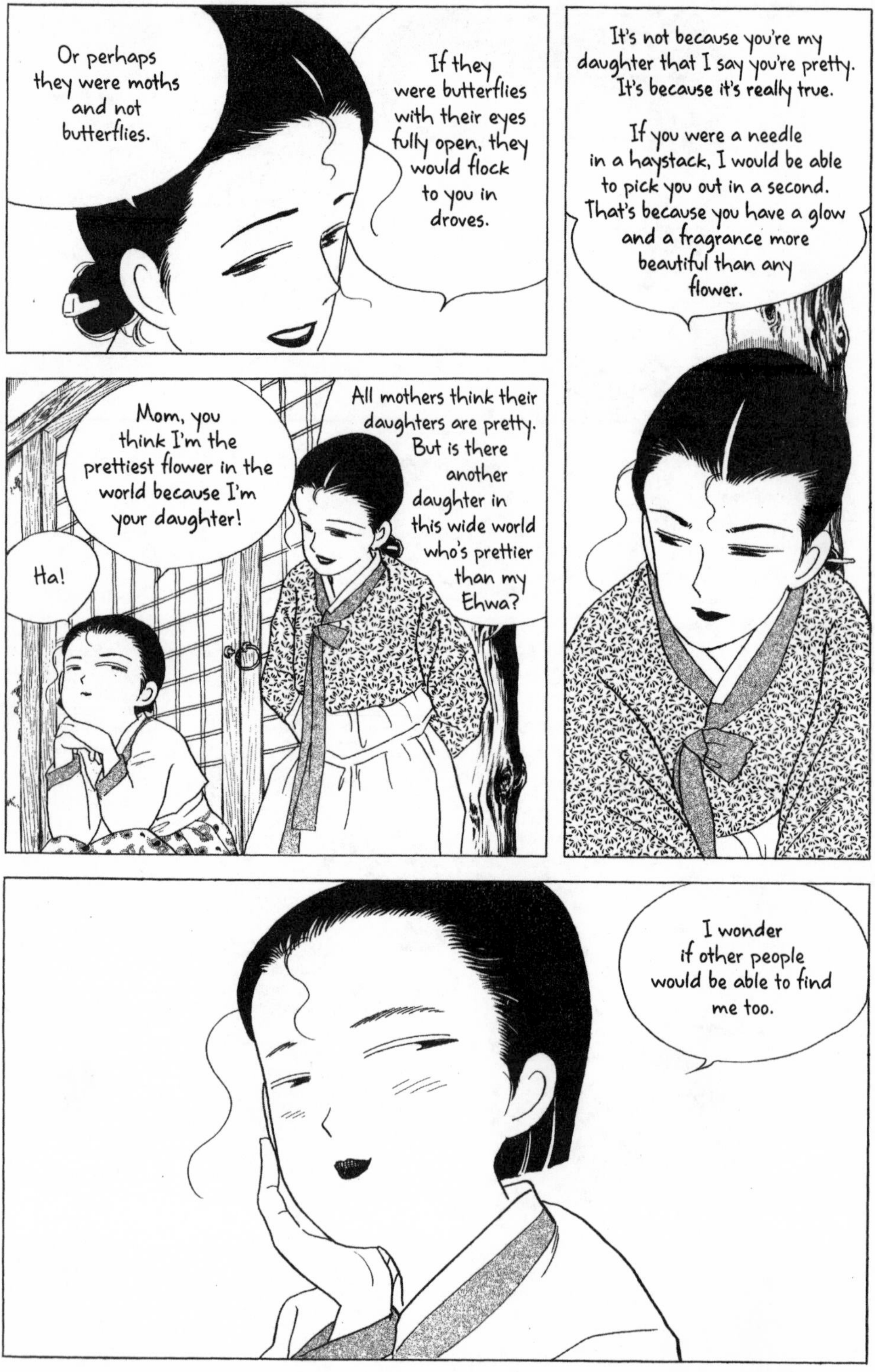
Or perhaps they were moths and not butterflies.
If they were butterflies with their eyes fully open, they would flock to you in droves.
It's not because you're my daughter that I say you're pretty. It's because it's really true.
If you were a needle in a haystack, I would be able to pick you out in a second. That's because you have a glow and a fragrance more beautiful than any flower.
Mom, you think I'm the prettiest flower in the world because I'm your daughter!
Ha!
All mothers think their daughters are pretty. But is there another daughter in this wide world who's prettier than my Ehwa?
I wonder if other people would be able to find me too.

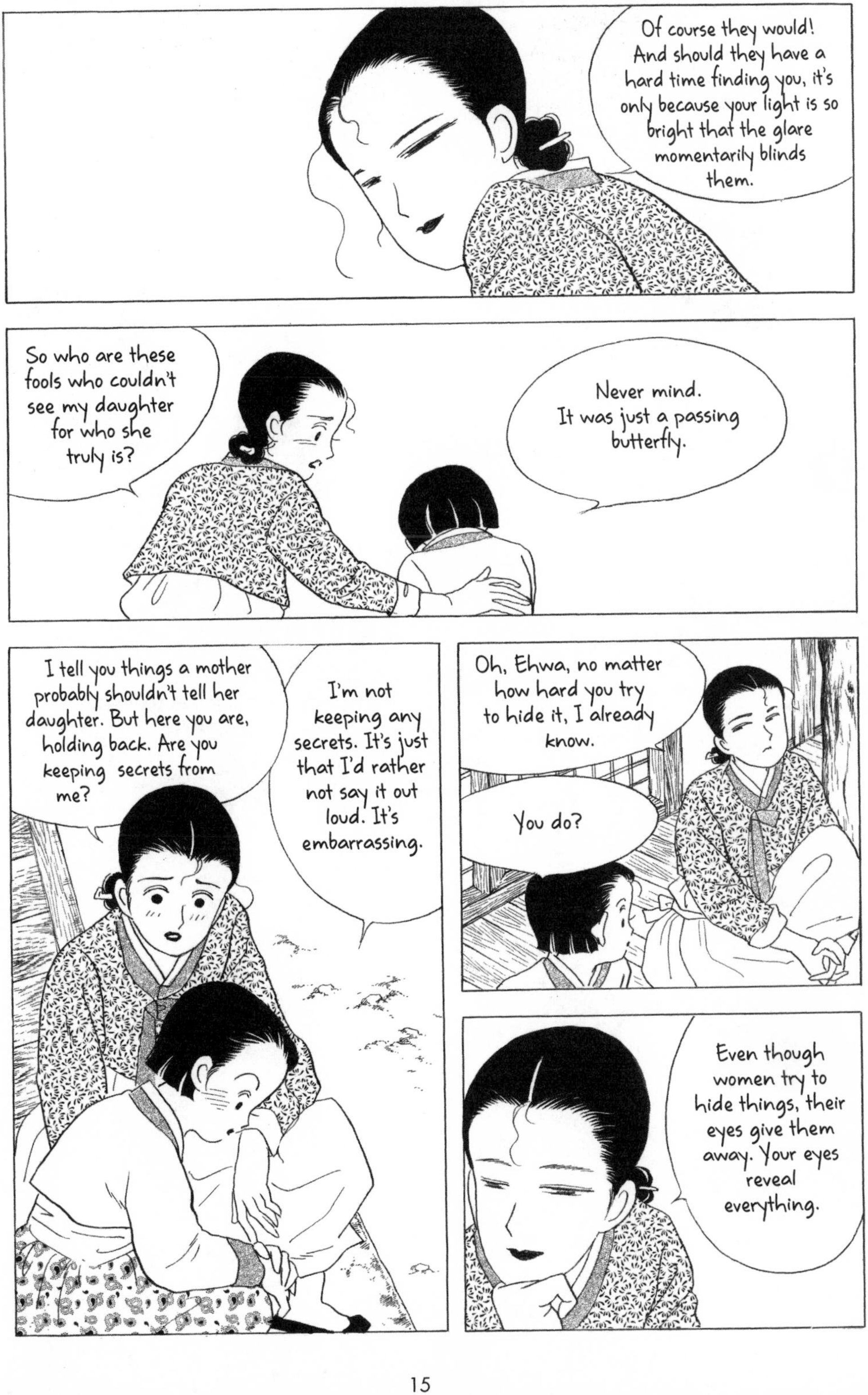
Of course they would! And should they have a hard time finding you, it's only because your light is so bright that the glare momentarily blinds them.
So who are these fools who couldn't see my daughter for who she truly is?
Never mind. It was just a passing butterfly.
I tell you things a mother probably shouldn't tell her daughter. But here you are, holding back. Are you keeping secrets from me?
I'm not keeping any secrets. It's just that I'd rather not say it out loud. It's embarrassing.
Oh, Ehwa, no matter how hard you try to hide it, I already know.
You do?
Even though women try to hide things, their eyes give them away. Your eyes reveal everything.

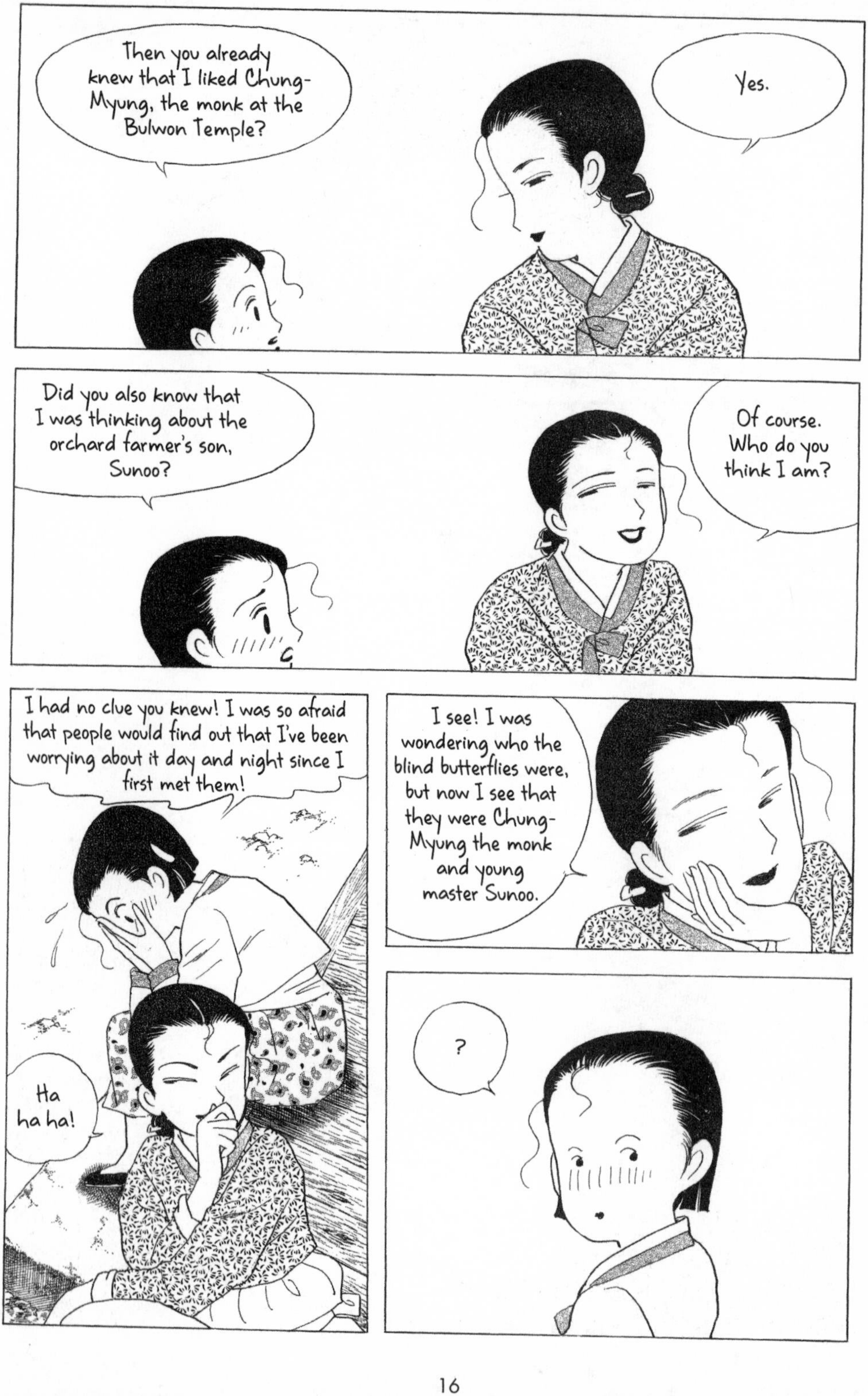
Then you already knew that I liked Chung-Myung, the monk at the Bulwon Temple?
Yes.
Did you also know that I was thinking about the orchard farmer's son, Sunoo?
Of course. Who do you think I am?
I had no clue you knew! I was so afraid that people would find out that I've been worrying about it day and night since I first met them!
Ha ha ha!
I see! I was wondering who the blind butterflies were, but now I see that they were Chung-Myung the monk and young master Sunoo.
?

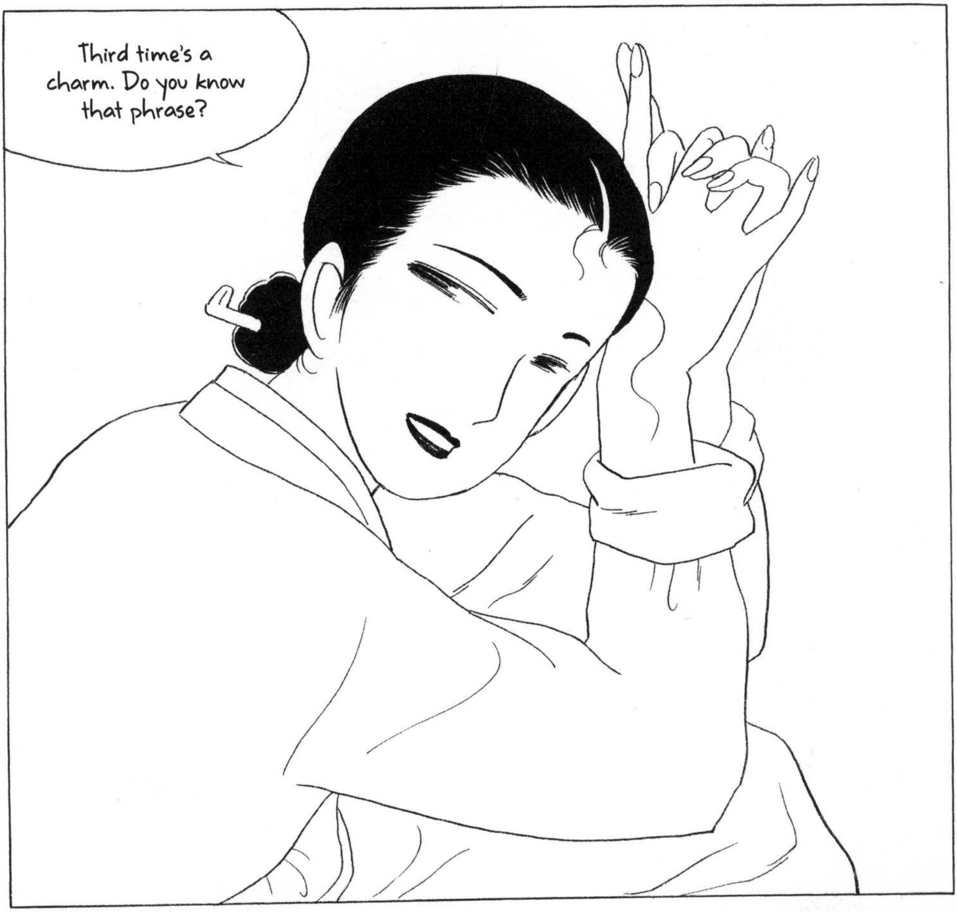
Third time's a charm. Do you know that phrase?

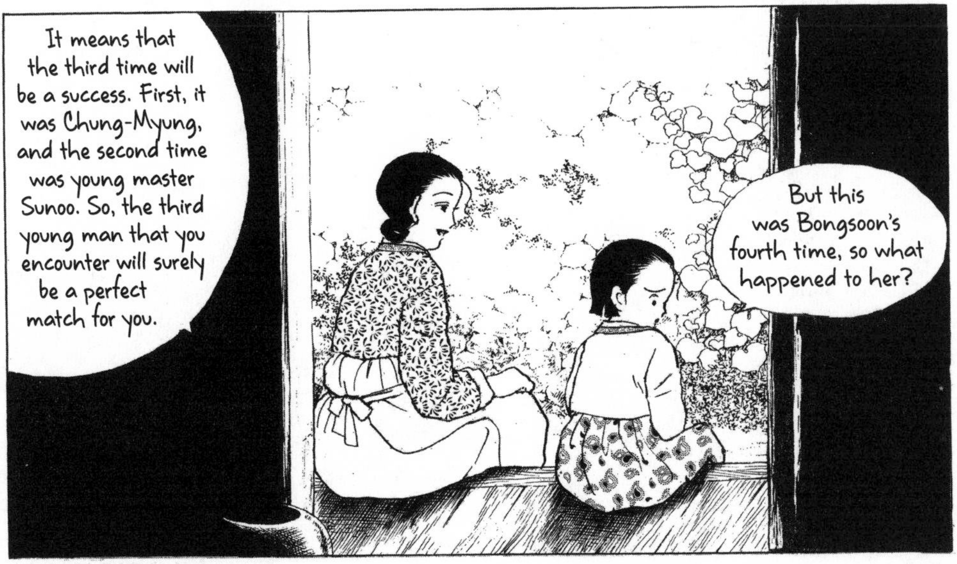
It means that the third time will be a success. First, it was Chung-Myung, and the second time was young master Sunoo. So, the third young man that you encounter will surely be a perfect match for you.
But this was Bongsoon's fourth time, so what happened to her?

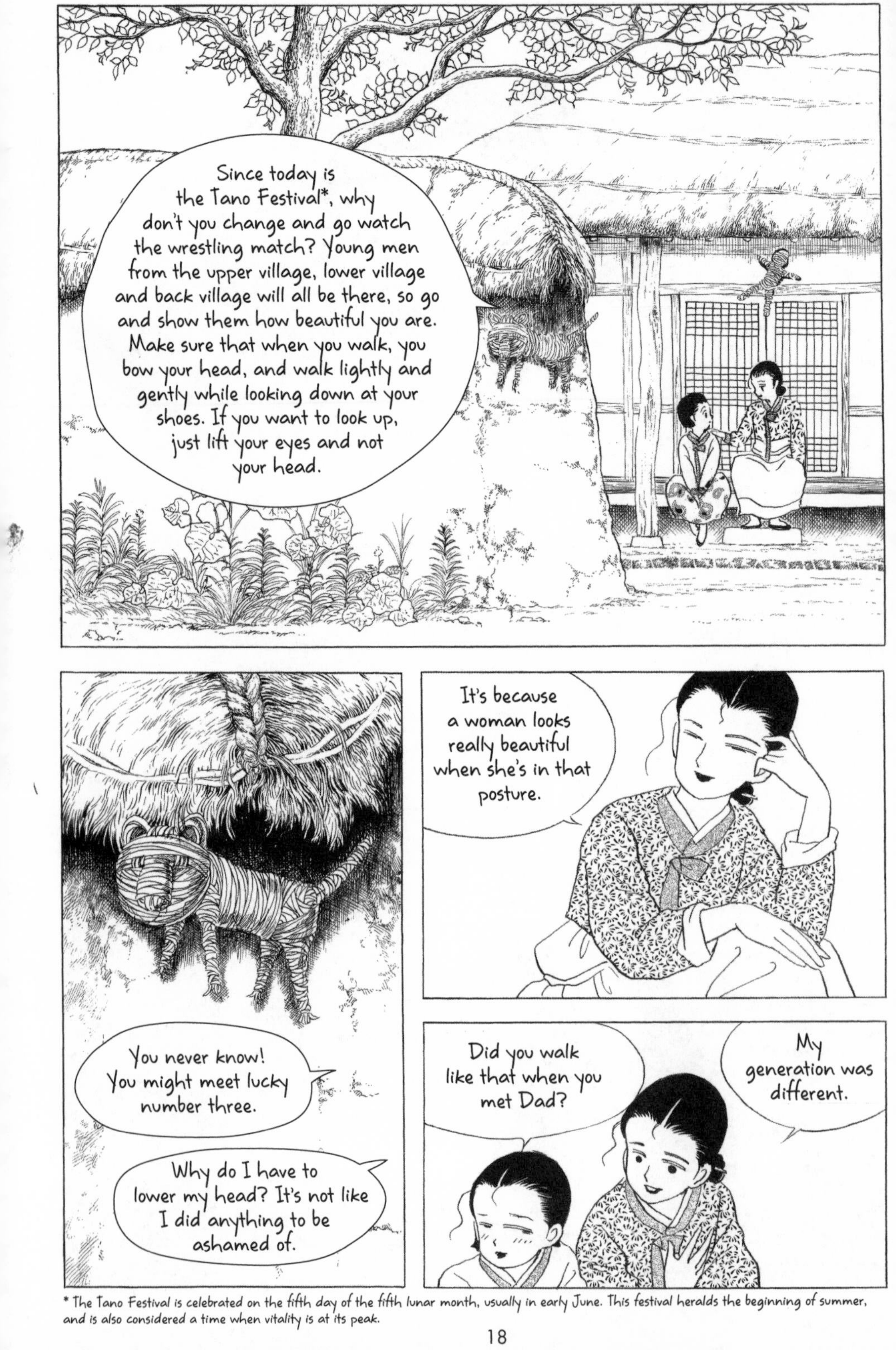
Since today is the Tano Festival*, why don't you change and go watch the wrestling match? Young men from the upper village, lower village and back village will all be there, so go and show them how beautiful you are. Make sure that when you walk, you bow your head, and walk lightly and gently while looking down at your shoes. If you want to look up, just lift your eyes and not your head.
You never know! You might meet lucky number three.
Why do I have to lower my head? It's not like I did anything to be ashamed of.
It's because a woman looks really beautiful when she's in that posture.
Did you walk like that when you met Dad?
My generation was different.

* The Tano Festival is celebrated on the fifth day of the fifth lunar month, usually in early June. This festival heralds the beginning of summer, and is also considered a time when vitality is at its peak.

Now you can meet people as you wish and fall in love as you wish. Times have changed for the better.

I boiled some sweet rush. Use the water to wash your hair. When you're done, rub camellia seed oil in your hair before you brush it.

I don't like sweet rush water. It's too salty.

Of all the things to not like! Sweet rush water is like medicine for a woman. It kills off bad energy and prevents all kinds of ailments.

Where are you going?

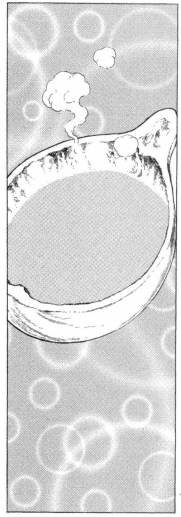

An enjoyable festival for others is a work day for me. It's one of my busiest days. I'm going to grind these mung beans so I can make pancakes.

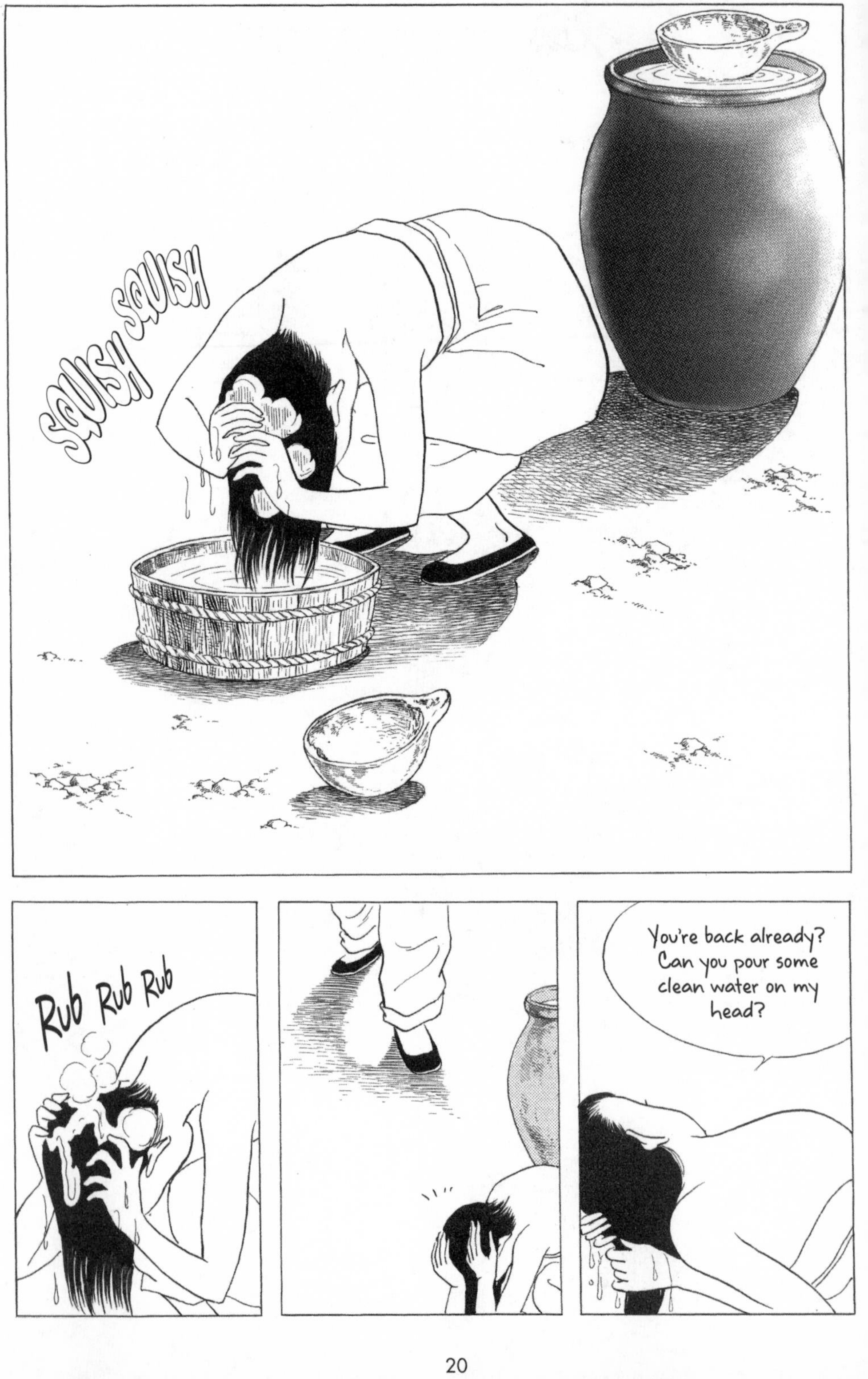
SQUISH SQUISH
Rub Rub Rub
You're back already? Can you pour some clean water on my head?

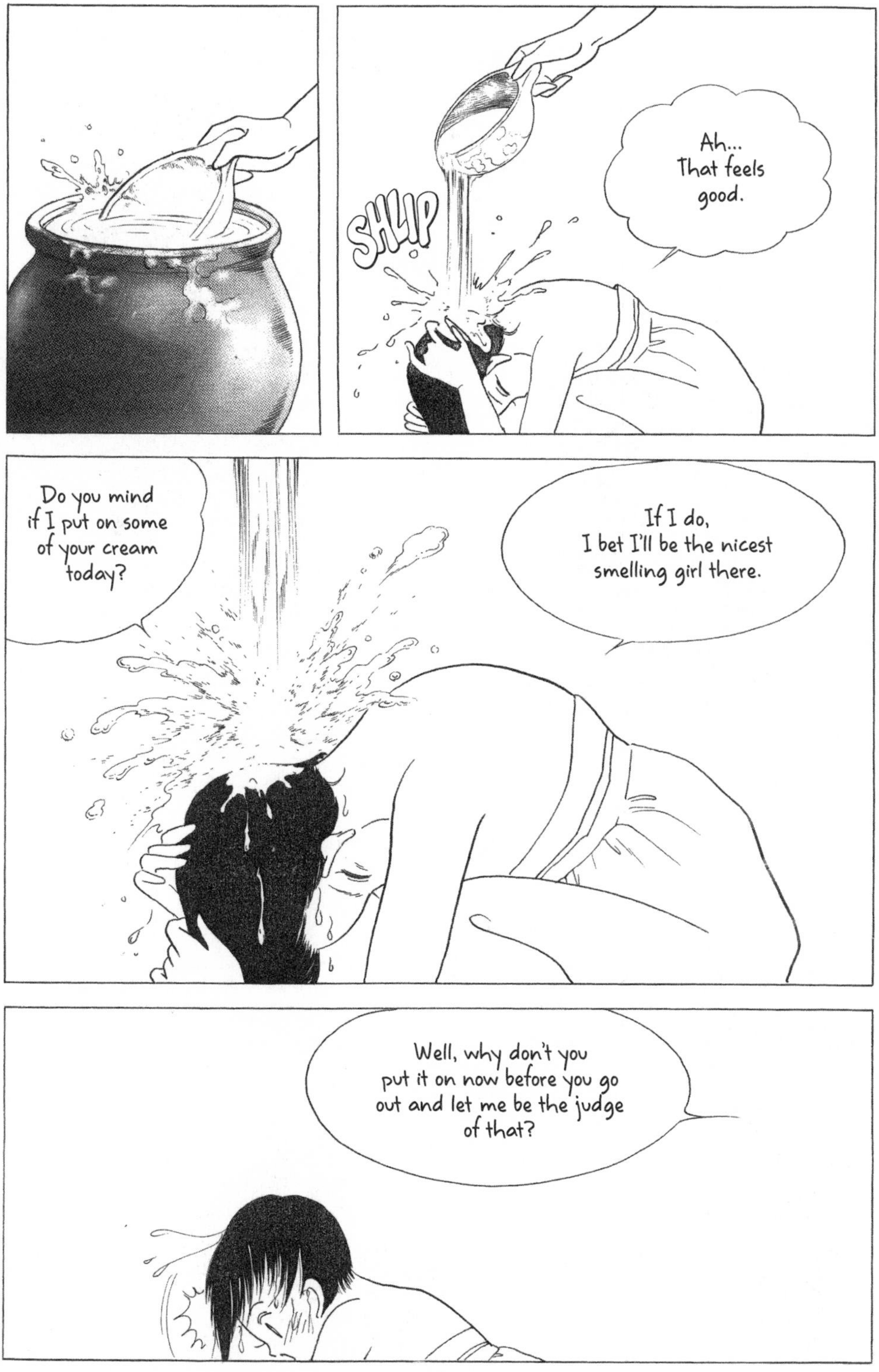
SHLIP
Ah... That feels good.
Do you mind if I put on some of your cream today?
If I do, I bet I'll be the nicest smelling girl there.
Well, why don't you put it on now before you go out and let me be the judge of that?

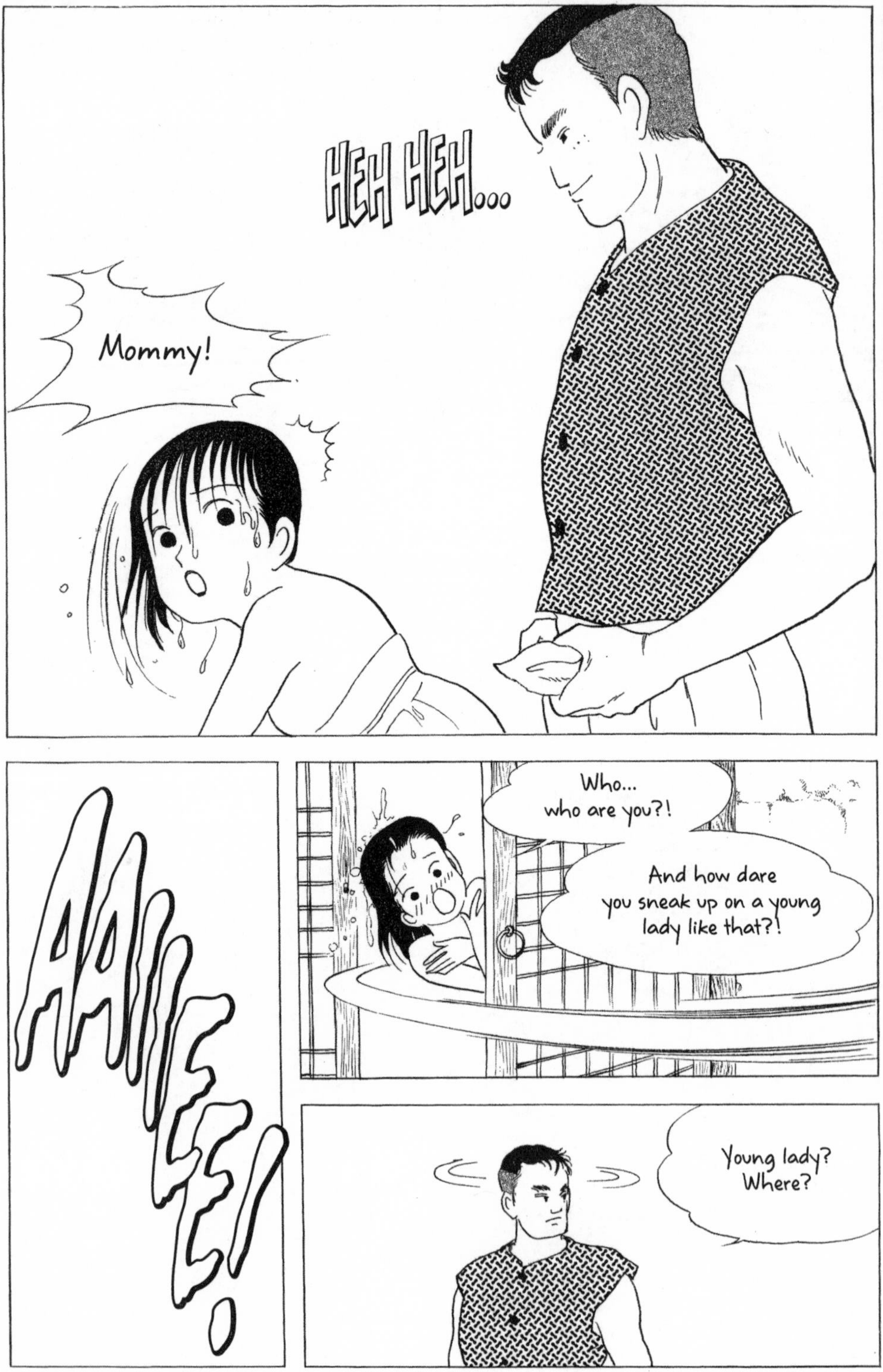
HEH HEH...
Mommy!
AAIIEEE!
Who... who are you?!
And how dare you sneak up on a young lady like that?!
Young lady? Where?

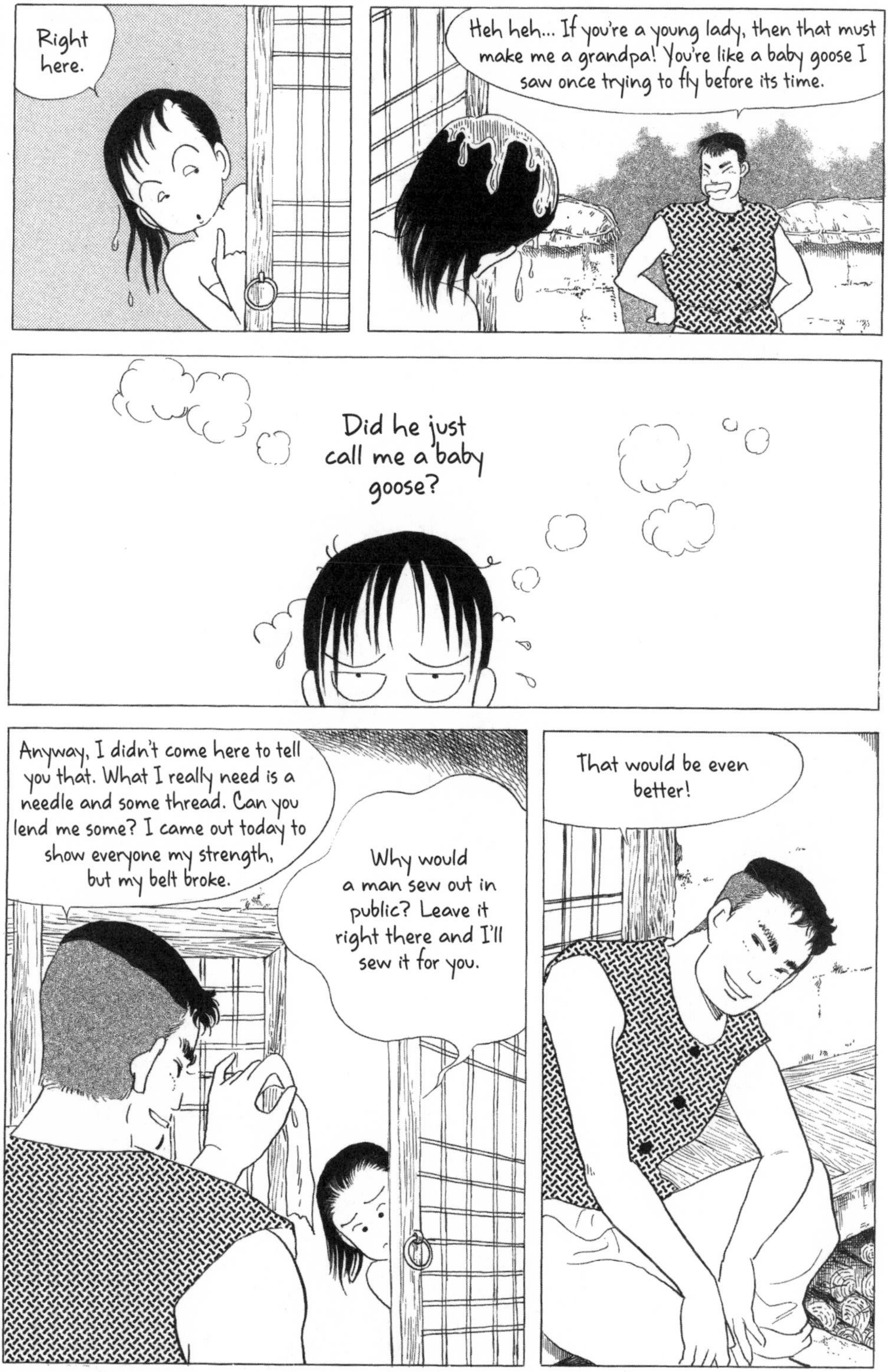
Right here.
Heh heh... If you're a young lady, then that must make me a grandpa! You're like a baby goose I saw once trying to fly before its time.
Did he just call me a baby goose?
Anyway, I didn't come here to tell you that. What I really need is a needle and some thread. Can you lend me some? I came out today to show everyone my strength, but my belt broke.
Why would a man sew out in public? Leave it right there and I'll sew it for you.
That would be even better!

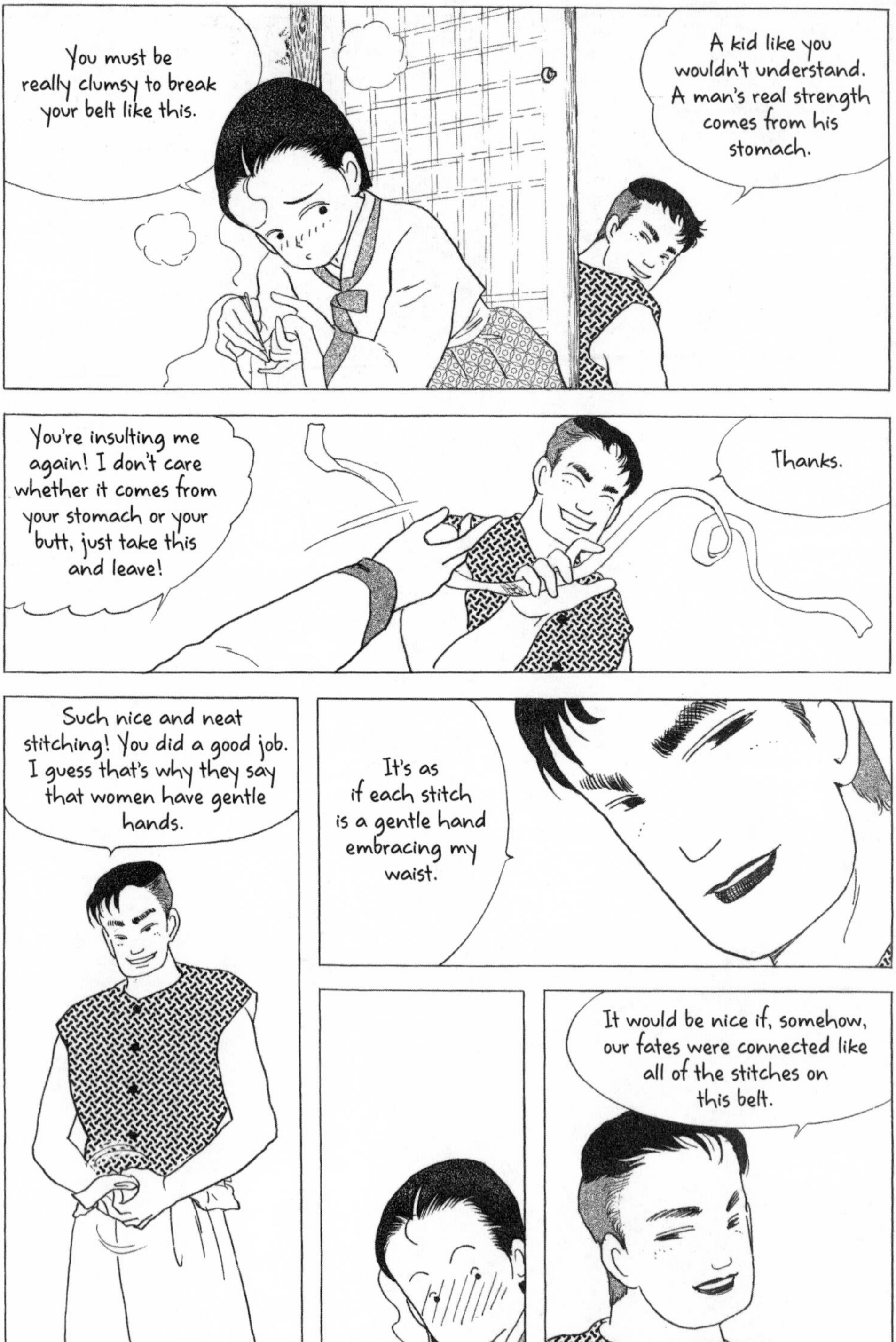
You must be really clumsy to break your belt like this.
A kid like you wouldn't understand. A man's real strength comes from his stomach.
You're insulting me again! I don't care whether it comes from your stomach or your butt, just take this and leave!
Thanks.
Such nice and neat stitching! You did a good job. I guess that's why they say that women have gentle hands.
It's as if each stitch is a gentle hand embracing my waist.
It would be nice if, somehow, our fates were connected like all of the stitches on this belt.

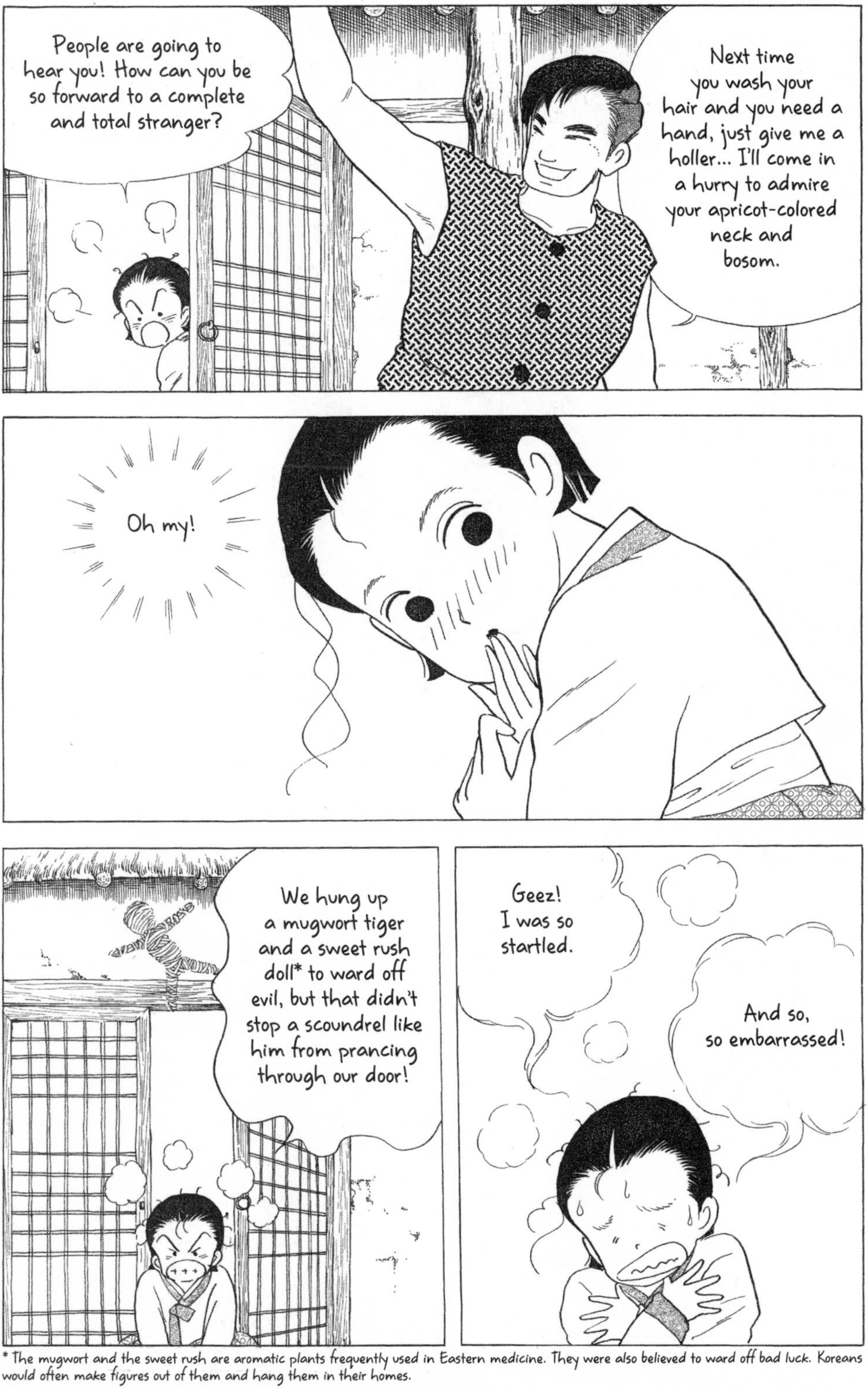
People are going to hear you! How can you be so forward to a complete and total stranger?
Next time you wash your hair and you need a hand, just give me a holler... I'll come in a hurry to admire your apricot-colored neck and bosom.
Oh my!
We hung up a mugwort tiger and a sweet rush doll* to ward off evil, but that didn't stop a scoundrel like him from prancing through our door!
Geez! I was so startled.
And so, so embarrassed!

* The mugwort and the sweet rush are aromatic plants frequently used in Eastern medicine. They were also believed to ward off bad luck. Koreans would often make figures out of them and hang them in their homes.

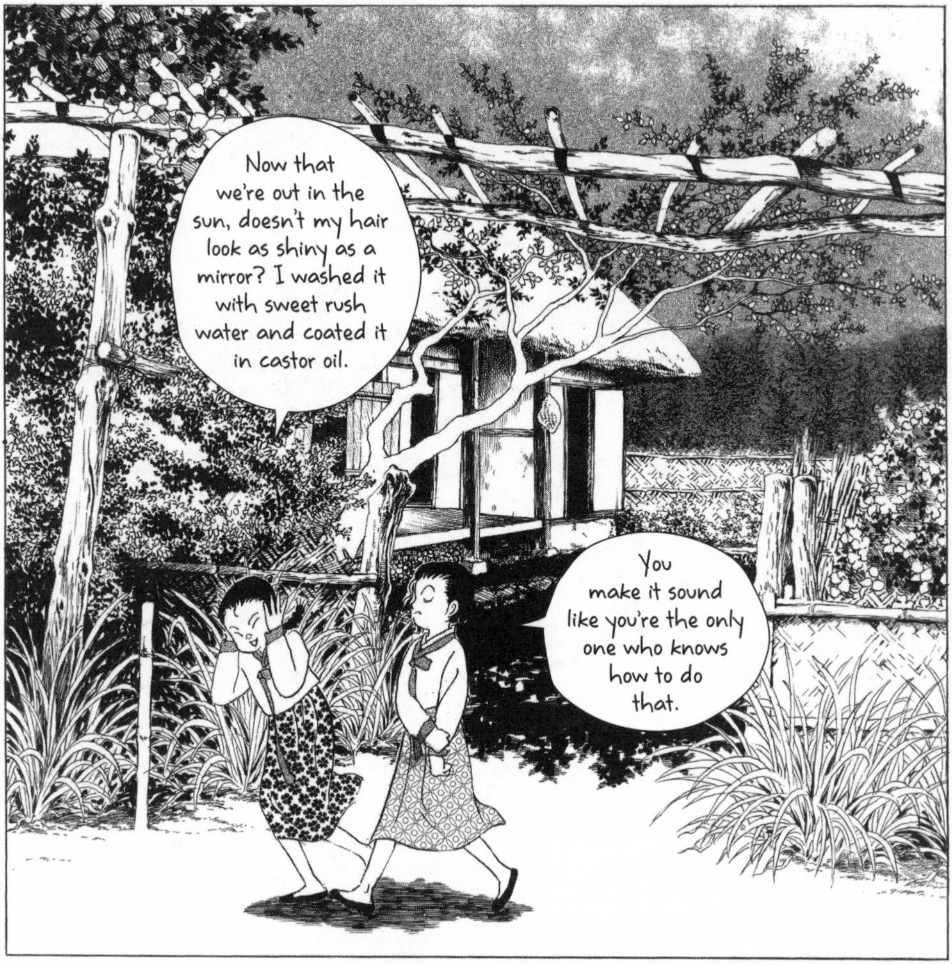
Now that we're out in the sun, doesn't my hair look as shiny as a mirror? I washed it with sweet rush water and coated it in castor oil.
You make it sound like you're the only one who knows how to do that.

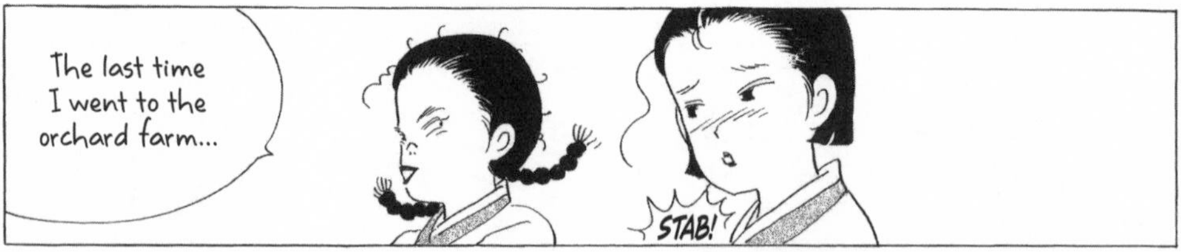
The last time I went to the orchard farm...
STAB!

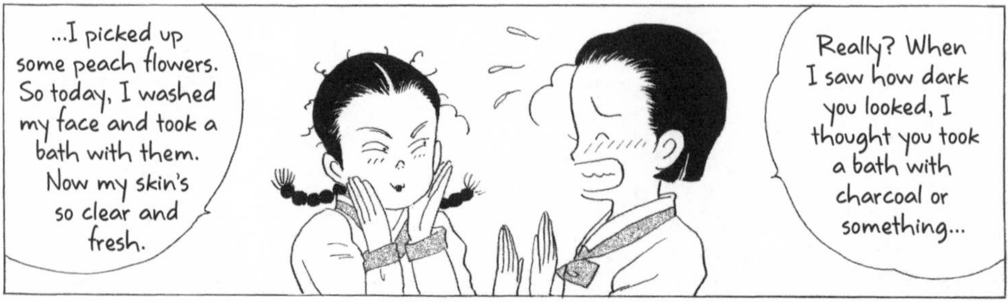
...I picked up some peach flowers. So today, I washed my face and took a bath with them. Now my skin's so clear and fresh.
Really? When I saw how dark you looked, I thought you took a bath with charcoal or something...

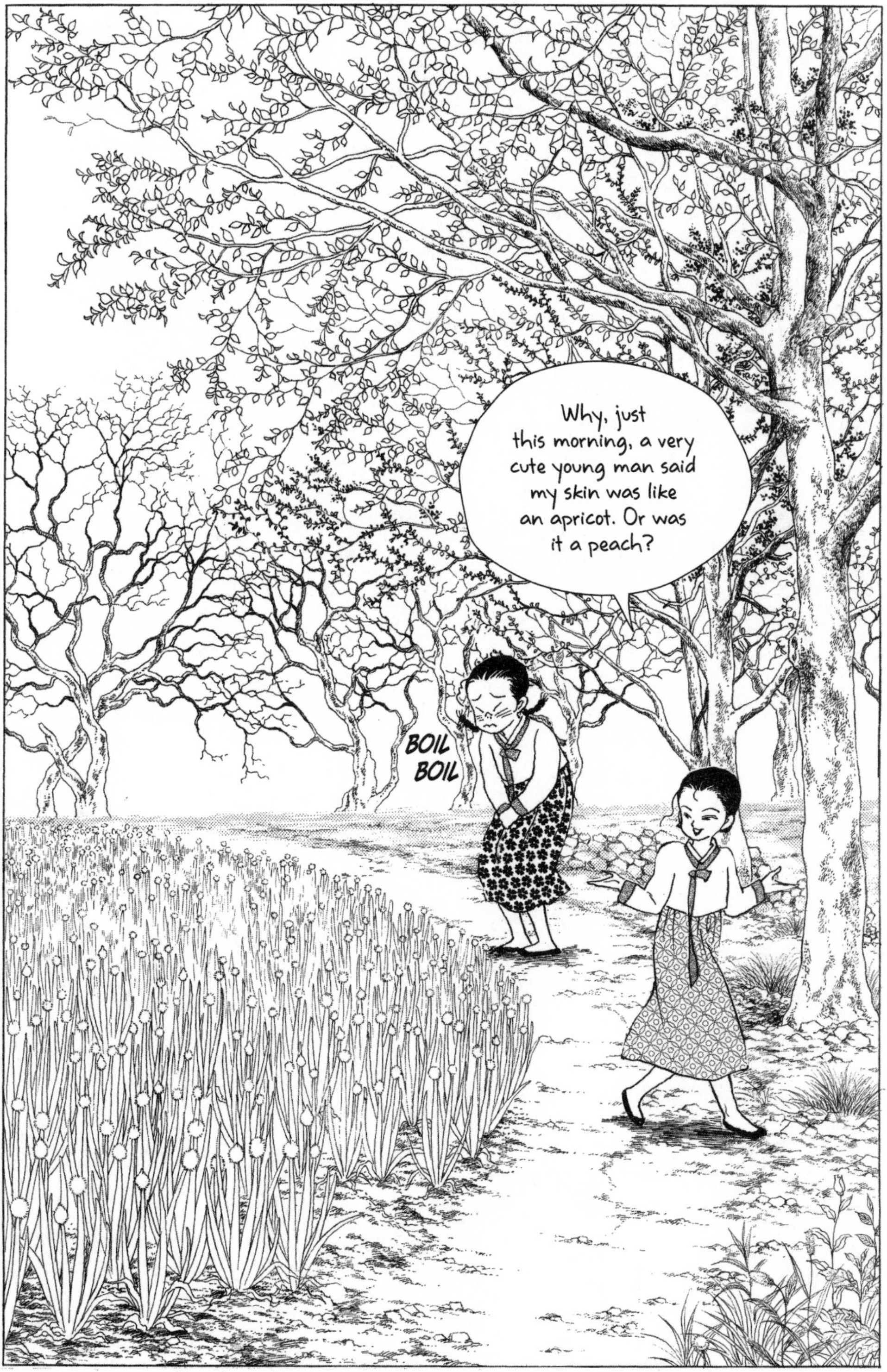
Why, just this morning, a very cute young man said my skin was like an apricot. Or was it a peach?
BOIL BOIL

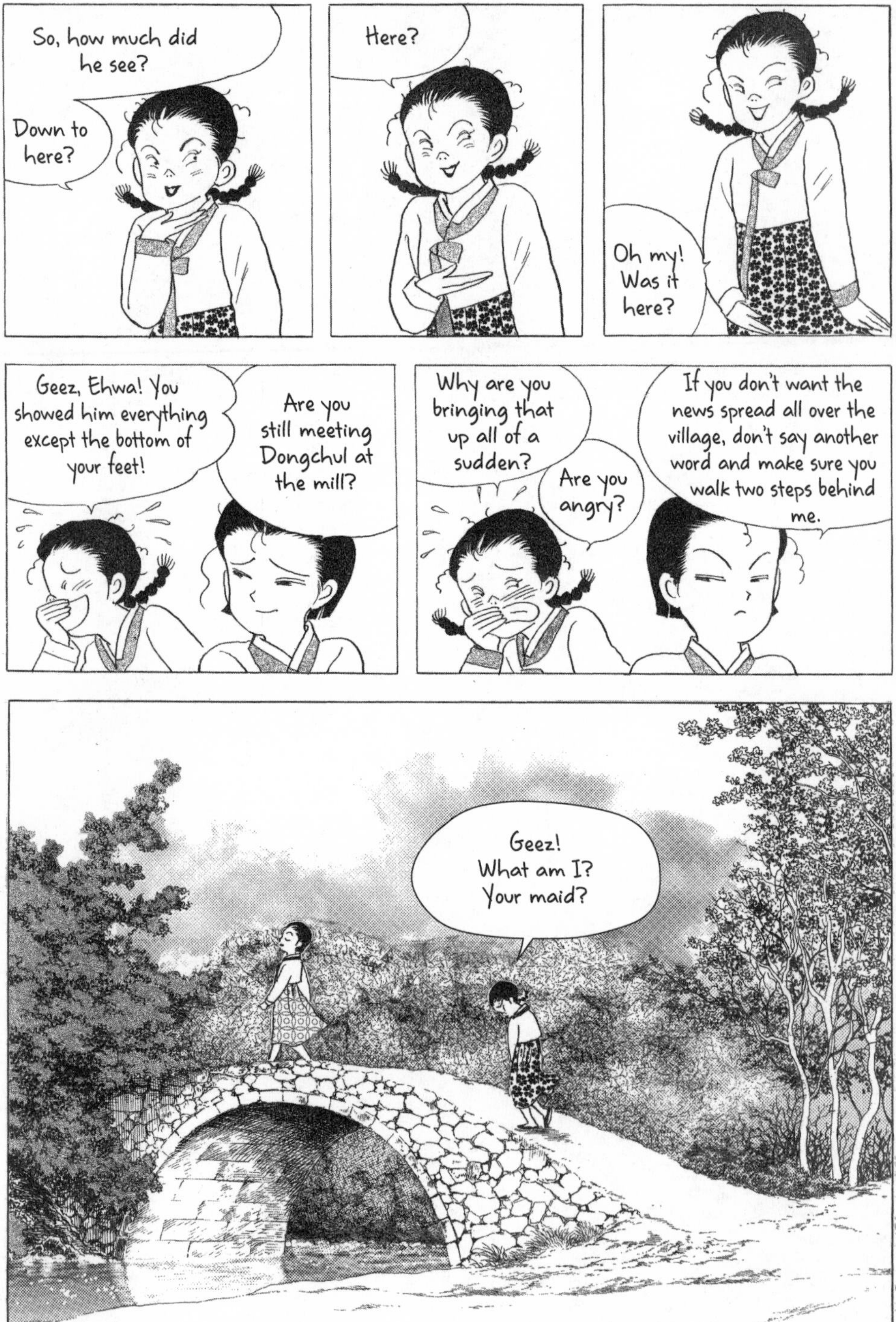
So, how much did he see?
Down to here?
Here?
Oh my! Was it here?
Geez, Ehwa! You showed him everything except the bottom of your feet!
Are you still meeting Dongchul at the mill?
Why are you bringing that up all of a sudden?
Are you angry?
If you don't want the news spread all over the village, don't say another word and make sure you walk two steps behind me.
Geez! What am I? Your maid?

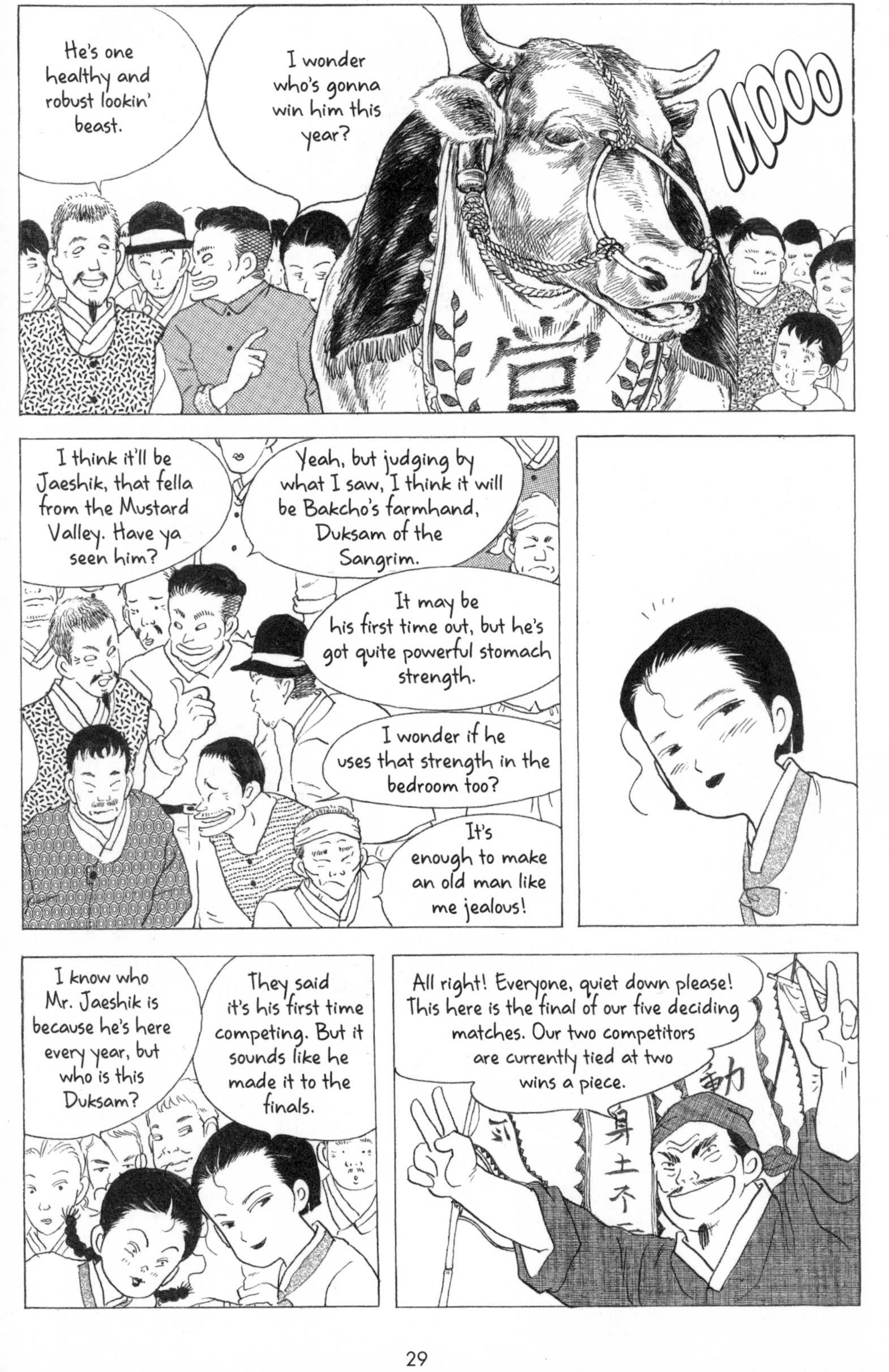
He's one healthy and robust lookin' beast.
I wonder who's gonna win him this year?
MOOO
I think it'll be Jaeshik, that fella from the Mustard Valley. Have ya seen him?
Yeah, but judging by what I saw, I think it will be Bakcho's farmhand, Duksam of the Sangrim.
It may be his first time out, but he's got quite powerful stomach strength.
I wonder if he uses that strength in the bedroom too?
It's enough to make an old man like me jealous!
I know who Mr. Jaeshik is because he's here every year, but who is this Duksam?
They said it's his first time competing. But it sounds like he made it to the finals.
All right! Everyone, quiet down please! This here is the final of our five deciding matches. Our two competitors are currently tied at two wins a piece.

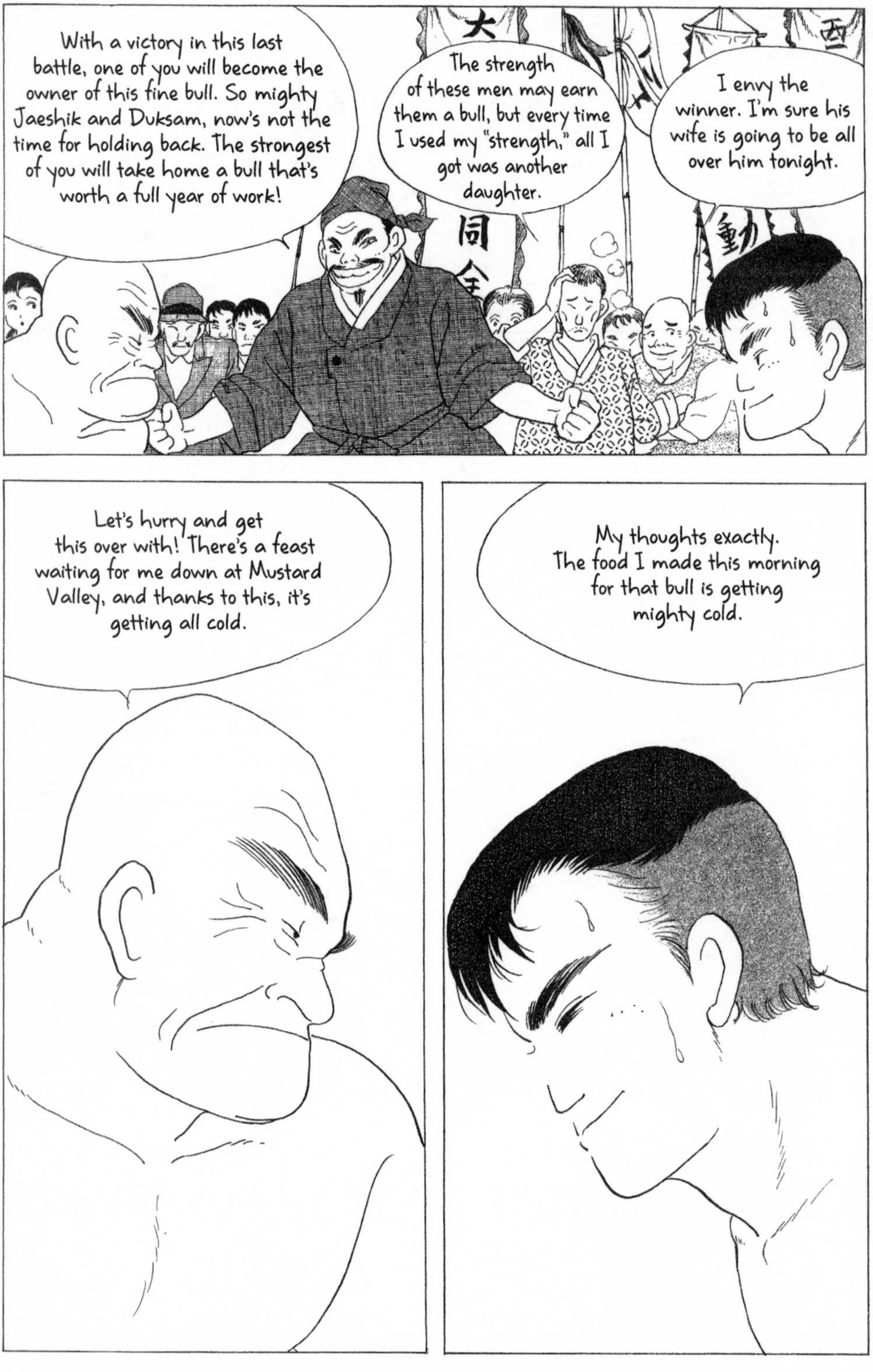
With a victory in this last battle, one of you will become the owner of this fine bull. So mighty Jaeshik and Duksam, now's not the time for holding back. The strongest of you will take home a bull that's worth a full year of work!
The strength of these men may earn them a bull, but every time I used my "strength," all I got was another daughter.
I envy the winner. I'm sure his wife is going to be all over him tonight.
Let's hurry and get this over with! There's a feast waiting for me down at Mustard Valley, and thanks to this, it's getting all cold.
My thoughts exactly. The food I made this morning for that bull is getting mighty cold.

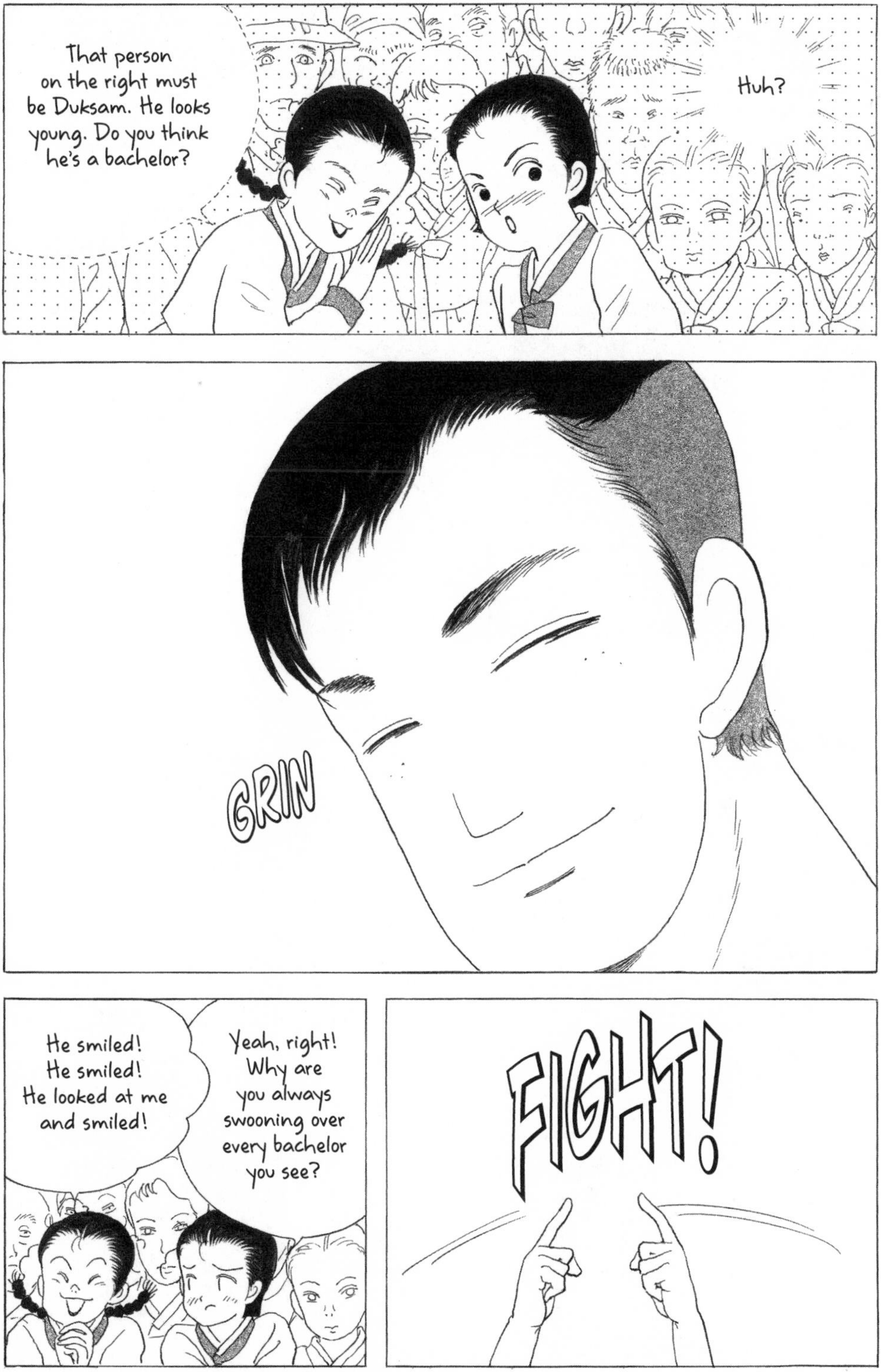
That person on the right must be Duksam. He looks young. Do you think he's a bachelor?
Huh?
GRIN
He smiled! He smiled! He looked at me and smiled!
Yeah, right! Why are you always swooning over every bachelor you see?
FIGHT!

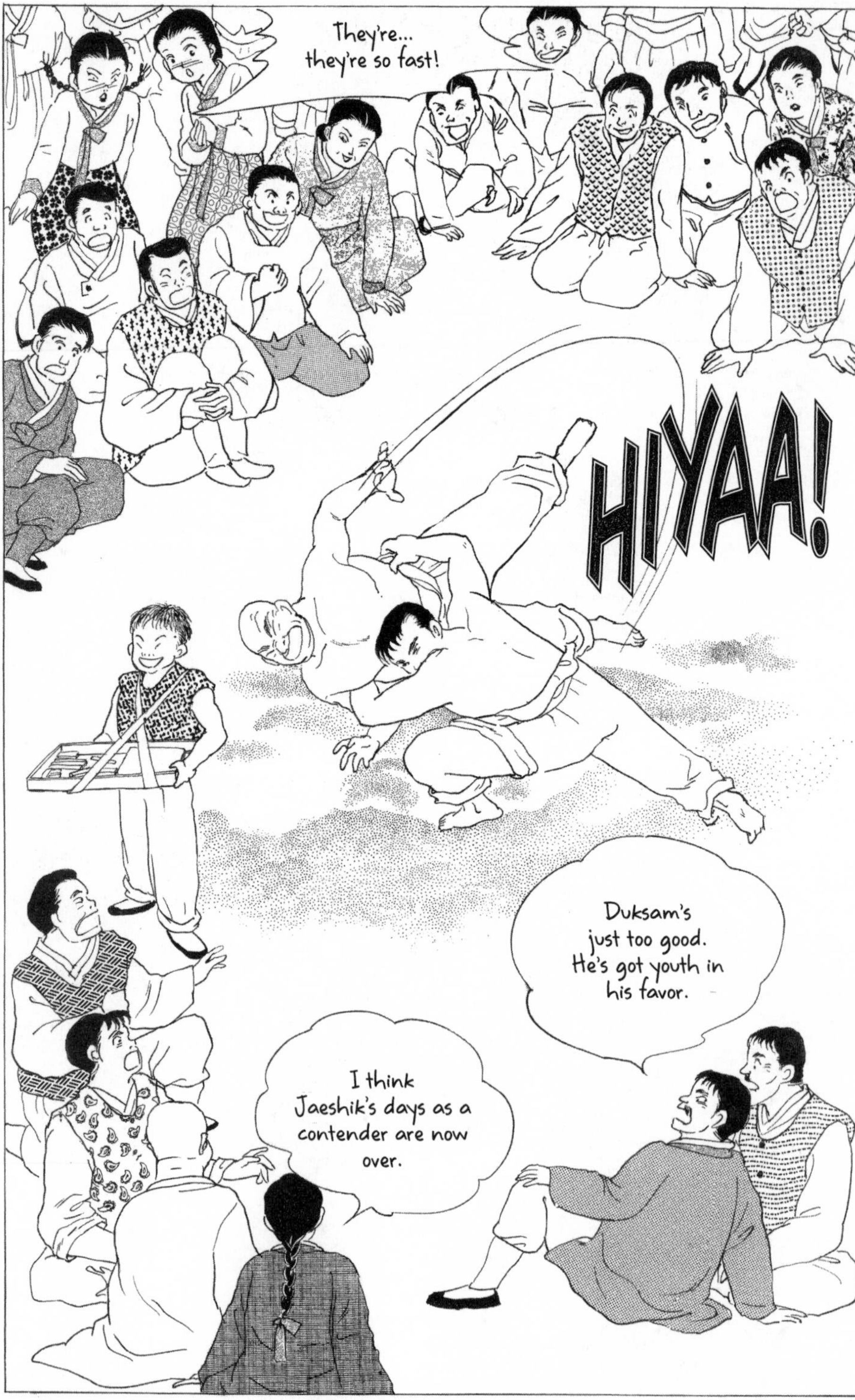
They're... they're so fast!
HIYAA!
Duksam's just too good. He's got youth in his favor.
I think Jaeshik's days as a contender are now over.

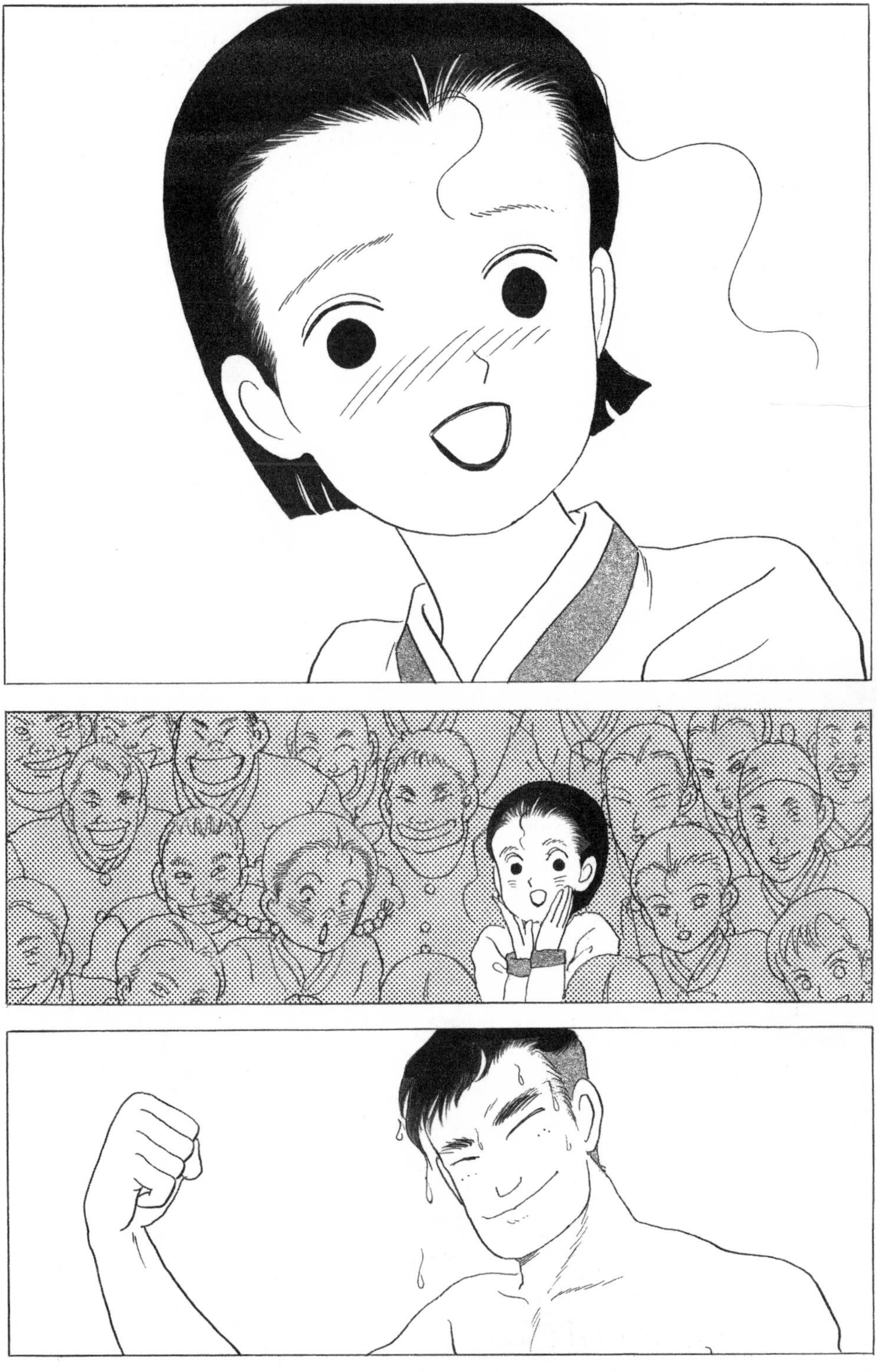

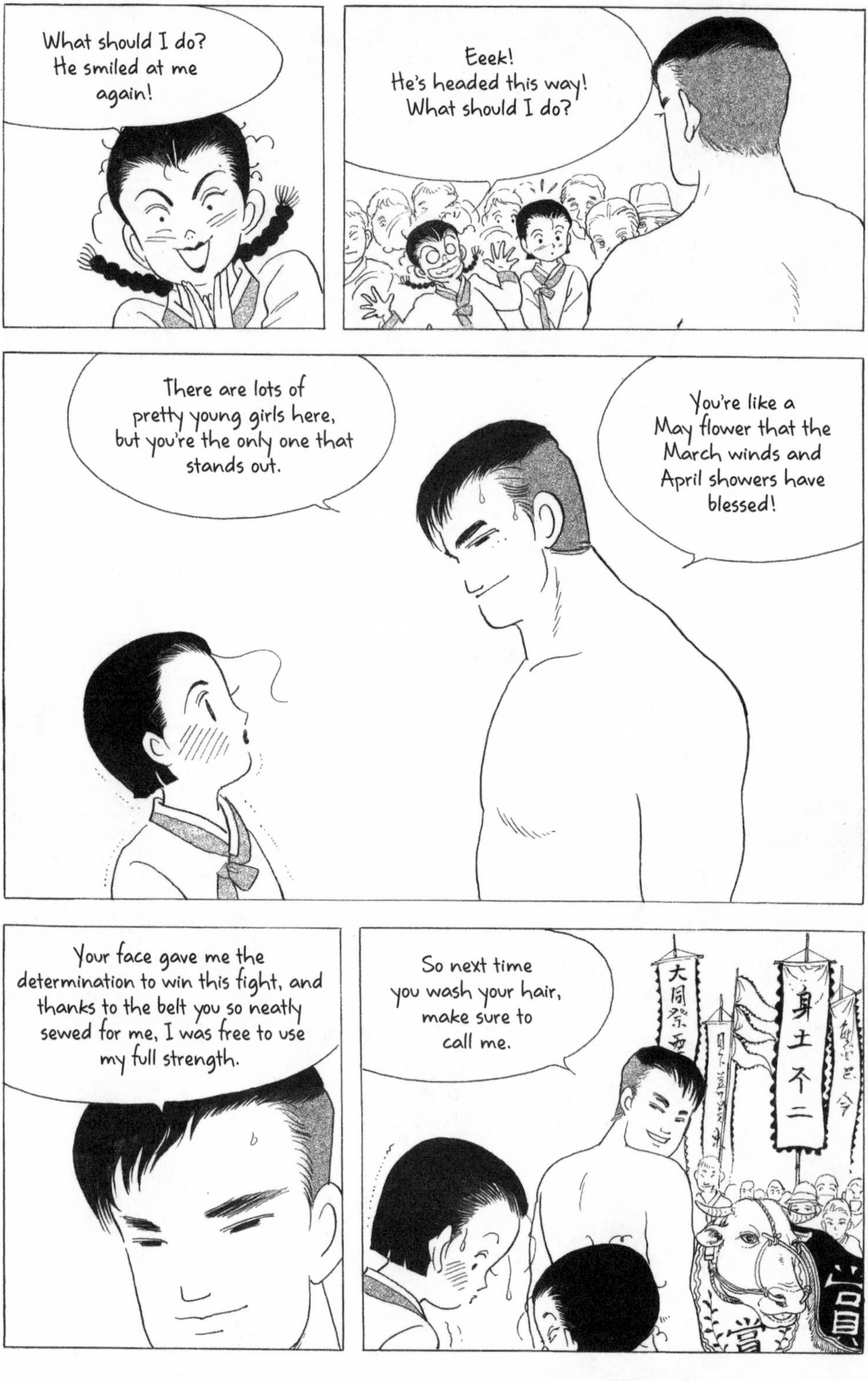
What should I do? He smiled at me again!
Eeek! He's headed this way! What should I do?
There are lots of pretty young girls here, but you're the only one that stands out.
You're like a May flower that the March winds and April showers have blessed!
Your face gave me the determination to win this fight, and thanks to the belt you so neatly sewed for me, I was free to use my full strength.
So next time you wash your hair, make sure to call me.
身土不二

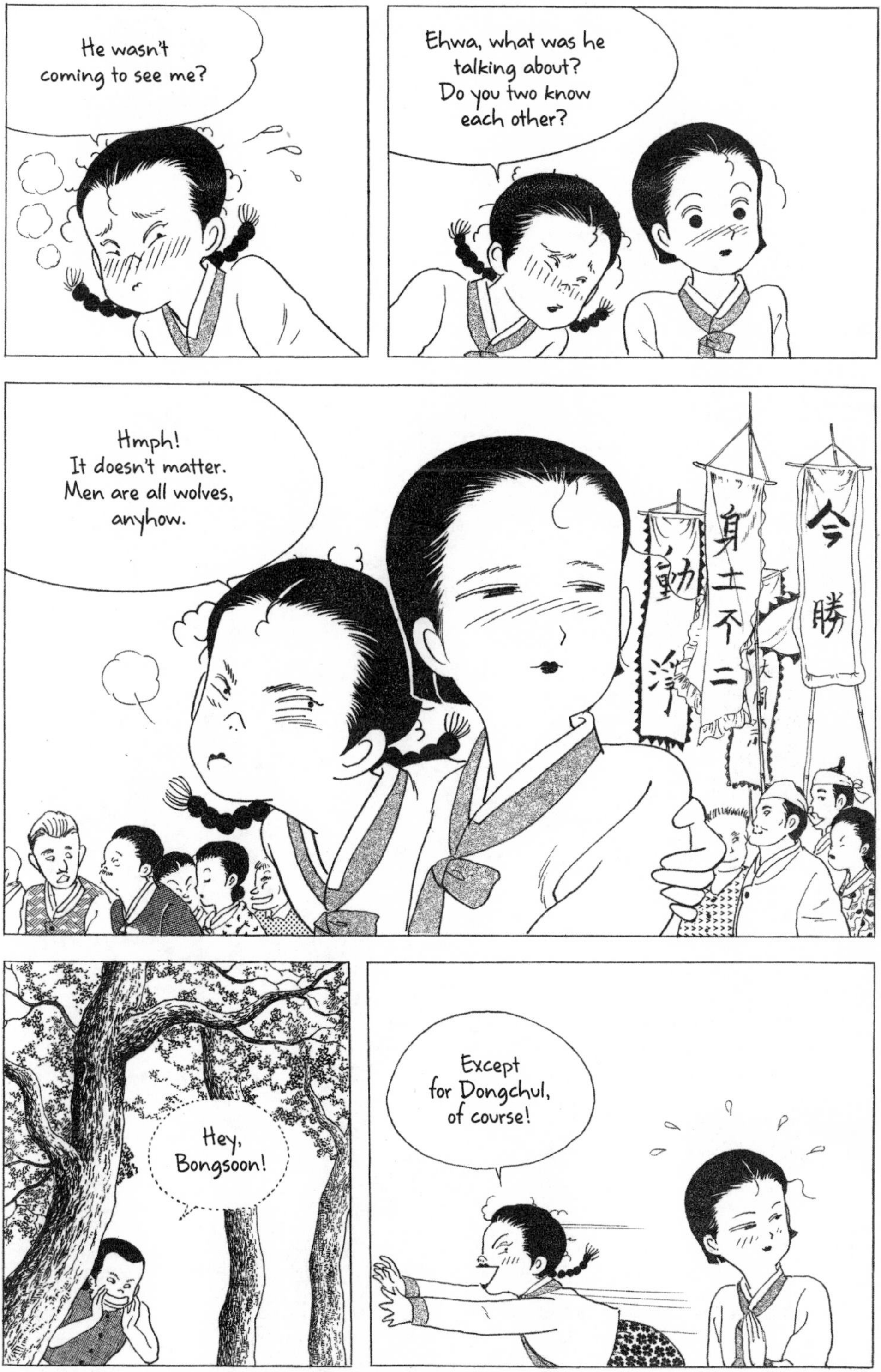
He wasn't coming to see me?
Ehwa, what was he talking about? Do you two know each other?
Hmph! It doesn't matter. Men are all wolves, anyhow.
身土不二
今勝
Hey, Bongsoon!
Except for Dongchul, of course!

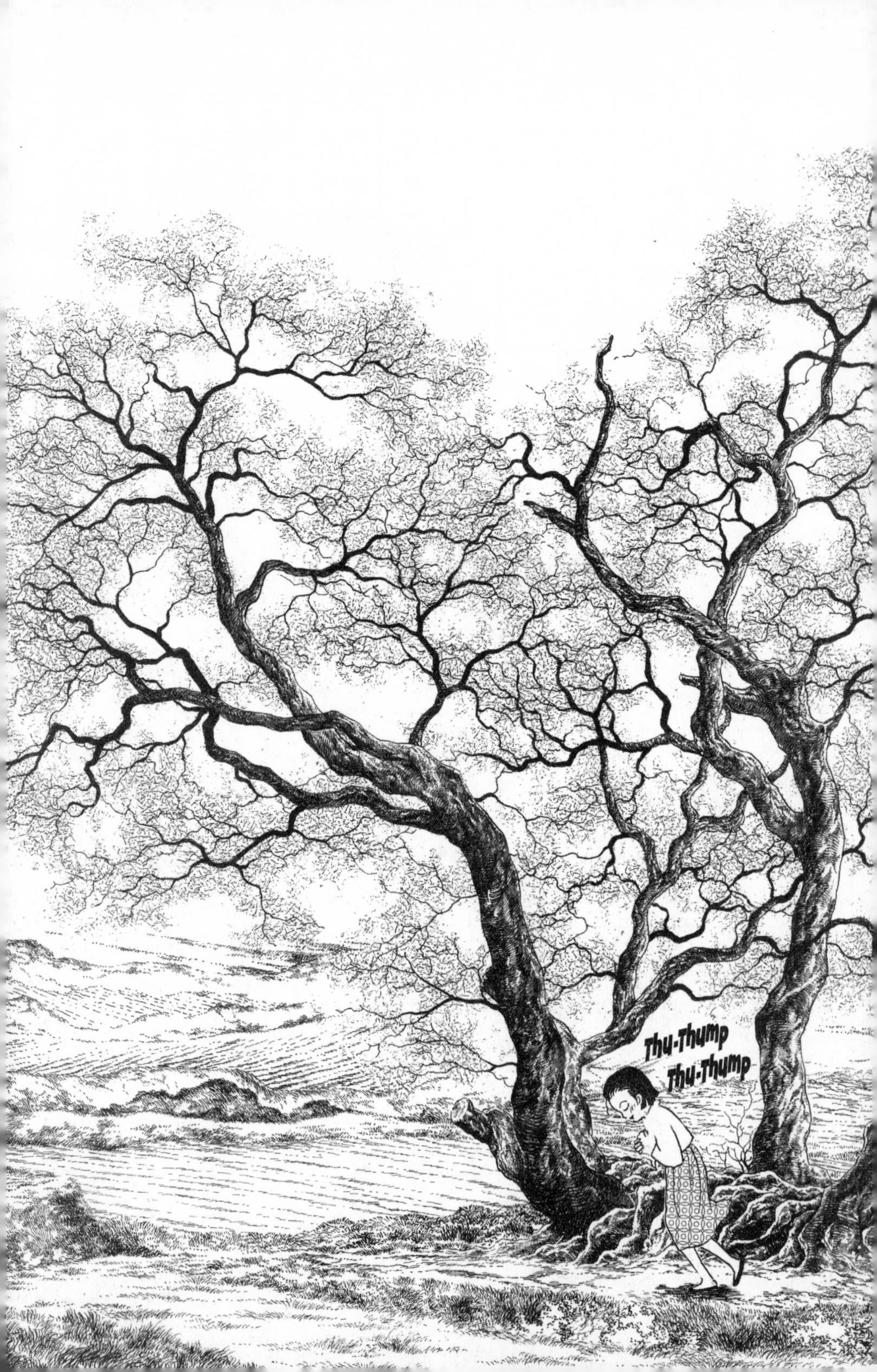
Thu-Thump
Thu-Thump

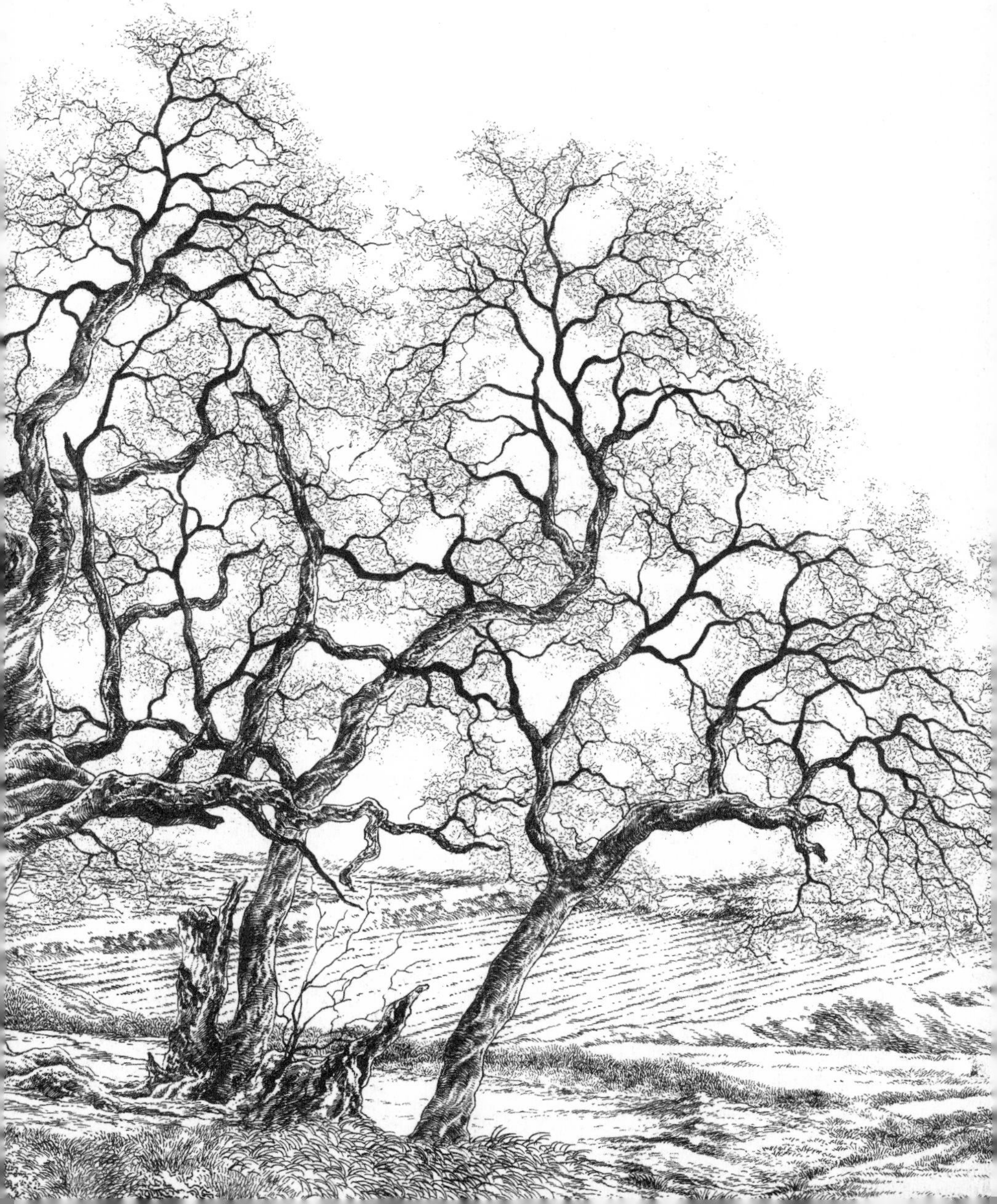

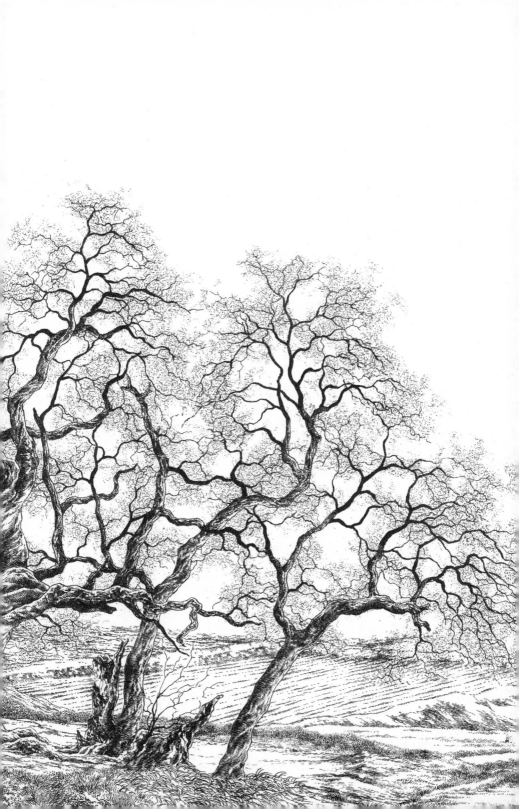

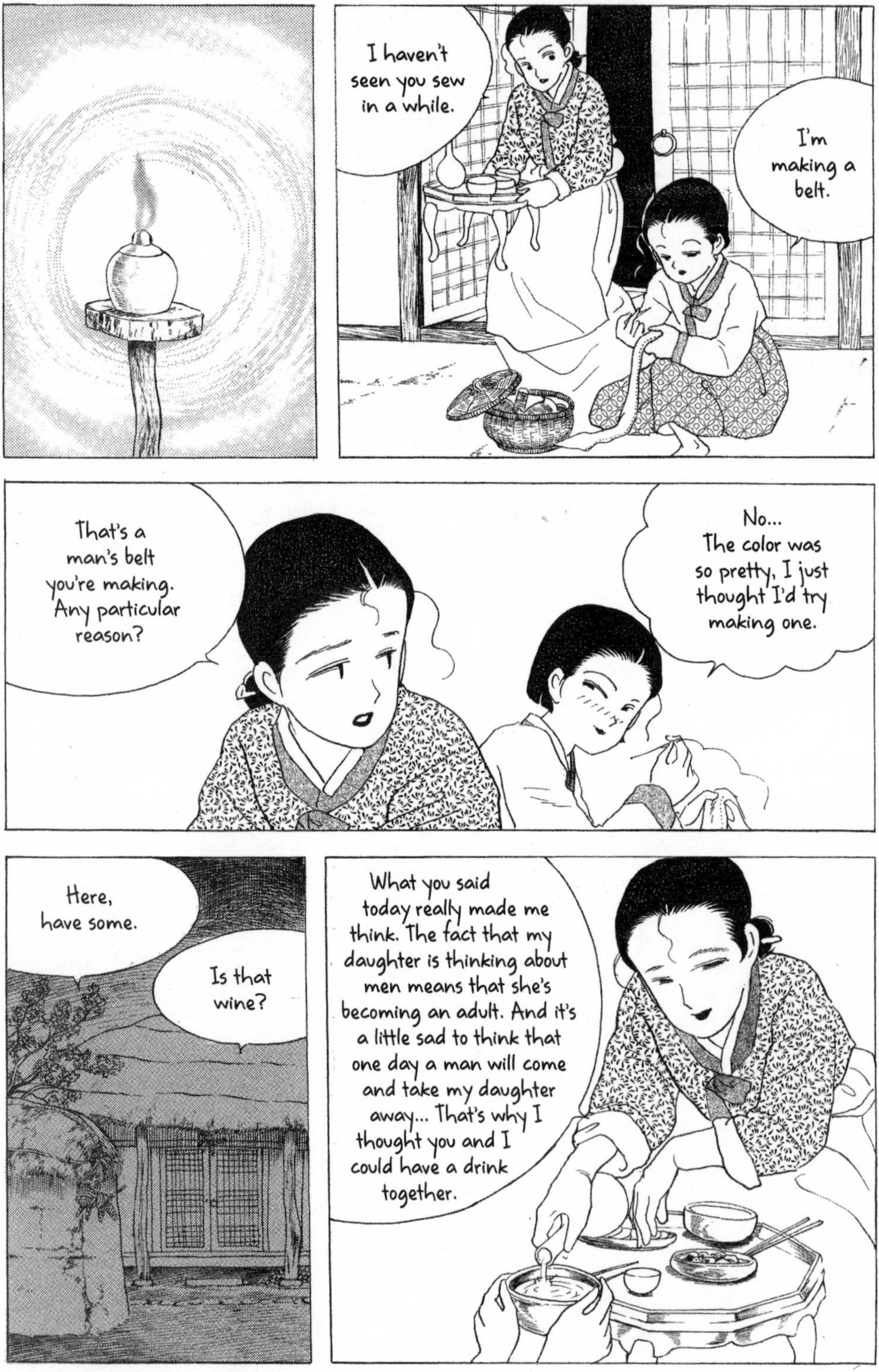
I haven't seen you sew in a while.
I'm making a belt.
That's a man's belt you're making. Any particular reason?
No... The color was so pretty, I just thought I'd try making one.
Here, have some.
Is that wine?
What you said today really made me think. The fact that my daughter is thinking about men means that she's becoming an adult. And it's a little sad to think that one day a man will come and take my daughter away... That's why I thought you and I could have a drink together.

In most households, it's the men who teach their sons how to drink. But we have no boys here, so I thought perhaps that I should teach you.

What if I get drunk?

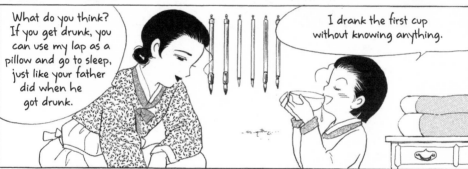

What do you think? If you get drunk, you can use my lap as a pillow and go to sleep, just like your father did when he got drunk.

I drank the first cup without knowing anything.

I drank the second cup because it's what the cup wanted.

May I have another cup?

Look at you! Are you sure this is your first time?

You said the third time's a charm, so this cup should be the best yet.

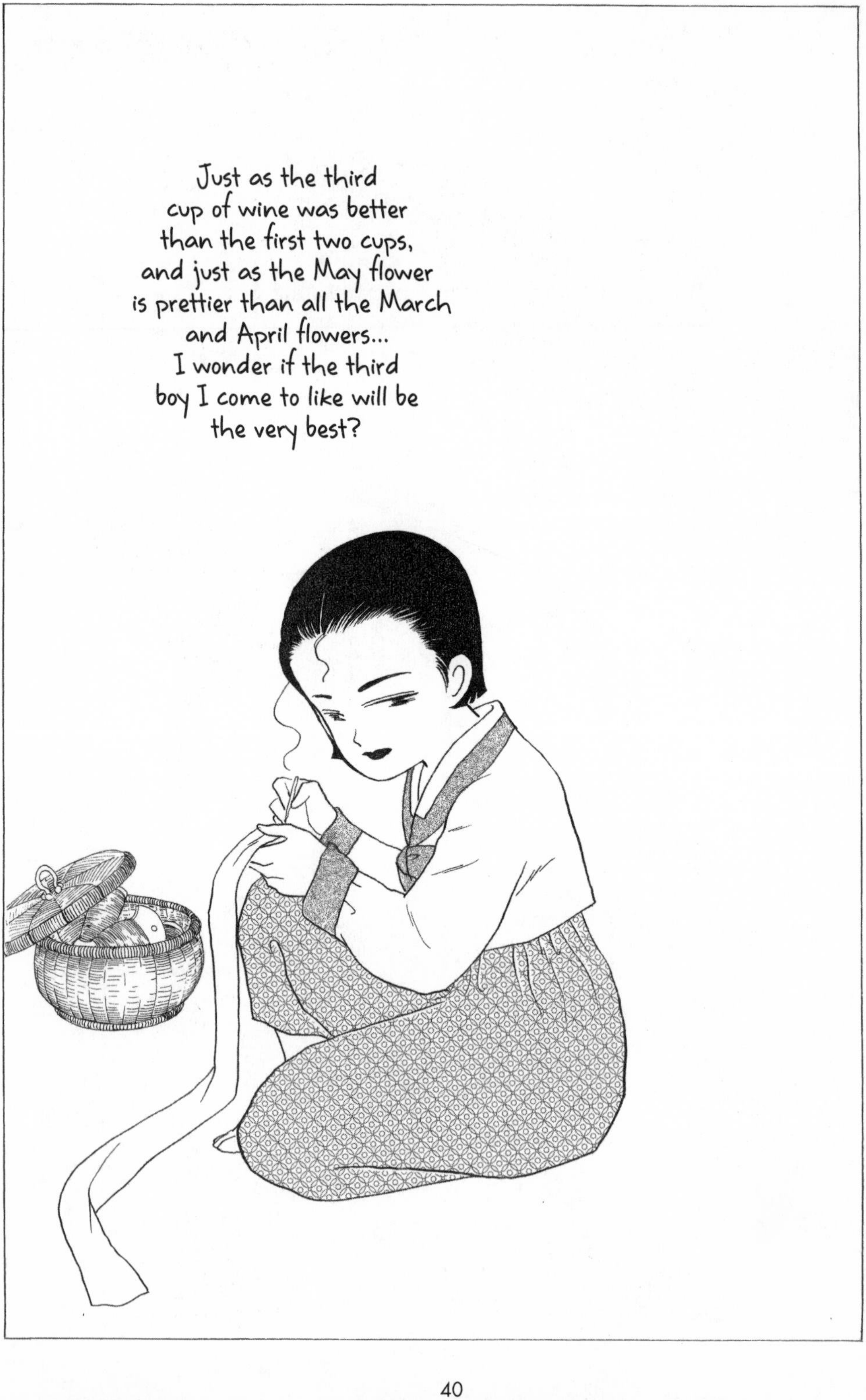
Just as the third cup of wine was better than the first two cups, and just as the May flower is prettier than all the March and April flowers... I wonder if the third boy I come to like will be the very best?

Chapter Two

DARK BLUE BELT

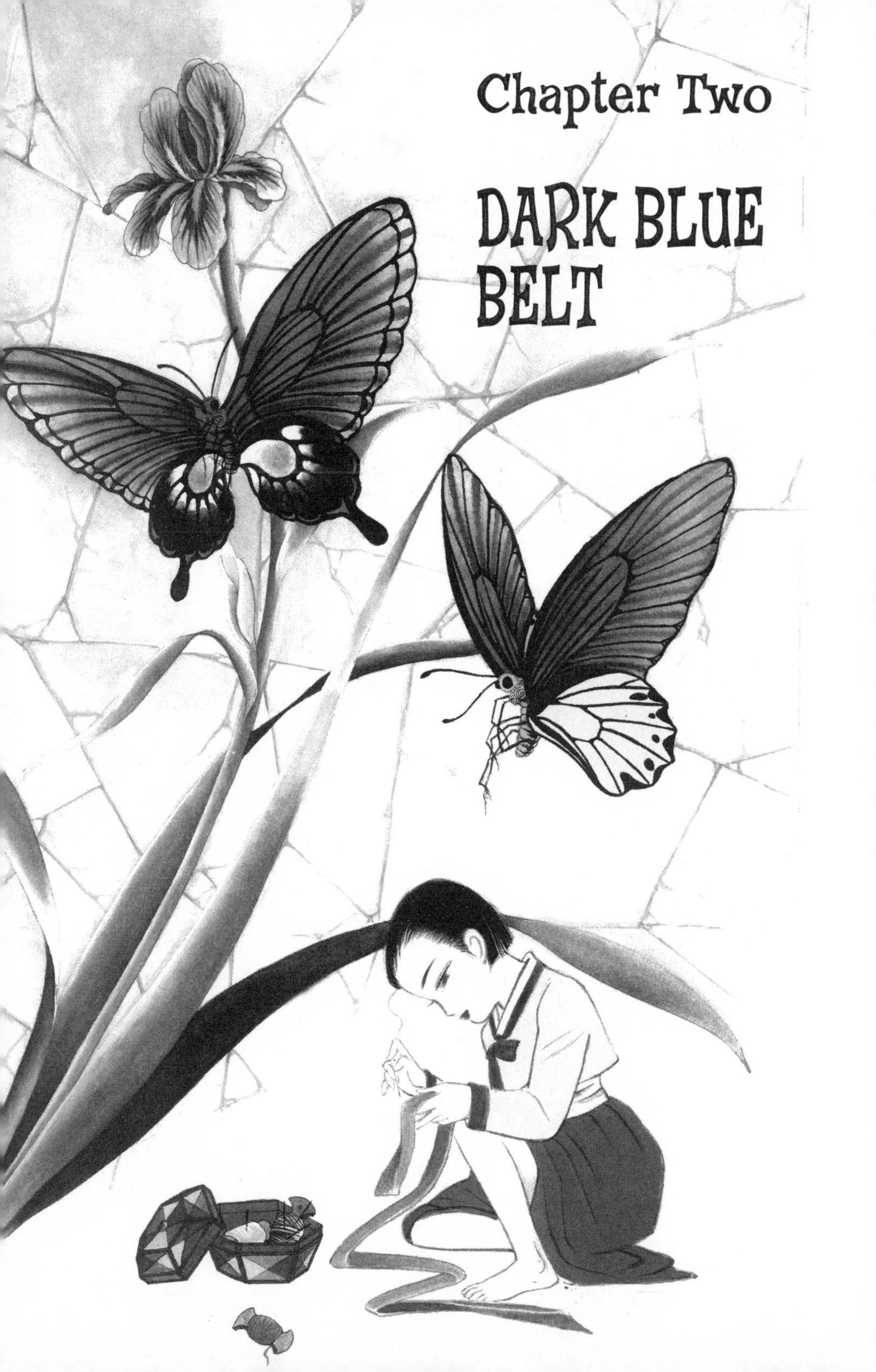

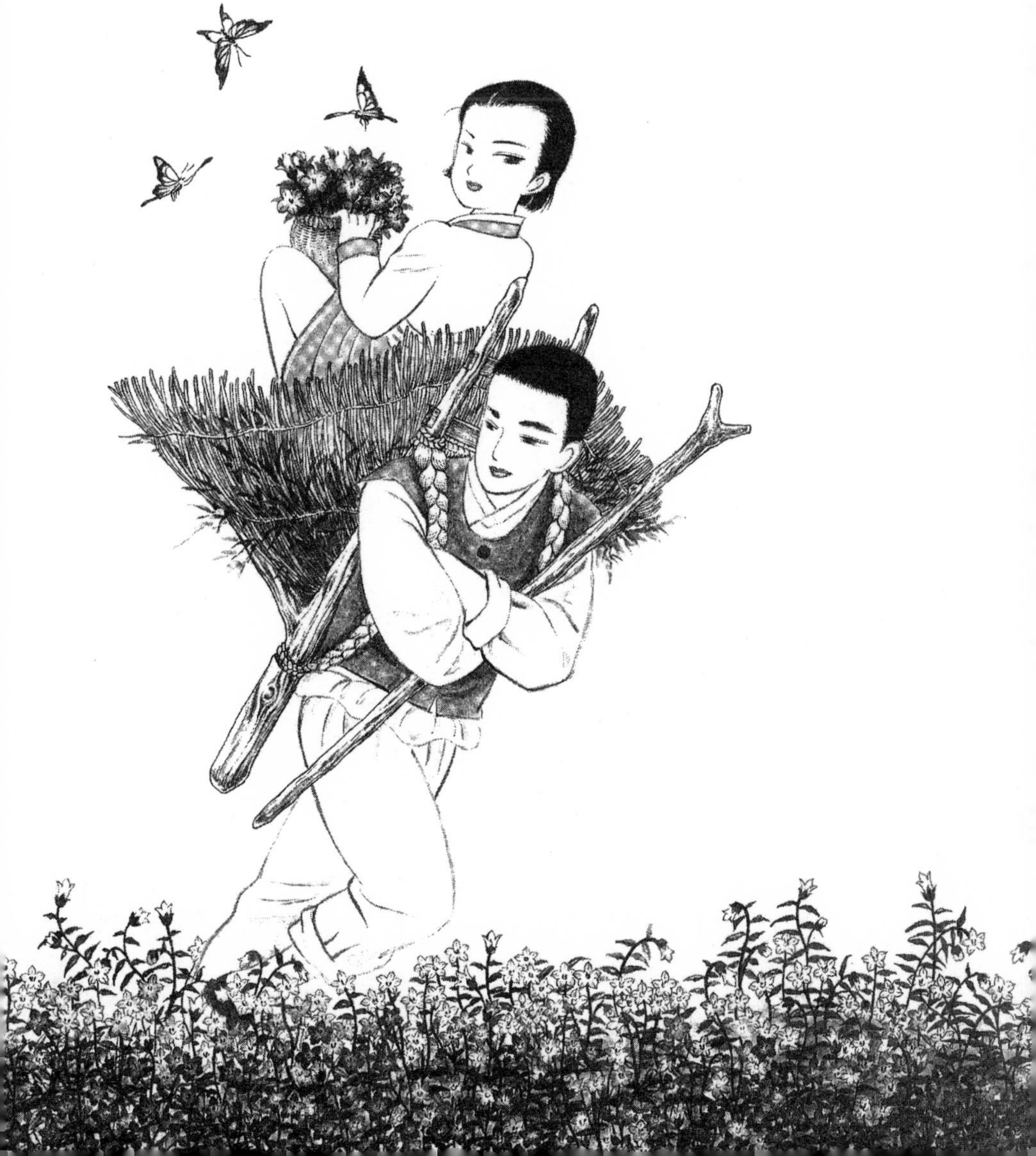

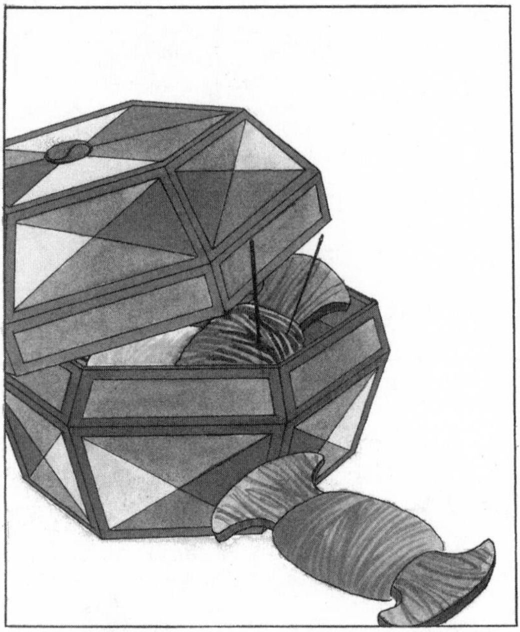

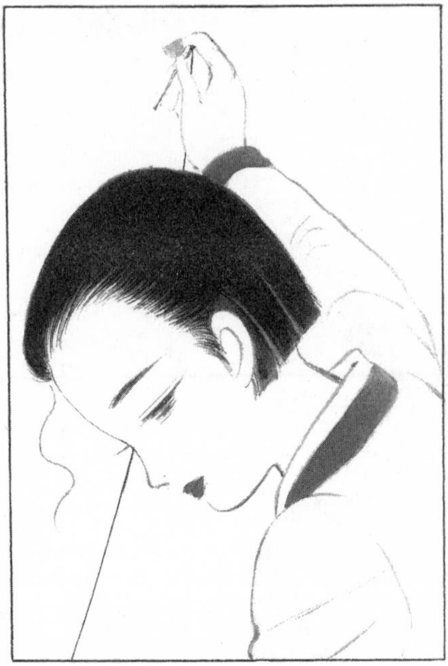

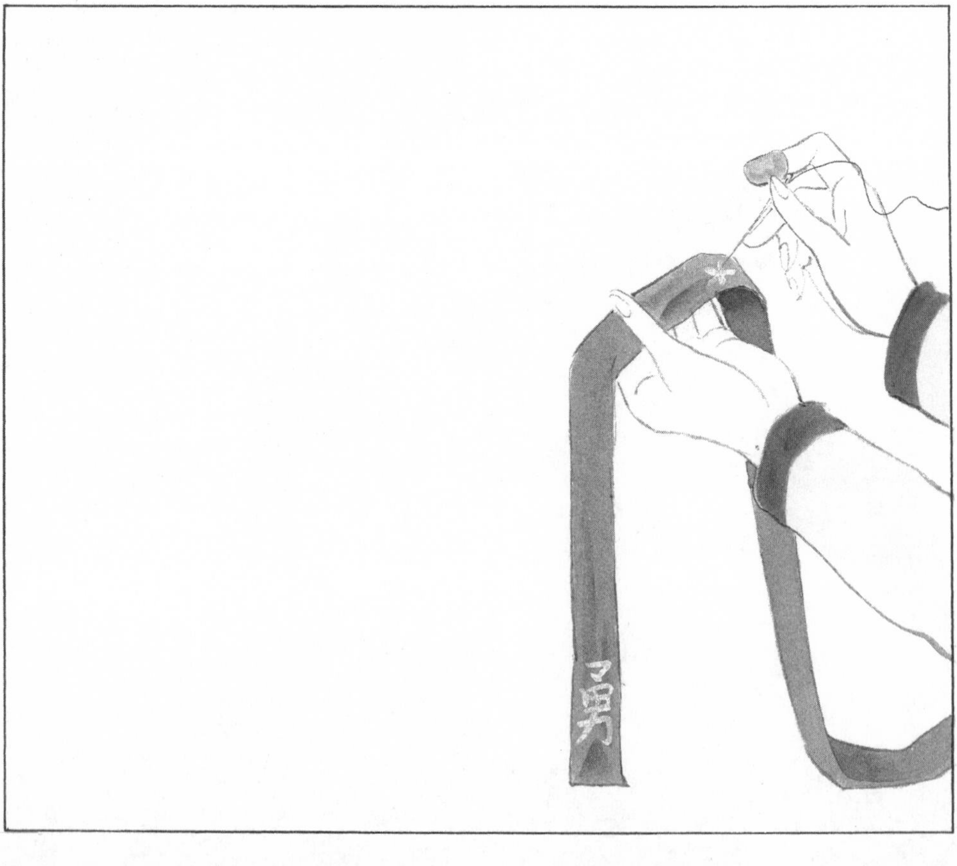
勇

Are you still working on that belt?

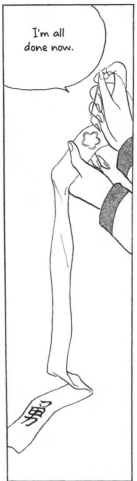

I'm all done now.

A belt doesn't need to be fancy to hold up a pair of pants, but you've embroidered words and design on it.

So who is the belt for?

Mom! I just made it because I was bored.

But why make a dark blue man's belt of all things?

45

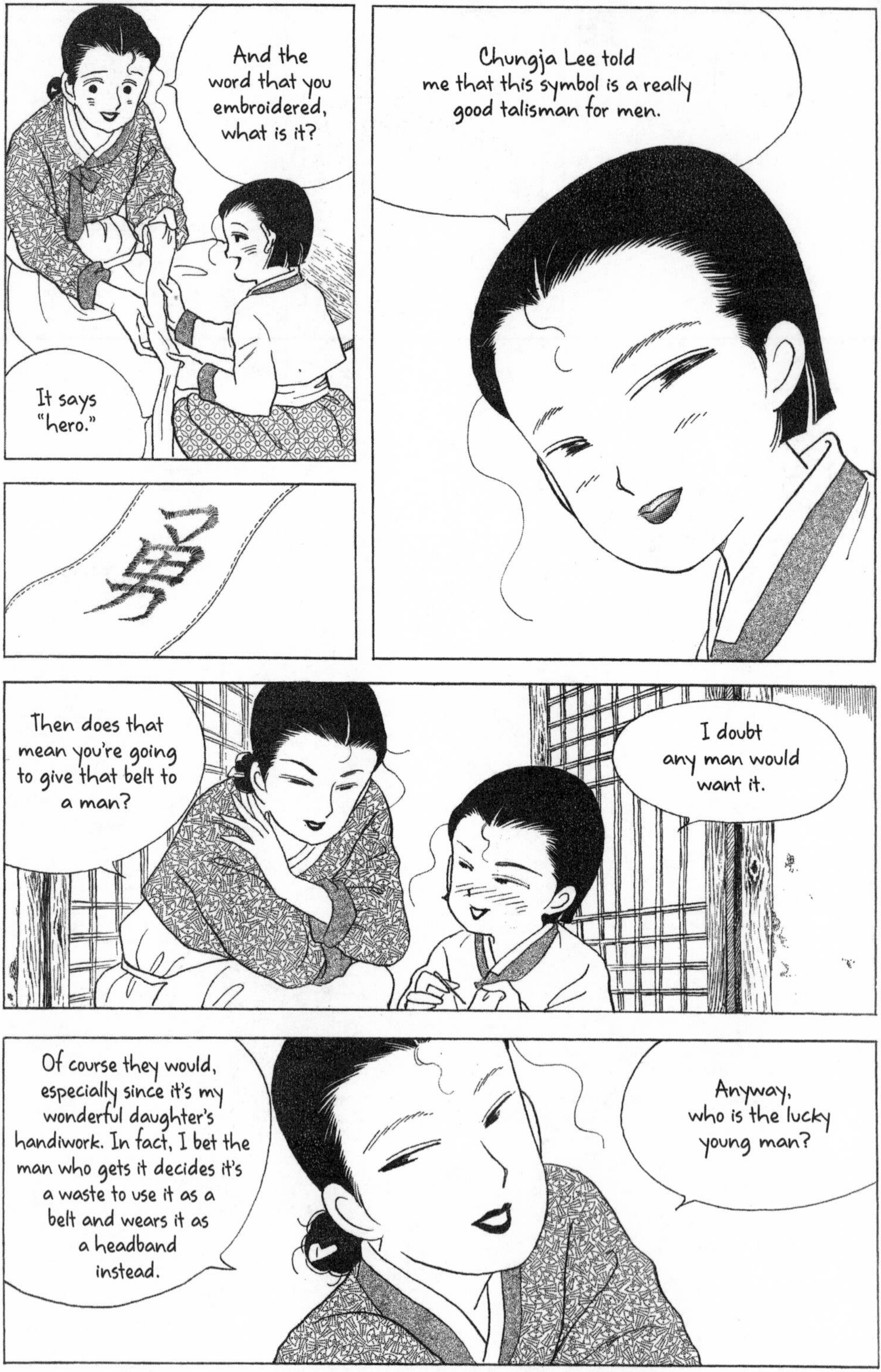
And the word that you embroidered, what is it?
It says "hero."
勇
Chungja Lee told me that this symbol is a really good talisman for men.
Then does that mean you're going to give that belt to a man?
I doubt any man would want it.
Of course they would, especially since it's my wonderful daughter's handiwork. In fact, I bet the man who gets it decides it's a waste to use it as a belt and wears it as a headband instead.
Anyway, who is the lucky young man?

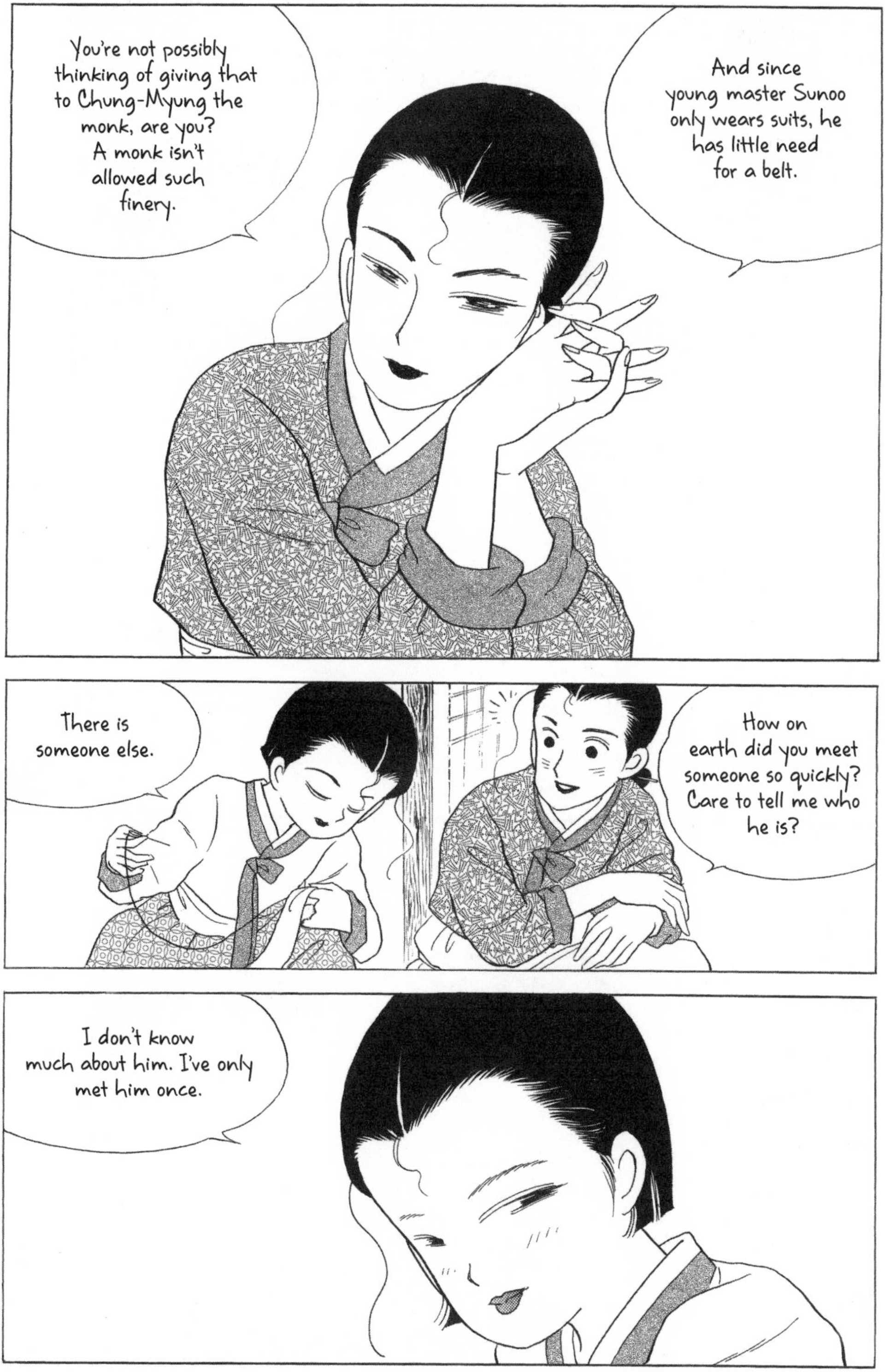
You're not possibly thinking of giving that to Chung-Myung the monk, are you? A monk isn't allowed such finery.
And since young master Sunoo only wears suits, he has little need for a belt.
There is someone else.
How on earth did you meet someone so quickly? Care to tell me who he is?
I don't know much about him. I've only met him once.

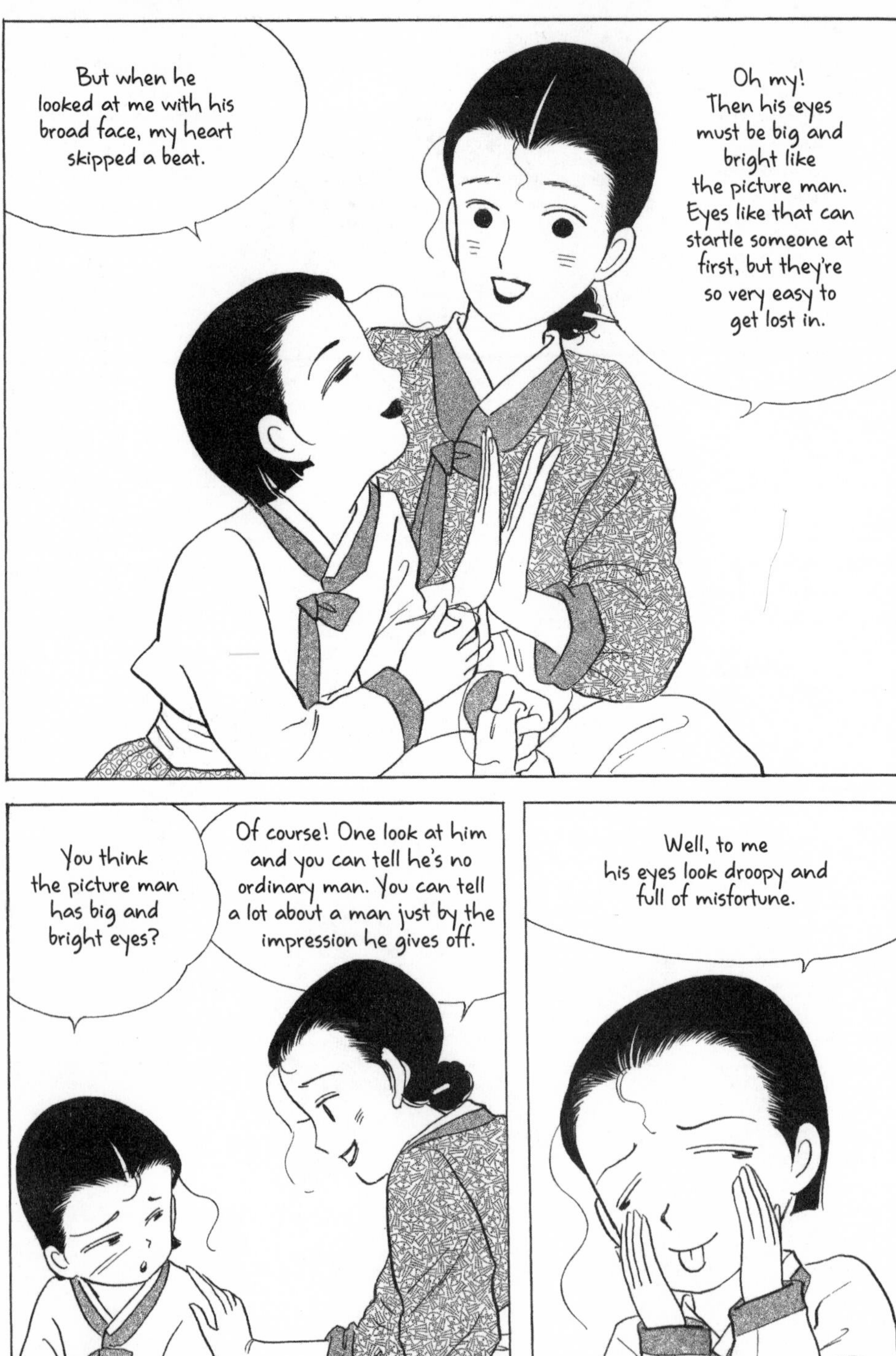
But when he looked at me with his broad face, my heart skipped a beat.
Oh my! Then his eyes must be big and bright like the picture man. Eyes like that can startle someone at first, but they're so very easy to get lost in.
You think the picture man has big and bright eyes?
Of course! One look at him and you can tell he's no ordinary man. You can tell a lot about a man just by the impression he gives off.
Well, to me his eyes look droopy and full of misfortune.

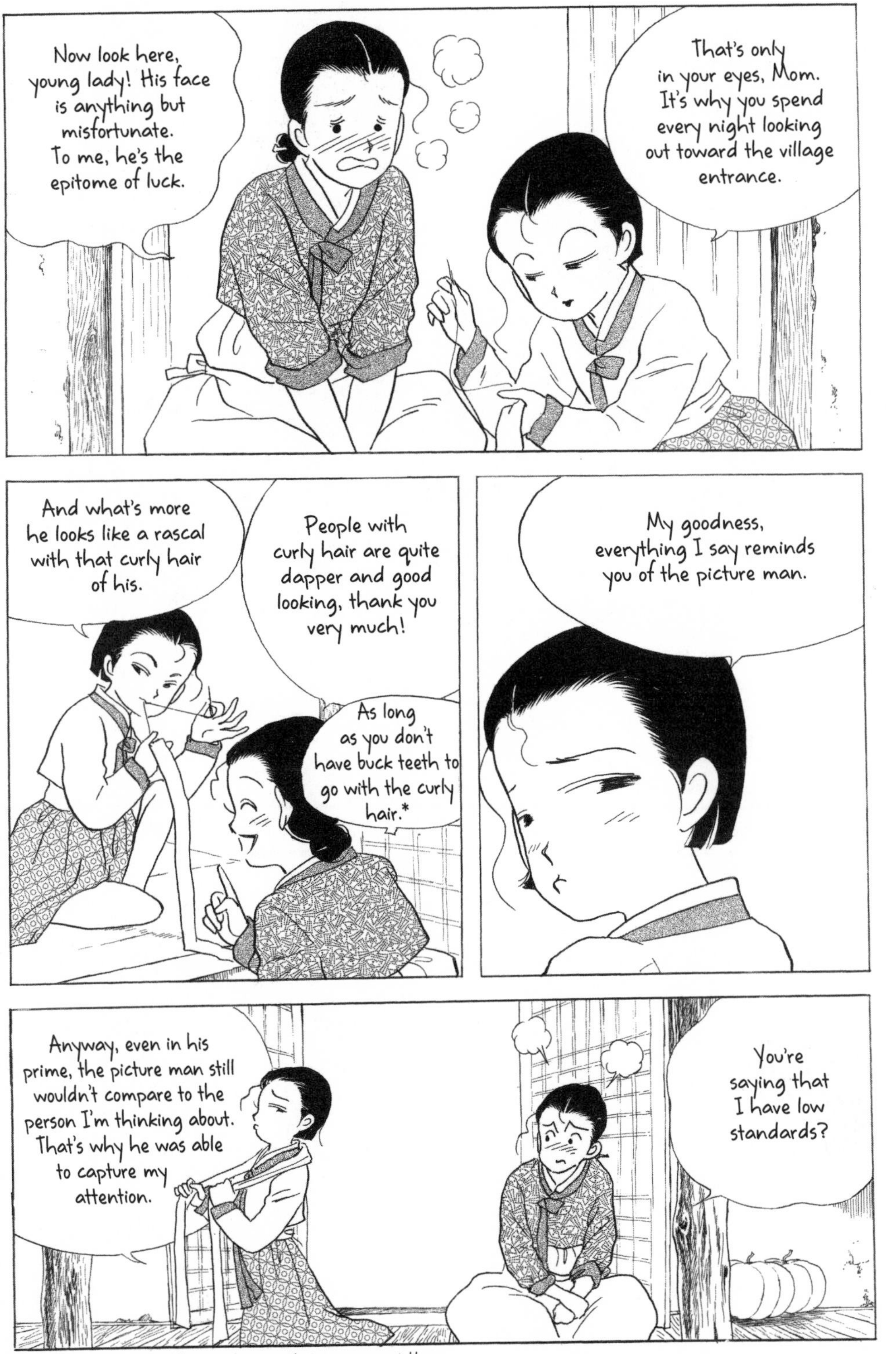
Now look here, young lady! His face is anything but misfortunate. To me, he's the epitome of luck.
That's only in your eyes, Mom. It's why you spend every night looking out toward the village entrance.
And what's more he looks like a rascal with that curly hair of his.
People with curly hair are quite dapper and good looking, thank you very much!
As long as you don't have buck teeth to go with the curly hair.*
My goodness, everything I say reminds you of the picture man.
Anyway, even in his prime, the picture man still wouldn't compare to the person I'm thinking about. That's why he was able to capture my attention.
You're saying that I have low standards?

*Having both curly hair and buck teeth means that you are very stubborn.

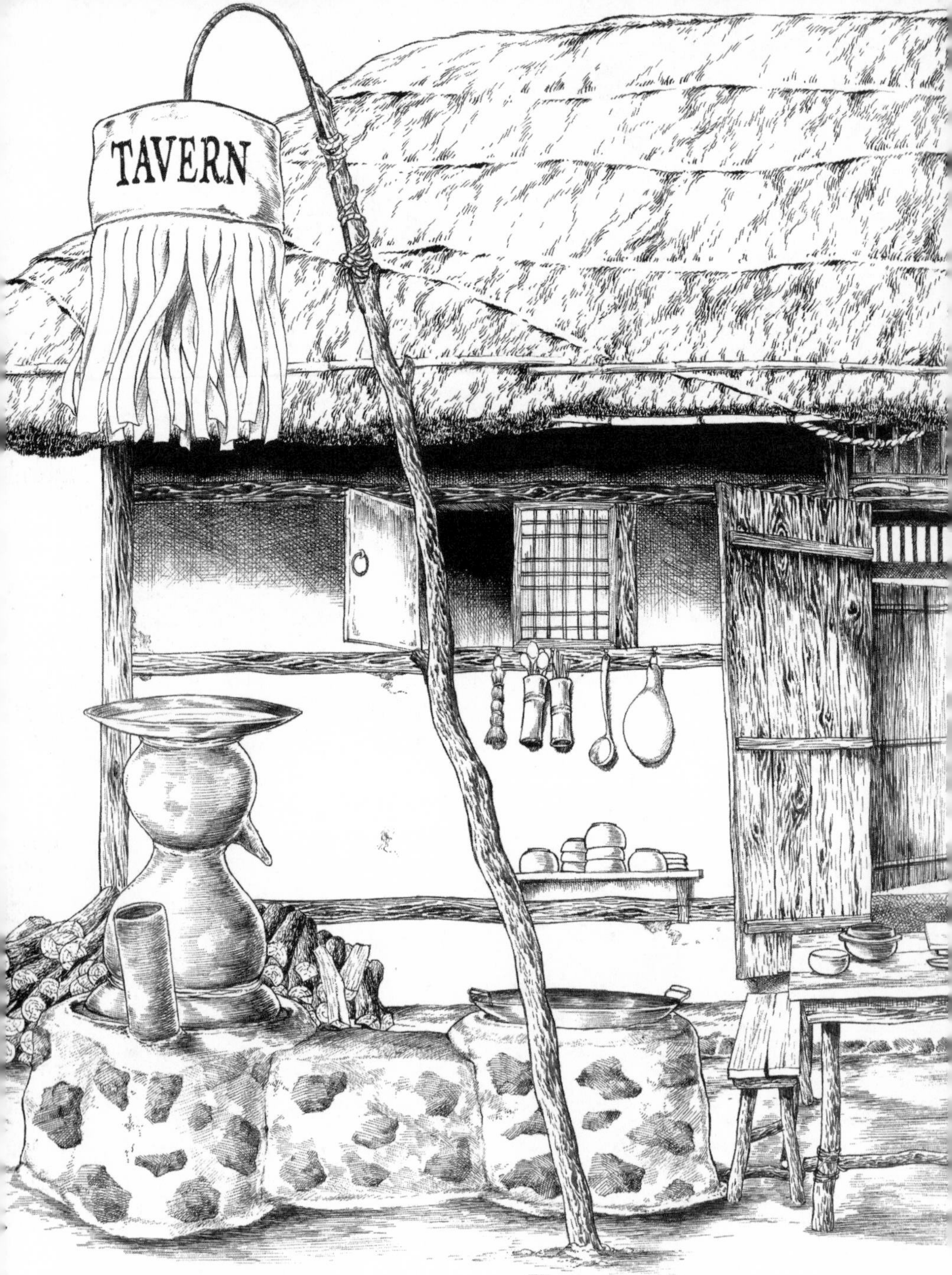
TAVERN

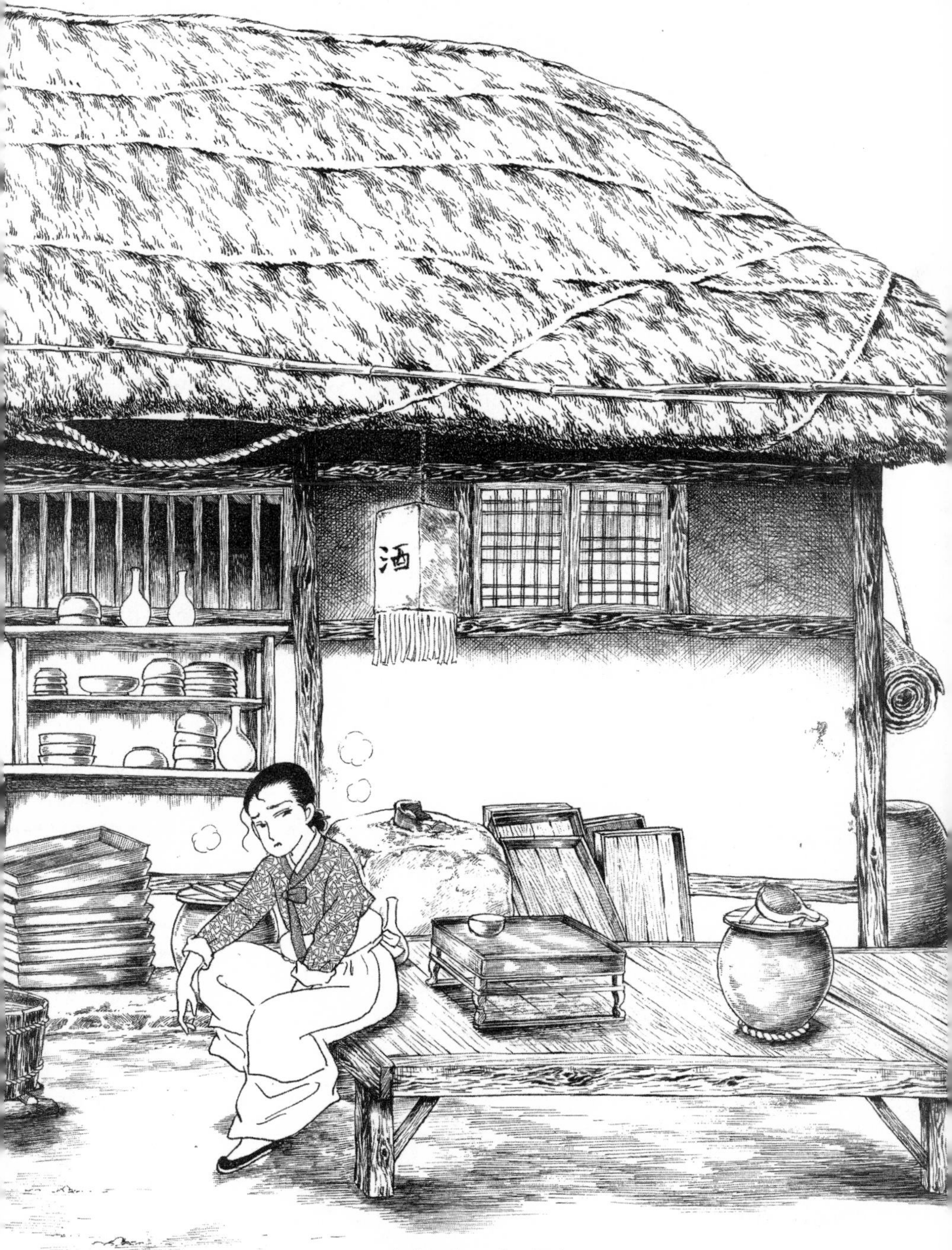
酒

What's so bad about my picture man?
I think he looks very good for his age.
What would she know? She's still just a little girl.
Child, I'll be keeping a close eye on you.
We'll see what kind of man you bring home.

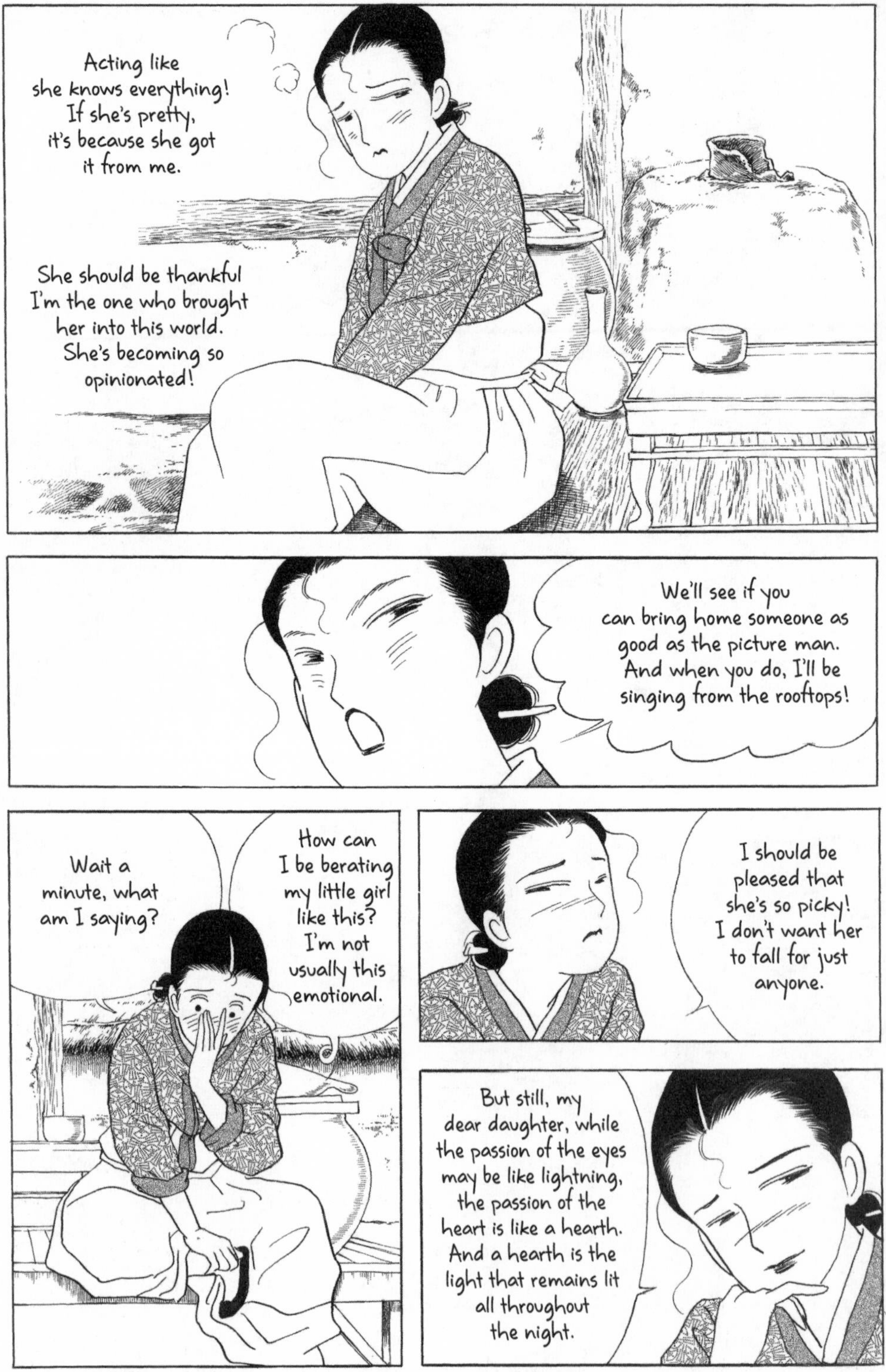
Acting like she knows everything! If she's pretty, it's because she got it from me.
She should be thankful I'm the one who brought her into this world. She's becoming so opinionated!
We'll see if you can bring home someone as good as the picture man. And when you do, I'll be singing from the rooftops!
Wait a minute, what am I saying?
How can I be berating my little girl like this? I'm not usually this emotional.
I should be pleased that she's so picky! I don't want her to fall for just anyone.
But still, my dear daughter, while the passion of the eyes may be like lightning, the passion of the heart is like a hearth. And a hearth is the light that remains lit all throughout the night.

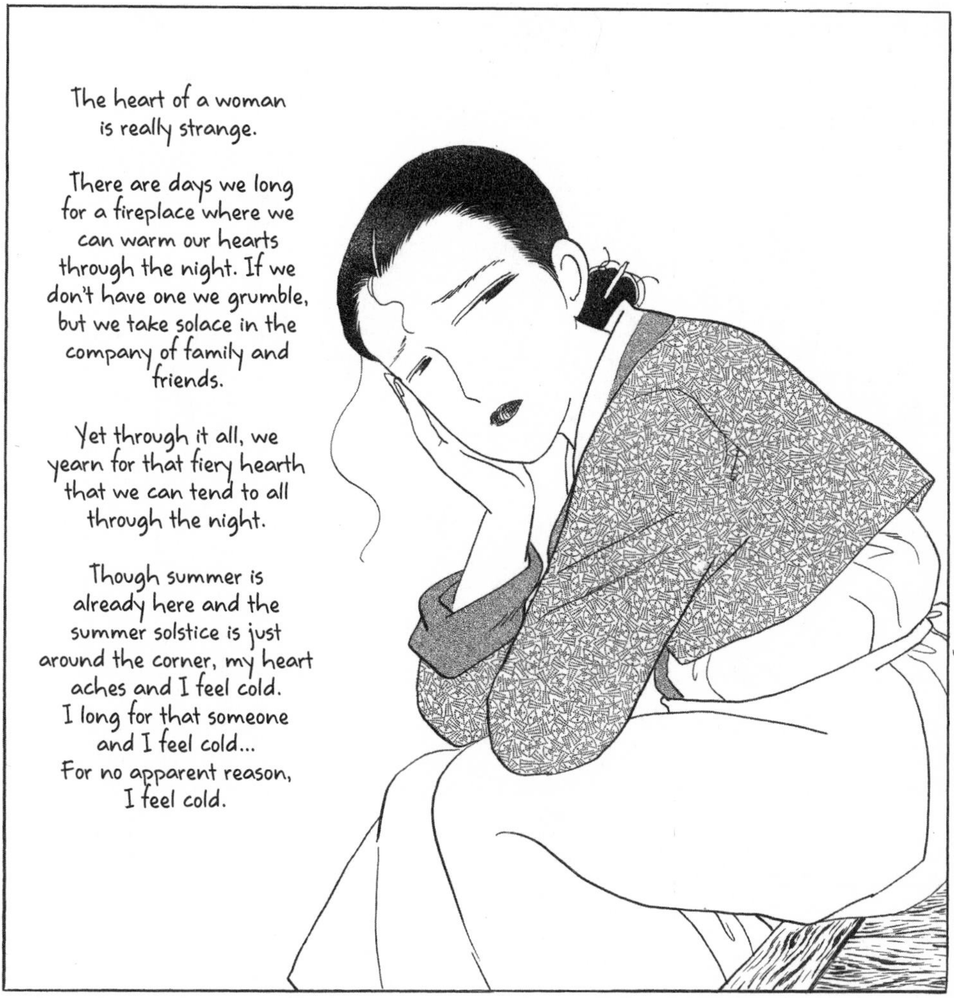
The heart of a woman is really strange.
There are days we long for a fireplace where we can warm our hearts through the night. If we don't have one we grumble, but we take solace in the company of family and friends.
Yet through it all, we yearn for that fiery hearth that we can tend to all through the night.
Though summer is already here and the summer solstice is just around the corner, my heart aches and I feel cold. I long for that someone and I feel cold... For no apparent reason, I feel cold.

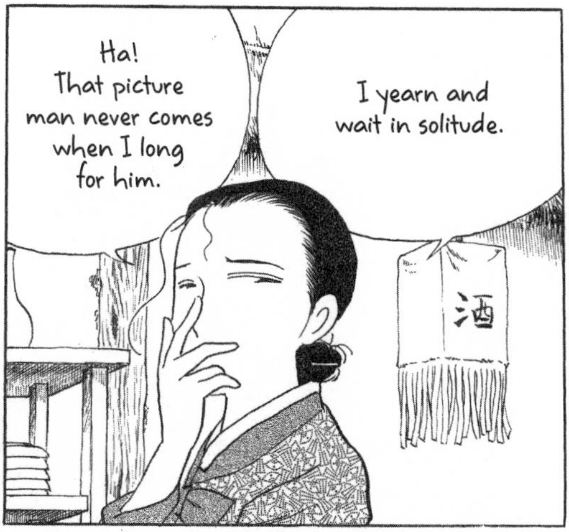
Ha! That picture man never comes when I long for him.
I yearn and wait in solitude.
酒

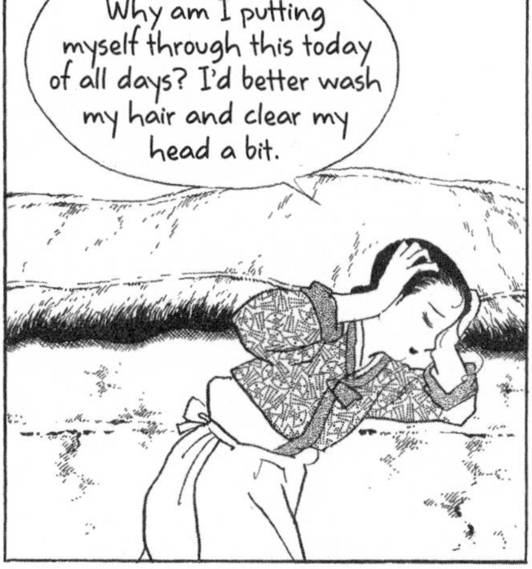
Why am I putting myself through this today of all days? I'd better wash my hair and clear my head a bit.

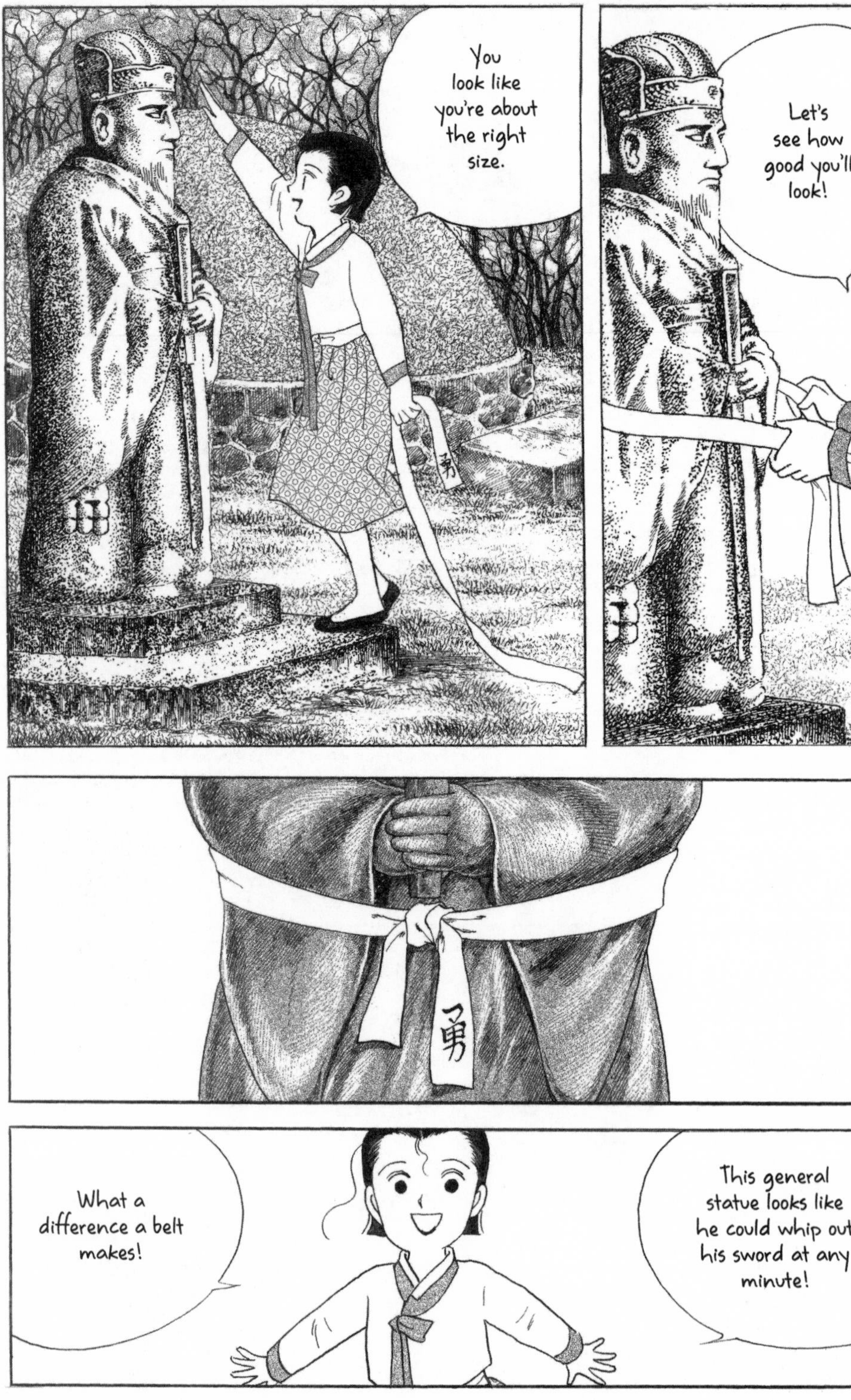
You look like you're about the right size.
勇
Let's see how good you'll look!
勇
What a difference a belt makes!
This general statue looks like he could whip out his sword at any minute!

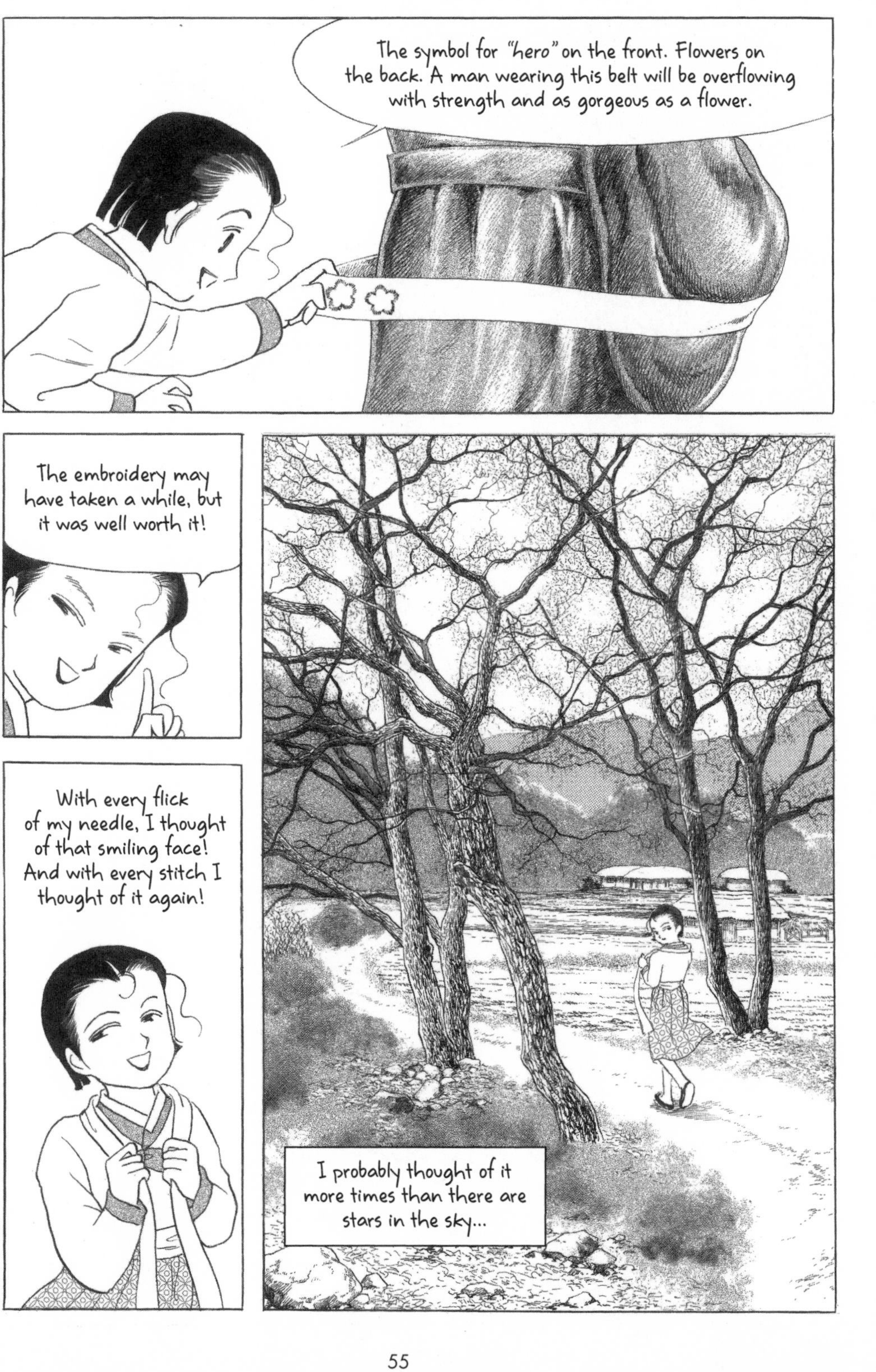
The symbol for "hero" on the front. Flowers on the back. A man wearing this belt will be overflowing with strength and as gorgeous as a flower.
The embroidery may have taken a while, but it was well worth it!
With every flick of my needle, I thought of that smiling face! And with every stitch I thought of it again!
I probably thought of it more times than there are stars in the sky...

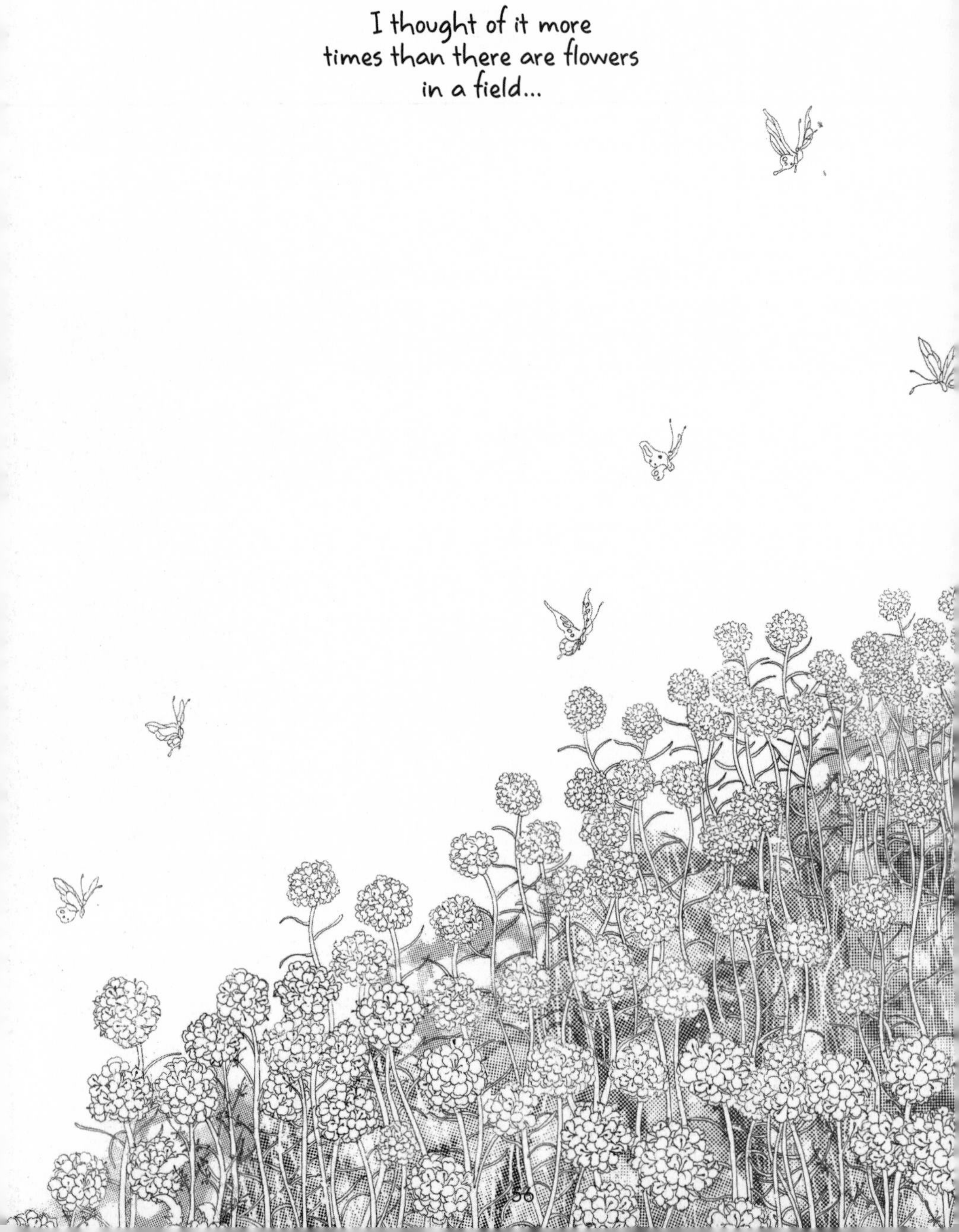
I thought of it more times than there are flowers in a field...

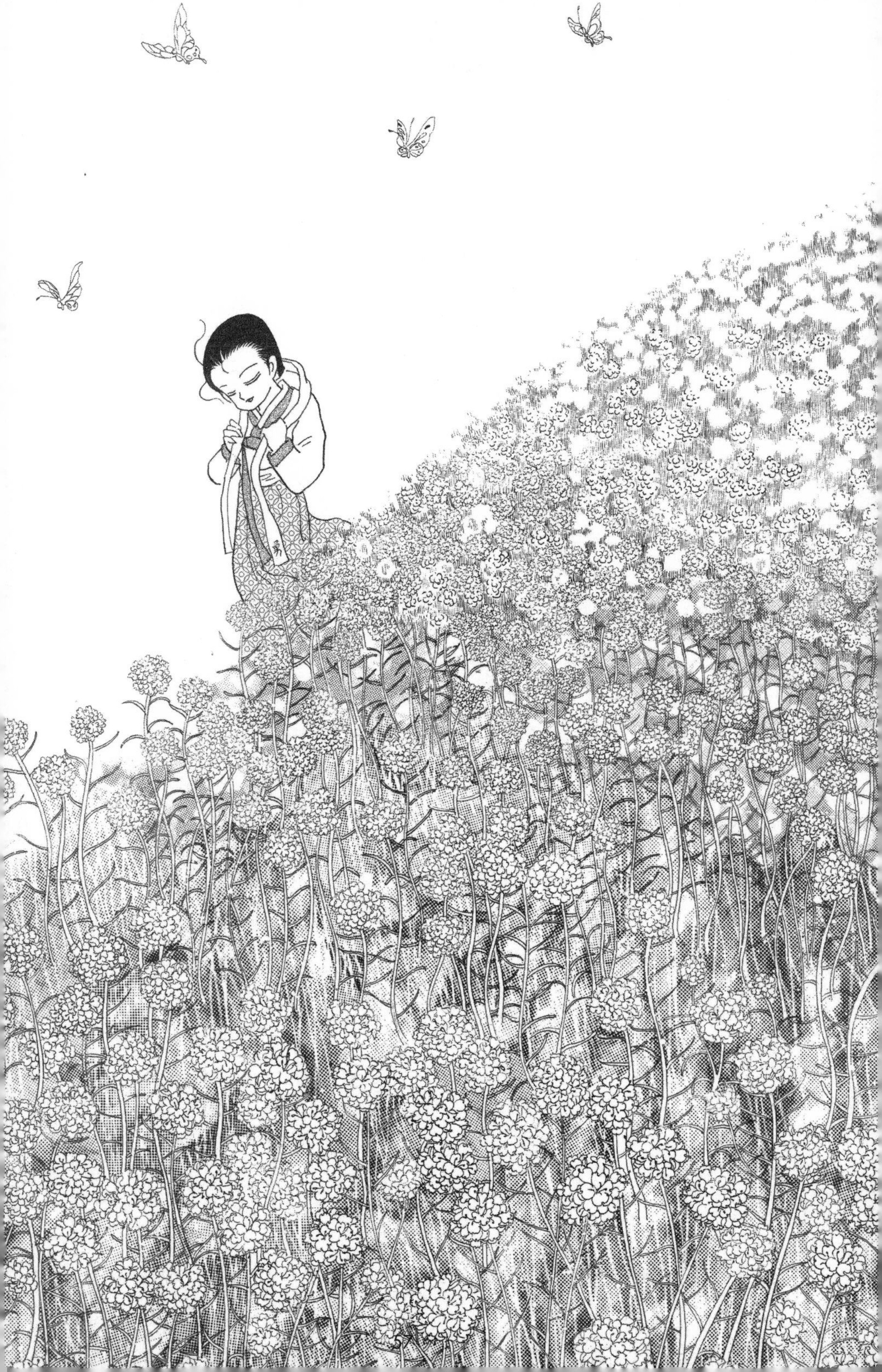

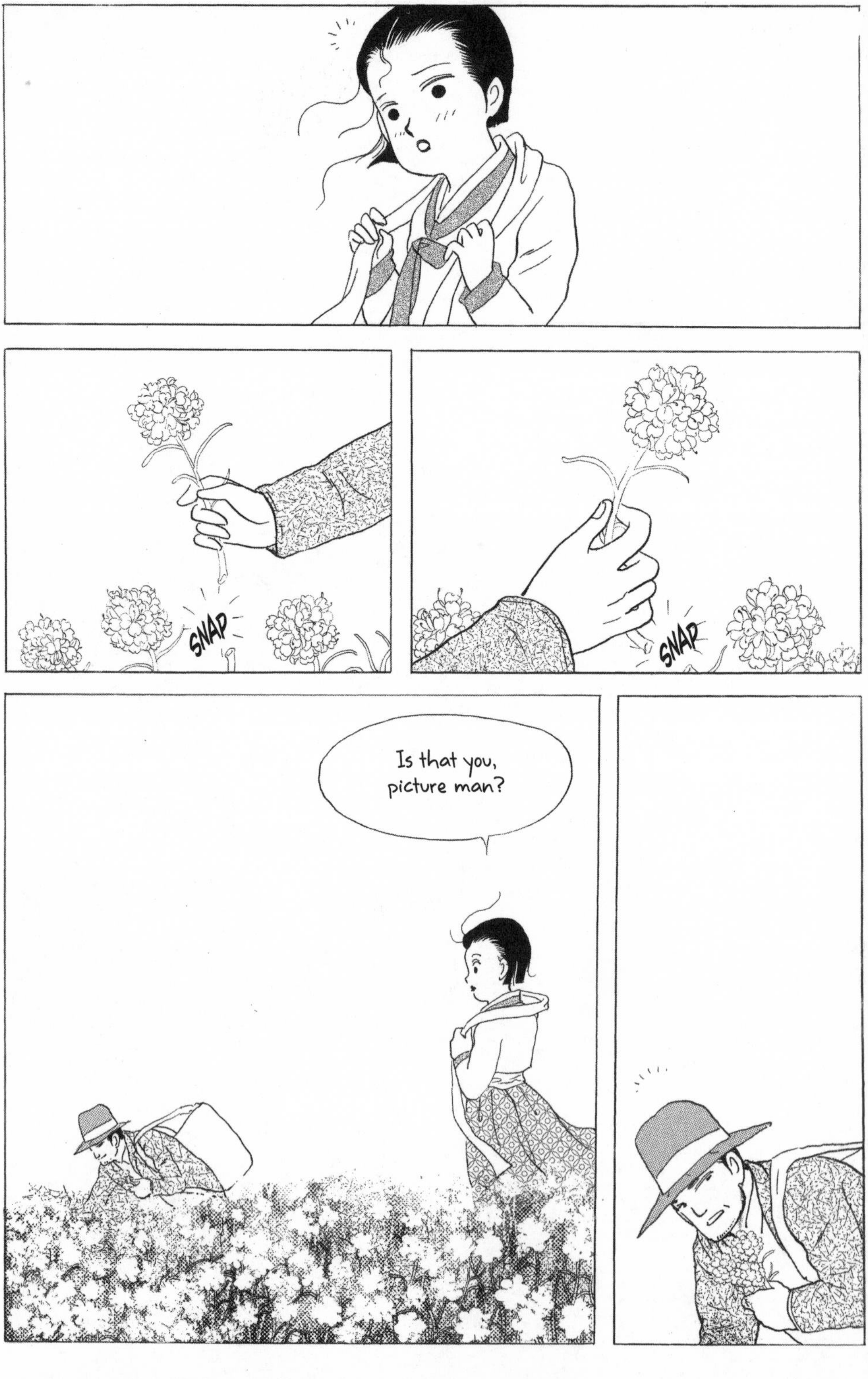
SNAP
SNAP
Is that you, picture man?

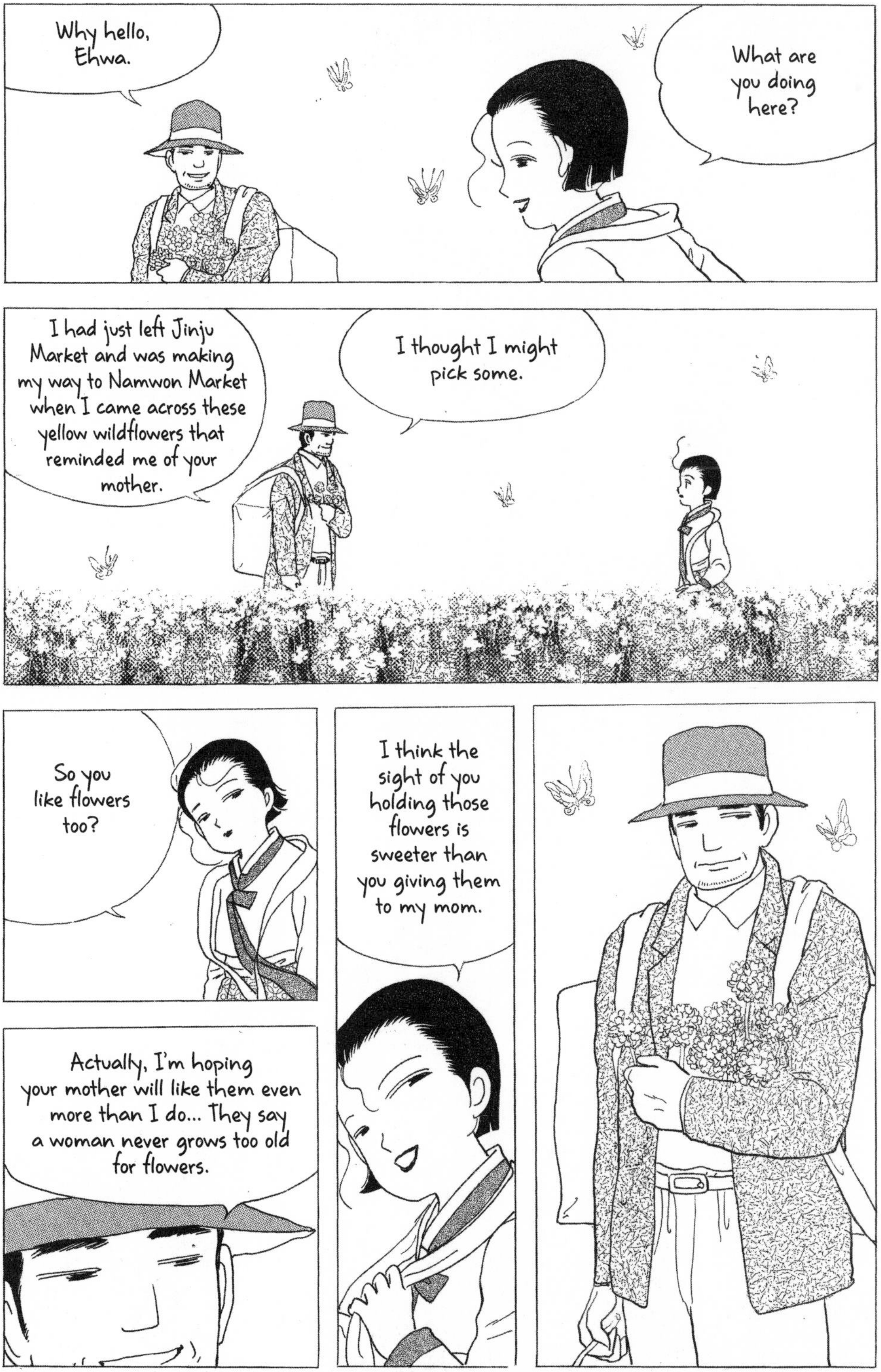
Why hello, Ehwa.
What are you doing here?
I had just left Jinju Market and was making my way to Namwon Market when I came across these yellow wildflowers that reminded me of your mother.
I thought I might pick some.
So you like flowers too?
Actually, I'm hoping your mother will like them even more than I do... They say a woman never grows too old for flowers.
I think the sight of you holding those flowers is sweeter than you giving them to my mom.

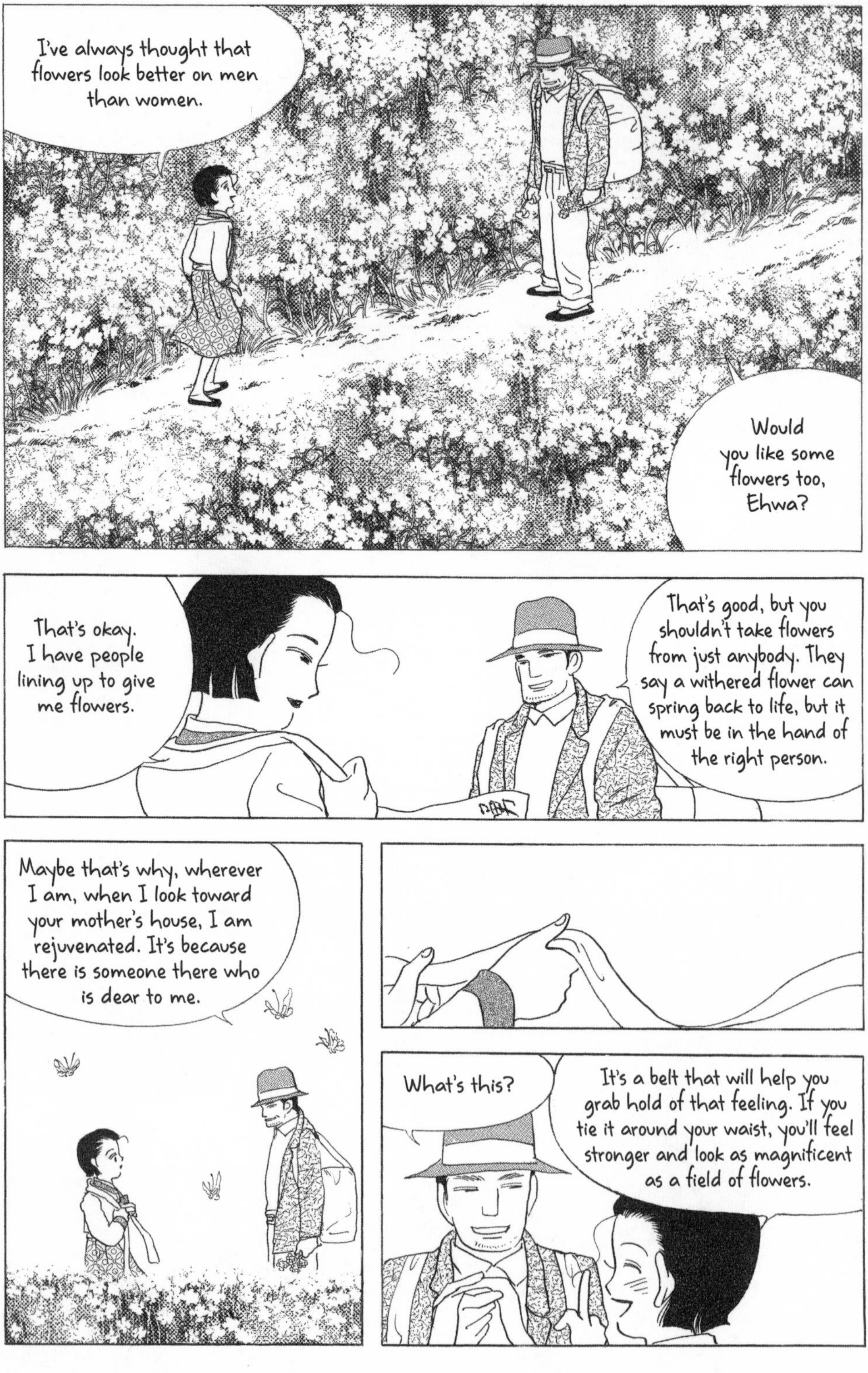
I've always thought that flowers look better on men than women.
Would you like some flowers too, Ehwa?
That's okay. I have people lining up to give me flowers.
That's good, but you shouldn't take flowers from just anybody. They say a withered flower can spring back to life, but it must be in the hand of the right person.
Maybe that's why, wherever I am, when I look toward your mother's house, I am rejuvenated. It's because there is someone there who is dear to me.
What's this?
It's a belt that will help you grab hold of that feeling. If you tie it around your waist, you'll feel stronger and look as magnificent as a field of flowers.

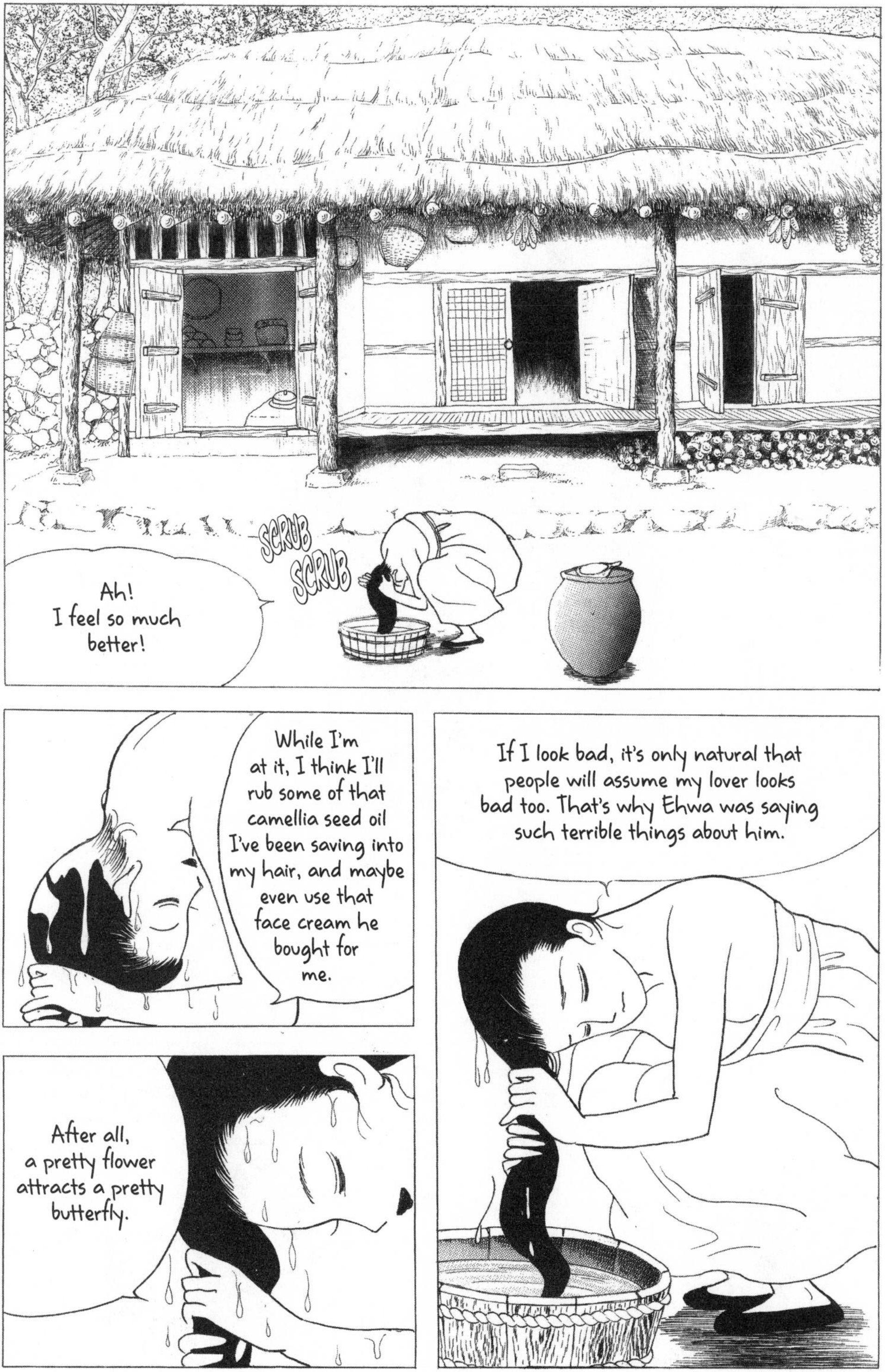
SCRUB SCRUB
Ah! I feel so much better!
While I'm at it, I think I'll rub some of that camellia seed oil I've been saving into my hair, and maybe even use that face cream he bought for me.
After all, a pretty flower attracts a pretty butterfly.
If I look bad, it's only natural that people will assume my lover looks bad too. That's why Ehwa was saying such terrible things about him.

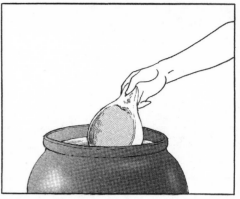

I told you to call me when you wash your hair.

How else can I pour clean water over it?

Who is that? How dare you?!

Huh?

62

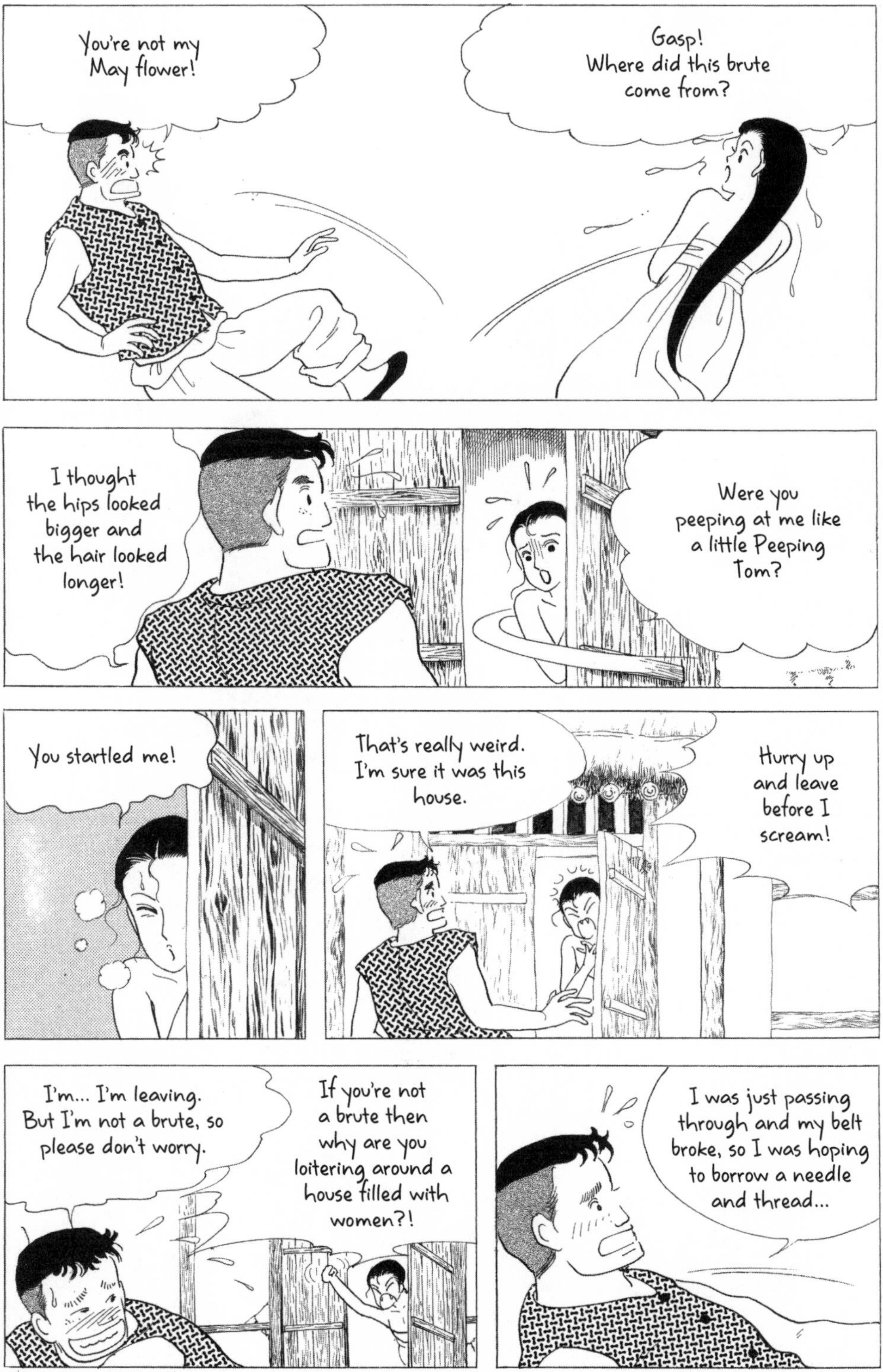
You're not my May flower!
Gasp! Where did this brute come from?
I thought the hips looked bigger and the hair looked longer!
Were you peeping at me like a little Peeping Tom?
You startled me!
That's really weird. I'm sure it was this house.
Hurry up and leave before I scream!
I'm... I'm leaving. But I'm not a brute, so please don't worry.
If you're not a brute then why are you loitering around a house filled with women?!
I was just passing through and my belt broke, so I was hoping to borrow a needle and thread...

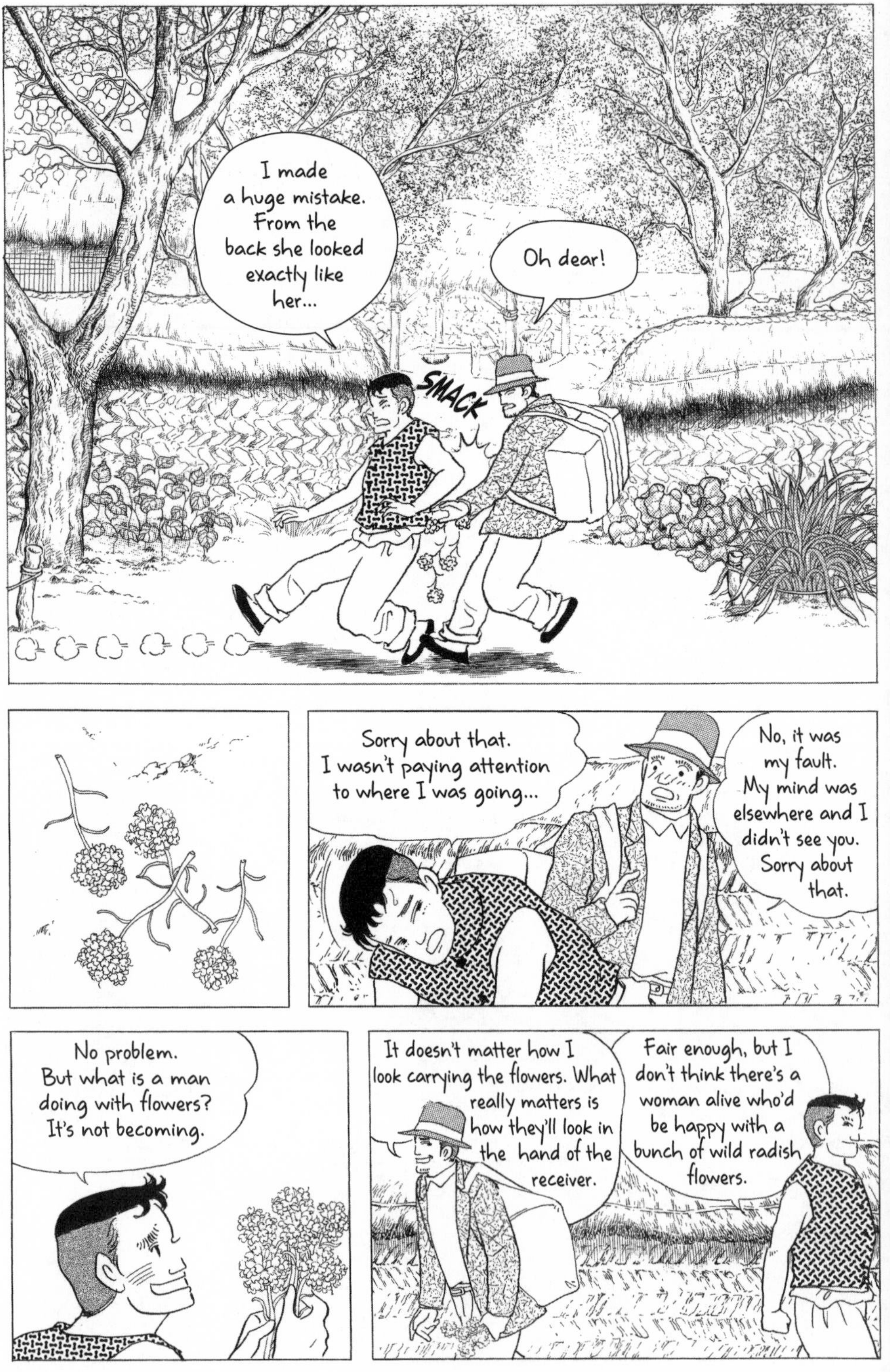
I made a huge mistake. From the back she looked exactly like her...
Oh dear!
SMACK
Sorry about that. I wasn't paying attention to where I was going...
No, it was my fault. My mind was elsewhere and I didn't see you. Sorry about that.
No problem. But what is a man doing with flowers? It's not becoming.
It doesn't matter how I look carrying the flowers. What really matters is how they'll look in the hand of the receiver.
Fair enough, but I don't think there's a woman alive who'd be happy with a bunch of wild radish flowers.

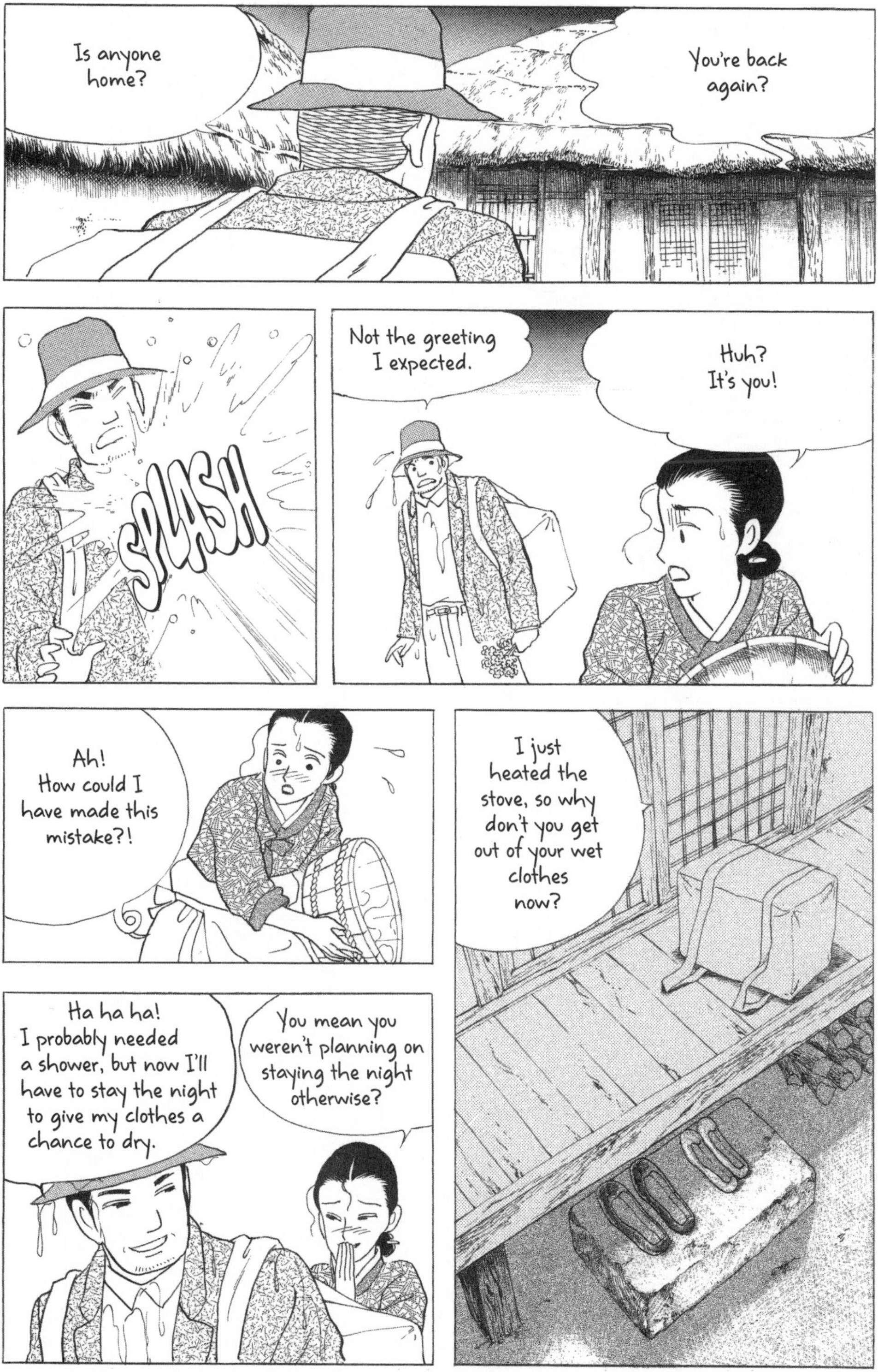
Is anyone home?
You're back again?
SPLASH
Not the greeting I expected.
Huh? It's you!
Ah! How could I have made this mistake?!
Ha ha ha! I probably needed a shower, but now I'll have to stay the night to give my clothes a chance to dry.
You mean you weren't planning on staying the night otherwise?
I just heated the stove, so why don't you get out of your wet clothes now?

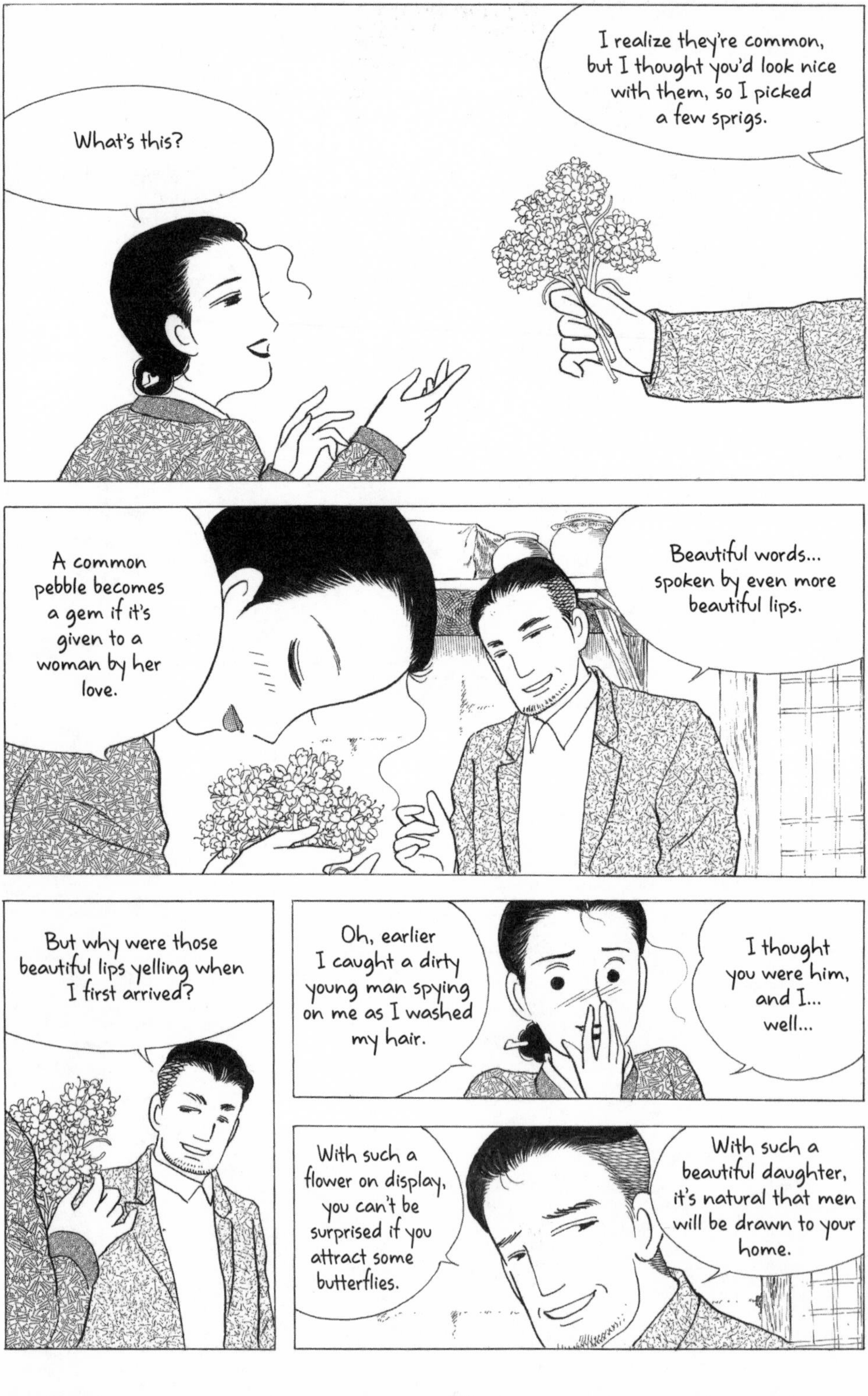
What's this?
I realize they're common, but I thought you'd look nice with them, so I picked a few sprigs.
A common pebble becomes a gem if it's given to a woman by her love.
Beautiful words... spoken by even more beautiful lips.
But why were those beautiful lips yelling when I first arrived?
Oh, earlier I caught a dirty young man spying on me as I washed my hair.
I thought you were him, and I... well...
With such a flower on display, you can't be surprised if you attract some butterflies.
With such a beautiful daughter, it's natural that men will be drawn to your home.

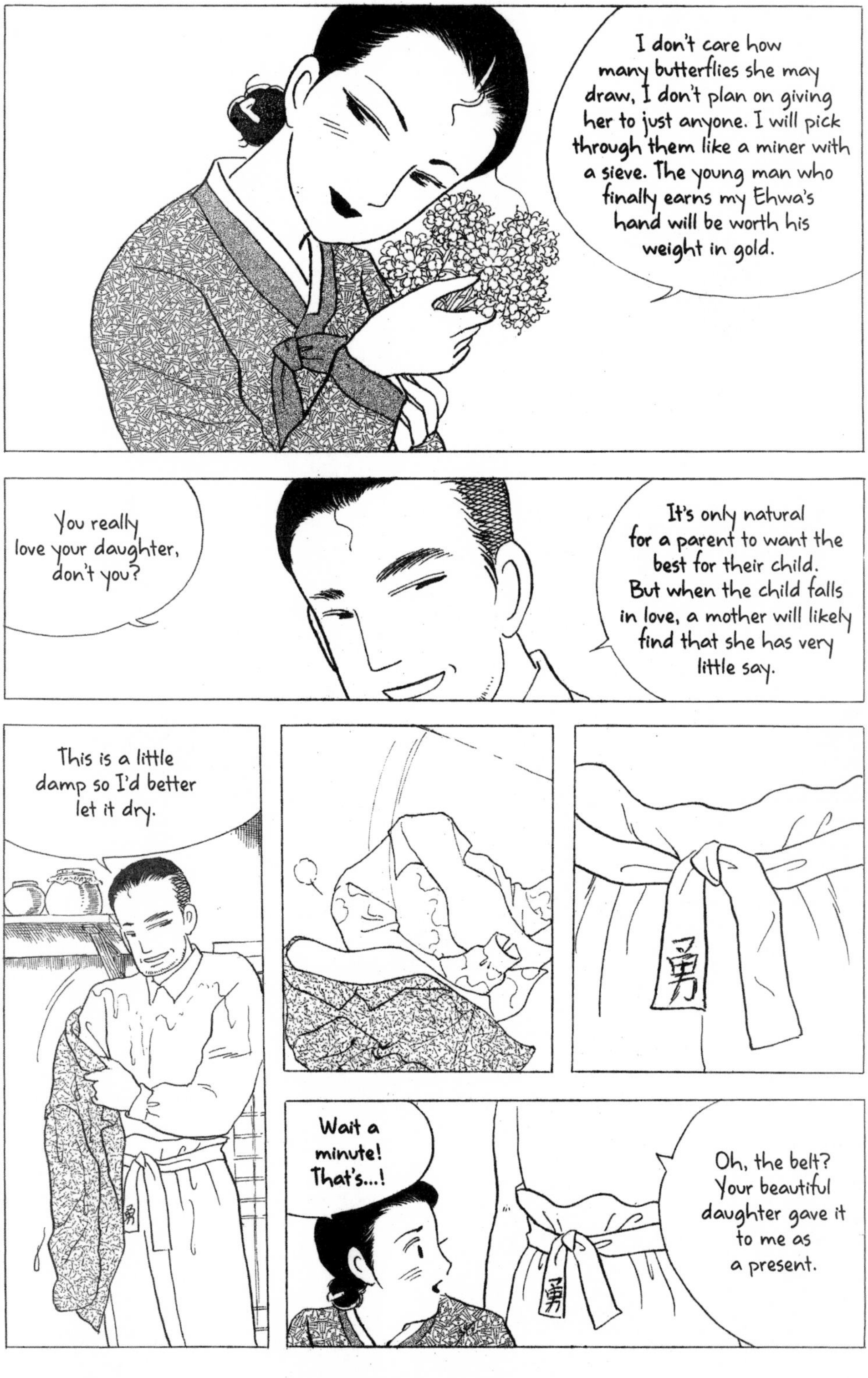
I don't care how many butterflies she may draw, I don't plan on giving her to just anyone. I will pick through them like a miner with a sieve. The young man who finally earns my Ehwa's hand will be worth his weight in gold.
You really love your daughter, don't you?
It's only natural for a parent to want the best for their child. But when the child falls in love, a mother will likely find that she has very little say.
This is a little damp so I'd better let it dry.
勇
勇
Wait a minute! That's...!
勇
Oh, the belt? Your beautiful daughter gave it to me as a present.

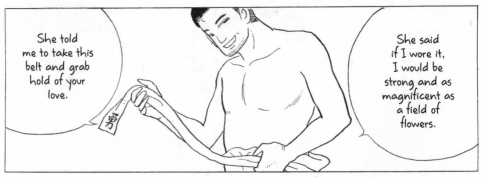

She told me to take this belt and grab hold of your love.

She said if I wore it, I would be strong and as magnificent as a field of flowers.

When a man brags about his strength, a woman can only assume he's trying to seduce her.

On a day like today, on a night like this...if I can't brag about my strength, then when can I?!

Audacious little girl!

Were you staying up nights to embroider that belt just to make me restless?

Are you also in love with a man with this kind of face, these kind of eyes, and this kind of voice? Is that why you were sewing a dark blue belt?

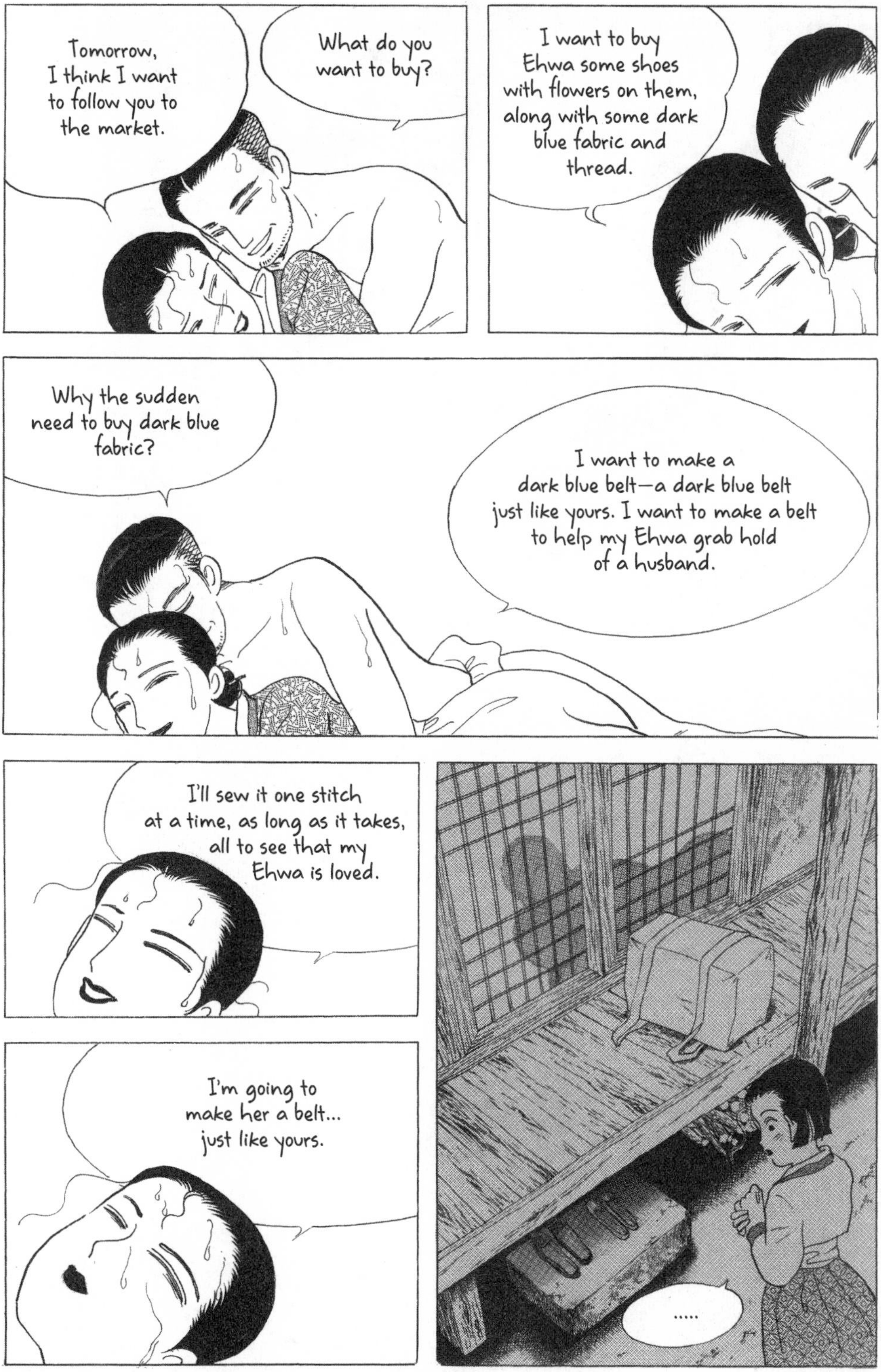
Tomorrow, I think I want to follow you to the market.
What do you want to buy?
I want to buy Ehwa some shoes with flowers on them, along with some dark blue fabric and thread.
Why the sudden need to buy dark blue fabric?
I want to make a dark blue belt—a dark blue belt just like yours. I want to make a belt to help my Ehwa grab hold of a husband.
I'll sew it one stitch at a time, as long as it takes, all to see that my Ehwa is loved.
I'm going to make her a belt... just like yours.
.....

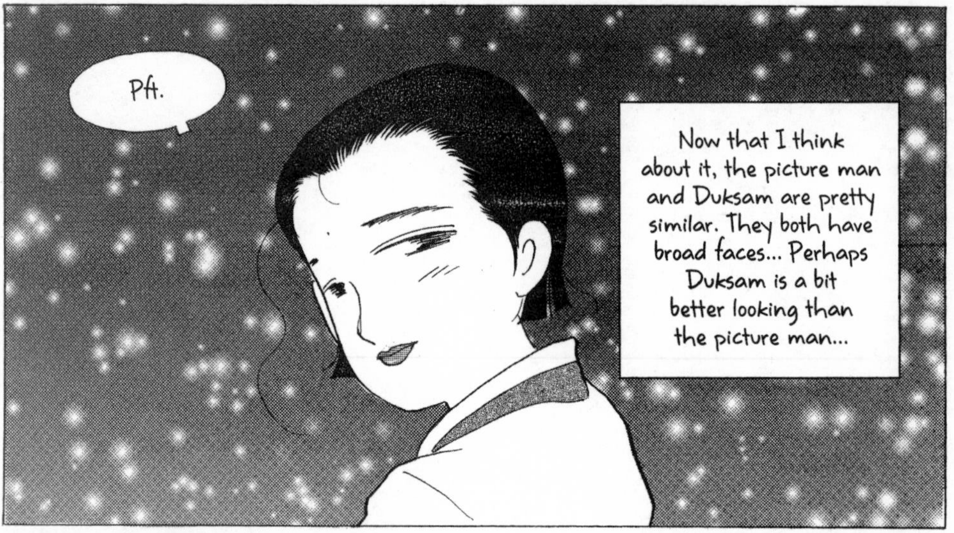
Pft.
Now that I think about it, the picture man and Duksam are pretty similar. They both have broad faces... Perhaps Duksam is a bit better looking than the picture man...

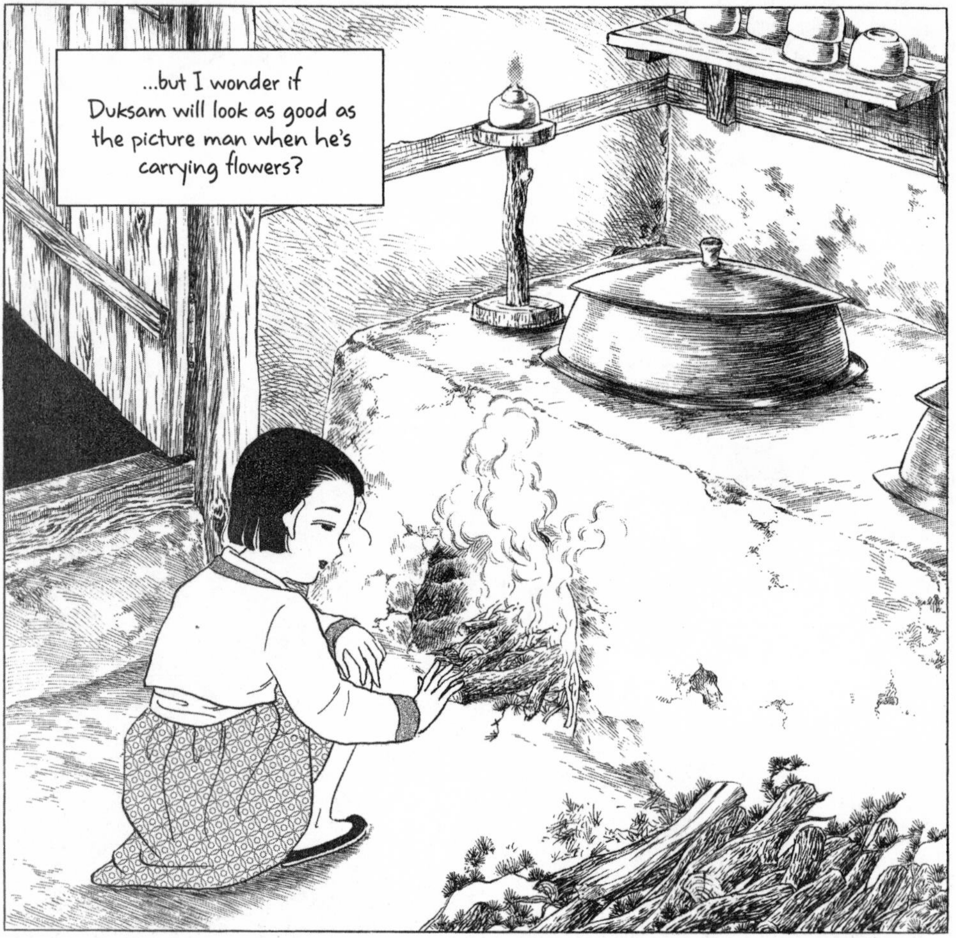
...but I wonder if Duksam will look as good as the picture man when he's carrying flowers?

Chapter Three
SECRET

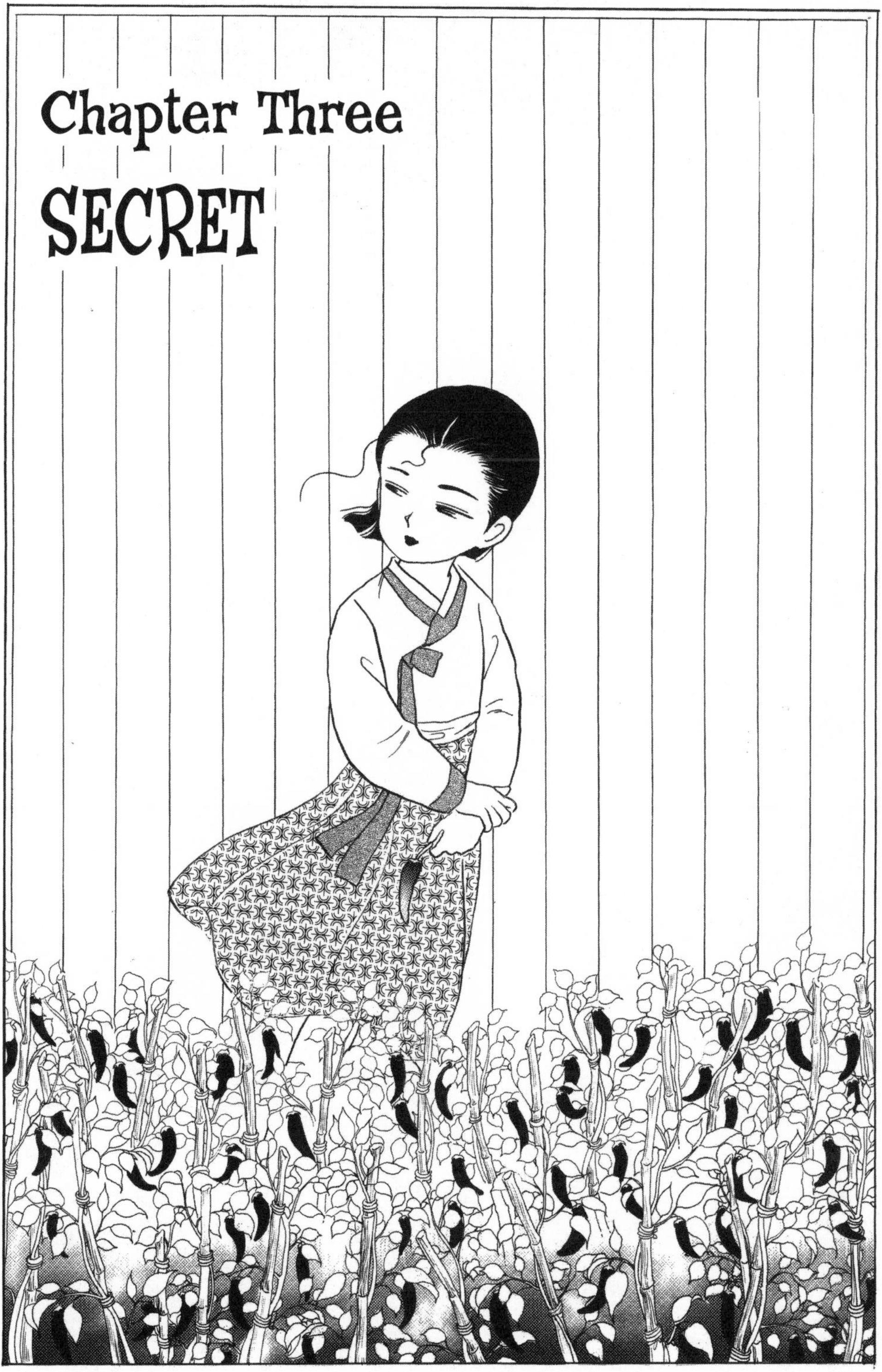

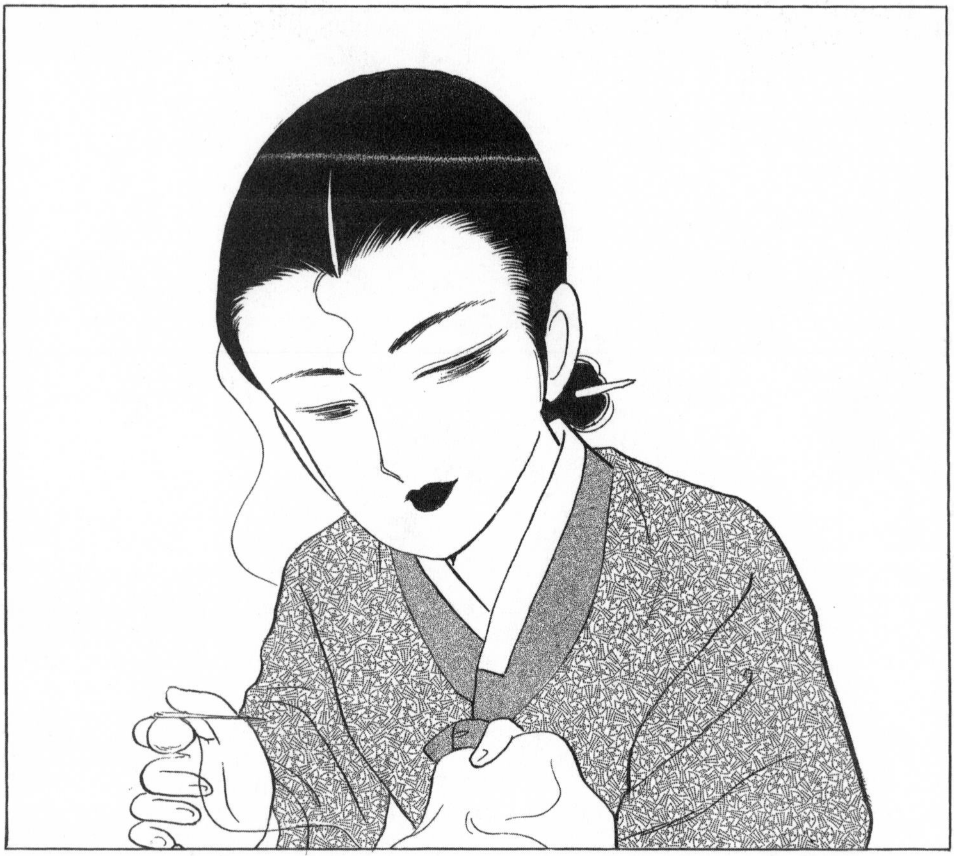

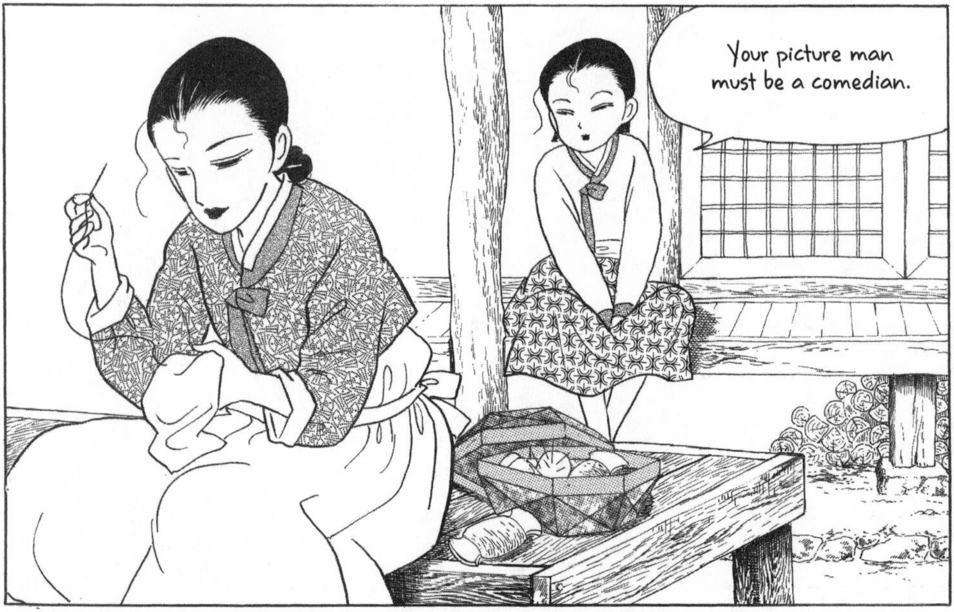
Your picture man must be a comedian.

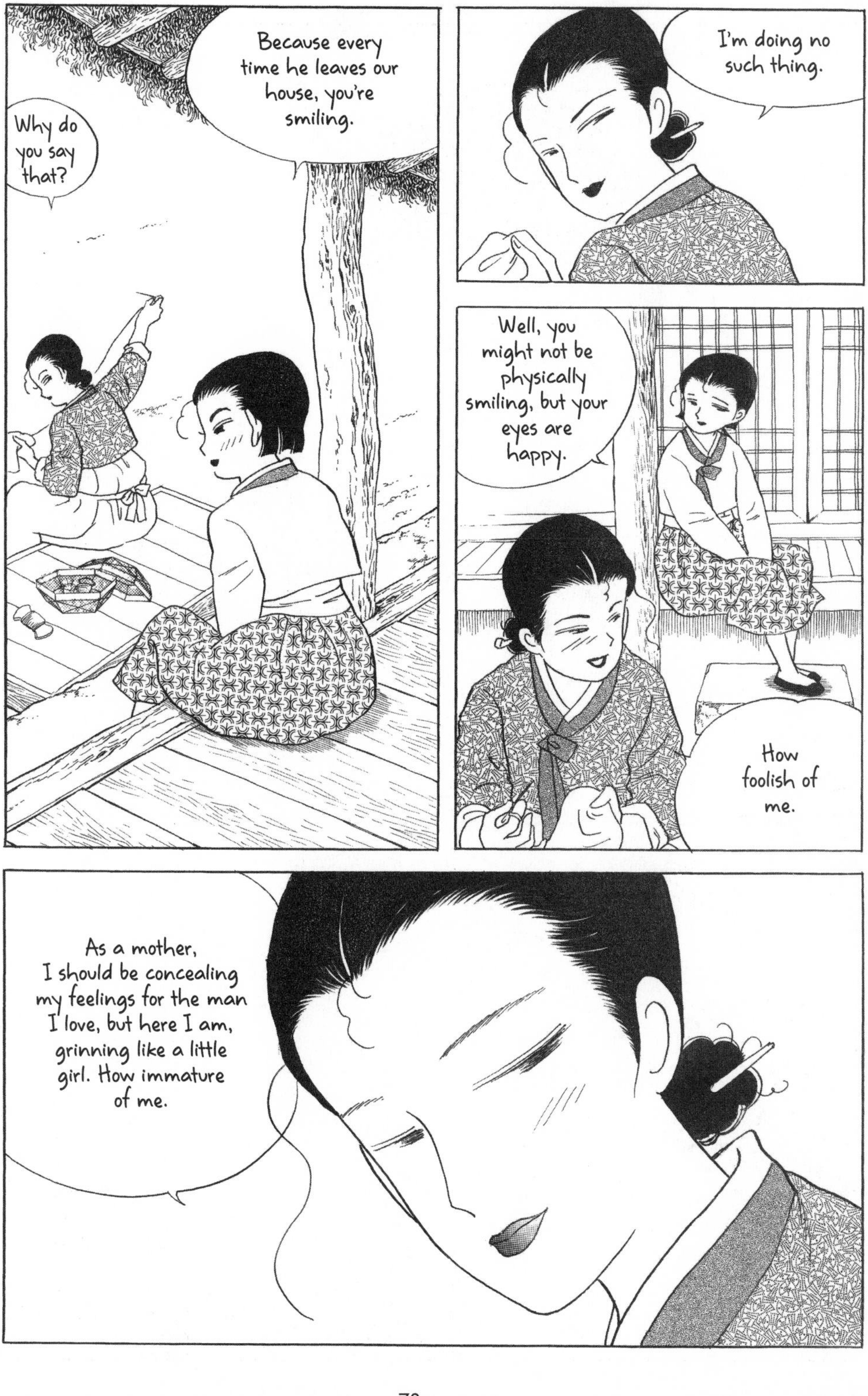

Why do you say that?
Because every time he leaves our house, you're smiling.
I'm doing no such thing.
Well, you might not be physically smiling, but your eyes are happy.
How foolish of me.
As a mother, I should be concealing my feelings for the man I love, but here I am, grinning like a little girl. How immature of me.

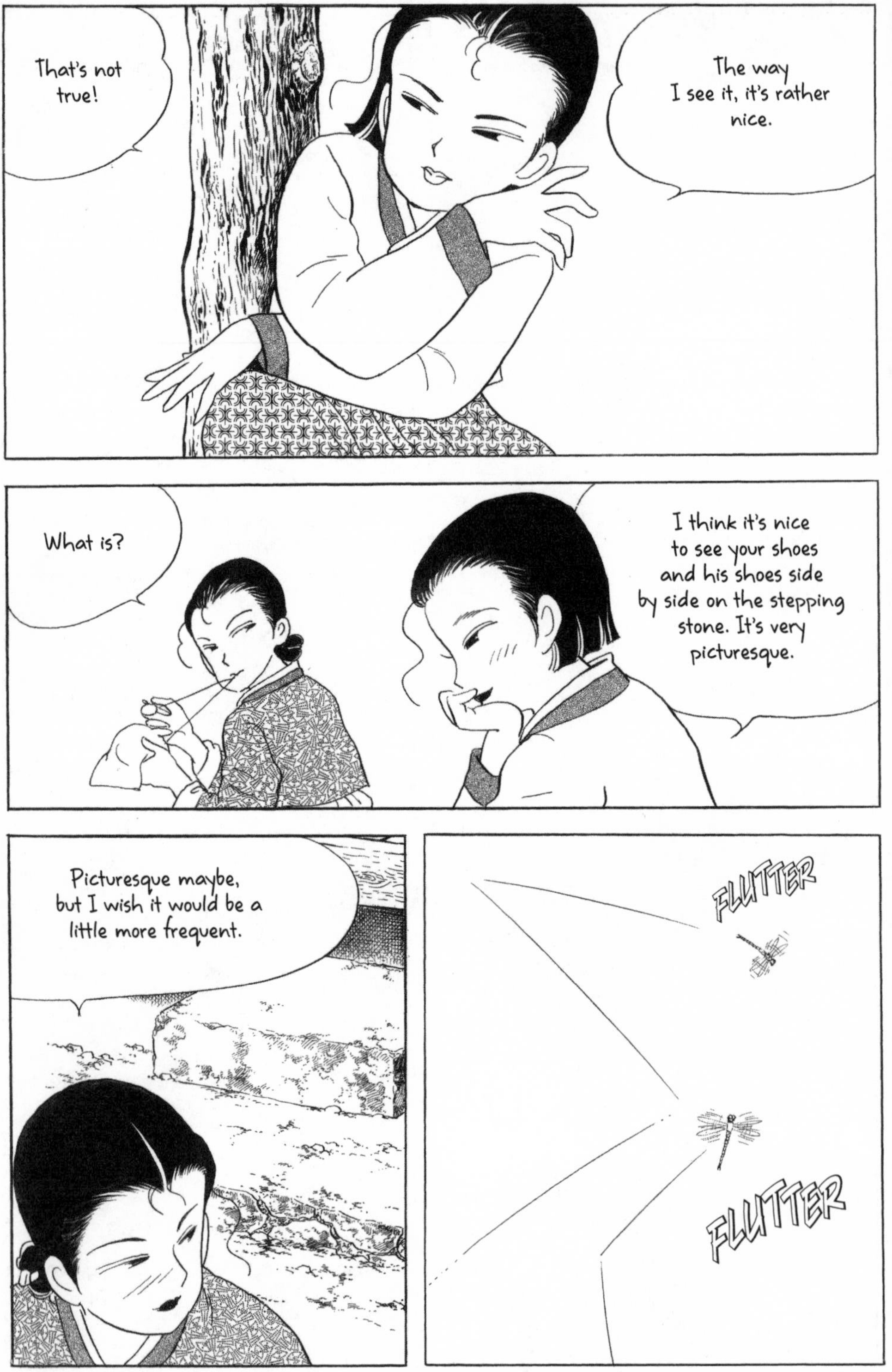
That's not true!
The way I see it, it's rather nice.
What is?
I think it's nice to see your shoes and his shoes side by side on the stepping stone. It's very picturesque.
Picturesque maybe, but I wish it would be a little more frequent.
FLUTTER
FLUTTER

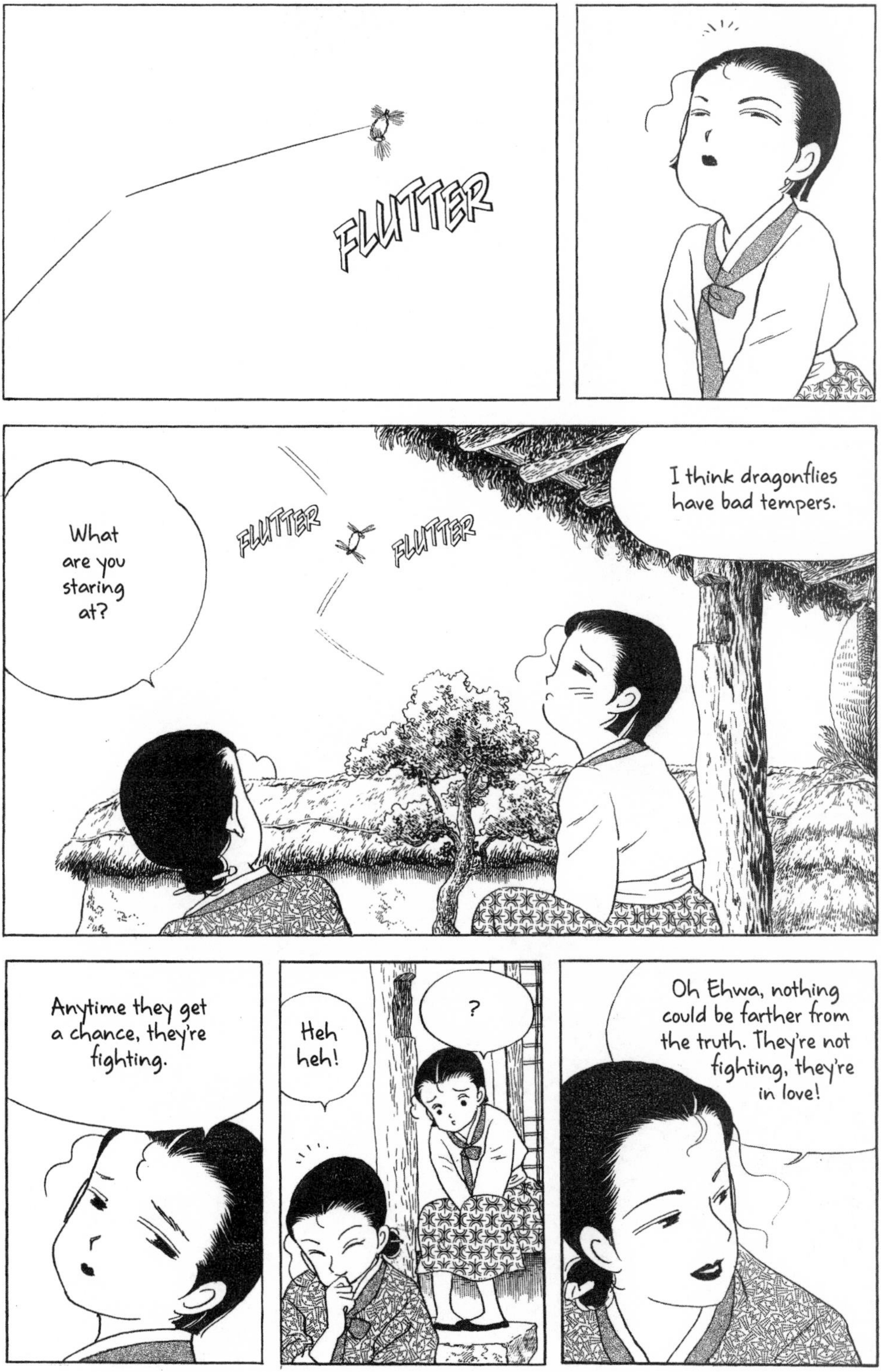
FLUTTER
What are you staring at?
FLUTTER
FLUTTER
I think dragonflies have bad tempers.
Anytime they get a chance, they're fighting.
Heh heh!
?
Oh Ehwa, nothing could be farther from the truth. They're not fighting, they're in love!

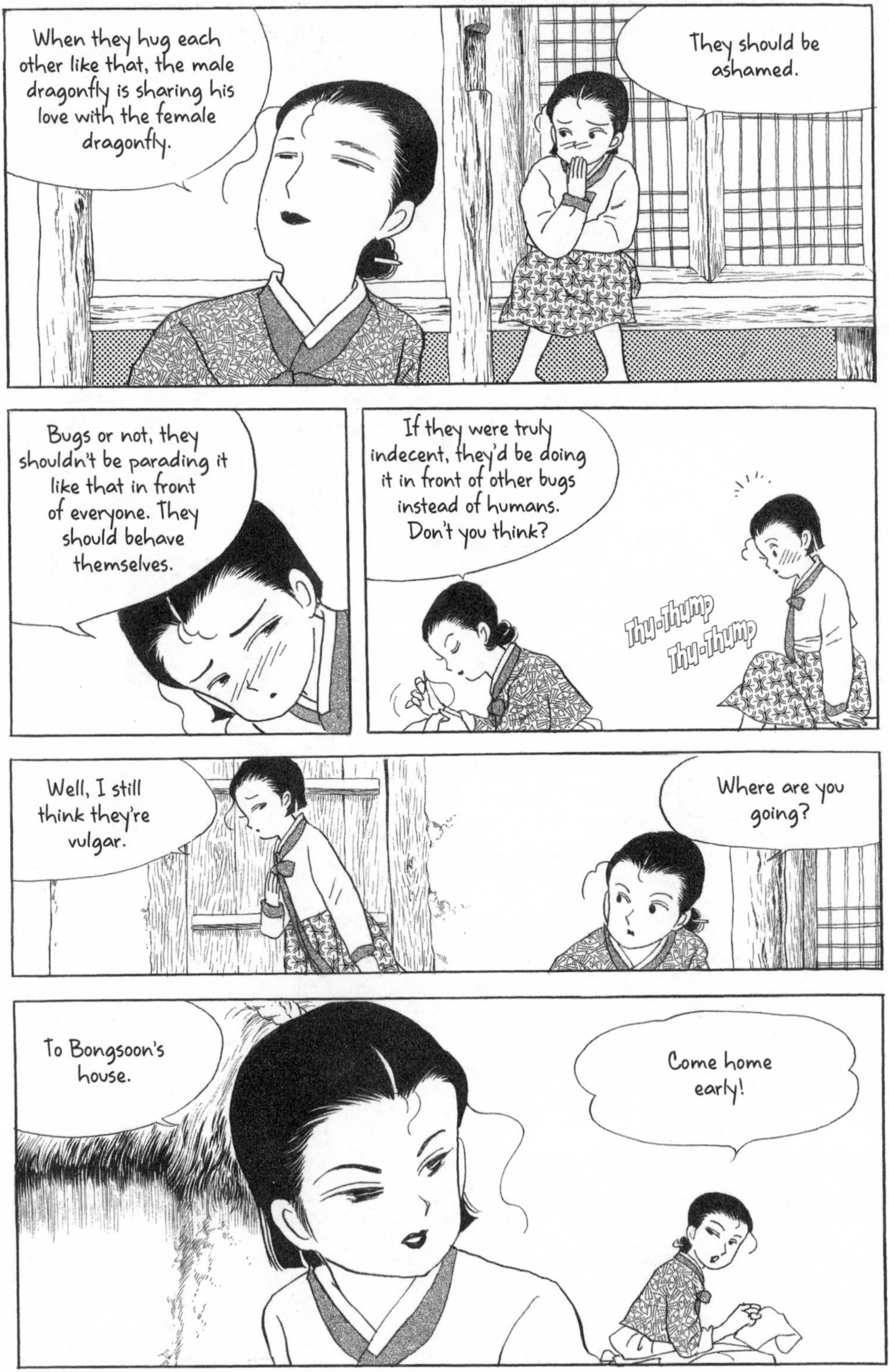
When they hug each other like that, the male dragonfly is sharing his love with the female dragonfly.
They should be ashamed.
Bugs or not, they shouldn't be parading it like that in front of everyone. They should behave themselves.
If they were truly indecent, they'd be doing it in front of other bugs instead of humans. Don't you think?
Thy-Thymp
Thy-Thymp
Well, I still think they're vulgar.
Where are you going?
To Bongsoon's house.
Come home early!

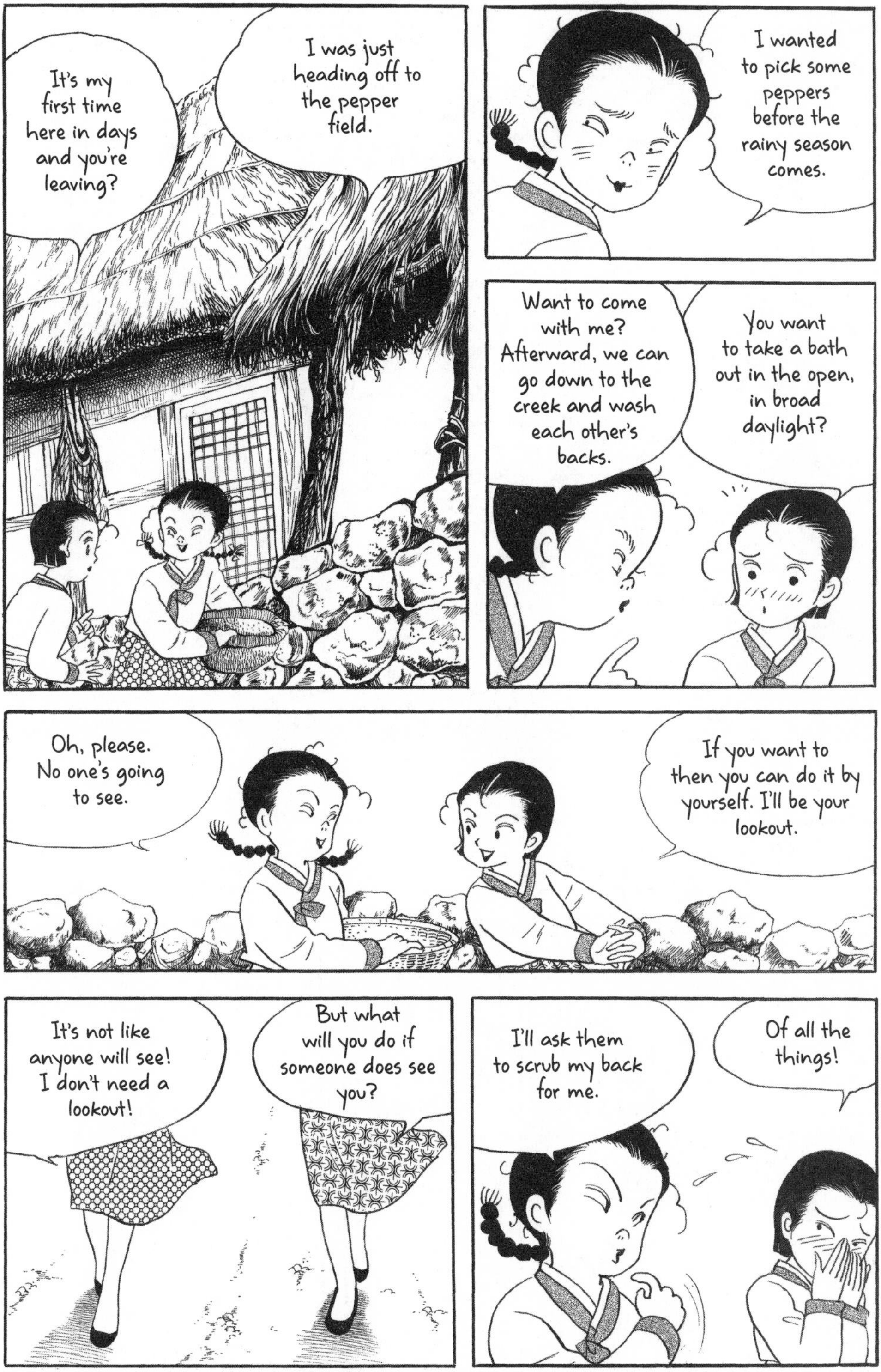
It's my first time here in days and you're leaving?
I was just heading off to the pepper field.
I wanted to pick some peppers before the rainy season comes.
Want to come with me? Afterward, we can go down to the creek and wash each other's backs.
You want to take a bath out in the open, in broad daylight?
Oh, please. No one's going to see.
If you want to then you can do it by yourself. I'll be your lookout.
It's not like anyone will see! I don't need a lookout!
But what will you do if someone does see you?
I'll ask them to scrub my back for me.
Of all the things!

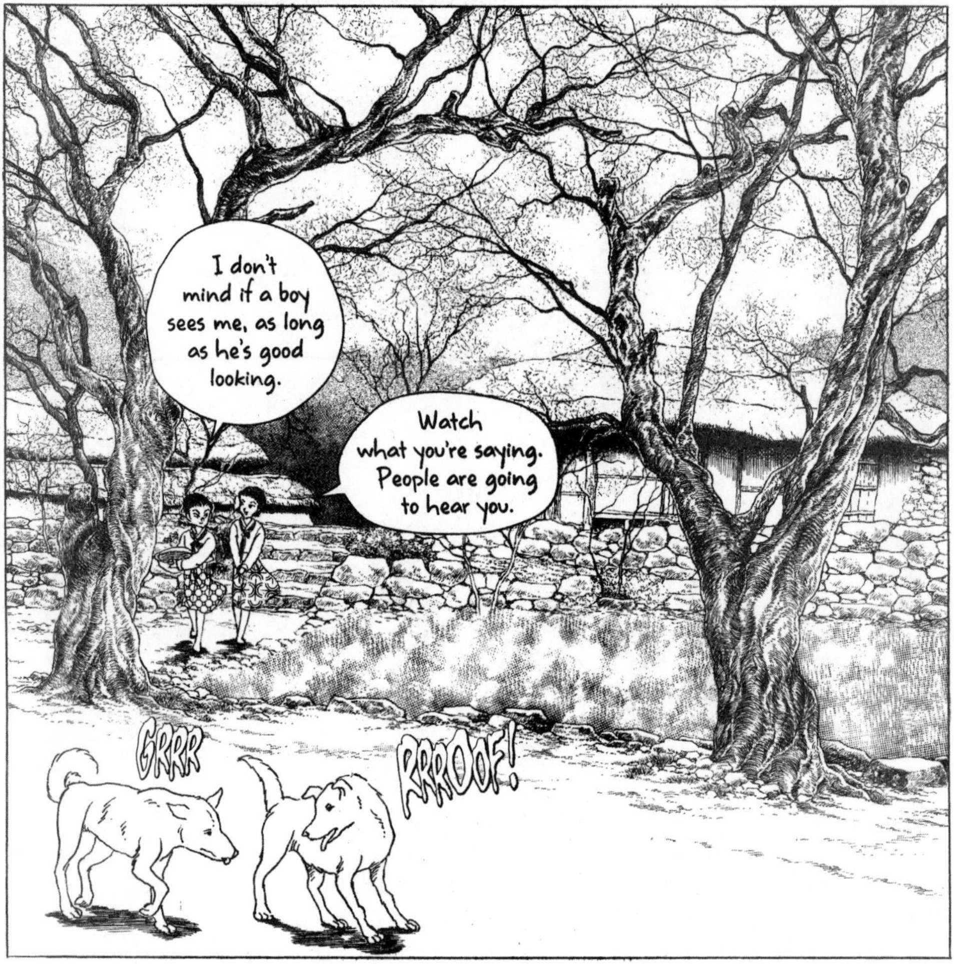
I don't mind if a boy sees me, as long as he's good looking.
Watch what you're saying. People are going to hear you.
GRRR
RRROOF!

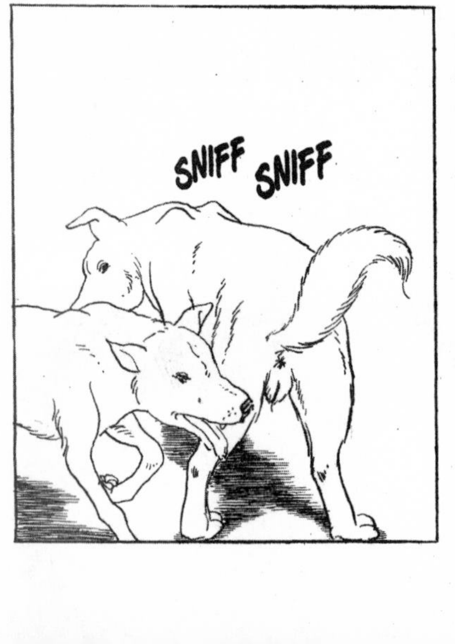
SNIFF SNIFF

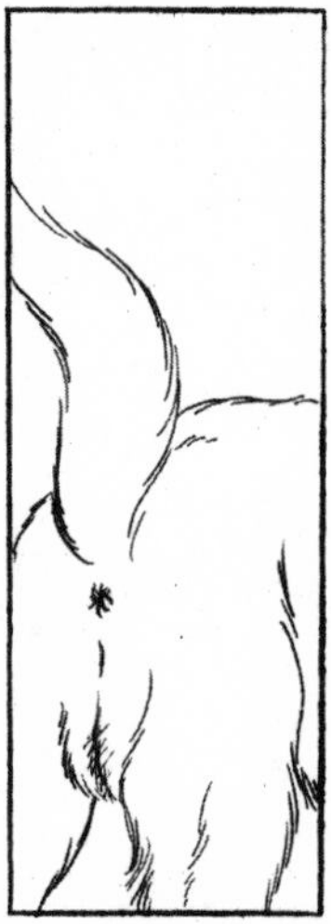

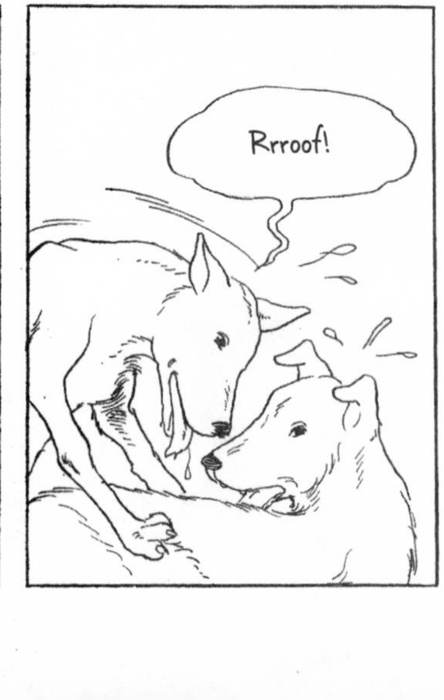
Rrroof!

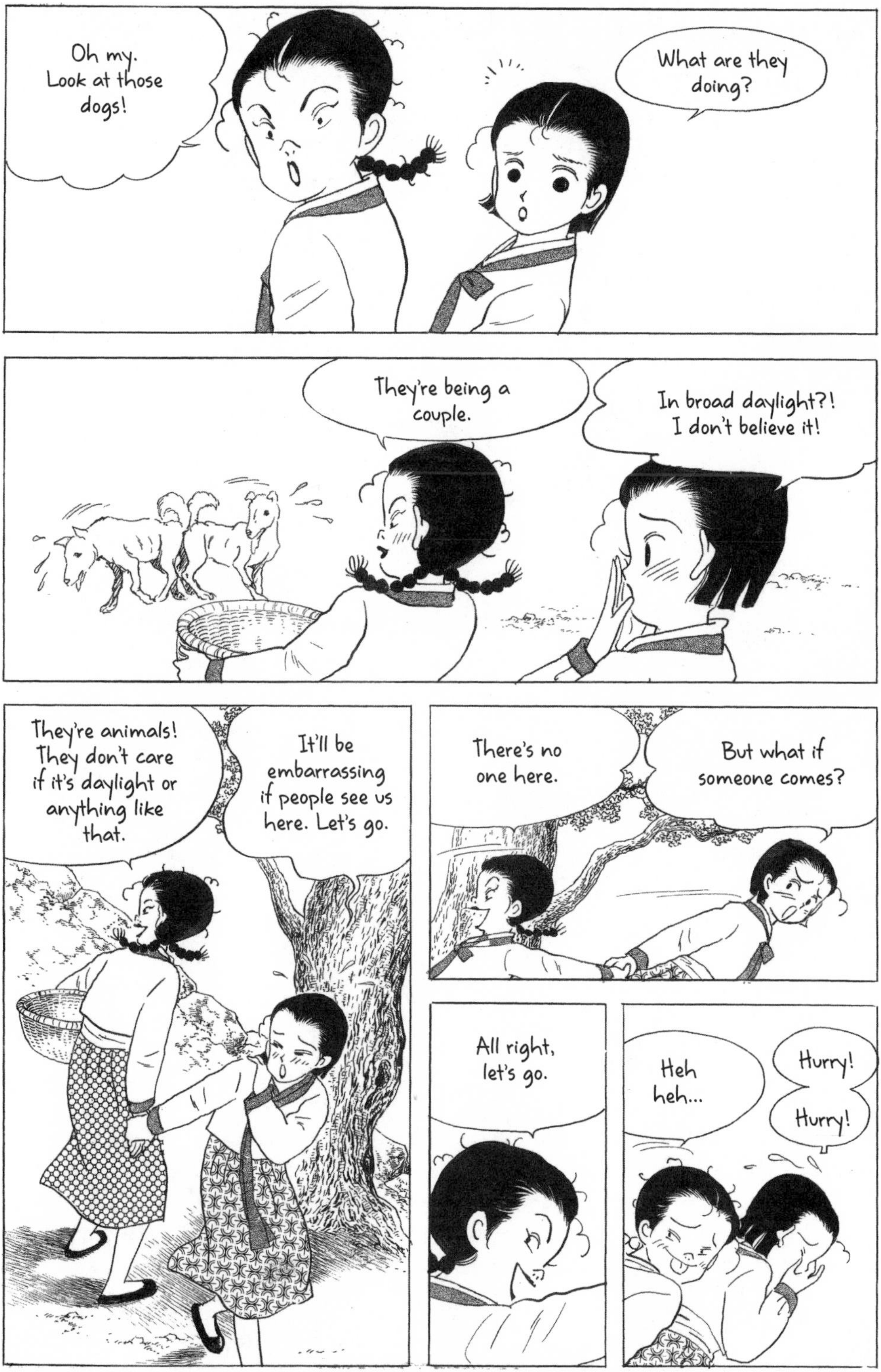
Oh my. Look at those dogs!
What are they doing?
They're being a couple.
In broad daylight?! I don't believe it!
They're animals! They don't care if it's daylight or anything like that.
It'll be embarrassing if people see us here. Let's go.
There's no one here.
But what if someone comes?
All right, let's go.
Heh heh...
Hurry!
Hurry!

You don't think anyone saw that besides us, do you?

I hope so! You don't see something like that too often!

Ahem!

Ahem!

What's wrong with that monk?

He must have seen them too.

Ahem!

Huh?

Ah!

Those two dogs are really putting on quite a show!

Oh my God!

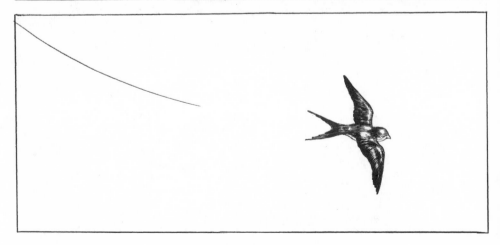

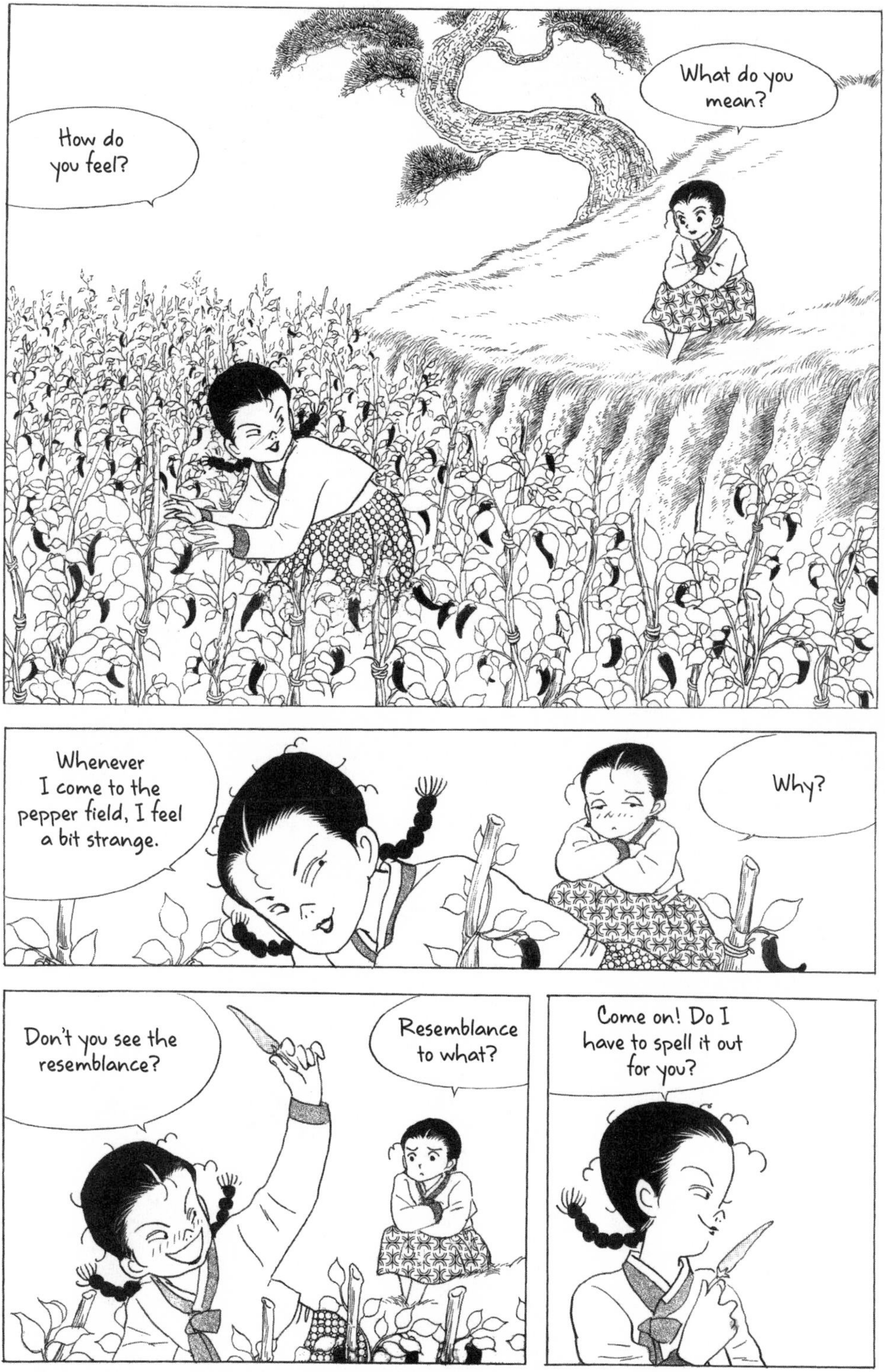
How do you feel?
What do you mean?
Whenever I come to the pepper field, I feel a bit strange.
Why?
Don't you see the resemblance?
Resemblance to what?
Come on! Do I have to spell it out for you?

Look!

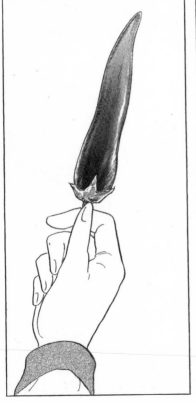

Bongsoon!

Stop acting like such a prude! I'm not saying anything you didn't already know!

What are you talking about?

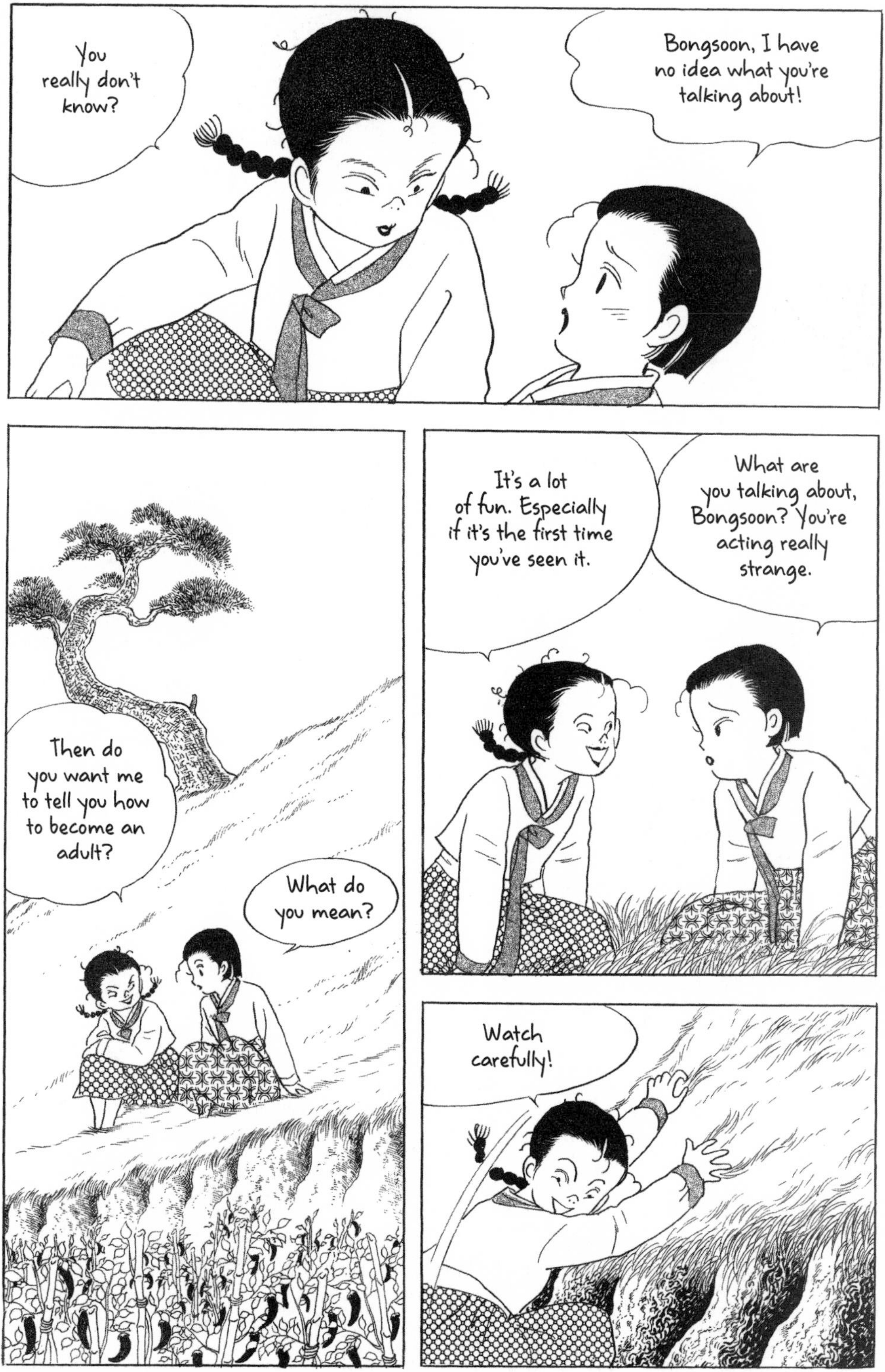
You really don't know?
Bongsoon, I have no idea what you're talking about!
Then do you want me to tell you how to become an adult?
What do you mean?
It's a lot of fun. Especially if it's the first time you've seen it.
What are you talking about, Bongsoon? You're acting really strange.
Watch carefully!

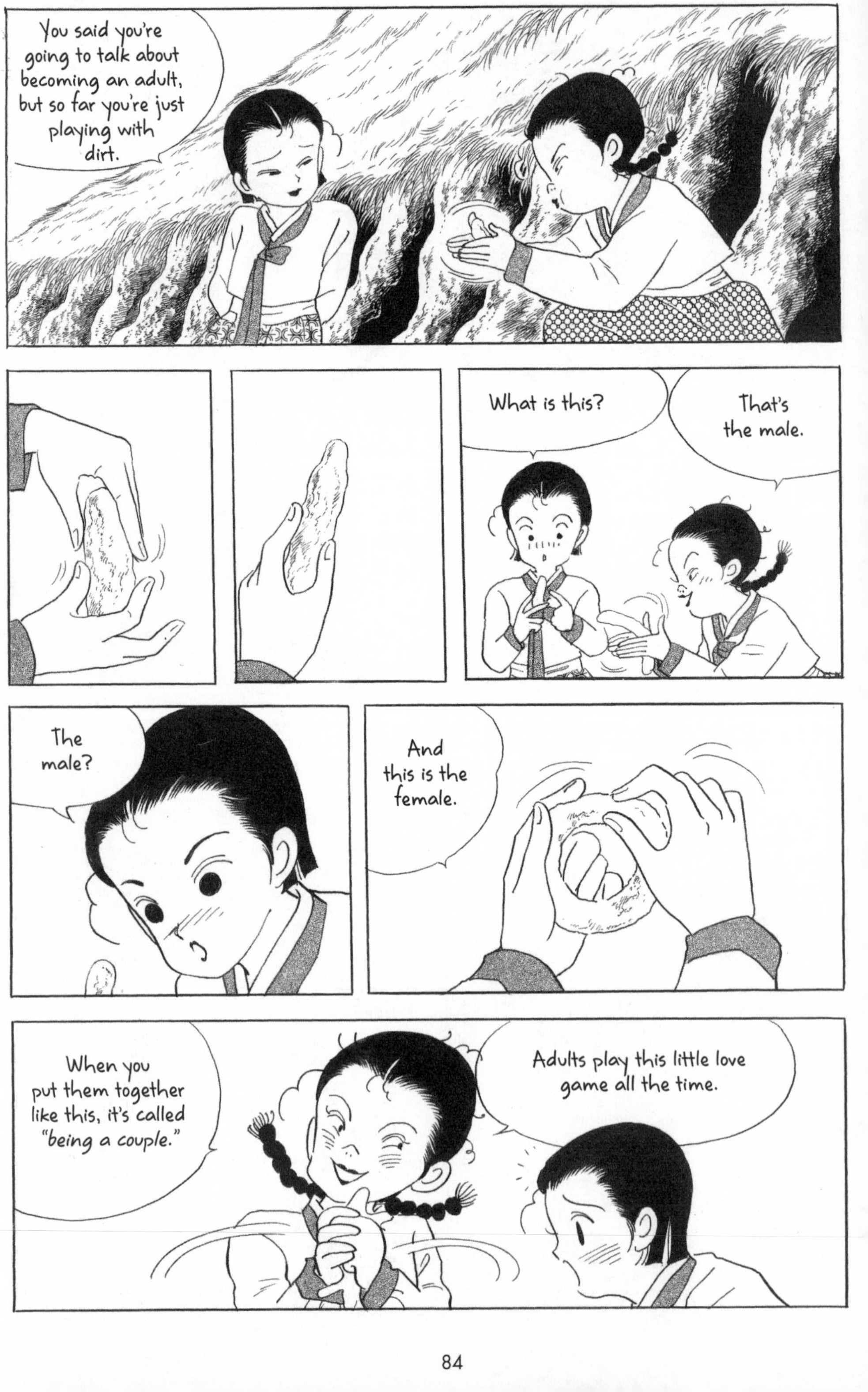
You said you're going to talk about becoming an adult, but so far you're just playing with dirt.
What is this?
That's the male.
The male?
And this is the female.
When you put them together like this, it's called "being a couple."
Adults play this little love game all the time.

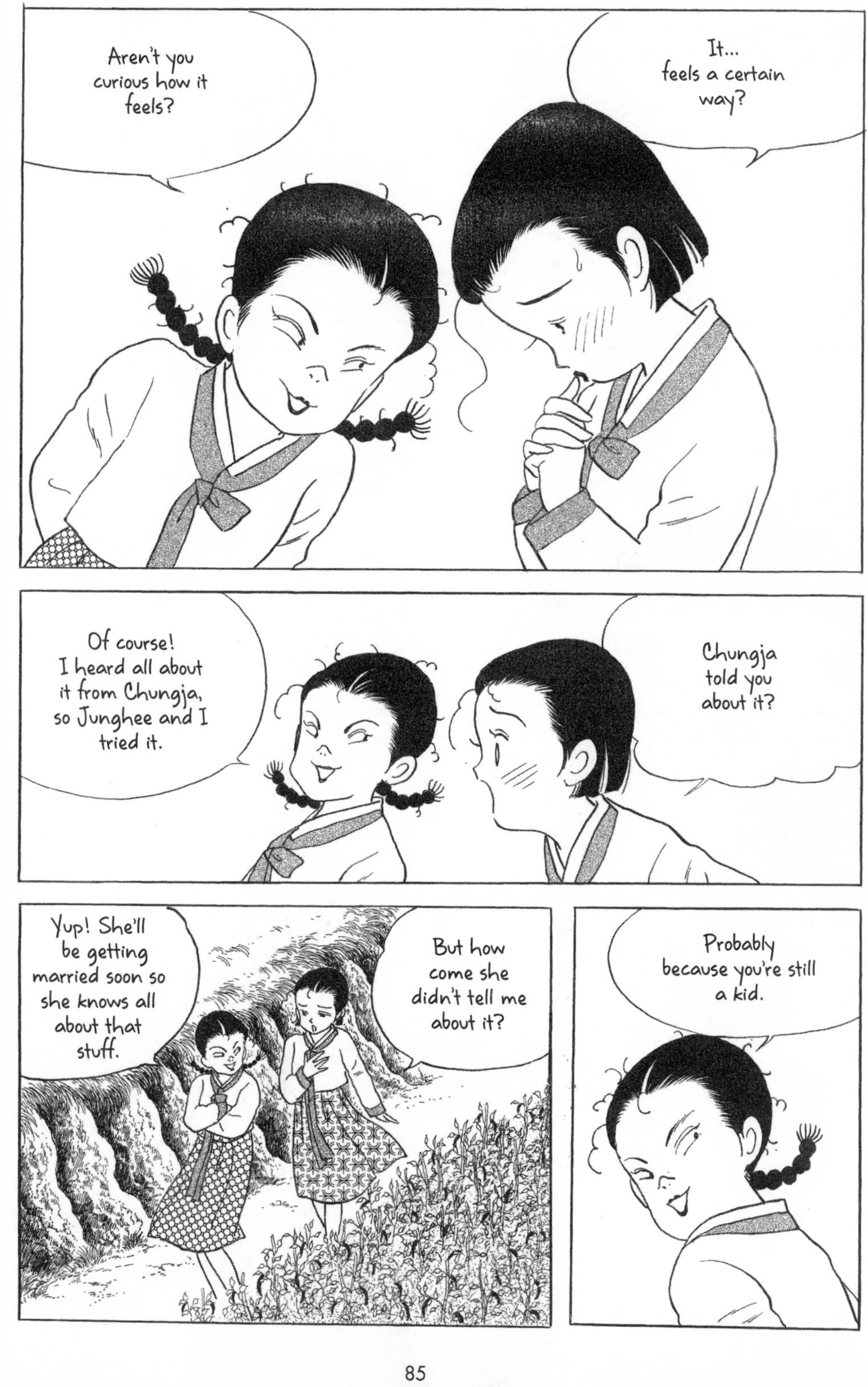
Aren't you curious how it feels?
It... feels a certain way?
Of course! I heard all about it from Chungja, so Junghee and I tried it.
Chungja told you about it?
Yup! She'll be getting married soon so she knows all about that stuff.
But how come she didn't tell me about it?
Probably because you're still a kid.

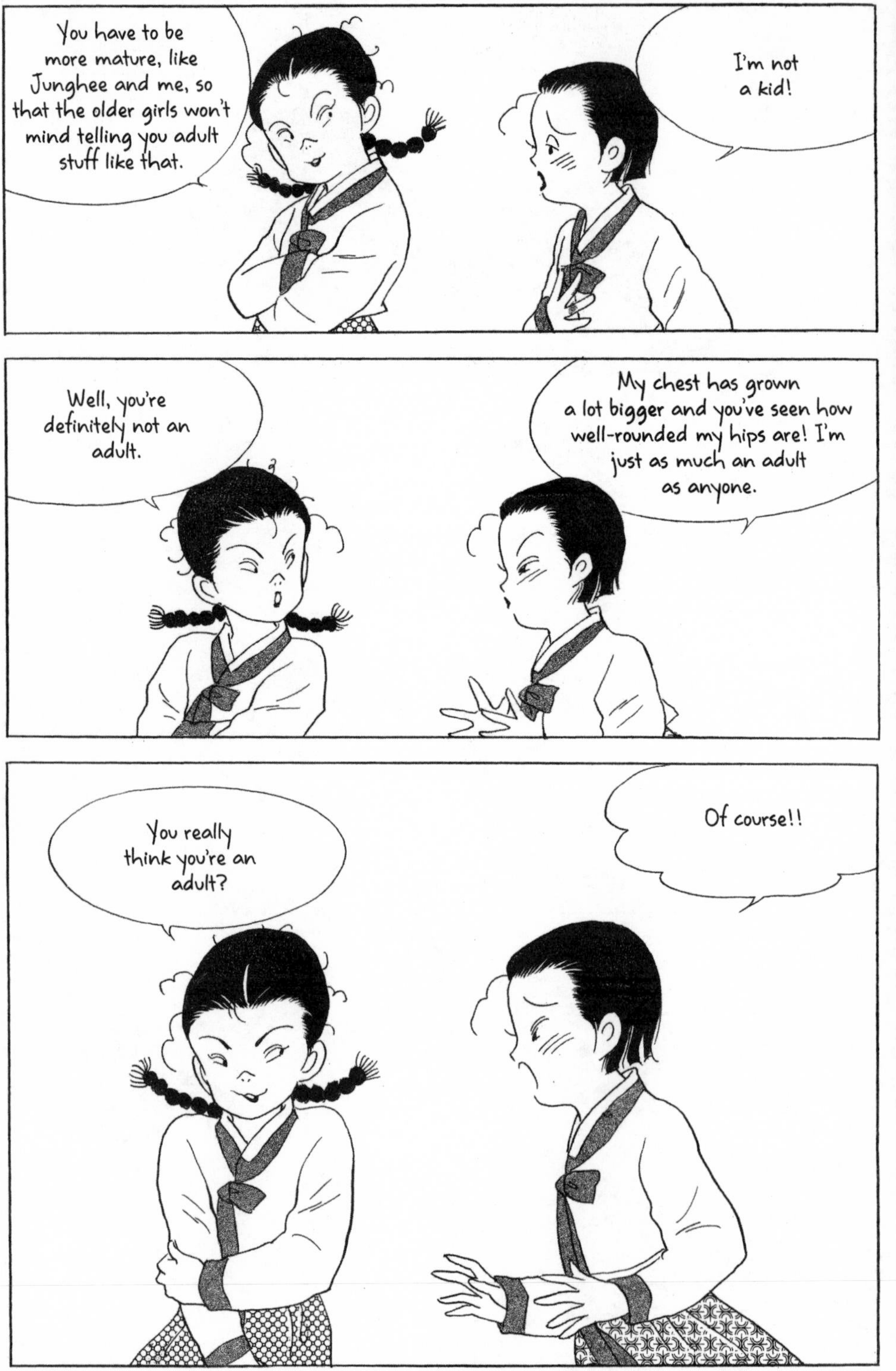
You have to be more mature, like Junghee and me, so that the older girls won't mind telling you adult stuff like that.
I'm not a kid!
Well, you're definitely not an adult.
My chest has grown a lot bigger and you've seen how well-rounded my hips are! I'm just as much an adult as anyone.
You really think you're an adult?
Of course!!

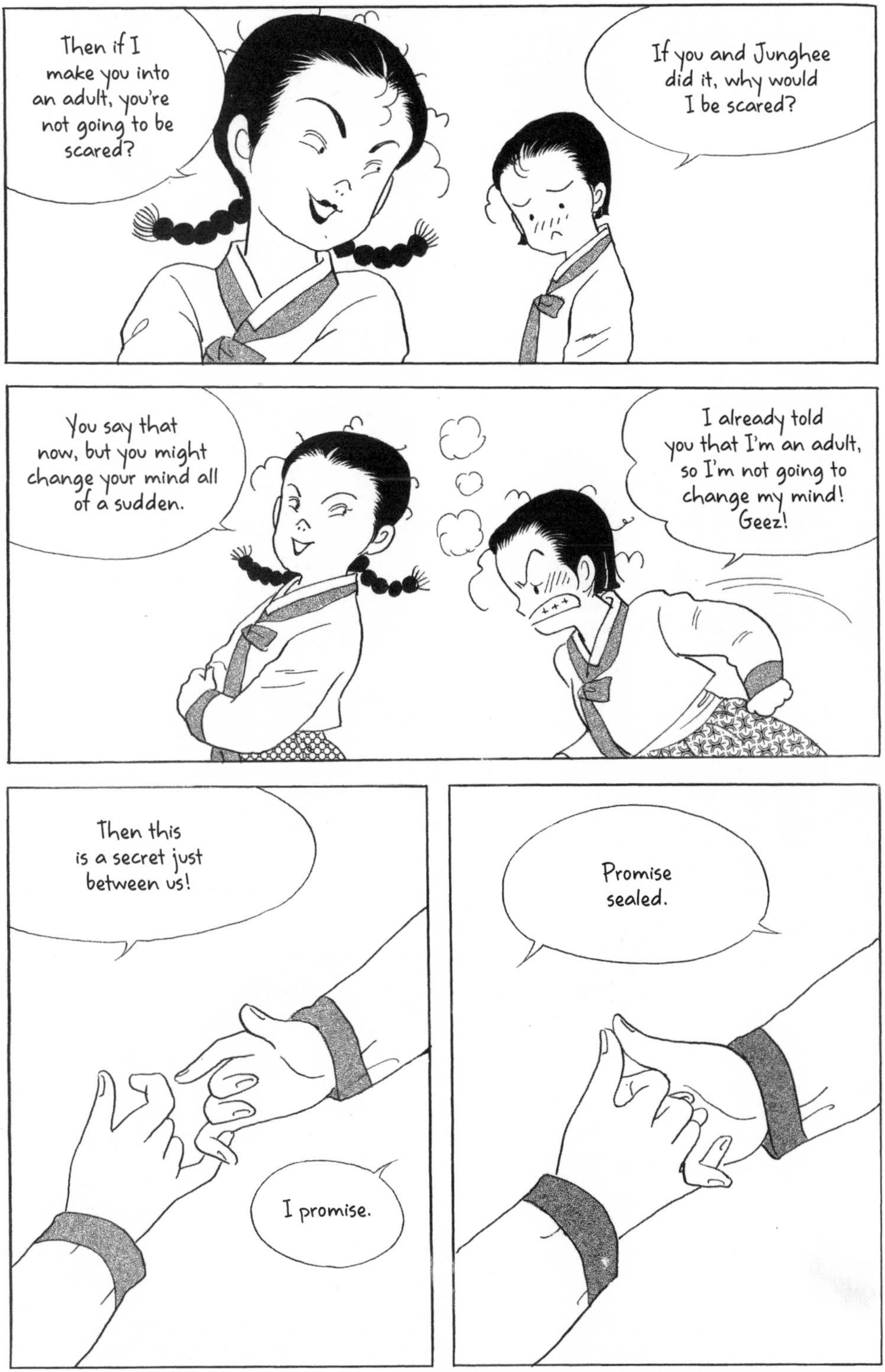
Then if I make you into an adult, you're not going to be scared?
If you and Junghee did it, why would I be scared?
You say that now, but you might change your mind all of a sudden.
I already told you that I'm an adult, so I'm not going to change my mind! Geez!
Then this is a secret just between us!
I promise.
Promise sealed.

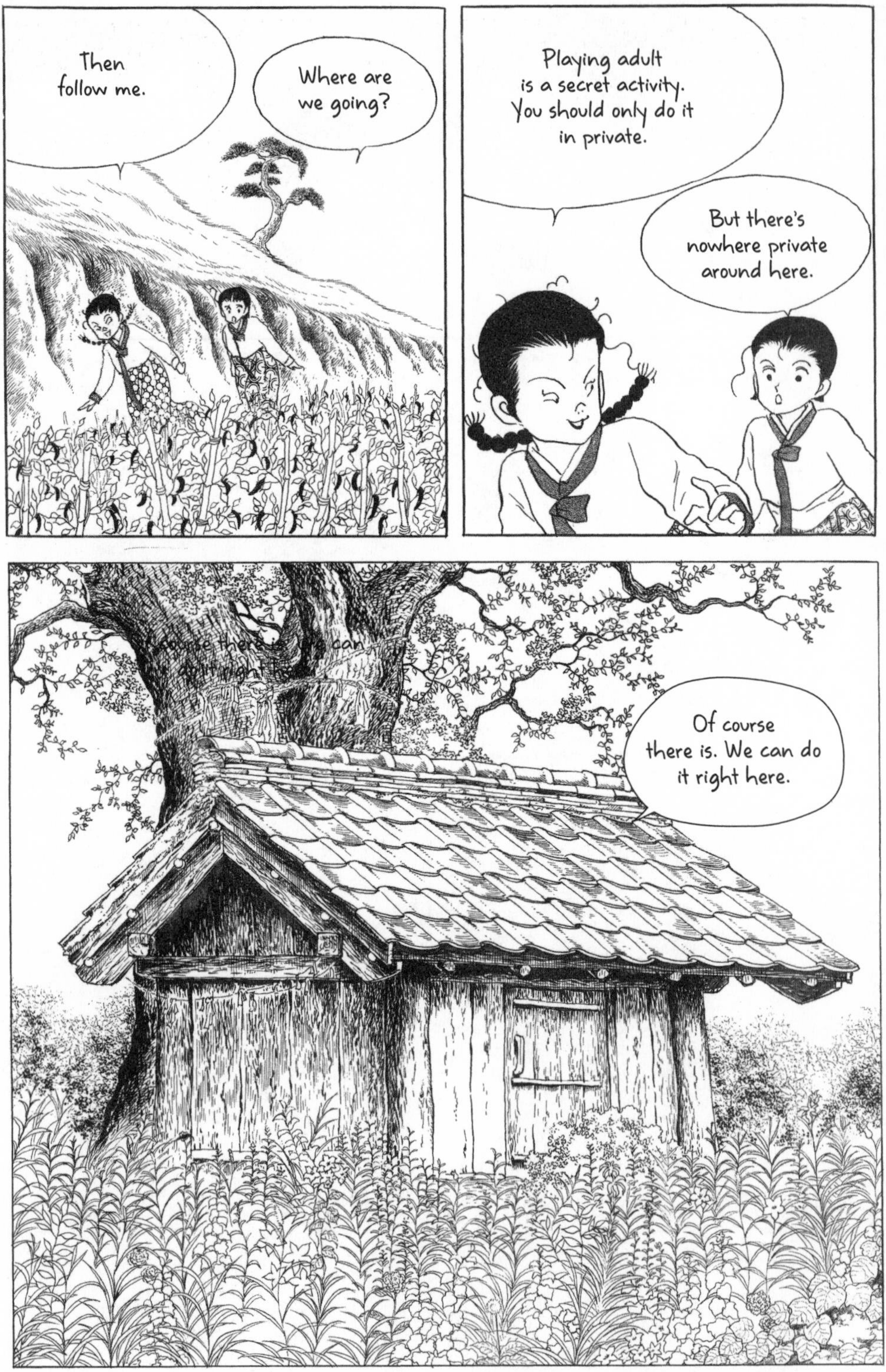
Then follow me.
Where are we going?
Playing adult is a secret activity. You should only do it in private.
But there's nowhere private around here.
Of course there is. We can do it right here.

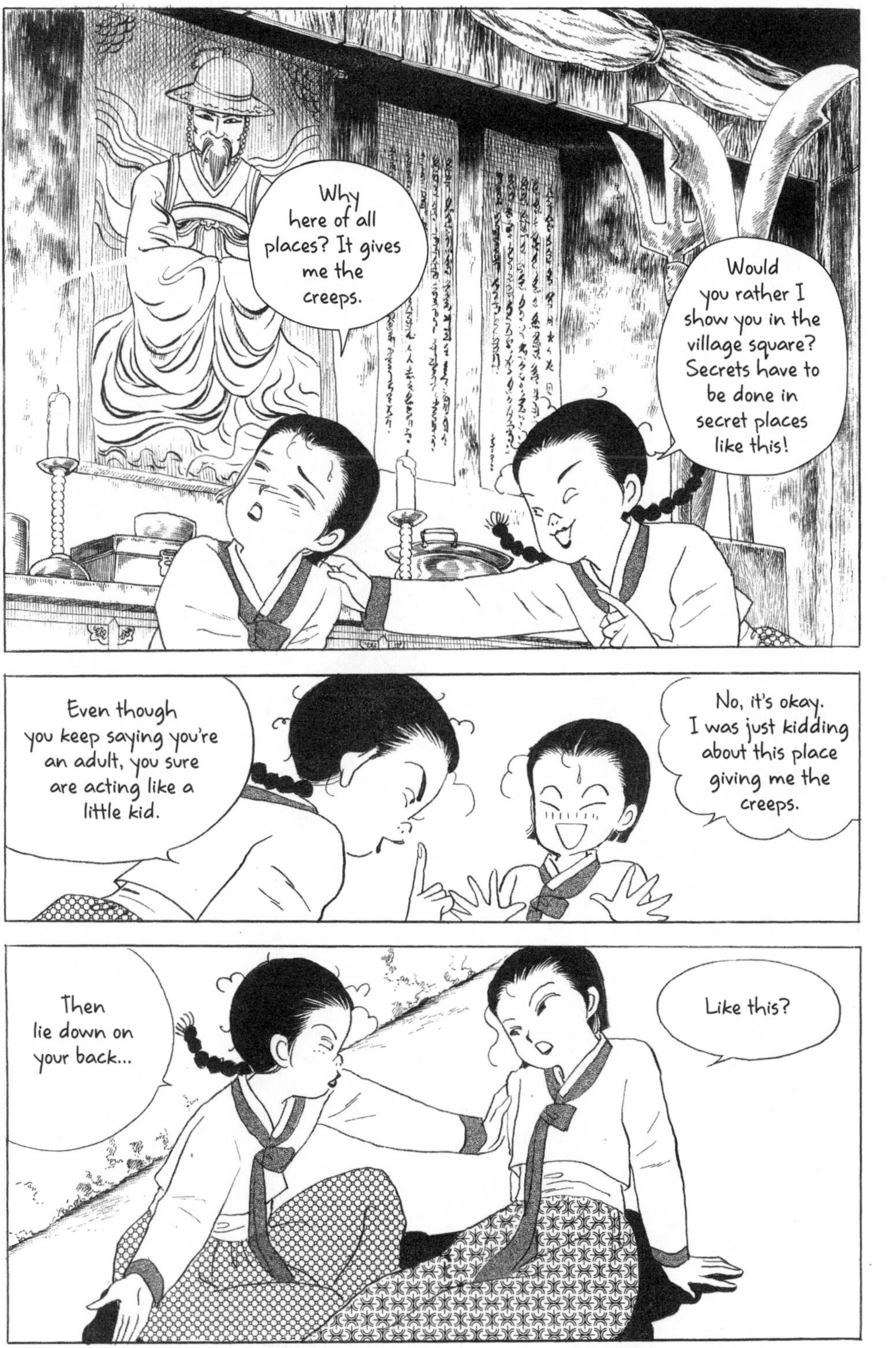
Why here of all places? It gives me the creeps.
Would you rather I show you in the village square? Secrets have to be done in secret places like this!
Even though you keep saying you're an adult, you sure are acting like a little kid.
No, it's okay. I was just kidding about this place giving me the creeps.
Then lie down on your back...
Like this?

Close your eyes.

And imagine that the hands touching you are the hands of the man you like.

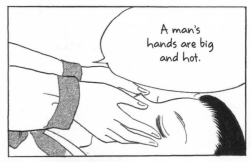

A man's hands are big and hot.

And where those hands touch you, you'll become hot too.

The hand caresses your cheek and moves to your lips...

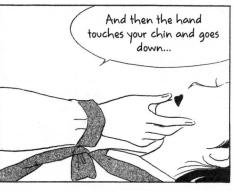

And then the hand touches your chin and goes down...

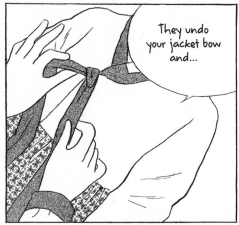

They undo your jacket bow and...

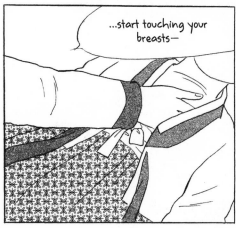

...start touching your breasts—

What... what are you doing?

You promised that you wouldn't get scared, remember? We haven't even gotten to the real part yet, so just stay still.

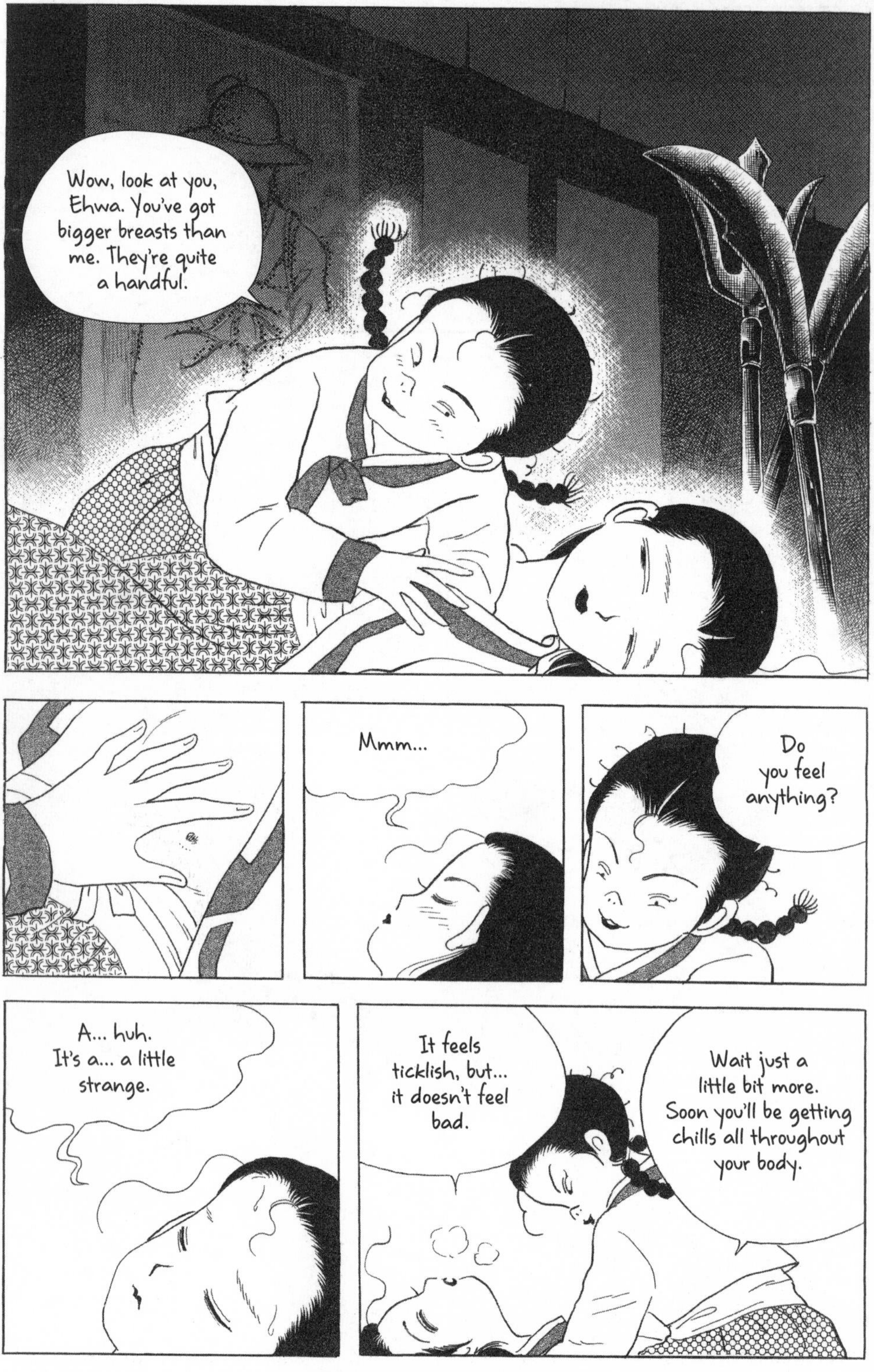
Wow, look at you, Ehwa. You've got bigger breasts than me. They're quite a handful.
Mmm...
Do you feel anything?
A... huh. It's a... a little strange.
It feels ticklish, but... it doesn't feel bad.
Wait just a little bit more. Soon you'll be getting chills all throughout your body.

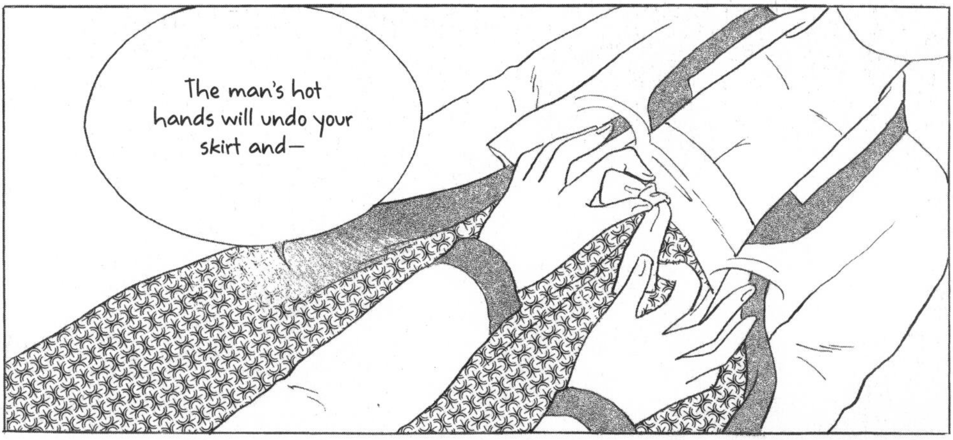
The man's hot hands will undo your skirt and—

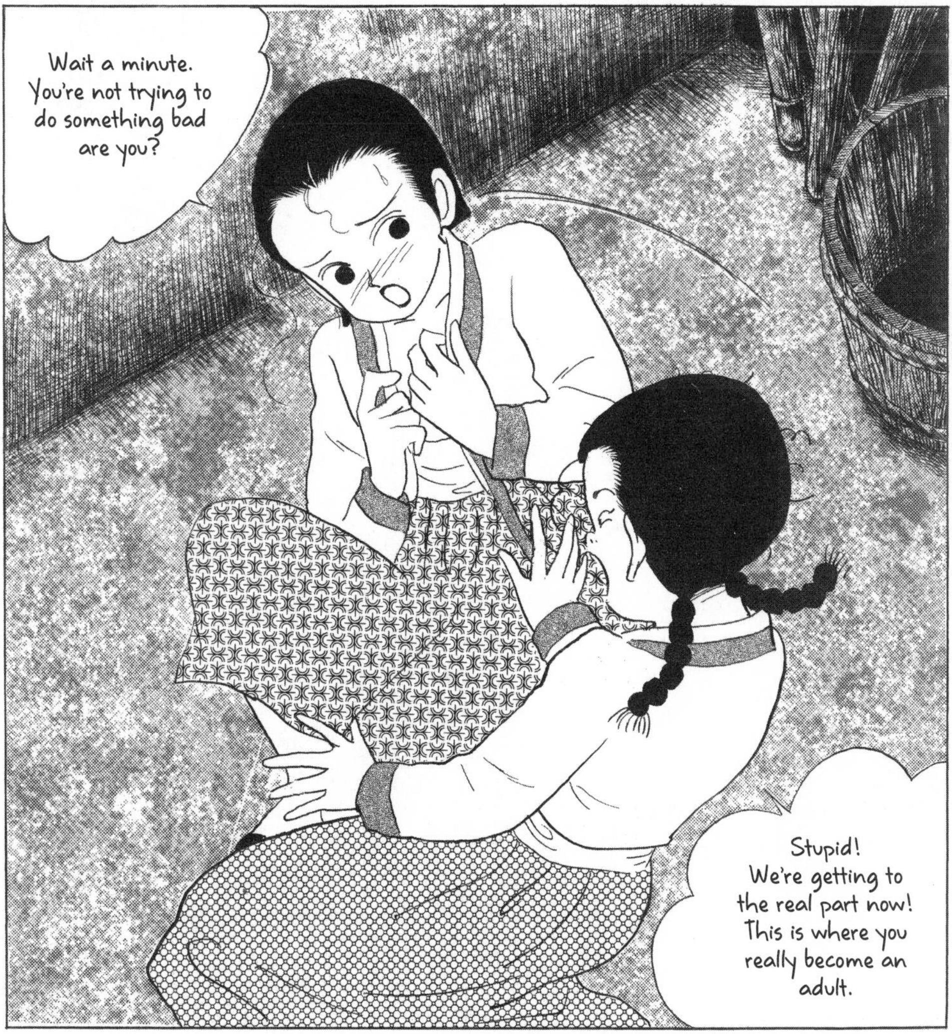
Wait a minute. You're not trying to do something bad are you?
Stupid! We're getting to the real part now! This is where you really become an adult.

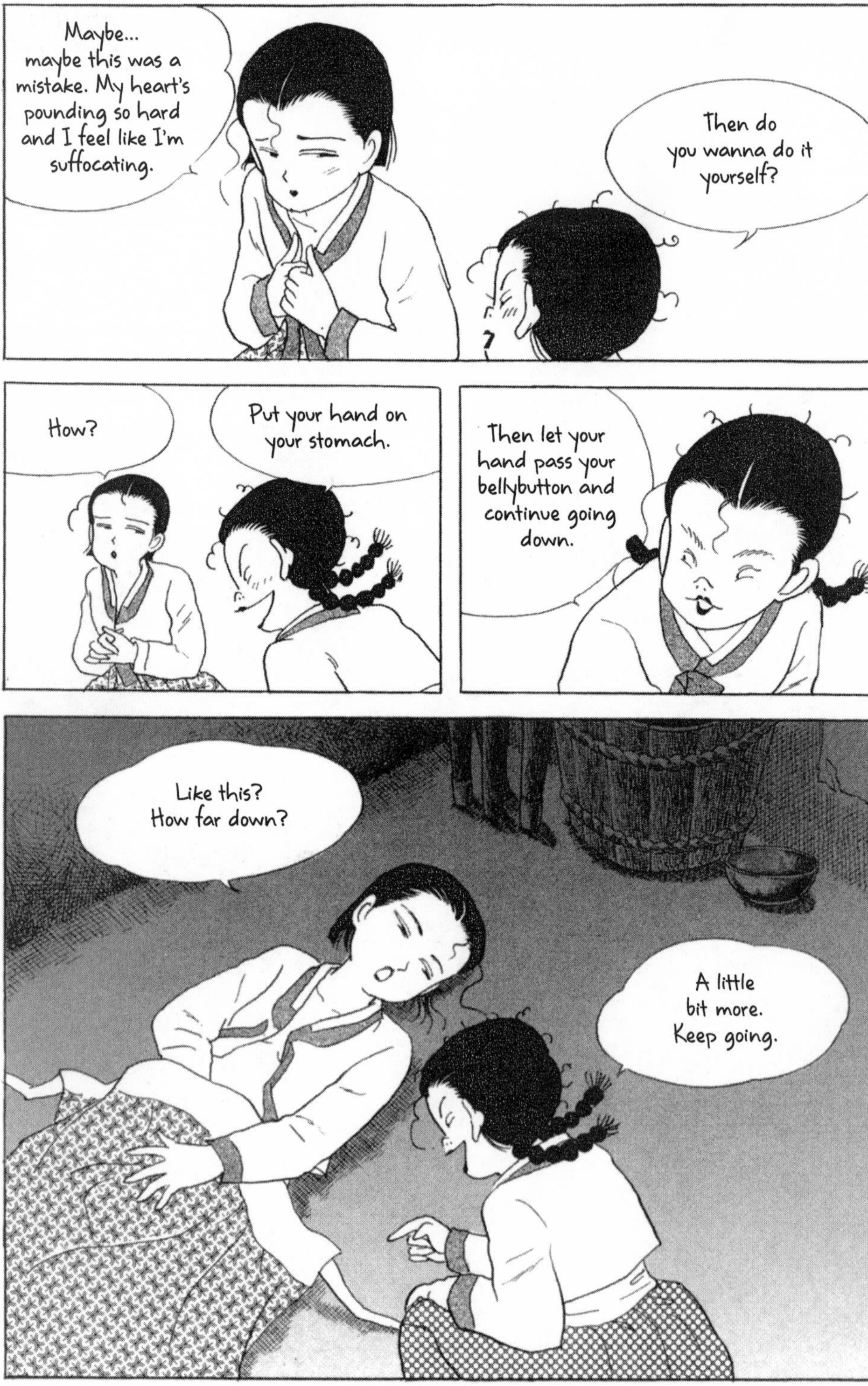
Maybe... maybe this was a mistake. My heart's pounding so hard and I feel like I'm suffocating.
Then do you wanna do it yourself?
How?
Put your hand on your stomach.
Then let your hand pass your bellybutton and continue going down.
Like this? How far down?
A little bit more. Keep going.

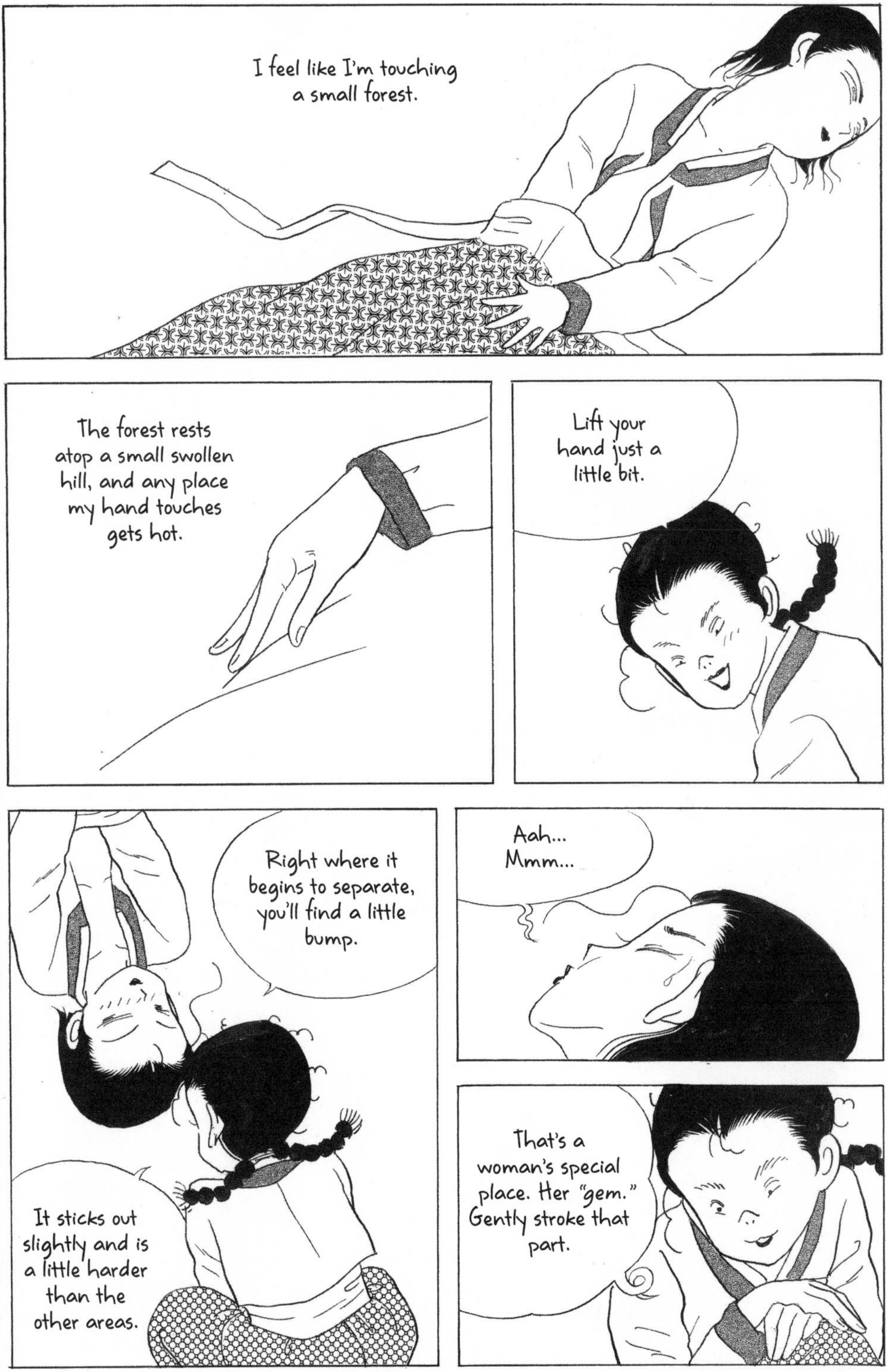
I feel like I'm touching a small forest.
The forest rests atop a small swollen hill, and any place my hand touches gets hot.
Lift your hand just a little bit.
Right where it begins to separate, you'll find a little bump.
It sticks out slightly and is a little harder than the other areas.
Aah... Mmm...
That's a woman's special place. Her "gem." Gently stroke that part.

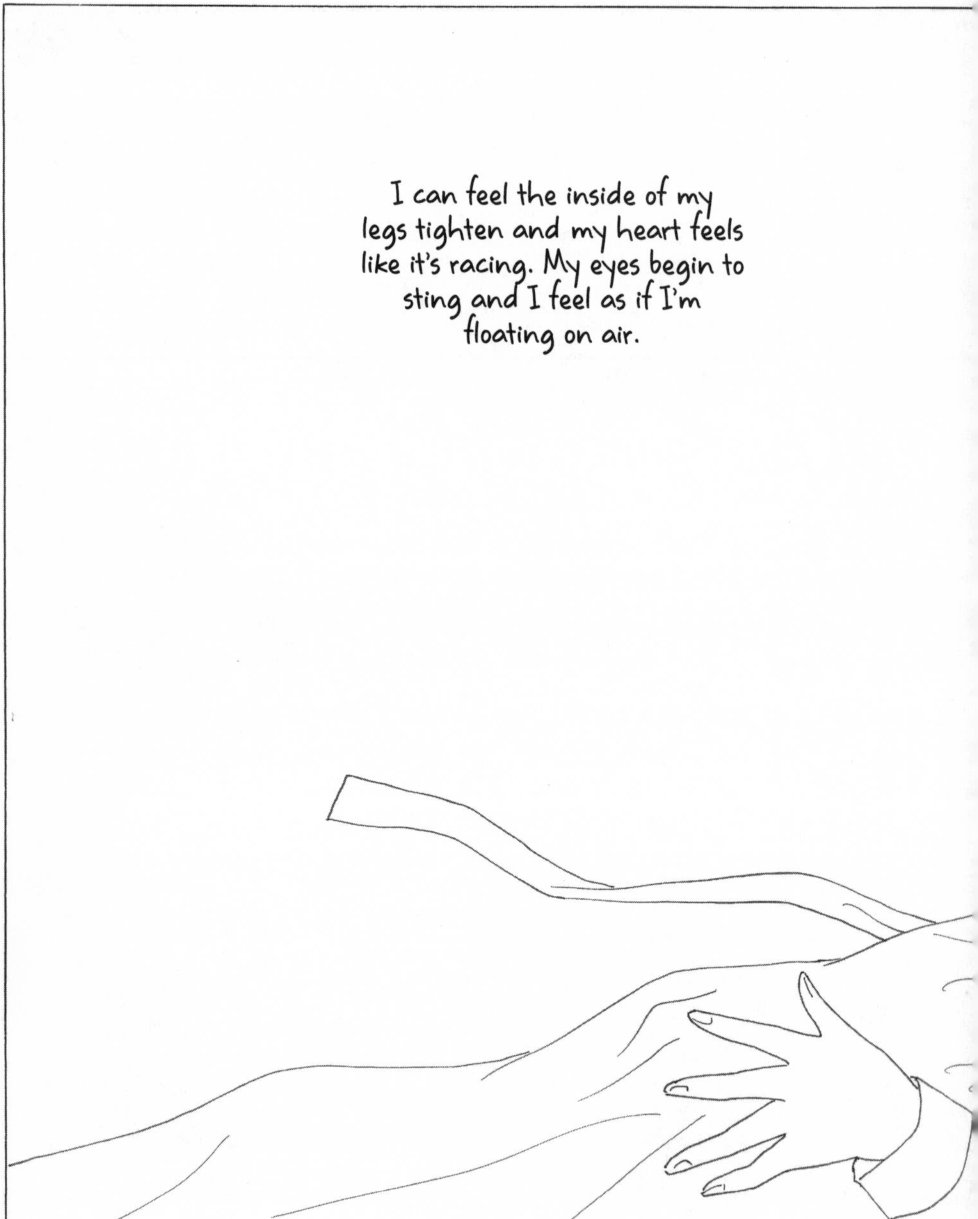
I can feel the inside of my legs tighten and my heart feels like it's racing. My eyes begin to sting and I feel as if I'm floating on air.

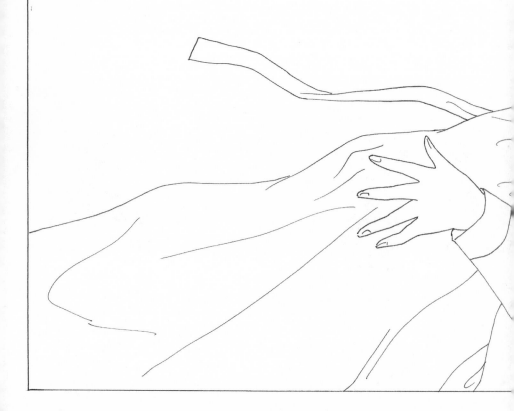

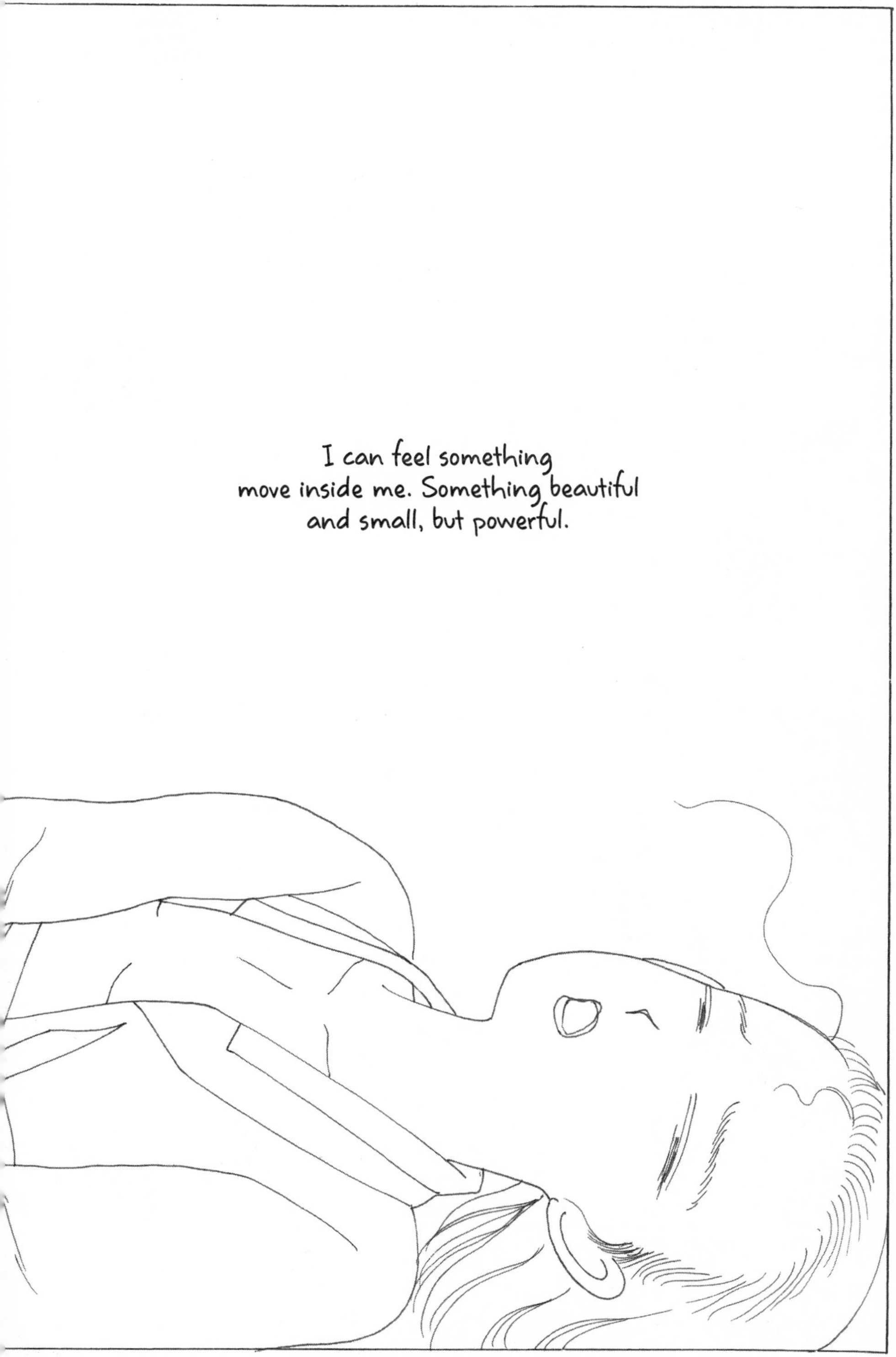
I can feel something move inside me. Something beautiful and small, but powerful.

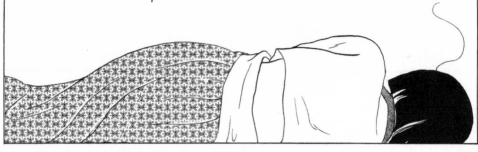

I feel good, even better than the time I became drunk from the wine Mom gave me. I'm out of breath, but I feel invigorated to the tips of my hair.

And now, a tiny spring is flowing, and my forest and fingertip are damp.

Look at you! For a girl who's always such a prude, you actually did it.

Now that you've "grown up," you're no longer a pear blossom and more like a peach—all rosy and pink. There's not a man alive who won't fall for you after seeing that face.

.....

Congratulations, Ehwa. That's the way of adults. And you've discovered the secret game that women play.

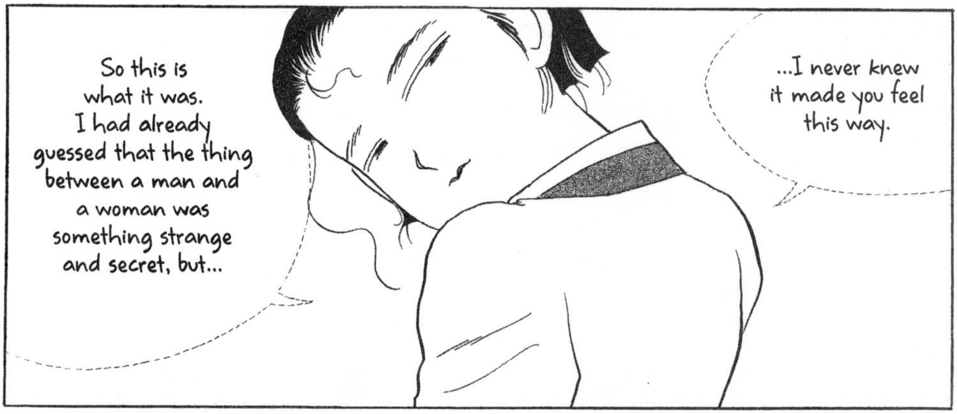
So this is what it was. I had already guessed that the thing between a man and a woman was something strange and secret, but...
...I never knew it made you feel this way.

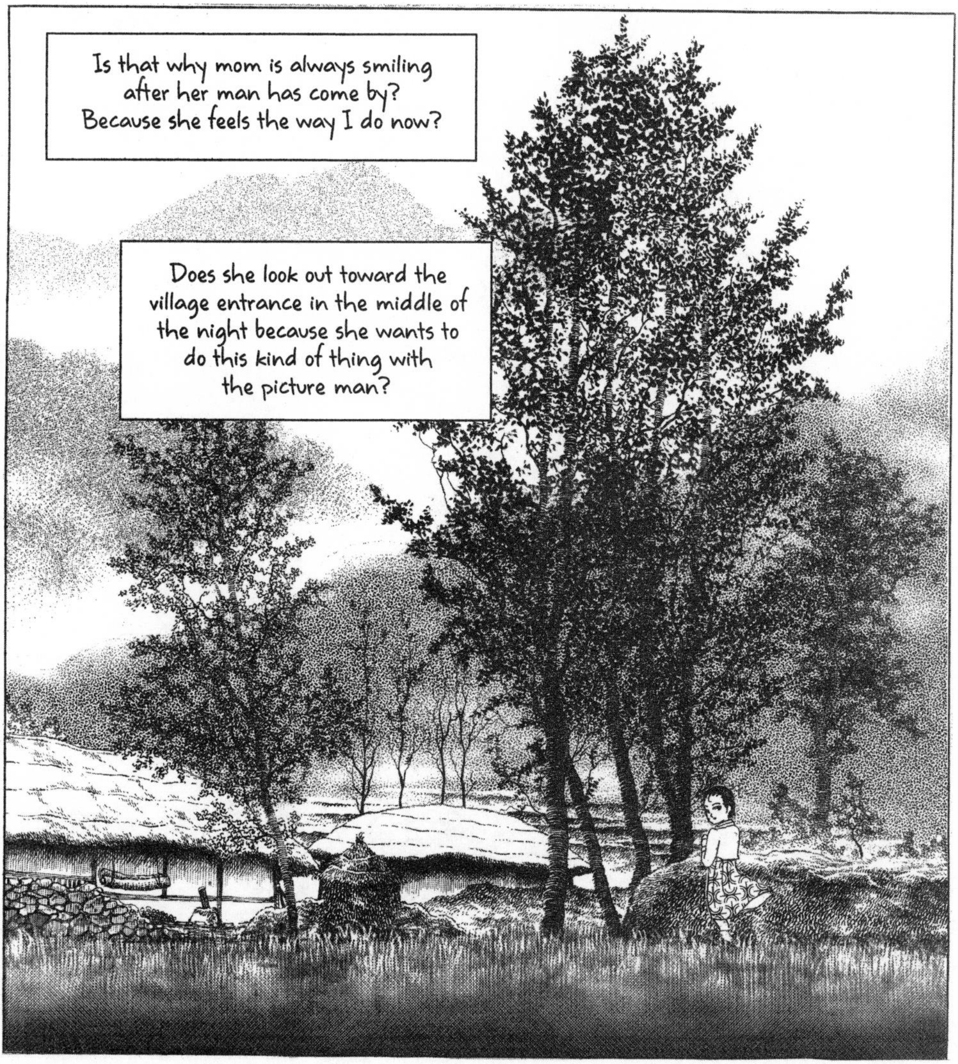
Is that why mom is always smiling after her man has come by? Because she feels the way I do now?
Does she look out toward the village entrance in the middle of the night because she wants to do this kind of thing with the picture man?

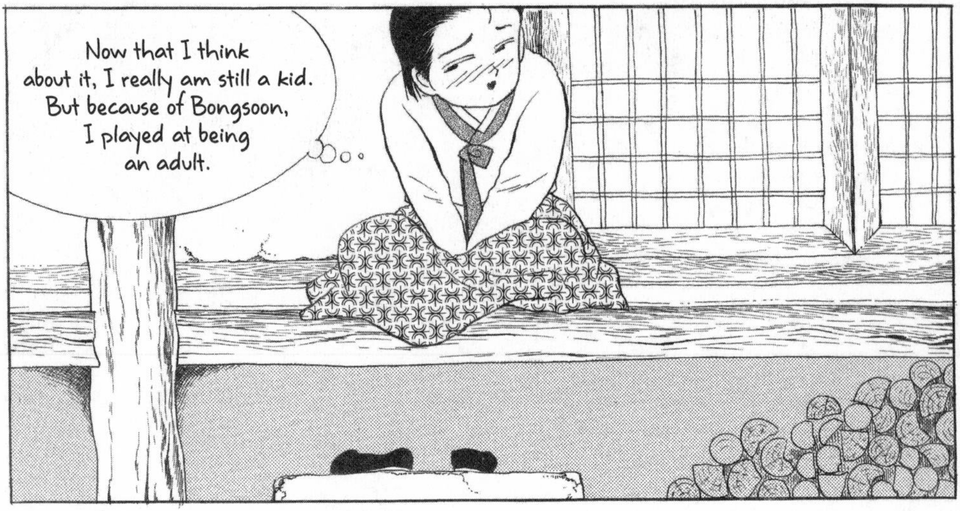
Now that I think about it, I really am still a kid. But because of Bongsoon, I played at being an adult.

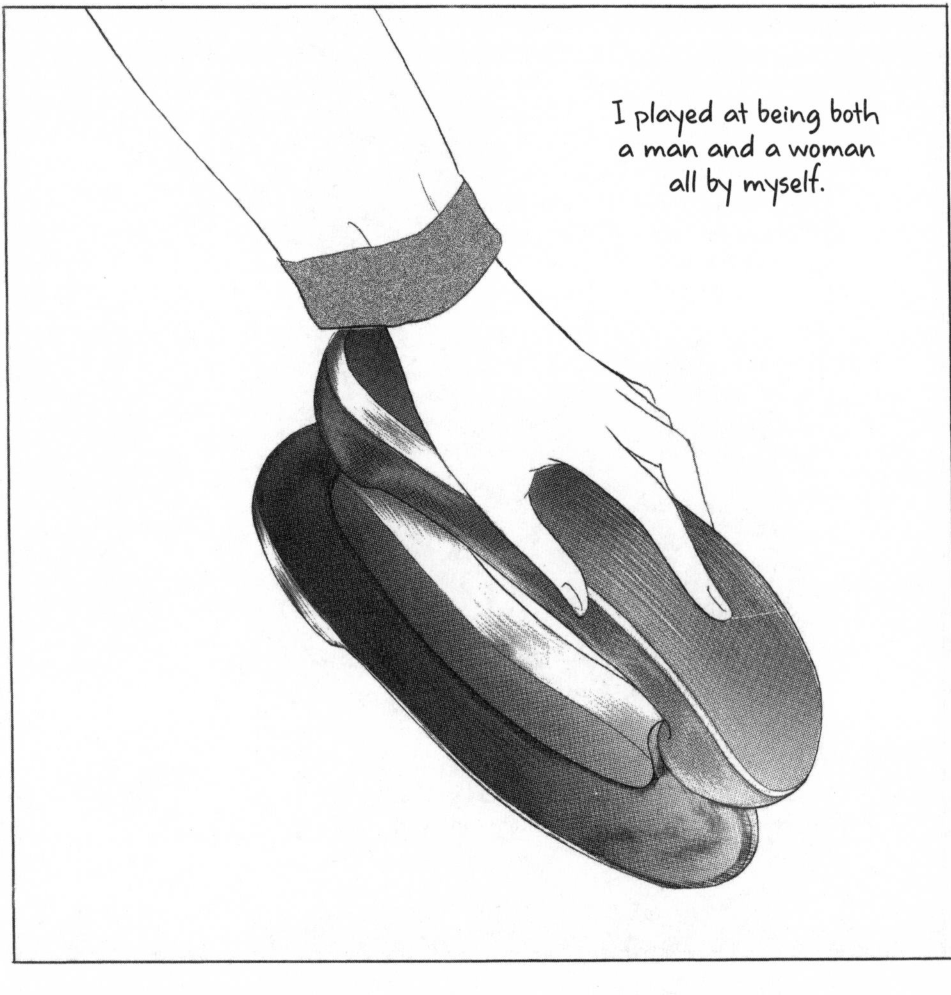
I played at being both a man and a woman all by myself.

Chapter Four

SCENT OF THE CHESTNUT FLOWER

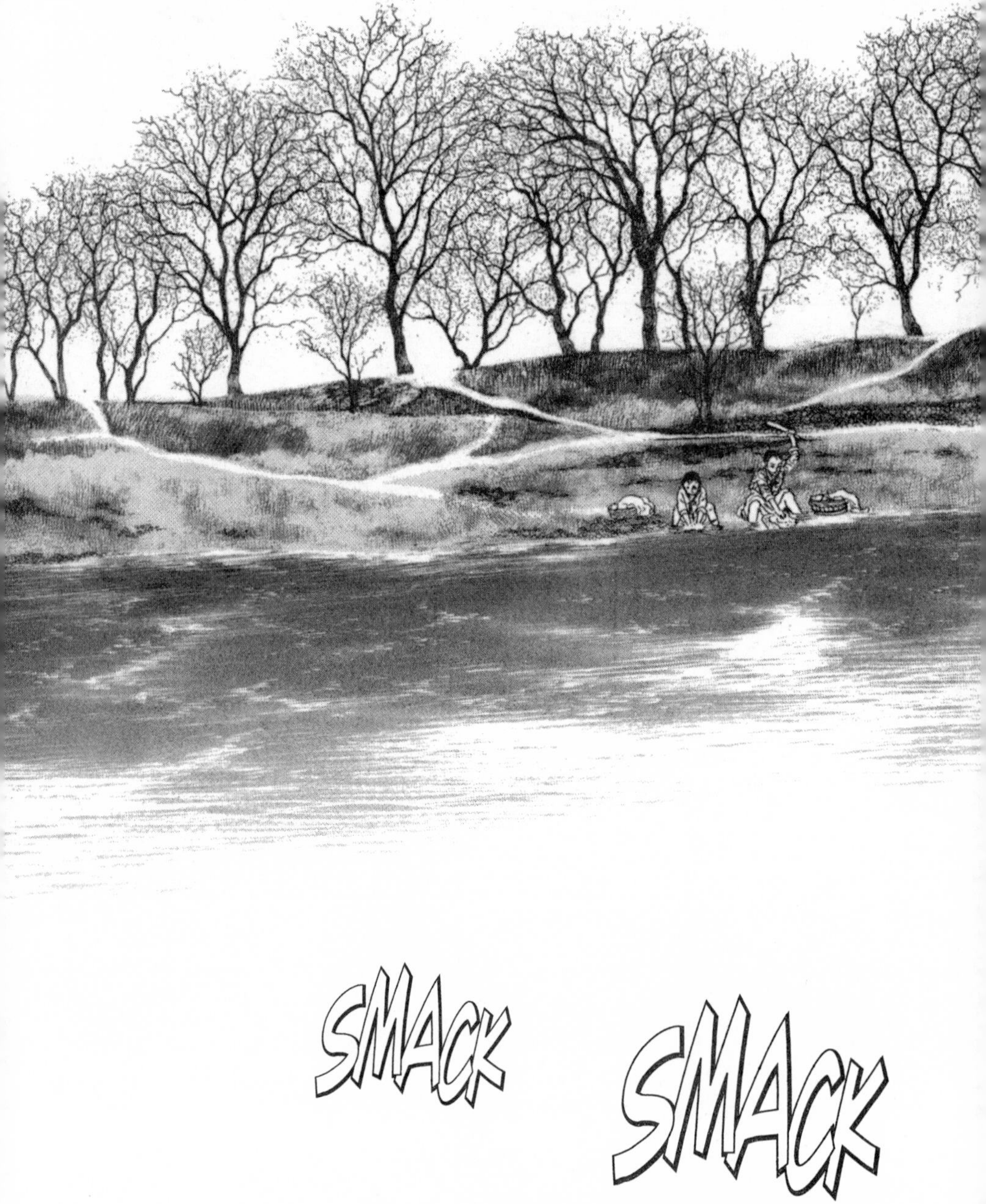
SMACK
SMACK

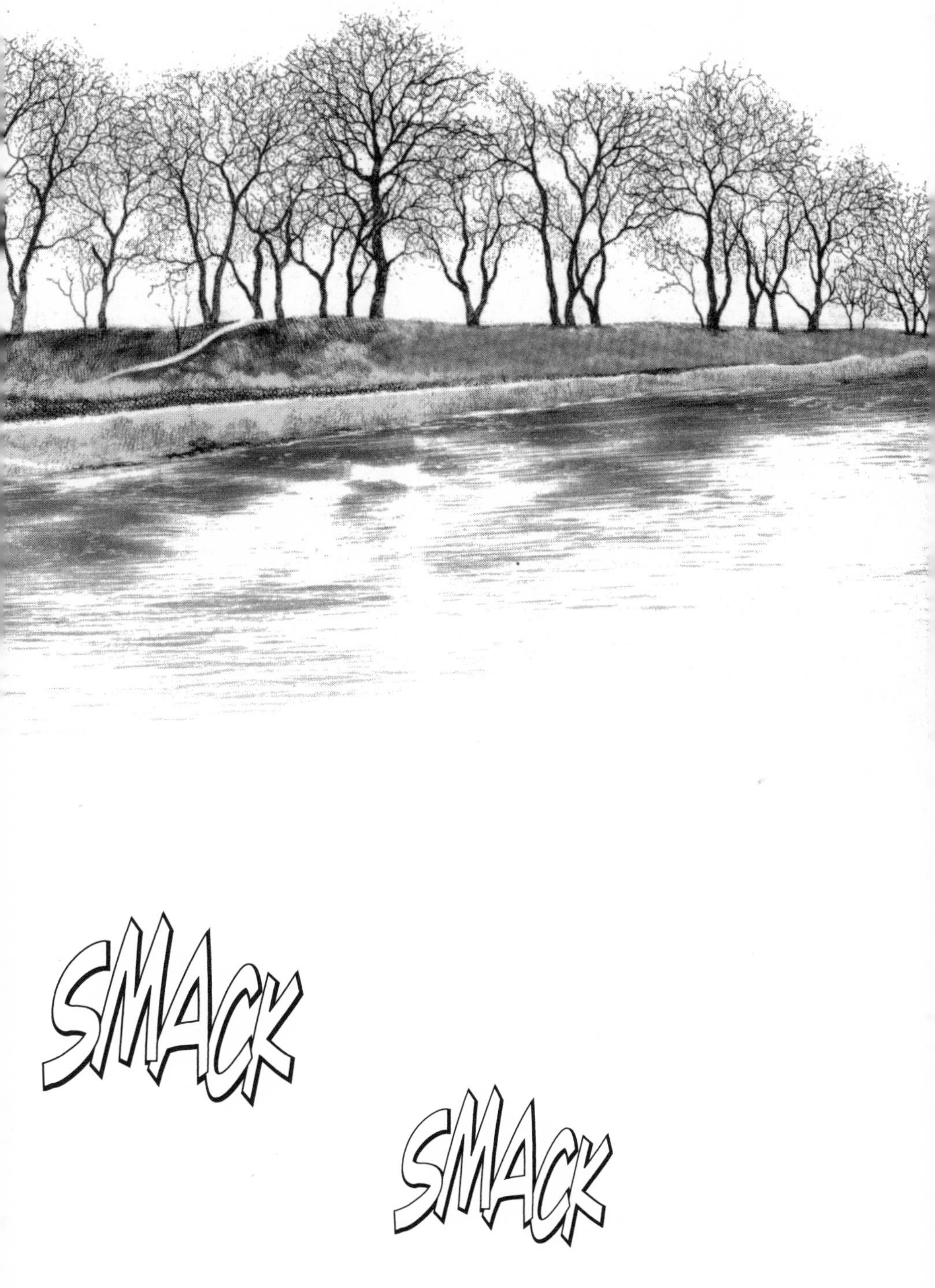
SMACK
SMACK

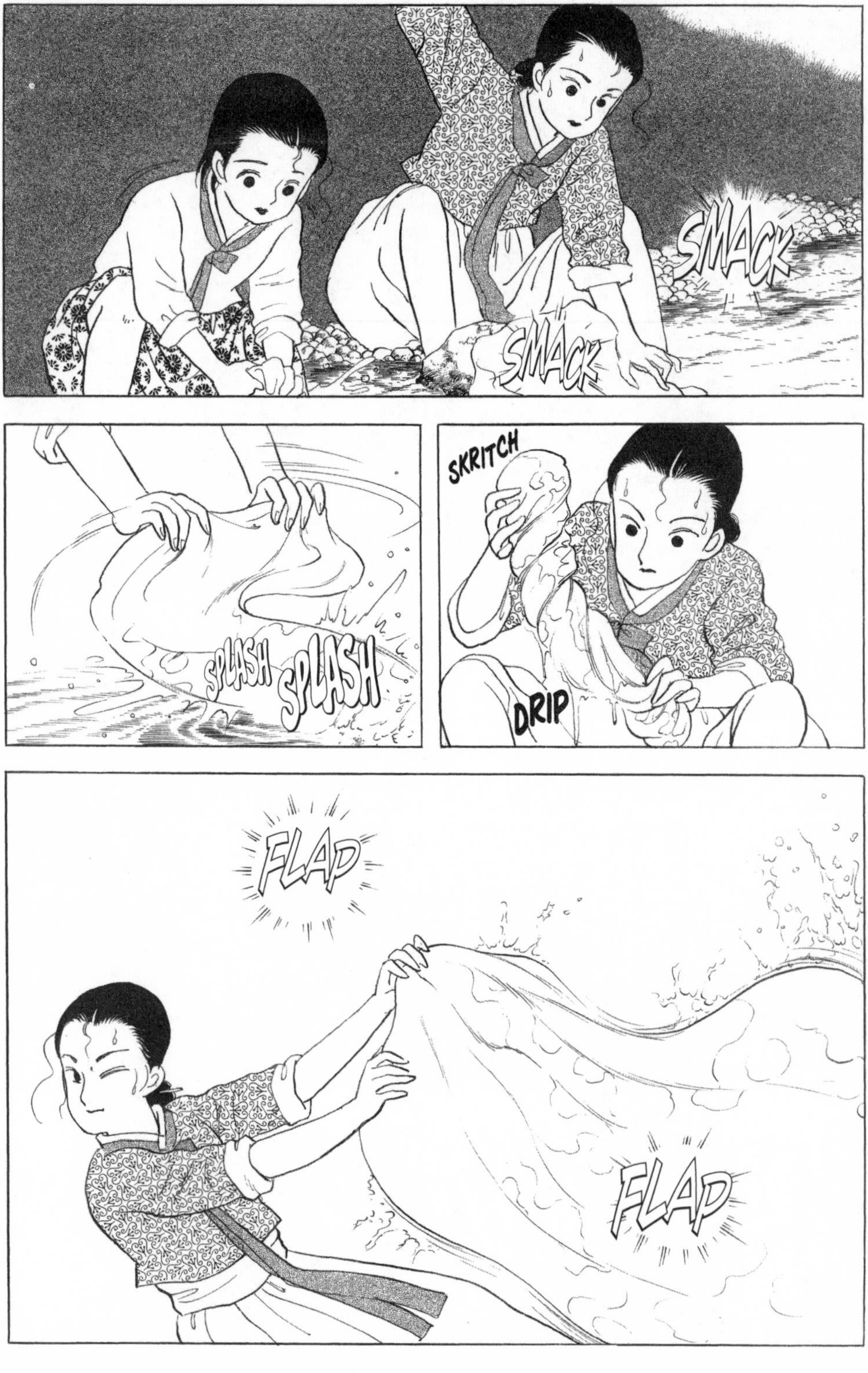
SMACK
SMACK
SPLASH
SPLASH
SKRITCH
DRIP
FLAP
FLAP

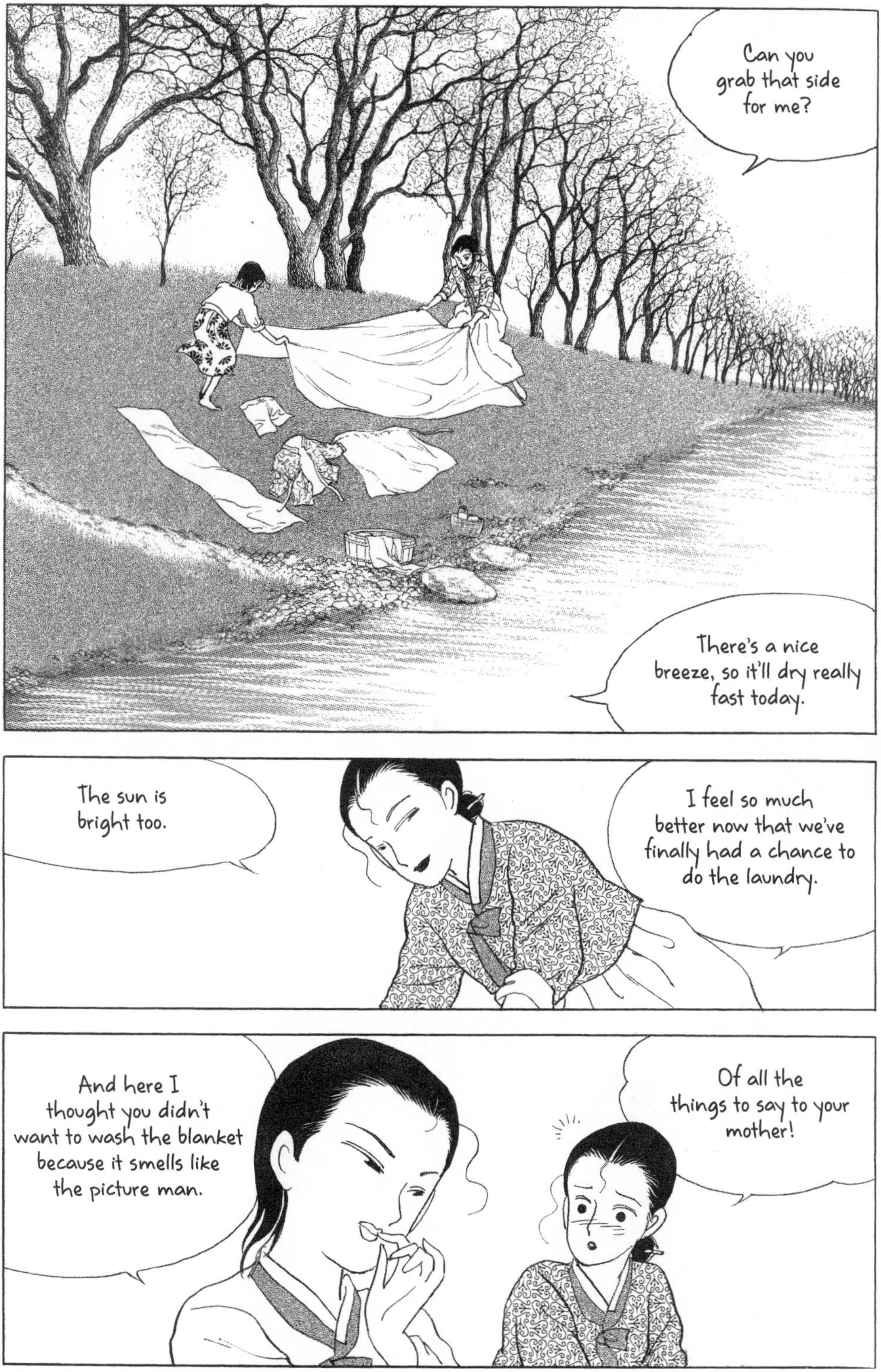
Can you grab that side for me?
There's a nice breeze, so it'll dry really fast today.
The sun is bright too.
I feel so much better now that we've finally had a chance to do the laundry.
And here I thought you didn't want to wash the blanket because it smells like the picture man.
Of all the things to say to your mother!

It's so peaceful here.

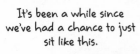

It's been a while since we've had a chance to just sit like this.

Every summer, when your father was still alive, we'd come out here to fish together. Then we'd cook what we caught by the riverbank.

He was such a thoughtful man. He would insist on cleaning the fish because he didn't want me to have to do such a dirty job.

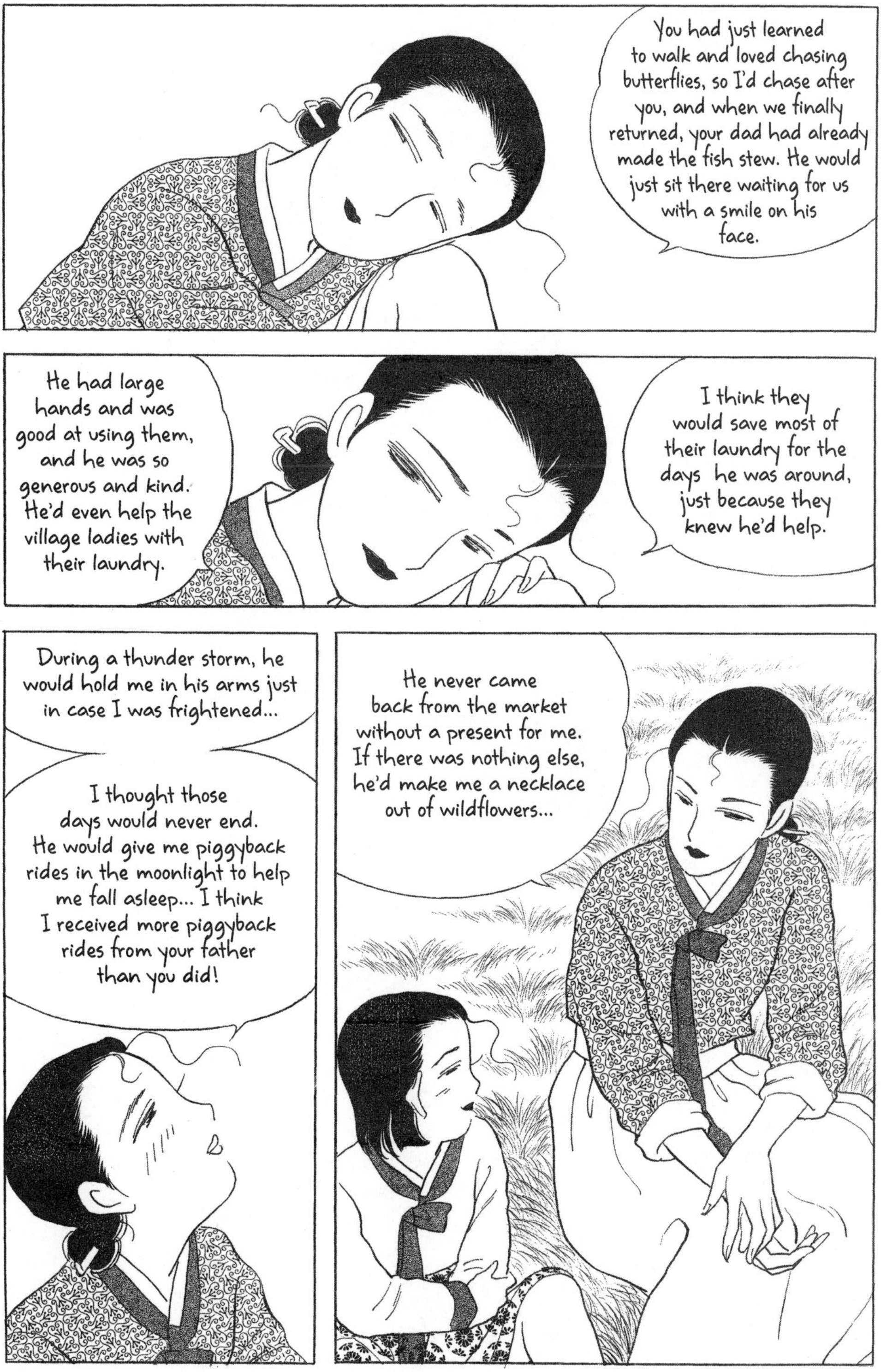
You had just learned to walk and loved chasing butterflies, so I'd chase after you, and when we finally returned, your dad had already made the fish stew. He would just sit there waiting for us with a smile on his face.
He had large hands and was good at using them, and he was so generous and kind. He'd even help the village ladies with their laundry.
I think they would save most of their laundry for the days he was around, just because they knew he'd help.
During a thunder storm, he would hold me in his arms just in case I was frightened...
I thought those days would never end. He would give me piggyback rides in the moonlight to help me fall asleep... I think I received more piggyback rides from your father than you did!
He never came back from the market without a present for me. If there was nothing else, he'd make me a necklace out of wildflowers...

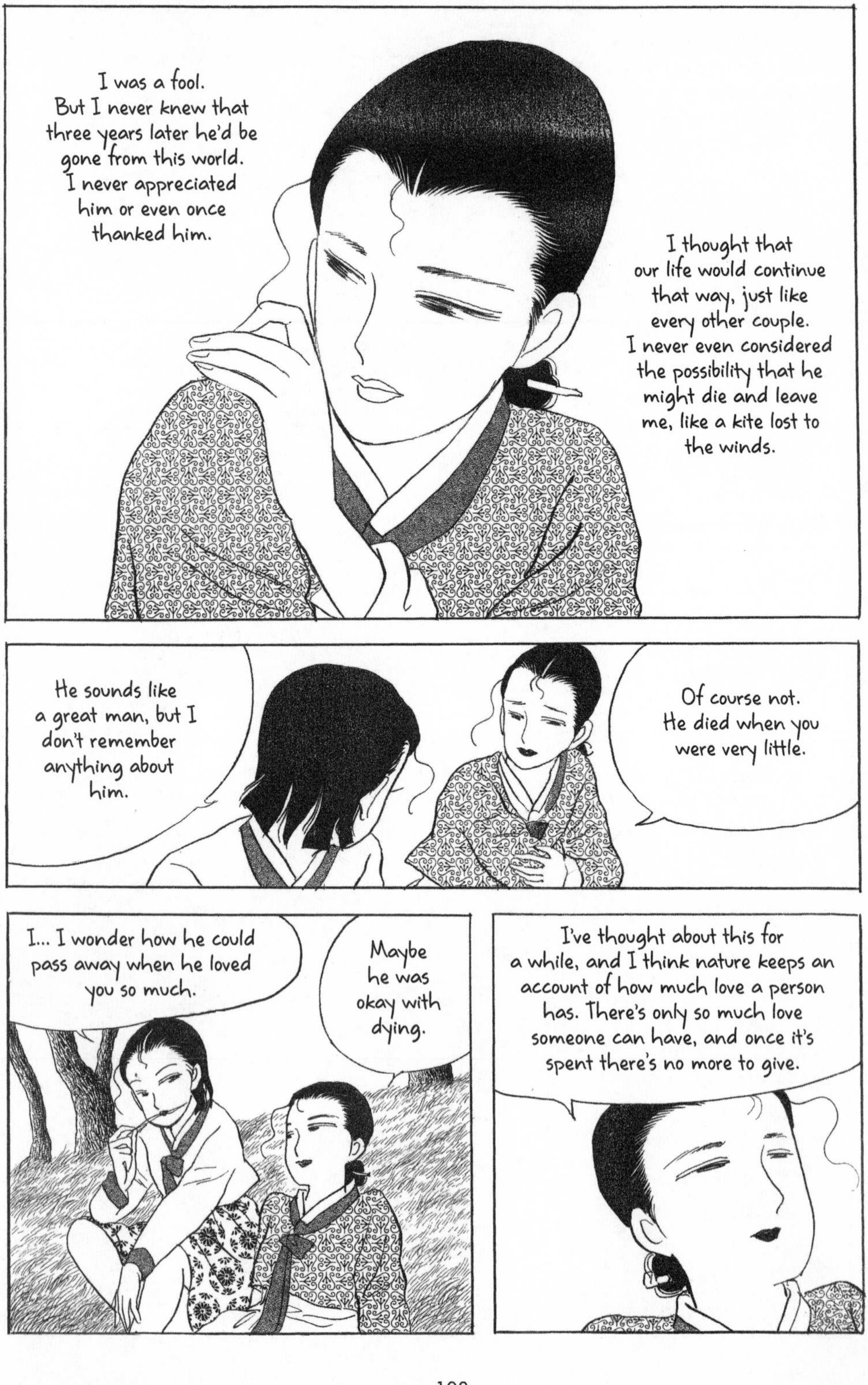
I was a fool. But I never knew that three years later he'd be gone from this world. I never appreciated him or even once thanked him.
I thought that our life would continue that way, just like every other couple. I never even considered the possibility that he might die and leave me, like a kite lost to the winds.
He sounds like a great man, but I don't remember anything about him.
Of course not. He died when you were very little.
I... I wonder how he could pass away when he loved you so much.
Maybe he was okay with dying.
I've thought about this for a while, and I think nature keeps an account of how much love a person has. There's only so much love someone can have, and once it's spent there's no more to give.

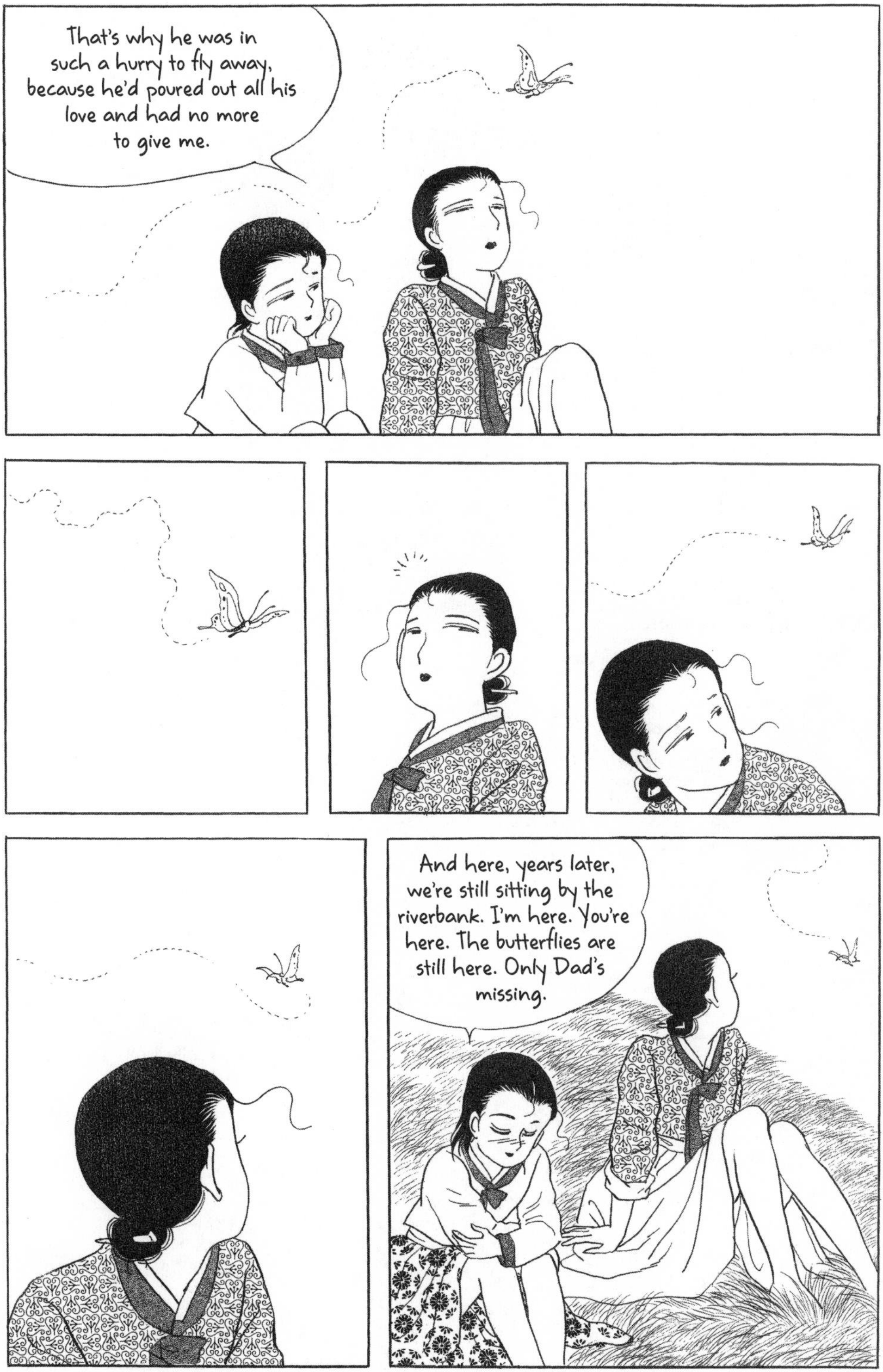
That's why he was in such a hurry to fly away, because he'd poured out all his love and had no more to give me.
And here, years later, we're still sitting by the riverbank. I'm here. You're here. The butterflies are still here. Only Dad's missing.

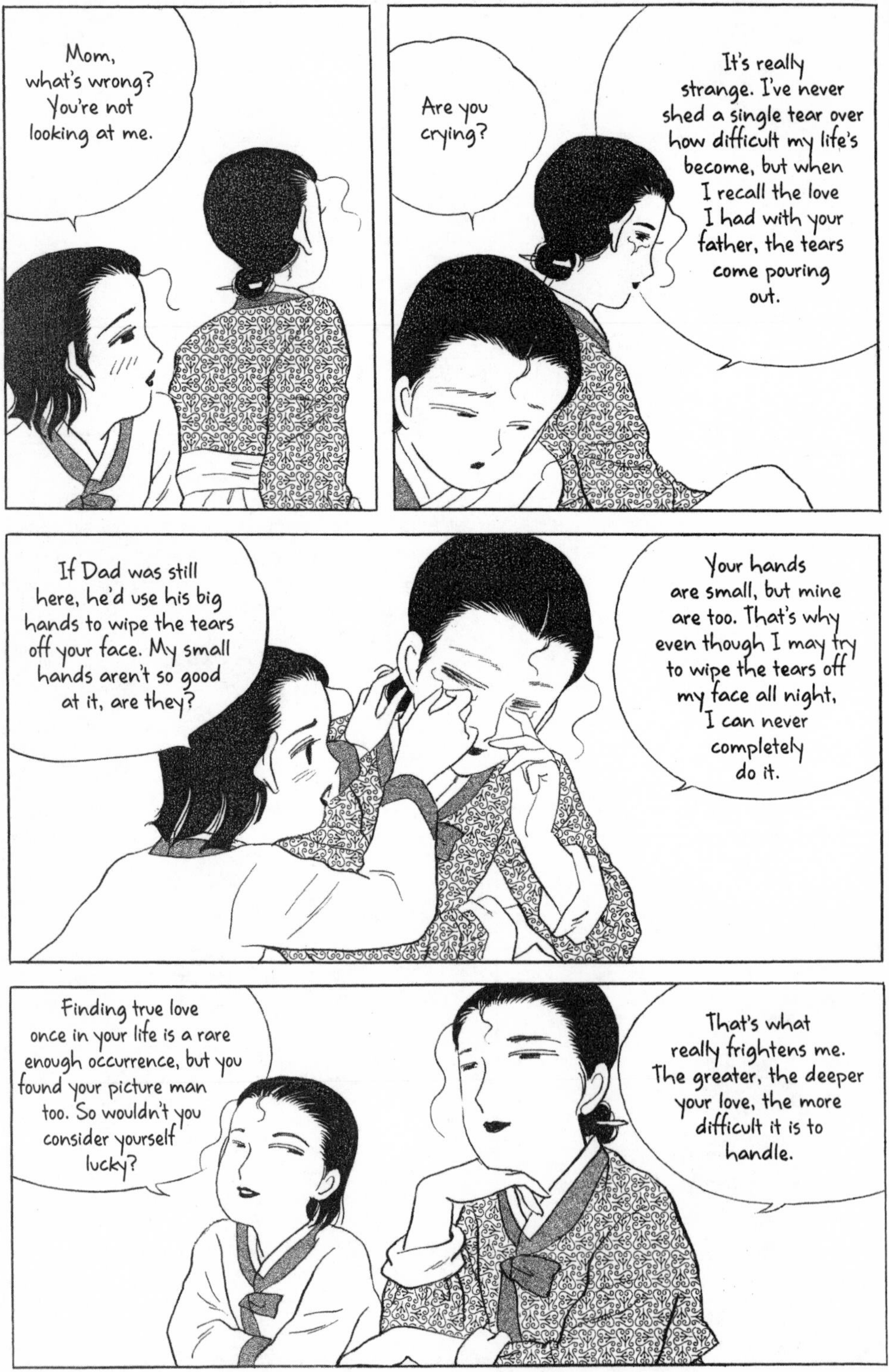
Mom, what's wrong? You're not looking at me.
Are you crying?
It's really strange. I've never shed a single tear over how difficult my life's become, but when I recall the love I had with your father, the tears come pouring out.
If Dad was still here, he'd use his big hands to wipe the tears off your face. My small hands aren't so good at it, are they?
Your hands are small, but mine are too. That's why even though I may try to wipe the tears off my face all night, I can never completely do it.
Finding true love once in your life is a rare enough occurrence, but you found your picture man too. So wouldn't you consider yourself lucky?
That's what really frightens me. The greater, the deeper your love, the more difficult it is to handle.

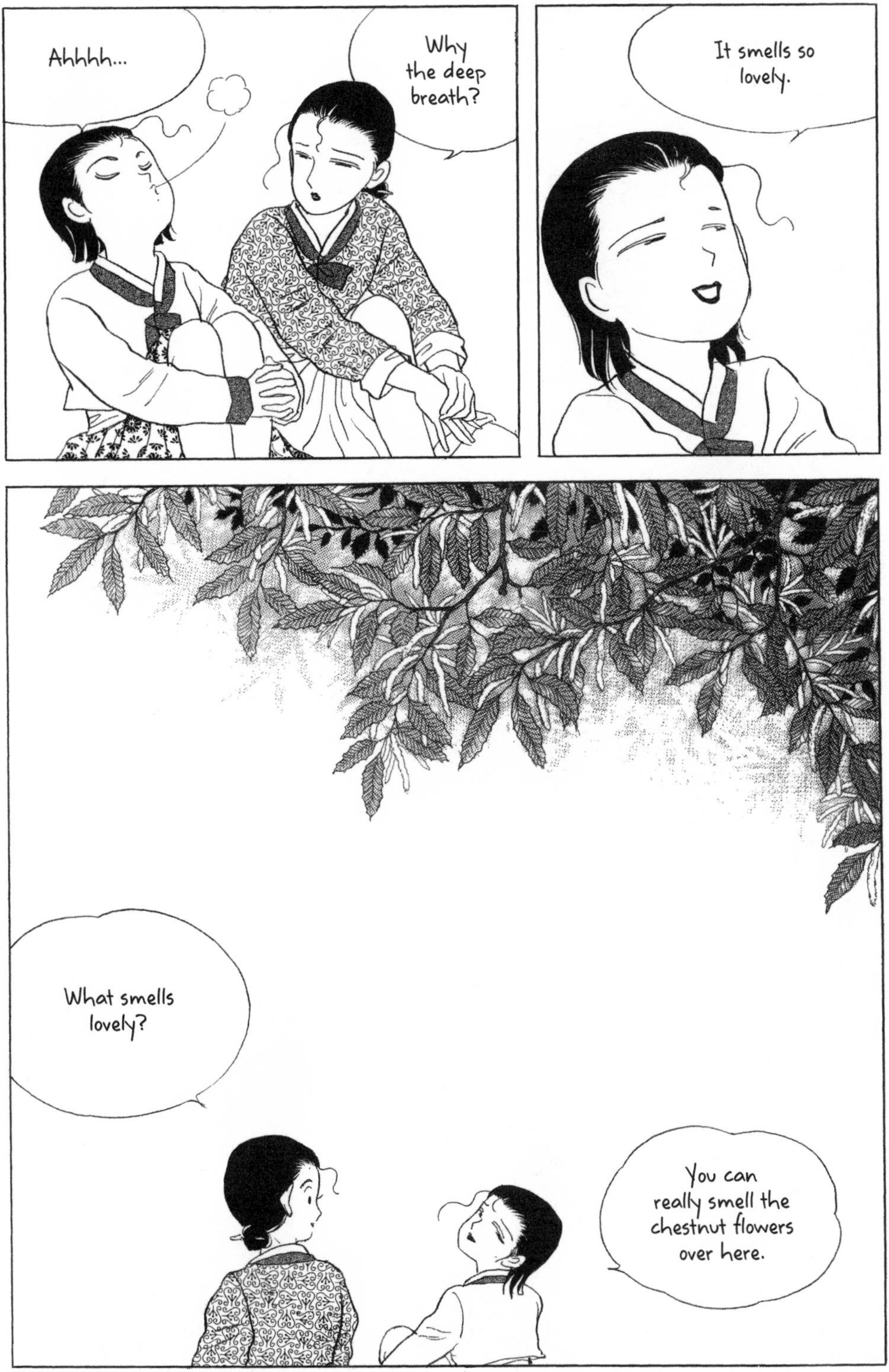
Ahhhh...
Why the deep breath?
It smells so lovely.
What smells lovely?
You can really smell the chestnut flowers over here.

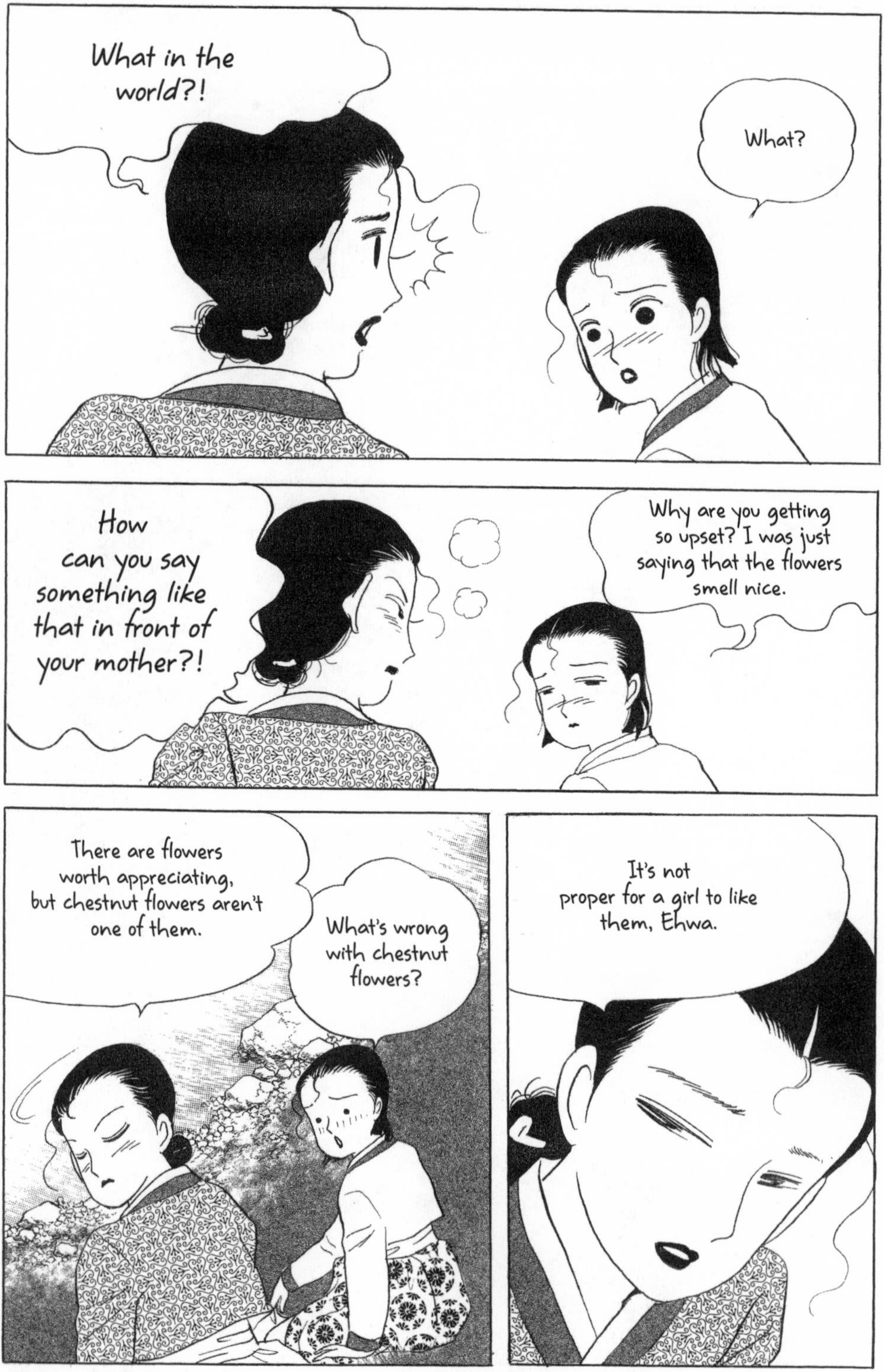
What in the world?!
What?
How can you say something like that in front of your mother?!
Why are you getting so upset? I was just saying that the flowers smell nice.
There are flowers worth appreciating, but chestnut flowers aren't one of them.
What's wrong with chestnut flowers?
It's not proper for a girl to like them, Ehwa.

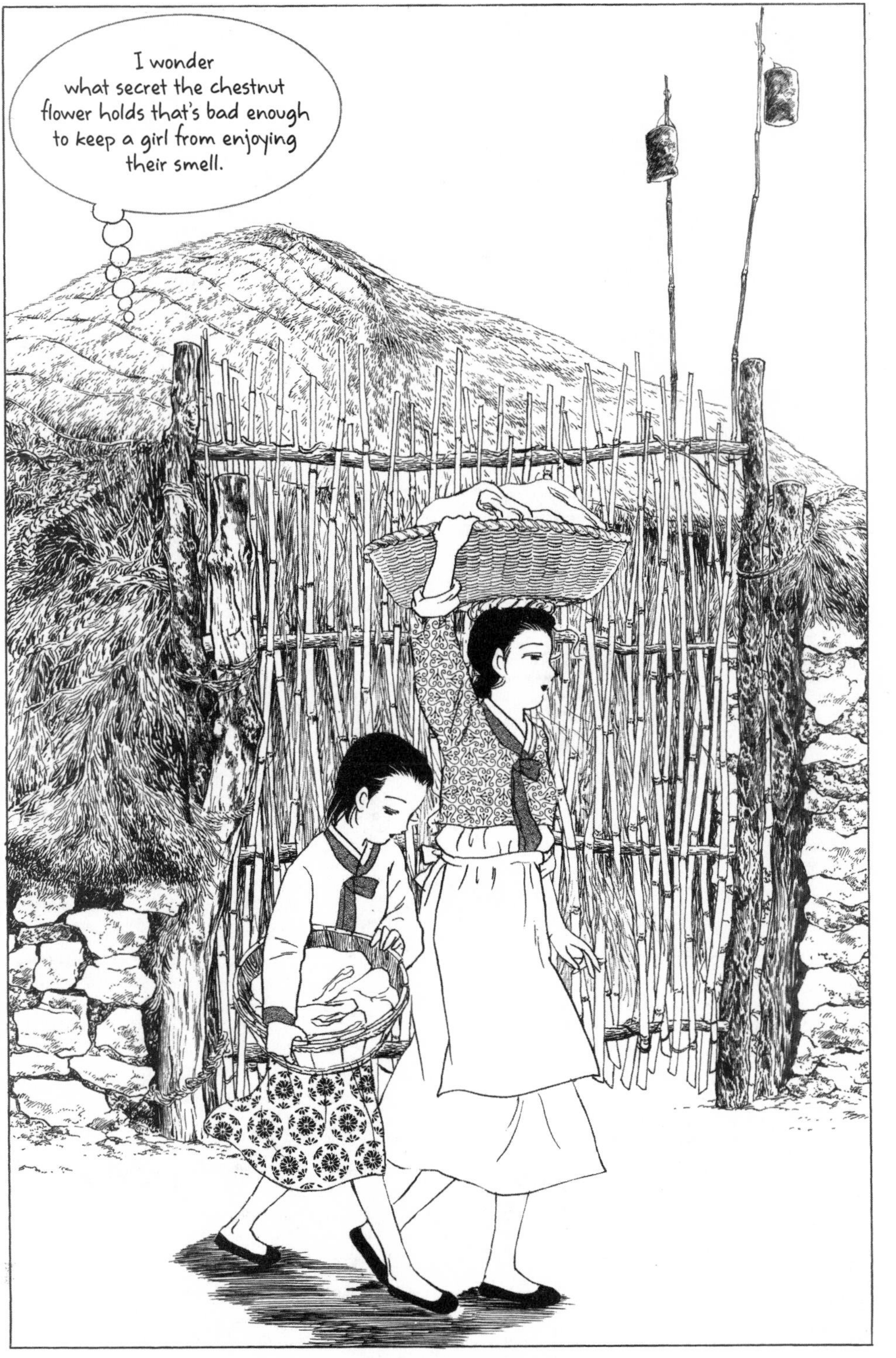
I wonder what secret the chestnut flower holds that's bad enough to keep a girl from enjoying their smell.

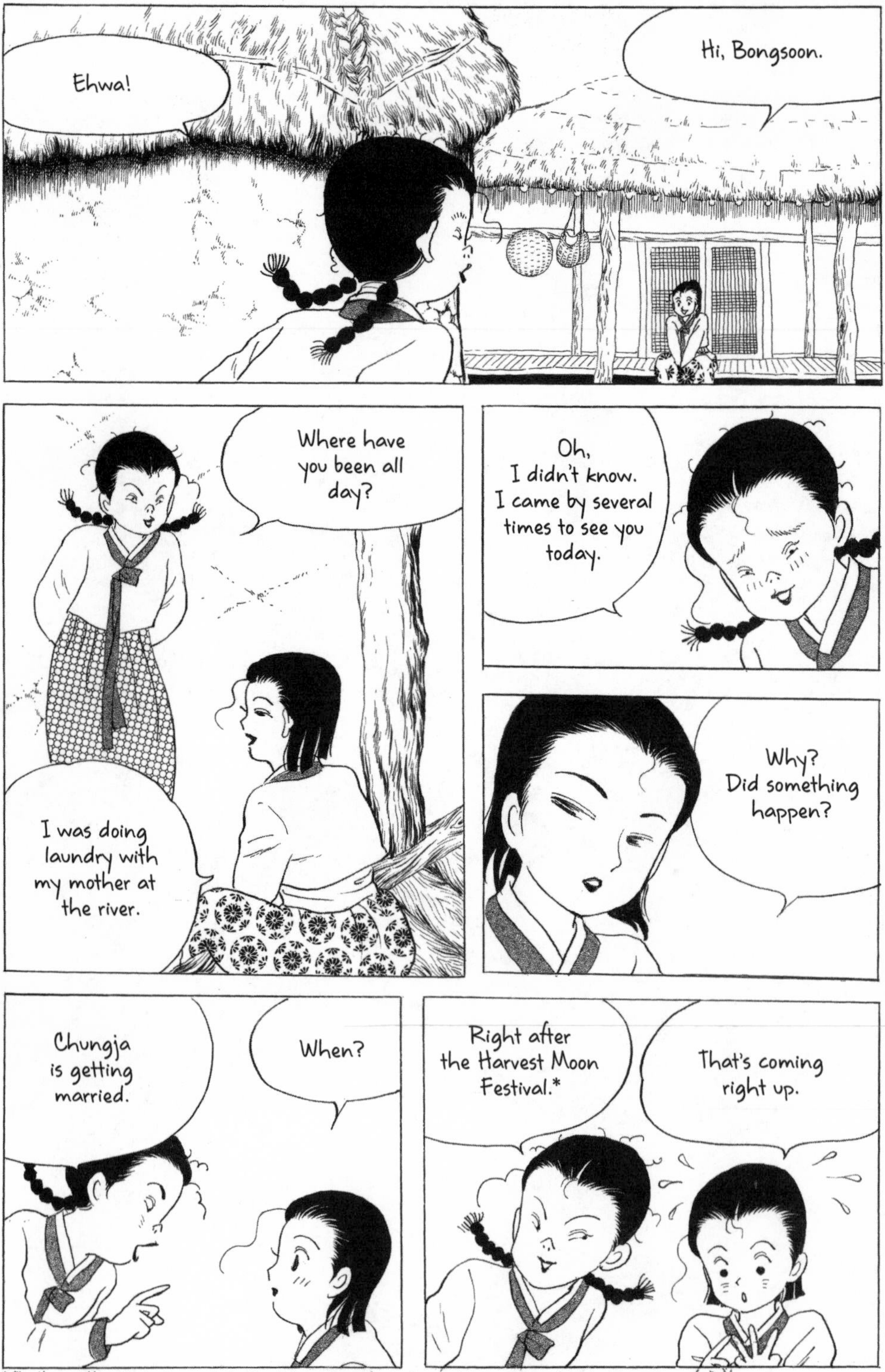
Ehwa!
Hi, Bongsoon.
Where have you been all day?
I was doing laundry with my mother at the river.
Oh, I didn't know. I came by several times to see you today.
Why? Did something happen?
Chungja is getting married.
When?
Right after the Harvest Moon Festival.*
That's coming right up.

* The Harvest Moon Festival is usually held mid-August to celebrate the year's harvest.

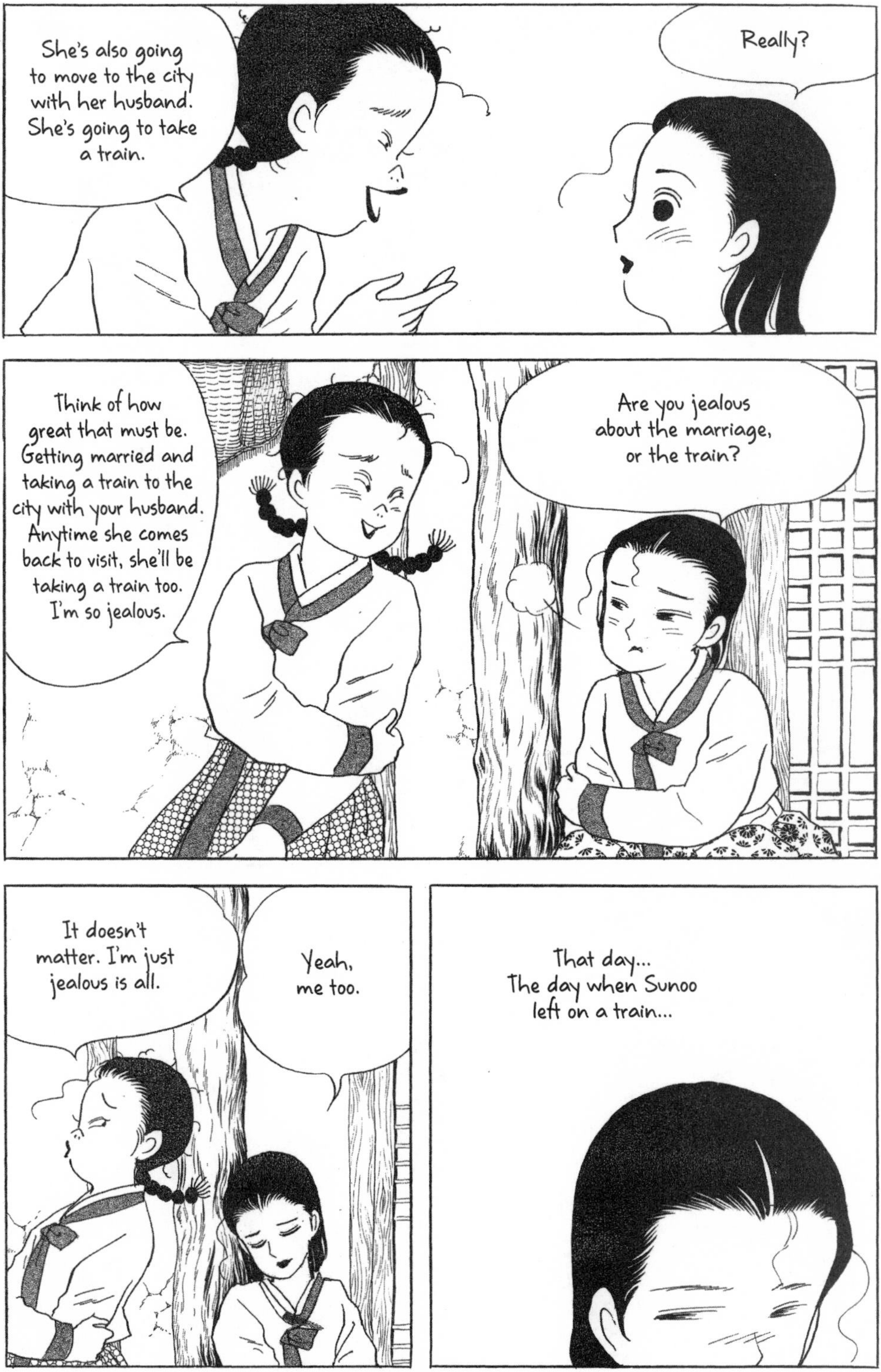
She's also going to move to the city with her husband. She's going to take a train.
Really?
Think of how great that must be. Getting married and taking a train to the city with your husband. Anytime she comes back to visit, she'll be taking a train too. I'm so jealous.
Are you jealous about the marriage, or the train?
It doesn't matter. I'm just jealous is all.
Yeah, me too.
That day... The day when Sunoo left on a train...

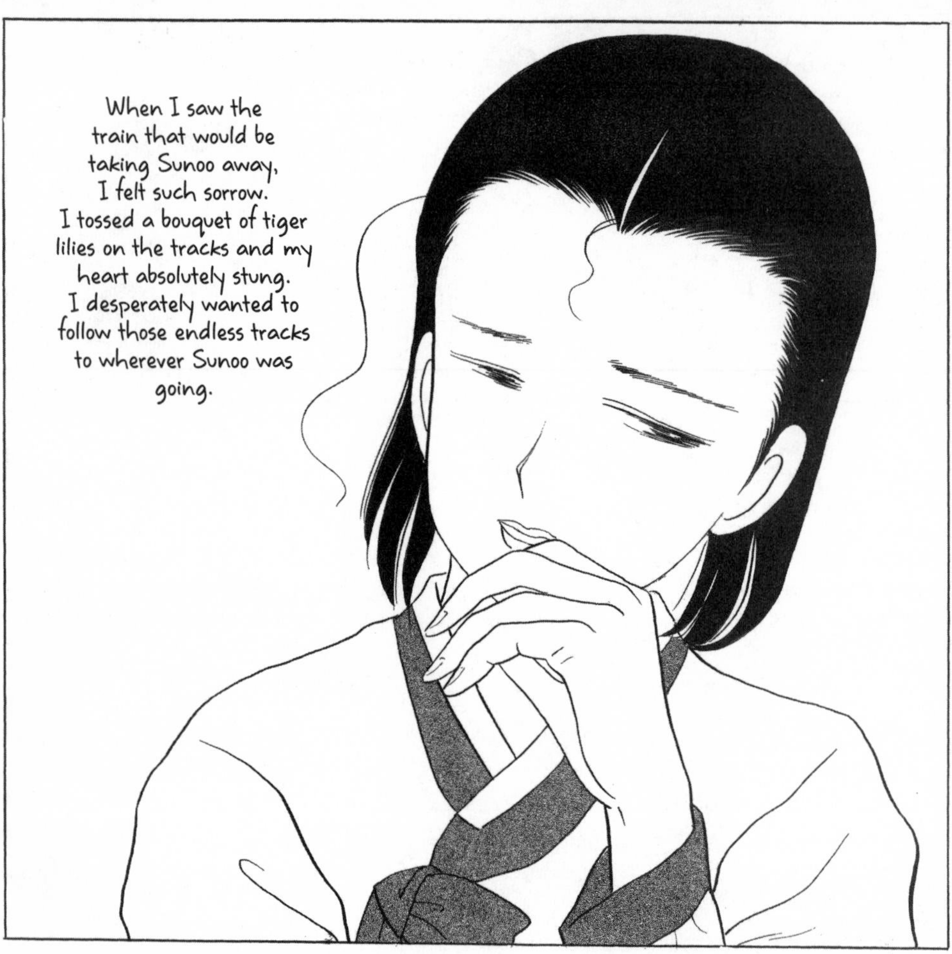
When I saw the train that would be taking Sunoo away, I felt such sorrow. I tossed a bouquet of tiger lilies on the tracks and my heart absolutely stung. I desperately wanted to follow those endless tracks to wherever Sunoo was going.
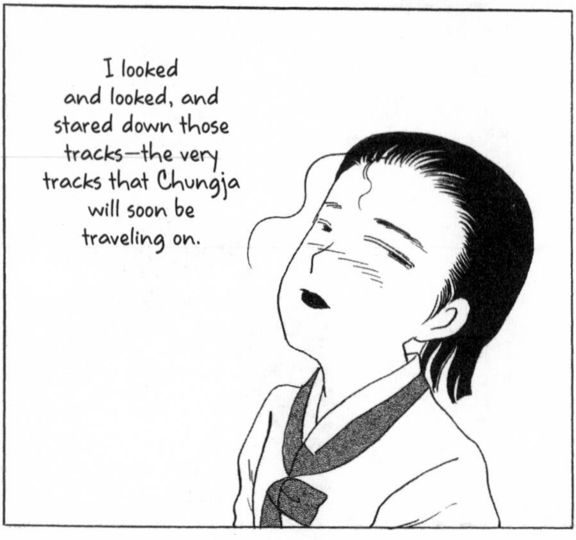
I looked and looked, and stared down those tracks—the very tracks that Chungja will soon be traveling on.
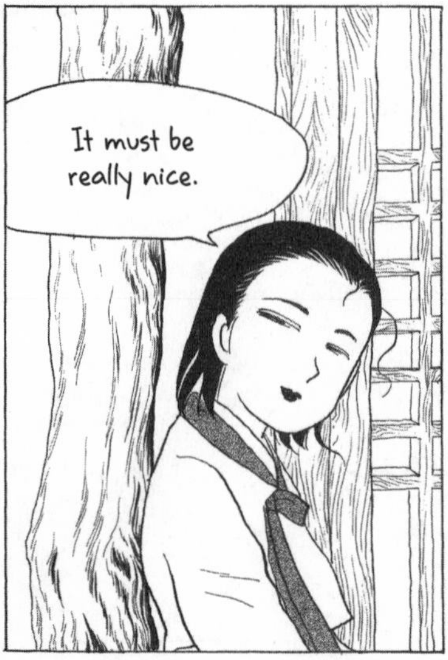
It must be really nice.

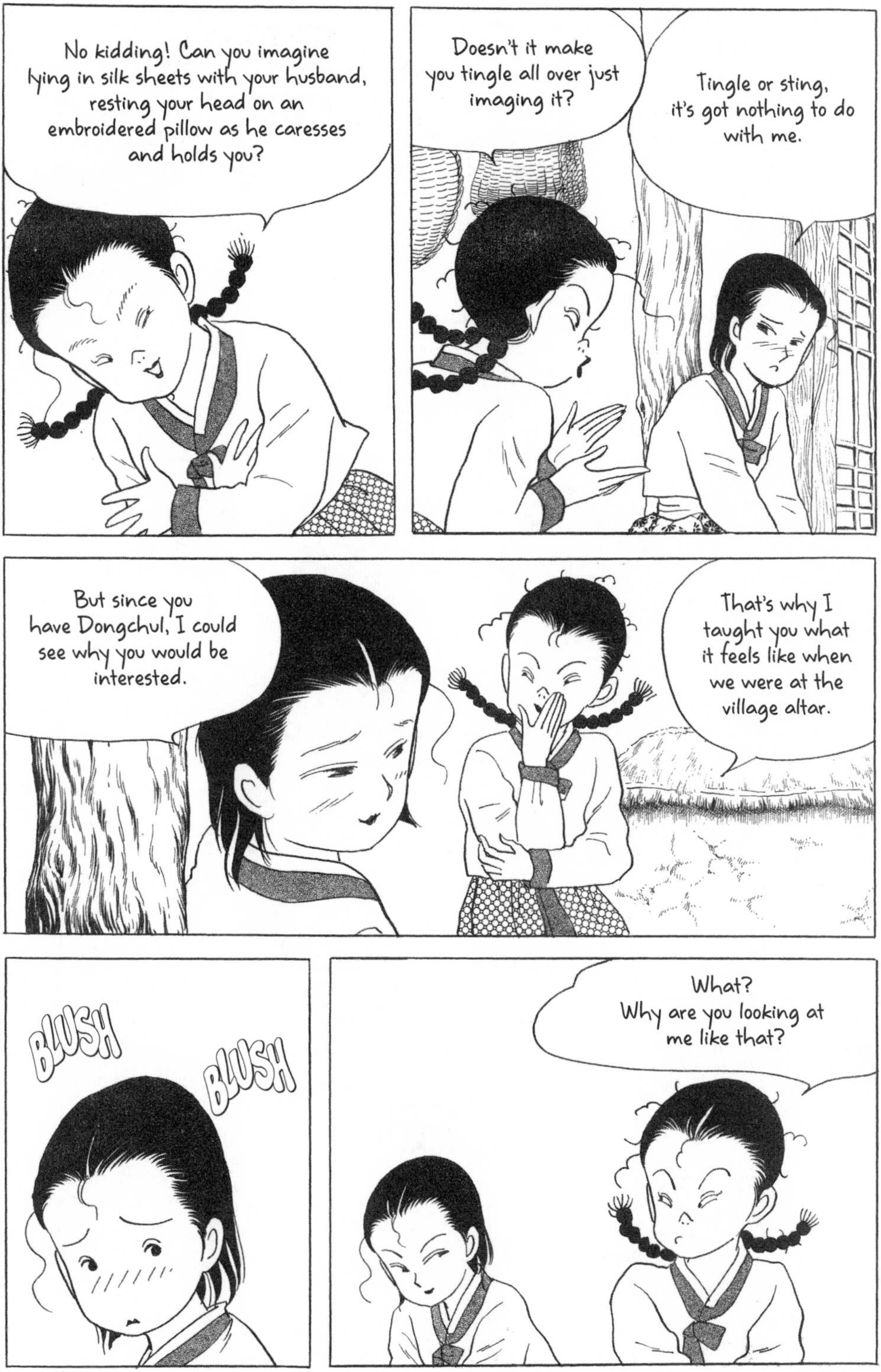
No kidding! Can you imagine lying in silk sheets with your husband, resting your head on an embroidered pillow as he caresses and holds you?
Doesn't it make you tingle all over just imaging it?
Tingle or sting, it's got nothing to do with me.
But since you have Dongchul, I could see why you would be interested.
That's why I taught you what it feels like when we were at the village altar.
BLUSH
BLUSH
What? Why are you looking at me like that?

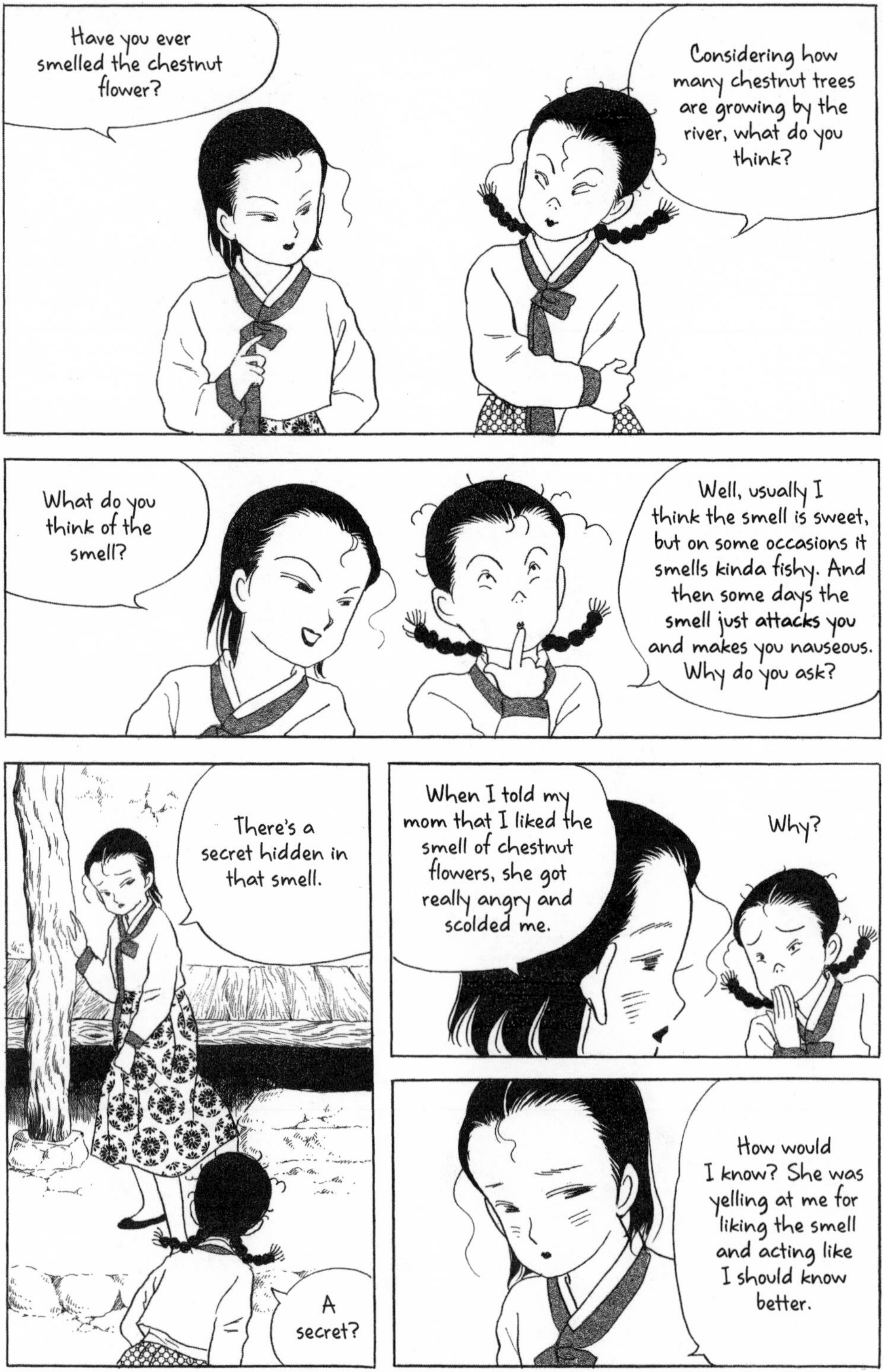
Have you ever smelled the chestnut flower?
Considering how many chestnut trees are growing by the river, what do you think?
What do you think of the smell?
Well, usually I think the smell is sweet, but on some occasions it smells kinda fishy. And then some days the smell just attacks you and makes you nauseous. Why do you ask?
There's a secret hidden in that smell.
A secret?
When I told my mom that I liked the smell of chestnut flowers, she got really angry and scolded me.
Why?
How would I know? She was yelling at me for liking the smell and acting like I should know better.

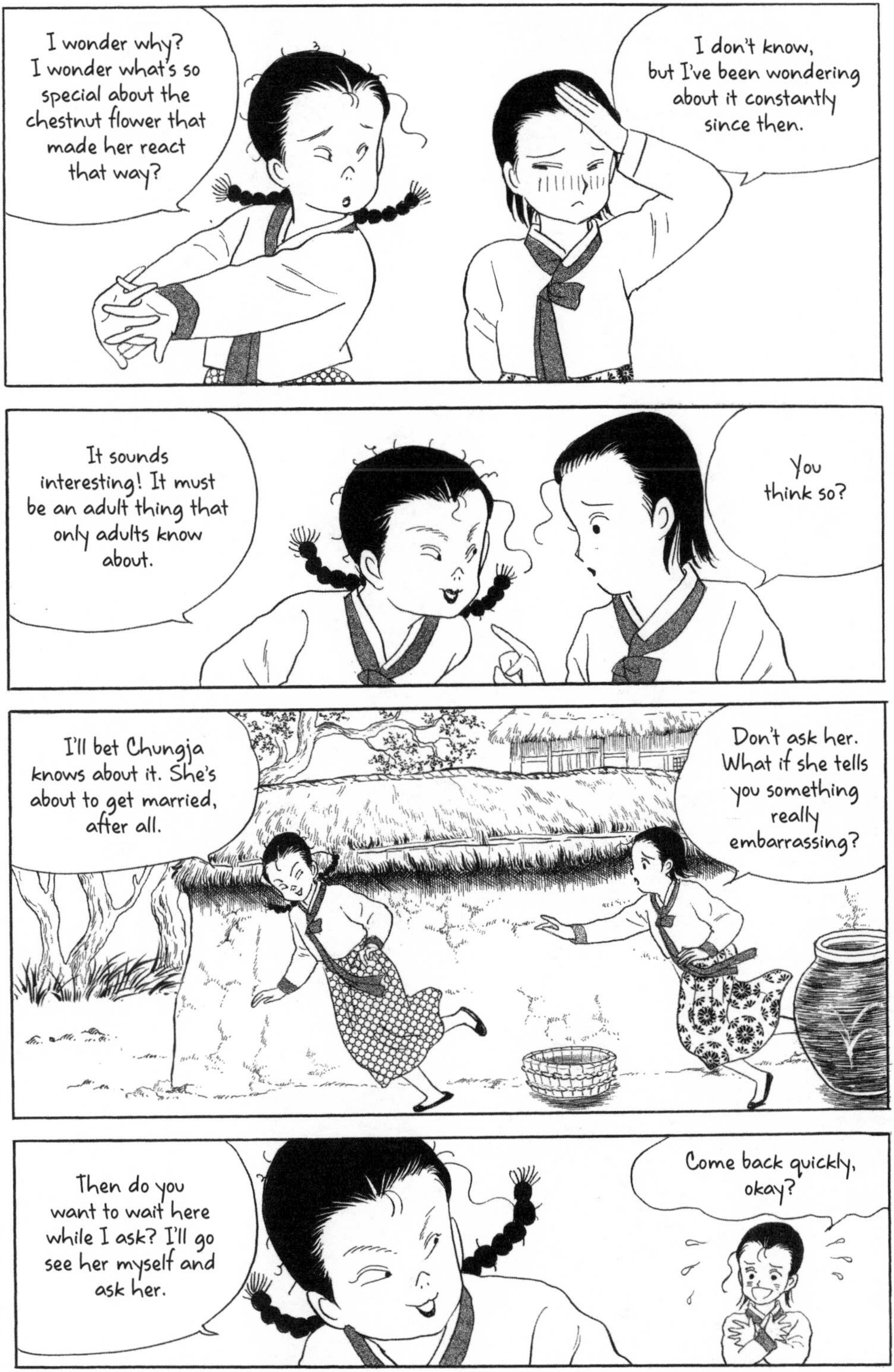
I wonder why? I wonder what's so special about the chestnut flower that made her react that way?
I don't know, but I've been wondering about it constantly since then.
It sounds interesting! It must be an adult thing that only adults know about.
You think so?
I'll bet Chungja knows about it. She's about to get married, after all.
Don't ask her. What if she tells you something really embarrassing?
Then do you want to wait here while I ask? I'll go see her myself and ask her.
Come back quickly, okay?

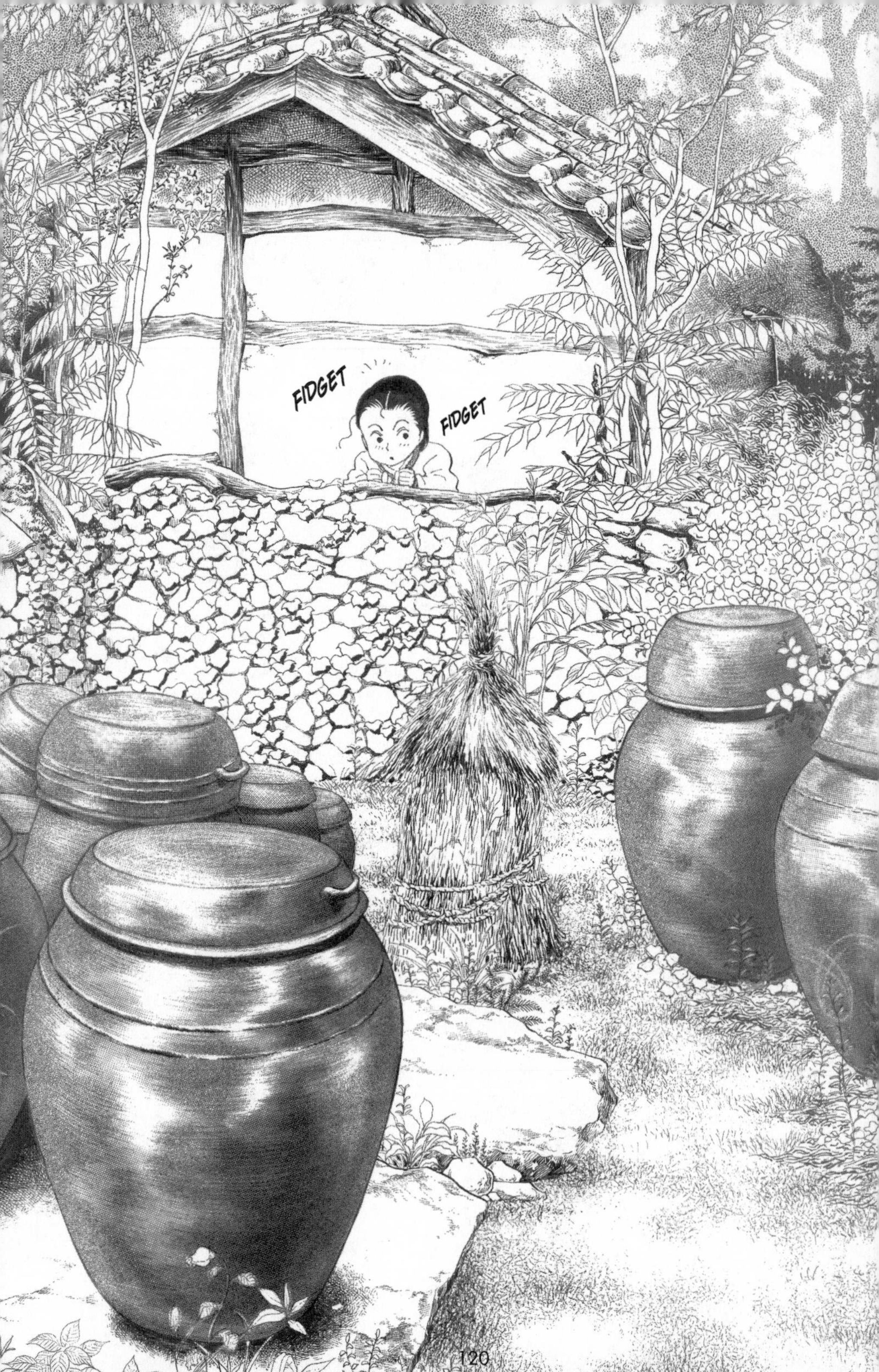
FIDGET
FIDGET

What's taking Bongsoon so long?! It must be that fat butt of hers. It's always slowing her down.
I'm dying of curiosity here and she's taking forever! What is she doing?

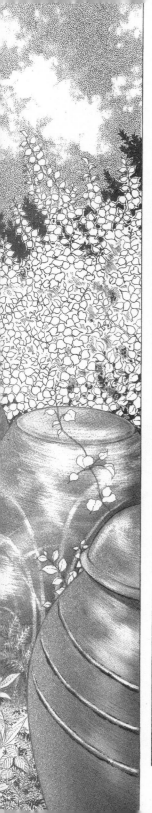

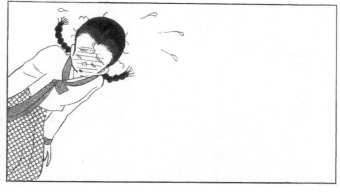

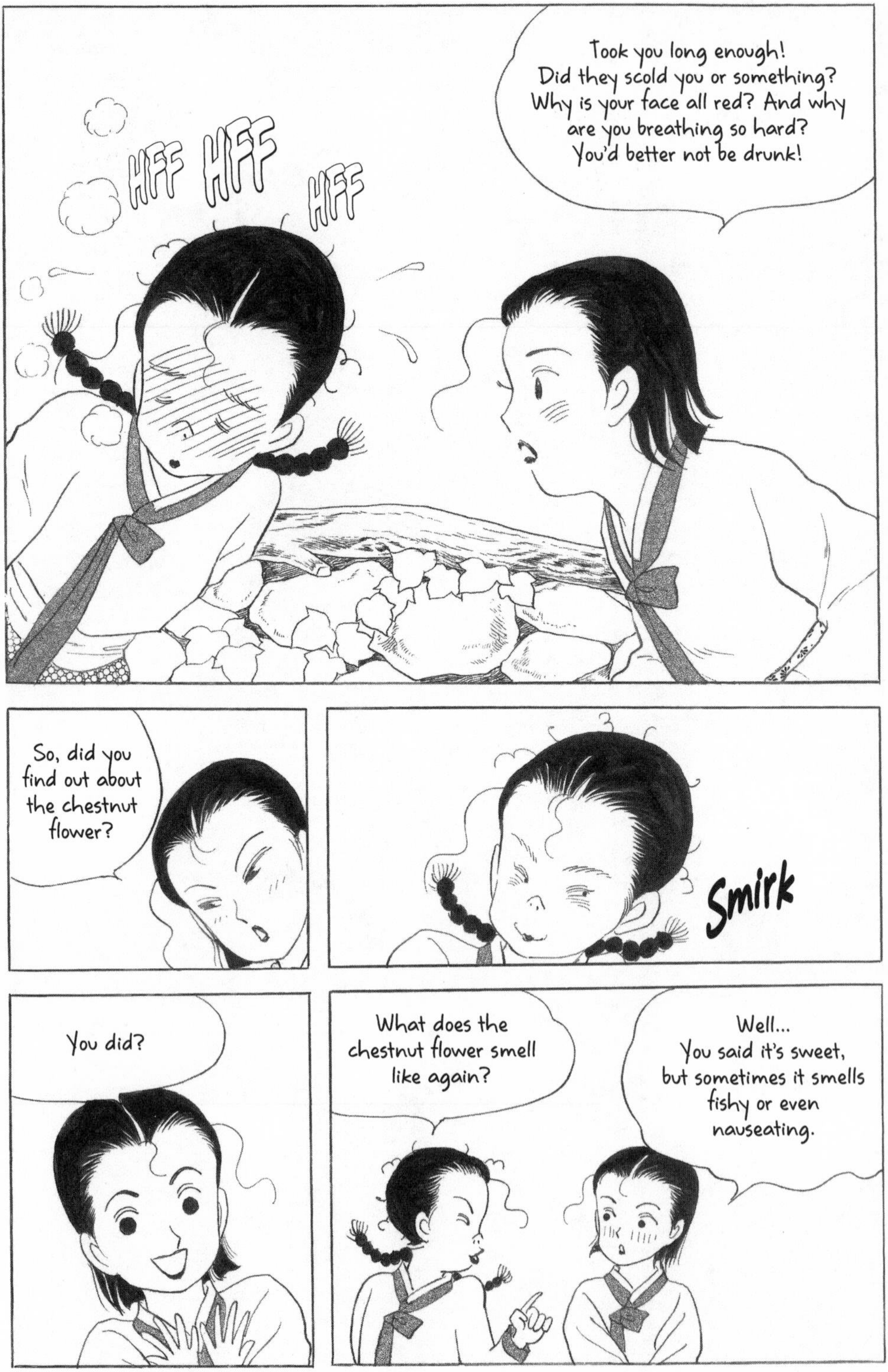
HFF HFF HFF
Took you long enough! Did they scold you or something? Why is your face all red? And why are you breathing so hard? You'd better not be drunk!
So, did you find out about the chestnut flower?
Smirk
You did?
What does the chestnut flower smell like again?
Well... You said it's sweet, but sometimes it smells fishy or even nauseating.

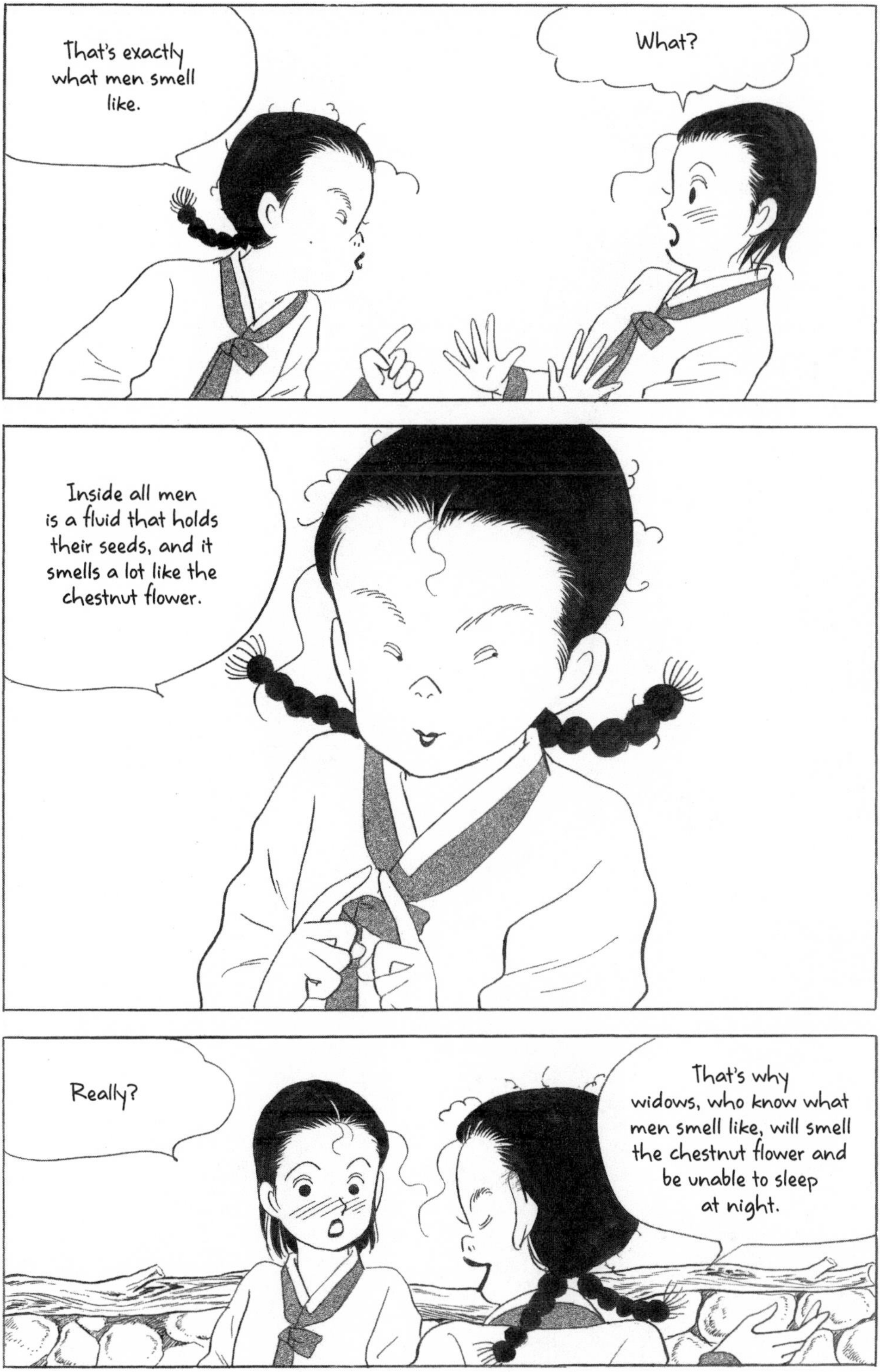
That's exactly what men smell like.
What?
Inside all men is a fluid that holds their seeds, and it smells a lot like the chestnut flower.
Really?
That's why widows, who know what men smell like, will smell the chestnut flower and be unable to sleep at night.

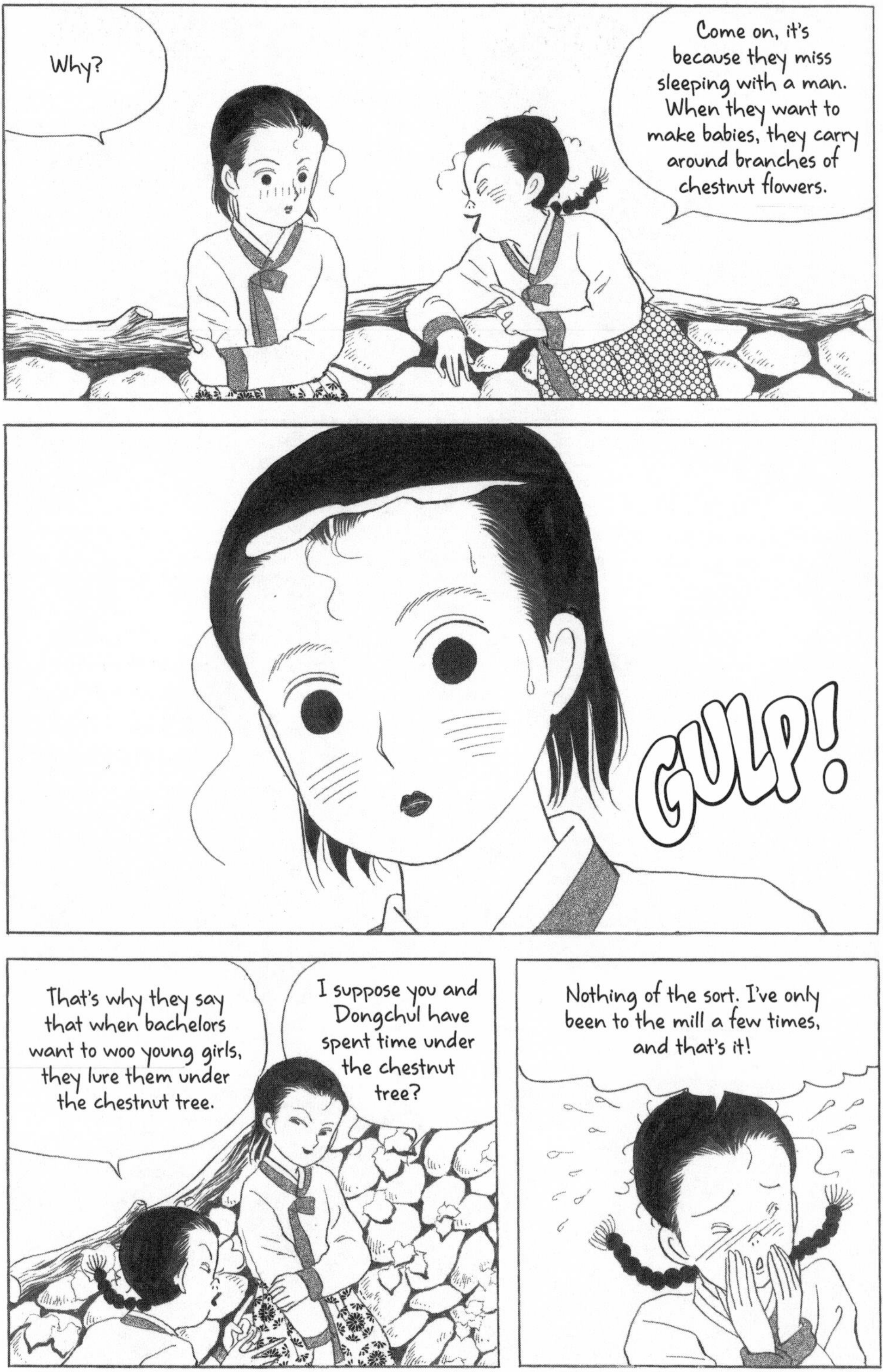

Why?
Come on, it's because they miss sleeping with a man. When they want to make babies, they carry around branches of chestnut flowers.
GULP!
That's why they say that when bachelors want to woo young girls, they lure them under the chestnut tree.
I suppose you and Dongchul have spent time under the chestnut tree?
Nothing of the sort. I've only been to the mill a few times, and that's it!

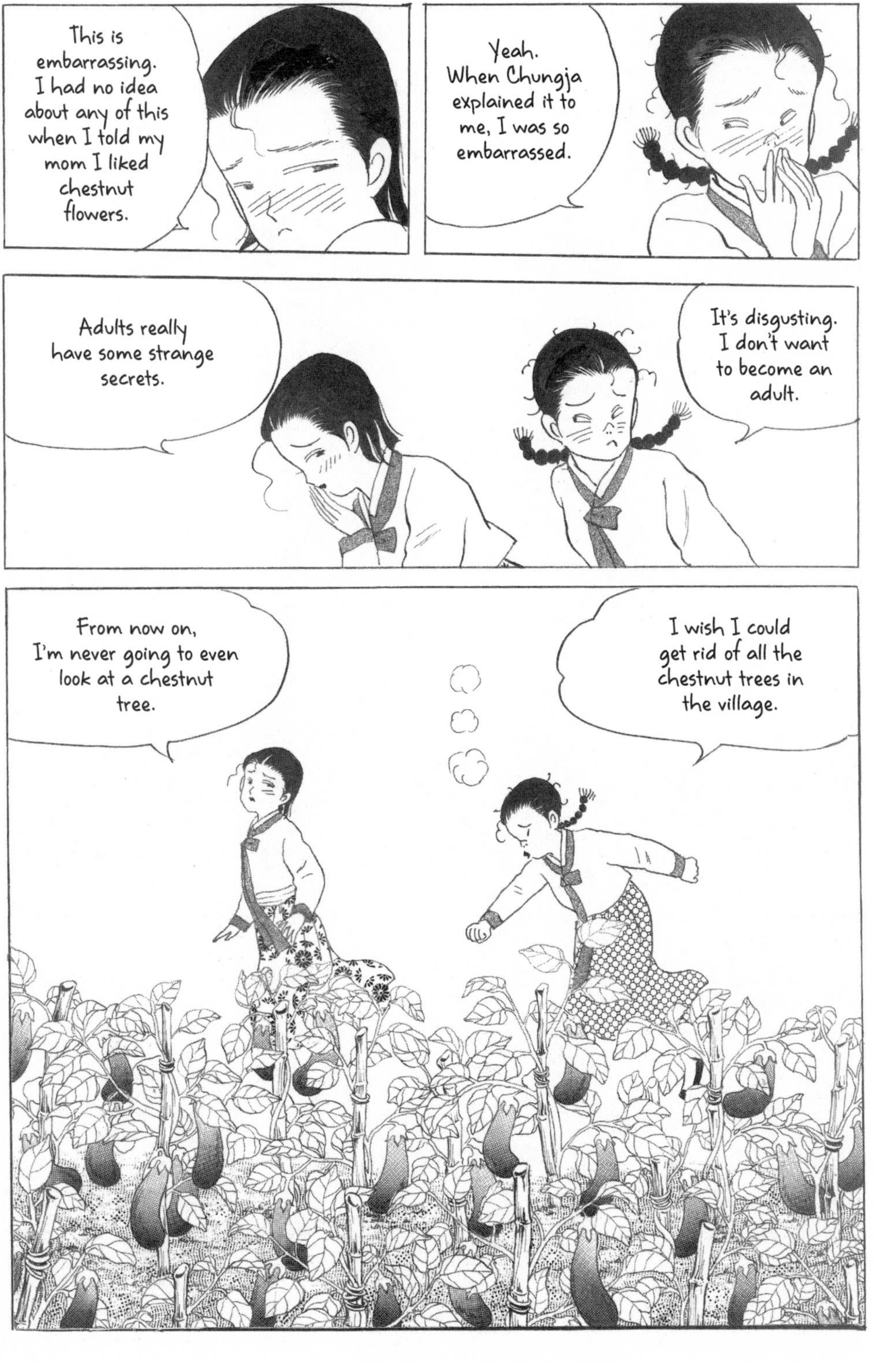
This is embarrassing. I had no idea about any of this when I told my mom I liked chestnut flowers.
Yeah. When Chungja explained it to me, I was so embarrassed.
Adults really have some strange secrets.
It's disgusting. I don't want to become an adult.
From now on, I'm never going to even look at a chestnut tree.
I wish I could get rid of all the chestnut trees in the village.

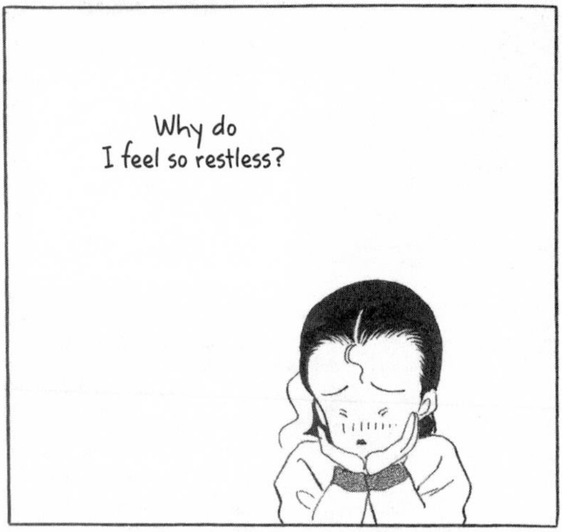
Why do
I feel so restless?

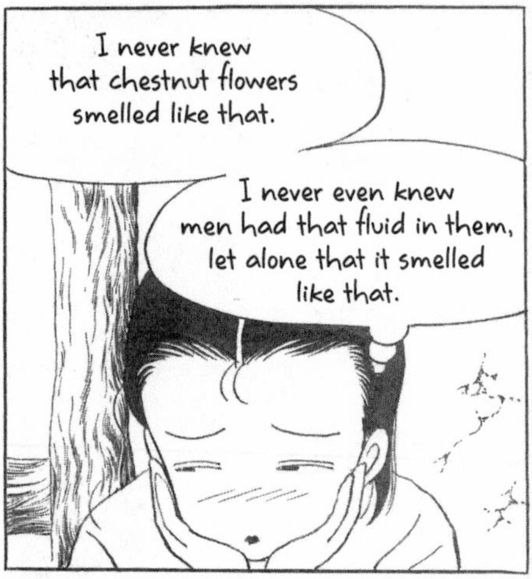
I never knew
that chestnut flowers
smelled like that.
I never even knew
men had that fluid in them,
let alone that it smelled
like that.

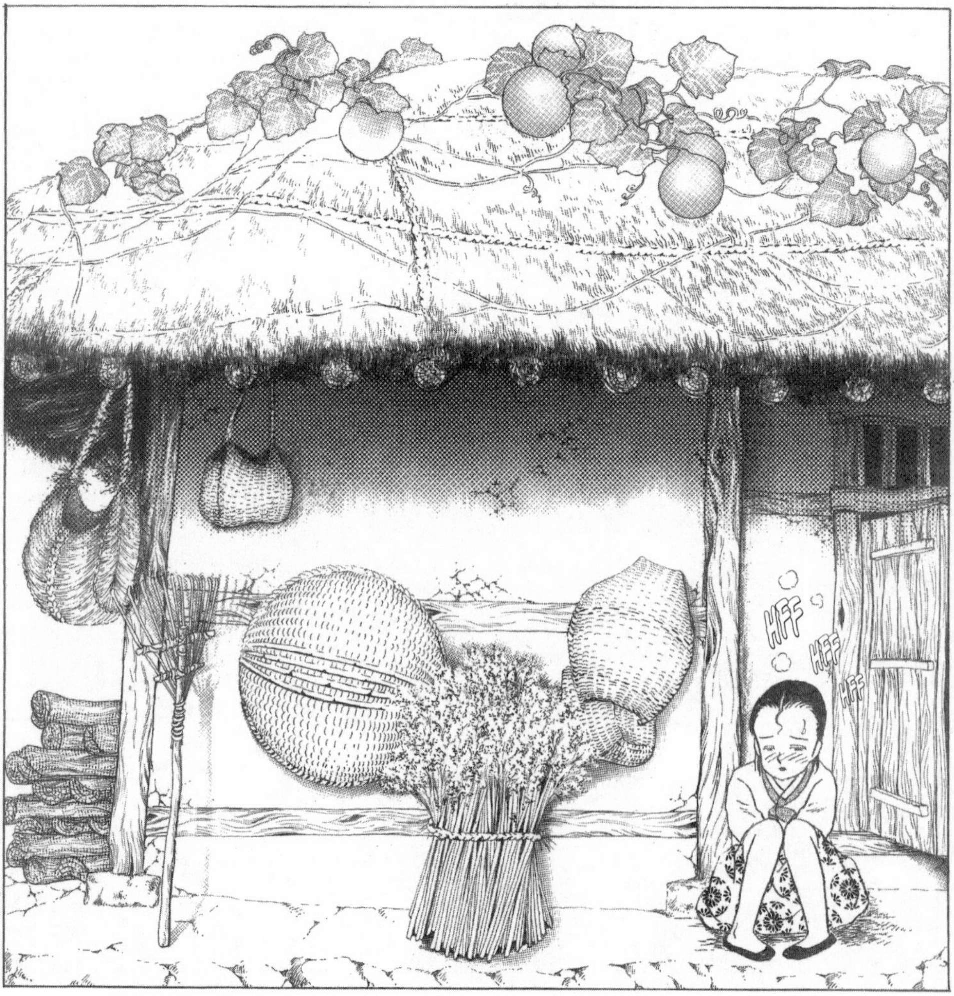
HFF
HFF
HFF

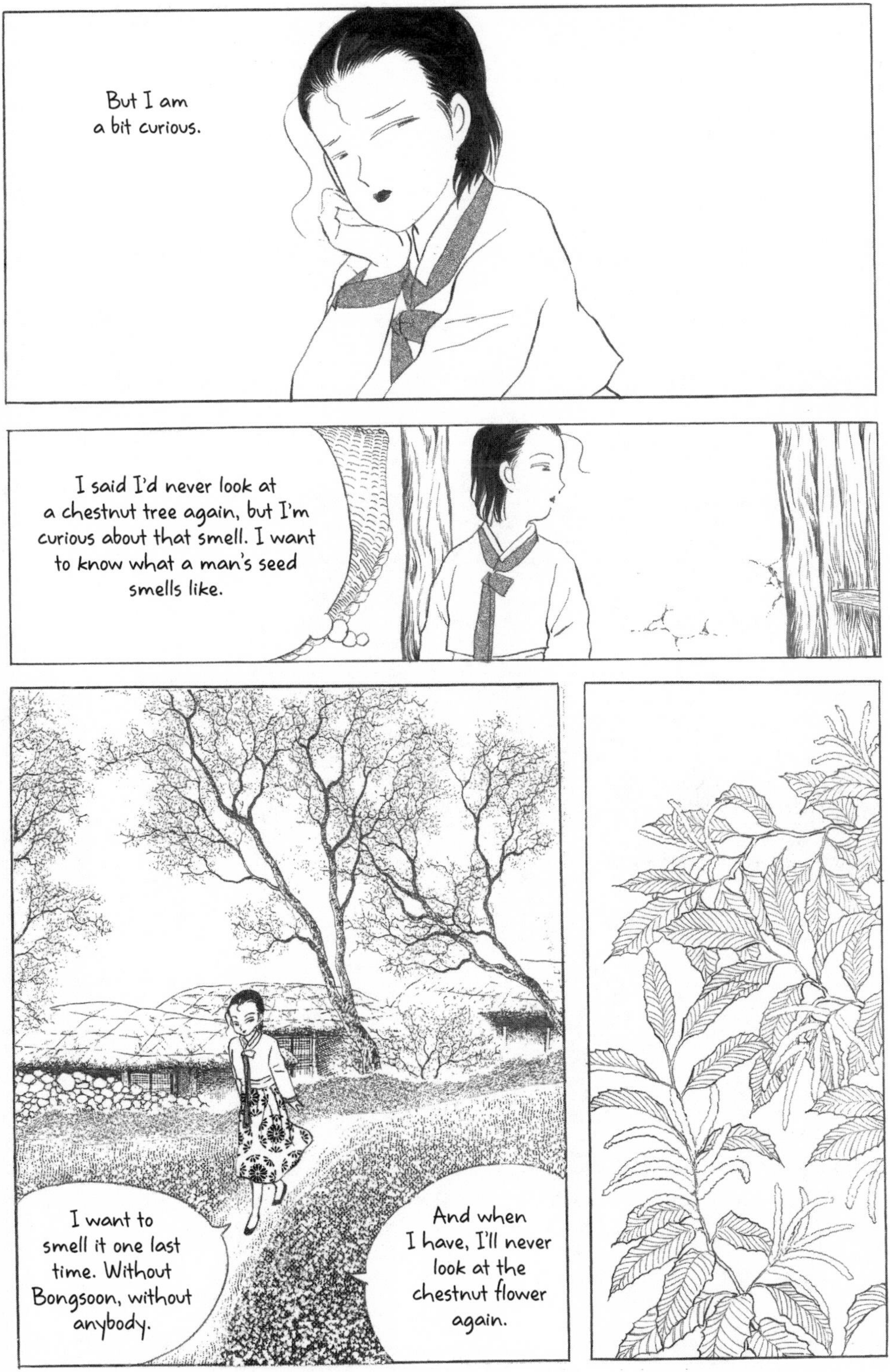
But I am a bit curious.
I said I'd never look at a chestnut tree again, but I'm curious about that smell. I want to know what a man's seed smells like.
I want to smell it one last time. Without Bongsoon, without anybody.
And when I have, I'll never look at the chestnut flower again.

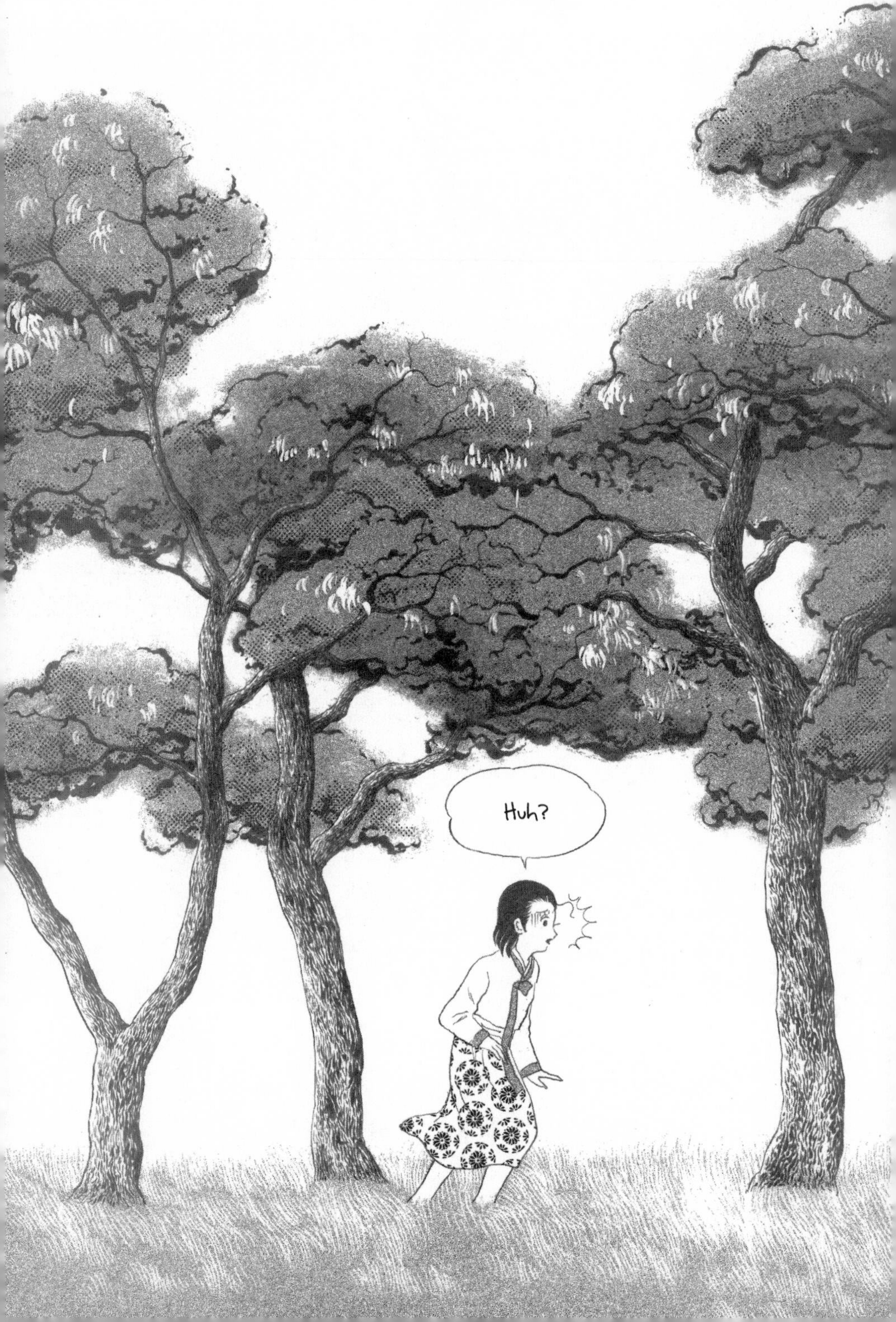
Huh?

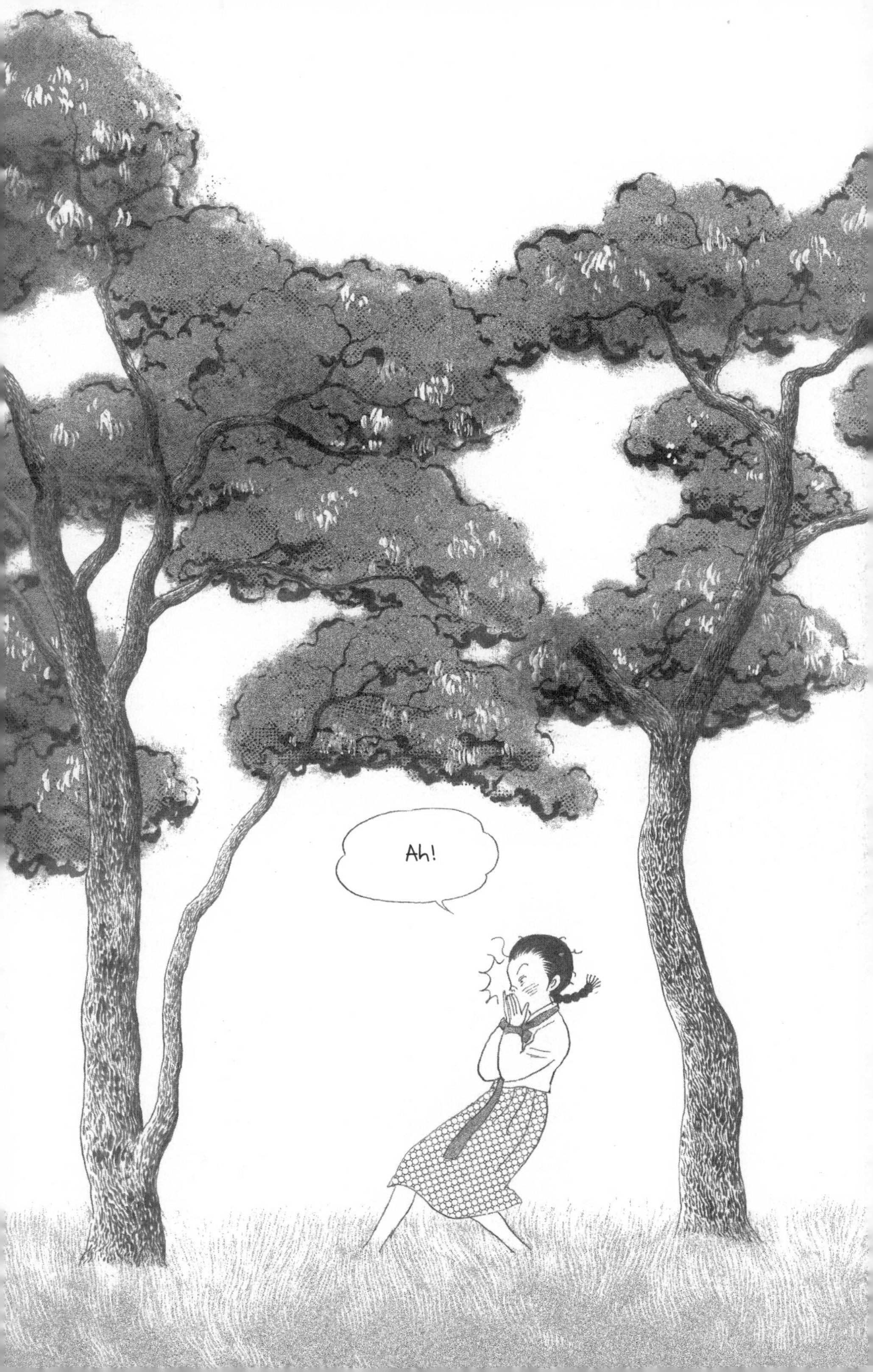
Ah!

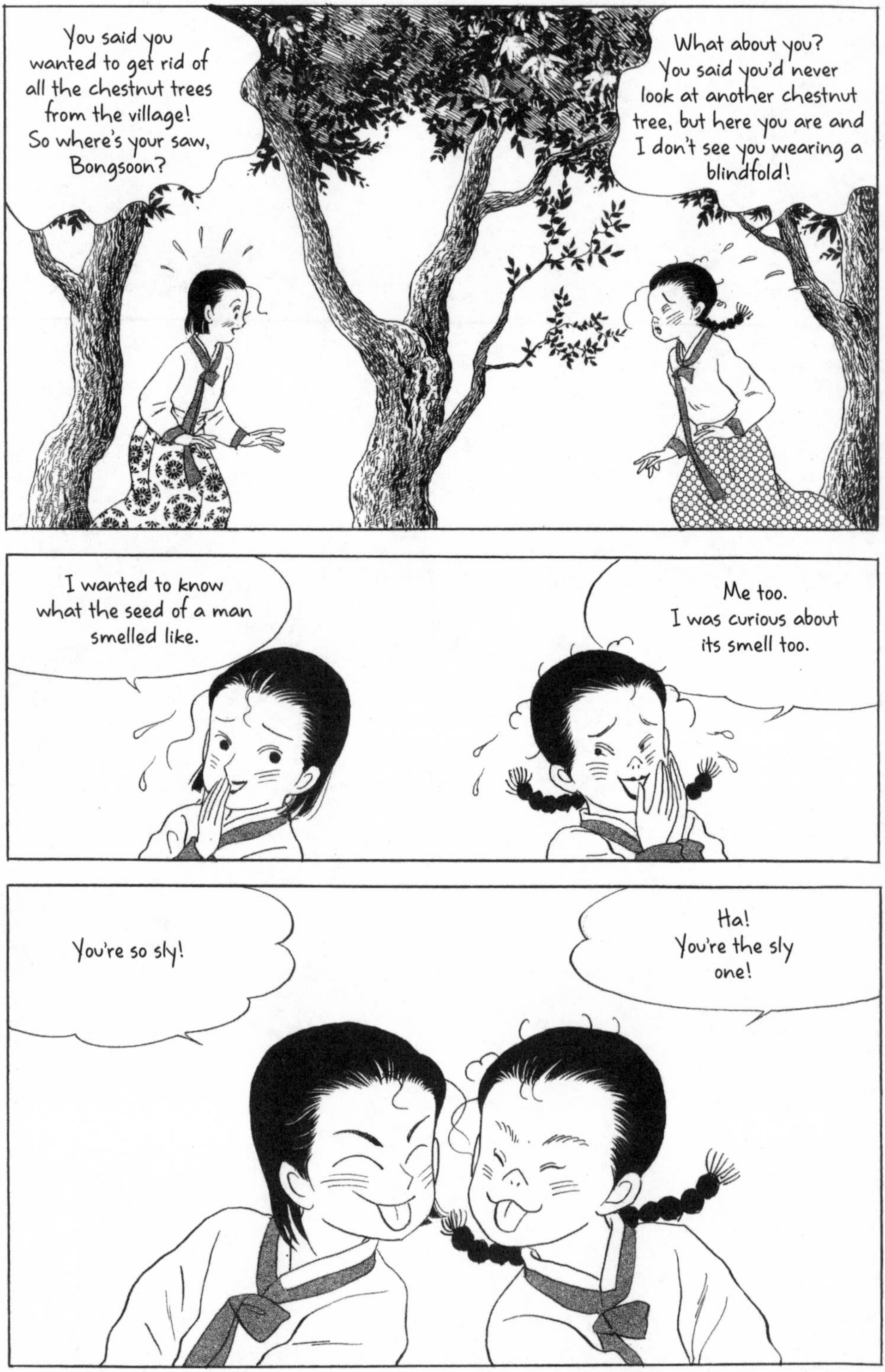
You said you wanted to get rid of all the chestnut trees from the village! So where's your saw, Bongsoon?
What about you? You said you'd never look at another chestnut tree, but here you are and I don't see you wearing a blindfold!
I wanted to know what the seed of a man smelled like.
Me too. I was curious about its smell too.
You're so sly!
Ha! You're the sly one!

Chapter Five

ONE HUNDRED DIFFERENT FLOWERS BLOOM WITHIN A WOMAN

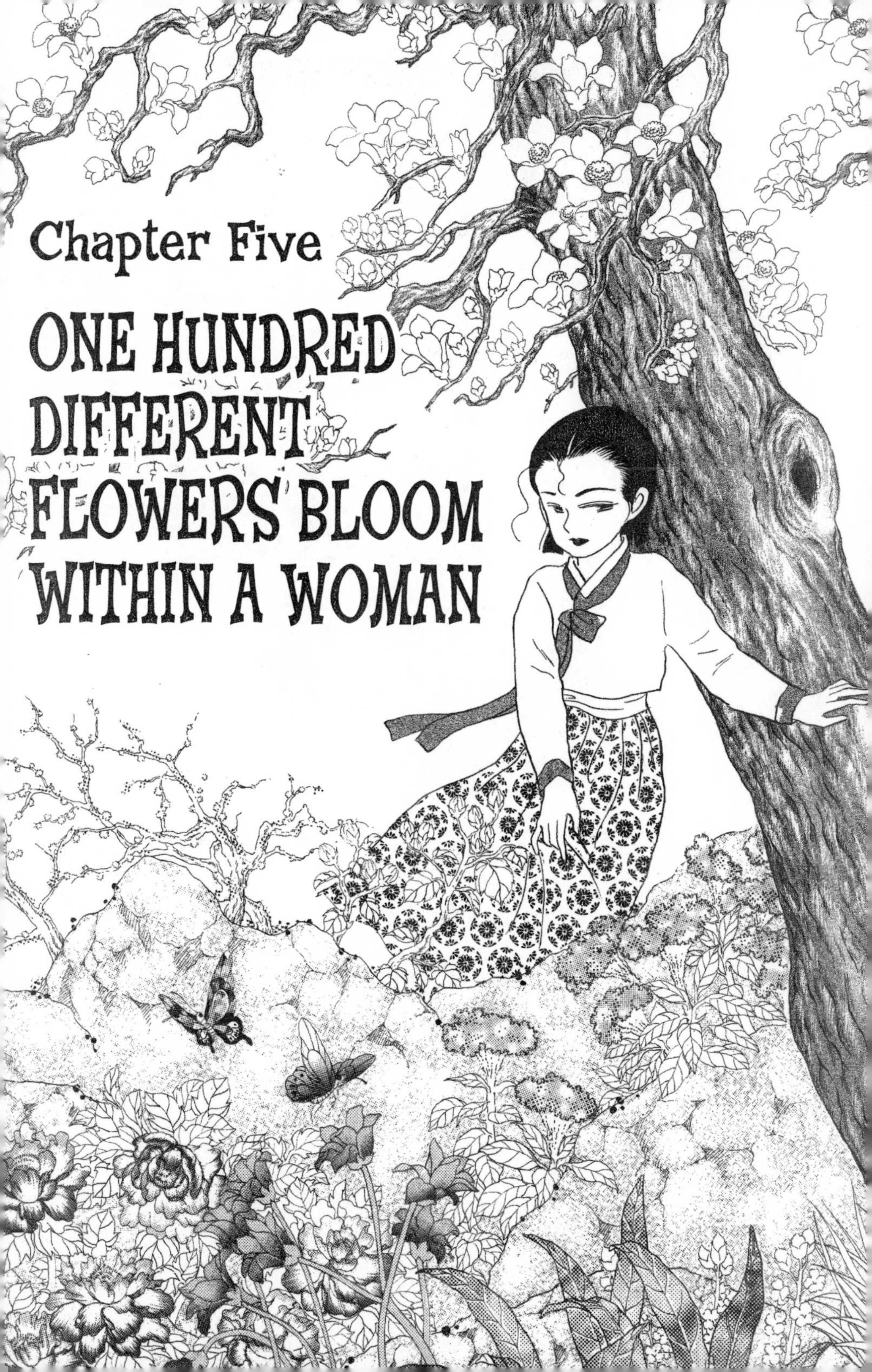

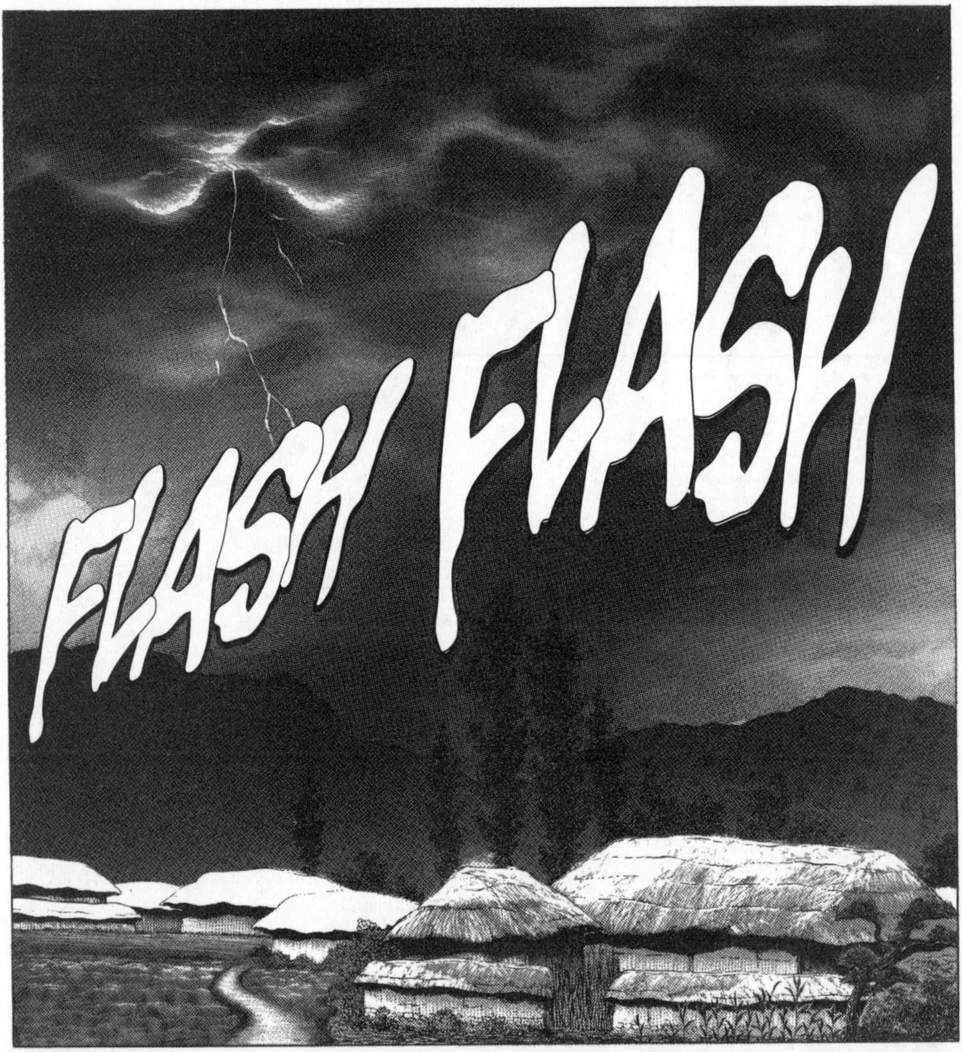
FLASH FLASH

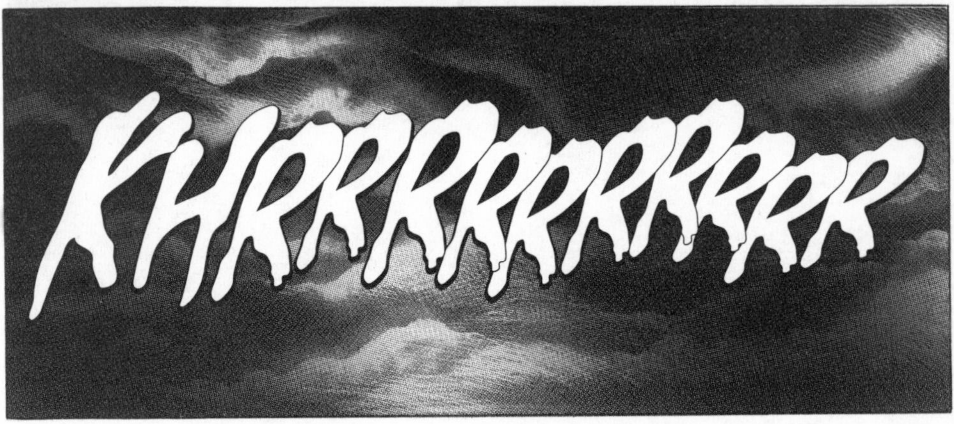
KHRRRRRRRRRRR

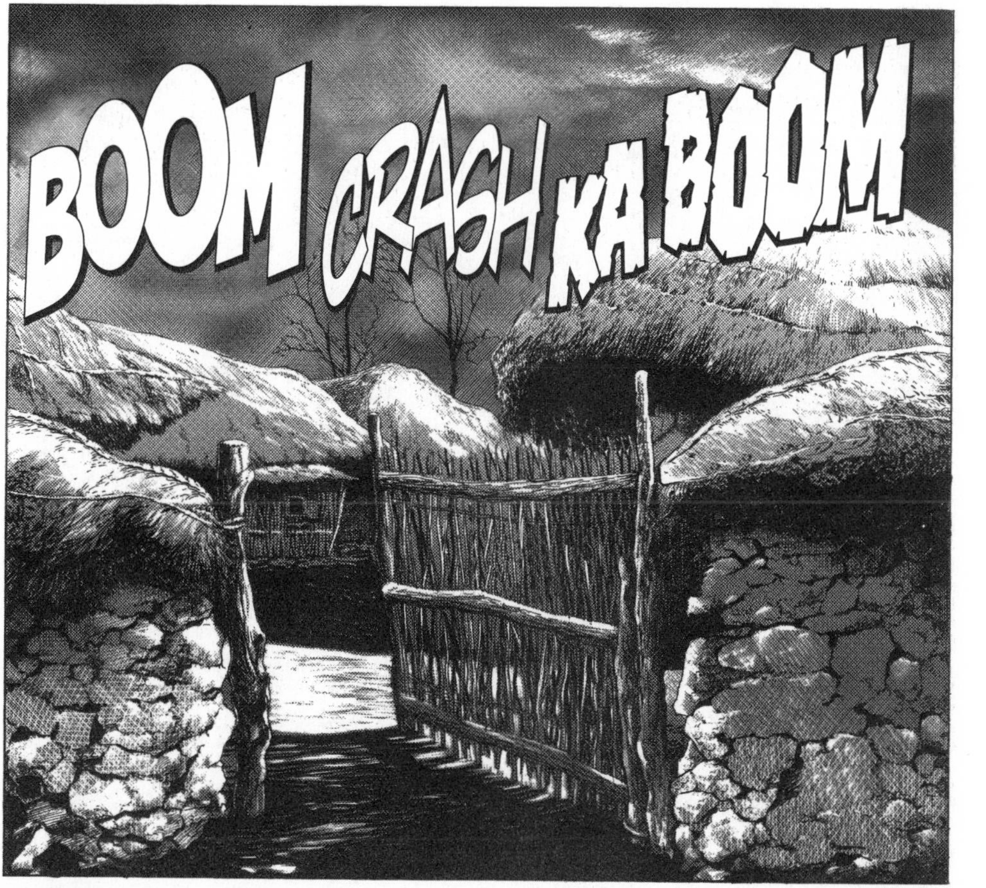
BOOM
CRASH
KA BOOM

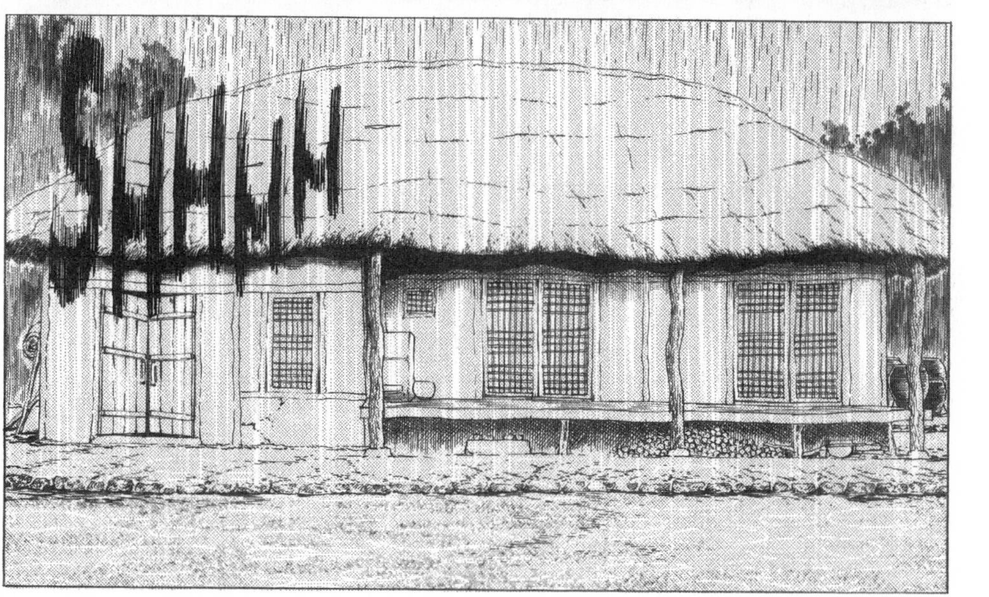
SHHH

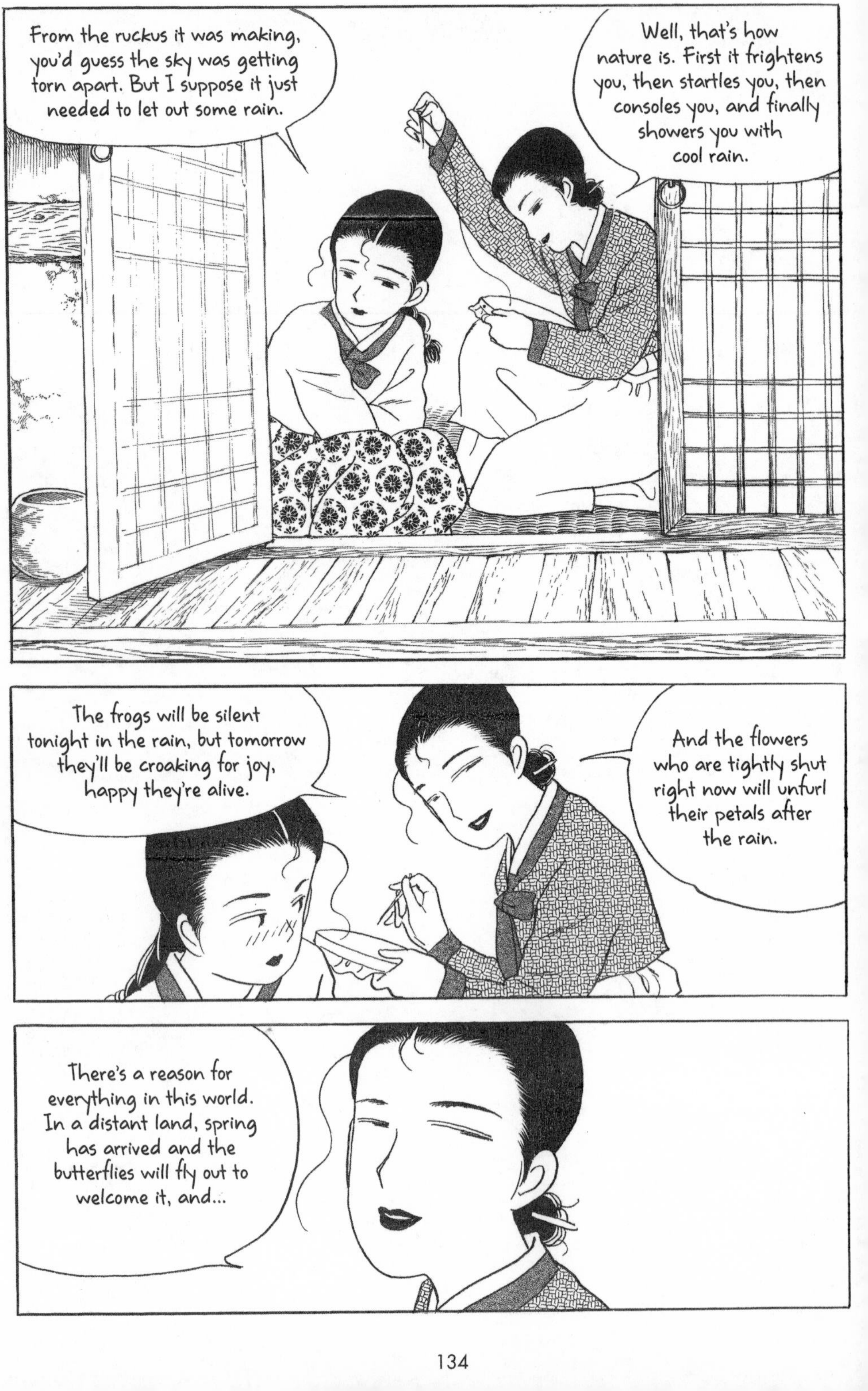
From the ruckus it was making, you'd guess the sky was getting torn apart. But I suppose it just needed to let out some rain.
Well, that's how nature is. First it frightens you, then startles you, then consoles you, and finally showers you with cool rain.
The frogs will be silent tonight in the rain, but tomorrow they'll be croaking for joy, happy they're alive.
And the flowers who are tightly shut right now will unfurl their petals after the rain.
There's a reason for everything in this world. In a distant land, spring has arrived and the butterflies will fly out to welcome it, and...

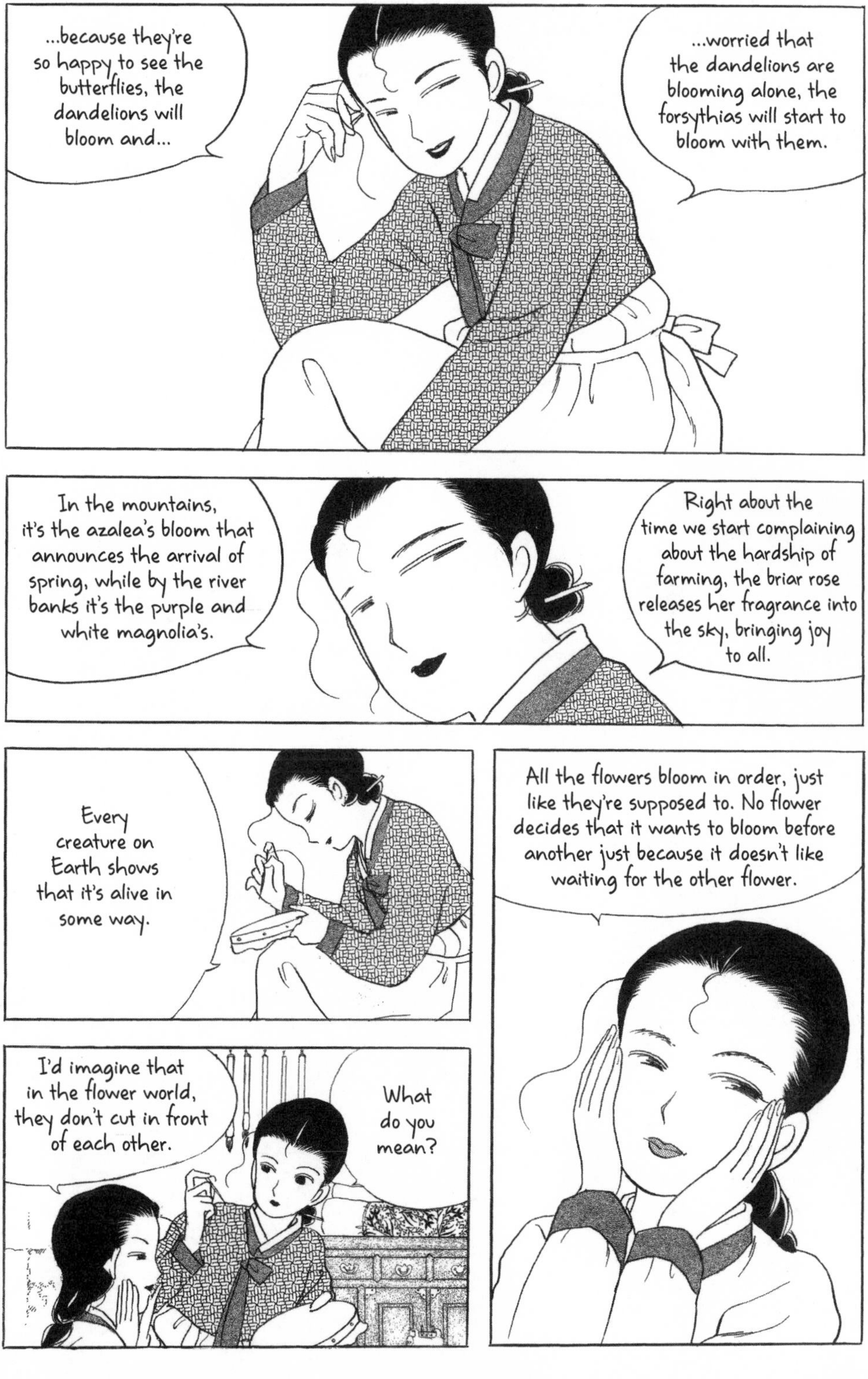
...because they're so happy to see the butterflies, the dandelions will bloom and...
...worried that the dandelions are blooming alone, the forsythias will start to bloom with them.
In the mountains, it's the azalea's bloom that announces the arrival of spring, while by the river banks it's the purple and white magnolia's.
Right about the time we start complaining about the hardship of farming, the briar rose releases her fragrance into the sky, bringing joy to all.
Every creature on Earth shows that it's alive in some way.
I'd imagine that in the flower world, they don't cut in front of each other.
What do you mean?
All the flowers bloom in order, just like they're supposed to. No flower decides that it wants to bloom before another just because it doesn't like waiting for the other flower.

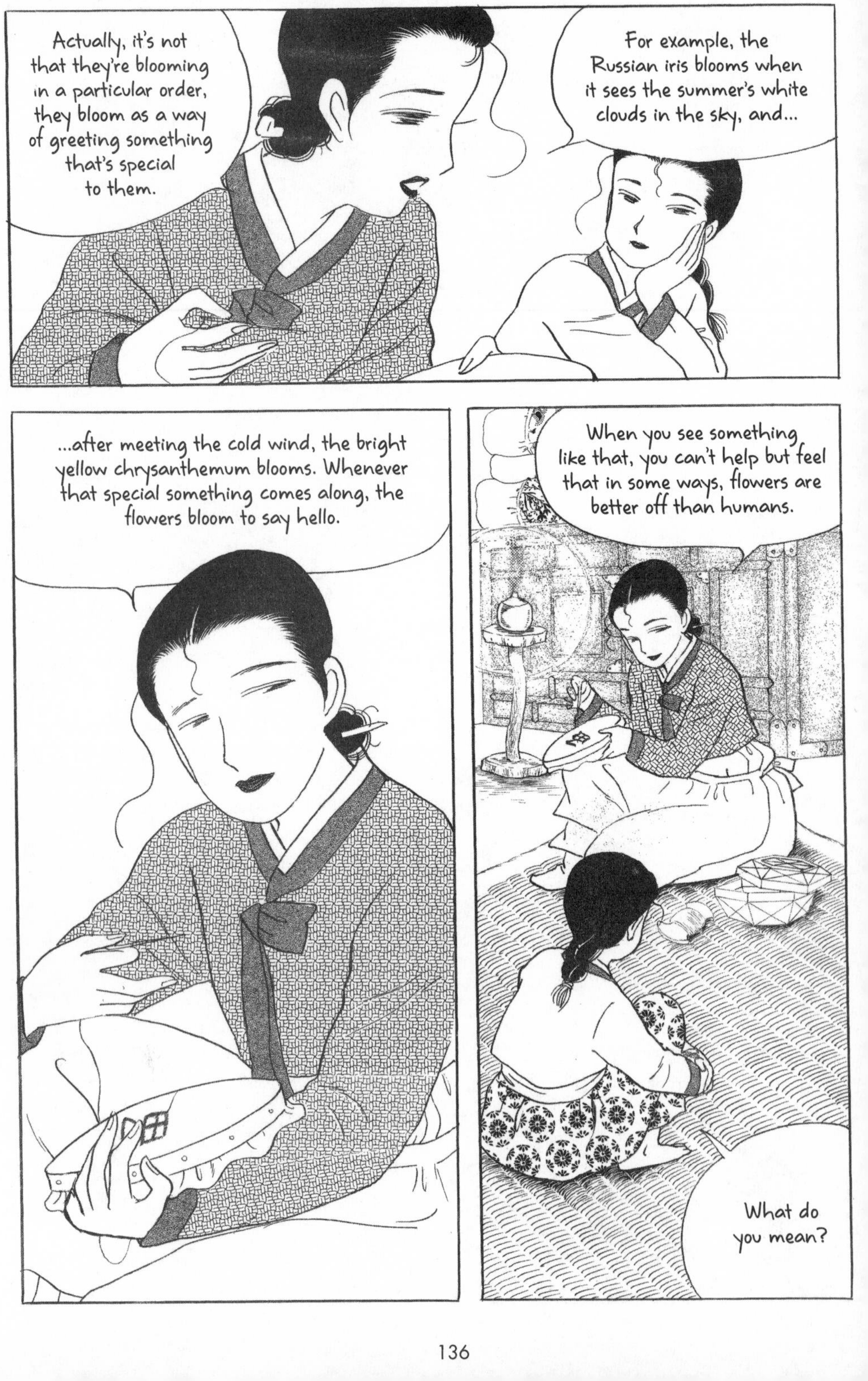
Actually, it's not that they're blooming in a particular order, they bloom as a way of greeting something that's special to them.
For example, the Russian iris blooms when it sees the summer's white clouds in the sky, and...
...after meeting the cold wind, the bright yellow chrysanthemum blooms. Whenever that special something comes along, the flowers bloom to say hello.
When you see something like that, you can't help but feel that in some ways, flowers are better off than humans.
What do you mean?

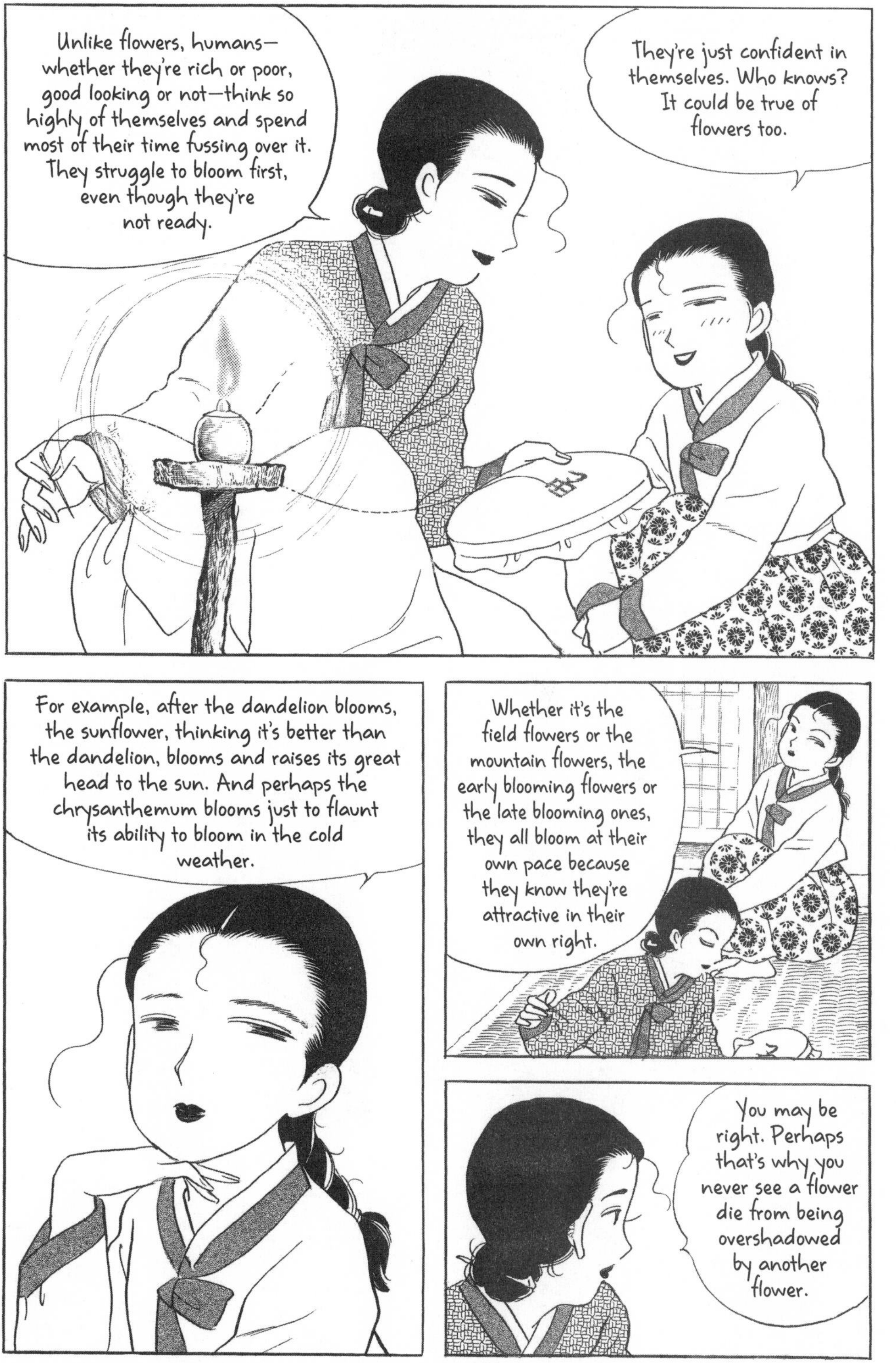
Unlike flowers, humans—whether they're rich or poor, good looking or not—think so highly of themselves and spend most of their time fussing over it. They struggle to bloom first, even though they're not ready.
They're just confident in themselves. Who knows? It could be true of flowers too.
For example, after the dandelion blooms, the sunflower, thinking it's better than the dandelion, blooms and raises its great head to the sun. And perhaps the chrysanthemum blooms just to flaunt its ability to bloom in the cold weather.
Whether it's the field flowers or the mountain flowers, the early blooming flowers or the late blooming ones, they all bloom at their own pace because they know they're attractive in their own right.
You may be right. Perhaps that's why you never see a flower die from being overshadowed by another flower.

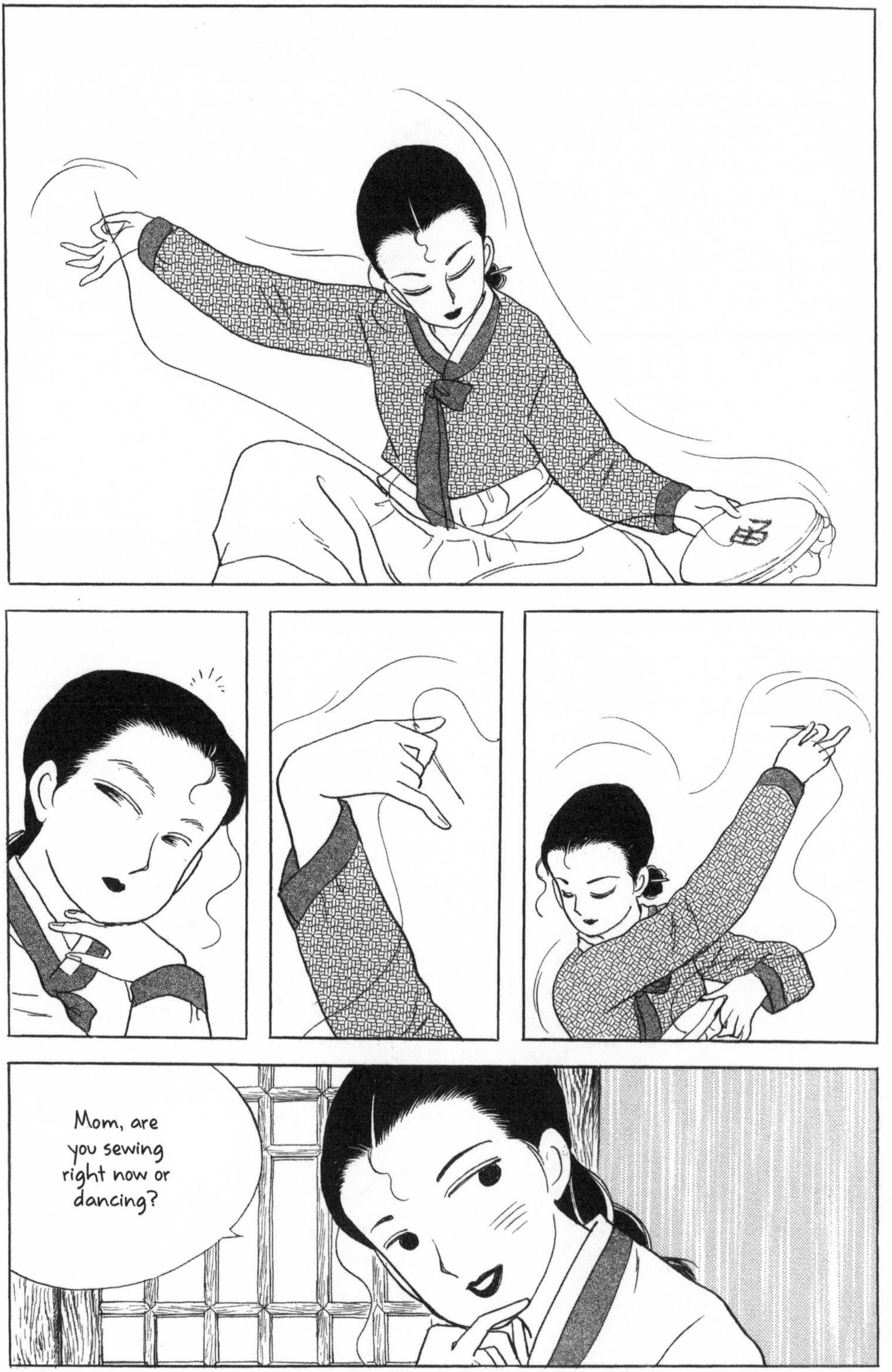
Mom, are you sewing right now or dancing?

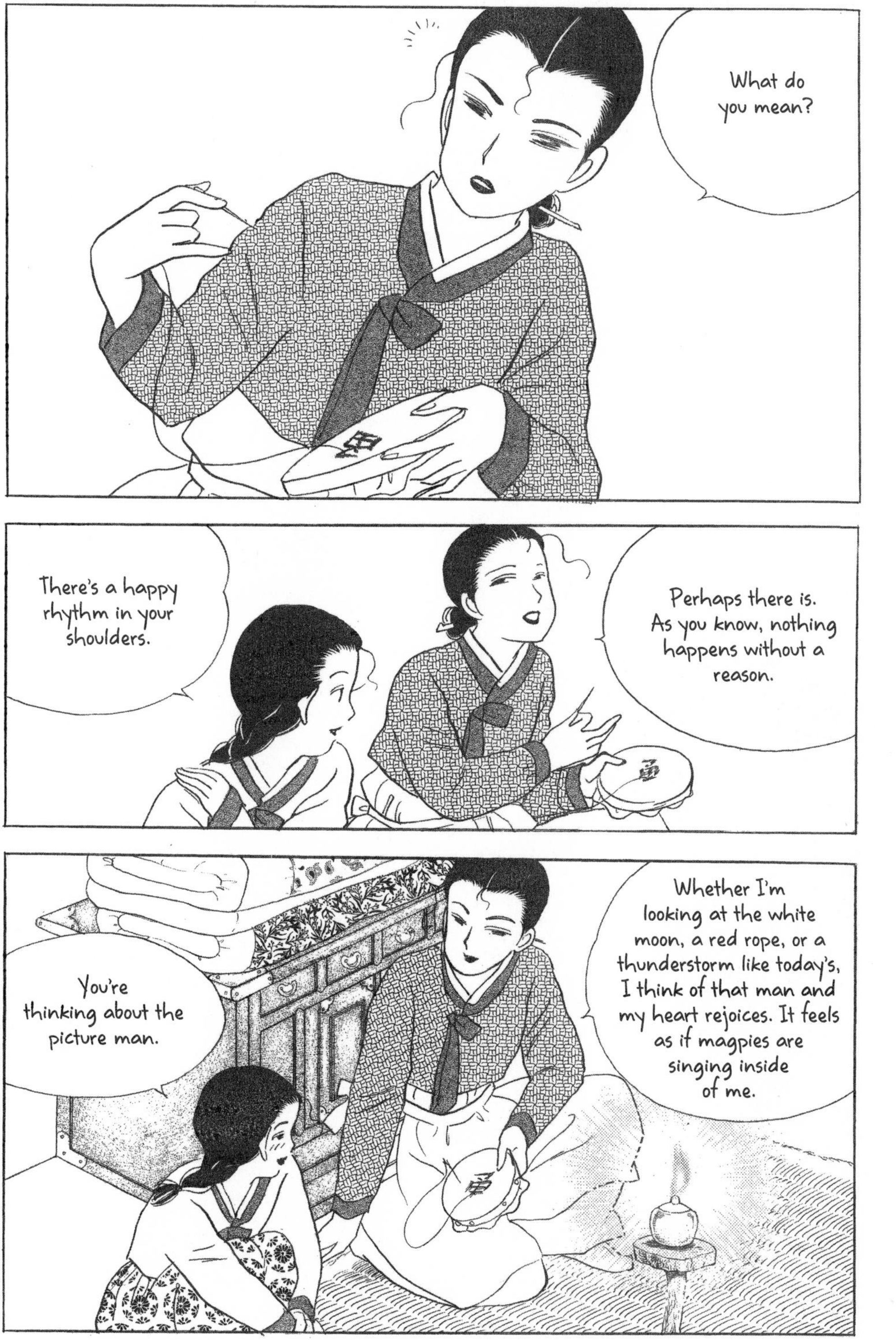
What do you mean?
There's a happy rhythm in your shoulders.
Perhaps there is. As you know, nothing happens without a reason.
You're thinking about the picture man.
Whether I'm looking at the white moon, a red rope, or a thunderstorm like today's, I think of that man and my heart rejoices. It feels as if magpies are singing inside of me.

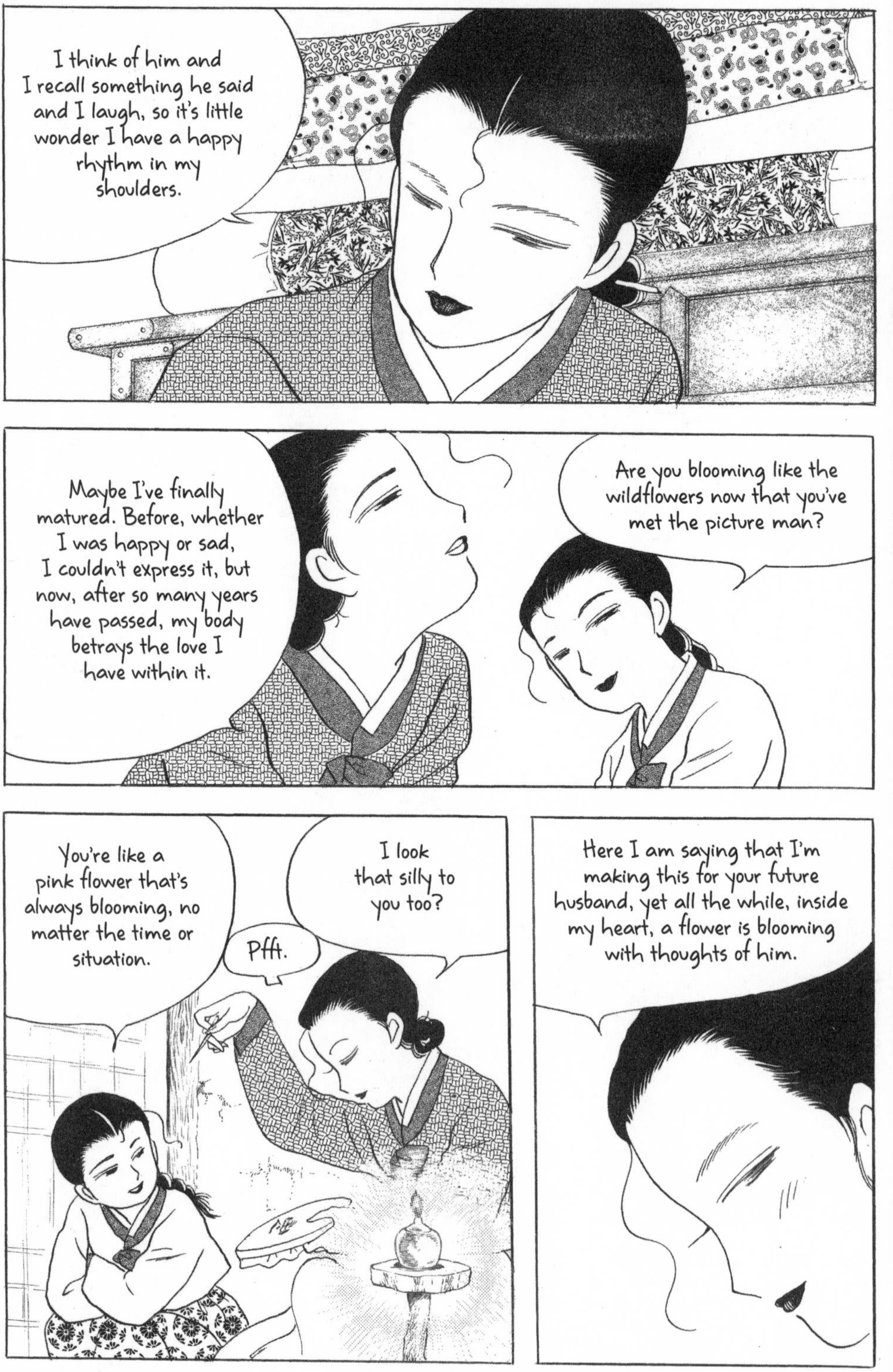
I think of him and I recall something he said and I laugh, so it's little wonder I have a happy rhythm in my shoulders.
Maybe I've finally matured. Before, whether I was happy or sad, I couldn't express it, but now, after so many years have passed, my body betrays the love I have within it.
Are you blooming like the wildflowers now that you've met the picture man?
You're like a pink flower that's always blooming, no matter the time or situation.
Pfft.
I look that silly to you too?
Here I am saying that I'm making this for your future husband, yet all the while, inside my heart, a flower is blooming with thoughts of him.

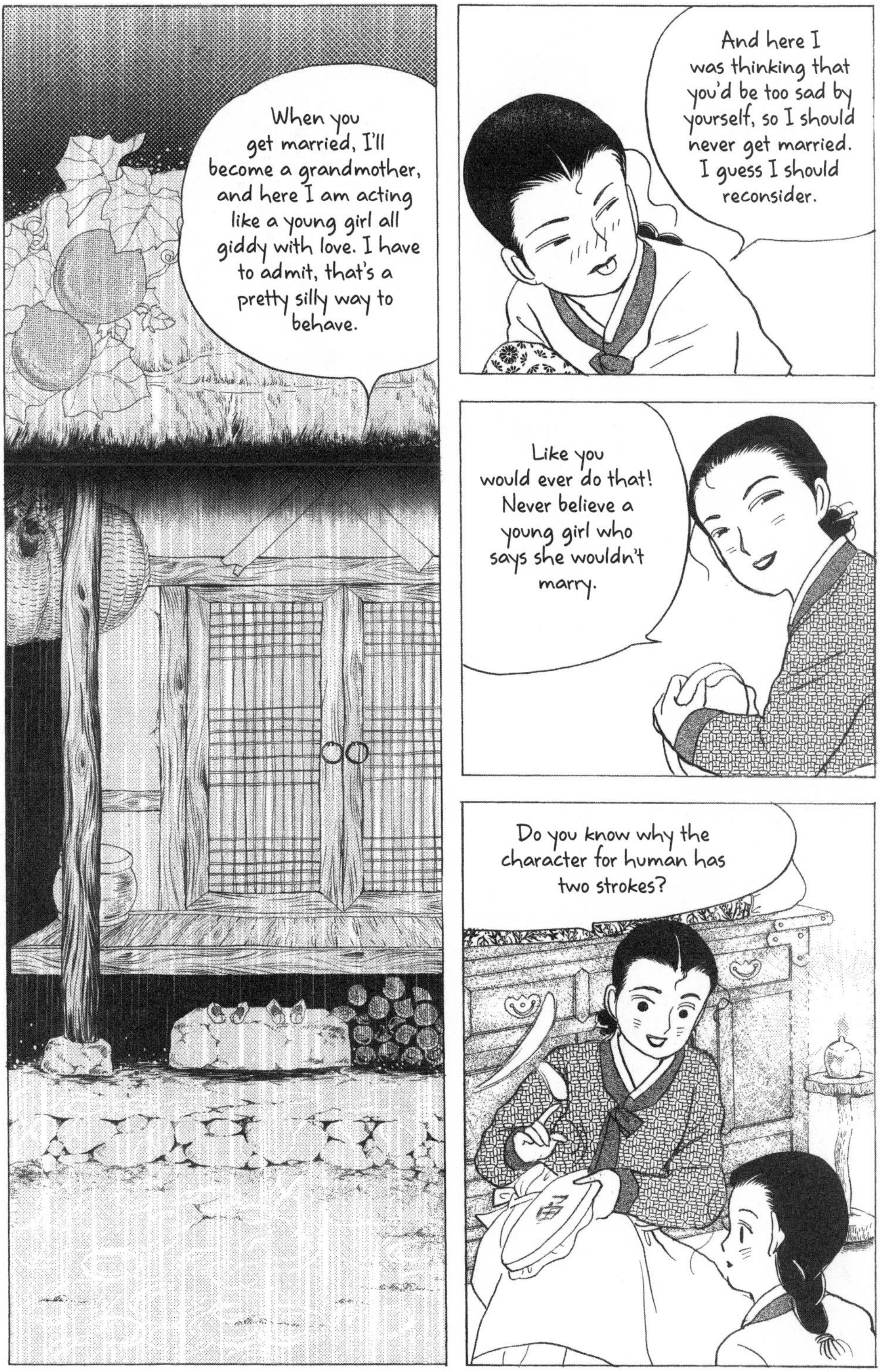
When you get married, I'll become a grandmother, and here I am acting like a young girl all giddy with love. I have to admit, that's a pretty silly way to behave.
And here I was thinking that you'd be too sad by yourself, so I should never get married. I guess I should reconsider.
Like you would ever do that! Never believe a young girl who says she wouldn't marry.
Do you know why the character for human has two strokes?

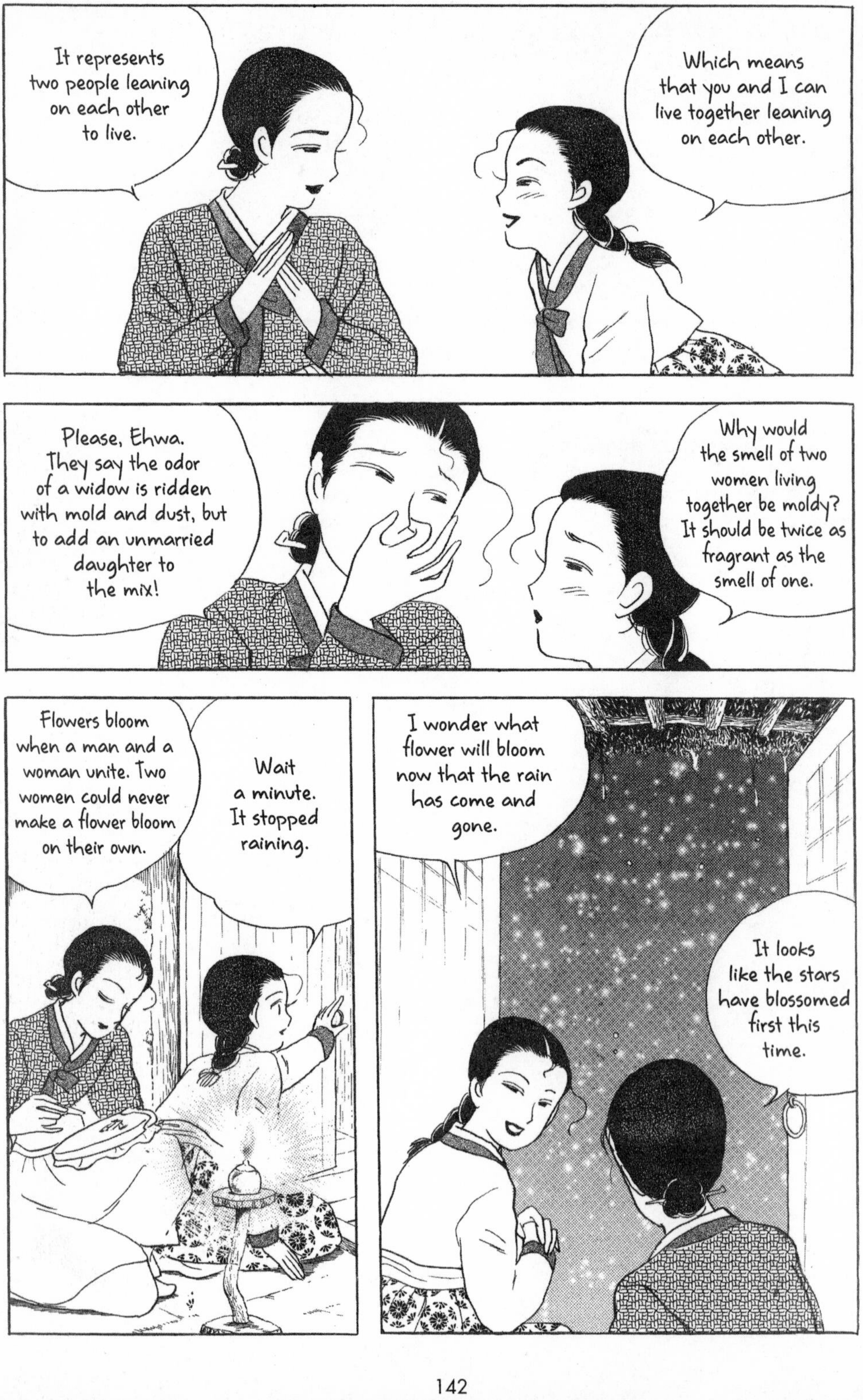
It represents two people leaning on each other to live.
Which means that you and I can live together leaning on each other.
Please, Ehwa. They say the odor of a widow is ridden with mold and dust, but to add an unmarried daughter to the mix!
Why would the smell of two women living together be moldy? It should be twice as fragrant as the smell of one.
Flowers bloom when a man and a woman unite. Two women could never make a flower bloom on their own.
Wait a minute. It stopped raining.
I wonder what flower will bloom now that the rain has come and gone.
It looks like the stars have blossomed first this time.

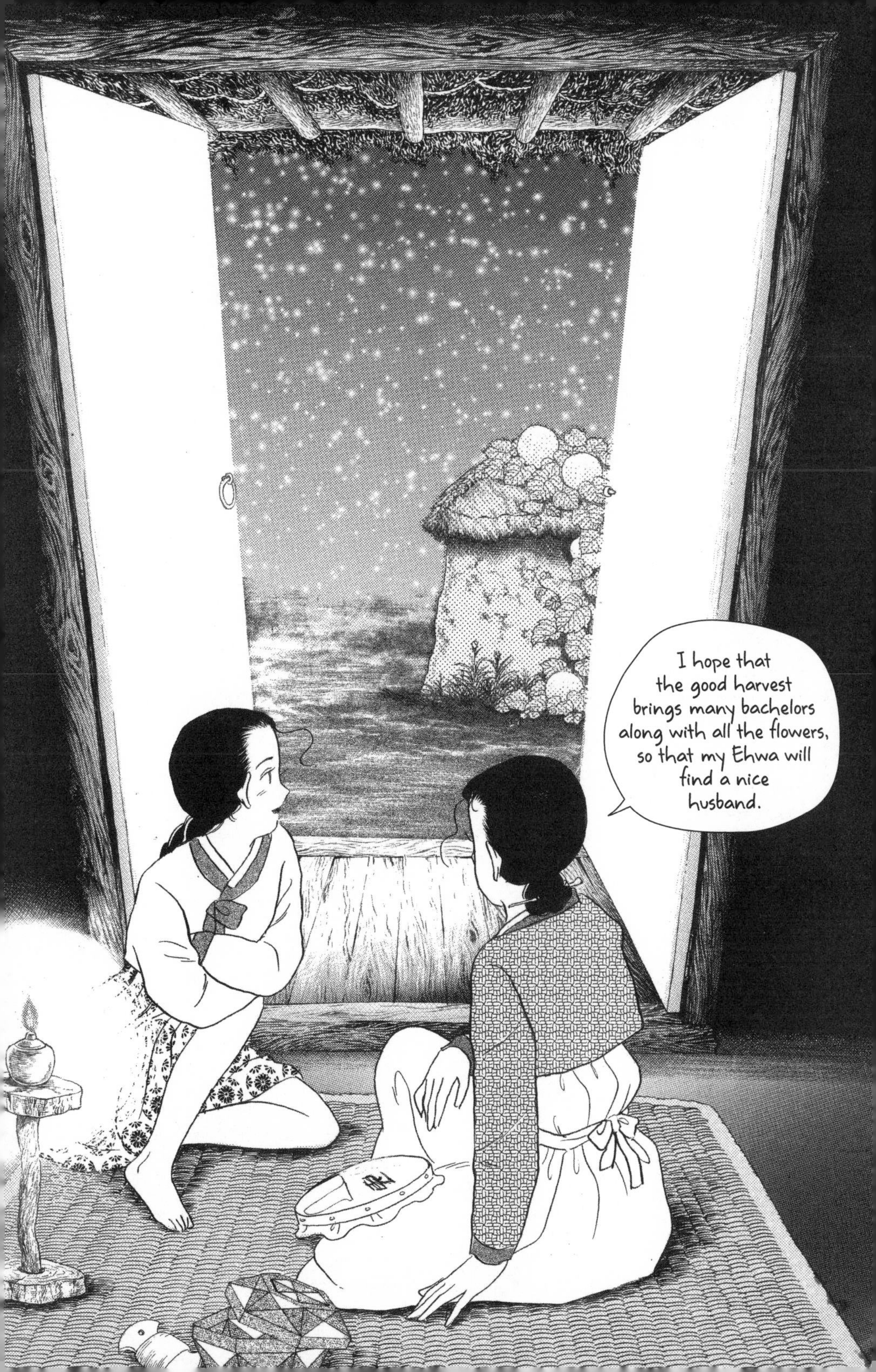
I hope that the good harvest brings many bachelors along with all the flowers, so that my Ehwa will find a nice husband.

RIBBIT

RIBBIT

RIBBIT

RIBBIT

RIBBIT

Those darn frogs didn't make a peep yesterday, but now that the rain is over they're croaking, happy to be alive.

It was really scary yesterday with all that thunder and lightning.

RIBBIT RIBBIT

Only someone with a guilty conscience would be too scared to sleep through a little thunderstorm.

Is that true? Maybe that's why I saw so many people headed for the temple this morning.

Do you think, because of the rain, all the chestnut flowers fell off their trees?

Geez! All that thunder and lightning yesterday, and *that's* what you're curious about?

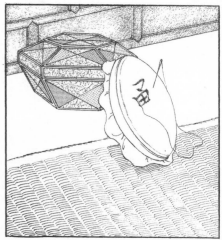

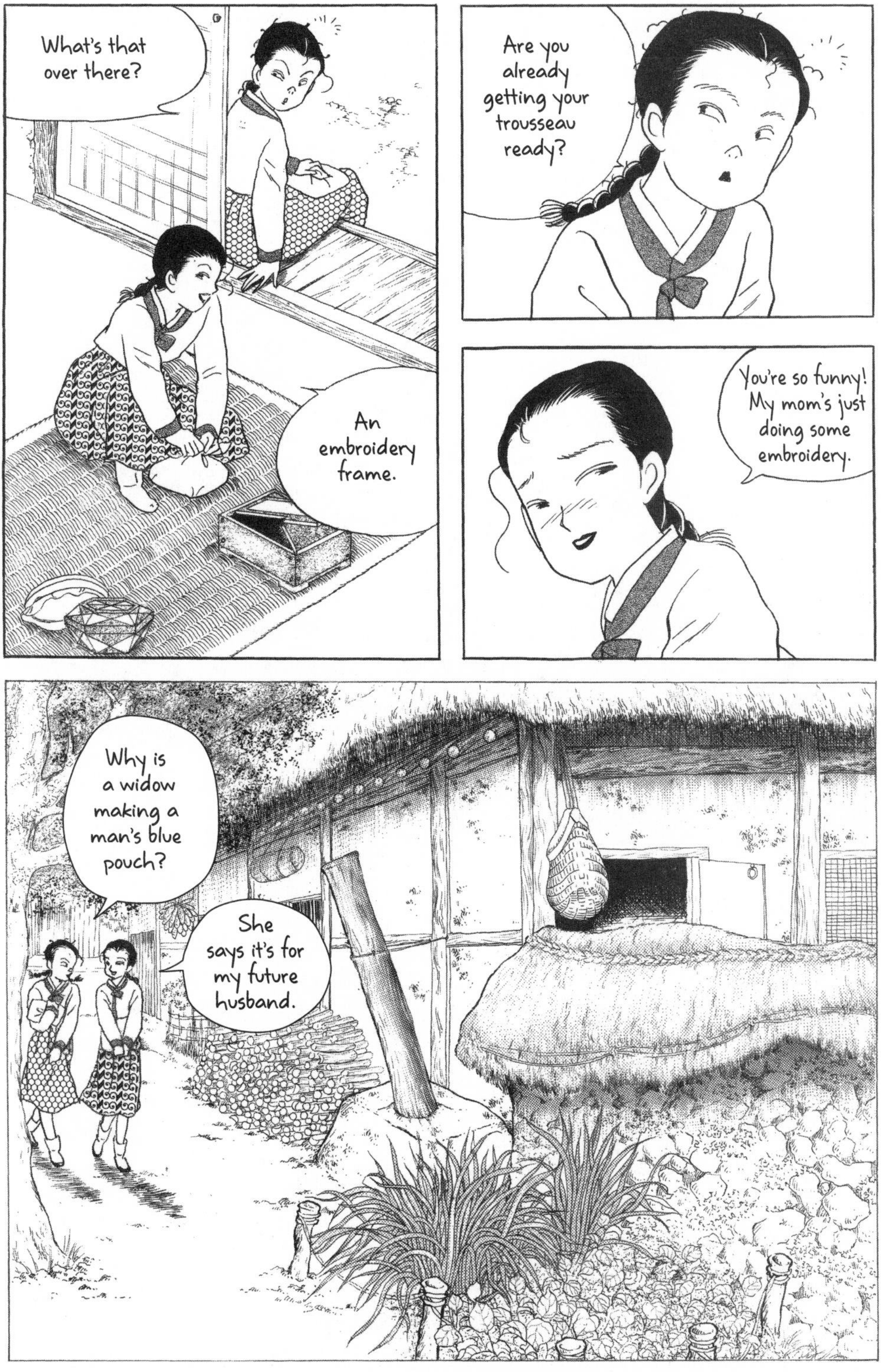
What's that over there?
An embroidery frame.
Are you already getting your trousseau ready?
You're so funny! My mom's just doing some embroidery.
Why is a widow making a man's blue pouch?
She says it's for my future husband.

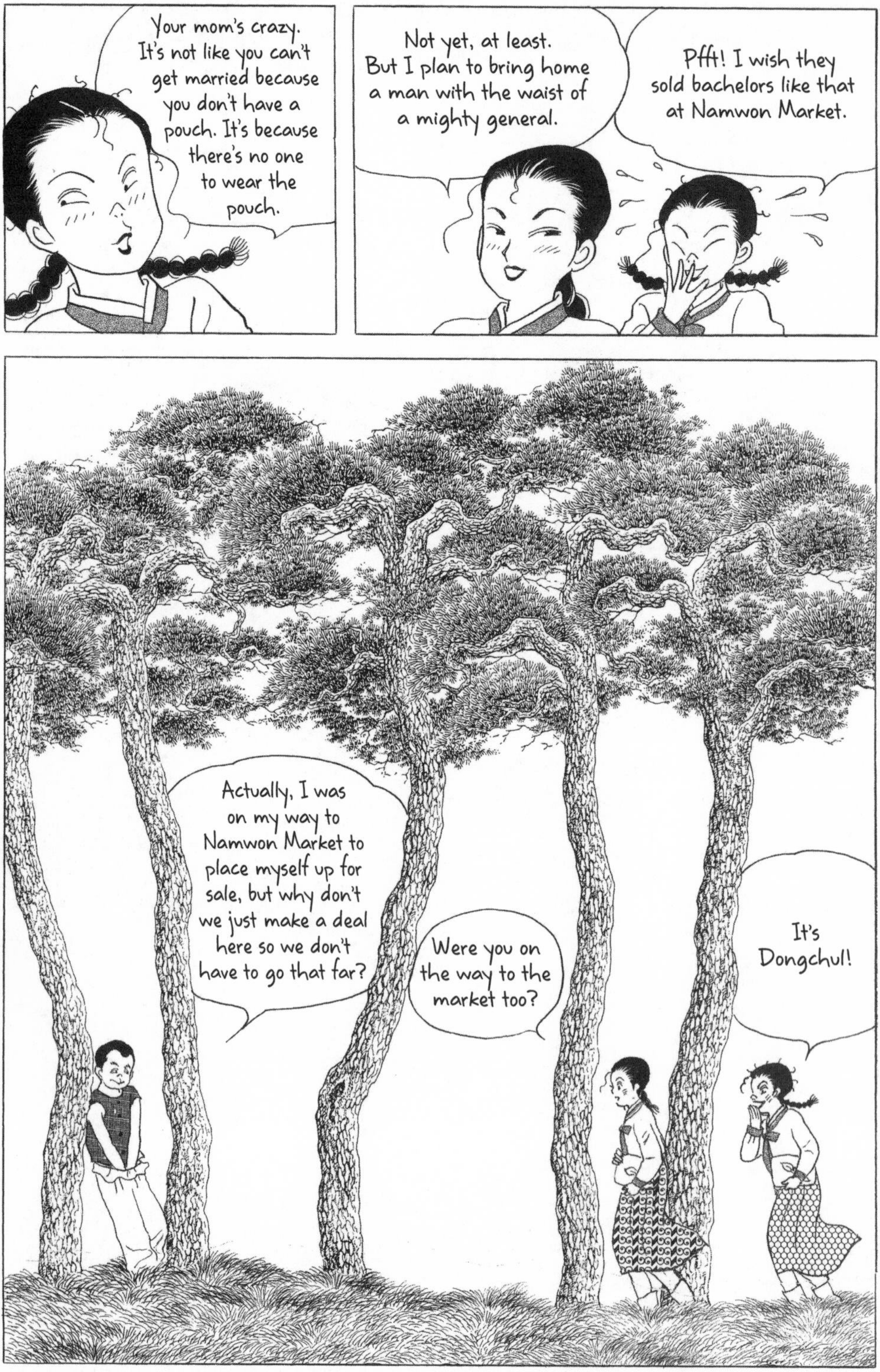
Your mom's crazy. It's not like you can't get married because you don't have a pouch. It's because there's no one to wear the pouch.
Not yet, at least. But I plan to bring home a man with the waist of a mighty general.
Pfft! I wish they sold bachelors like that at Namwon Market.
Actually, I was on my way to Namwon Market to place myself up for sale, but why don't we just make a deal here so we don't have to go that far?
Were you on the way to the market too?
It's Dongchul!

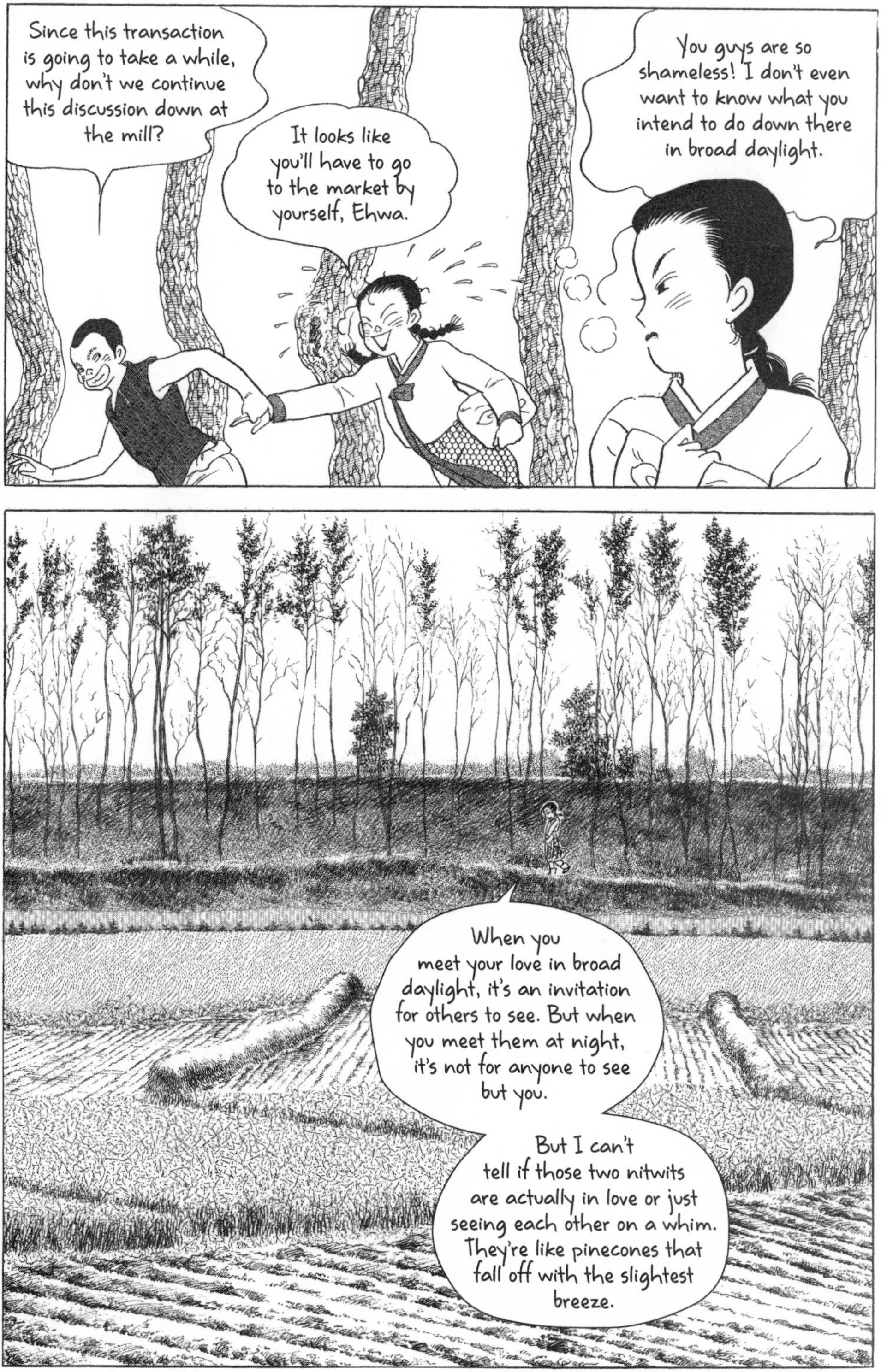
Since this transaction is going to take a while, why don't we continue this discussion down at the mill?
It looks like you'll have to go to the market by yourself, Ehwa.
You guys are so shameless! I don't even want to know what you intend to do down there in broad daylight.
When you meet your love in broad daylight, it's an invitation for others to see. But when you meet them at night, it's not for anyone to see but you.
But I can't tell if those two nitwits are actually in love or just seeing each other on a whim. They're like pinecones that fall off with the slightest breeze.

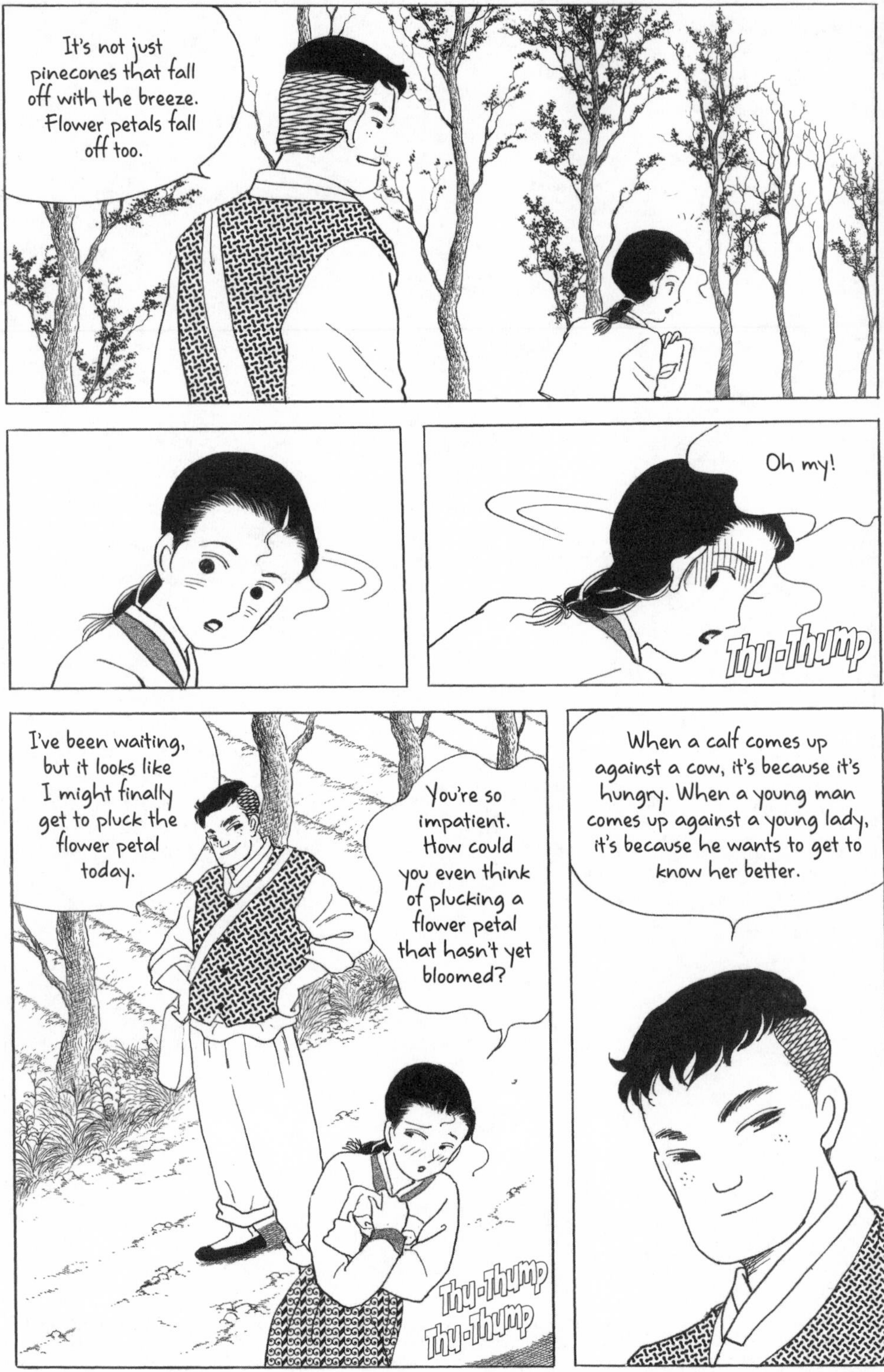

It's not just pinecones that fall off with the breeze. Flower petals fall off too.
Oh my!
Thu-Thump
I've been waiting, but it looks like I might finally get to pluck the flower petal today.
You're so impatient. How could you even think of plucking a flower petal that hasn't yet bloomed?
Thu-Thump Thu-Thump
When a calf comes up against a cow, it's because it's hungry. When a young man comes up against a young lady, it's because he wants to get to know her better.

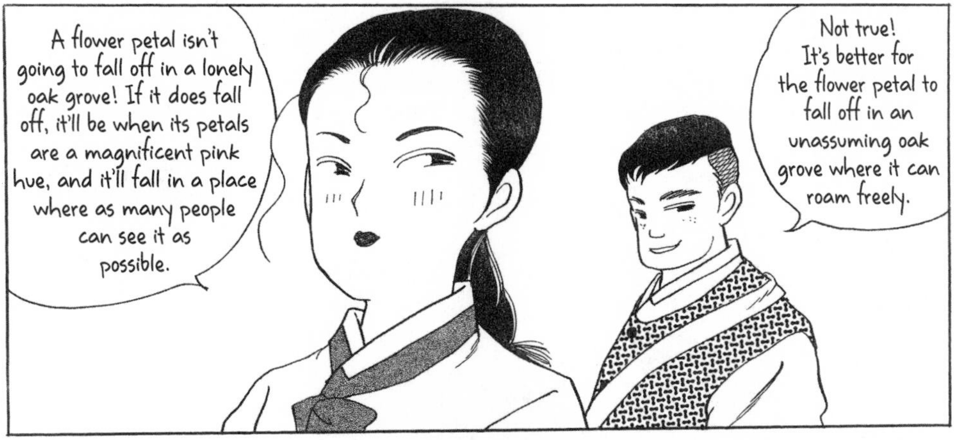
A flower petal isn't going to fall off in a lonely oak grove! If it does fall off, it'll be when its petals are a magnificent pink hue, and it'll fall in a place where as many people can see it as possible.
Not true! It's better for the flower petal to fall off in an unassuming oak grove where it can roam freely.

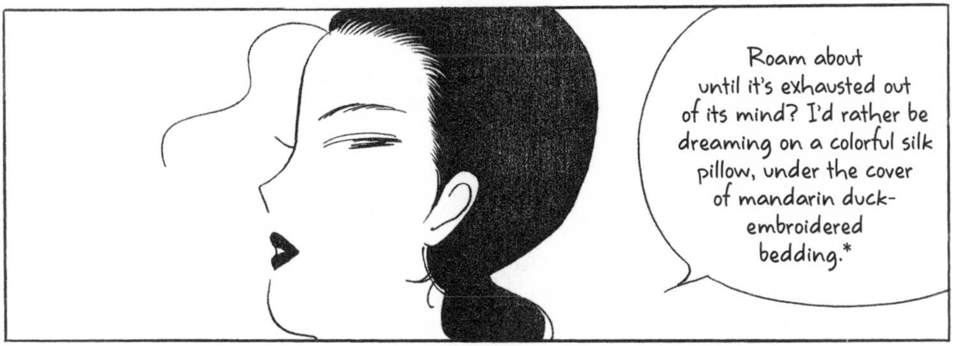
Roam about until it's exhausted out of its mind? I'd rather be dreaming on a colorful silk pillow, under the cover of mandarin duck-embroidered bedding.*

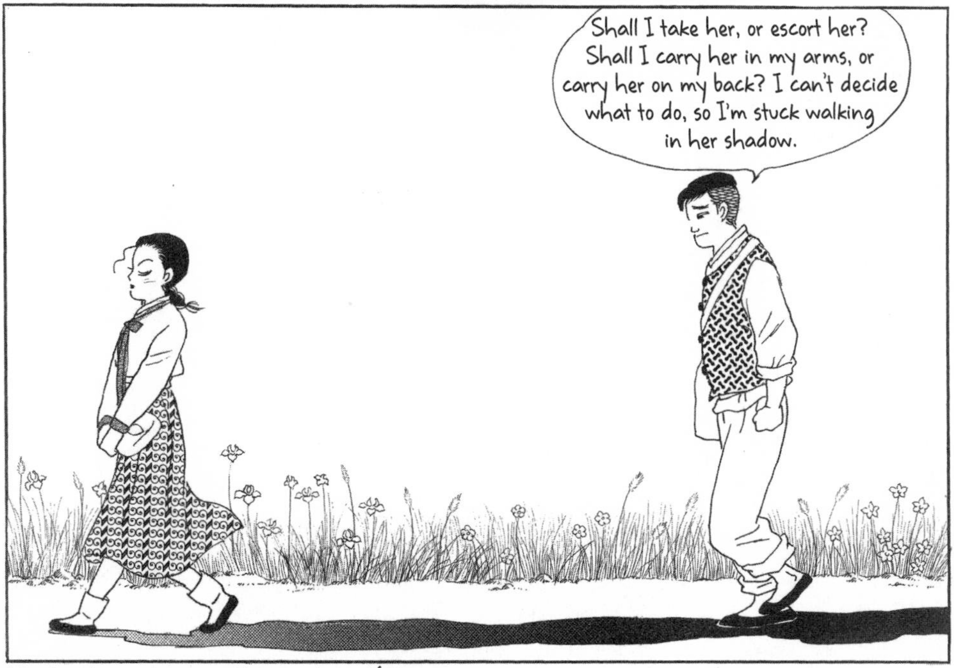
Shall I take her, or escort her? Shall I carry her in my arms, or carry her on my back? I can't decide what to do, so I'm stuck walking in her shadow.

* Mandarin ducks symbolize marital happiness, love and fidelity.

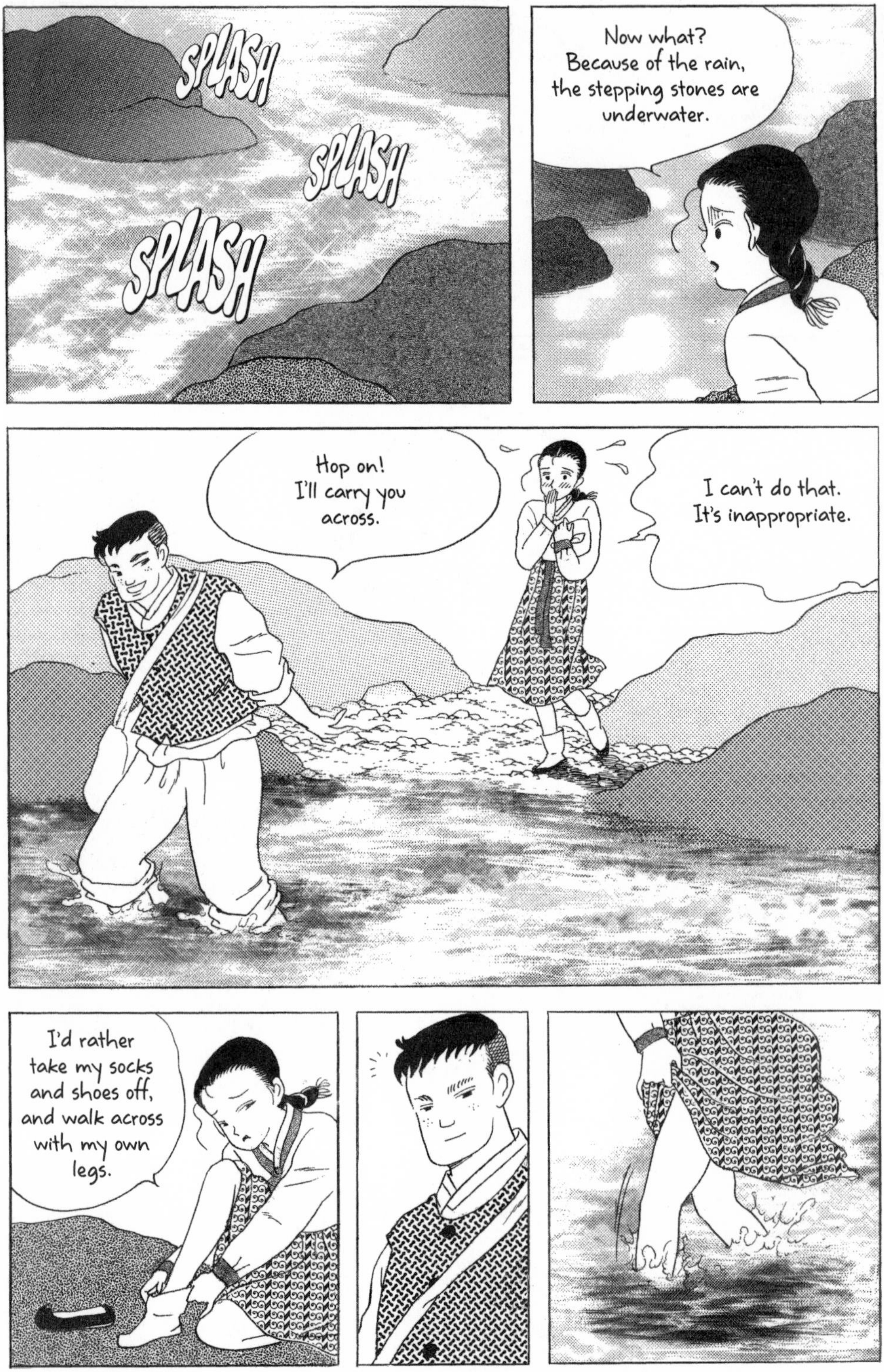
SPLASH
SPLASH
SPLASH
Now what? Because of the rain, the stepping stones are underwater.
Hop on! I'll carry you across.
I can't do that. It's inappropriate.
I'd rather take my socks and shoes off, and walk across with my own legs.

Since the water is deep, you might just have to take off your undergarments as well.

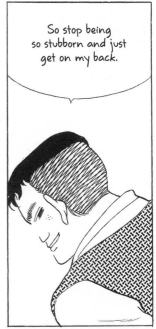

So stop being so stubborn and just get on my back.

What am I going to do if people see me?

What are they going to say? We're just a boy and a girl getting to know each other.

Since I already have you on my back, shall I announce it to everyone in the village?

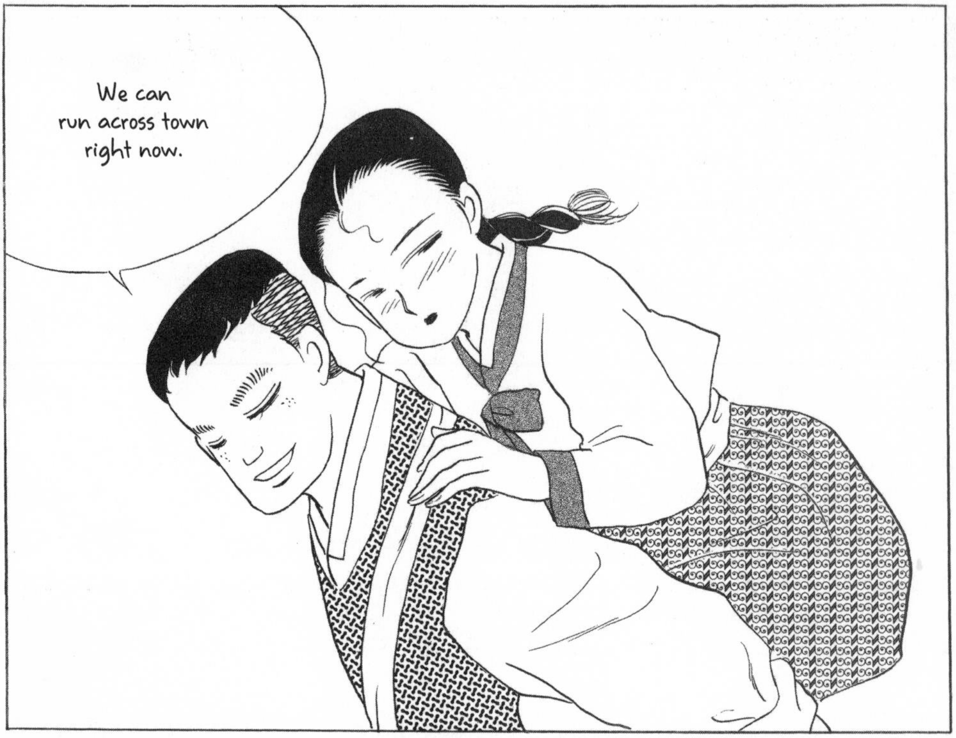
We can run across town right now.
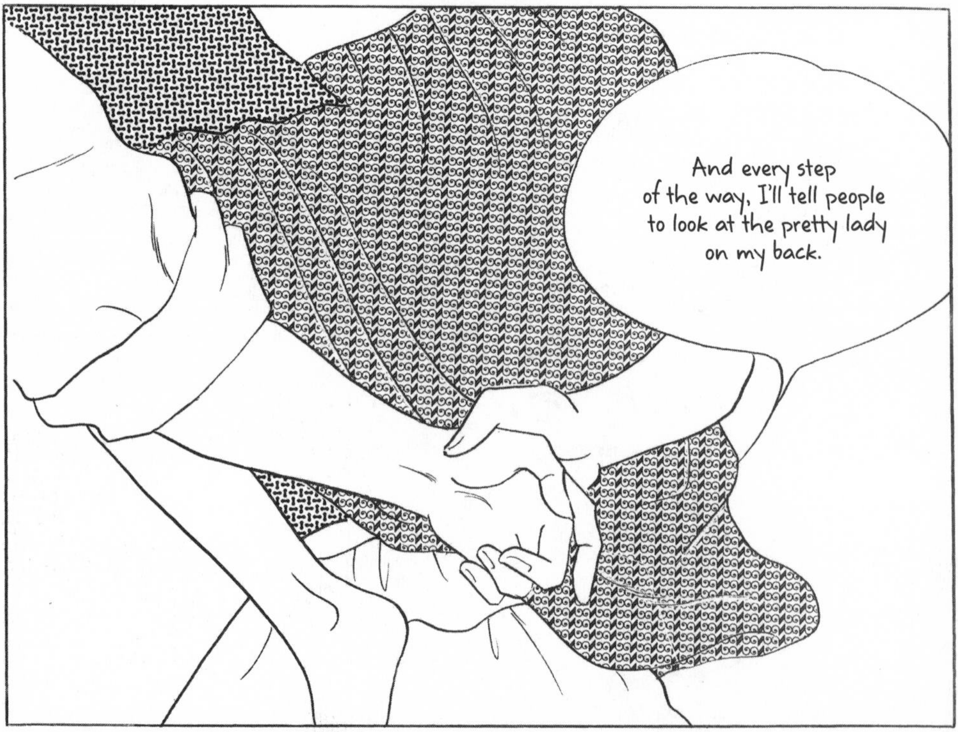
And every step of the way, I'll tell people to look at the pretty lady on my back.

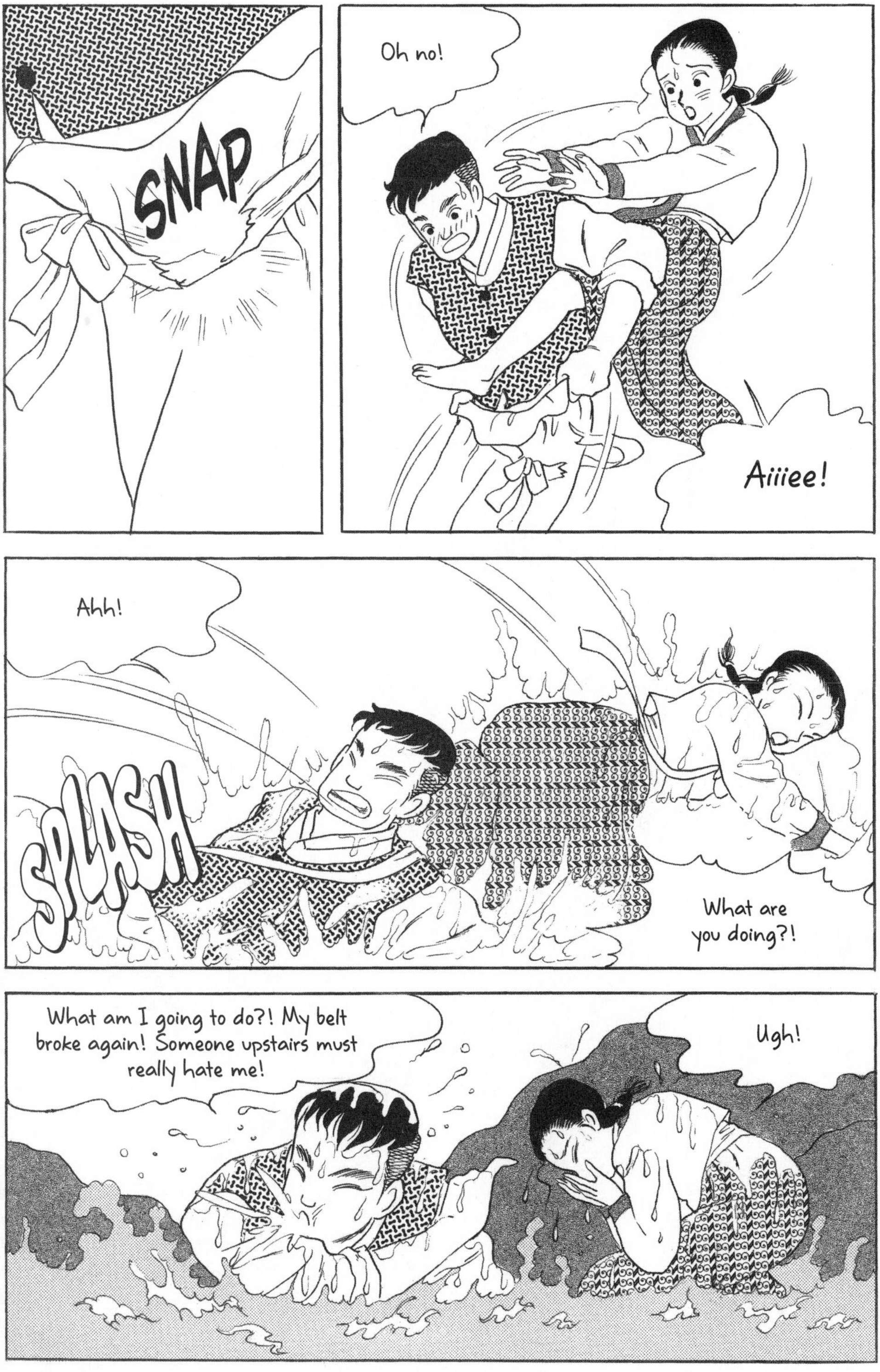
SNAP
Oh no!
Aiiiee!
Ahh!
SPLASH
What are you doing?!
What am I going to do?! My belt broke again! Someone upstairs must really hate me!
Ugh!

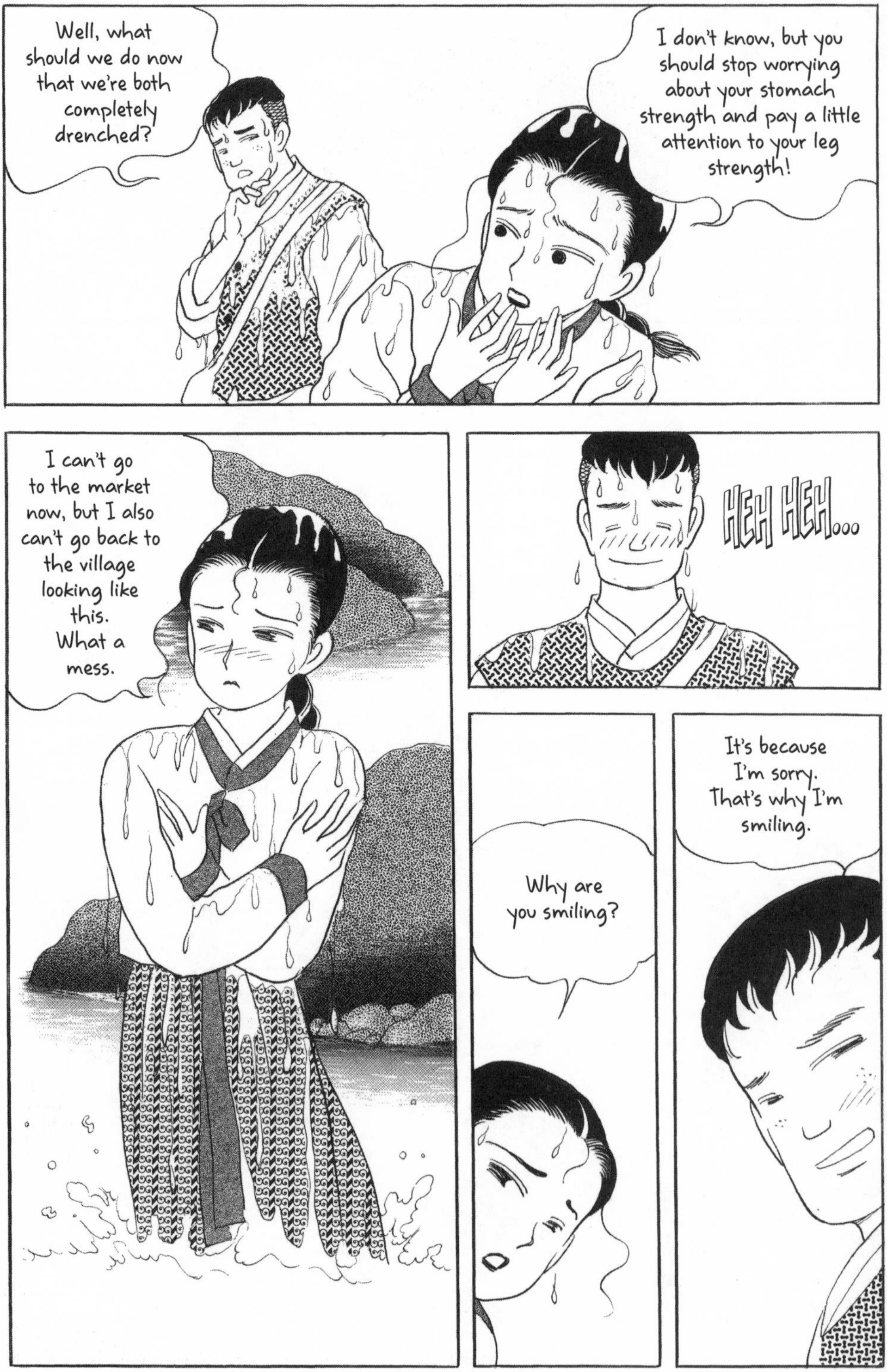

Well, what should we do now that we're both completely drenched?
I don't know, but you should stop worrying about your stomach strength and pay a little attention to your leg strength!
I can't go to the market now, but I also can't go back to the village looking like this. What a mess.
HEH HEH...
Why are you smiling?
It's because I'm sorry. That's why I'm smiling.

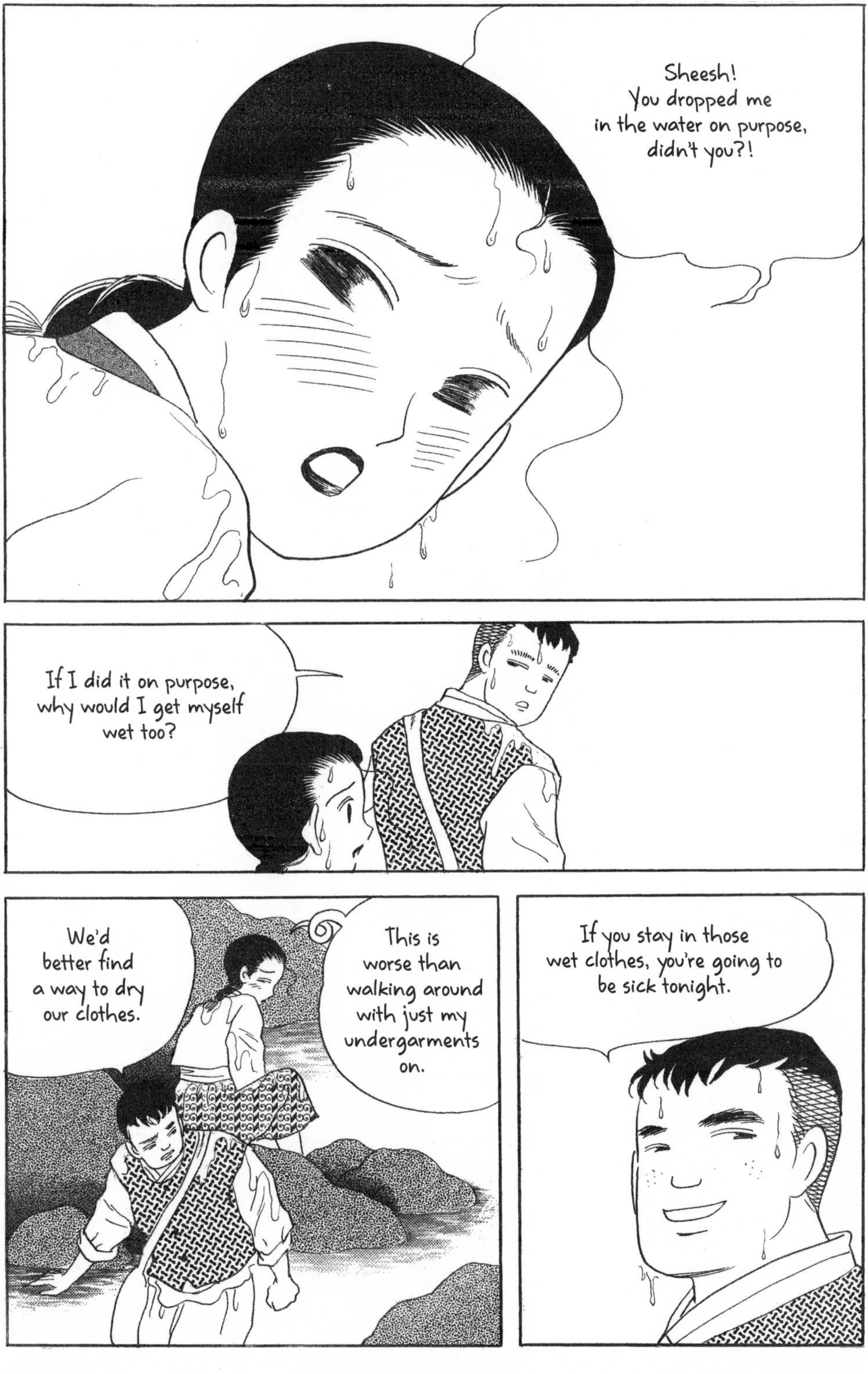
Sheesh! You dropped me in the water on purpose, didn't you?!
If I did it on purpose, why would I get myself wet too?
We'd better find a way to dry our clothes.
This is worse than walking around with just my undergarments on.
If you stay in those wet clothes, you're going to be sick tonight.

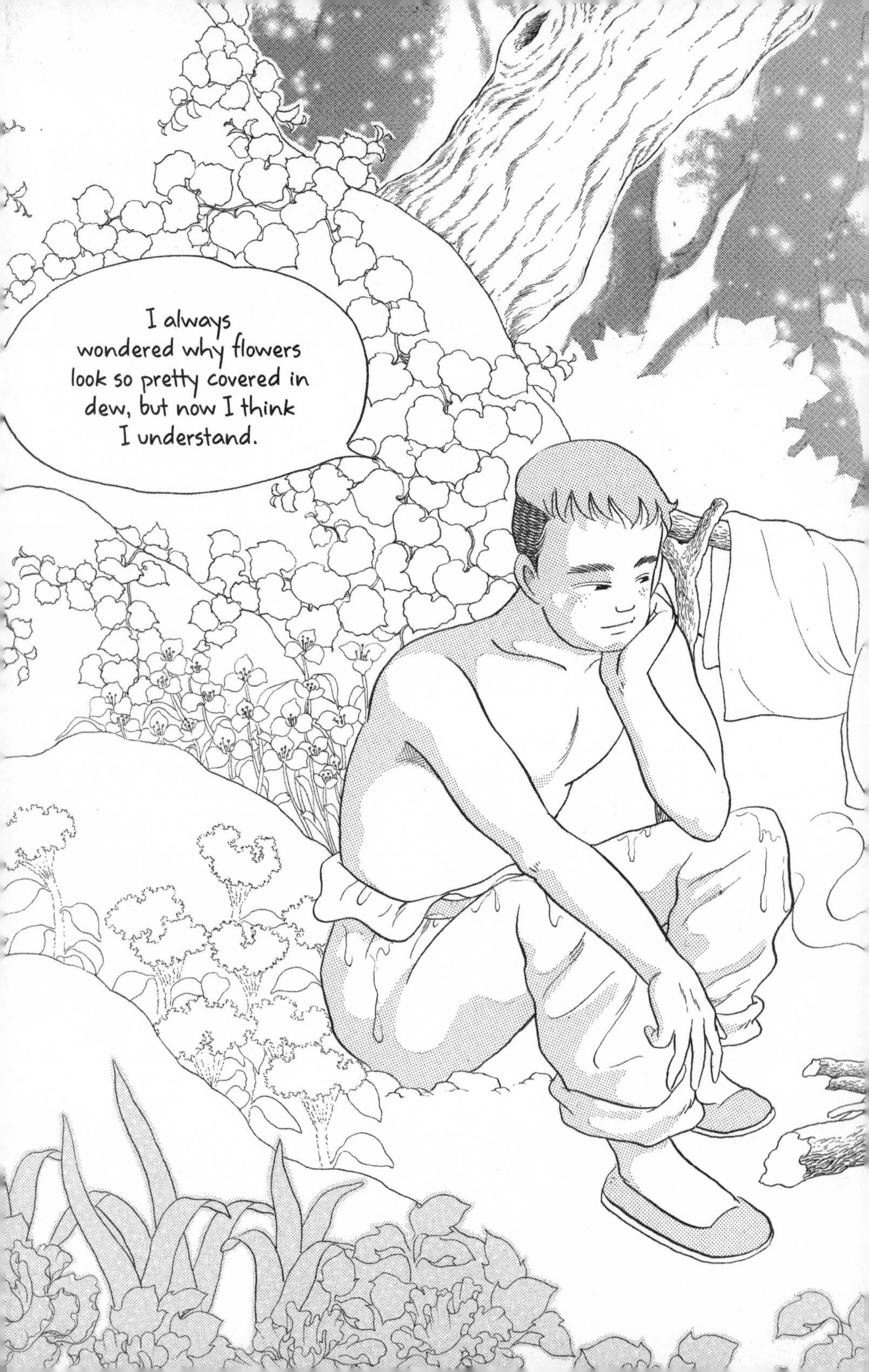
I always wondered why flowers look so pretty covered in dew, but now I think I understand.

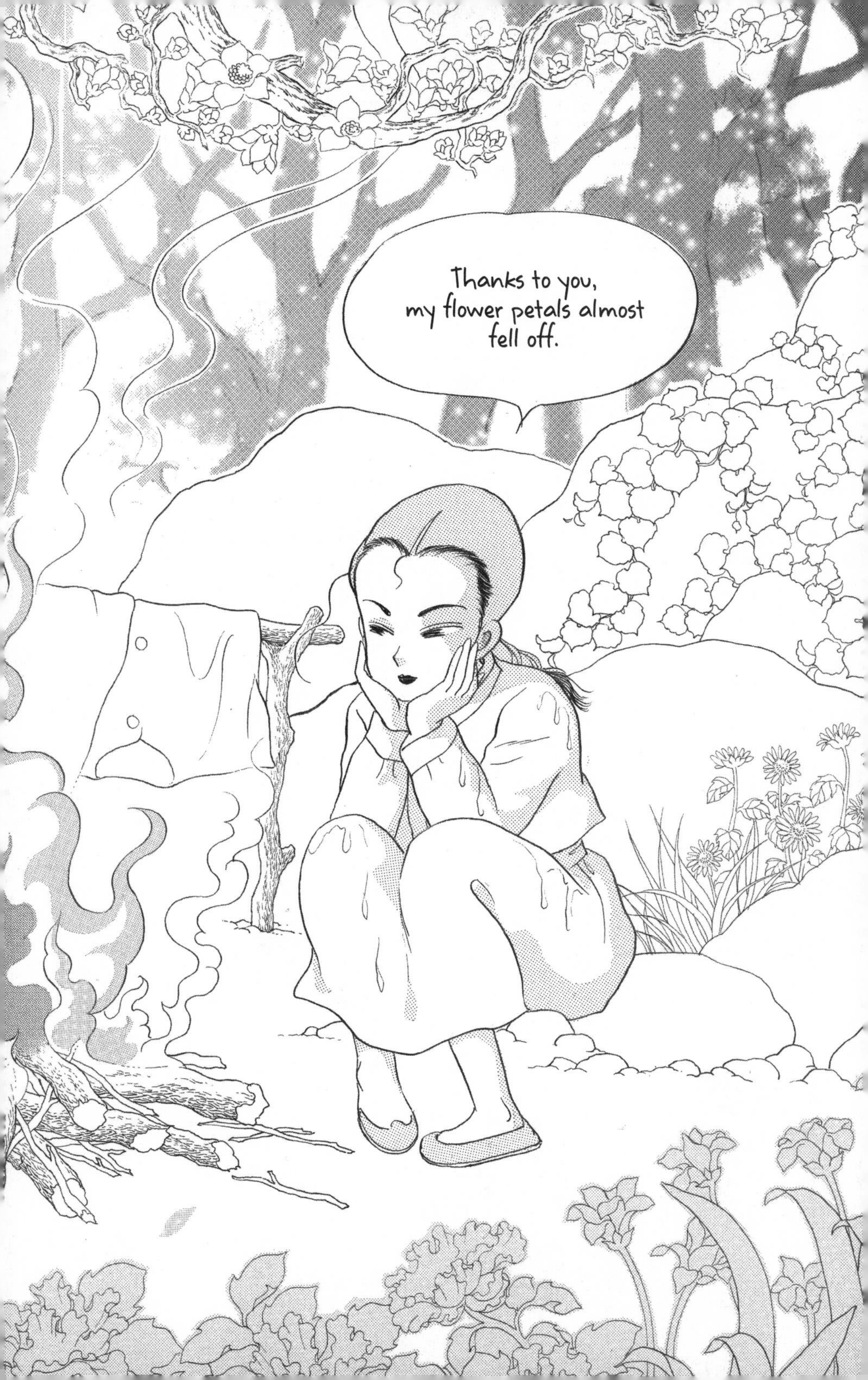
Thanks to you, my flower petals almost fell off.

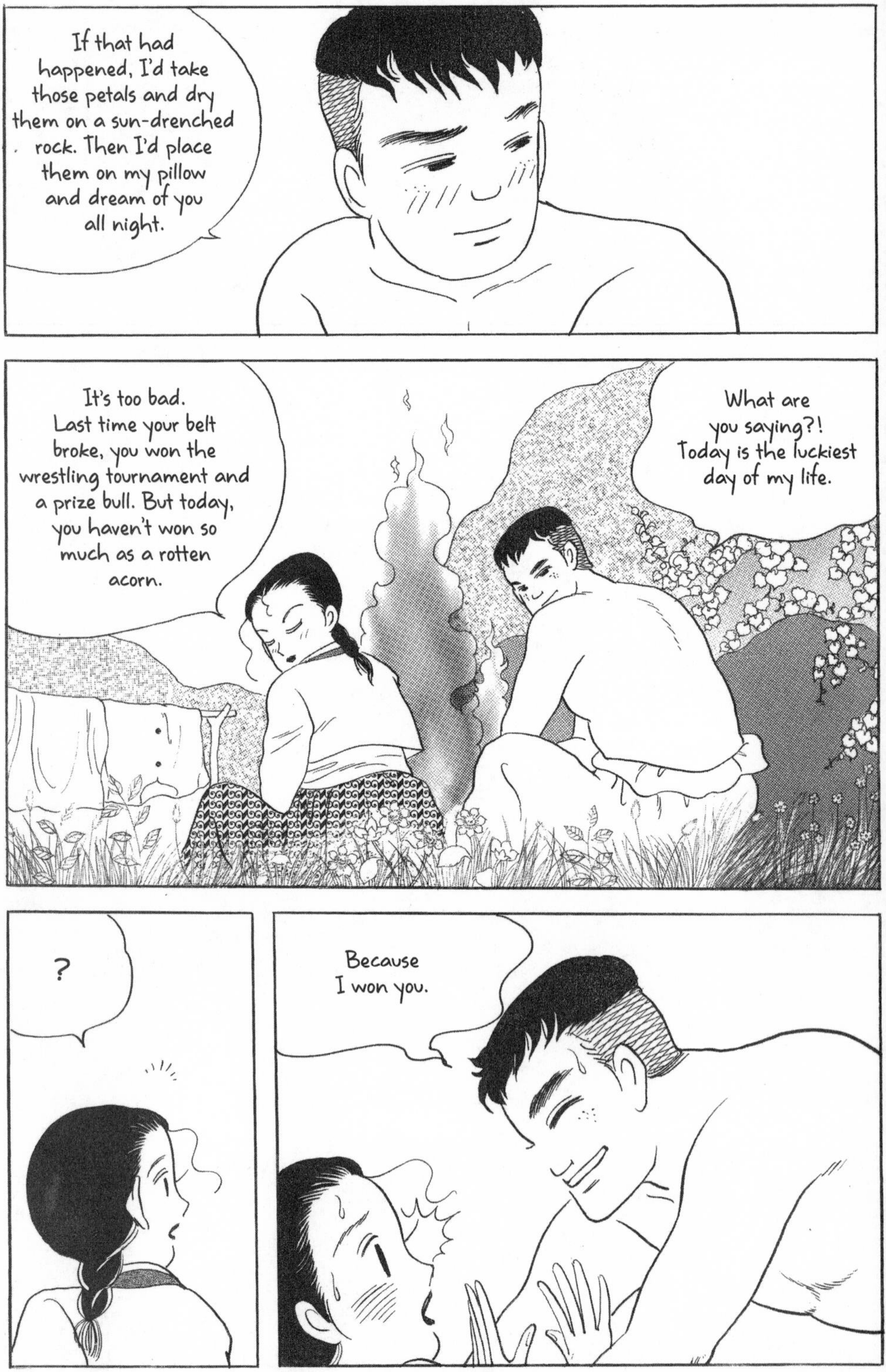
If that had happened, I'd take those petals and dry them on a sun-drenched rock. Then I'd place them on my pillow and dream of you all night.
It's too bad. Last time your belt broke, you won the wrestling tournament and a prize bull. But today, you haven't won so much as a rotten acorn.
What are you saying?! Today is the luckiest day of my life.
?
Because I won you.

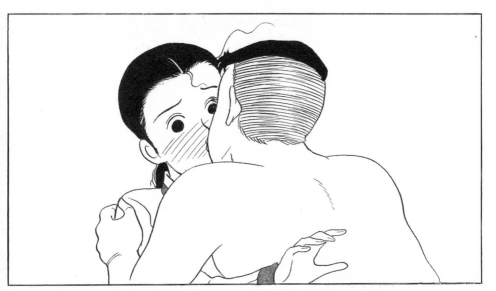

You're supposed to close your eyes.

Mmm...

This is one lucky belt. Every time it breaks, I win a treasure.

That's why, until I get married, I'm going to continue using it.

Then I guess I don't have to go to the market today. I had planned on getting some more fabric and embroidery thread...

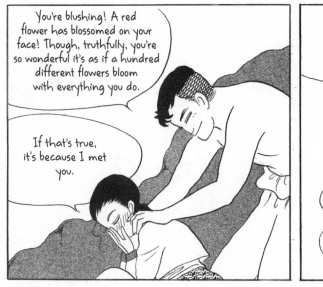

You're blushing! A red flower has blossomed on your face! Though, truthfully, you're so wonderful it's as if a hundred different flowers bloom with everything you do.

If that's true, it's because I met you.

That's why a hundred different flowers have bloomed within me.

Chapter Six

THE WIND THAT CALLS OUT TO A WOMAN

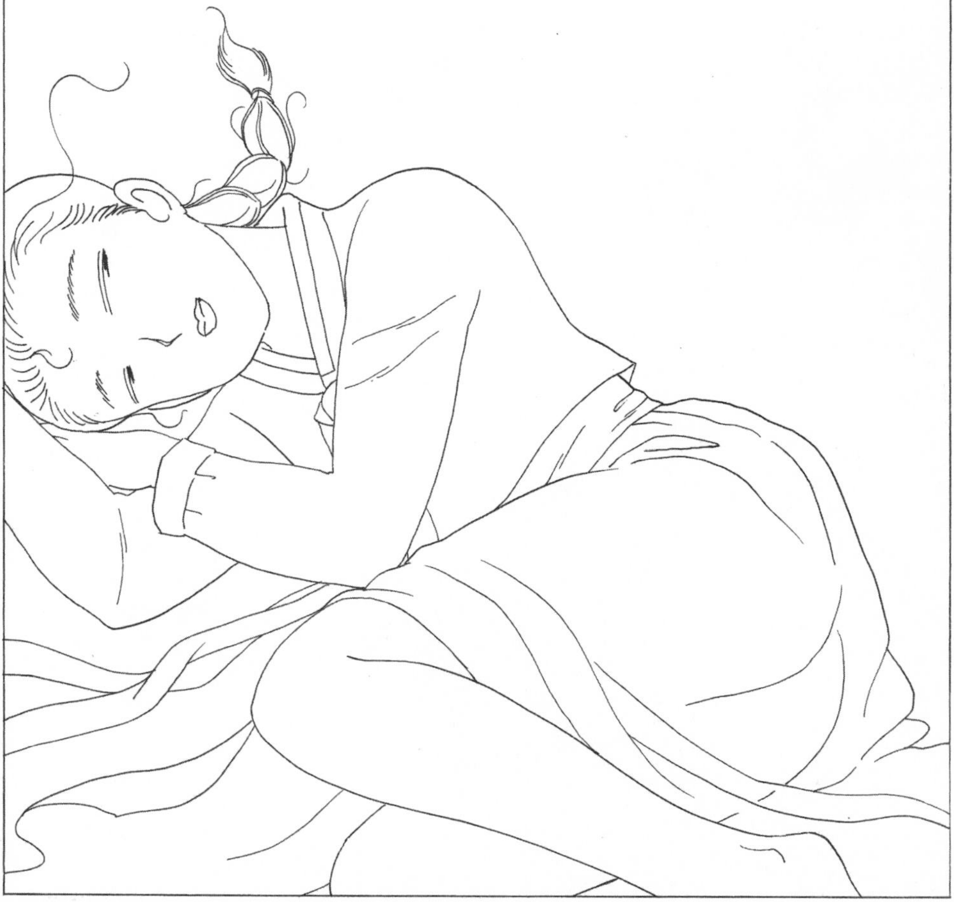

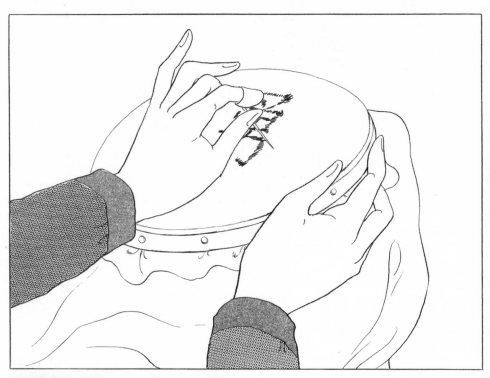

You said you're going to give that pouch to my future husband, right?

That's right.

The way you're wielding that needle, I'd guess that you're trying to tie me down to you.

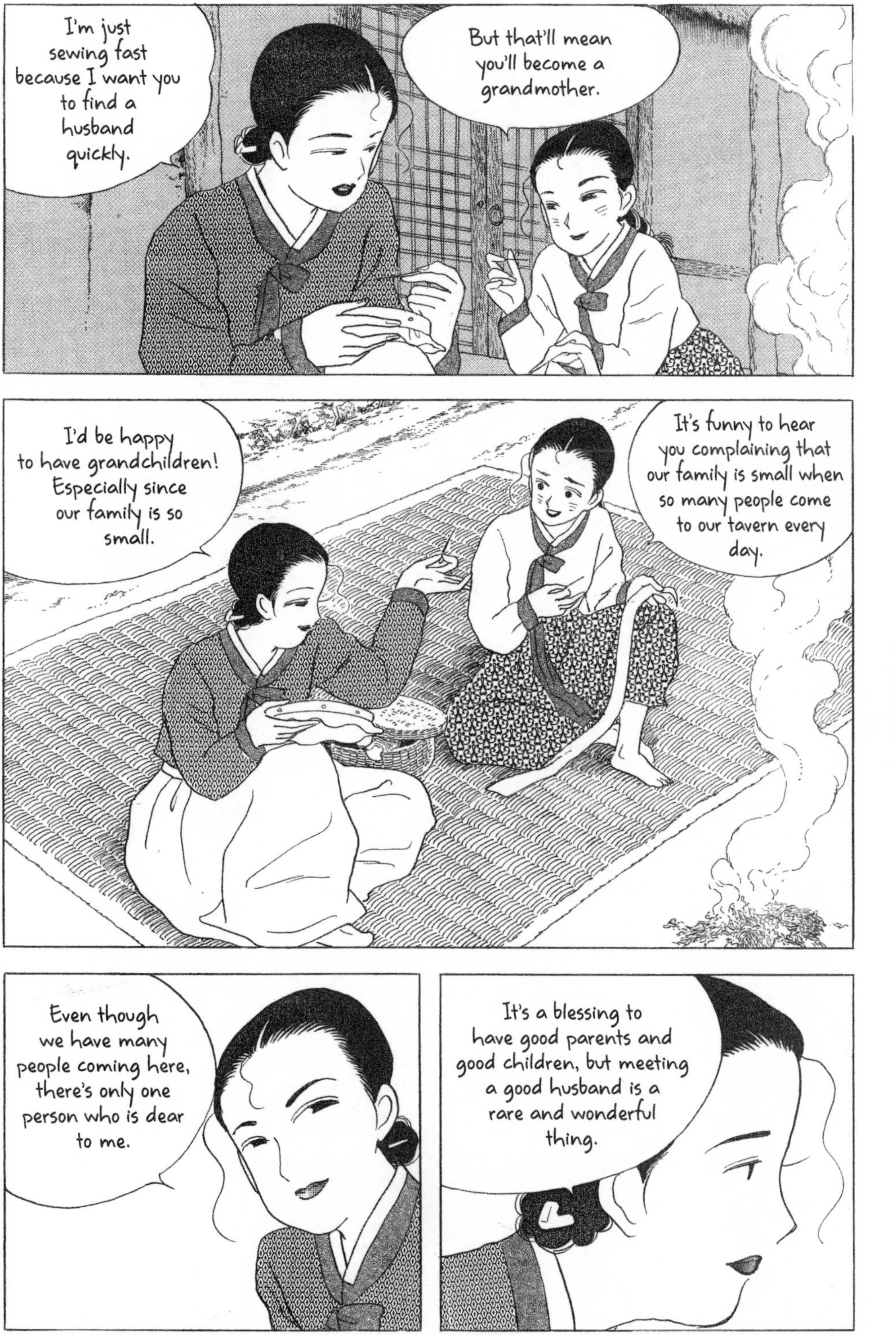
I'm just sewing fast because I want you to find a husband quickly.
But that'll mean you'll become a grandmother.
I'd be happy to have grandchildren! Especially since our family is so small.
It's funny to hear you complaining that our family is small when so many people come to our tavern every day.
Even though we have many people coming here, there's only one person who is dear to me.
It's a blessing to have good parents and good children, but meeting a good husband is a rare and wonderful thing.

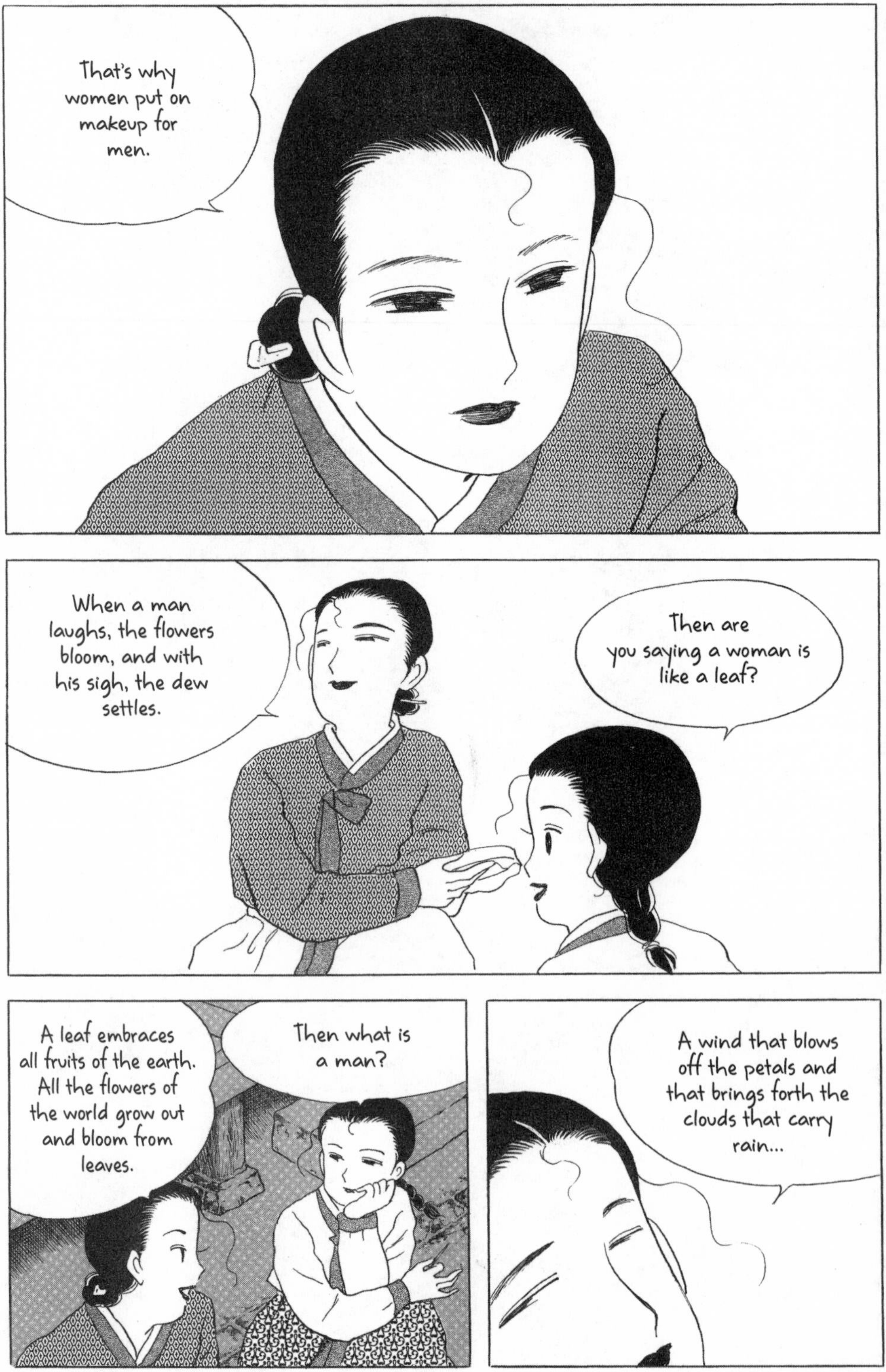
That's why women put on makeup for men.
When a man laughs, the flowers bloom, and with his sigh, the dew settles.
Then are you saying a woman is like a leaf?
A leaf embraces all fruits of the earth. All the flowers of the world grow out and bloom from leaves.
Then what is a man?
A wind that blows off the petals and that brings forth the clouds that carry rain...

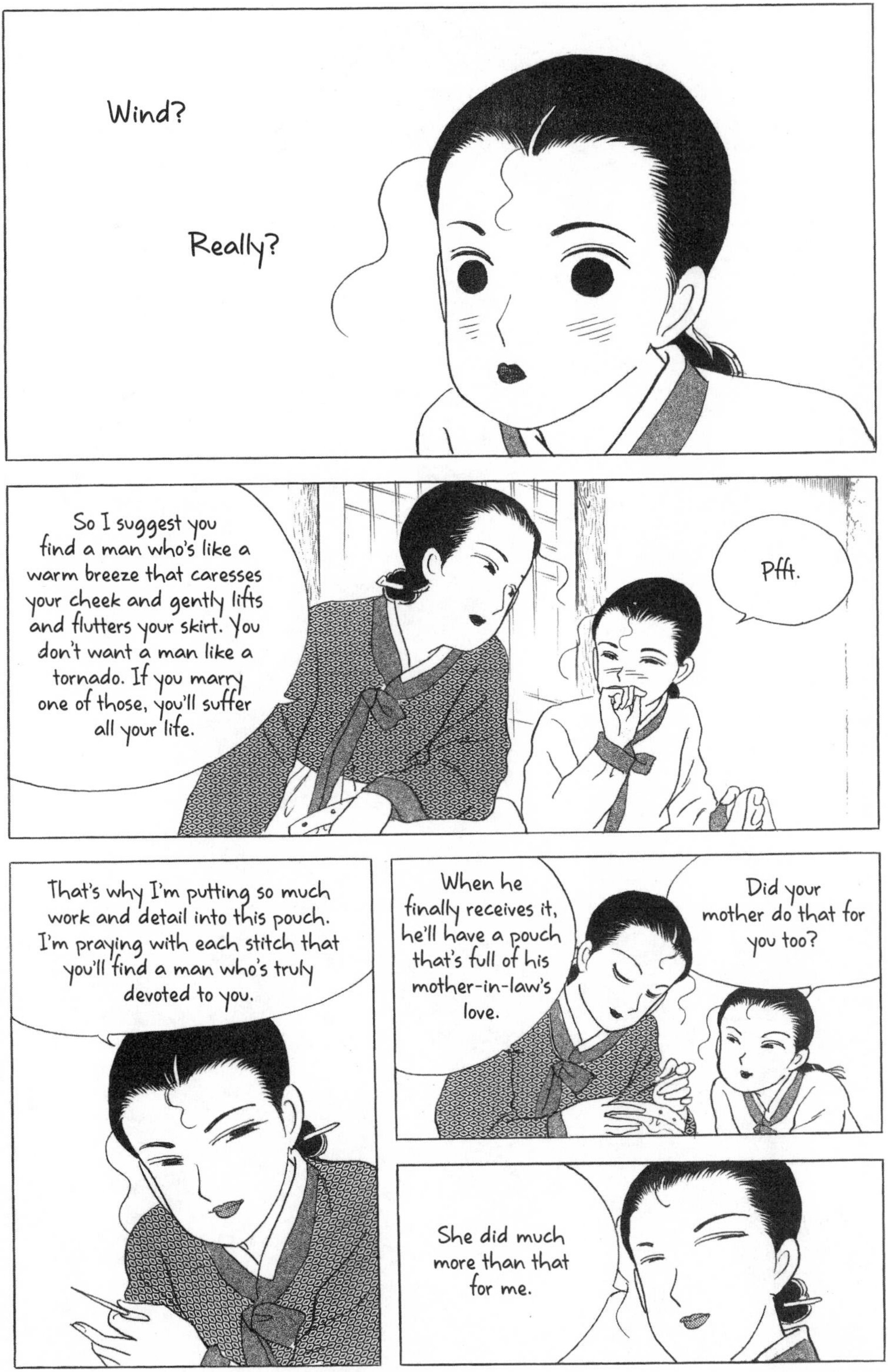
Wind?
Really?
So I suggest you find a man who's like a warm breeze that caresses your cheek and gently lifts and flutters your skirt. You don't want a man like a tornado. If you marry one of those, you'll suffer all your life.
Pfft.
That's why I'm putting so much work and detail into this pouch. I'm praying with each stitch that you'll find a man who's truly devoted to you.
When he finally receives it, he'll have a pouch that's full of his mother-in-law's love.
Did your mother do that for you too?
She did much more than that for me.

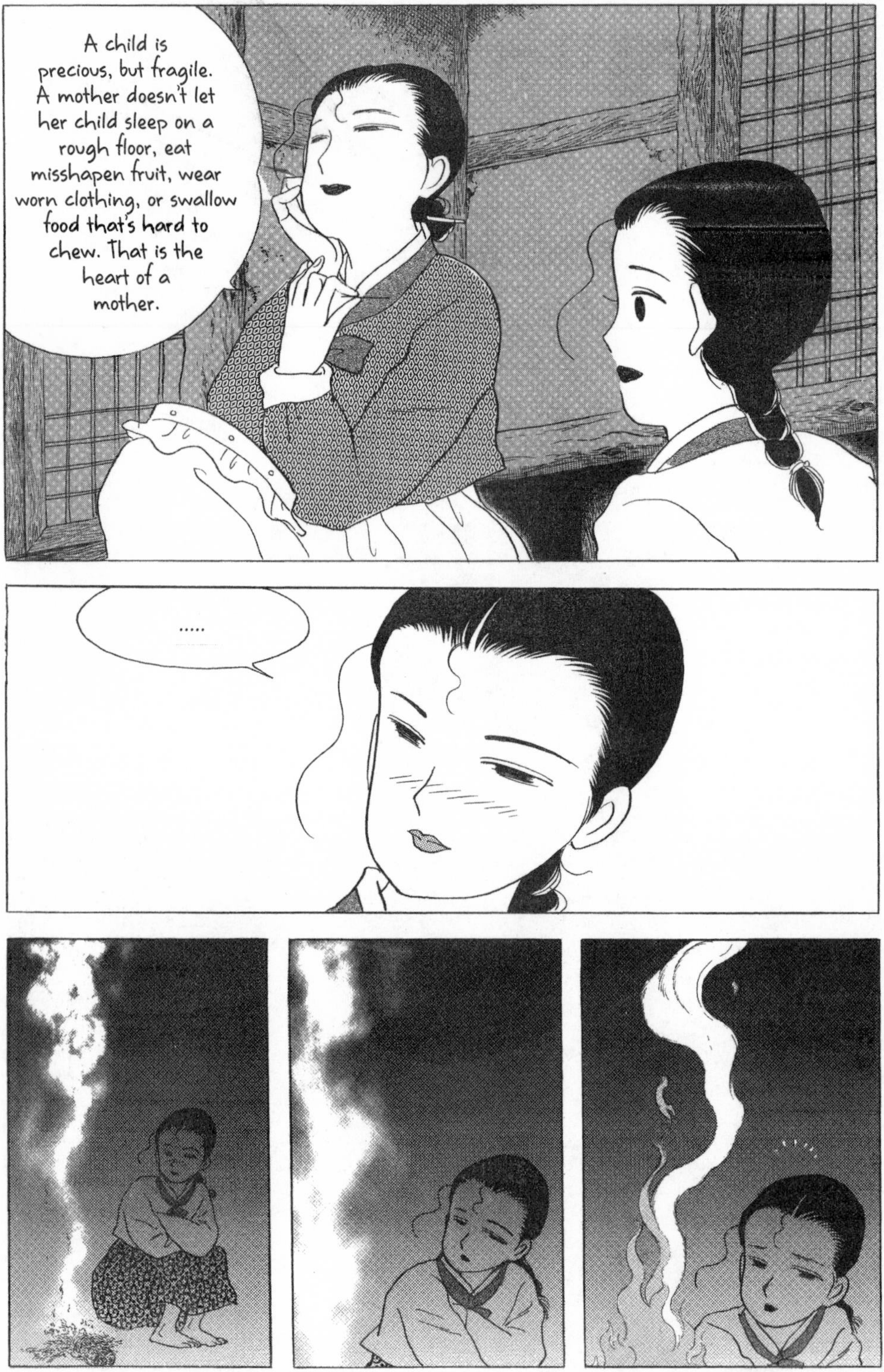
A child is precious, but fragile. A mother doesn't let her child sleep on a rough floor, eat misshapen fruit, wear worn clothing, or swallow food that's hard to chew. That is the heart of a mother.
.....

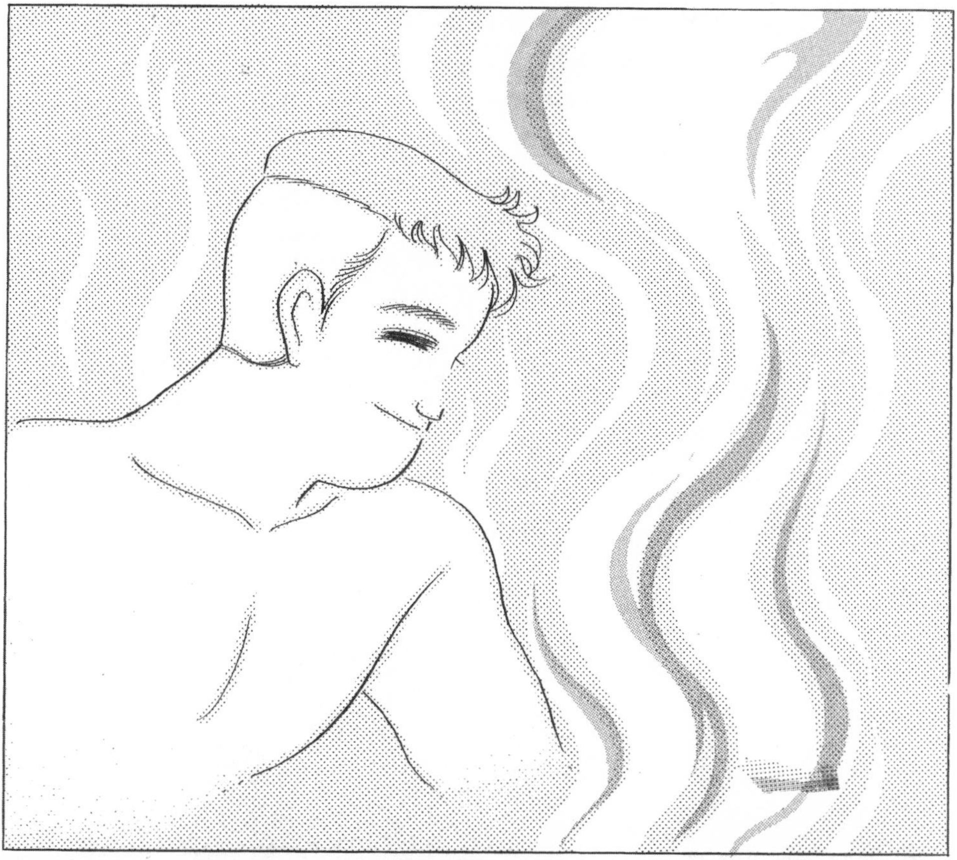

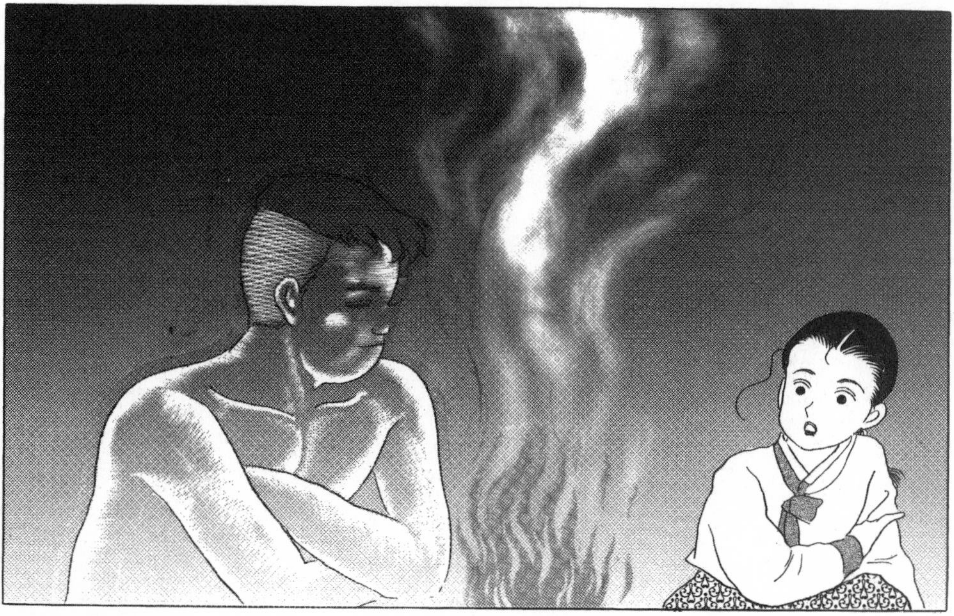

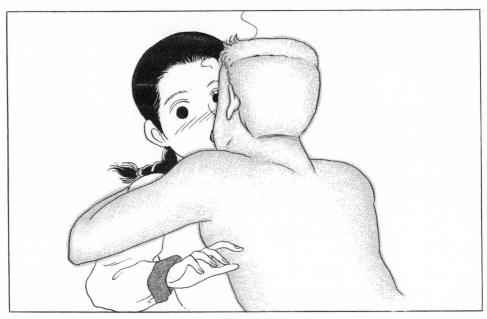

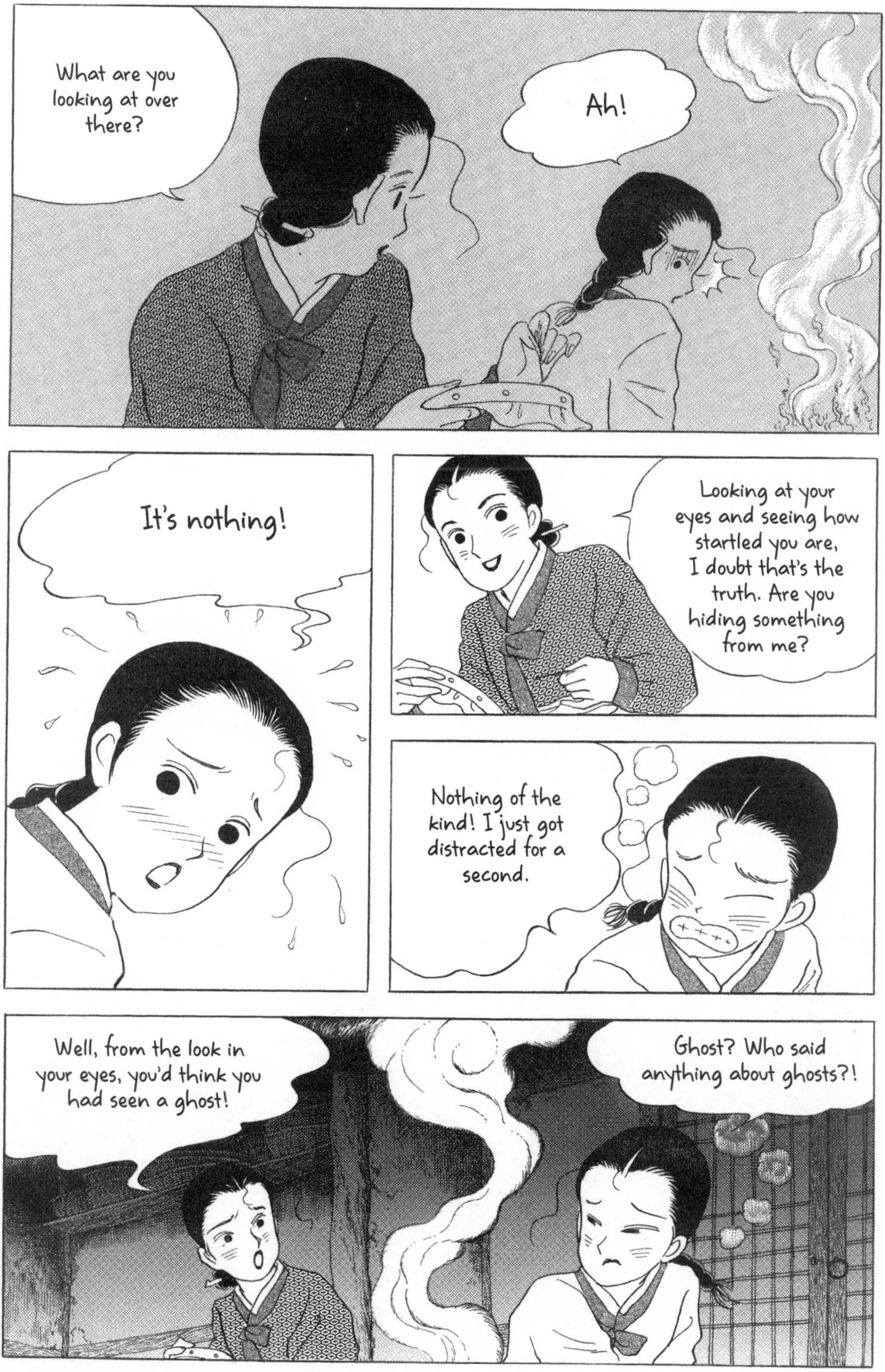
What are you looking at over there?
Ah!
It's nothing!
Looking at your eyes and seeing how startled you are, I doubt that's the truth. Are you hiding something from me?
Nothing of the kind! I just got distracted for a second.
Well, from the look in your eyes, you'd think you had seen a ghost!
Ghost? Who said anything about ghosts?!

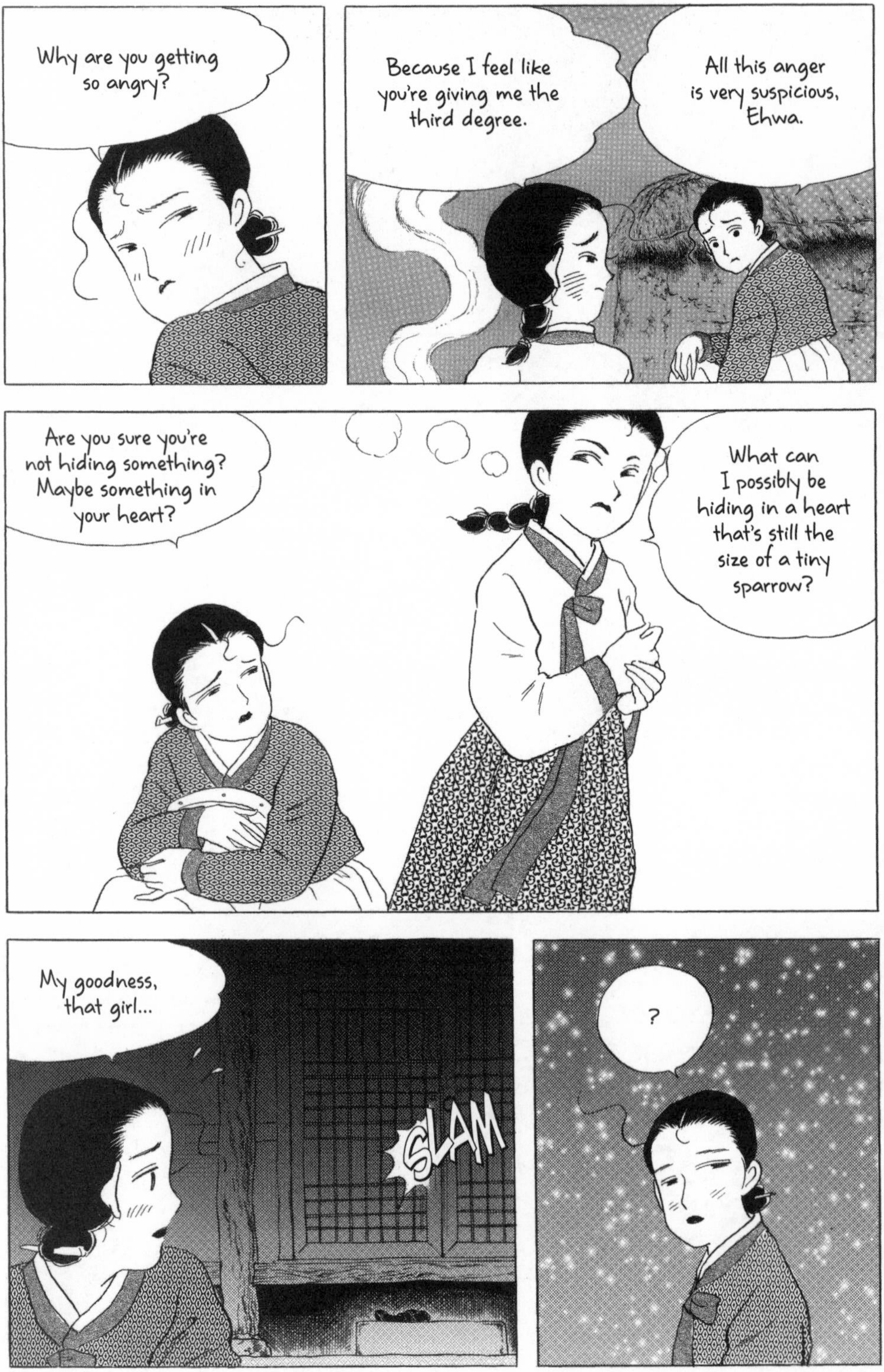

Why are you getting so angry?
Because I feel like you're giving me the third degree.
All this anger is very suspicious, Ehwa.
Are you sure you're not hiding something? Maybe something in your heart?
What can I possibly be hiding in a heart that's still the size of a tiny sparrow?
My goodness, that girl...
SLAM
?

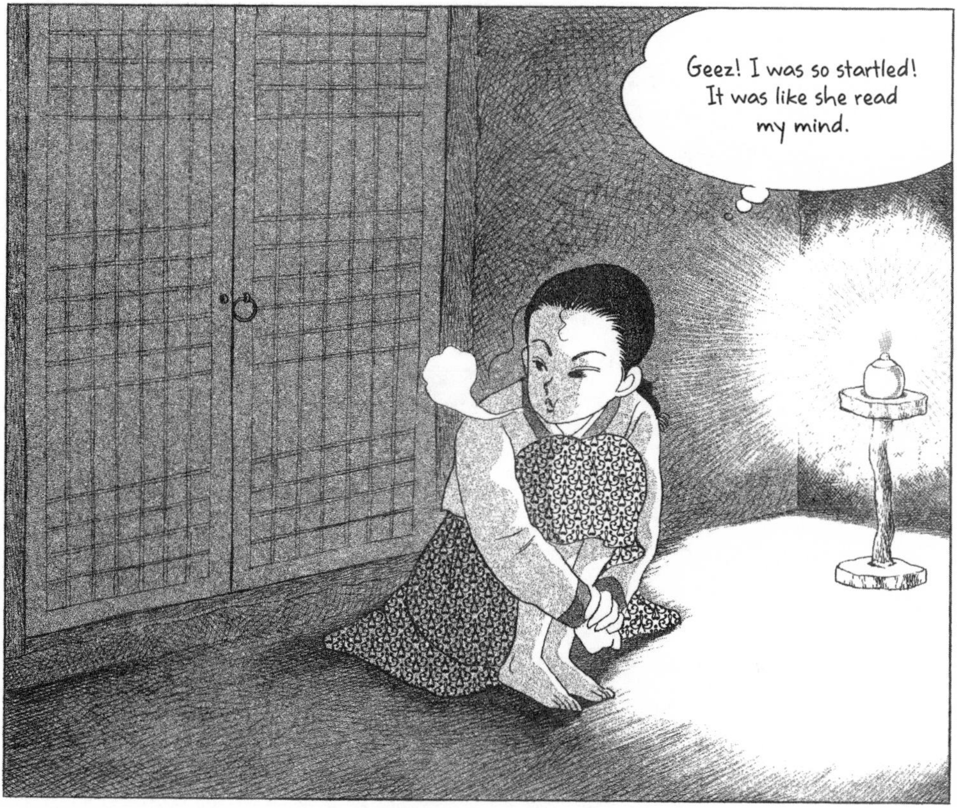
Geez! I was so startled! It was like she read my mind.
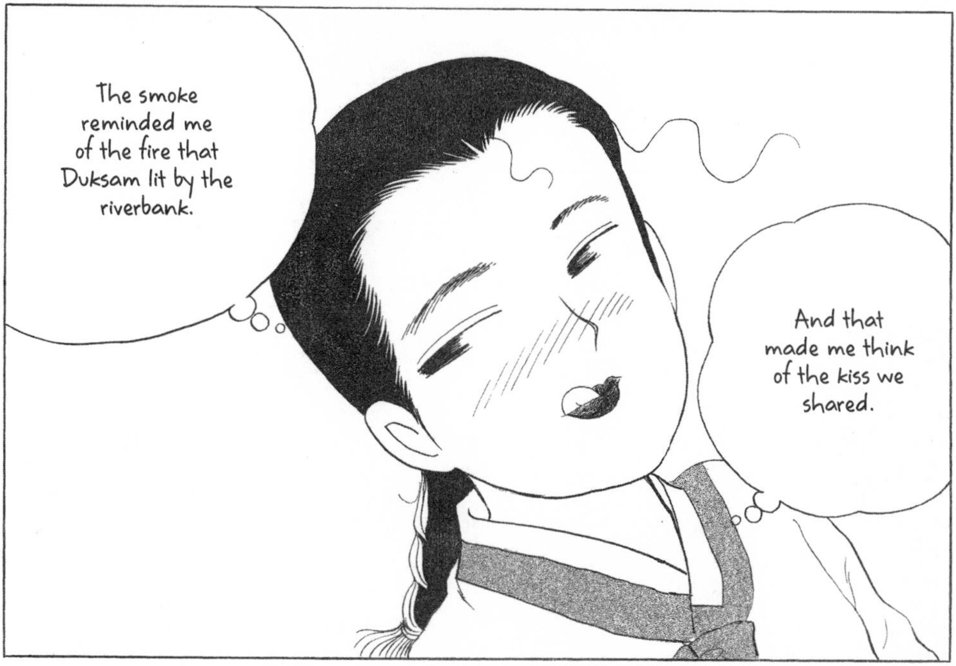
The smoke reminded me of the fire that Duksam lit by the riverbank.
And that made me think of the kiss we shared.

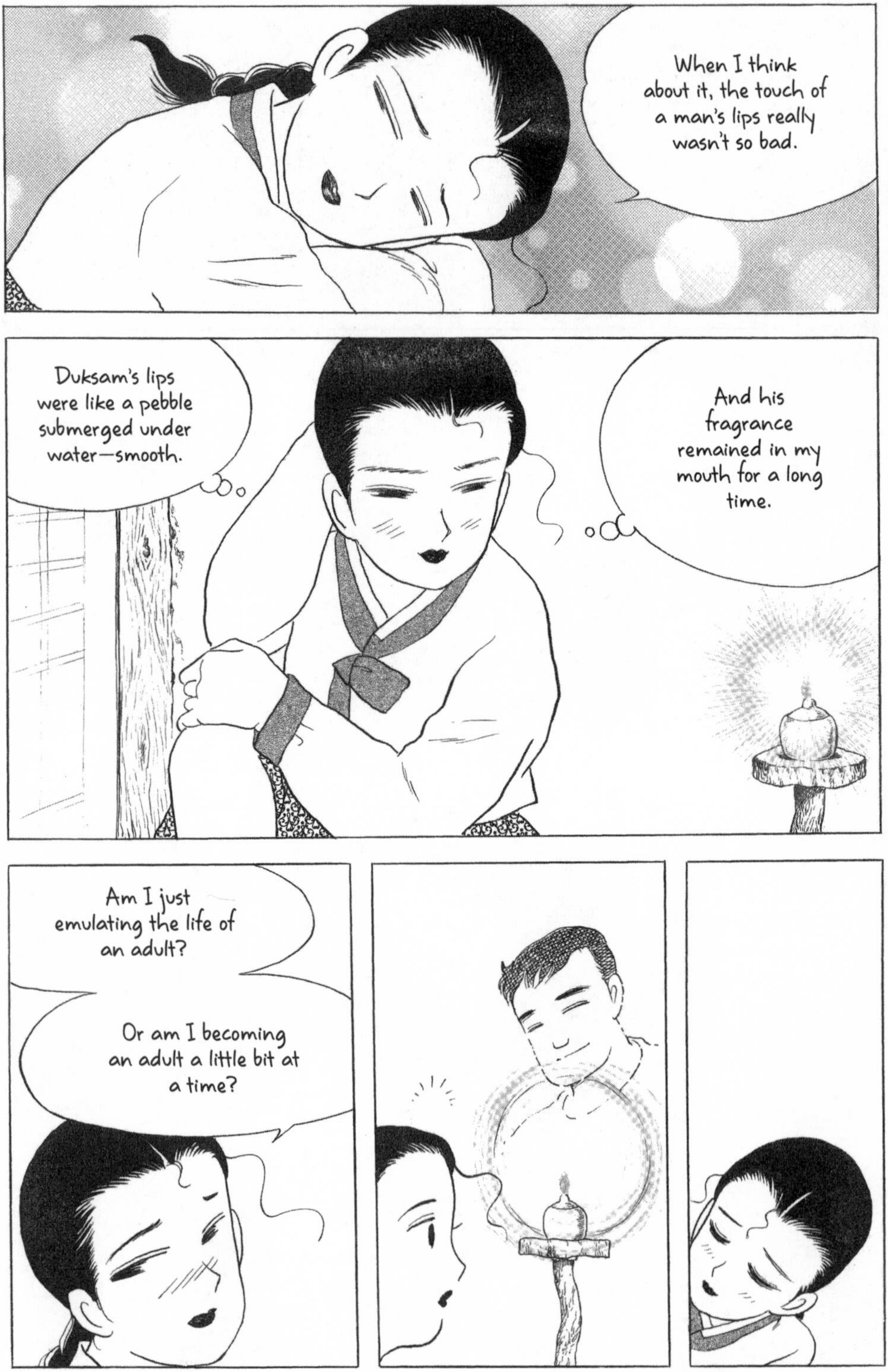
When I think about it, the touch of a man's lips really wasn't so bad.
Duksam's lips were like a pebble submerged under water—smooth.
And his fragrance remained in my mouth for a long time.
Am I just emulating the life of an adult?
Or am I becoming an adult a little bit at a time?

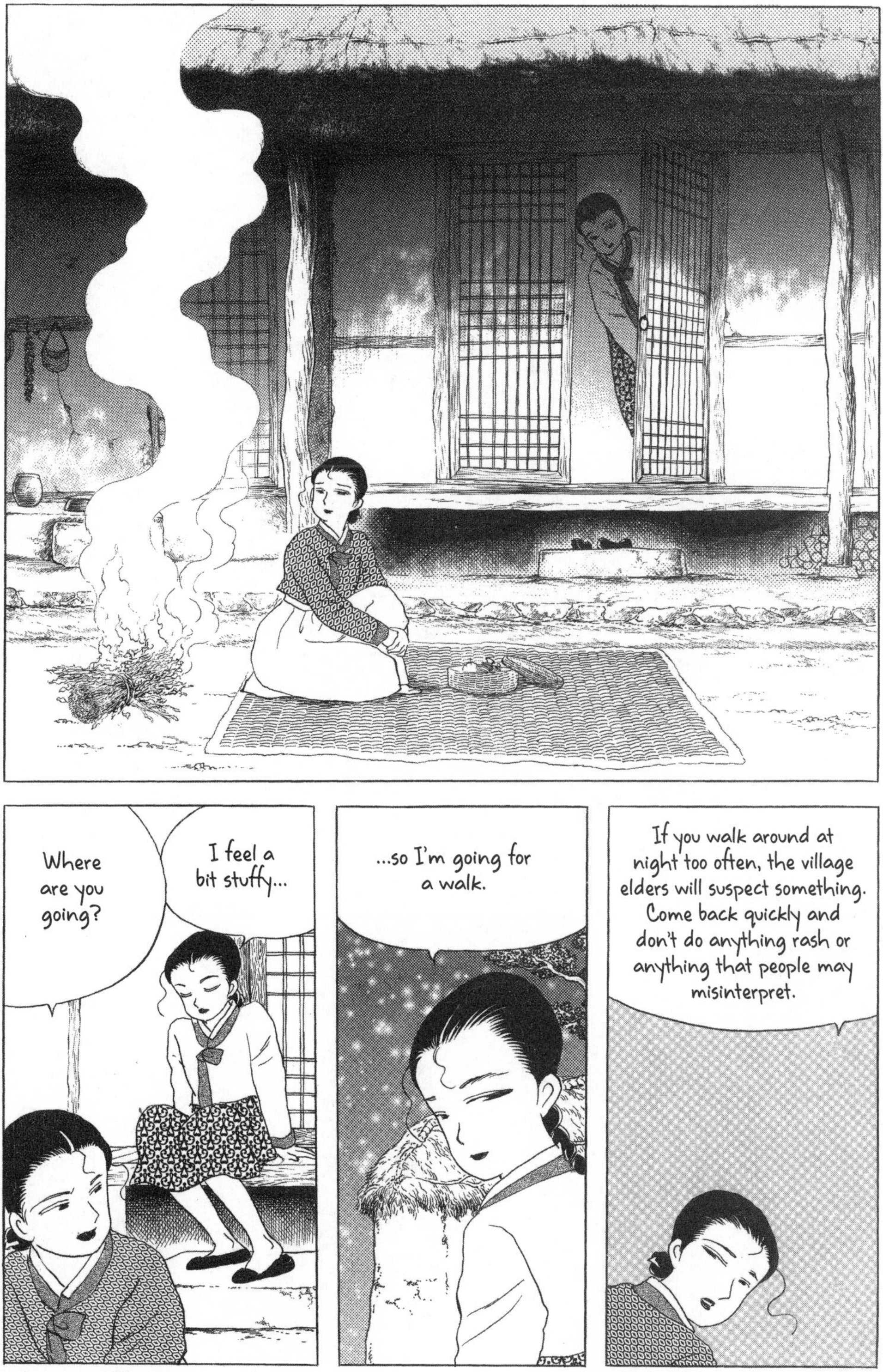
Where are you going?
I feel a bit stuffy...
...so I'm going for a walk.
If you walk around at night too often, the village elders will suspect something. Come back quickly and don't do anything rash or anything that people may misinterpret.

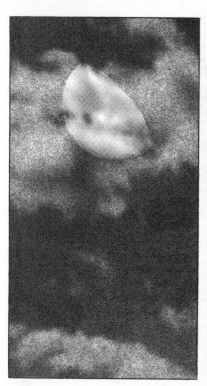

I must really have it bad. Even a misshapen moon looks like Duksam to me.

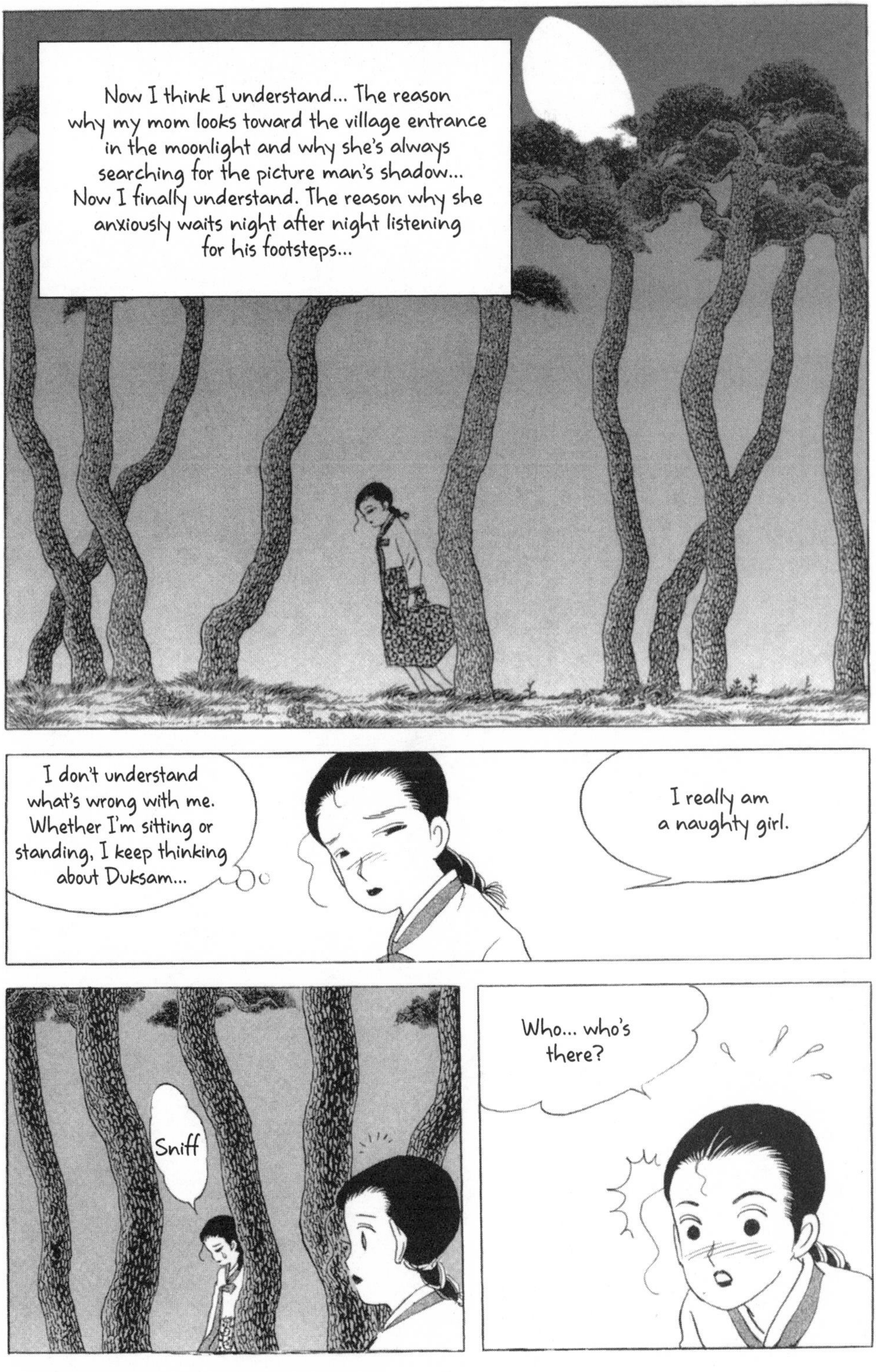
Now I think I understand... The reason why my mom looks toward the village entrance in the moonlight and why she's always searching for the picture man's shadow... Now I finally understand. The reason why she anxiously waits night after night listening for his footsteps...
I don't understand what's wrong with me. Whether I'm sitting or standing, I keep thinking about Duksam...
I really am a naughty girl.
Sniff
Who... who's there?

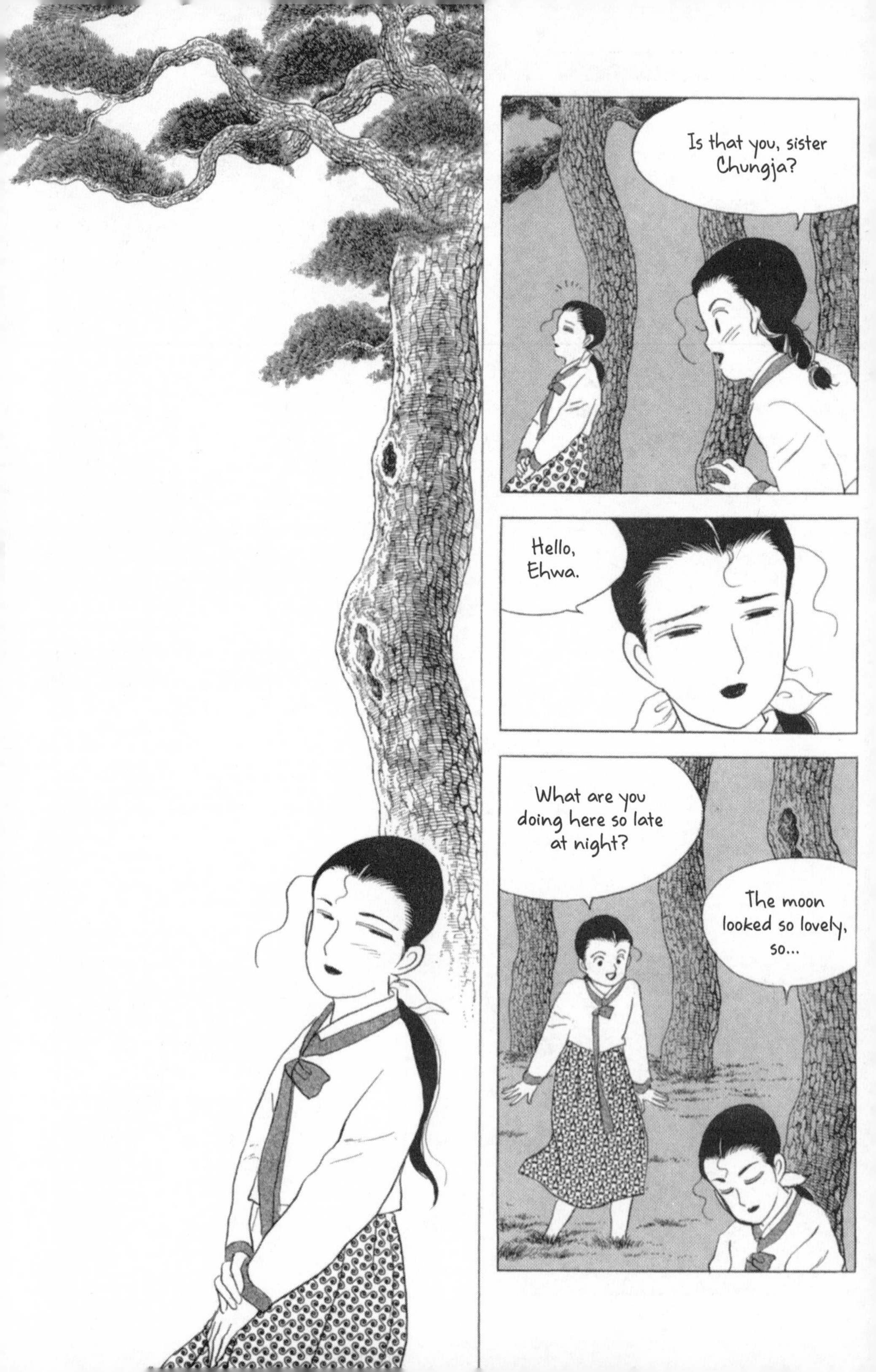
Is that you, sister Chungja?
Hello, Ehwa.
What are you doing here so late at night?
The moon looked so lovely, so...

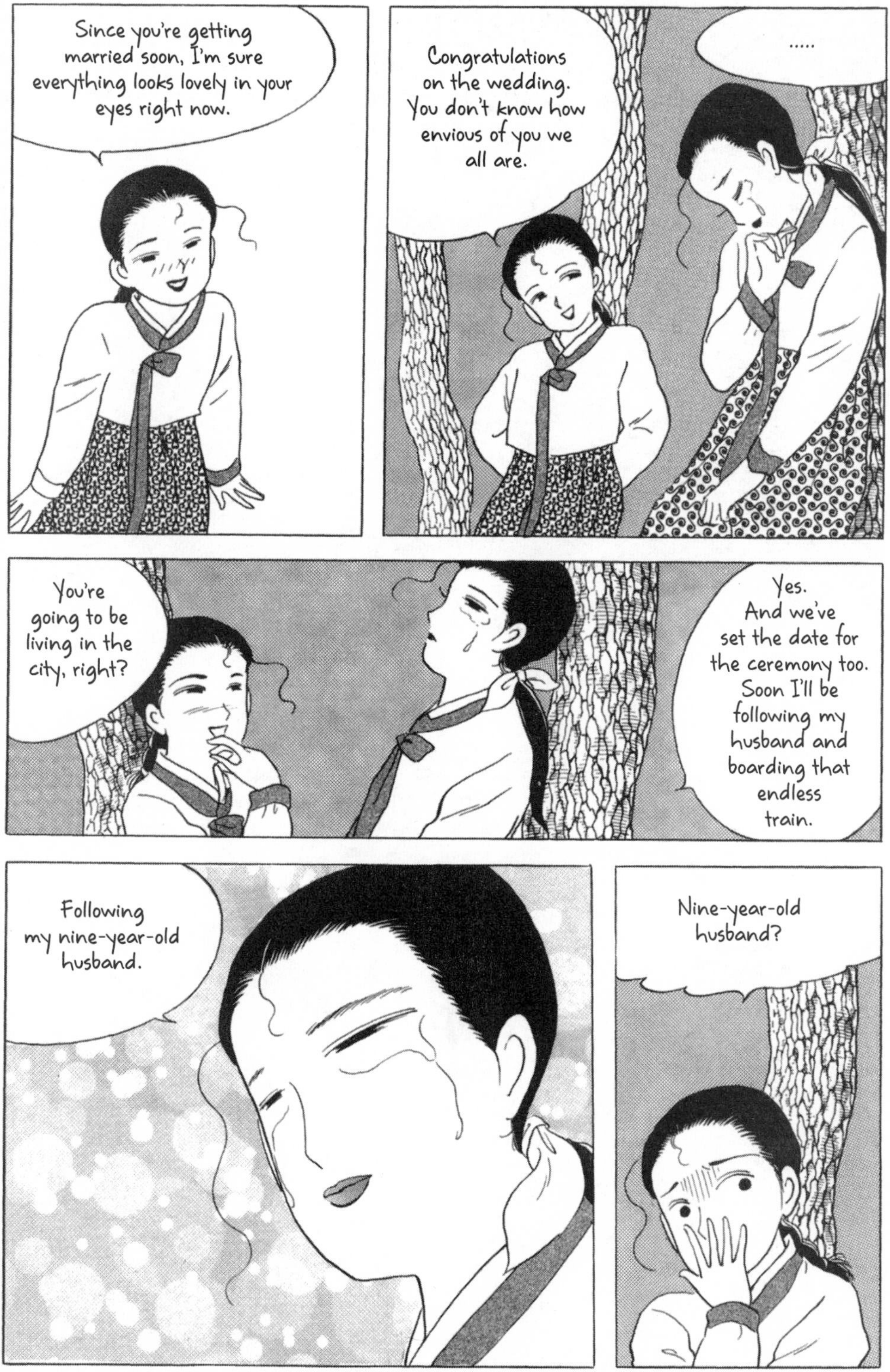

Since you're getting married soon, I'm sure everything looks lovely in your eyes right now.
Congratulations on the wedding. You don't know how envious of you we all are.
.....
You're going to be living in the city, right?
Yes. And we've set the date for the ceremony too. Soon I'll be following my husband and boarding that endless train.
Following my nine-year-old husband.
Nine-year-old husband?

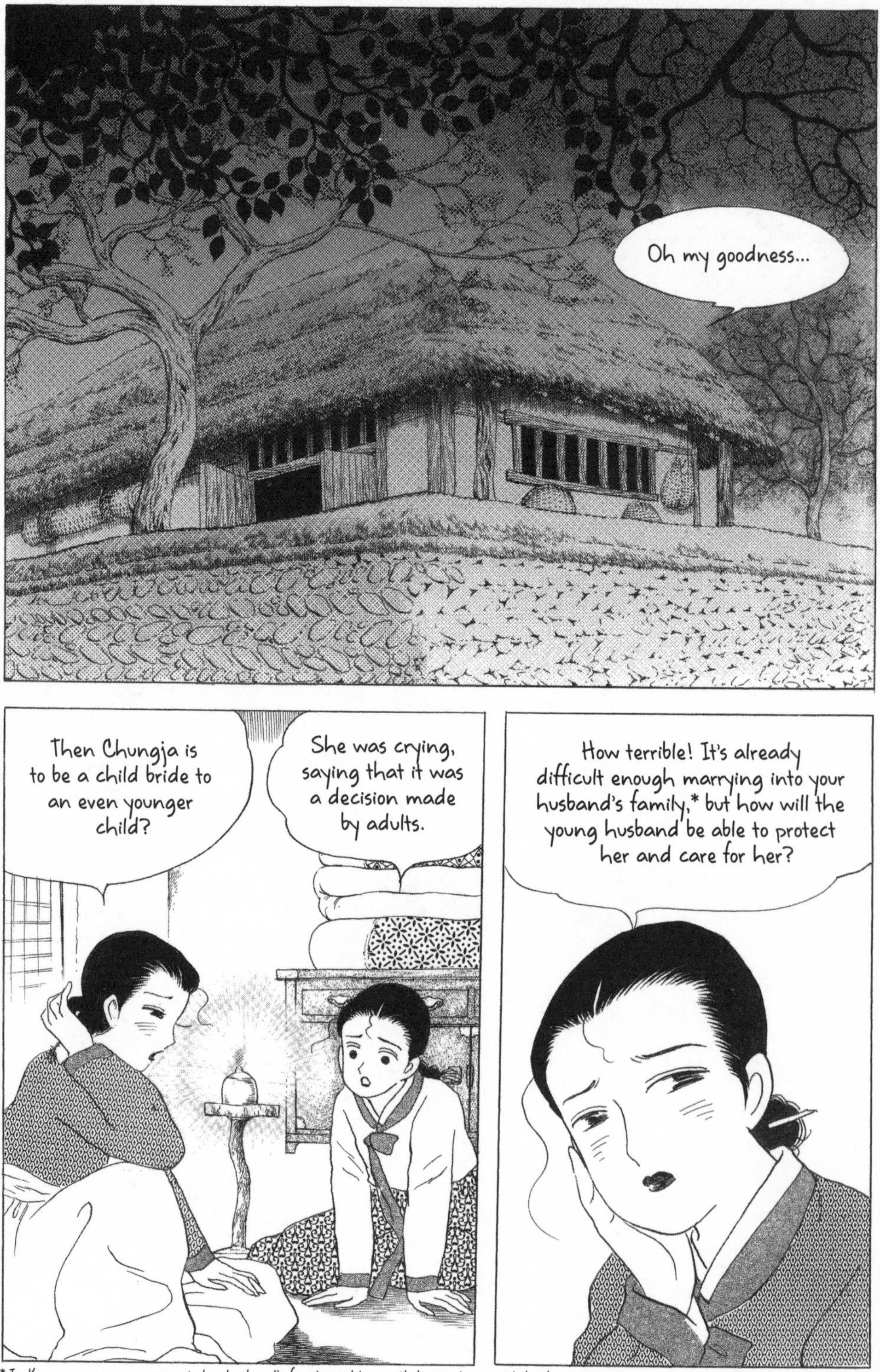

Oh my goodness...
Then Chungja is to be a child bride to an even younger child?
She was crying, saying that it was a decision made by adults.
How terrible! It's already difficult enough marrying into your husband's family,* but how will the young husband be able to protect her and care for her?

* In Korea, a woman marries into her husband's family and lives with her in-laws until death.

Rather than protecting and caring for her, she'll have to carry him, put him to bed, wash him, dress him and actually run the household.

Even a woman with the most wonderful married life, with great in-laws, still needs the comfort of her husband's arms every now and then. But it looks like she'll have to tend to her husband's every whim. I feel so sorry for her.

She looked so frustrated and sad crying by herself under the moon in the pine grove.

Do you know why pickled food is so spicy and salty? It's because it's been made by hands that have experienced married life with in-laws.

You have to live three years as a mute, three years as a deaf person, and three years groping around like you're blind before you can expect to receive any comfort from your in-laws.

That's not the only thing! She's marrying the oldest son and the grandmother is going to live with them, too.*

Oh, my! Oh, my!

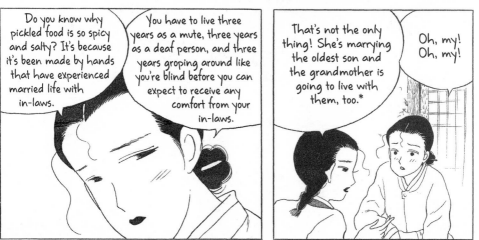

* In Korea at the time this story takes place, the role of the eldest daughter-in-law was considered to be prestigious, but also full of responsibilities. It was her role to teach the younger daughter-in-laws and to set the tone of the household.

An only daughter with an only daughter
Raises her child like a precious treasure
Upon her wedding day
She offers words of wisdom
Married life is not easy
Though you see, act as if you don't
Though you hear, act as if you don't
The less you say, the better your
married life will be
Hearing those words, the only daughter
Rides the palanquin and enters her
in-laws' home
First, she lives mute for three years
Then blind for three years
And finally deaf for three years
After living like this for nine years
Dropwort flowers are in full bloom

The father-in-law watching all this
Considers her to be a mute
One day, as they approach the house
She hears an echo and says
"Listen, the mountain is speaking"
The father-in-law hears her speak
Words spoken by the "mute"
He is delighted
He calls a servant and tells him
"Let go of the palanquin
And quickly catch a pheasant"
When the servants bring the pheasant
The father-in-law says
"Let's quickly, quickly return home"

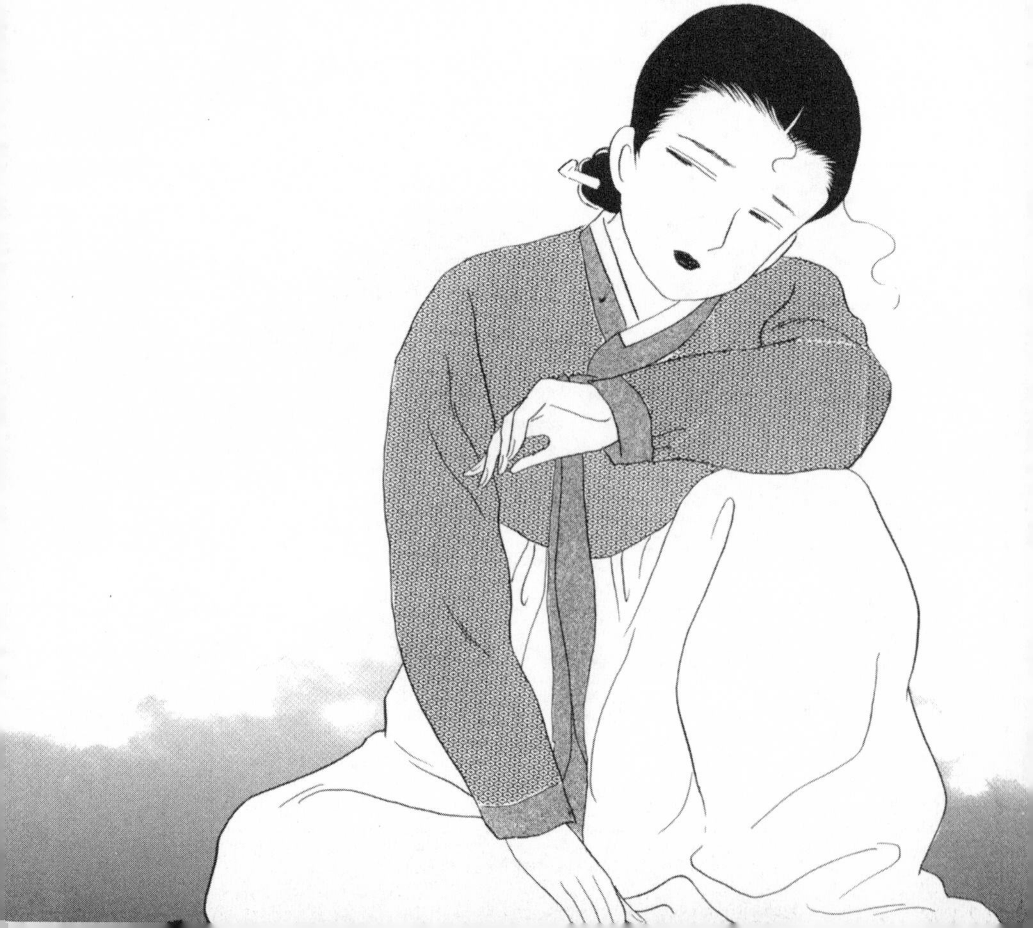

The once-mute daughter-in-law
Has no choice but to return
And begins to pluck the
freshly caught pheasant
She lights the stove, grills
the pheasant
And as she serves the meat, she says
Father-in-law, father-in-law,
please eat
The wings that once used to conceal
Mother-in-law, mother-in-law,
please eat
The beak that once used to mock
The eyes that so slyly peered
Are for grandmother-in-law to eat
And the flapping tail
Is for grandfather-in-law to eat...

The "delicate" liver
Is for sister-in-law to eat
Husband, husband, please eat
The legs, the strong little legs
Heart, heart, full of heartache
Is what I have eaten
Onerous, onerous
Onerous is the life living with in-laws
A ten-strand cloth, a skirt ten
times wide
Are useless in catching all the tears.
Futile, futile
Futile is a life living with in-laws
She wears her shirt crooked
The ribbon permanently droops
Wet from her tears

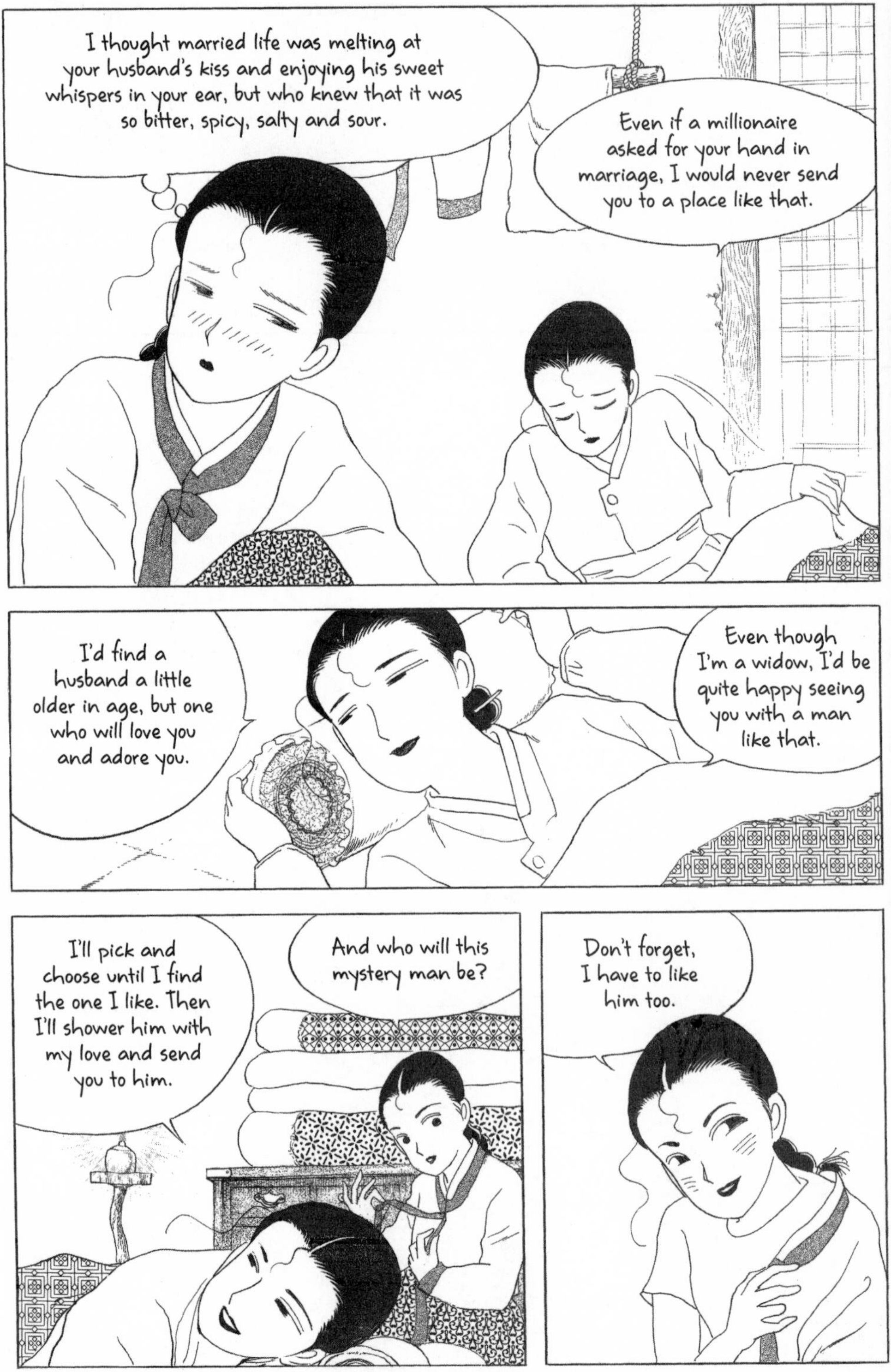
I thought married life was melting at your husband's kiss and enjoying his sweet whispers in your ear, but who knew that it was so bitter, spicy, salty and sour.
Even if a millionaire asked for your hand in marriage, I would never send you to a place like that.
I'd find a husband a little older in age, but one who will love you and adore you.
Even though I'm a widow, I'd be quite happy seeing you with a man like that.
I'll pick and choose until I find the one I like. Then I'll shower him with my love and send you to him.
And who will this mystery man be?
Don't forget, I have to like him too.

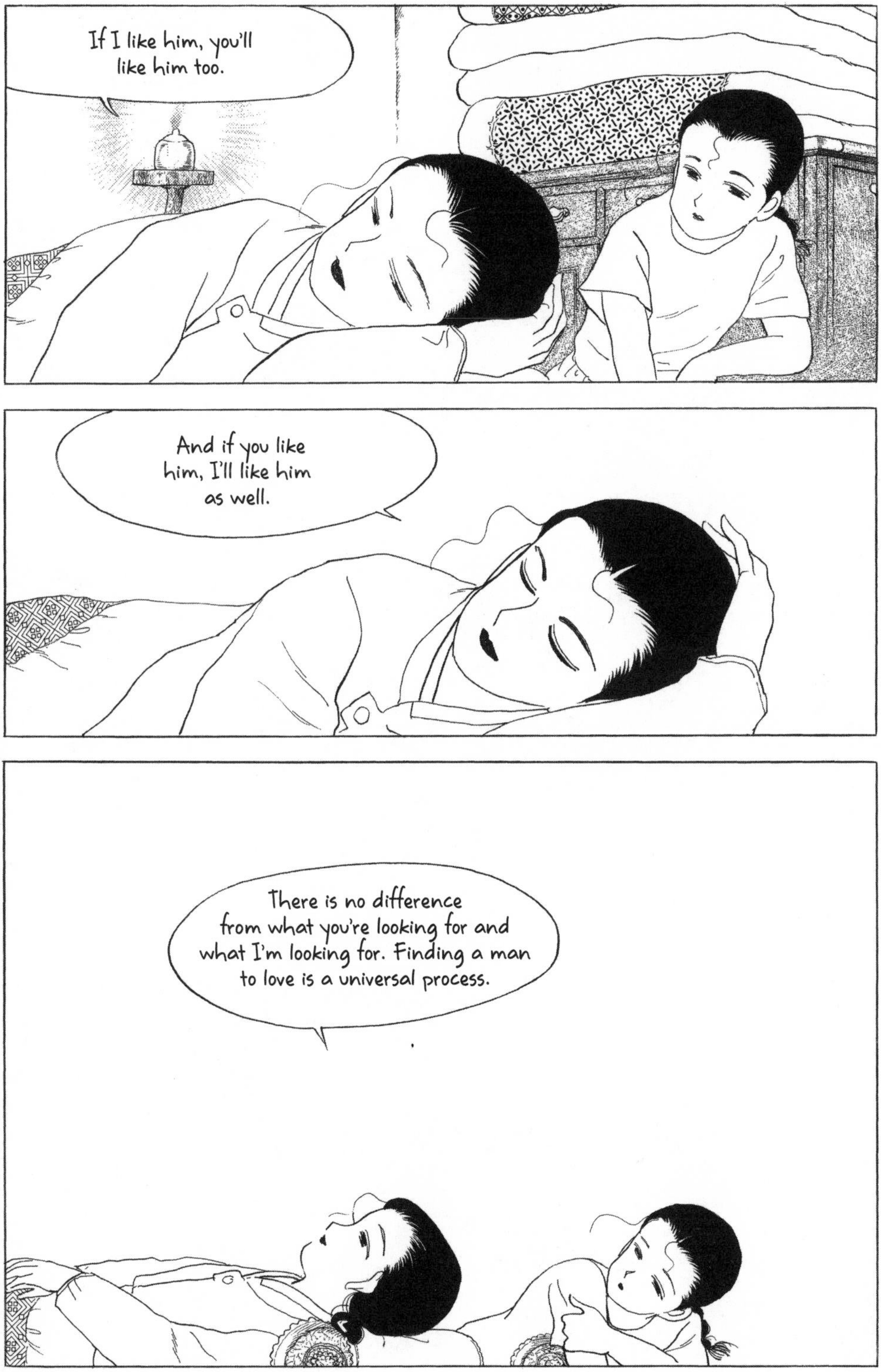
If I like him, you'll like him too.
And if you like him, I'll like him as well.
There is no difference from what you're looking for and what I'm looking for. Finding a man to love is a universal process.

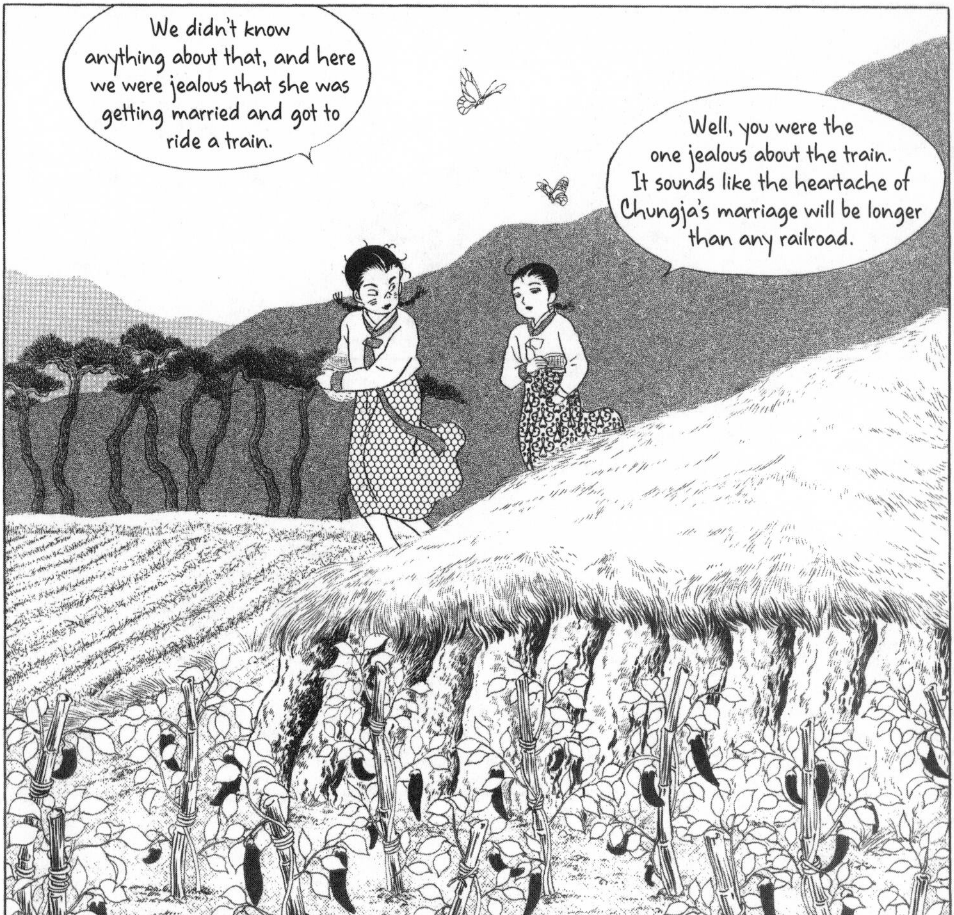
We didn't know anything about that, and here we were jealous that she was getting married and got to ride a train.
Well, you were the one jealous about the train. It sounds like the heartache of Chungja's marriage will be longer than any railroad.
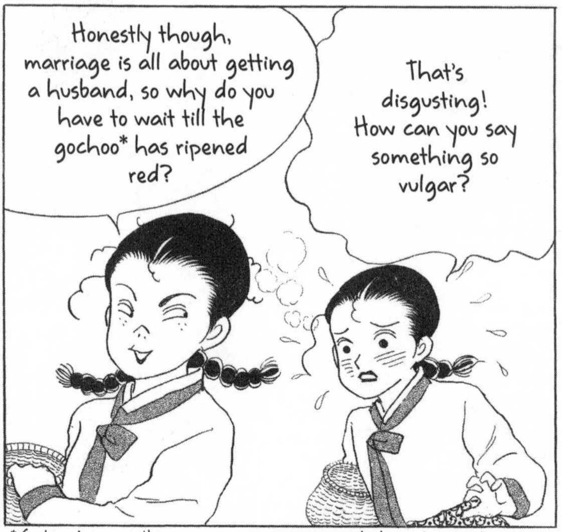
Honestly though, marriage is all about getting a husband, so why do you have to wait till the gochoo* has ripened red?
That's disgusting! How can you say something so vulgar?
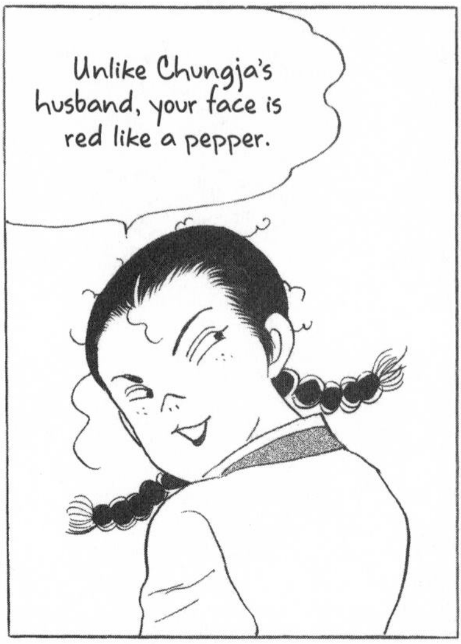
Unlike Chungja's husband, your face is red like a pepper.

* Gochoo: A pepper. Here, peppers are synonymous with the male genitalia.

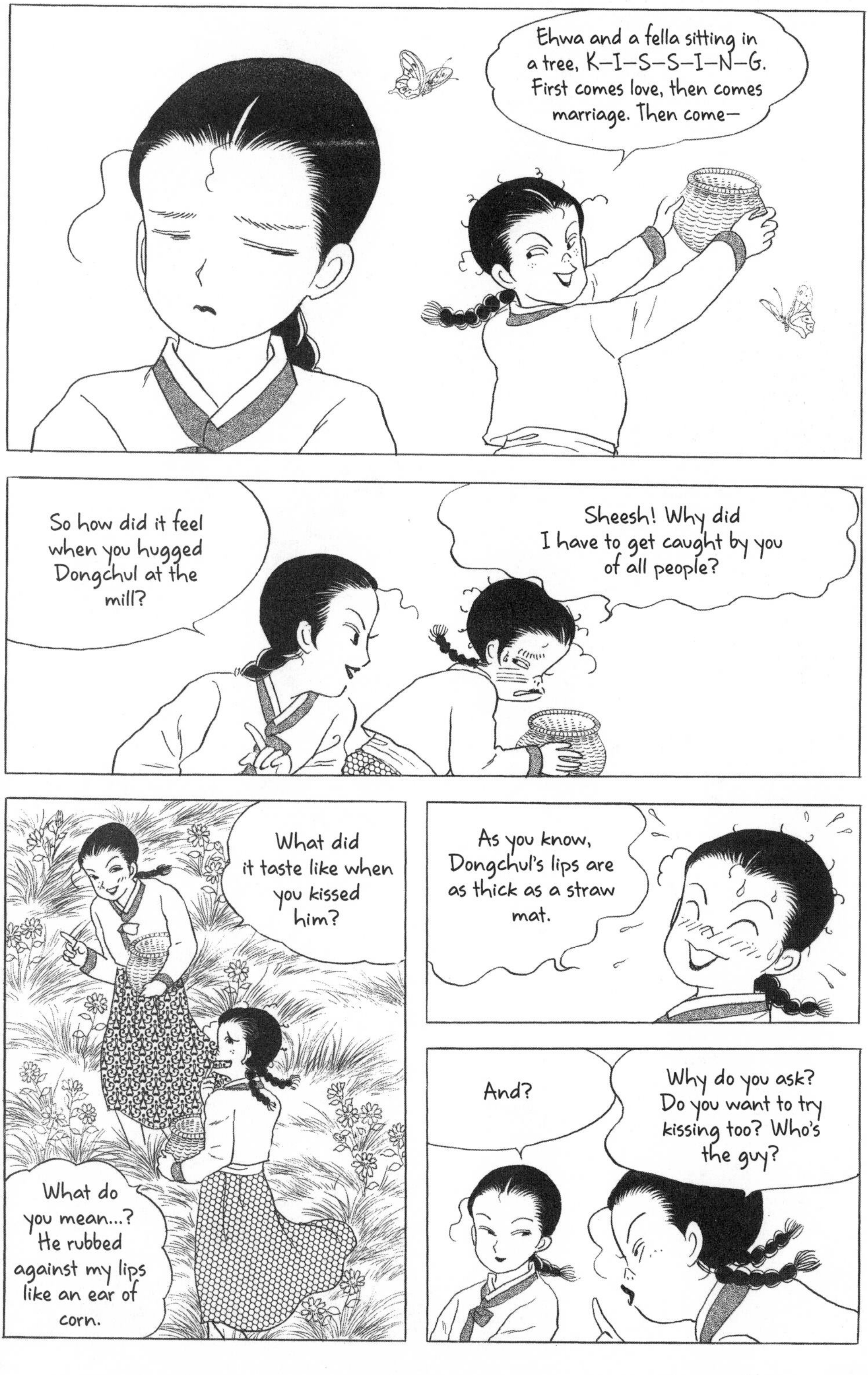
Ehwa and a fella sitting in a tree, K-I-S-S-I-N-G. First comes love, then comes marriage. Then come—
So how did it feel when you hugged Dongchul at the mill?
Sheesh! Why did I have to get caught by you of all people?
What did it taste like when you kissed him?
What do you mean...? He rubbed against my lips like an ear of corn.
As you know, Dongchul's lips are as thick as a straw mat.
And?
Why do you ask? Do you want to try kissing too? Who's the guy?

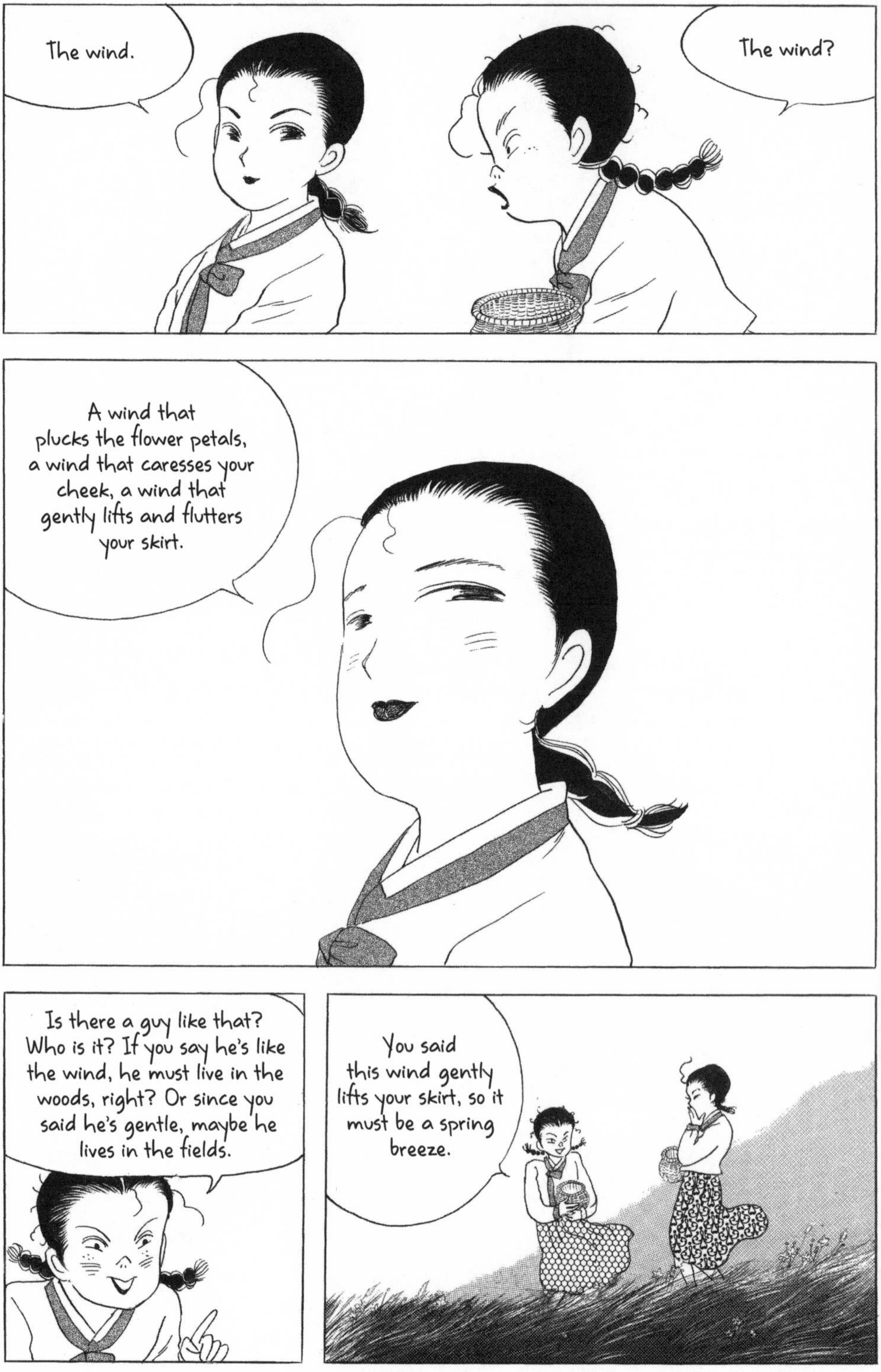
The wind.
The wind?
A wind that plucks the flower petals, a wind that caresses your cheek, a wind that gently lifts and flutters your skirt.
Is there a guy like that? Who is it? If you say he's like the wind, he must live in the woods, right? Or since you said he's gentle, maybe he lives in the fields.
You said this wind gently lifts your skirt, so it must be a spring breeze.

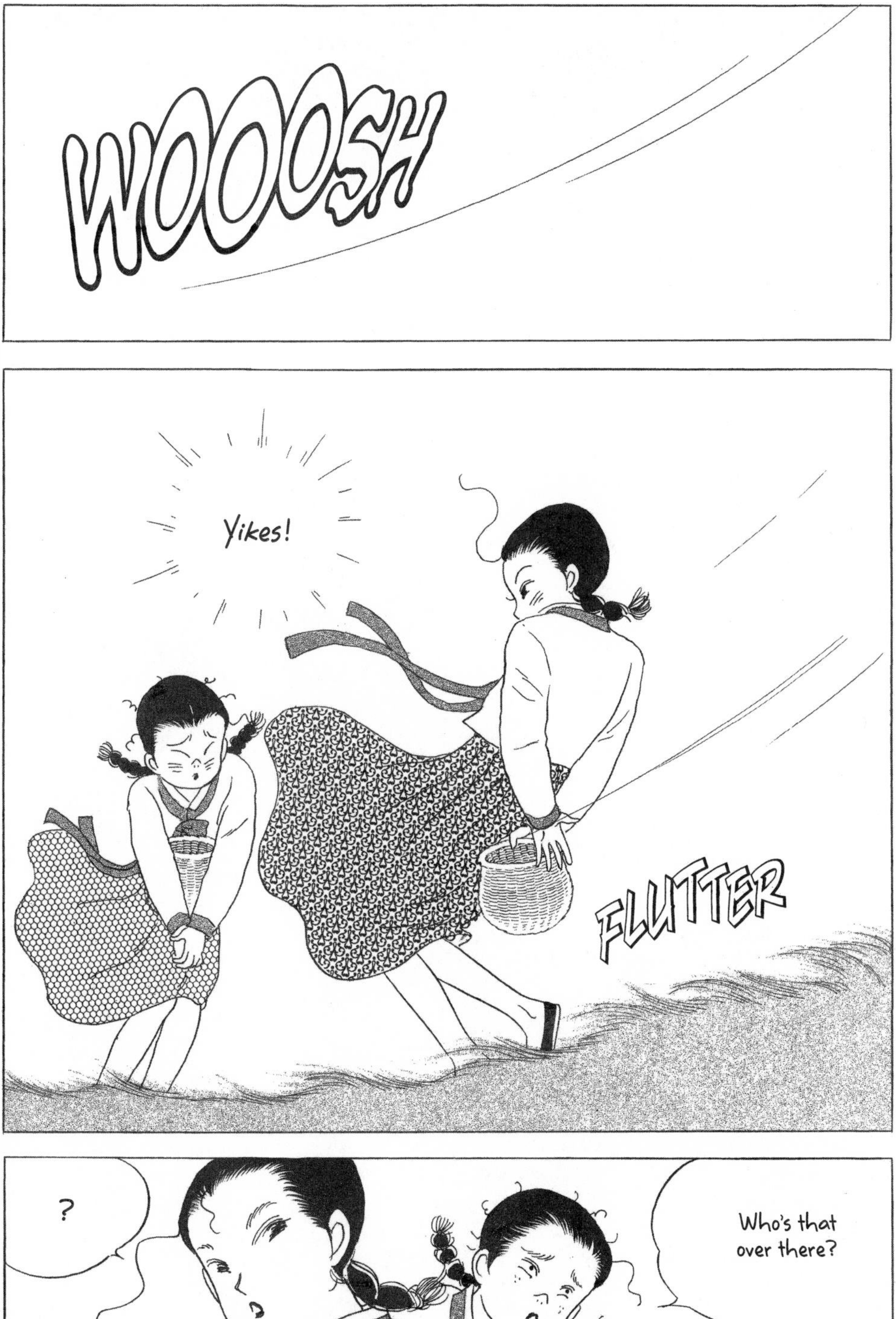
WOOOSH
Yikes!
FLUTTER
?
Who's that over there?

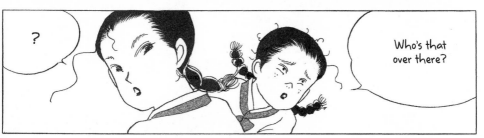

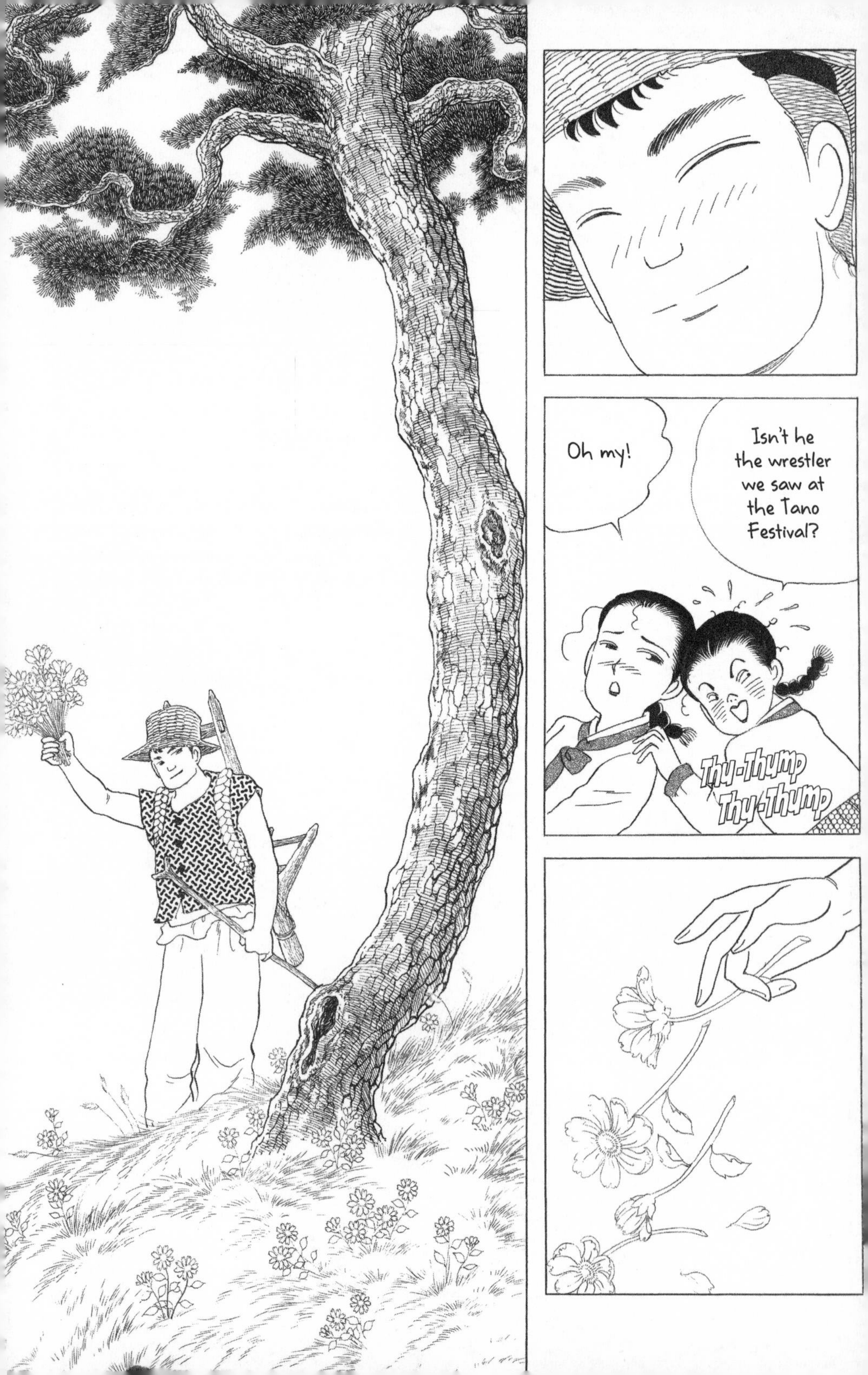

Oh my!
Isn't he the wrestler we saw at the Tano Festival?
Thy-Thump
Thy-Thump

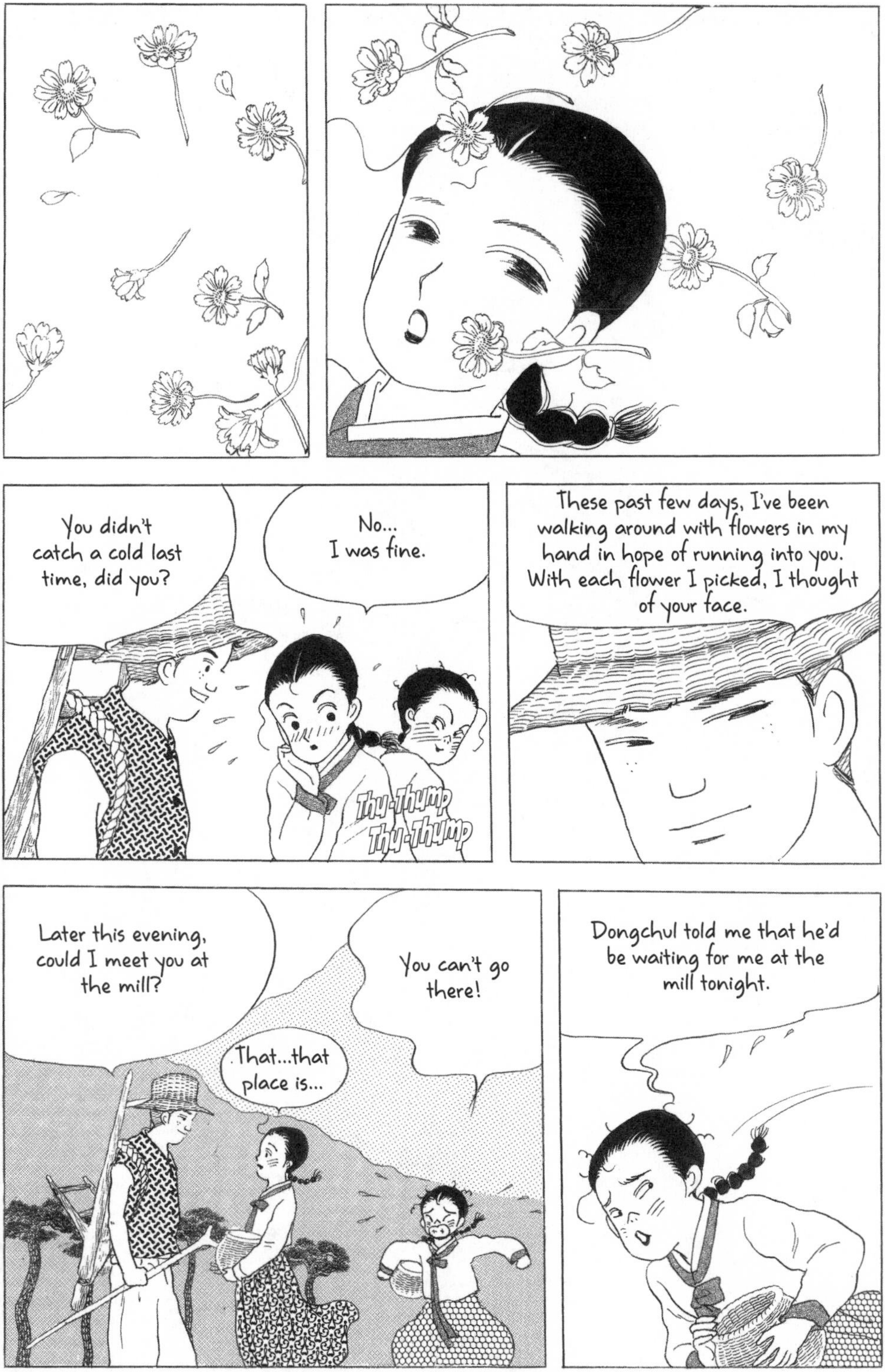

You didn't catch a cold last time, did you?
No... I was fine.
Thu-Thump Thu-Thump
These past few days, I've been walking around with flowers in my hand in hope of running into you. With each flower I picked, I thought of your face.
Later this evening, could I meet you at the mill?
You can't go there!
That...that place is...
Dongchul told me that he'd be waiting for me at the mill tonight.

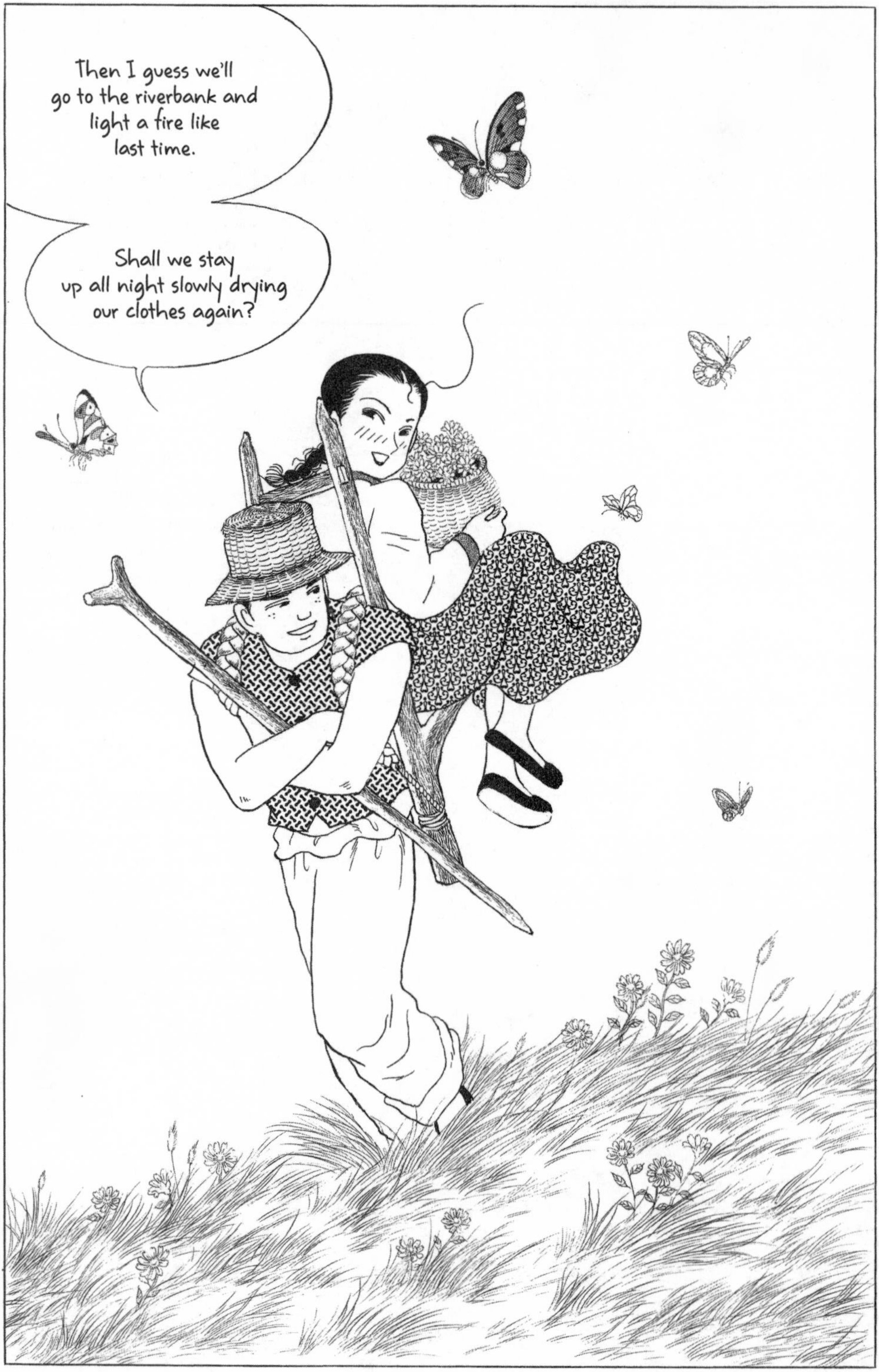
Then I guess we'll go to the riverbank and light a fire like last time.
Shall we stay up all night slowly drying our clothes again?

Chapter Seven

FLOWER INSIDE THE FENCE, BUTTERFLY OUTSIDE THE FENCE

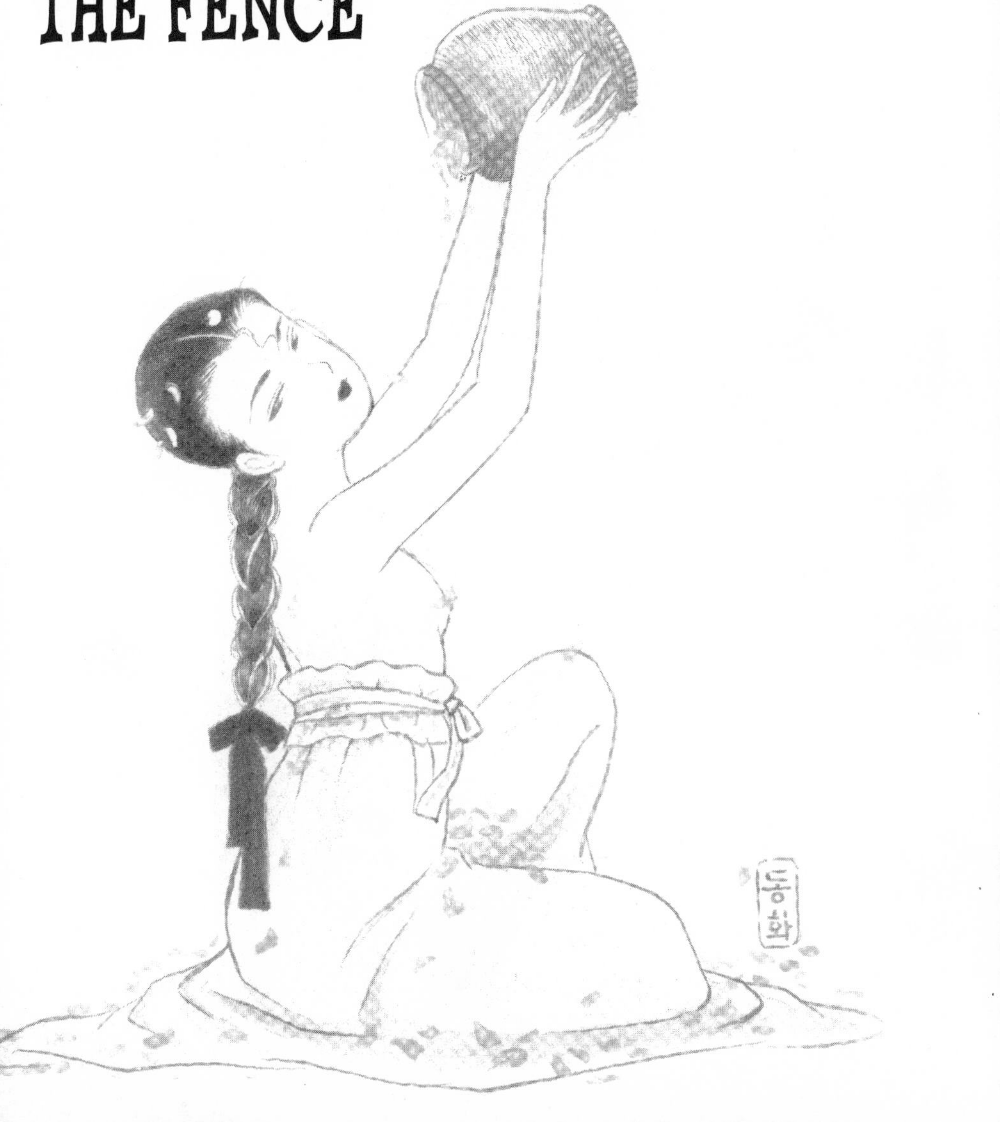
동화

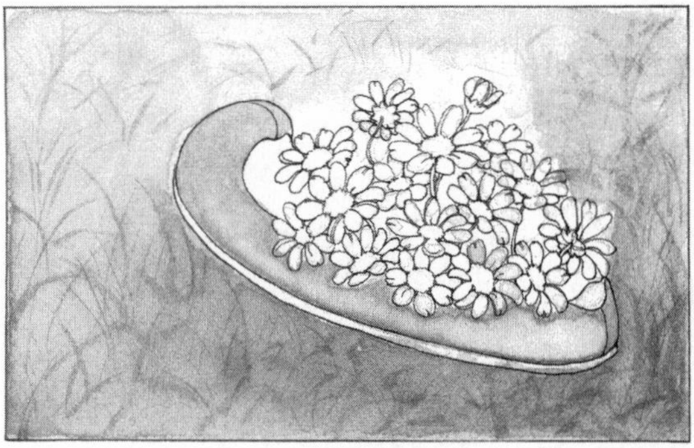
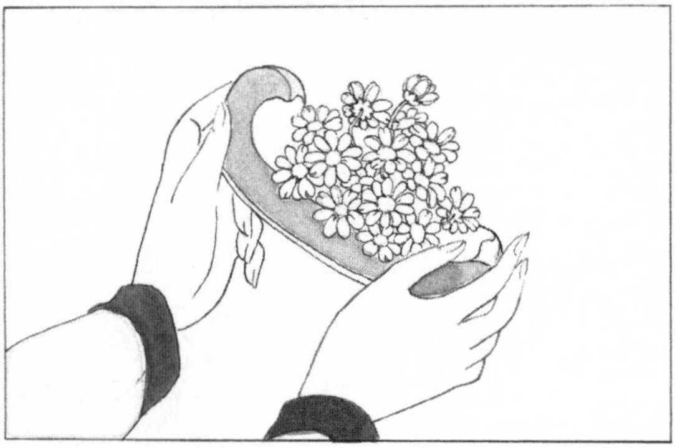
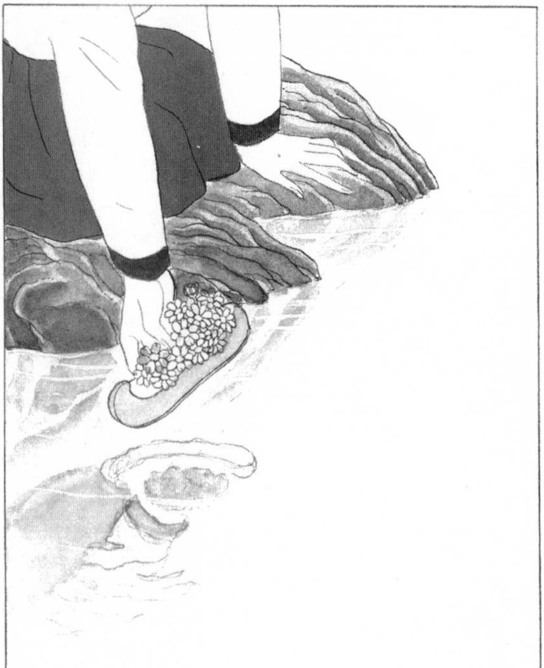
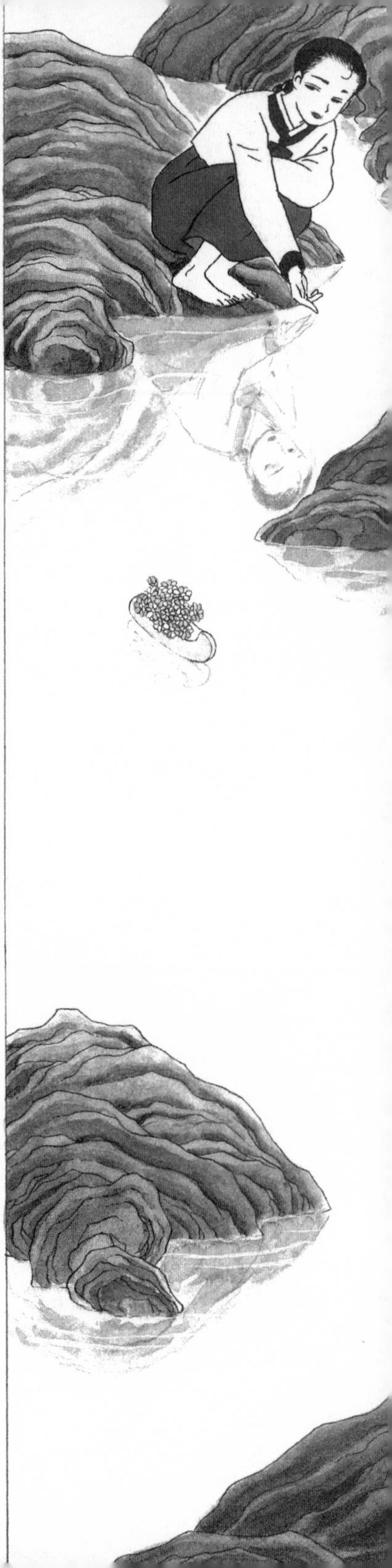

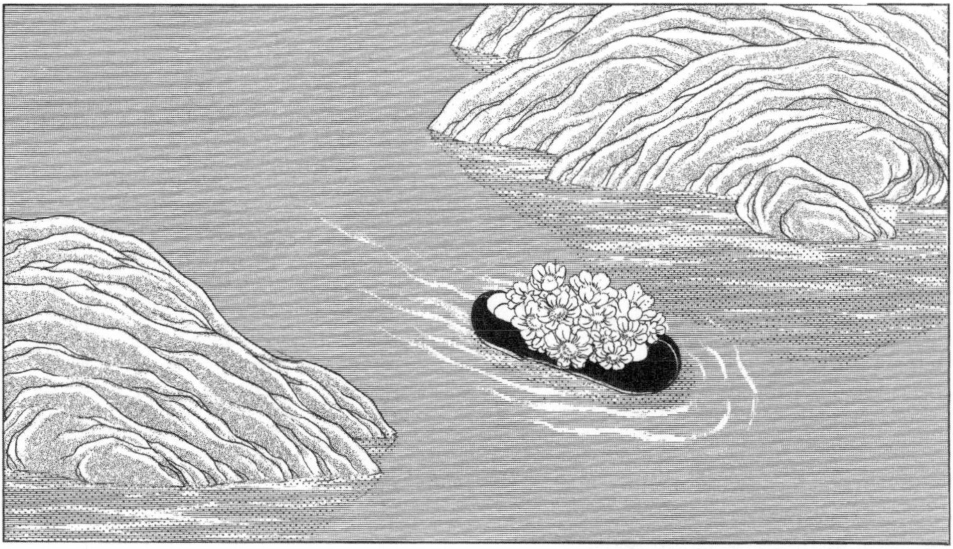
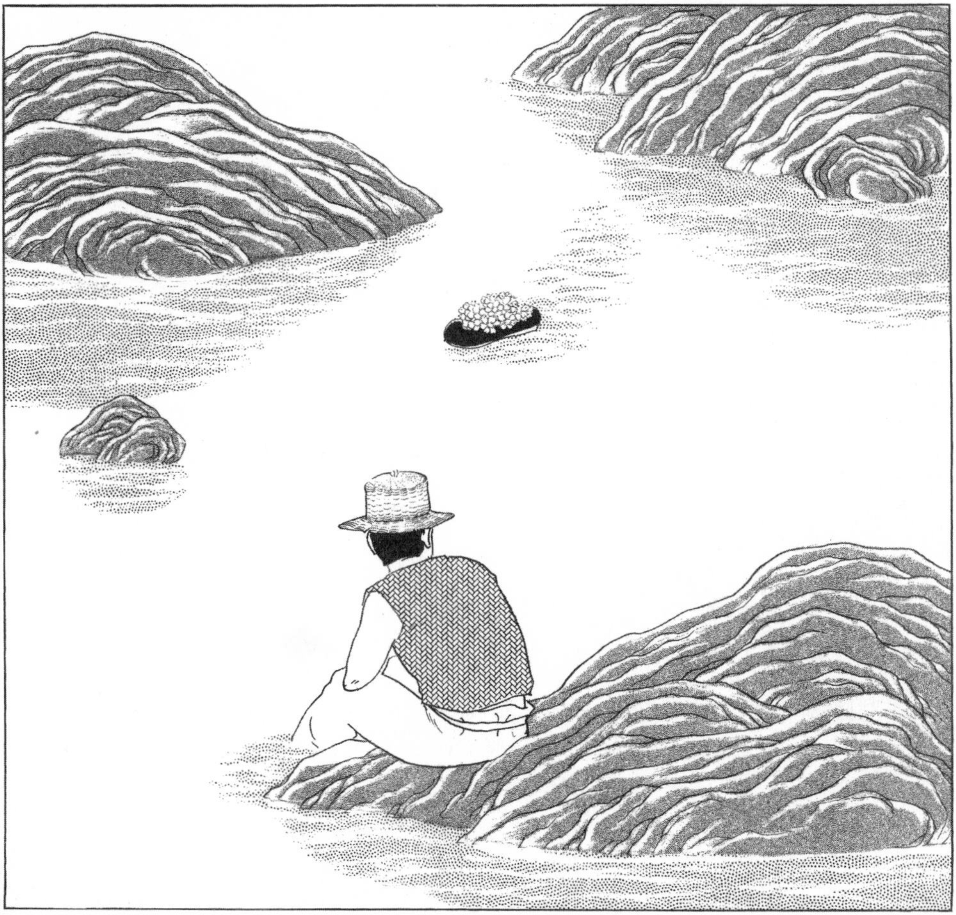

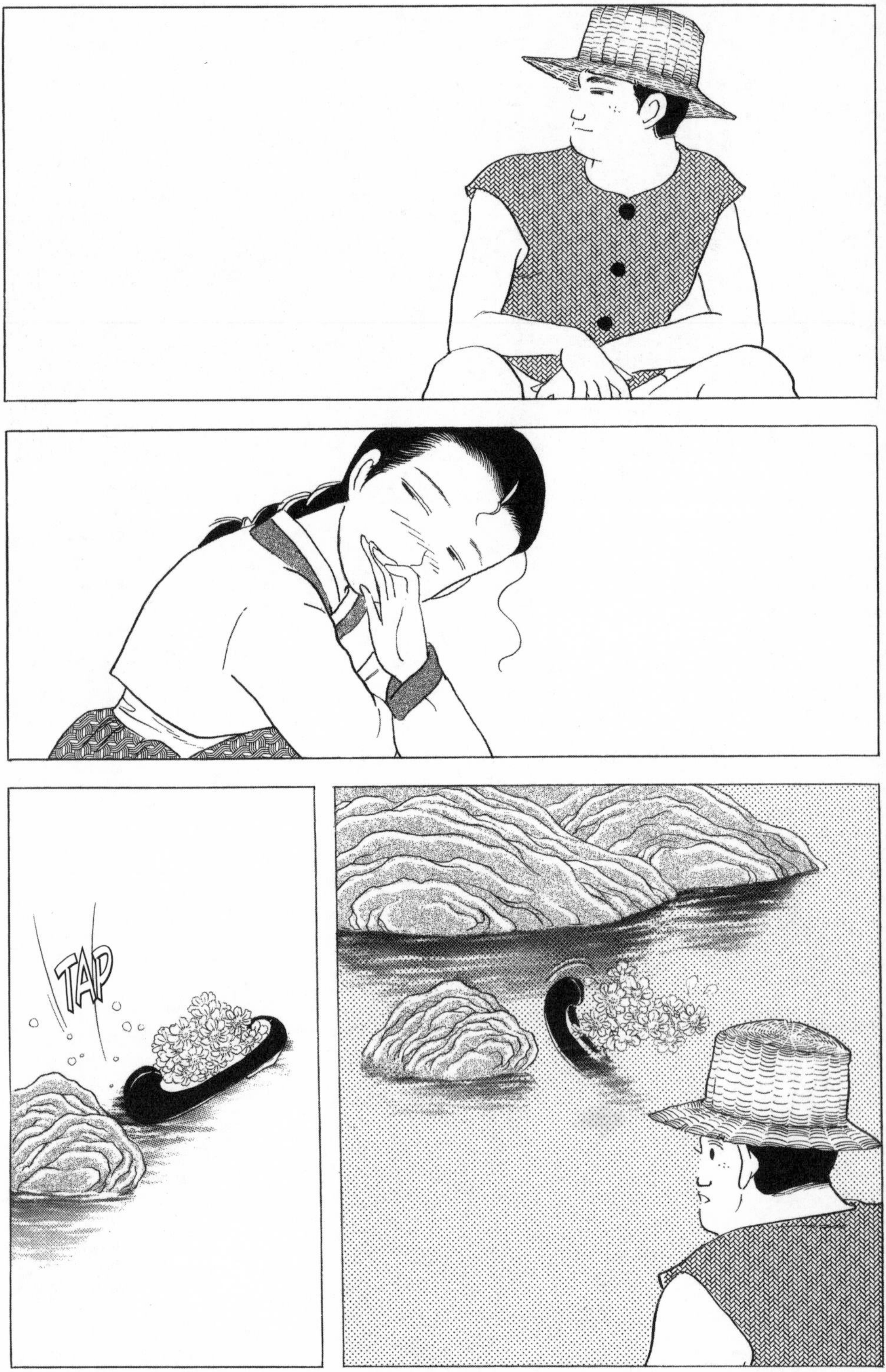
TAP

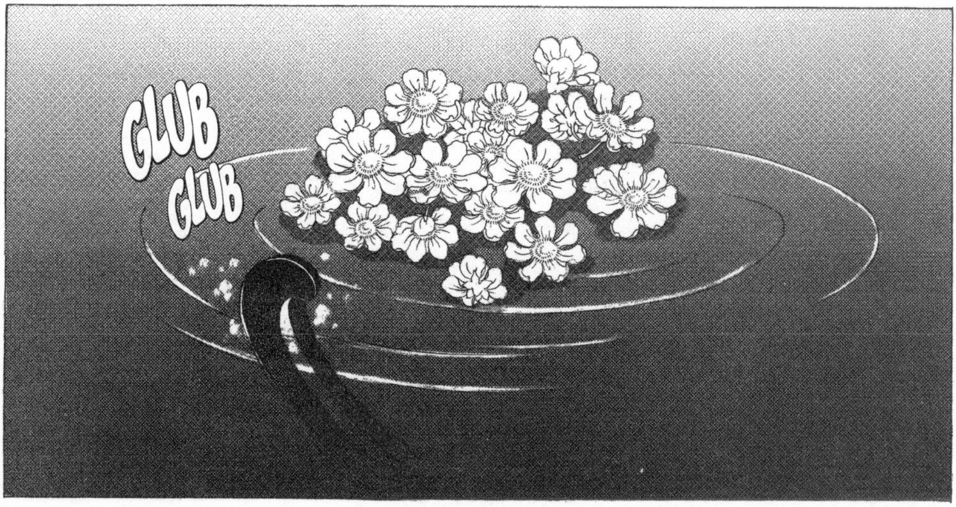
GLUB
GLUB
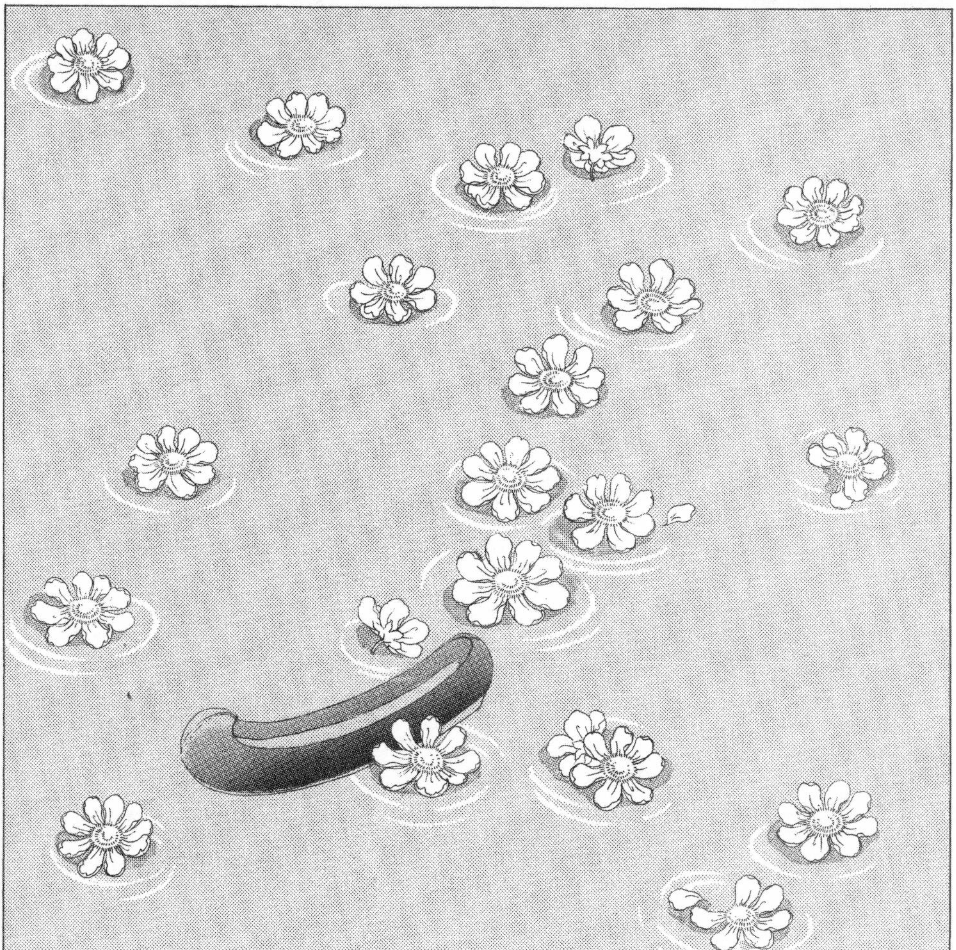

Heh heh...

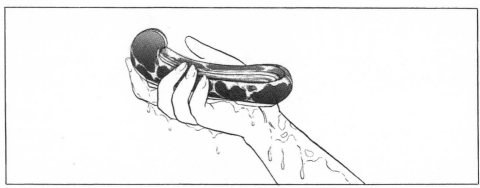

GULP
GULP

I wonder what this vessel held that made the water taste so sweet.

Blush

Blush

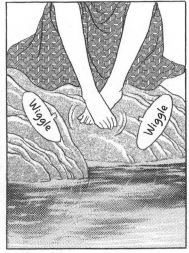

Wiggle

Wiggle

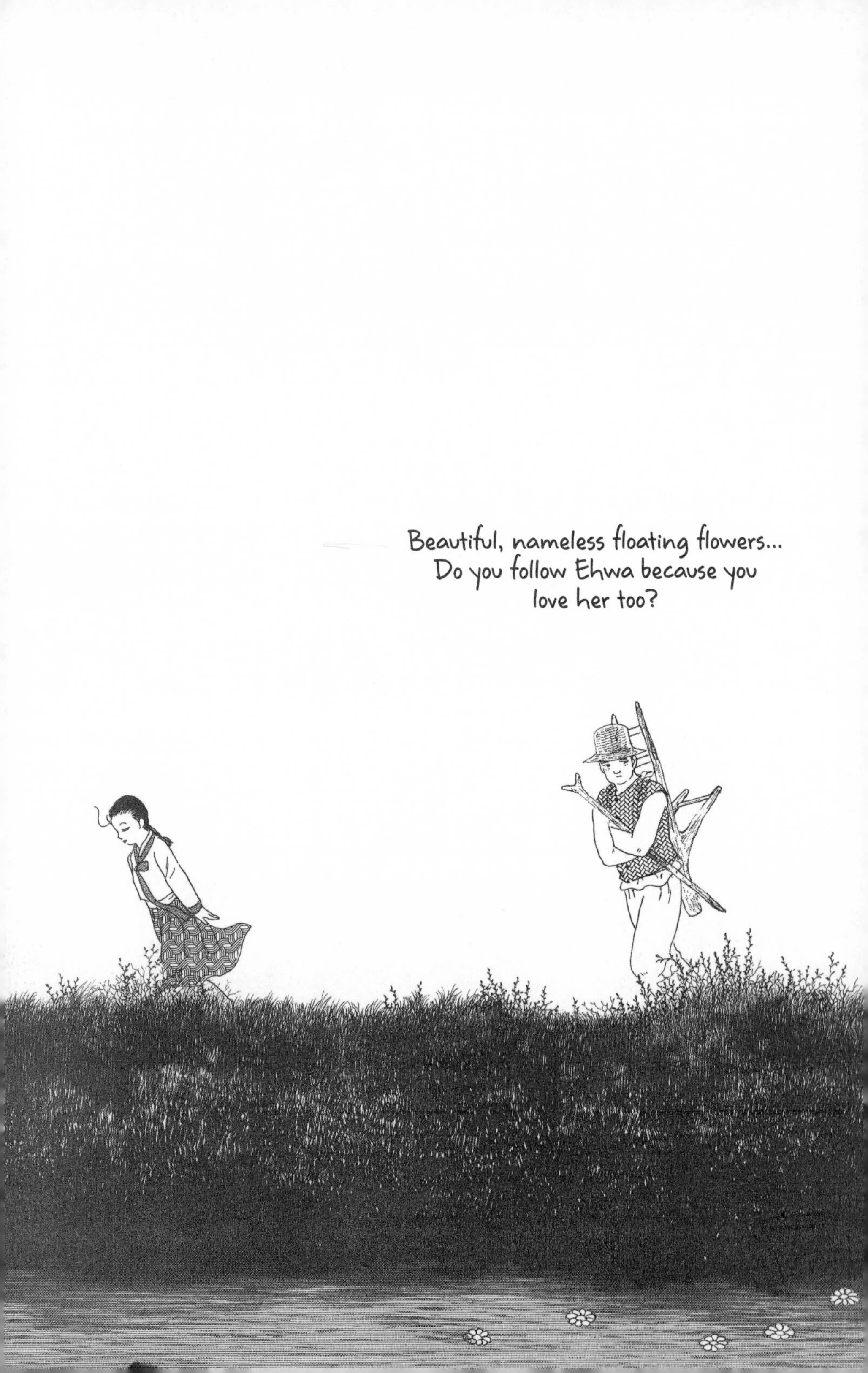
Beautiful, nameless floating flowers... Do you follow Ehwa because you love her too?

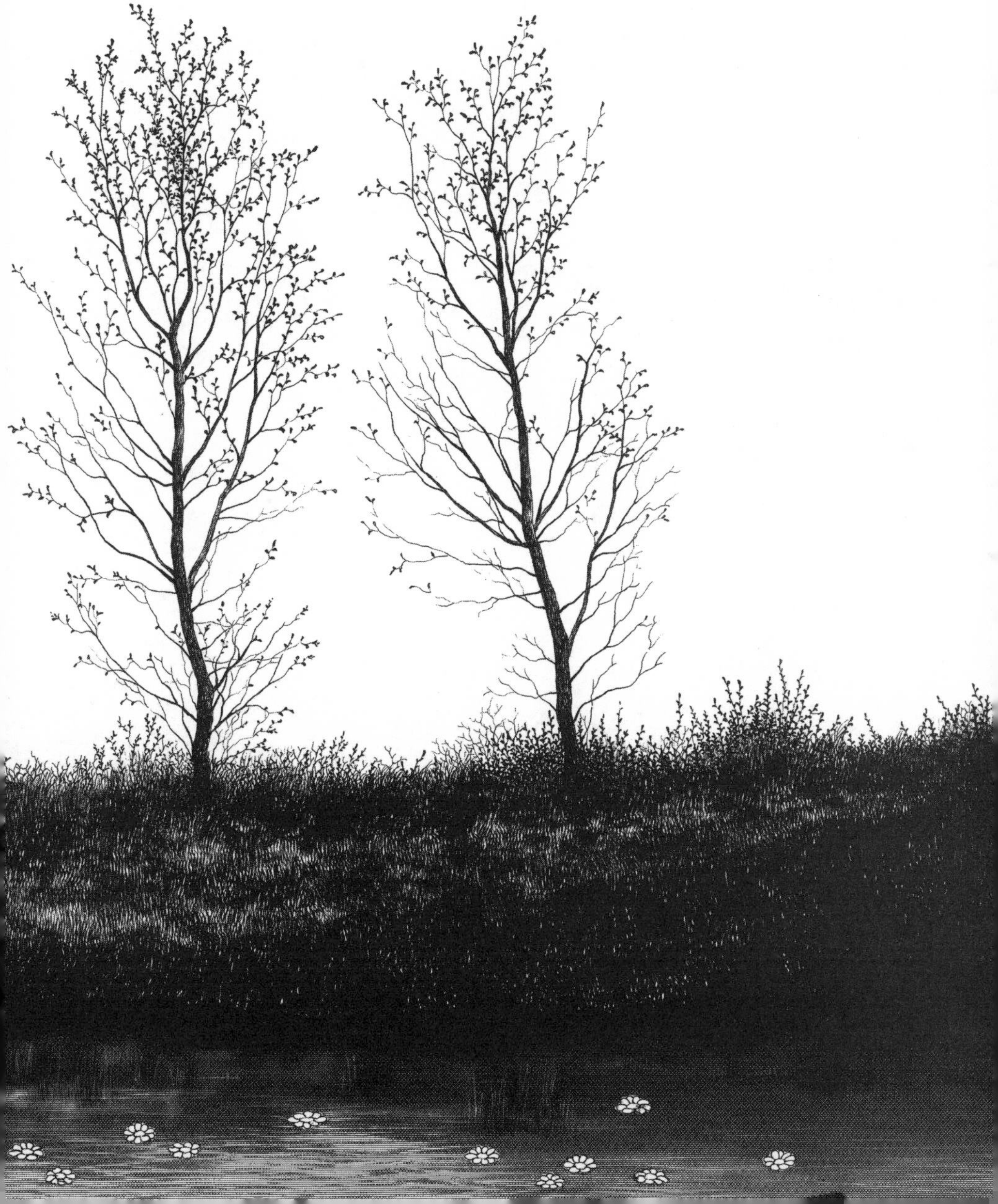

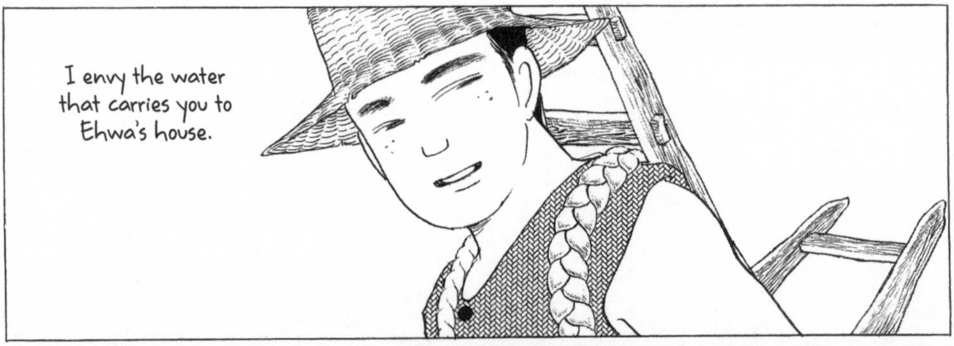
I envy the water that carries you to Ehwa's house.

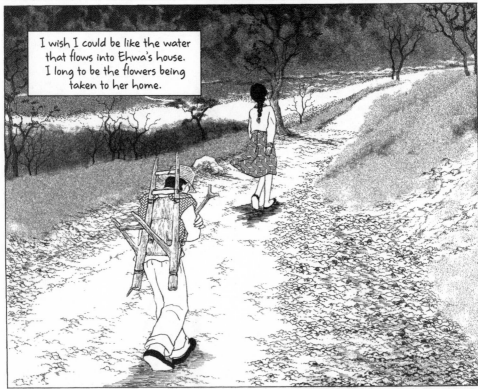

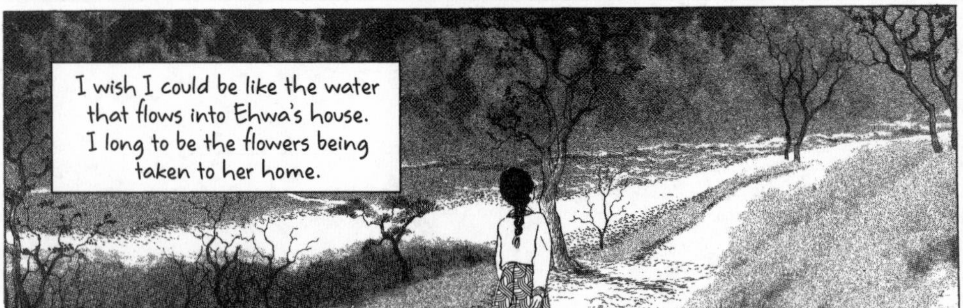
I wish I could be like the water that flows into Ehwa's house. I long to be the flowers being taken to her home.

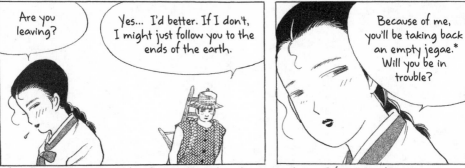

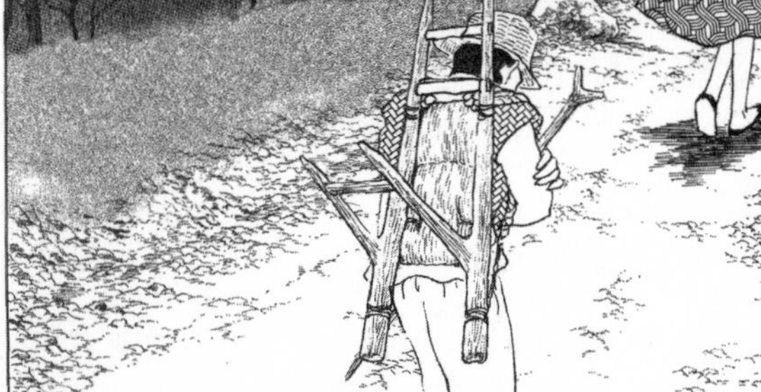
Are you leaving?
Yes... I'd better. If I don't, I might just follow you to the ends of the earth.

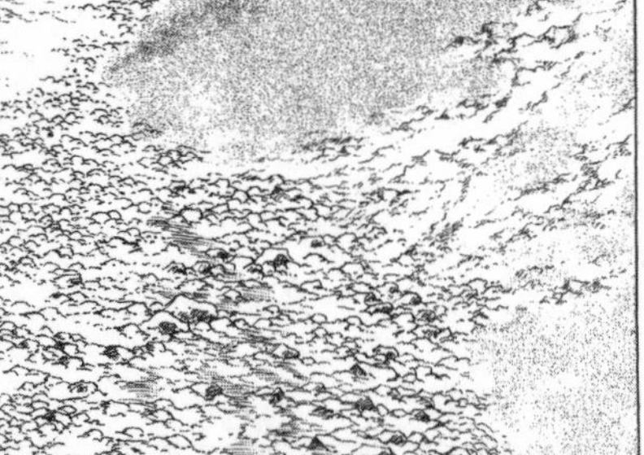
Because of me, you'll be taking back an empty jegae.* Will you be in trouble?

* Jegae: The wooden item on Duksam's back. People tie whatever they wish to carry onto the jegae. It functions like a backpack.

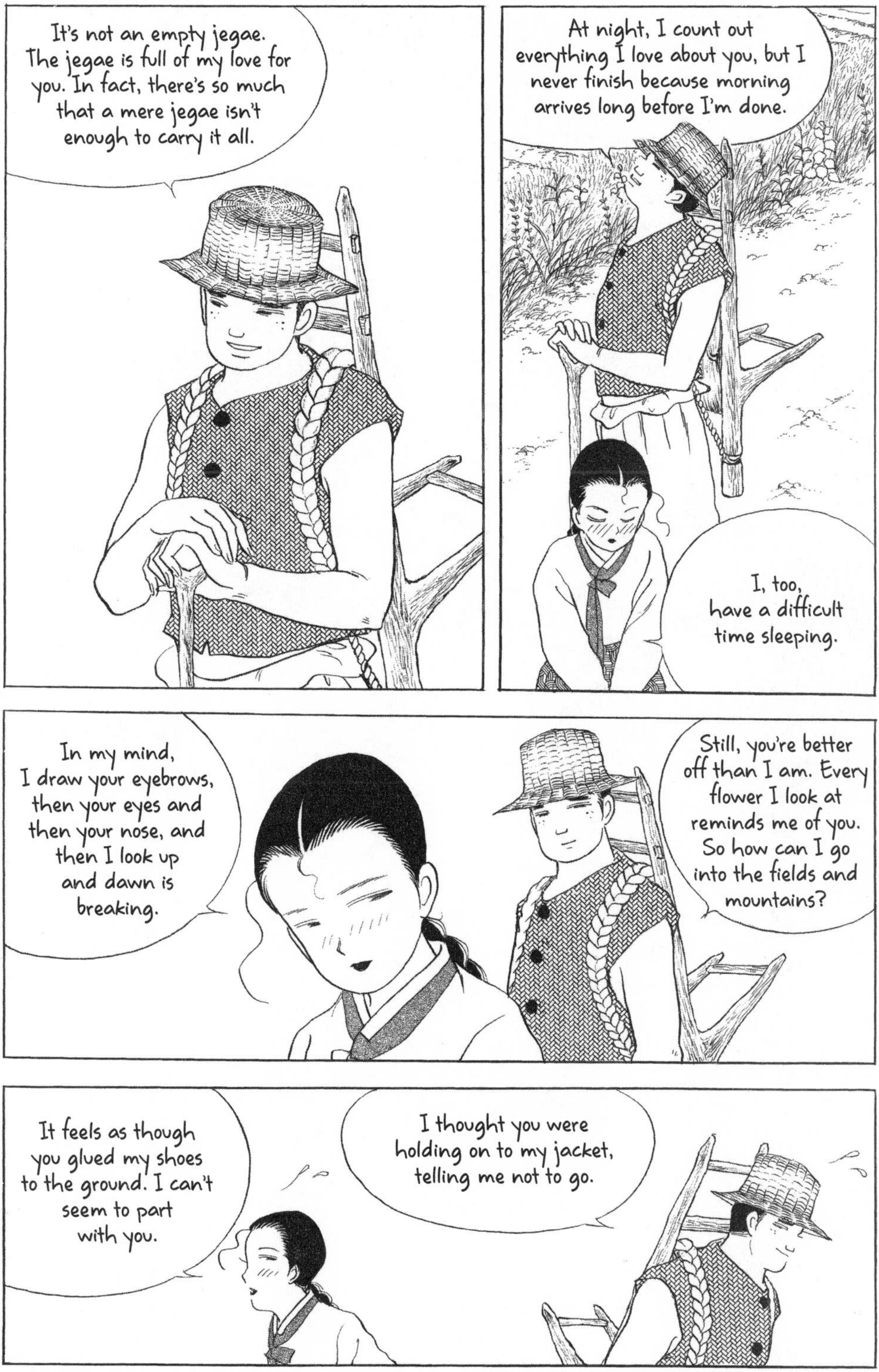
It's not an empty jegae. The jegae is full of my love for you. In fact, there's so much that a mere jegae isn't enough to carry it all.
At night, I count out everything I love about you, but I never finish because morning arrives long before I'm done.
I, too, have a difficult time sleeping.
In my mind, I draw your eyebrows, then your eyes and then your nose, and then I look up and dawn is breaking.
Still, you're better off than I am. Every flower I look at reminds me of you. So how can I go into the fields and mountains?
It feels as though you glued my shoes to the ground. I can't seem to part with you.
I thought you were holding on to my jacket, telling me not to go.

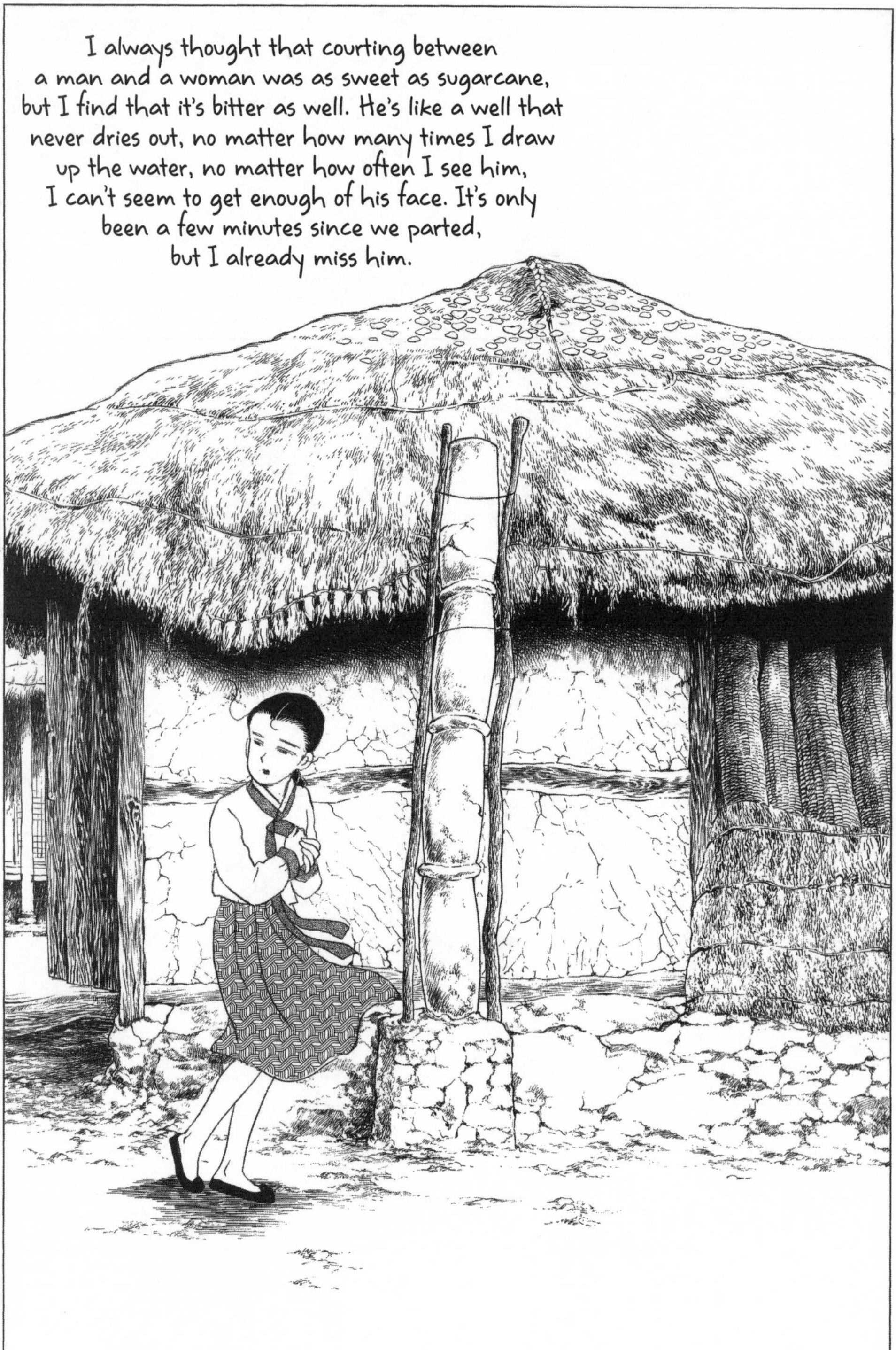
I always thought that courting between a man and a woman was as sweet as sugarcane, but I find that it's bitter as well. He's like a well that never dries out, no matter how many times I draw up the water, no matter how often I see him, I can't seem to get enough of his face. It's only been a few minutes since we parted, but I already miss him.

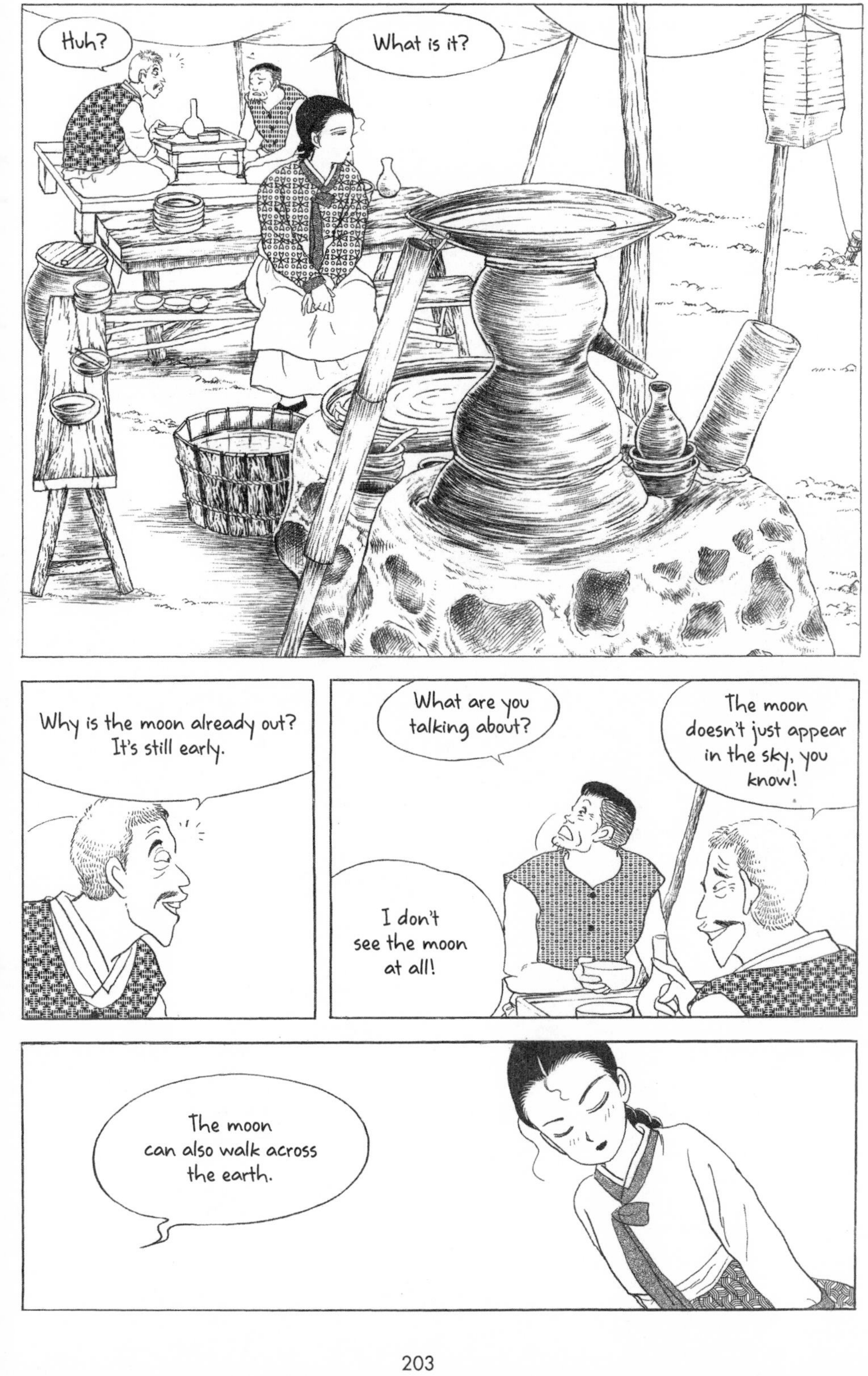
Huh?
What is it?
Why is the moon already out? It's still early.
What are you talking about?
The moon doesn't just appear in the sky, you know!
I don't see the moon at all!
The moon can also walk across the earth.

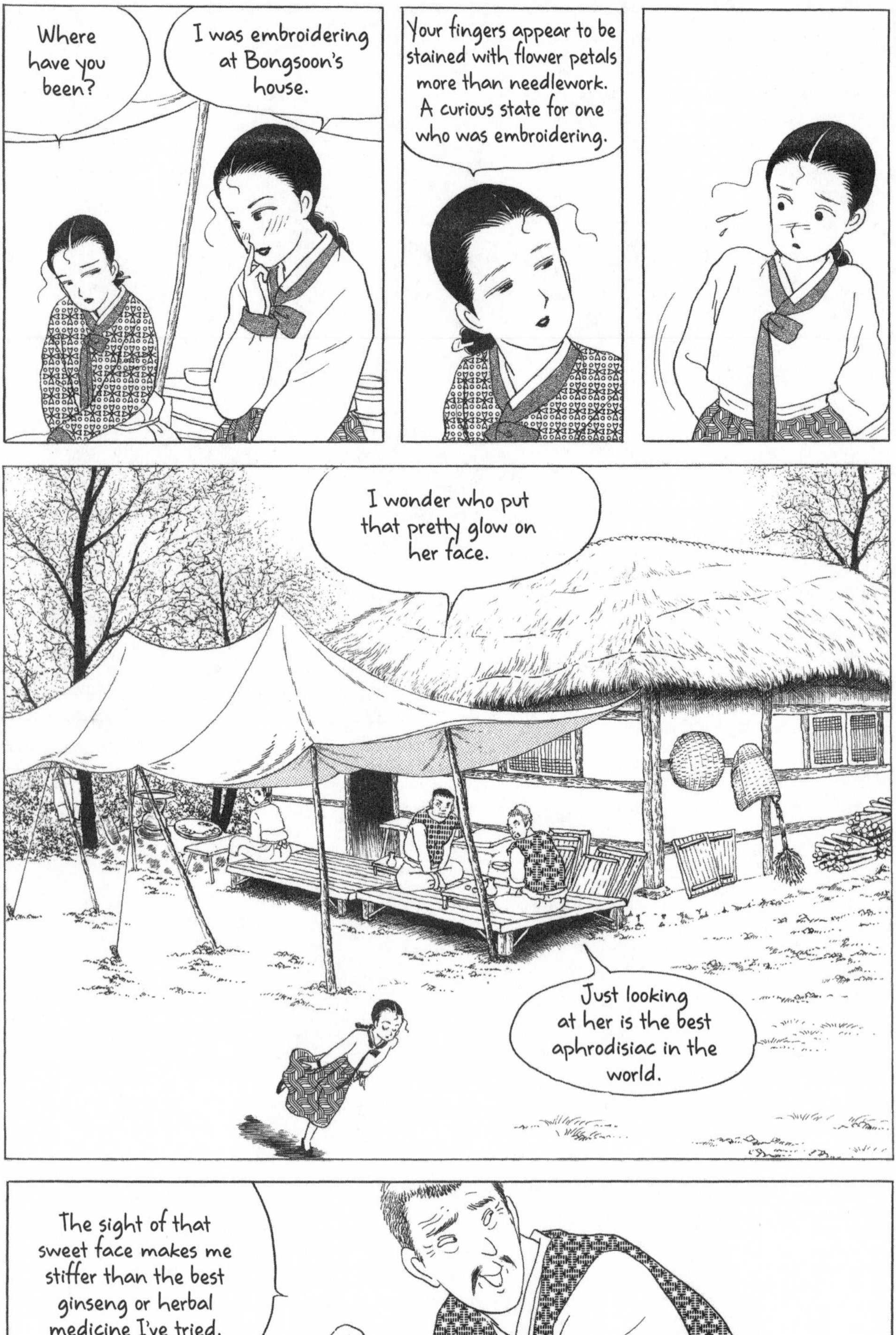
Where have you been?
I was embroidering at Bongsoon's house.
Your fingers appear to be stained with flower petals more than needlework. A curious state for one who was embroidering.
I wonder who put that pretty glow on her face.
Just looking at her is the best aphrodisiac in the world.
The sight of that sweet face makes me stiffer than the best ginseng or herbal medicine I've tried.

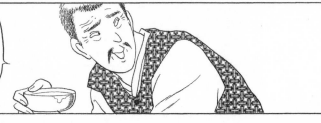

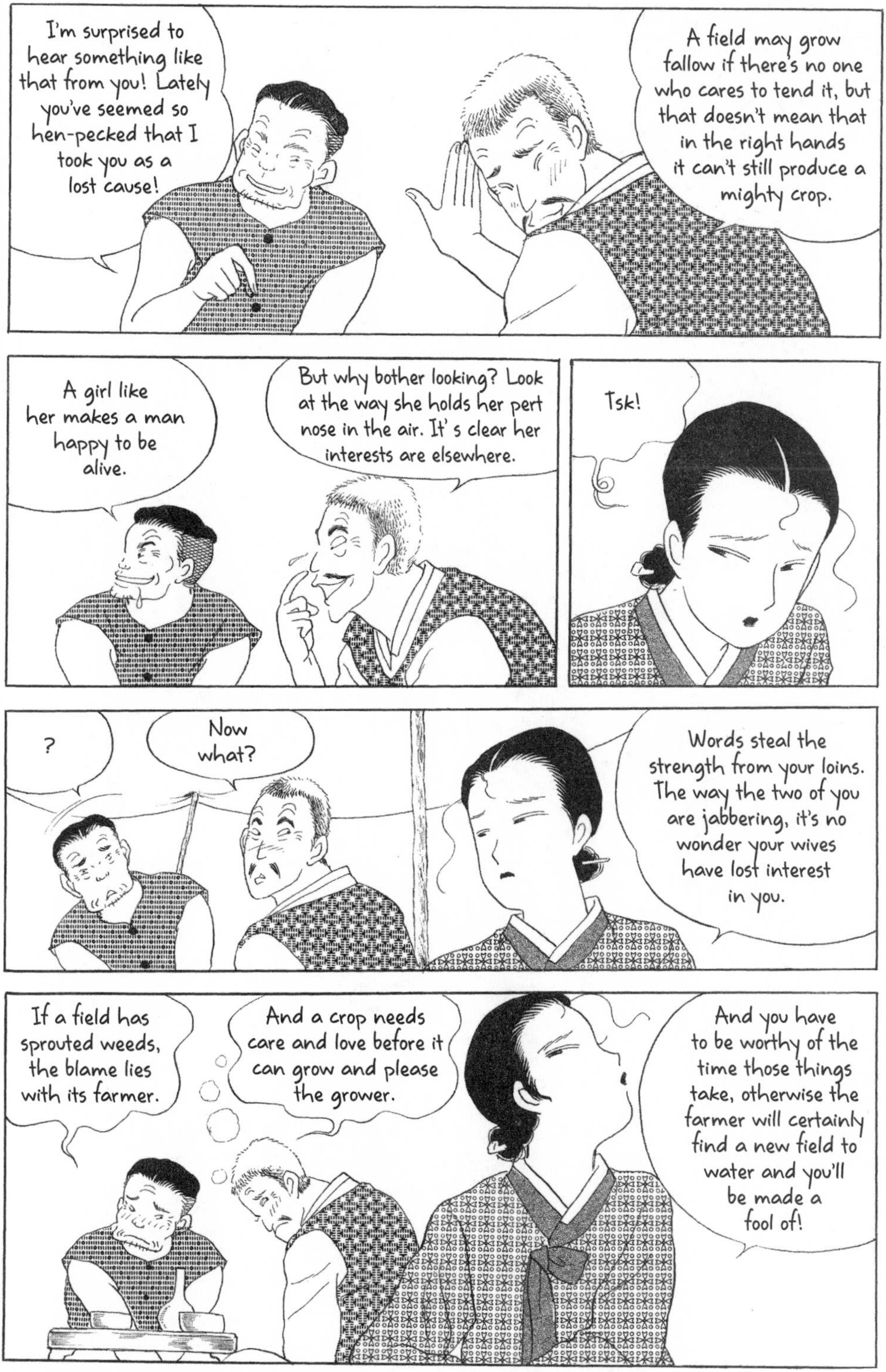
I'm surprised to hear something like that from you! Lately you've seemed so hen-pecked that I took you as a lost cause!
A field may grow fallow if there's no one who cares to tend it, but that doesn't mean that in the right hands it can't still produce a mighty crop.
A girl like her makes a man happy to be alive.
But why bother looking? Look at the way she holds her pert nose in the air. It's clear her interests are elsewhere.
Tsk!
?
Now what?
Words steal the strength from your loins. The way the two of you are jabbering, it's no wonder your wives have lost interest in you.
If a field has sprouted weeds, the blame lies with its farmer.
And a crop needs care and love before it can grow and please the grower.
And you have to be worthy of the time those things take, otherwise the farmer will certainly find a new field to water and you'll be made a fool of!

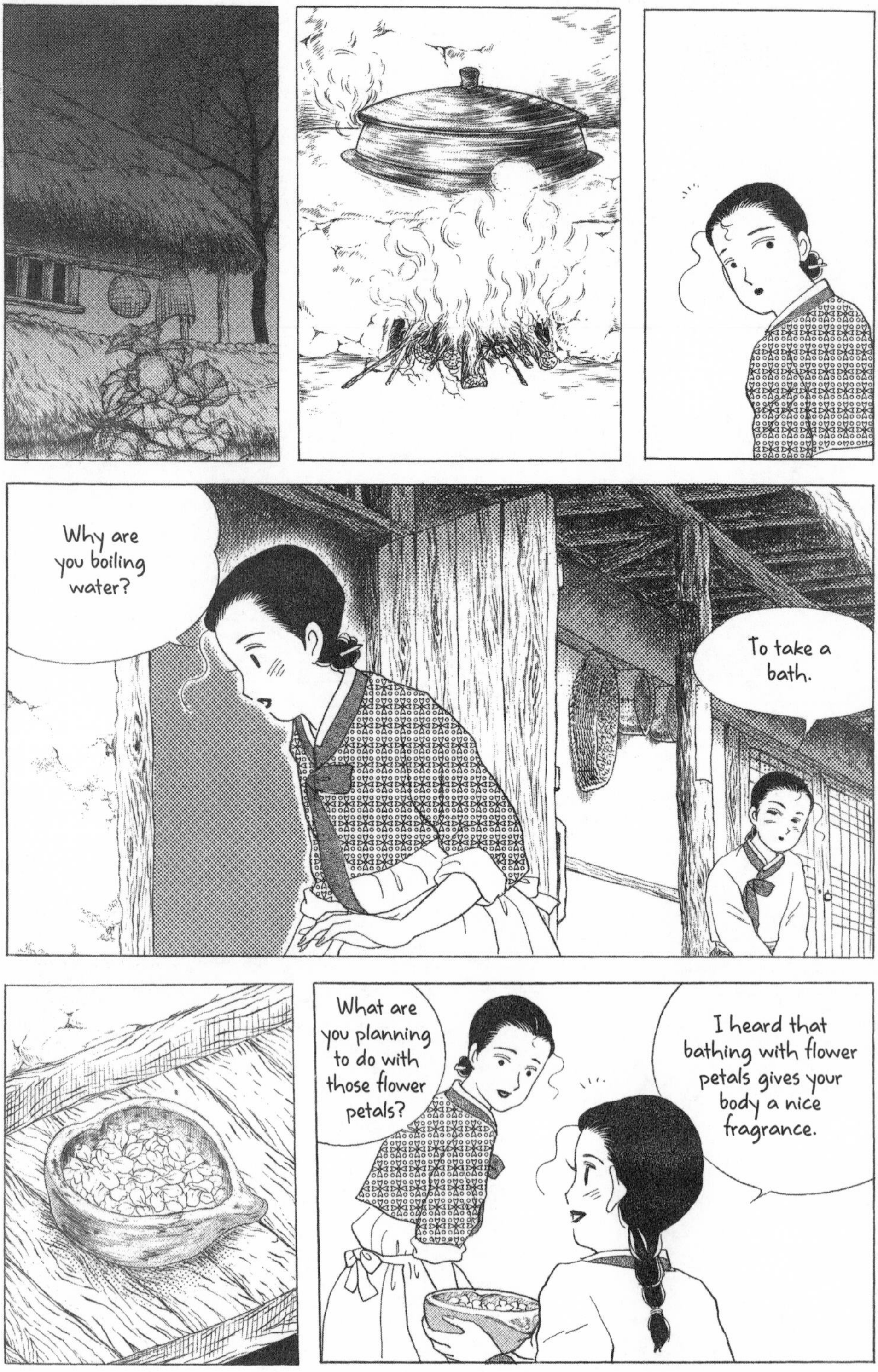
Why are you boiling water?
To take a bath.
What are you planning to do with those flower petals?
I heard that bathing with flower petals gives your body a nice fragrance.

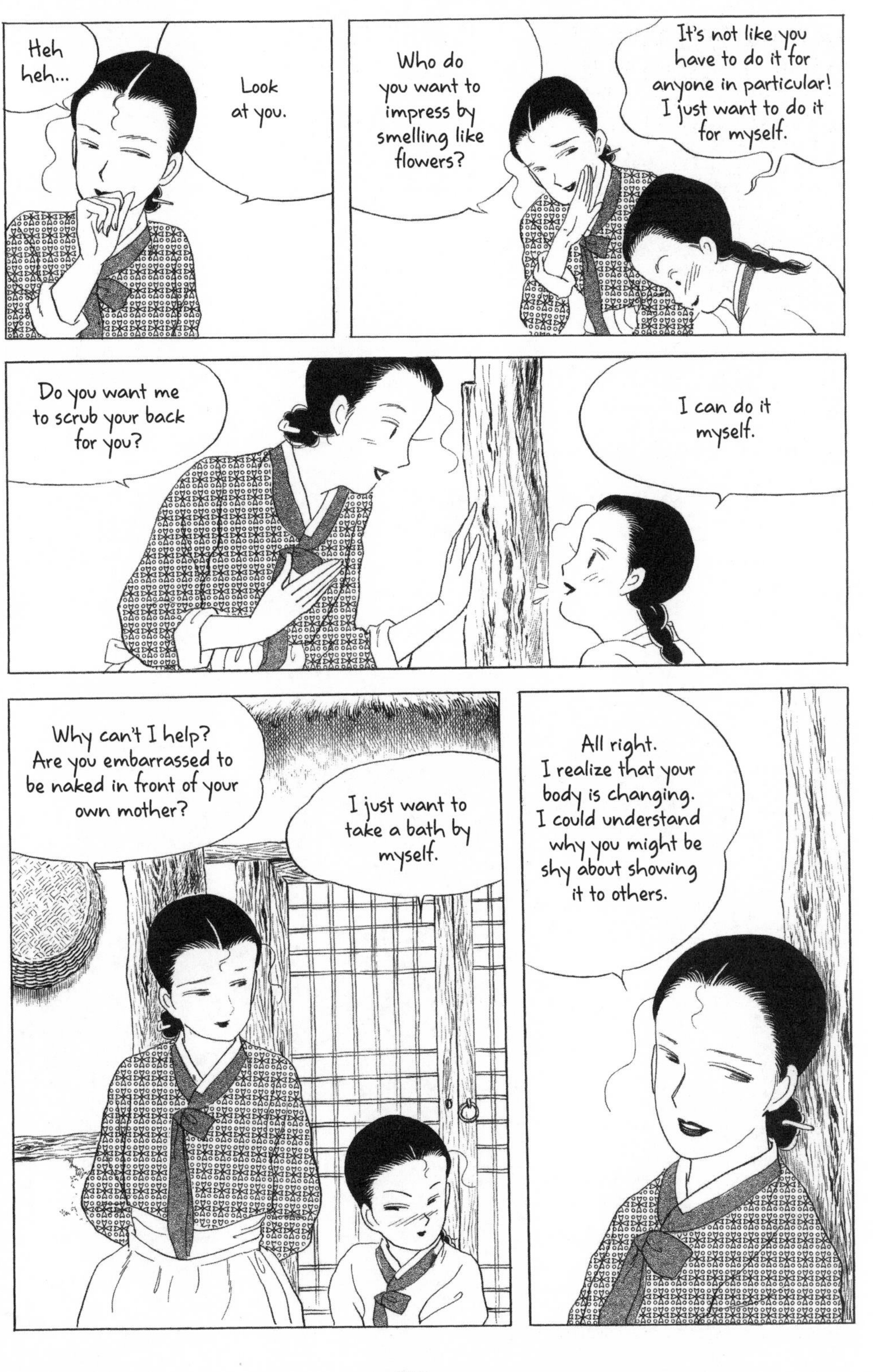

Heh heh...
Look at you.
Who do you want to impress by smelling like flowers?
It's not like you have to do it for anyone in particular! I just want to do it for myself.
Do you want me to scrub your back for you?
I can do it myself.
Why can't I help? Are you embarrassed to be naked in front of your own mother?
I just want to take a bath by myself.
All right. I realize that your body is changing. I could understand why you might be shy about showing it to others.

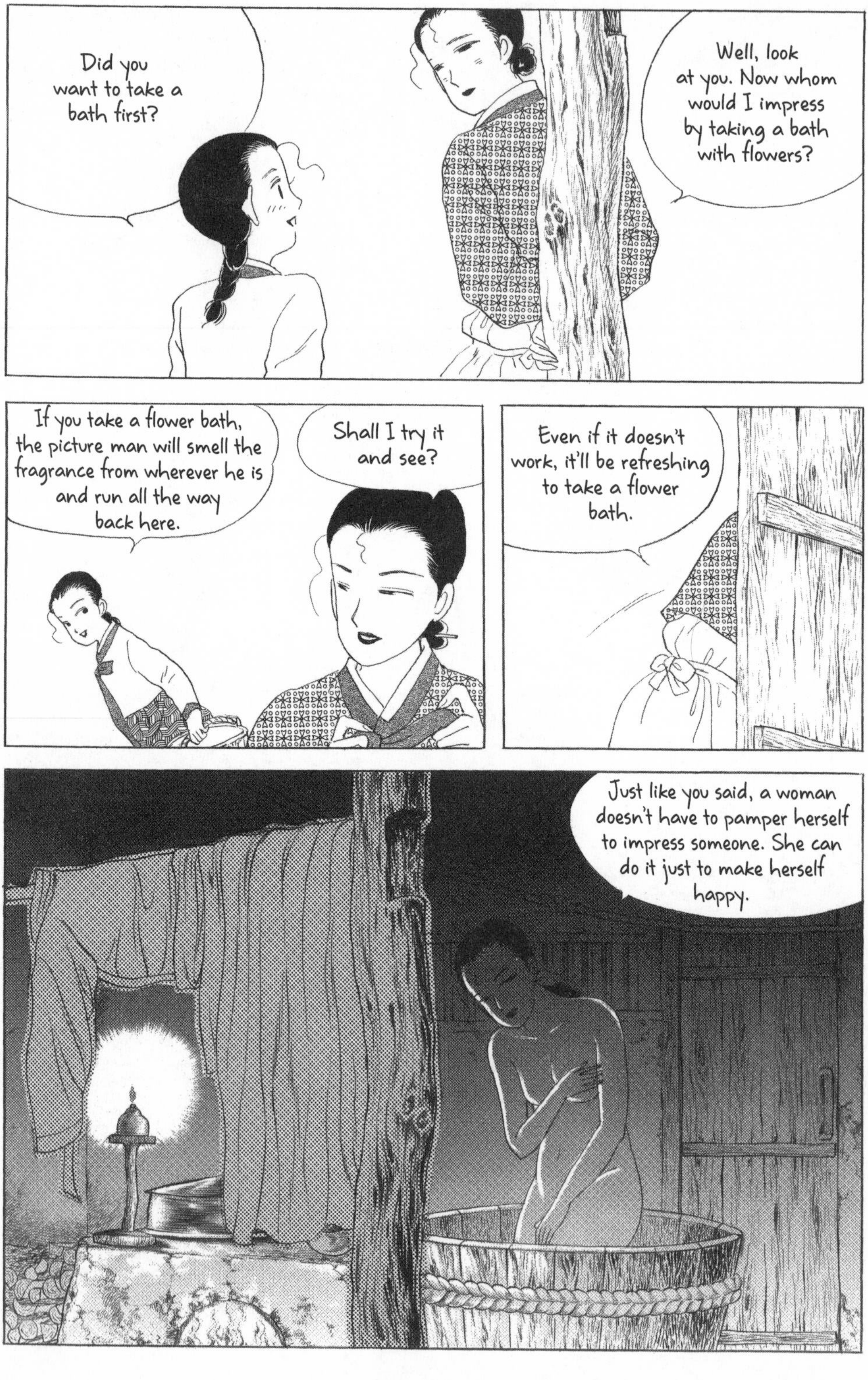

Did you want to take a bath first?
Well, look at you. Now whom would I impress by taking a bath with flowers?
If you take a flower bath, the picture man will smell the fragrance from wherever he is and run all the way back here.
Shall I try it and see?
Even if it doesn't work, it'll be refreshing to take a flower bath.
Just like you said, a woman doesn't have to pamper herself to impress someone. She can do it just to make herself happy.

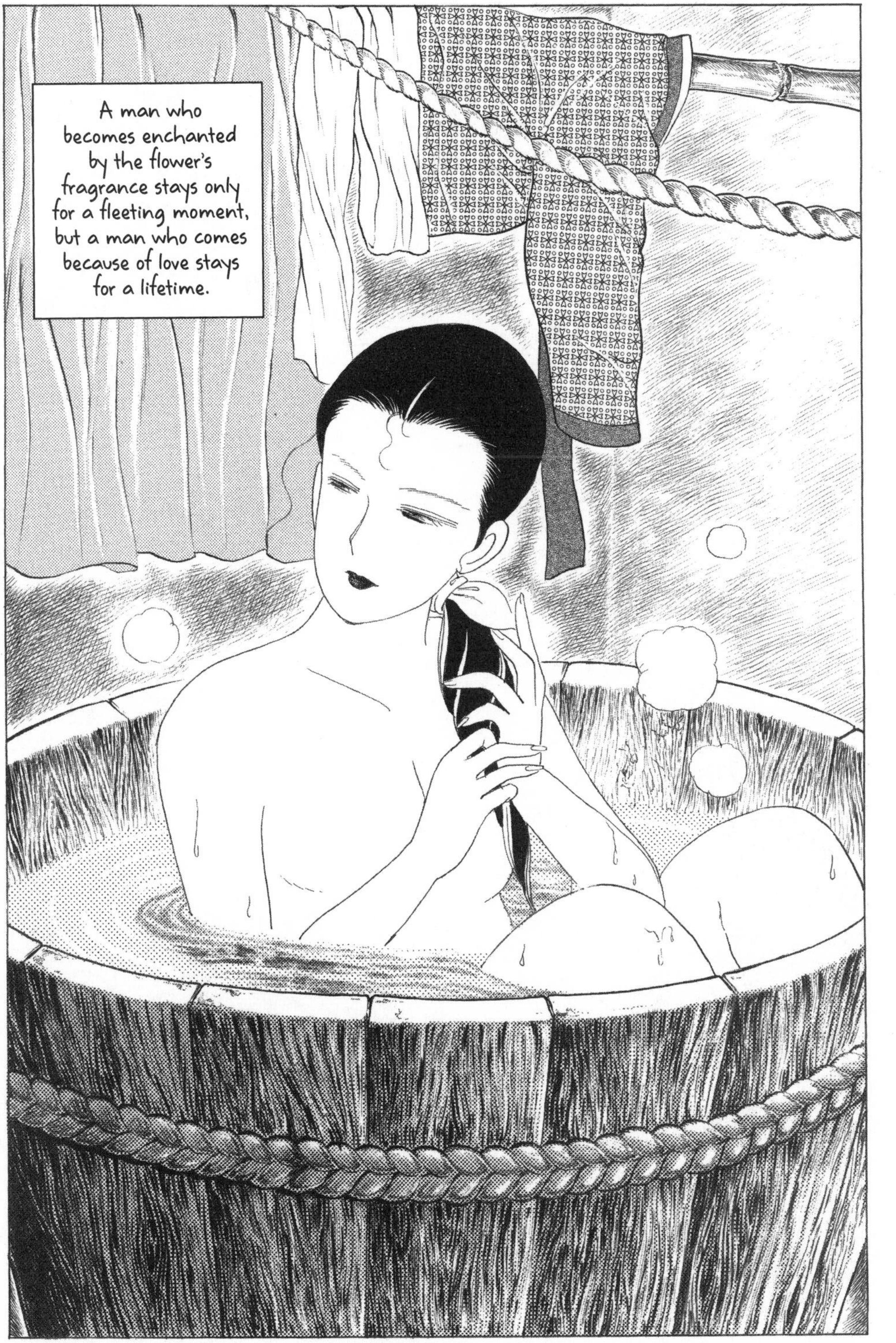
A man who becomes enchanted by the flower's fragrance stays only for a fleeting moment, but a man who comes because of love stays for a lifetime.

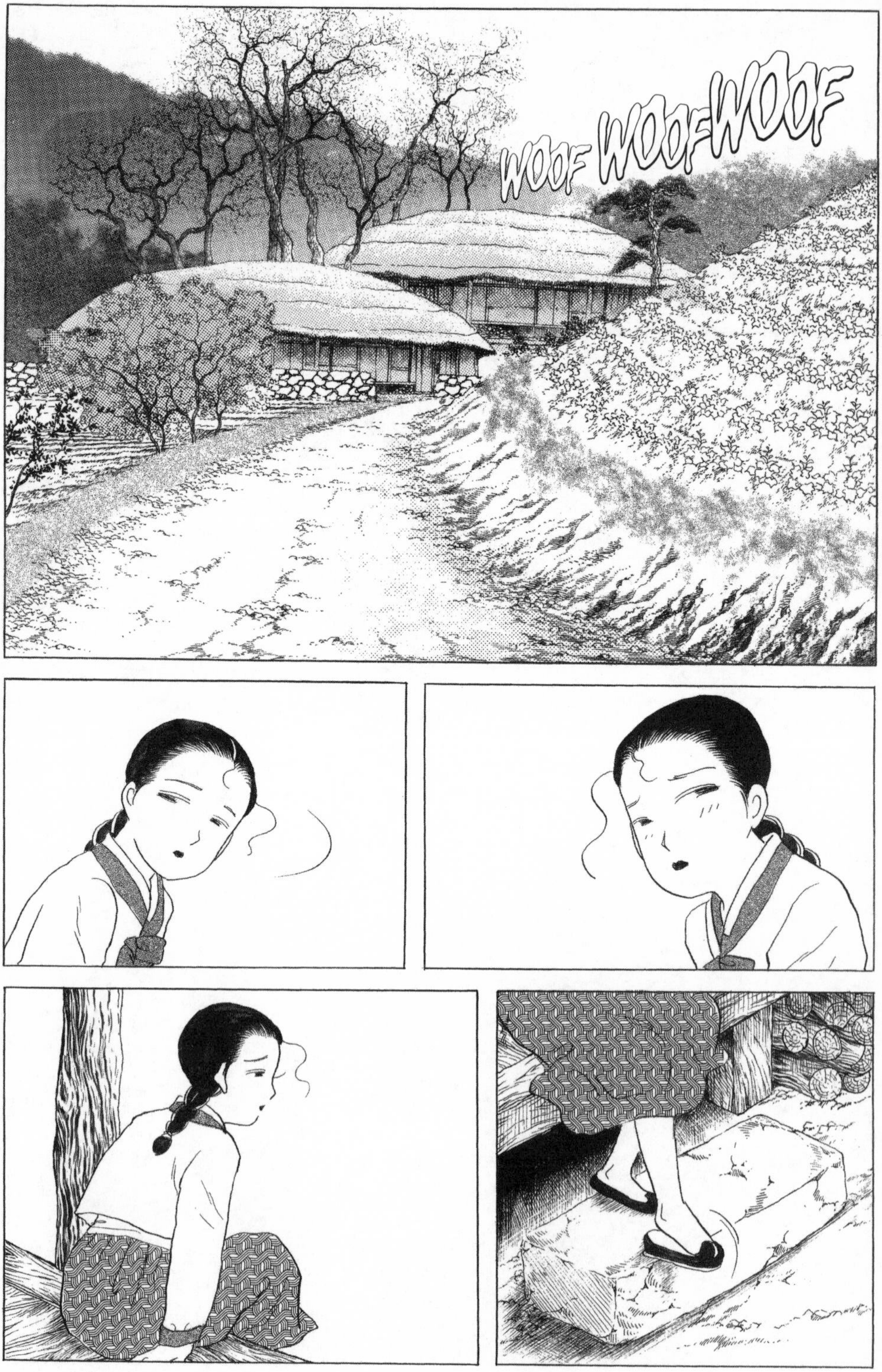
WOOF WOOF WOOF

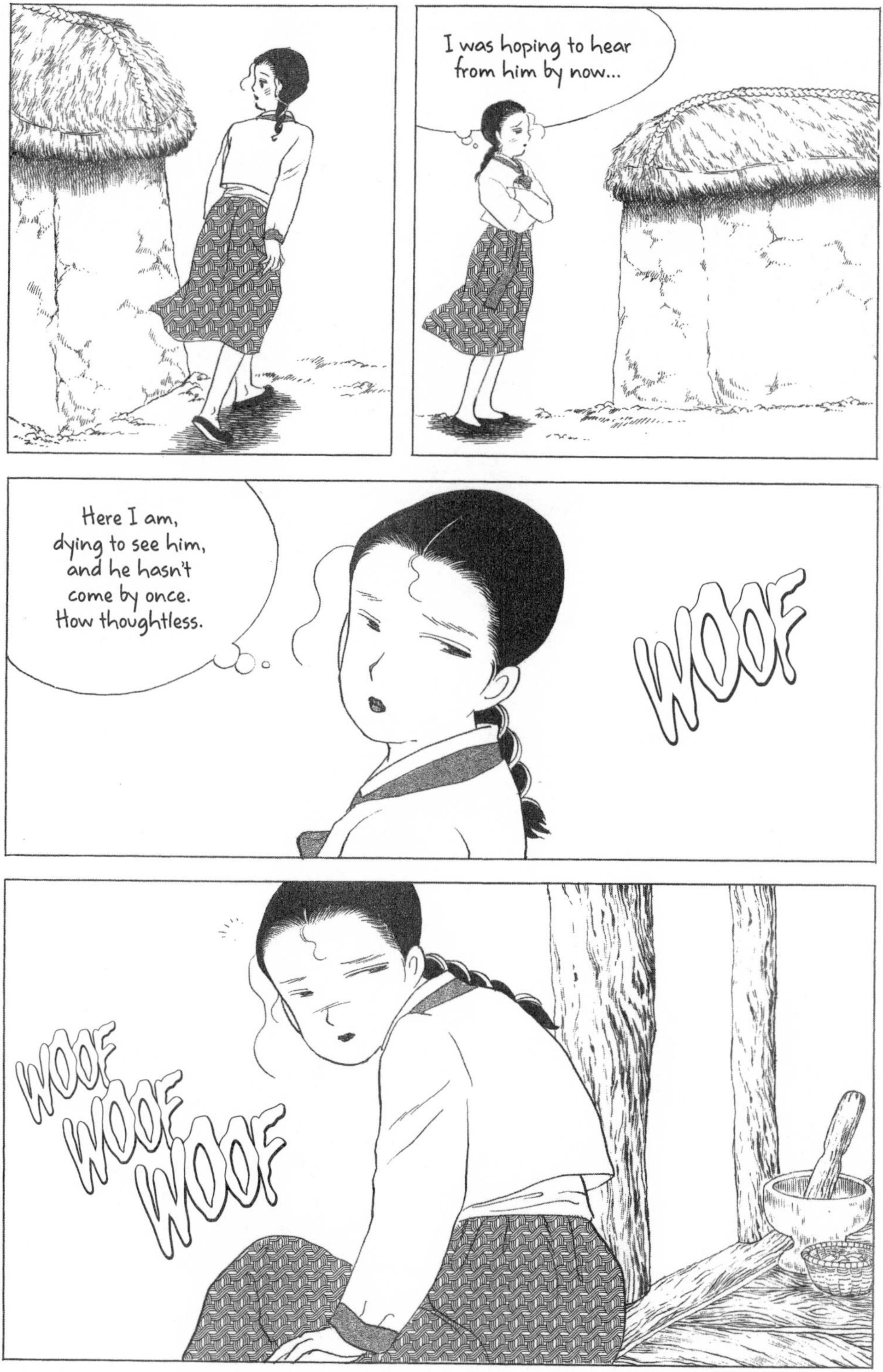
I was hoping to hear from him by now...
Here I am, dying to see him, and he hasn't come by once. How thoughtless.
WOOF
WOOF
WOOF
WOOF

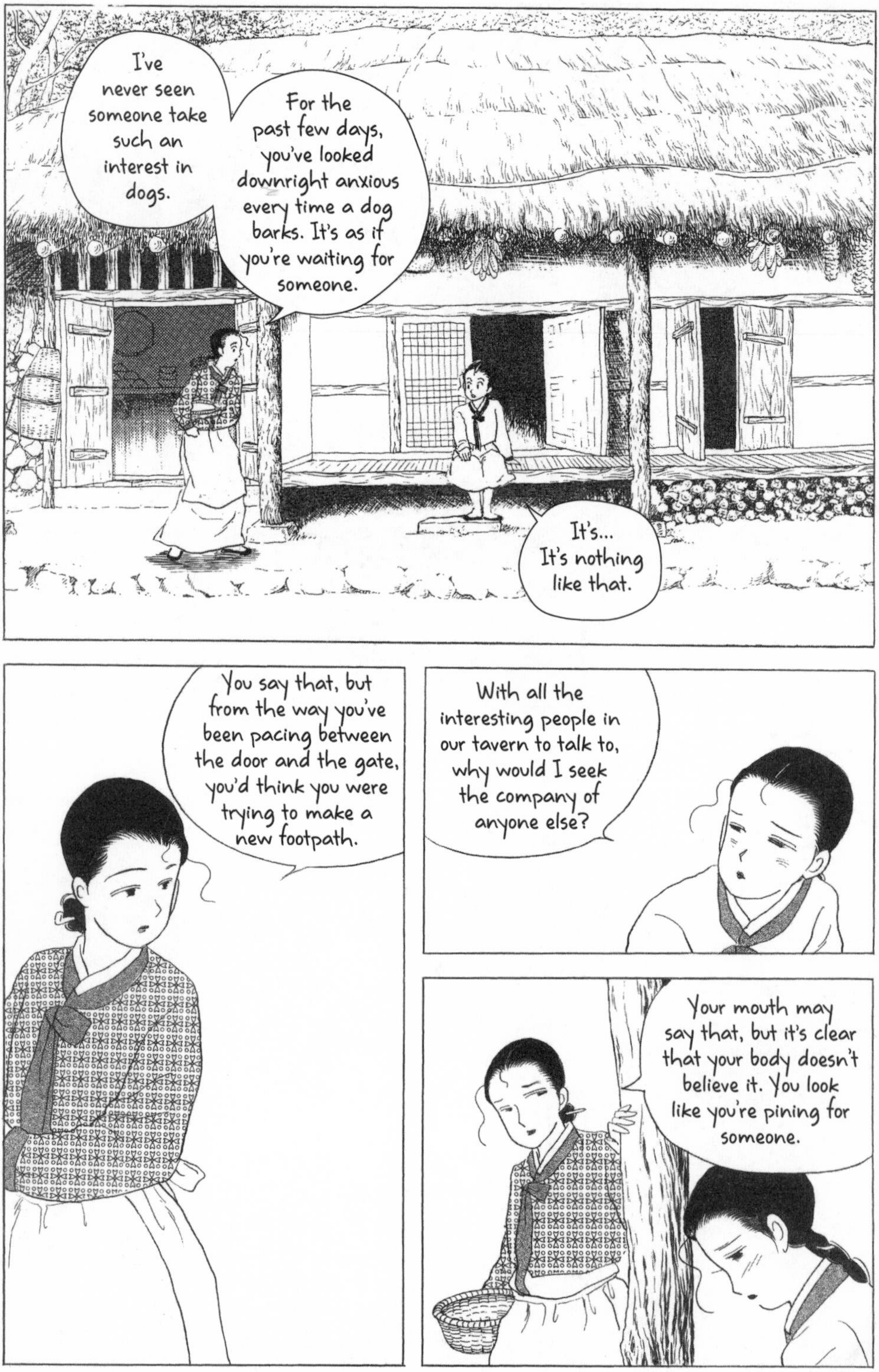
I've never seen someone take such an interest in dogs.
For the past few days, you've looked downright anxious every time a dog barks. It's as if you're waiting for someone.
It's... It's nothing like that.
You say that, but from the way you've been pacing between the door and the gate, you'd think you were trying to make a new footpath.
With all the interesting people in our tavern to talk to, why would I seek the company of anyone else?
Your mouth may say that, but it's clear that your body doesn't believe it. You look like you're pining for someone.

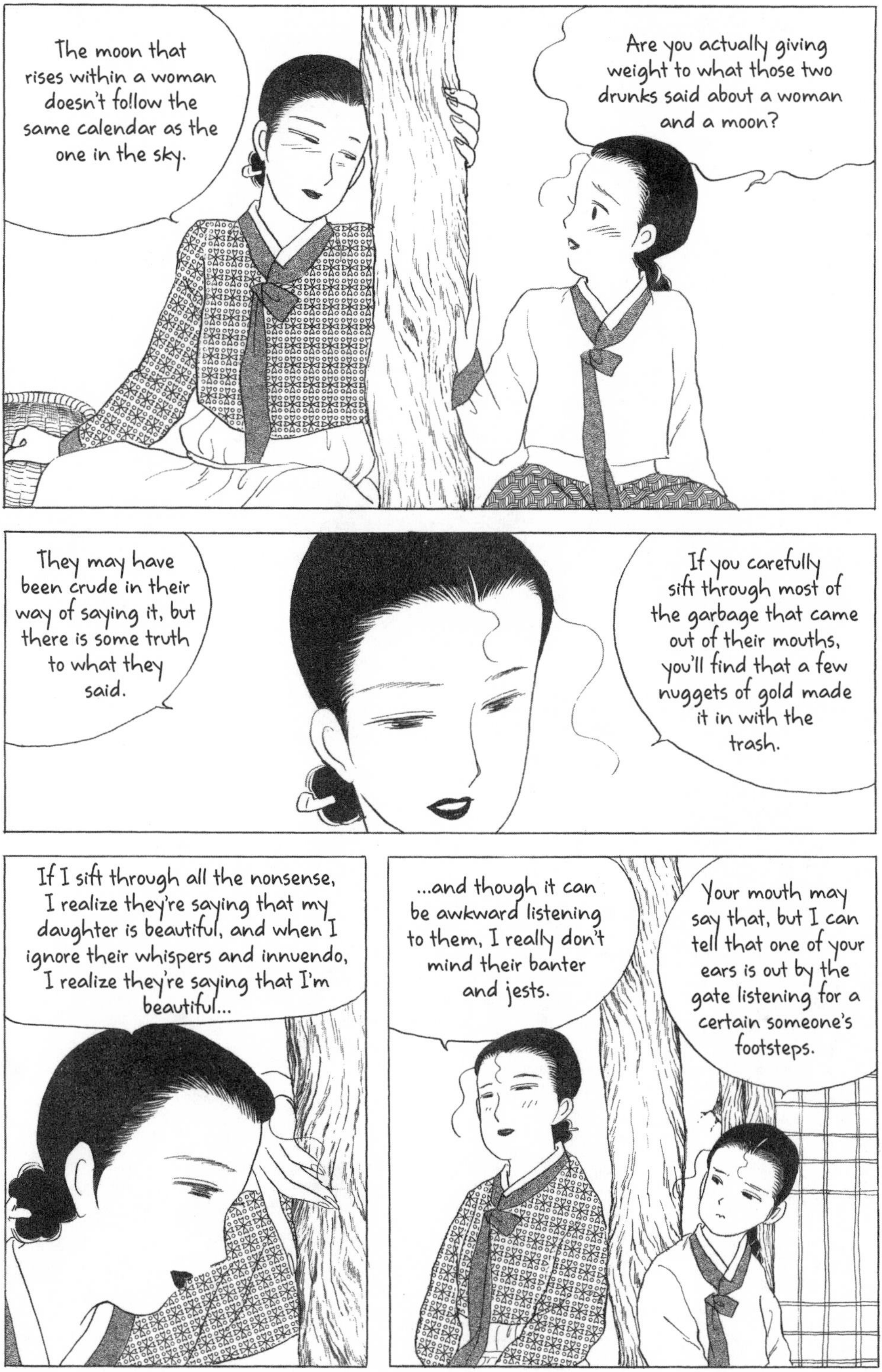
The moon that rises within a woman doesn't follow the same calendar as the one in the sky.
Are you actually giving weight to what those two drunks said about a woman and a moon?
They may have been crude in their way of saying it, but there is some truth to what they said.
If you carefully sift through most of the garbage that came out of their mouths, you'll find that a few nuggets of gold made it in with the trash.
If I sift through all the nonsense, I realize they're saying that my daughter is beautiful, and when I ignore their whispers and innuendo, I realize they're saying that I'm beautiful...
...and though it can be awkward listening to them, I really don't mind their banter and jests.
Your mouth may say that, but I can tell that one of your ears is out by the gate listening for a certain someone's footsteps.

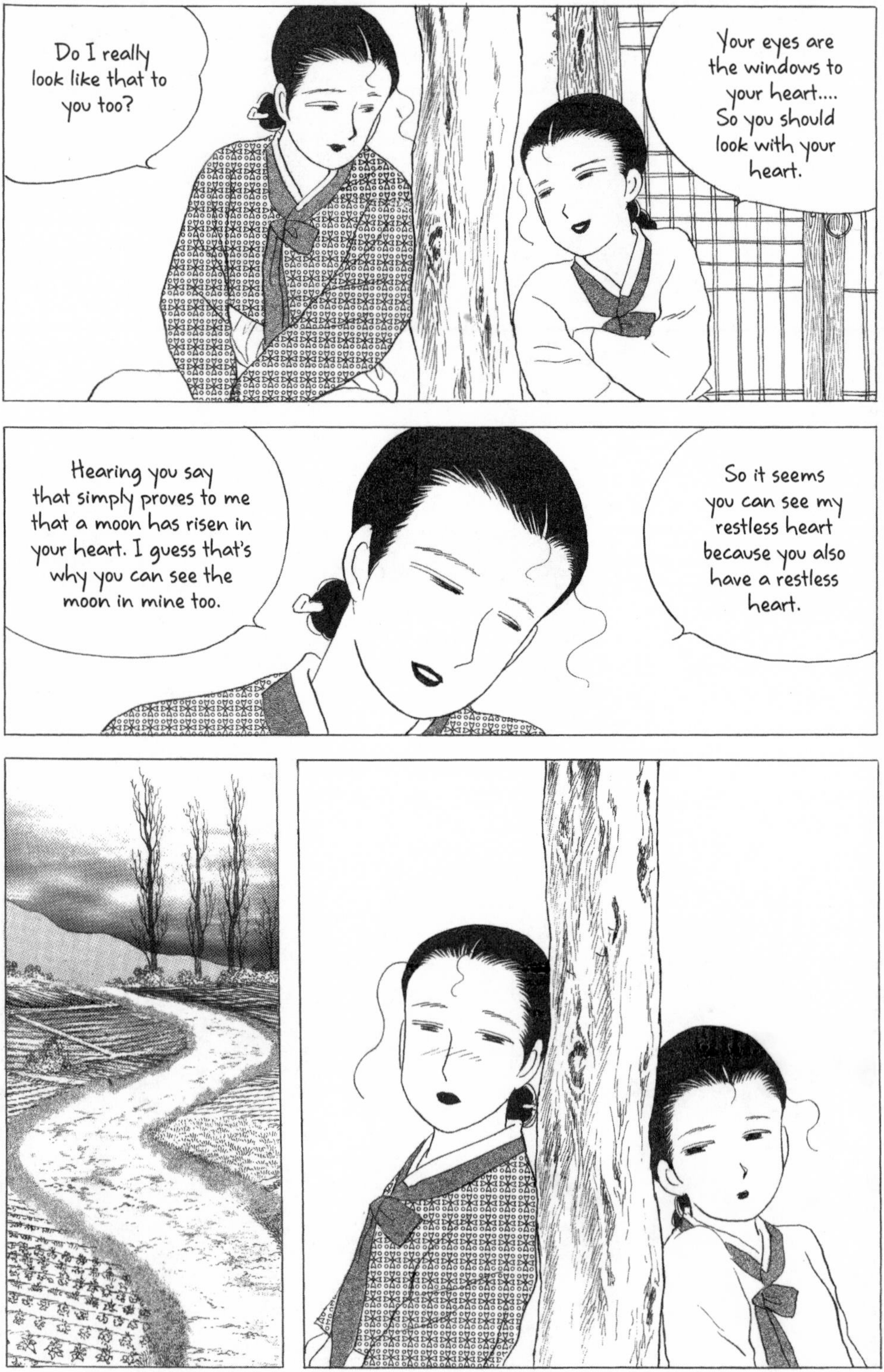
Do I really look like that to you too?
Your eyes are the windows to your heart.... So you should look with your heart.
Hearing you say that simply proves to me that a moon has risen in your heart. I guess that's why you can see the moon in mine too.
So it seems you can see my restless heart because you also have a restless heart.

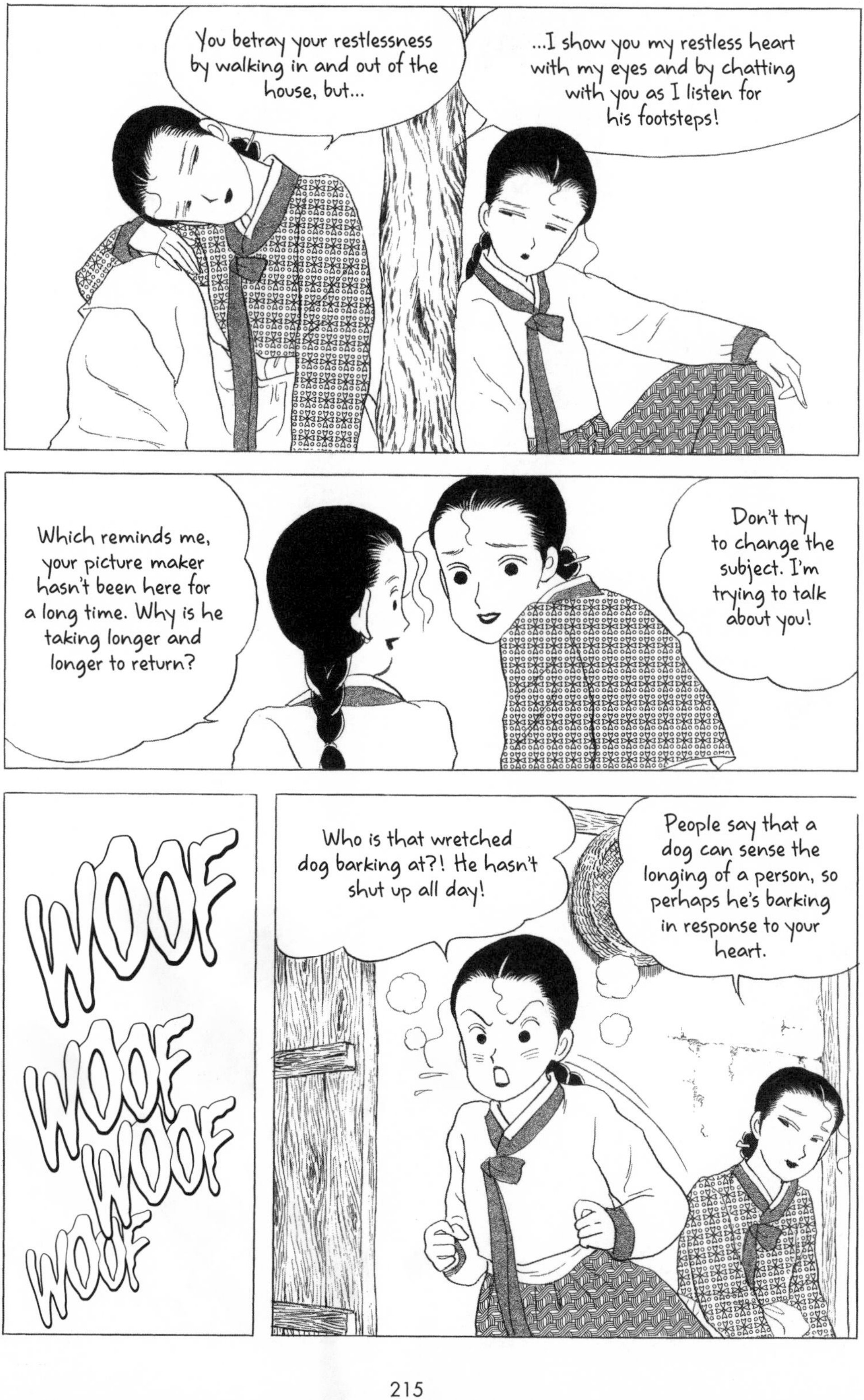
You betray your restlessness by walking in and out of the house, but...
...I show you my restless heart with my eyes and by chatting with you as I listen for his footsteps!
Which reminds me, your picture maker hasn't been here for a long time. Why is he taking longer and longer to return?
Don't try to change the subject. I'm trying to talk about you!
WOOF
WOOF WOOF WOOF
WOOF
Who is that wretched dog barking at?! He hasn't shut up all day!
People say that a dog can sense the longing of a person, so perhaps he's barking in response to your heart.

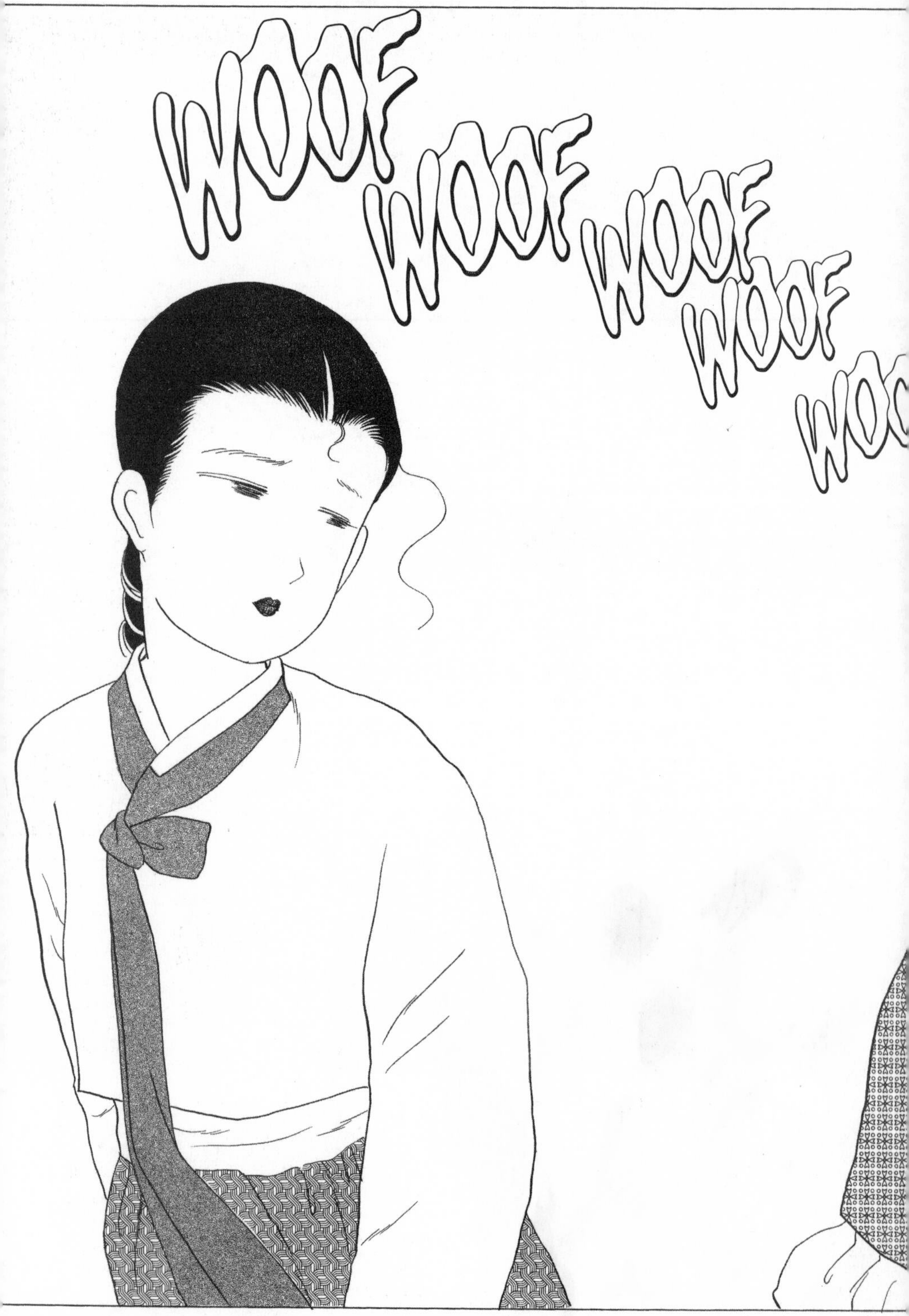
WOOF
WOOF
WOOF
WOOF

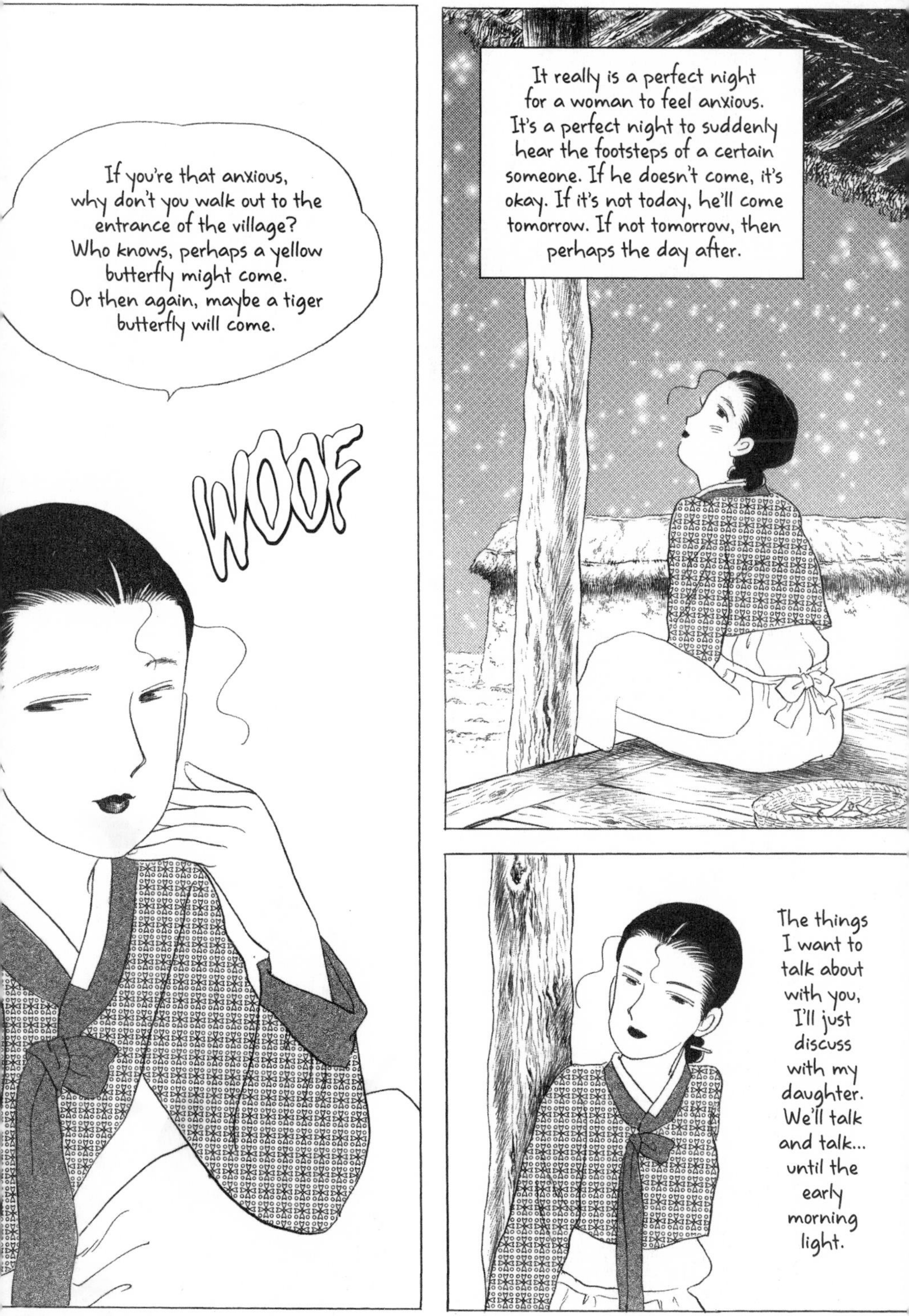
If you're that anxious, why don't you walk out to the entrance of the village? Who knows, perhaps a yellow butterfly might come. Or then again, maybe a tiger butterfly will come.
WOOF
It really is a perfect night for a woman to feel anxious. It's a perfect night to suddenly hear the footsteps of a certain someone. If he doesn't come, it's okay. If it's not today, he'll come tomorrow. If not tomorrow, then perhaps the day after.
The things I want to talk about with you, I'll just discuss with my daughter. We'll talk and talk... until the early morning light.

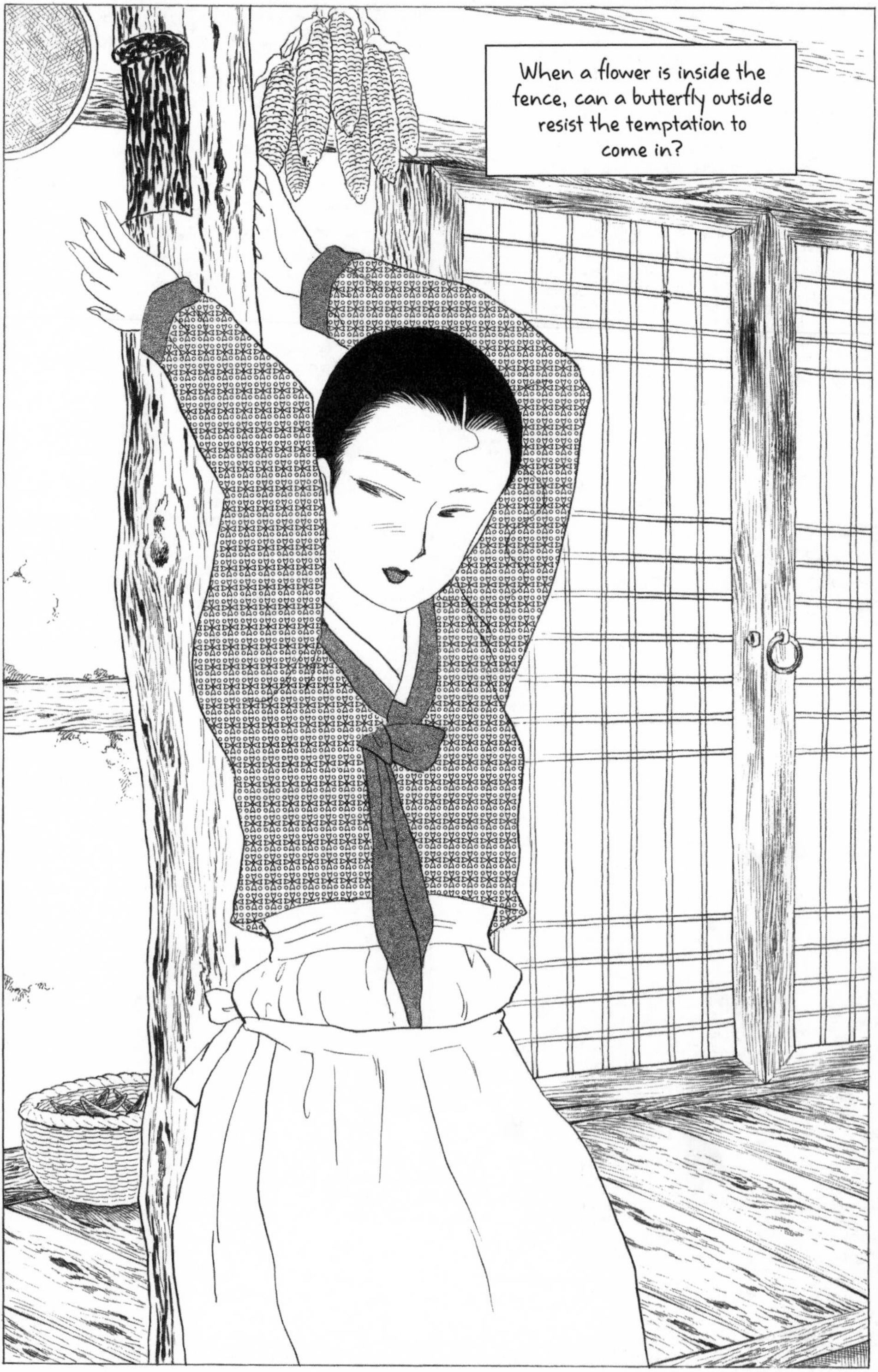
When a flower is inside the fence, can a butterfly outside resist the temptation to come in?

Chapter Eight

WHITE
BELLFLOWER

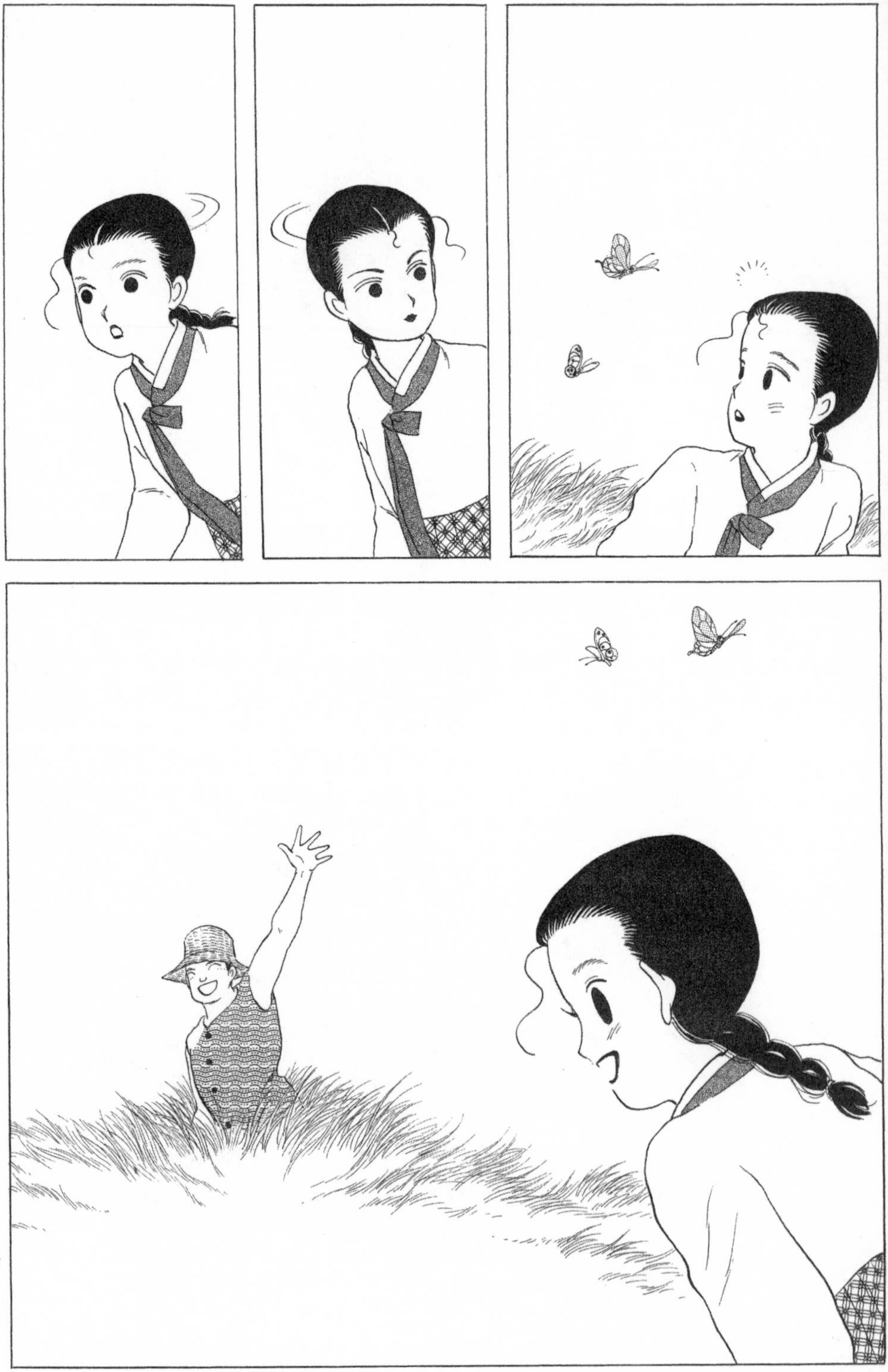

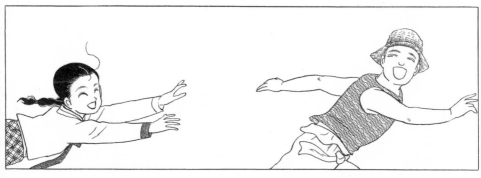

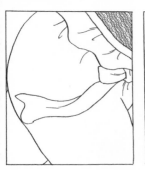
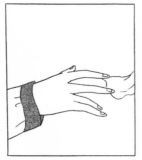
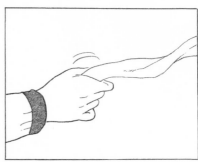

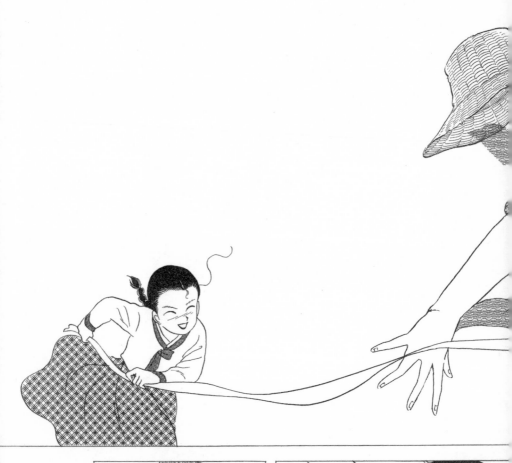

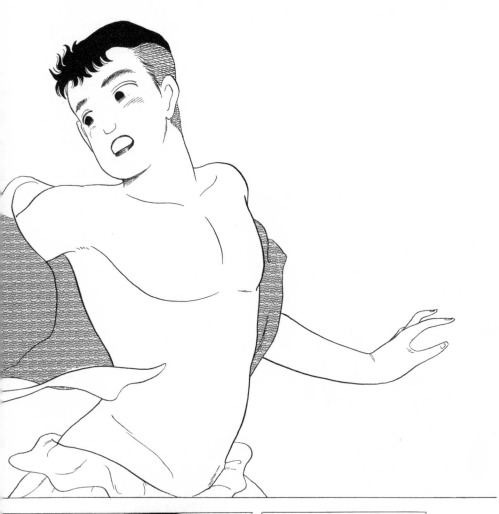

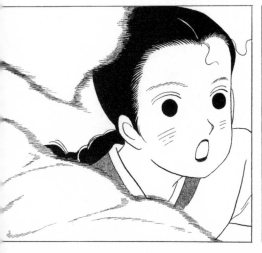

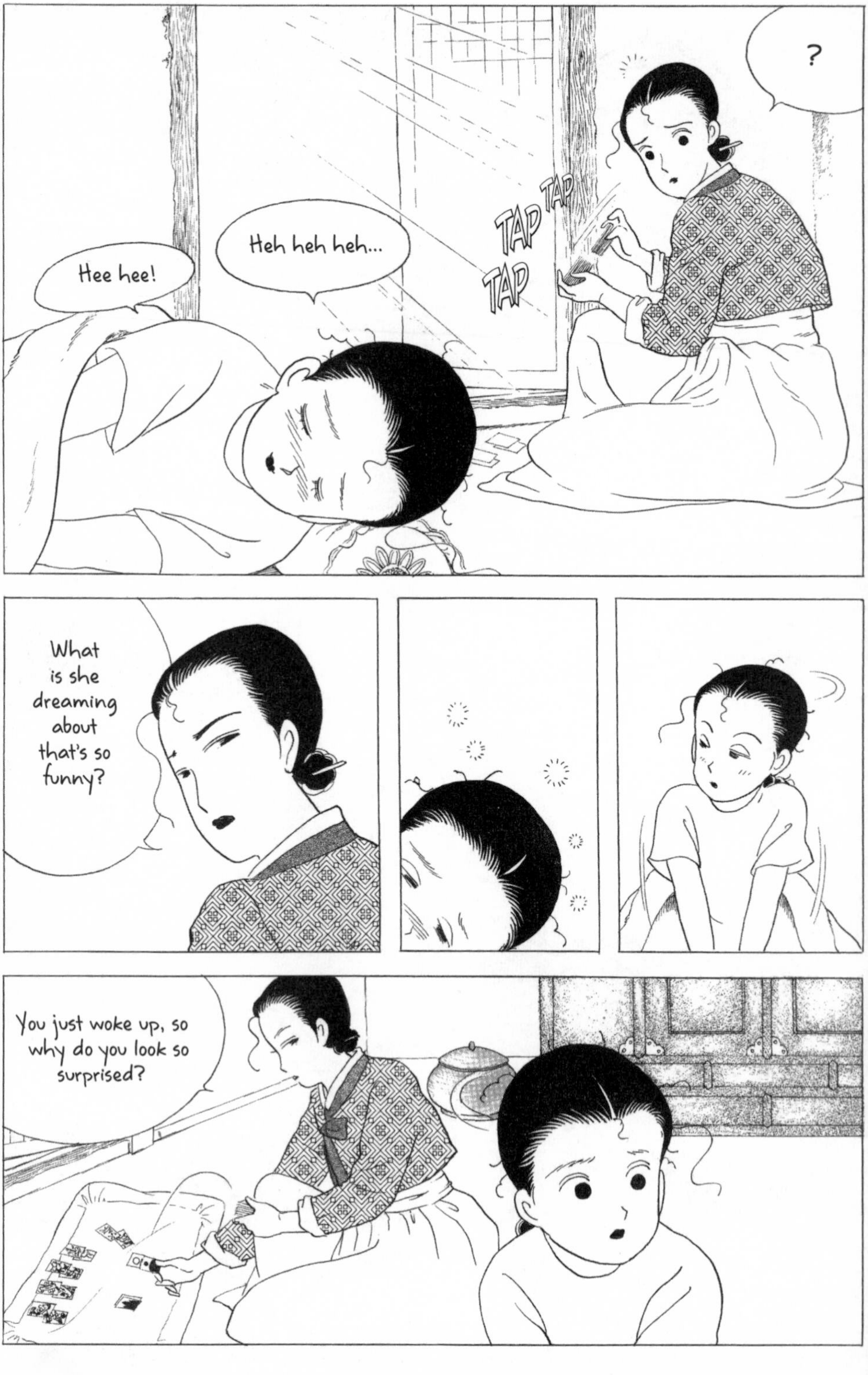
Hee hee!
Heh heh heh...
TAP TAP TAP
?
What is she dreaming about that's so funny?
You just woke up, so why do you look so surprised?

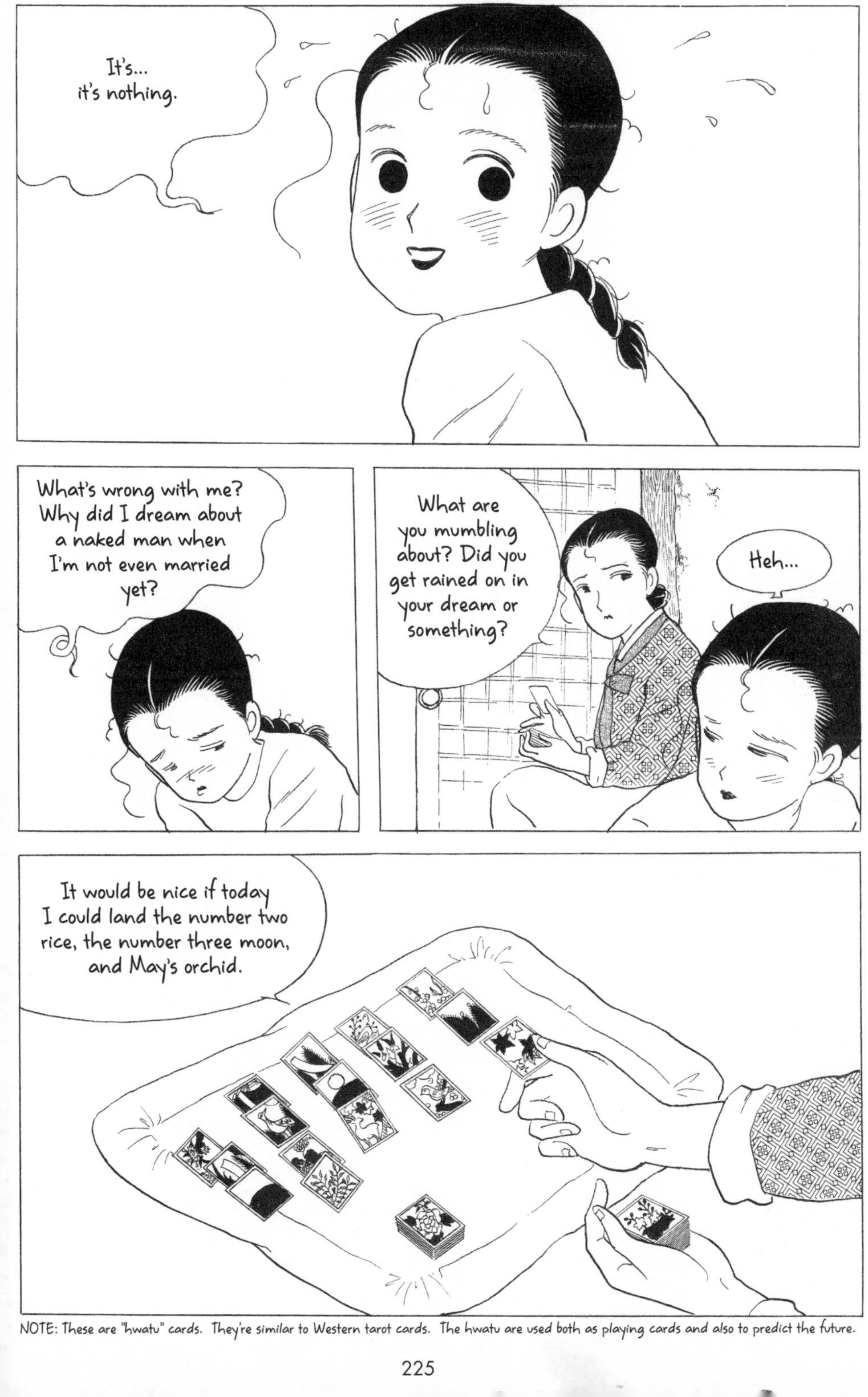
It's... it's nothing.
What's wrong with me? Why did I dream about a naked man when I'm not even married yet?
What are you mumbling about? Did you get rained on in your dream or something?
Heh...
It would be nice if today I could land the number two rice, the number three moon, and May's orchid.

NOTE: These are "hwatu" cards. They're similar to Western tarot cards. The hwatu are used both as playing cards and also to predict the future.

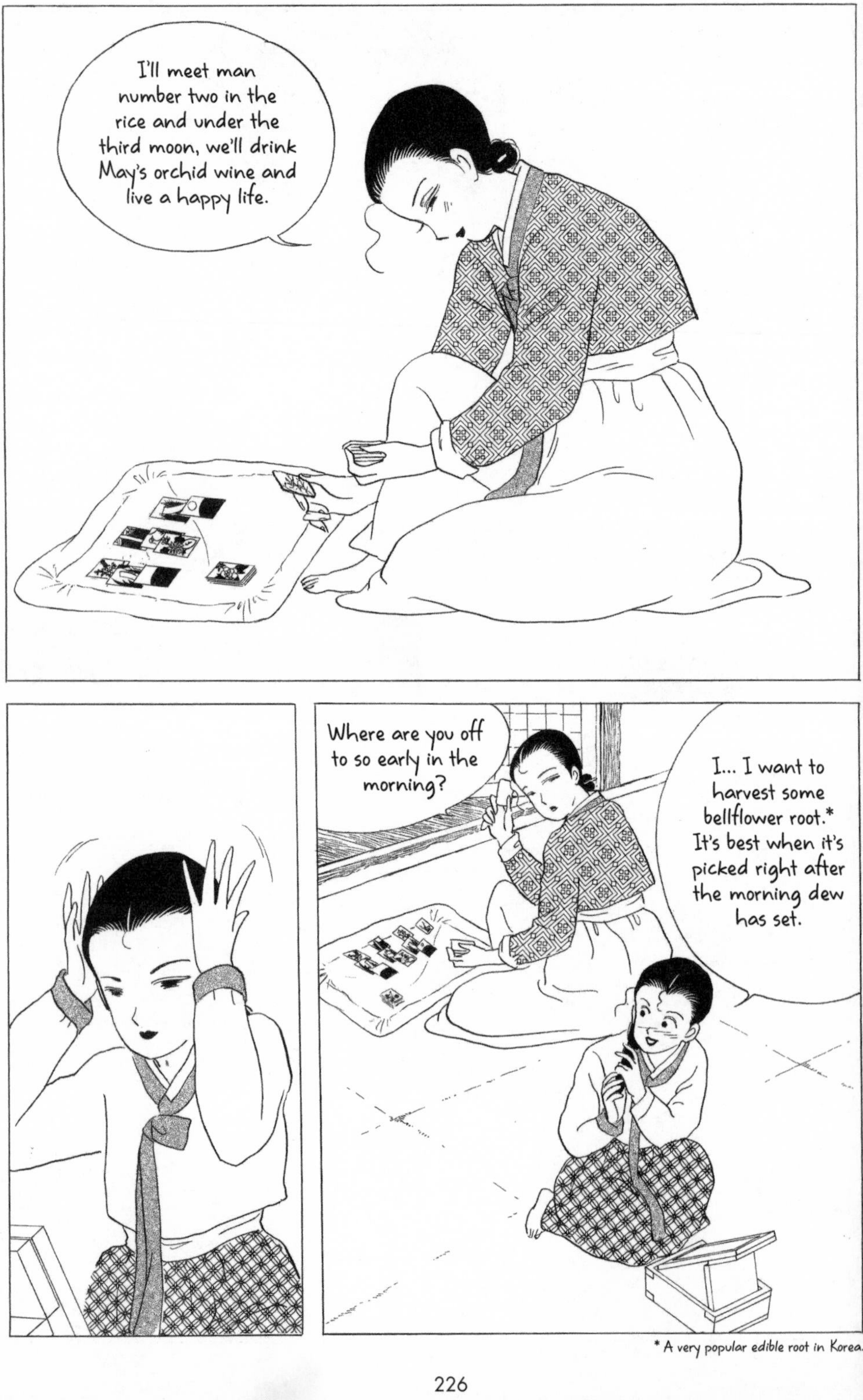

I'll meet man number two in the rice and under the third moon, we'll drink May's orchid wine and live a happy life.
Where are you off to so early in the morning?
I... I want to harvest some bellflower root.* It's best when it's picked right after the morning dew has set.

* A very popular edible root in Korea.

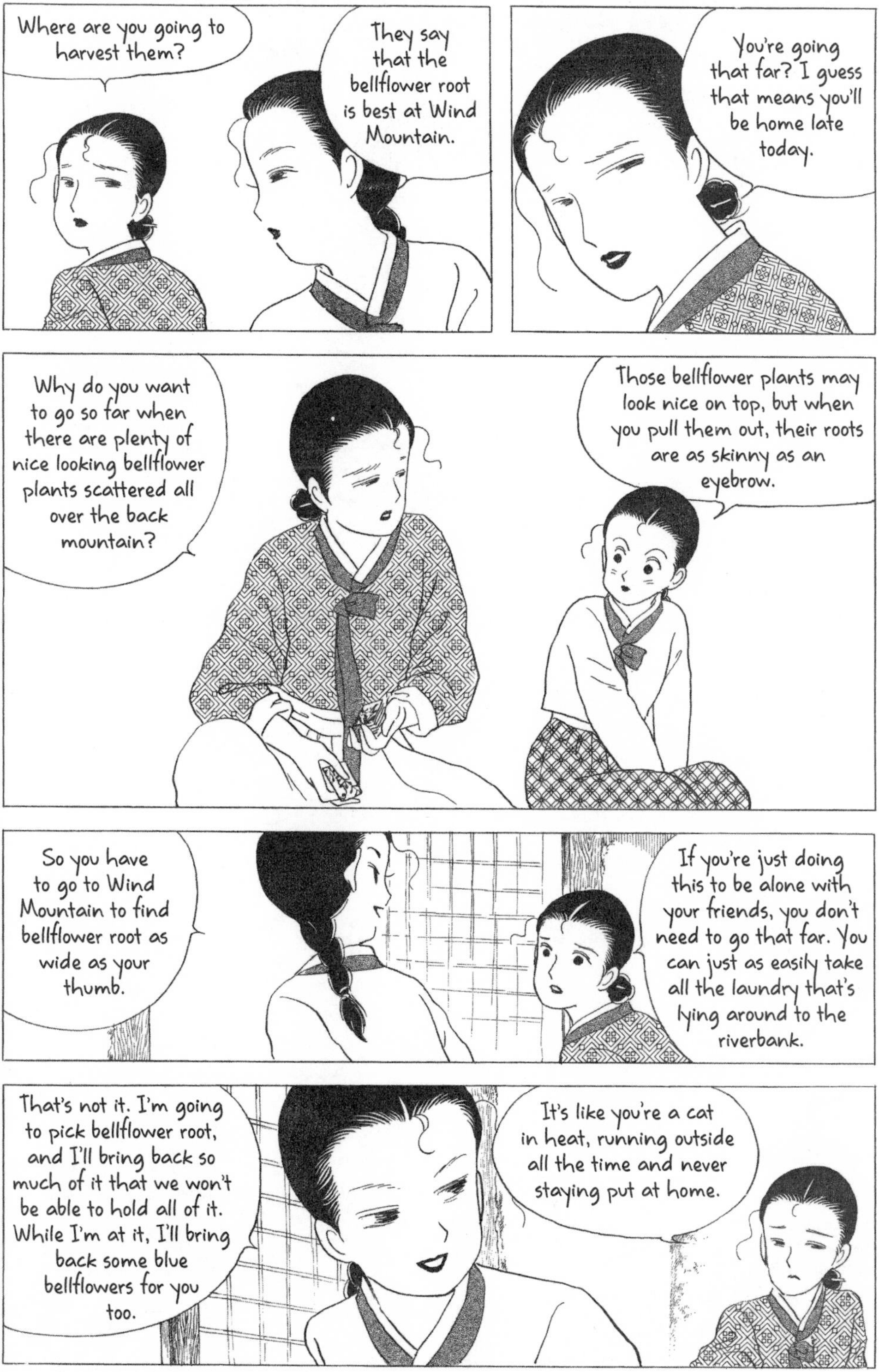
Where are you going to harvest them?
They say that the bellflower root is best at Wind Mountain.
You're going that far? I guess that means you'll be home late today.
Why do you want to go so far when there are plenty of nice looking bellflower plants scattered all over the back mountain?
Those bellflower plants may look nice on top, but when you pull them out, their roots are as skinny as an eyebrow.
So you have to go to Wind Mountain to find bellflower root as wide as your thumb.
If you're just doing this to be alone with your friends, you don't need to go that far. You can just as easily take all the laundry that's lying around to the riverbank.
That's not it. I'm going to pick bellflower root, and I'll bring back so much of it that we won't be able to hold all of it. While I'm at it, I'll bring back some blue bellflowers for you too.
It's like you're a cat in heat, running outside all the time and never staying put at home.

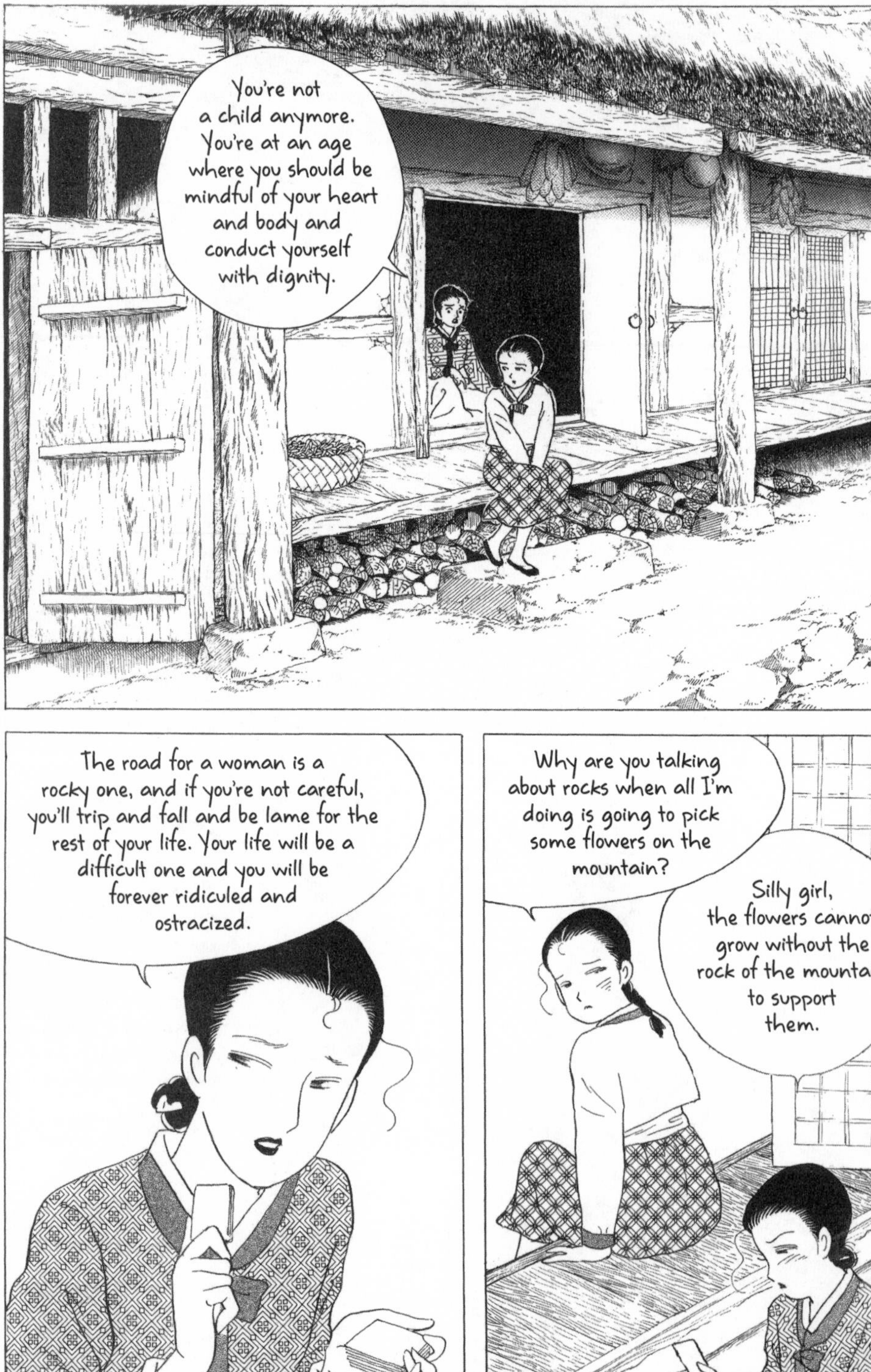
You're not a child anymore. You're at an age where you should be mindful of your heart and body and conduct yourself with dignity.
The road for a woman is a rocky one, and if you're not careful, you'll trip and fall and be lame for the rest of your life. Your life will be a difficult one and you will be forever ridiculed and ostracized.
Why are you talking about rocks when all I'm doing is going to pick some flowers on the mountain?
Silly girl, the flowers cannot grow without the rock of the mountain to support them.

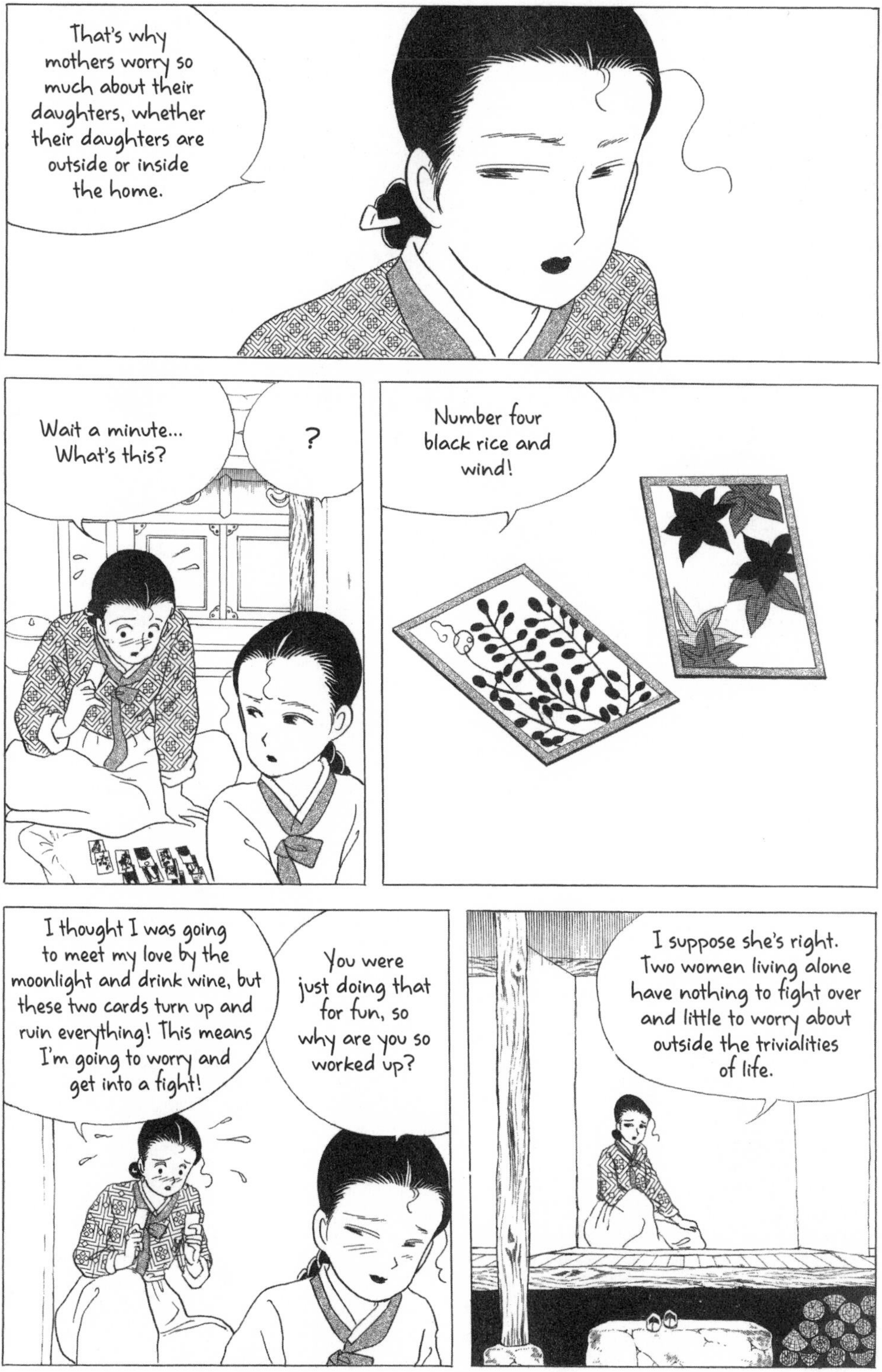

That's why mothers worry so much about their daughters, whether their daughters are outside or inside the home.
Wait a minute... What's this?
?
Number four black rice and wind!
I thought I was going to meet my love by the moonlight and drink wine, but these two cards turn up and ruin everything! This means I'm going to worry and get into a fight!
You were just doing that for fun, so why are you so worked up?
I suppose she's right. Two women living alone have nothing to fight over and little to worry about outside the trivialities of life.

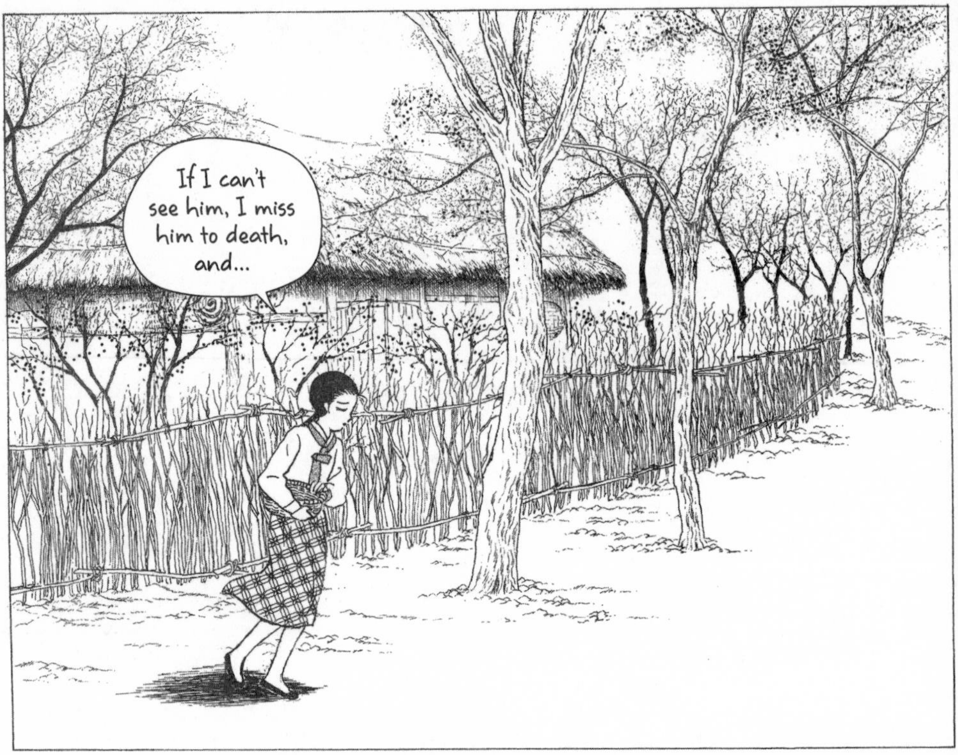
If I can't see him, I miss him to death, and...
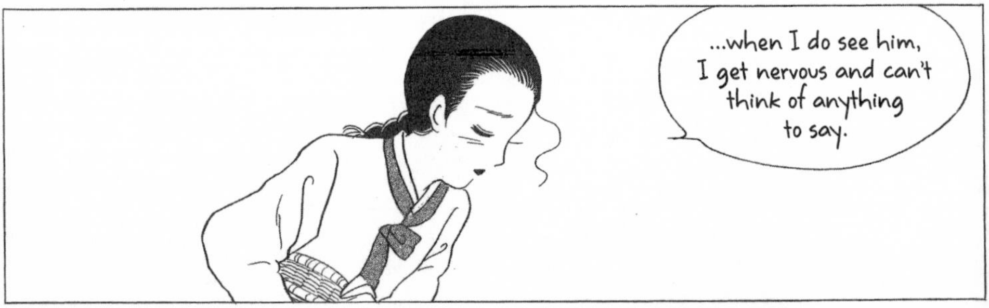
...when I do see him, I get nervous and can't think of anything to say.
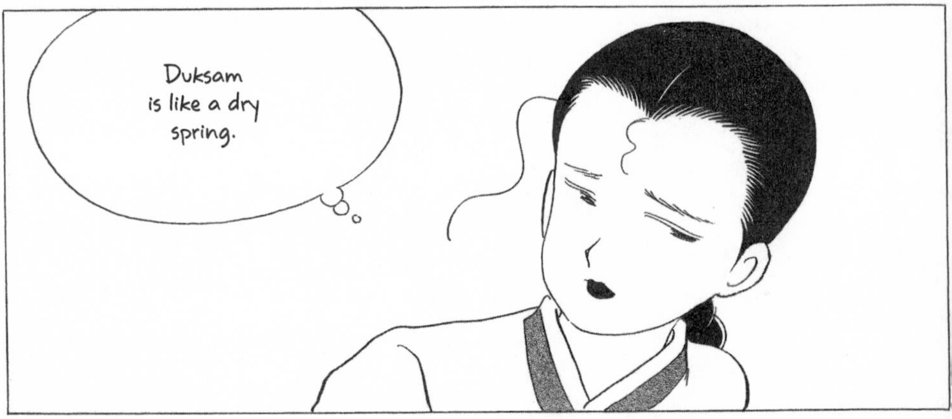
Duksam is like a dry spring.

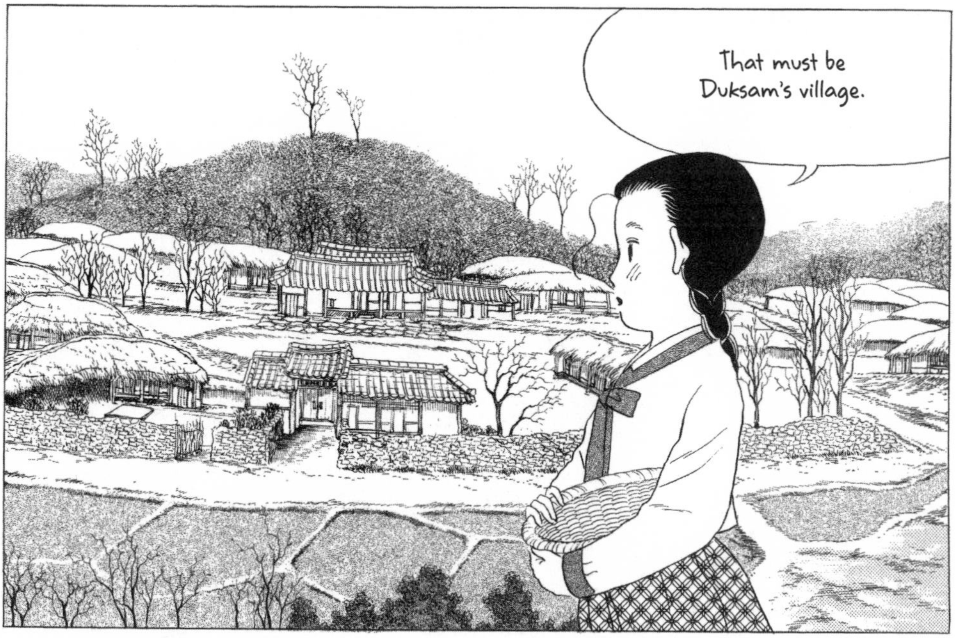
That must be Duksam's village.

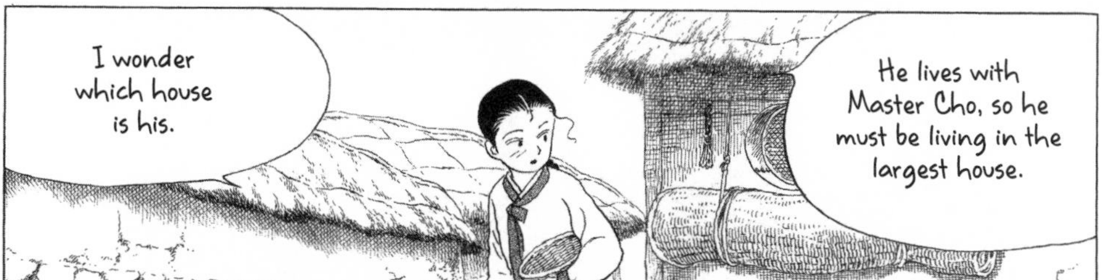
I wonder which house is his.
He lives with Master Cho, so he must be living in the largest house.

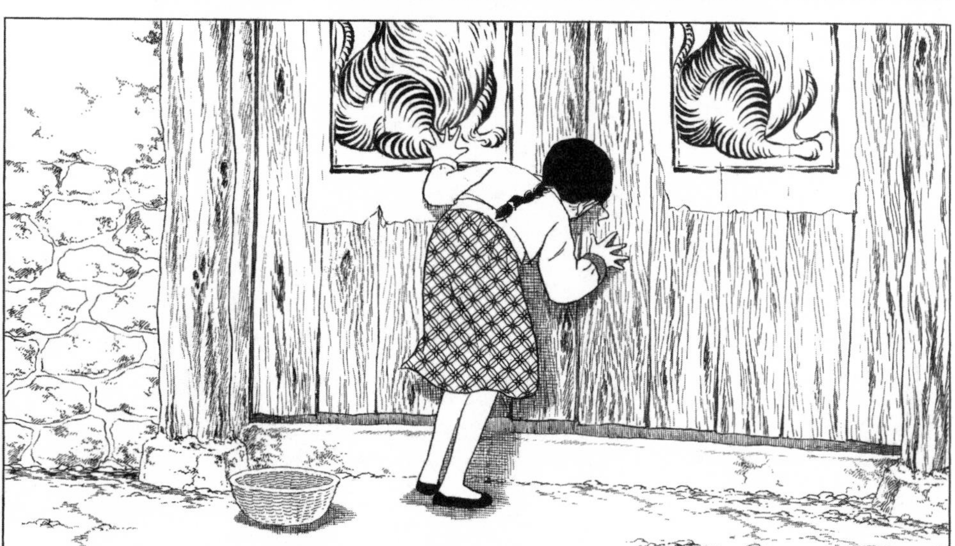

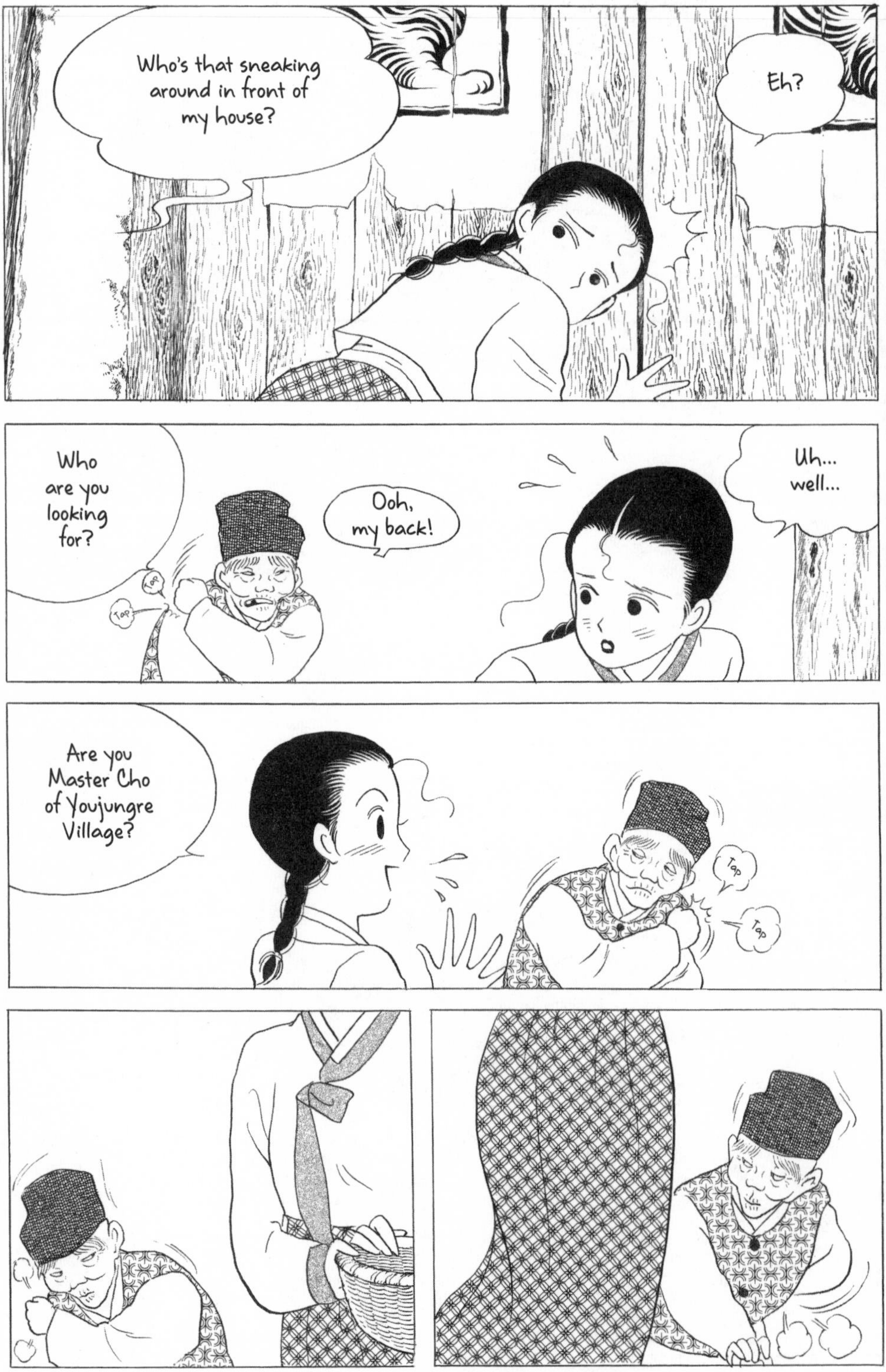
Who's that sneaking around in front of my house?
Eh?
Who are you looking for?
Tap
Tap
Ooh, my back!
Uh... well...
Are you Master Cho of Youjungre Village?
Tap
Tap

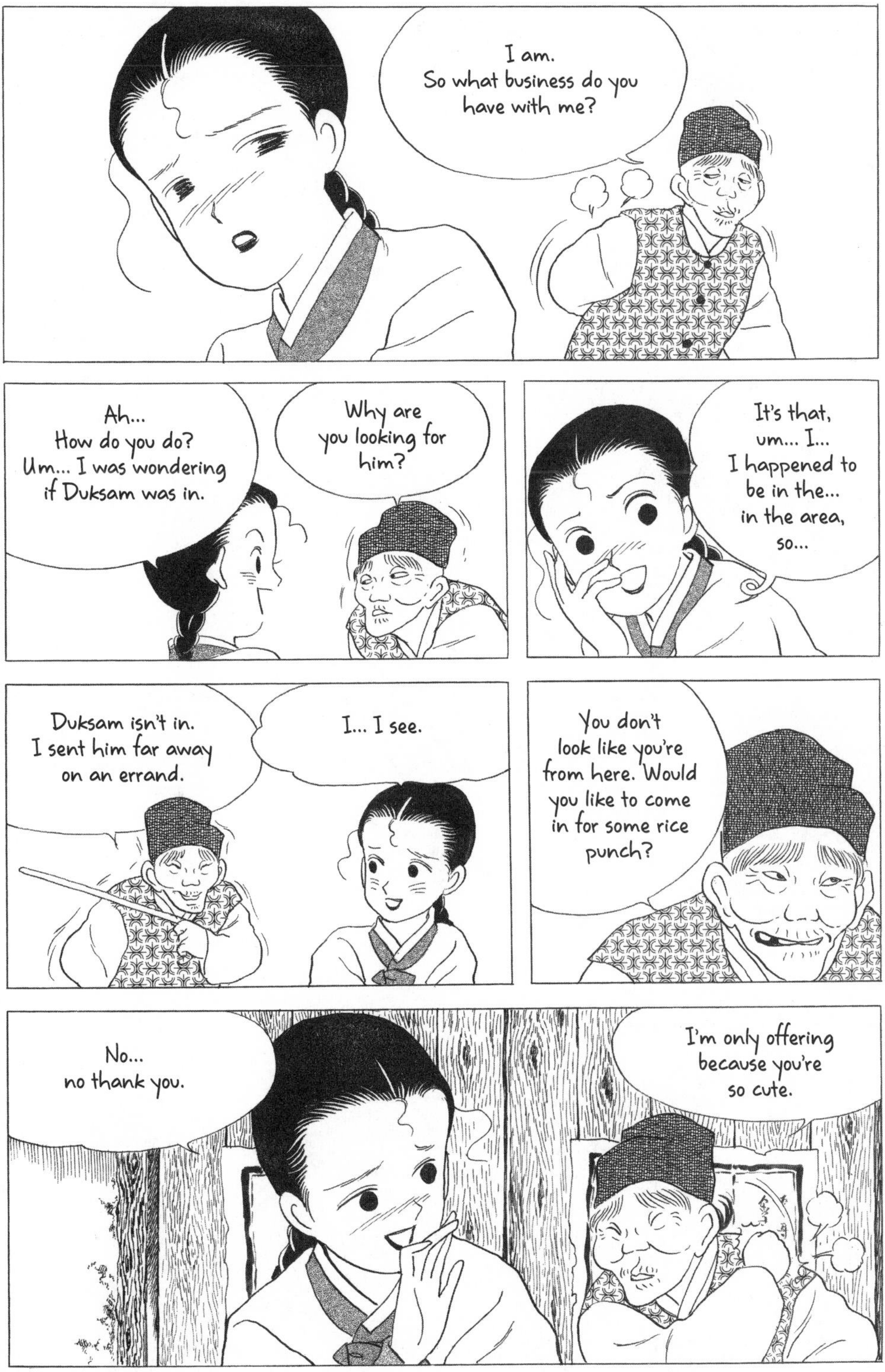
I am.
So what business do you have with me?
Ah... How do you do? Um... I was wondering if Duksam was in.
Why are you looking for him?
It's that, um... I... I happened to be in the... in the area, so...
Duksam isn't in. I sent him far away on an errand.
I... I see.
You don't look like you're from here. Would you like to come in for some rice punch?
No... no thank you.
I'm only offering because you're so cute.

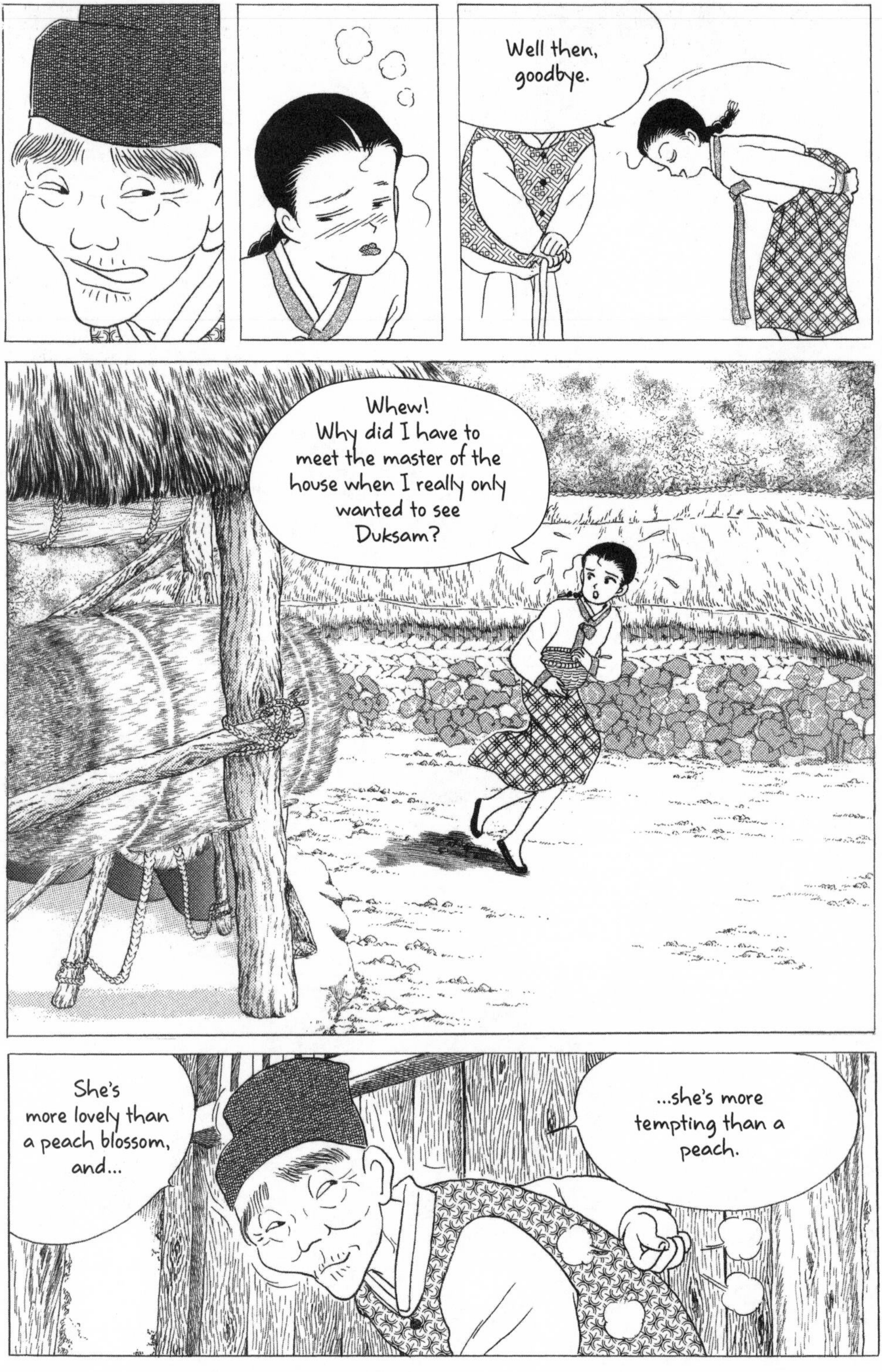
Well then, goodbye.
Whew! Why did I have to meet the master of the house when I really only wanted to see Duksam?
She's more lovely than a peach blossom, and...
...she's more tempting than a peach.

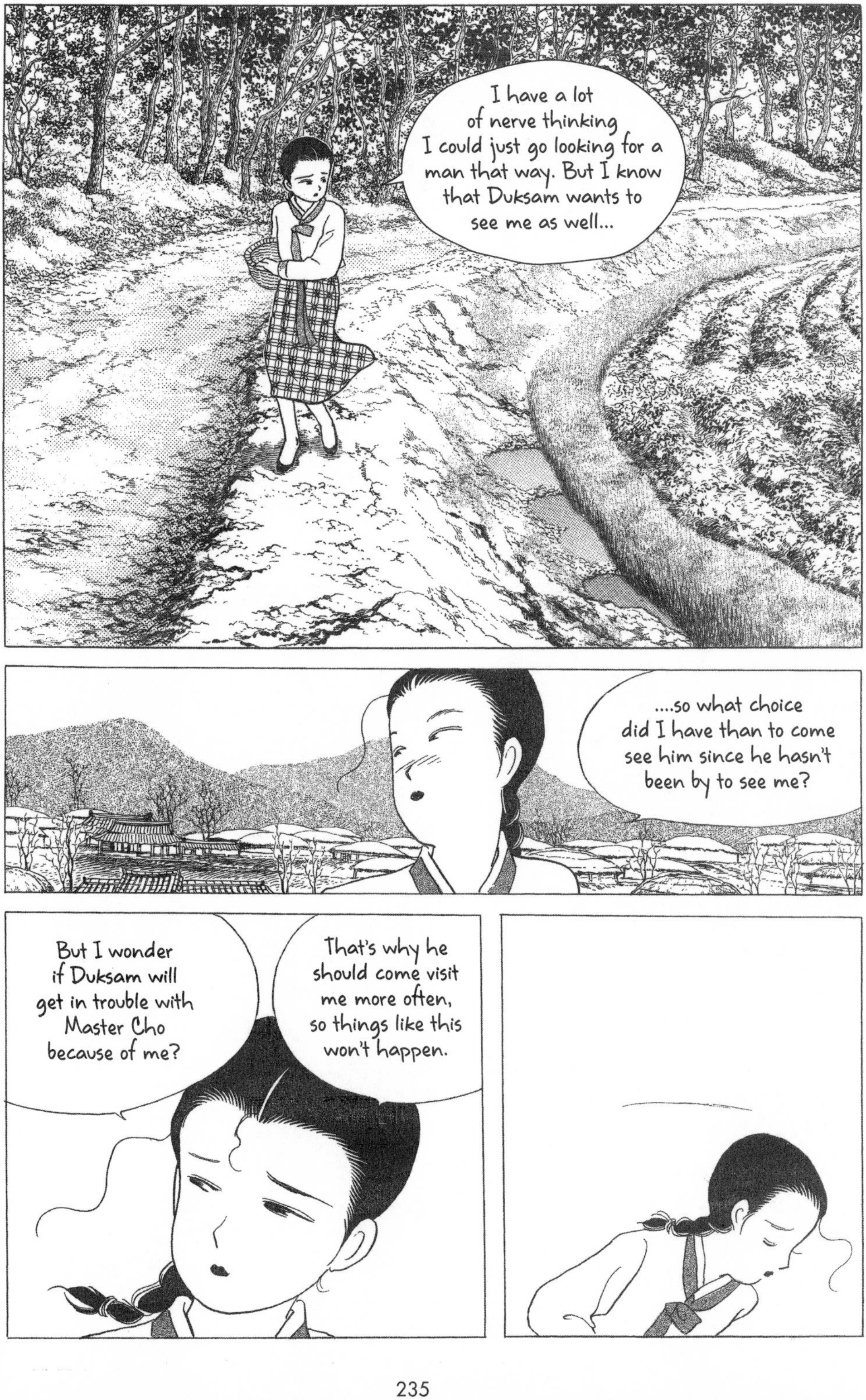
I have a lot of nerve thinking I could just go looking for a man that way. But I know that Duksam wants to see me as well...
....so what choice did I have than to come see him since he hasn't been by to see me?
But I wonder if Duksam will get in trouble with Master Cho because of me?
That's why he should come visit me more often, so things like this won't happen.

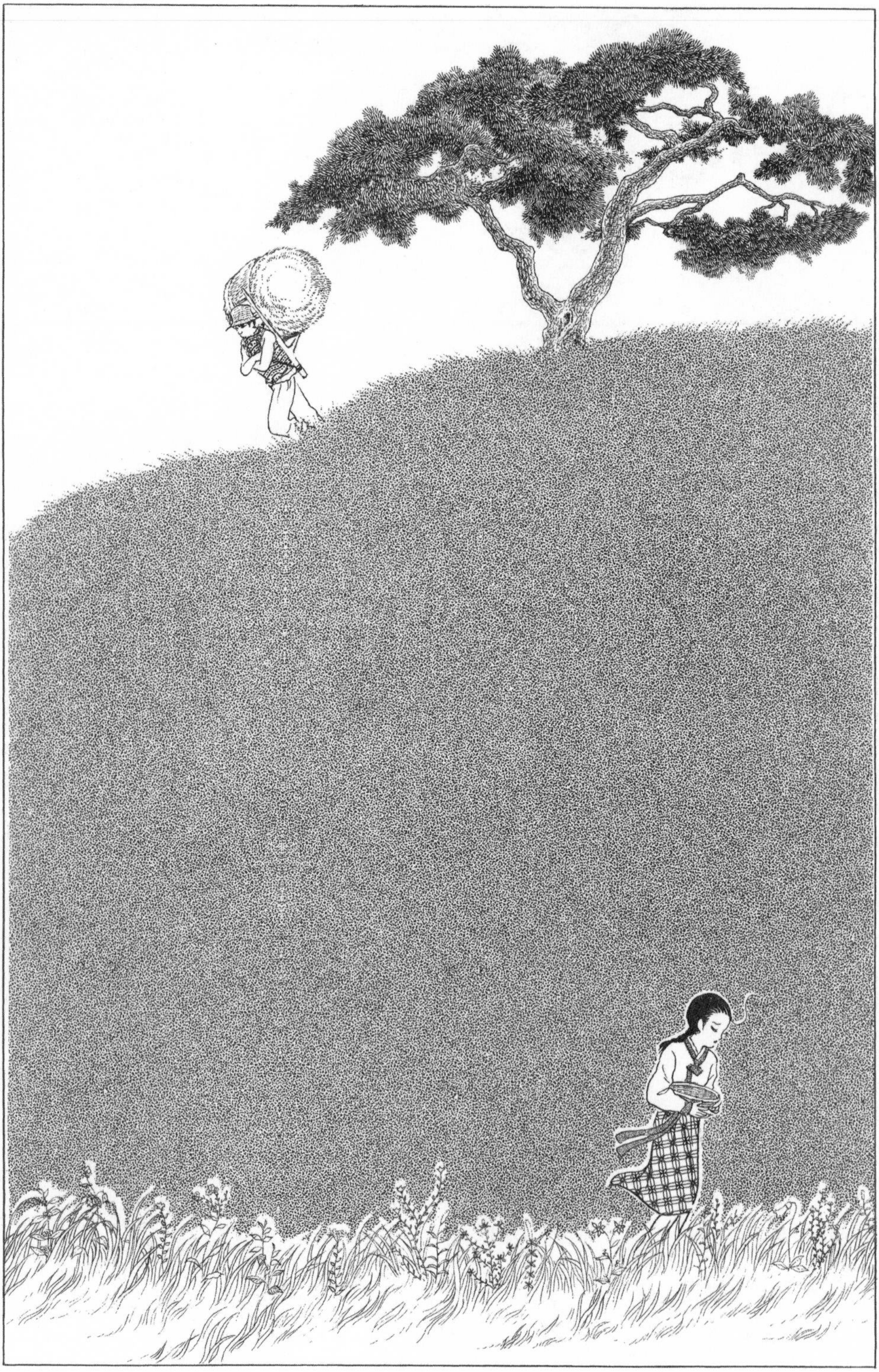

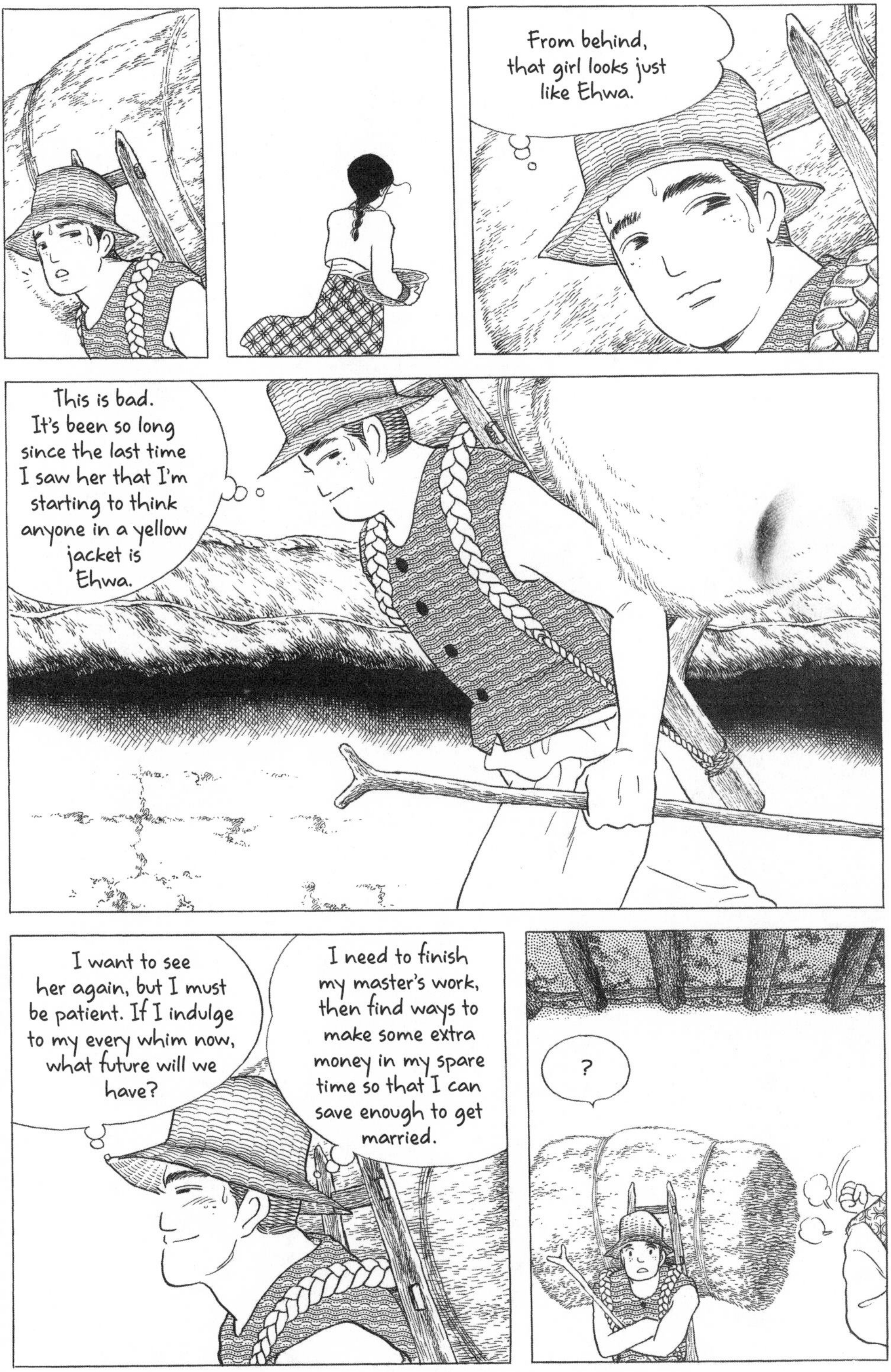
From behind, that girl looks just like Ehwa.
This is bad. It's been so long since the last time I saw her that I'm starting to think anyone in a yellow jacket is Ehwa.
I want to see her again, but I must be patient. If I indulge to my every whim now, what future will we have?
I need to finish my master's work, then find ways to make some extra money in my spare time so that I can save enough to get married.
?

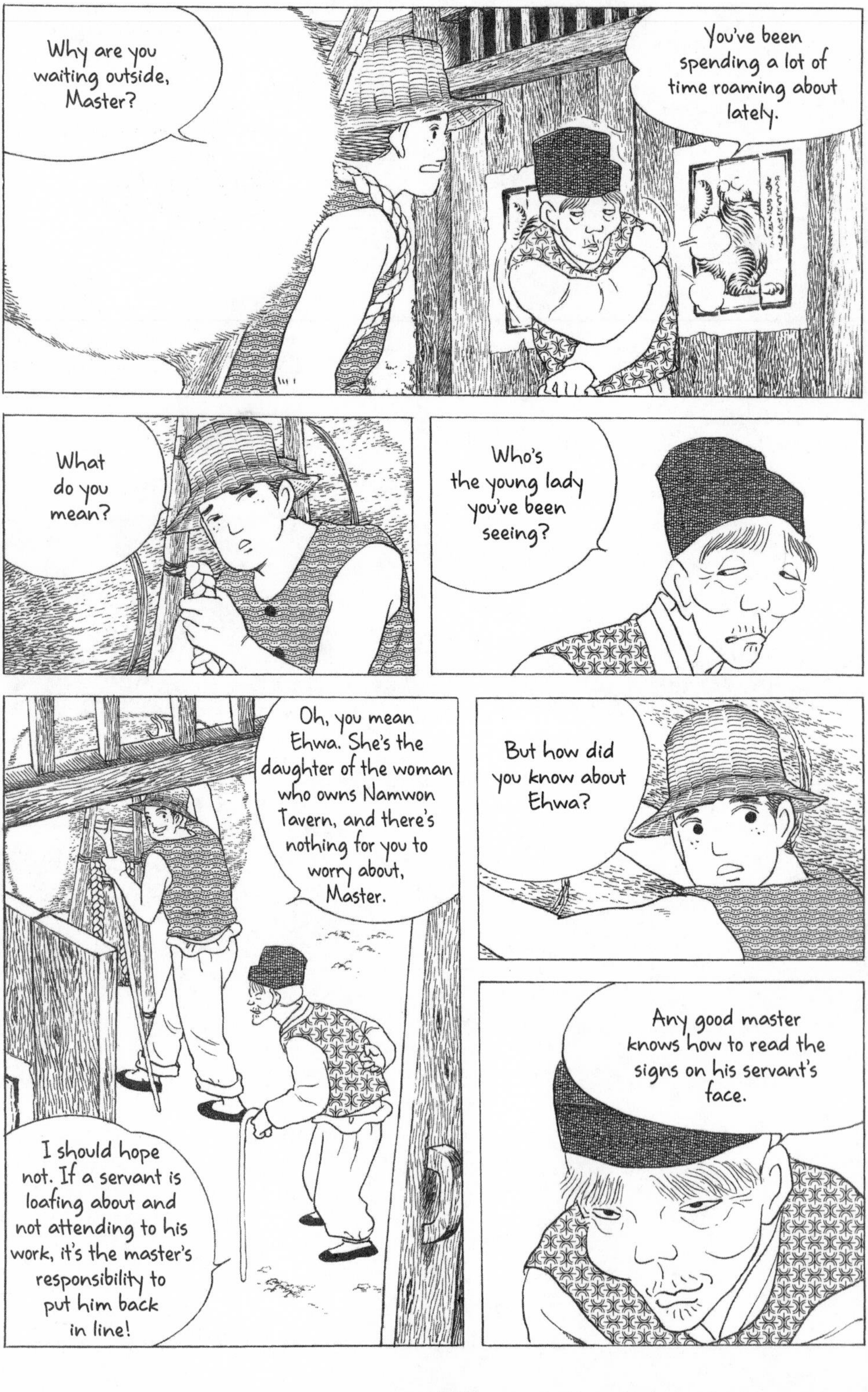
Why are you waiting outside, Master?
You've been spending a lot of time roaming about lately.
What do you mean?
Who's the young lady you've been seeing?
Oh, you mean Ehwa. She's the daughter of the woman who owns Namwon Tavern, and there's nothing for you to worry about, Master.
I should hope not. If a servant is loafing about and not attending to his work, it's the master's responsibility to put him back in line!
But how did you know about Ehwa?
Any good master knows how to read the signs on his servant's face.

The sesame field near the rock quarry is a mess. I'd like you to spend a few nights there to attend to it.

But Master, why send me away when there's so much work to be done here?

I'm sending you there because you're diligent and good with your hands. It looks like we'll have an abundant sesame seed harvest, so I need someone good minding the field.

I've prepared a pot and some food on the back porch, so take it with you and leave immediately.

Yes, sir.

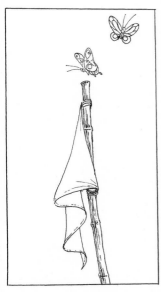

Oh my, what brings Master Cho to my humble abode?

What do you think? I have a favor to request of you, the village shaman.

239

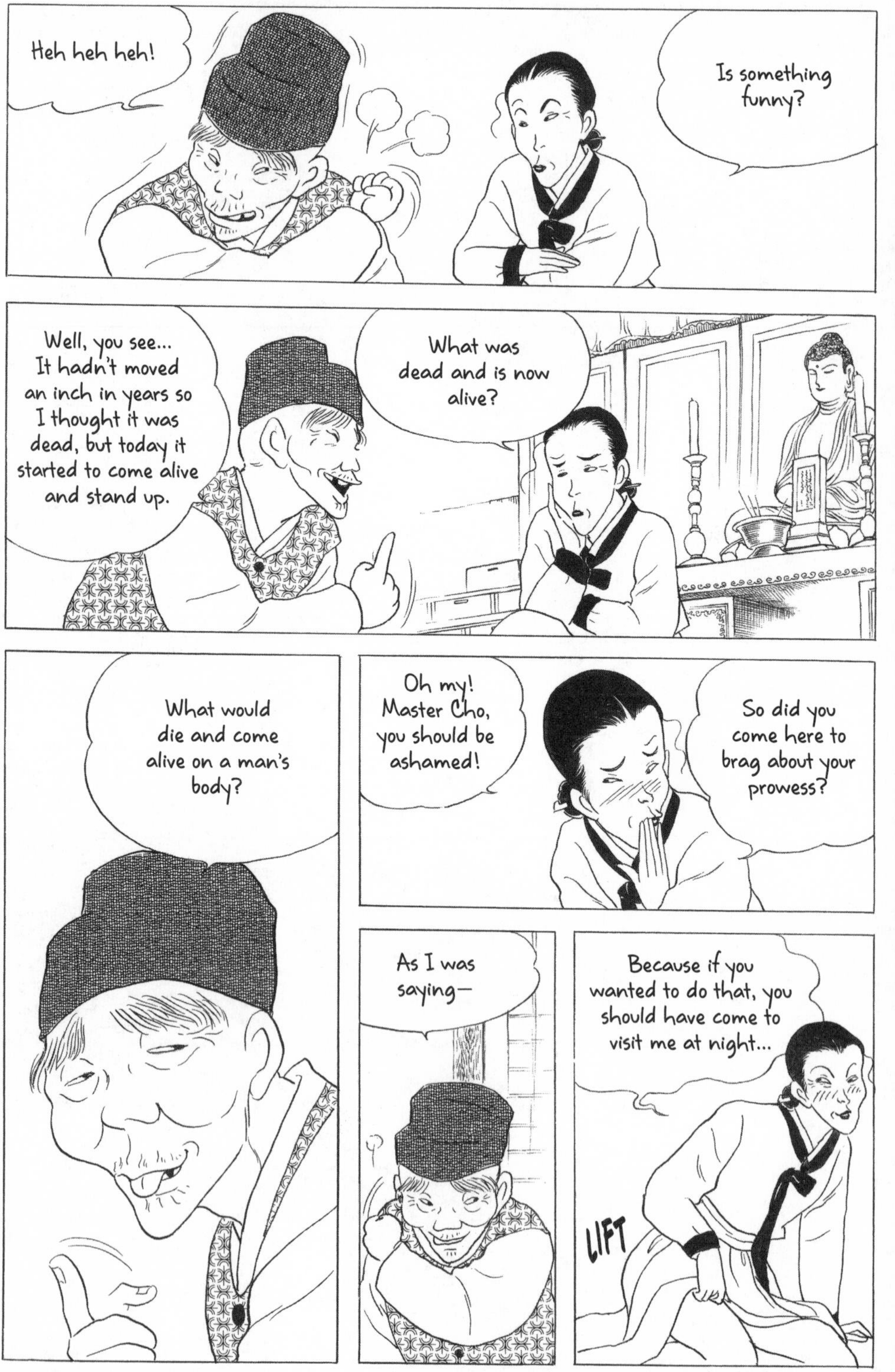
Heh heh heh!
Is something funny?
Well, you see... It hadn't moved an inch in years so I thought it was dead, but today it started to come alive and stand up.
What was dead and is now alive?
What would die and come alive on a man's body?
Oh my! Master Cho, you should be ashamed!
So did you come here to brag about your prowess?
As I was saying—
Because if you wanted to do that, you should have come to visit me at night...
LIFT

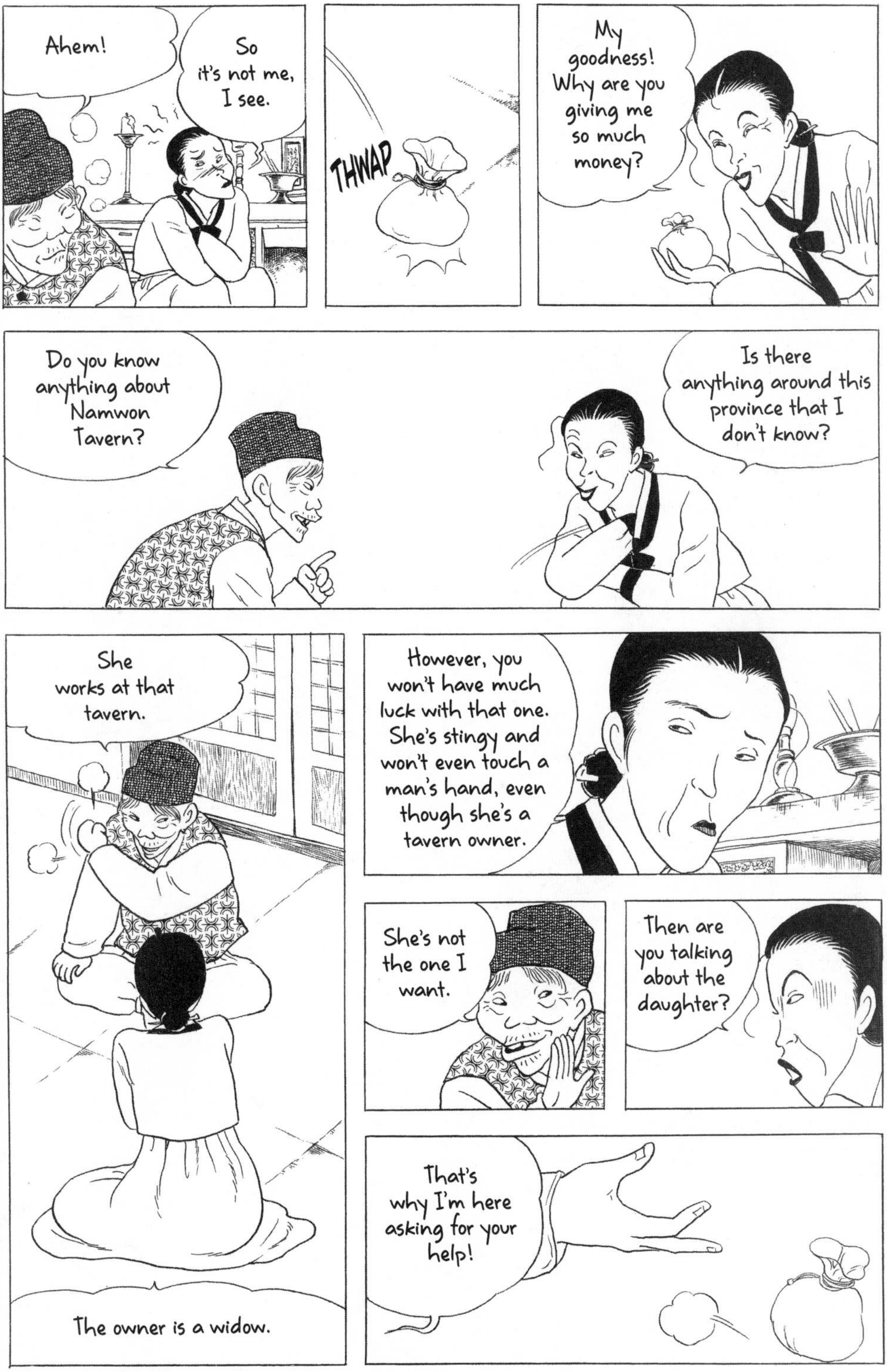
Ahem!
So it's not me, I see.
THWAP
My goodness! Why are you giving me so much money?
Do you know anything about Namwon Tavern?
Is there anything around this province that I don't know?
She works at that tavern.
The owner is a widow.
However, you won't have much luck with that one. She's stingy and won't even touch a man's hand, even though she's a tavern owner.
She's not the one I want.
Then are you talking about the daughter?
That's why I'm here asking for your help!

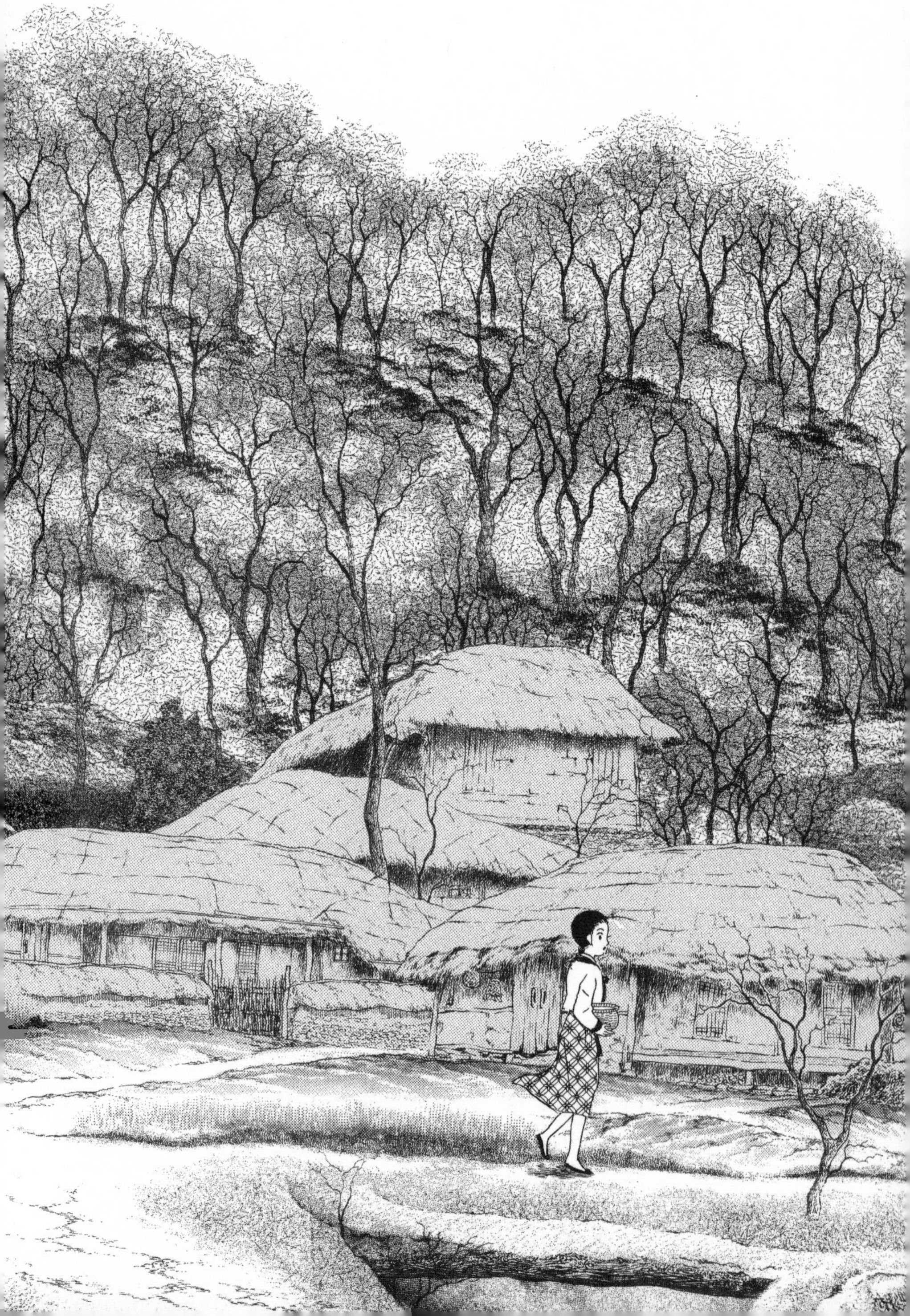

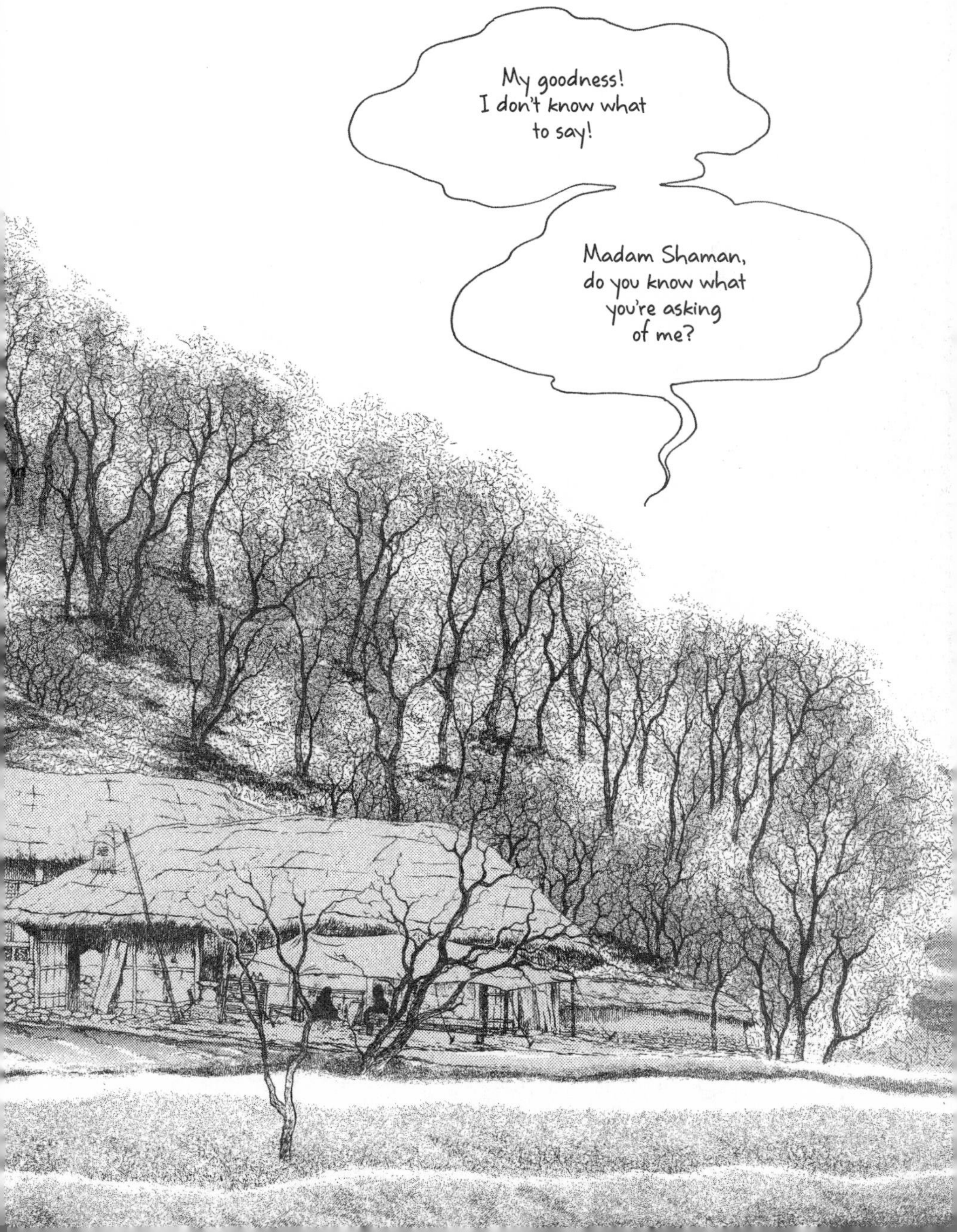
My goodness! I don't know what to say!
Madam Shaman, do you know what you're asking of me?

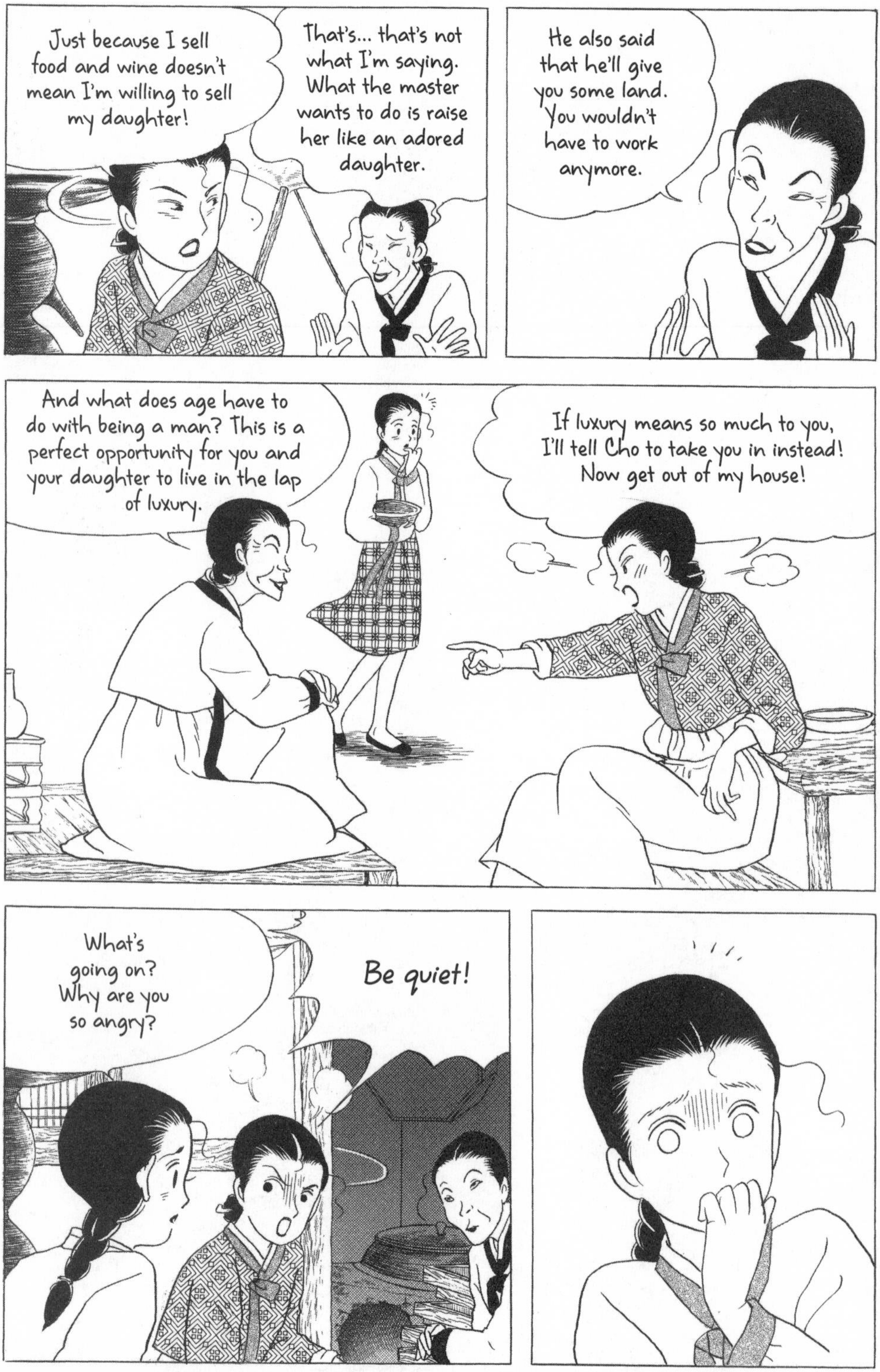
Just because I sell food and wine doesn't mean I'm willing to sell my daughter!
That's... that's not what I'm saying. What the master wants to do is raise her like an adored daughter.
He also said that he'll give you some land. You wouldn't have to work anymore.
And what does age have to do with being a man? This is a perfect opportunity for you and your daughter to live in the lap of luxury.
If luxury means so much to you, I'll tell Cho to take you in instead! Now get out of my house!
What's going on? Why are you so angry?
Be quiet!

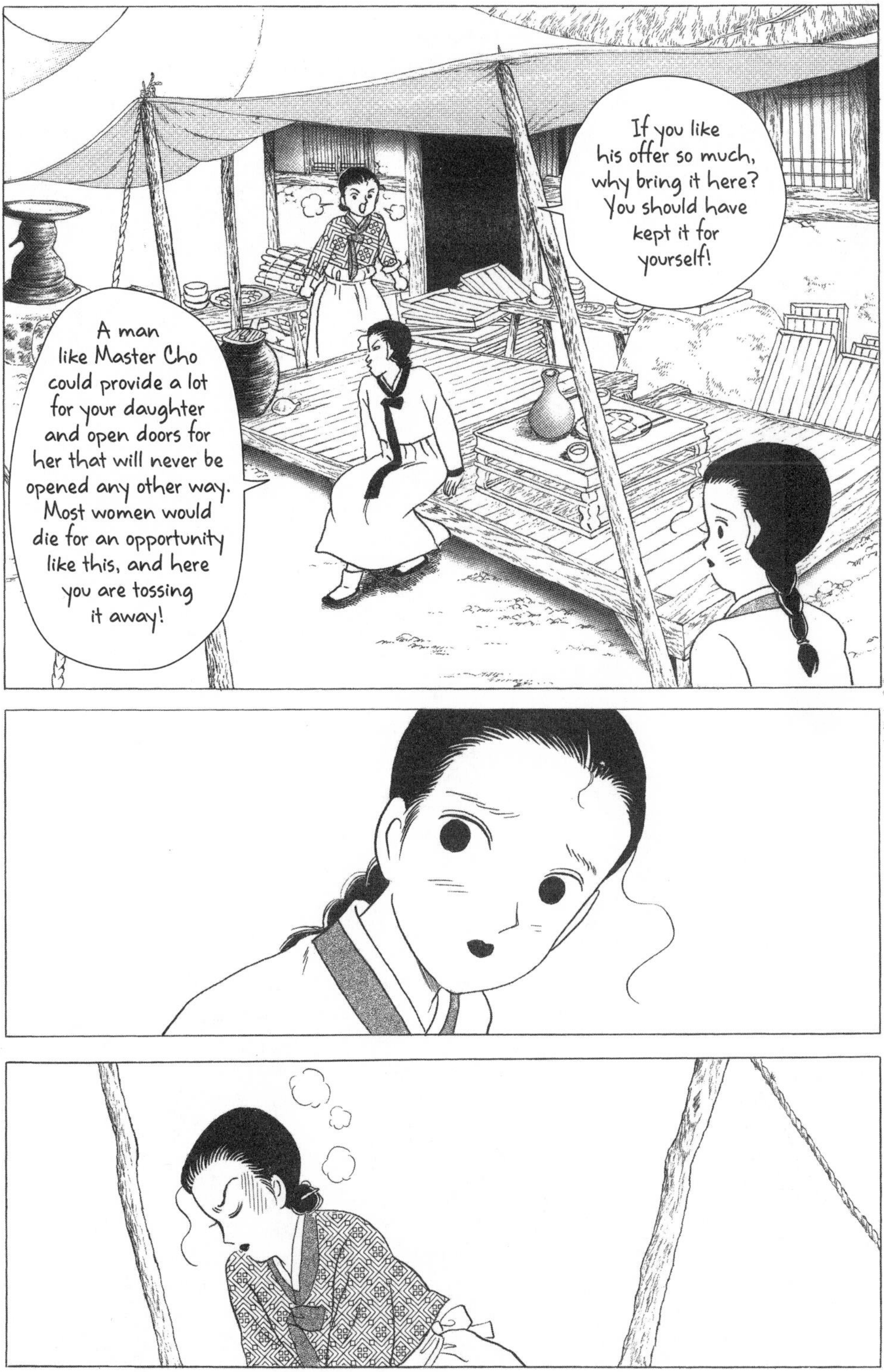
A man like Master Cho could provide a lot for your daughter and open doors for her that will never be opened any other way. Most women would die for an opportunity like this, and here you are tossing it away!
If you like his offer so much, why bring it here? You should have kept it for yourself!

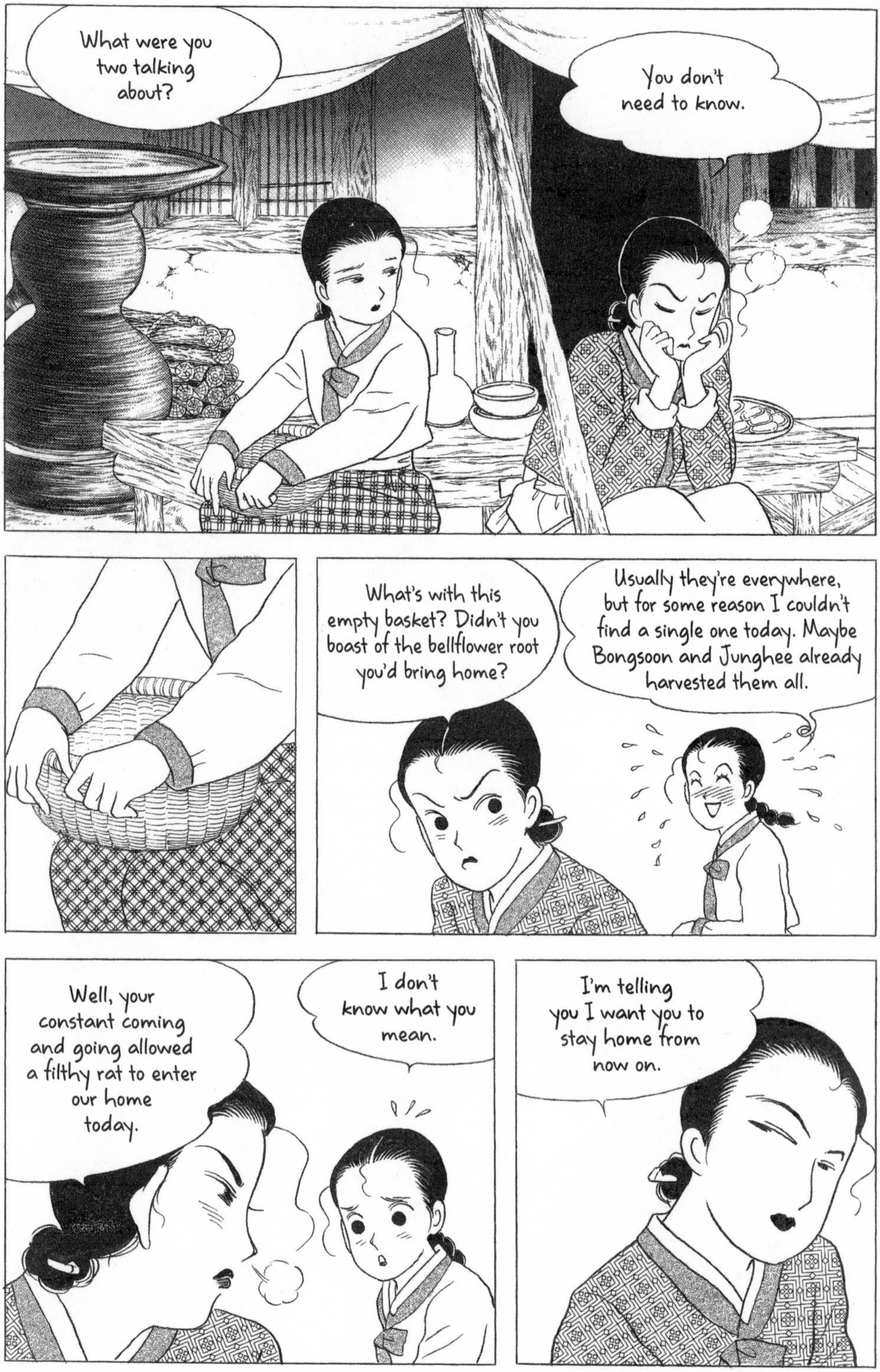
What were you two talking about?
You don't need to know.
What's with this empty basket? Didn't you boast of the bellflower root you'd bring home?
Usually they're everywhere, but for some reason I couldn't find a single one today. Maybe Bongsoon and Junghee already harvested them all.
Well, your constant coming and going allowed a filthy rat to enter our home today.
I don't know what you mean.
I'm telling you I want you to stay home from now on.

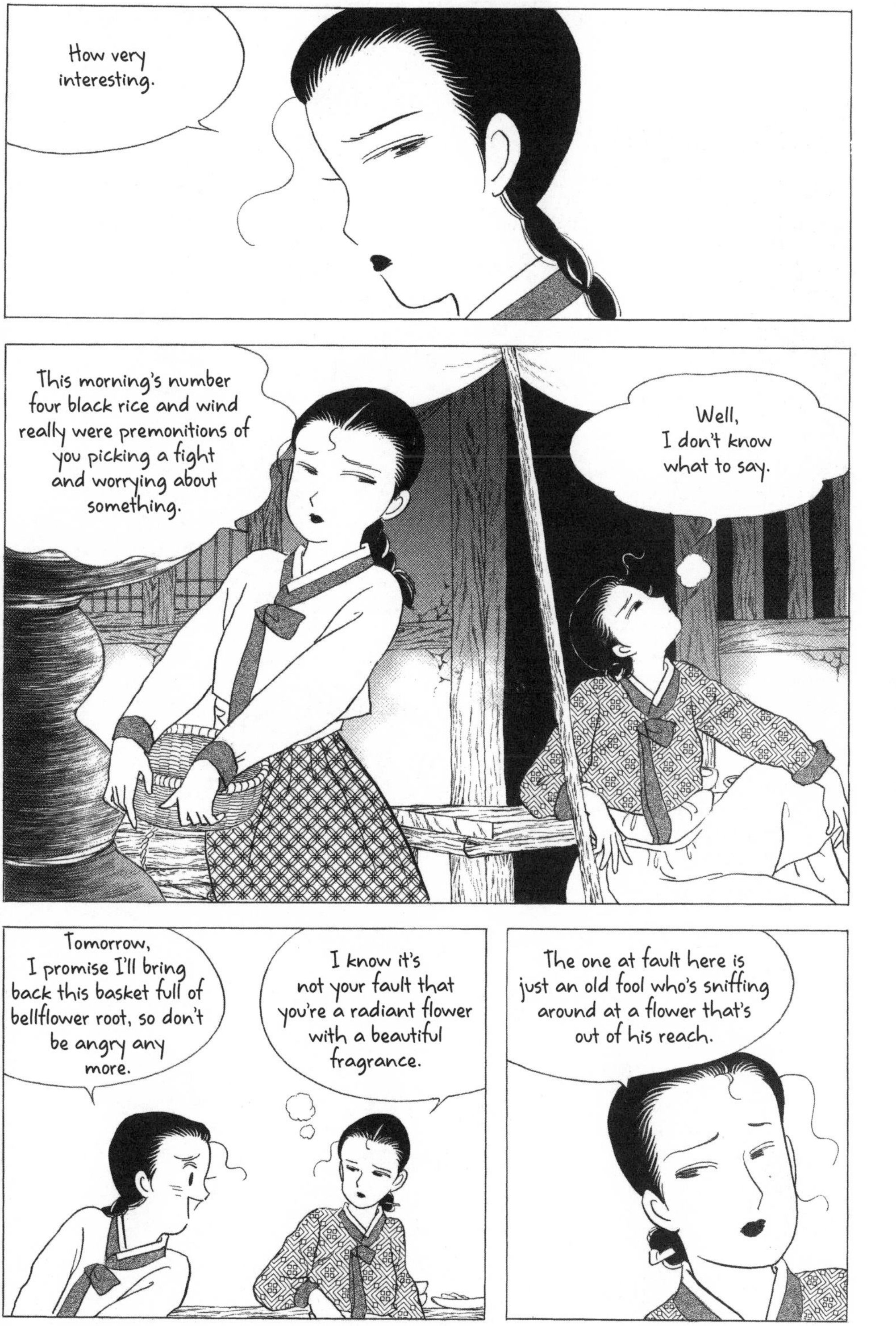
How very interesting.
This morning's number four black rice and wind really were premonitions of you picking a fight and worrying about something.
Well, I don't know what to say.
Tomorrow, I promise I'll bring back this basket full of bellflower root, so don't be angry any more.
I know it's not your fault that you're a radiant flower with a beautiful fragrance.
The one at fault here is just an old fool who's sniffing around at a flower that's out of his reach.

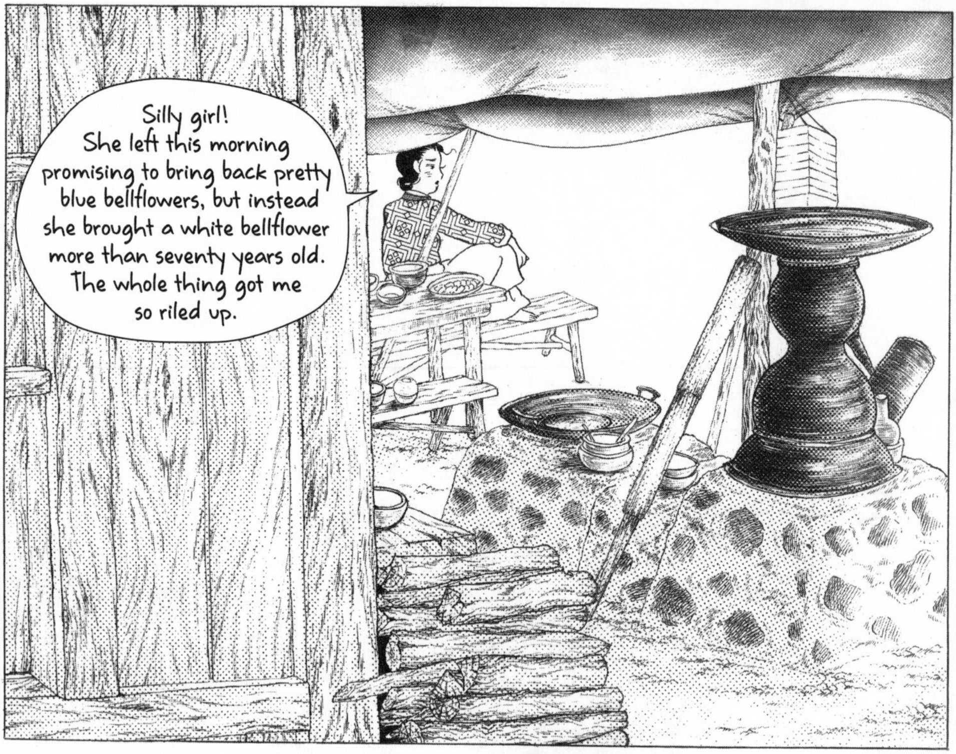
Silly girl! She left this morning promising to bring back pretty blue bellflowers, but instead she brought a white bellflower more than seventy years old. The whole thing got me so riled up.

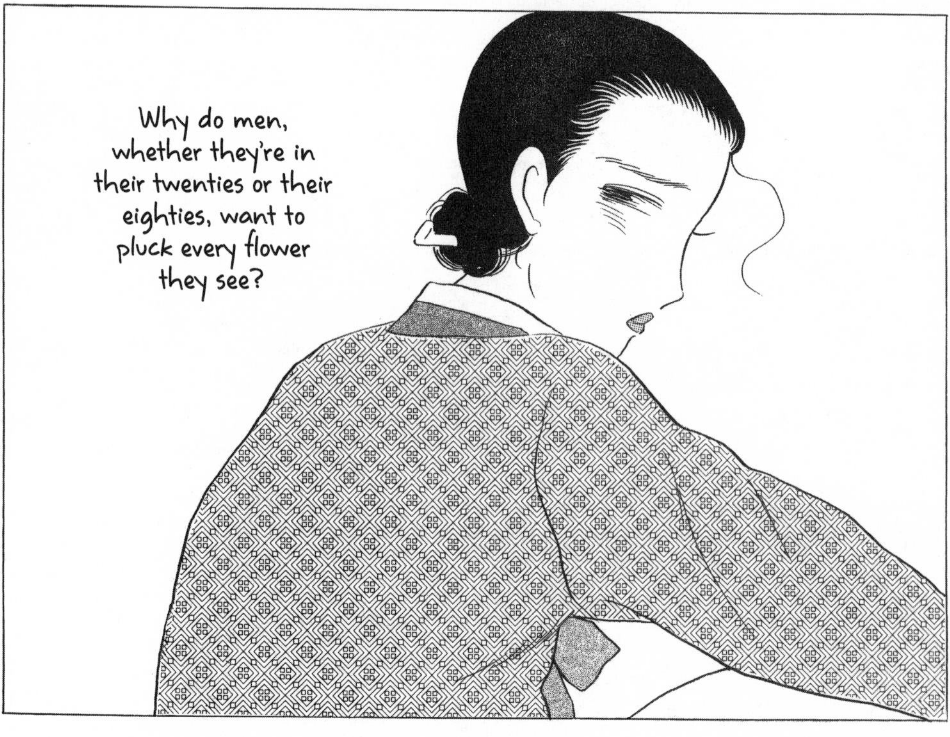
Why do men, whether they're in their twenties or their eighties, want to pluck every flower they see?

Chapter Nine
FORTUNATE LIFE

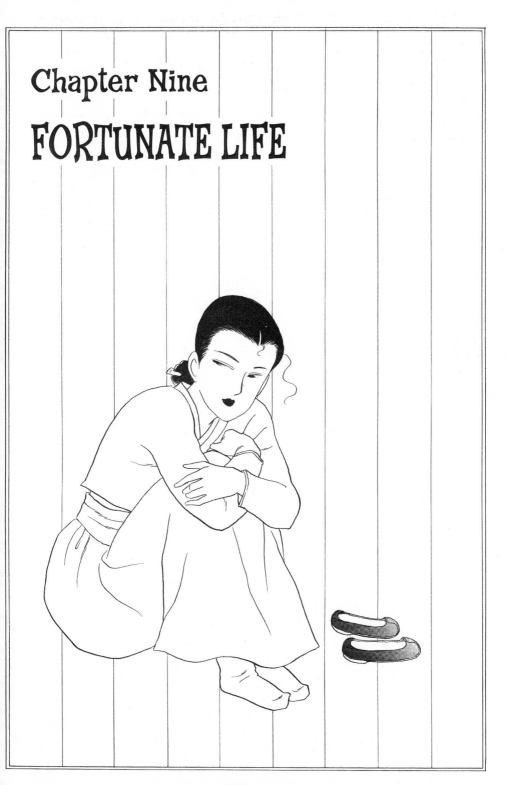

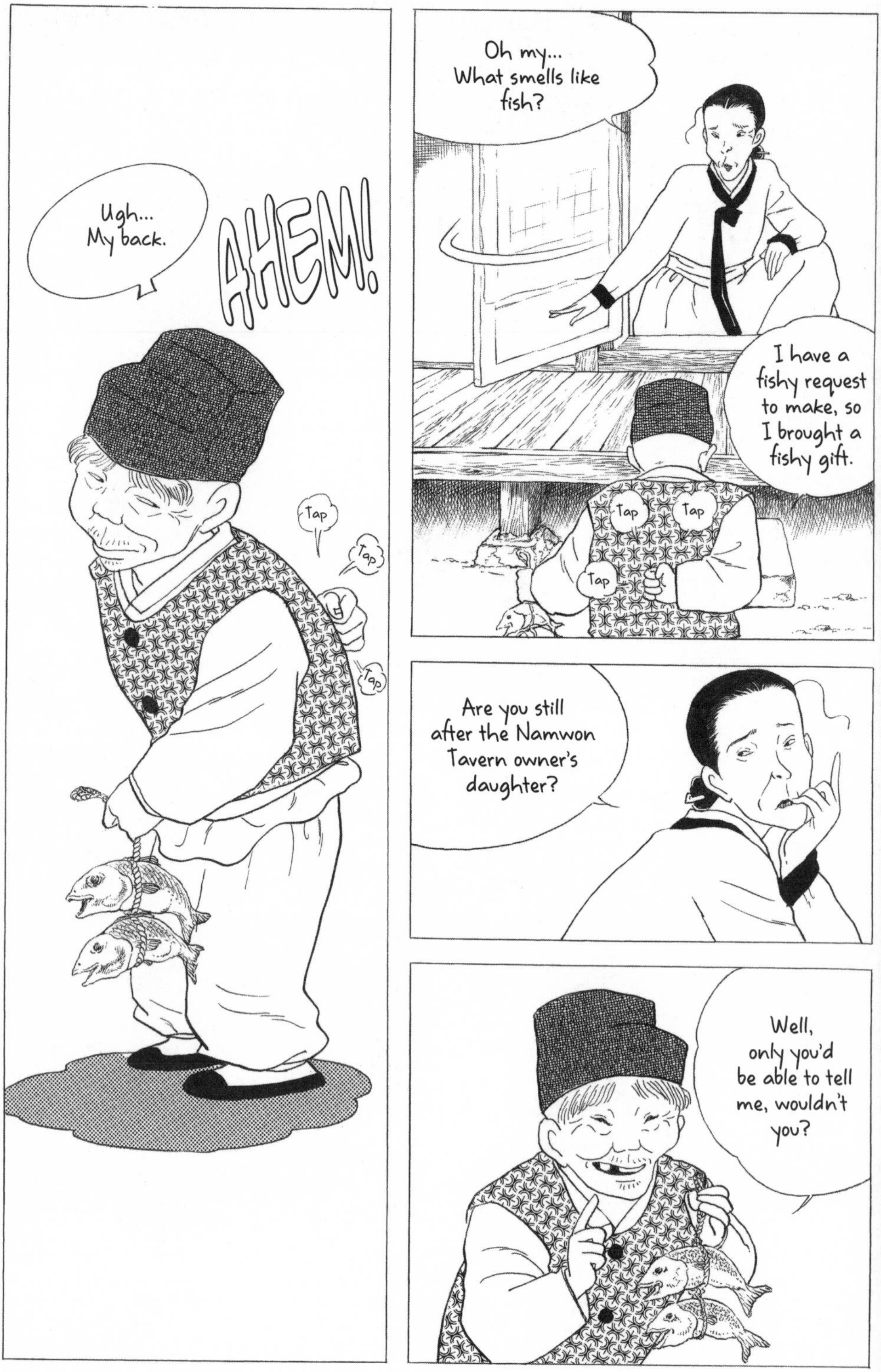
Ugh... My back.
AHEM!
Tap
Tap
Tap
Oh my... What smells like fish?
I have a fishy request to make, so I brought a fishy gift.
Tap
Tap
Tap
Are you still after the Namwon Tavern owner's daughter?
Well, only you'd be able to tell me, wouldn't you?

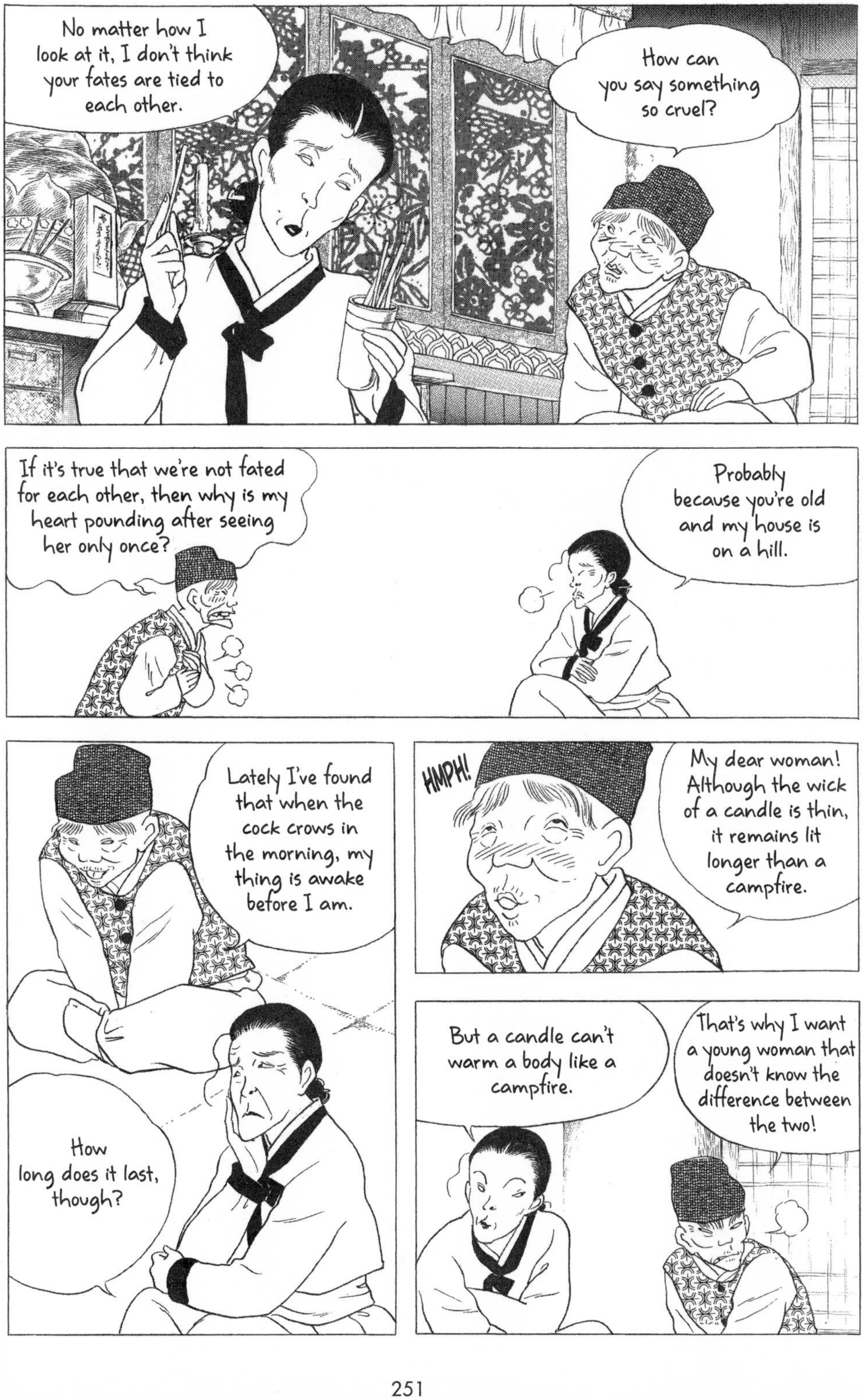
No matter how I look at it, I don't think your fates are tied to each other.
How can you say something so cruel?
If it's true that we're not fated for each other, then why is my heart pounding after seeing her only once?
Probably because you're old and my house is on a hill.
Lately I've found that when the cock crows in the morning, my thing is awake before I am.
How long does it last, though?
HMPH!
My dear woman! Although the wick of a candle is thin, it remains lit longer than a campfire.
But a candle can't warm a body like a campfire.
That's why I want a young woman that doesn't know the difference between the two!

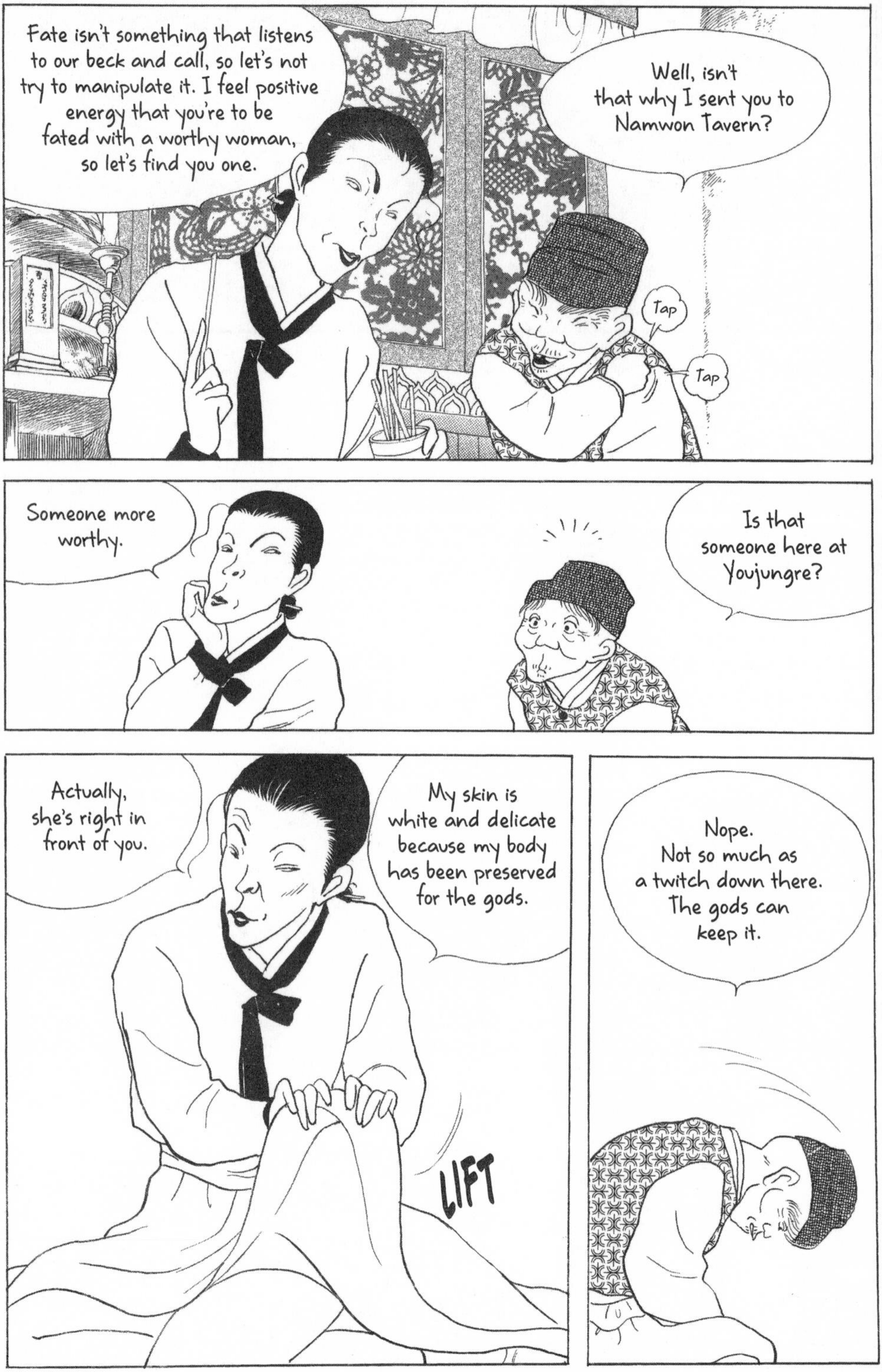
Fate isn't something that listens to our beck and call, so let's not try to manipulate it. I feel positive energy that you're to be fated with a worthy woman, so let's find you one.
Well, isn't that why I sent you to Namwon Tavern?
Tap
Tap
Someone more worthy.
Is that someone here at Youjungre?
Actually, she's right in front of you.
My skin is white and delicate because my body has been preserved for the gods.
LIFT
Nope. Not so much as a twitch down there. The gods can keep it.

I guess arousal isn't contagious.

I'm not giving up so easily. Take her this gold and silver, as well as this deed to the tobacco field next to the mill, and bring the girl to me.

SSSK

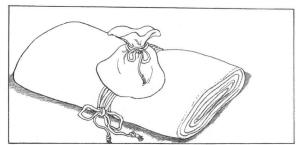

Apparently, no one told his groin that he's no longer a young man.

I'll watch your house for you! You just hurry up and get going now!

253

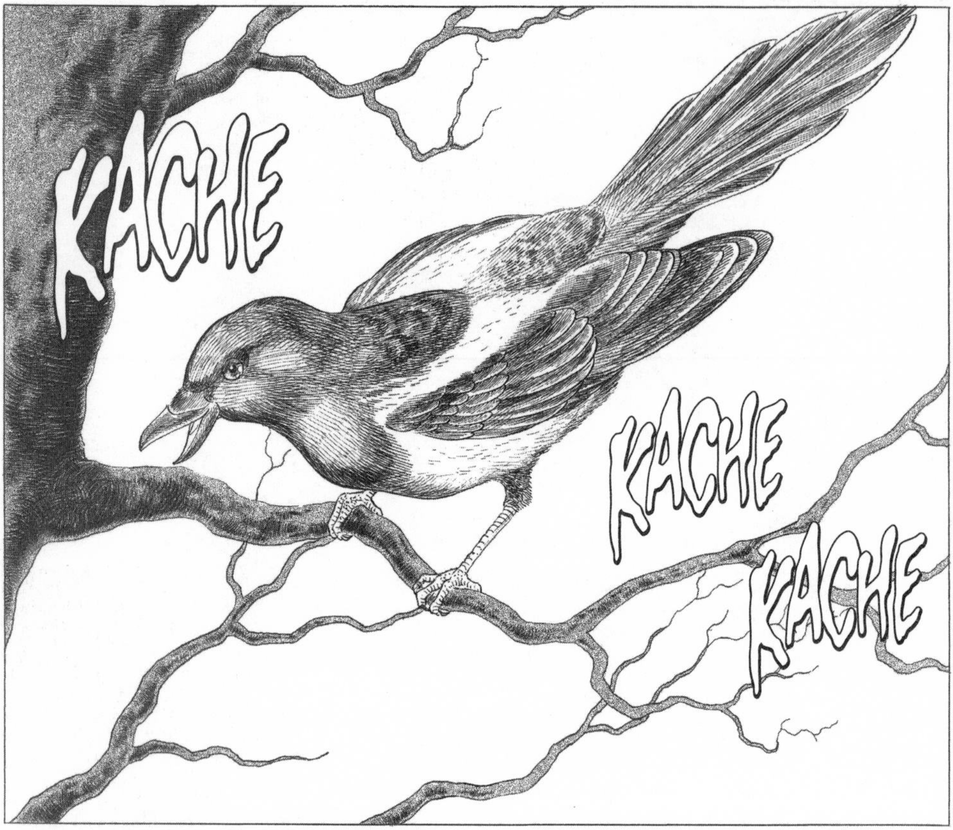
KACHE
KACHE
KACHE

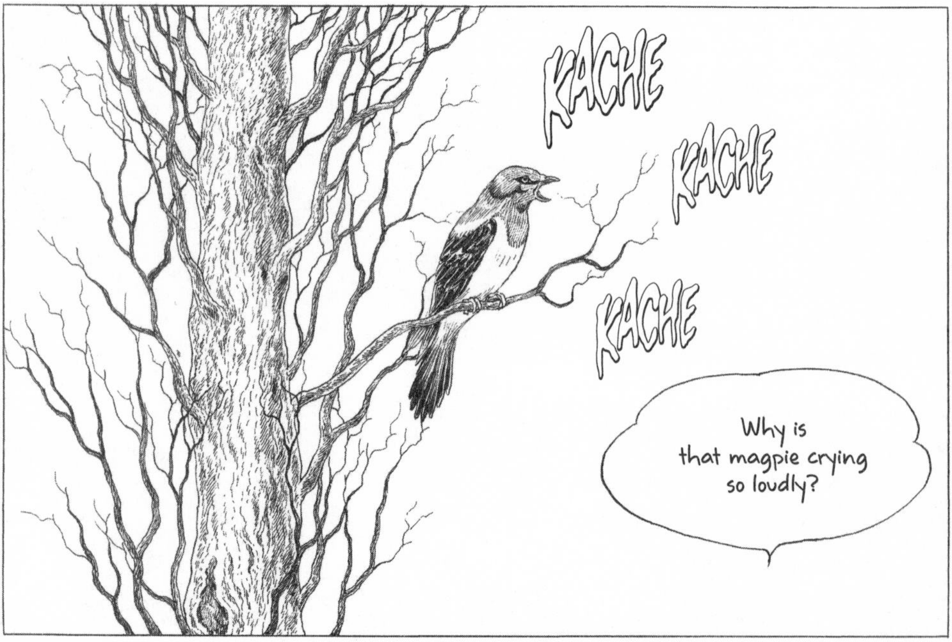
KACHE
KACHE
KACHE
Why is that magpie crying so loudly?

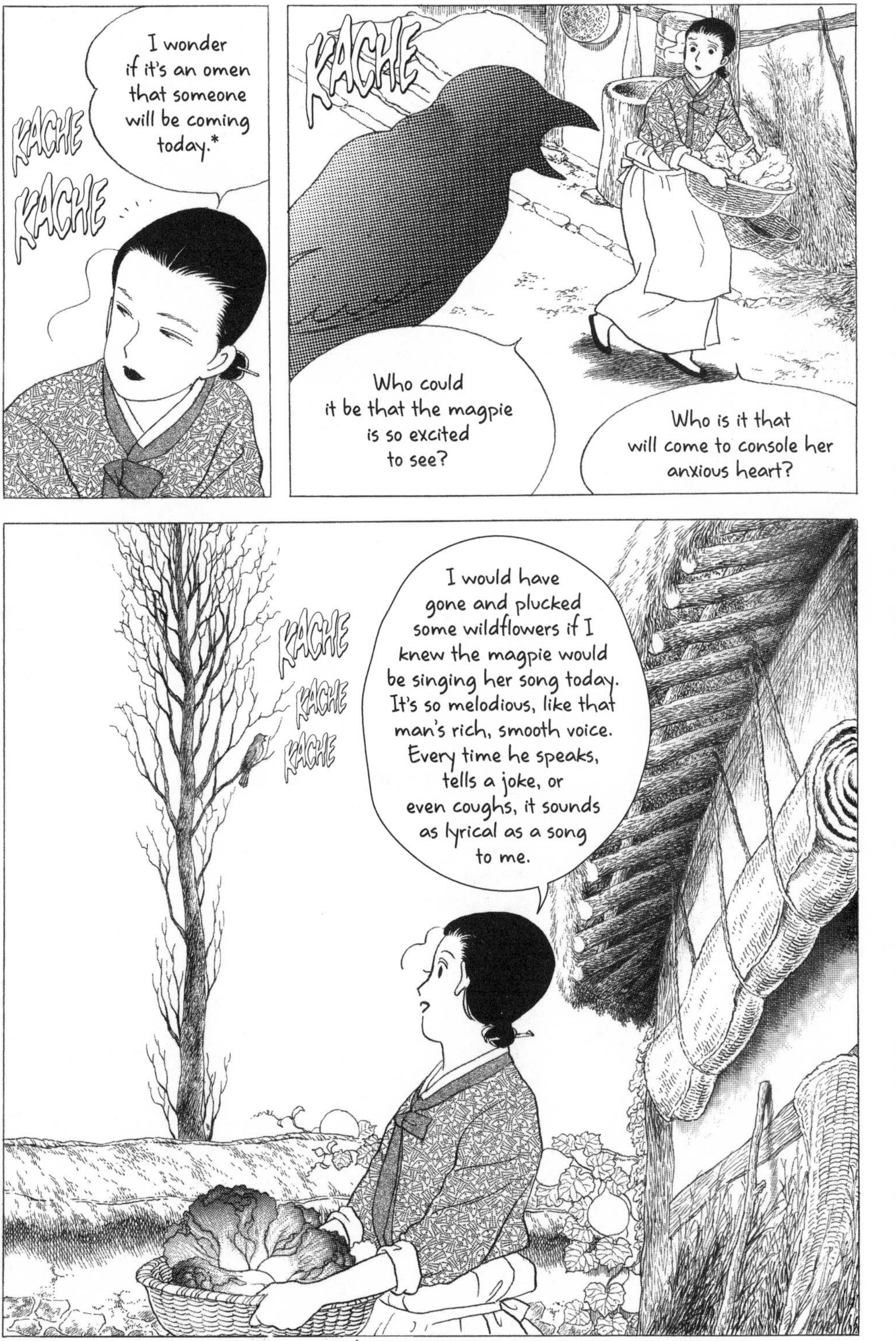
I wonder if it's an omen that someone will be coming today.*
KACHE
KACHE
KACHE
Who could it be that the magpie is so excited to see?
Who is it that will come to console her anxious heart?
KACHE
KACHE
KACHE
I would have gone and plucked some wildflowers if I knew the magpie would be singing her song today. It's so melodious, like that man's rich, smooth voice. Every time he speaks, tells a joke, or even coughs, it sounds as lyrical as a song to me.

* The magpie is believed to herald good news or the arrival of an important person.

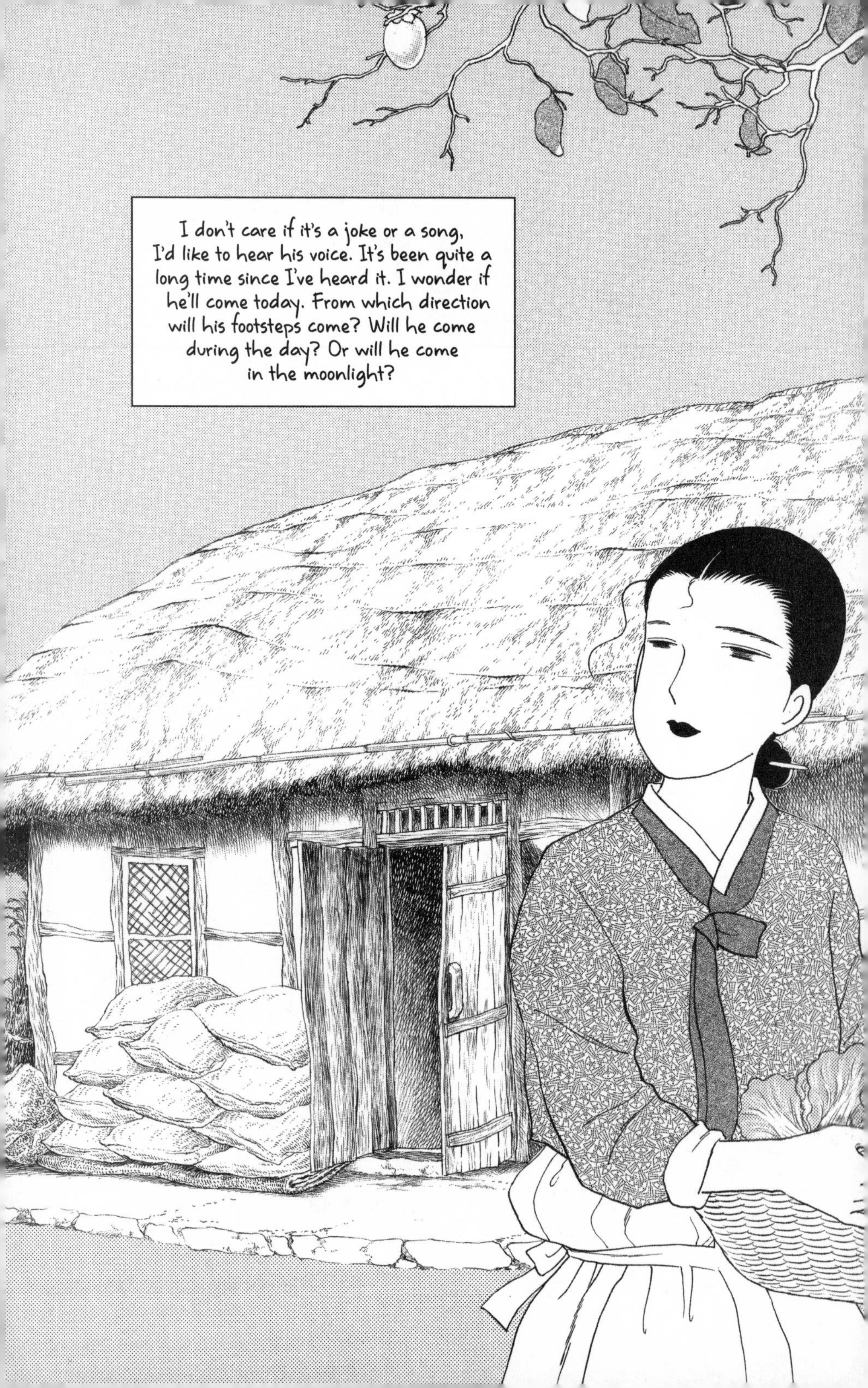
I don't care if it's a joke or a song, I'd like to hear his voice. It's been quite a long time since I've heard it. I wonder if he'll come today. From which direction will his footsteps come? Will he come during the day? Or will he come in the moonlight?

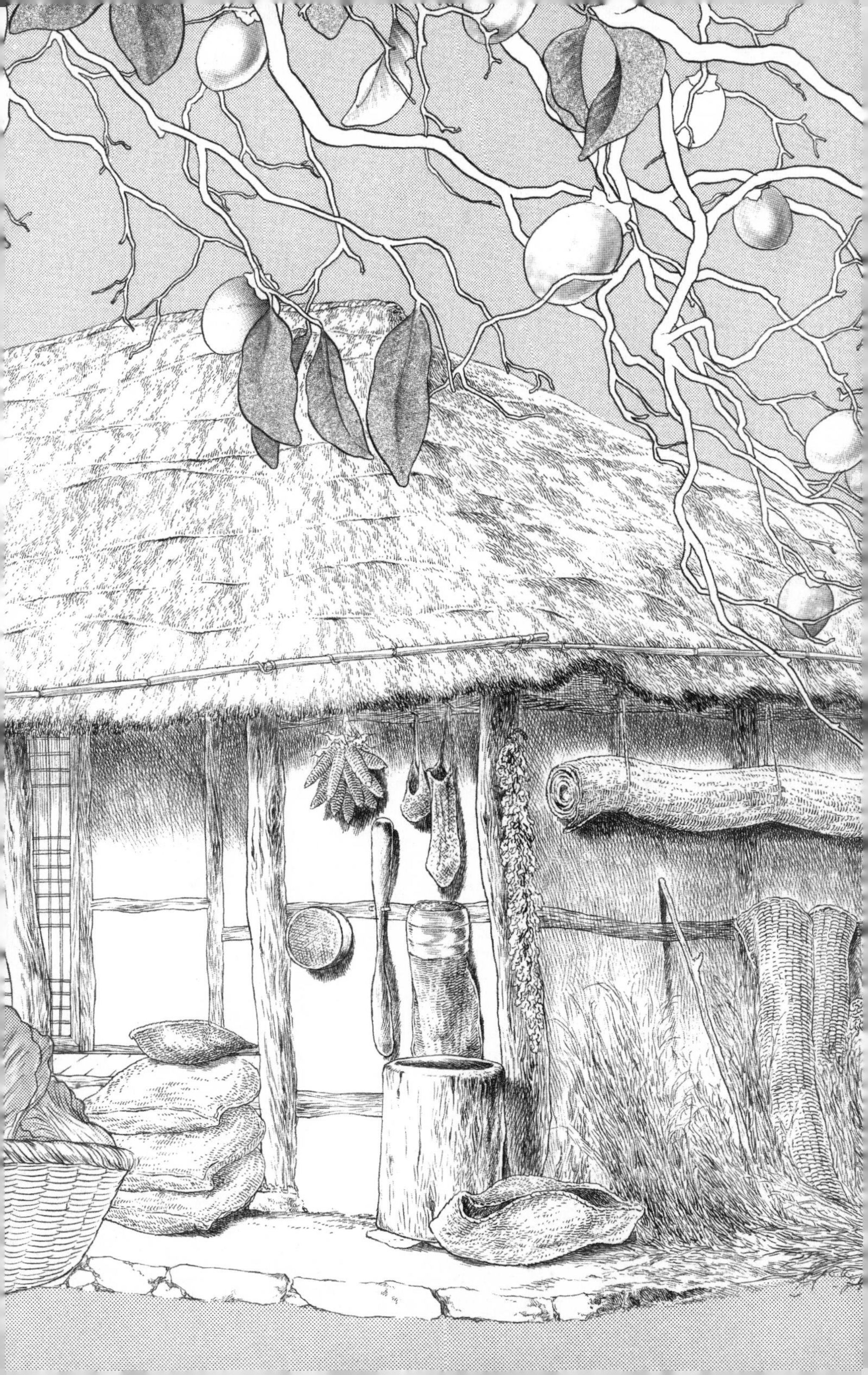

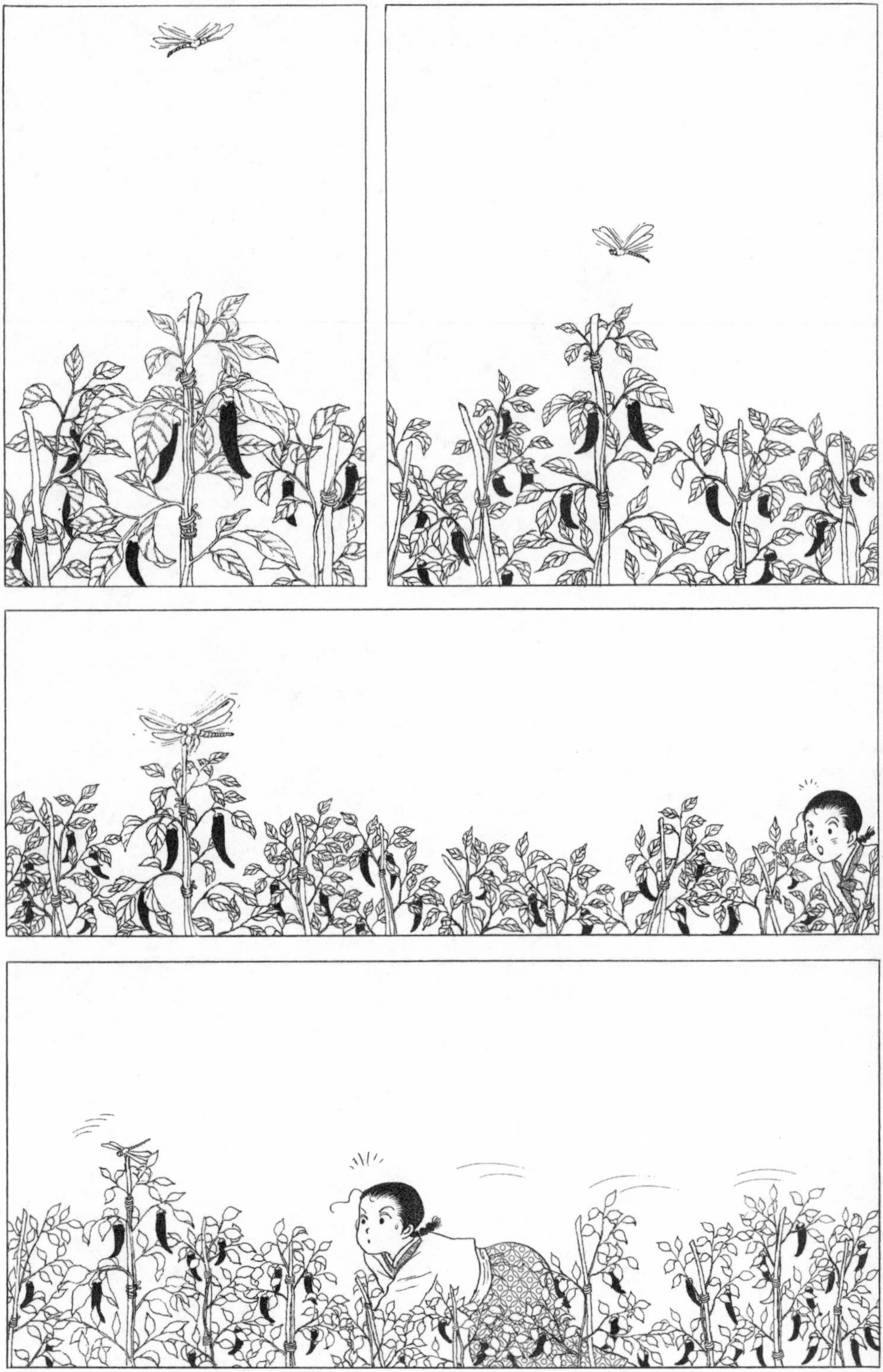

Did you catch it?

FLUTTER FLUTTER

Seeing how she's been loitering in the pepper field, she must be really anxious to get married.

Then I guess we should marry her off.

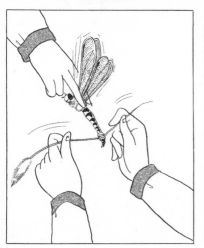

Who shall we marry her off to?

If she flies east, we'll marry her off to an egg merchant. If she flies west, then we'll marry her off to a wig merchant.

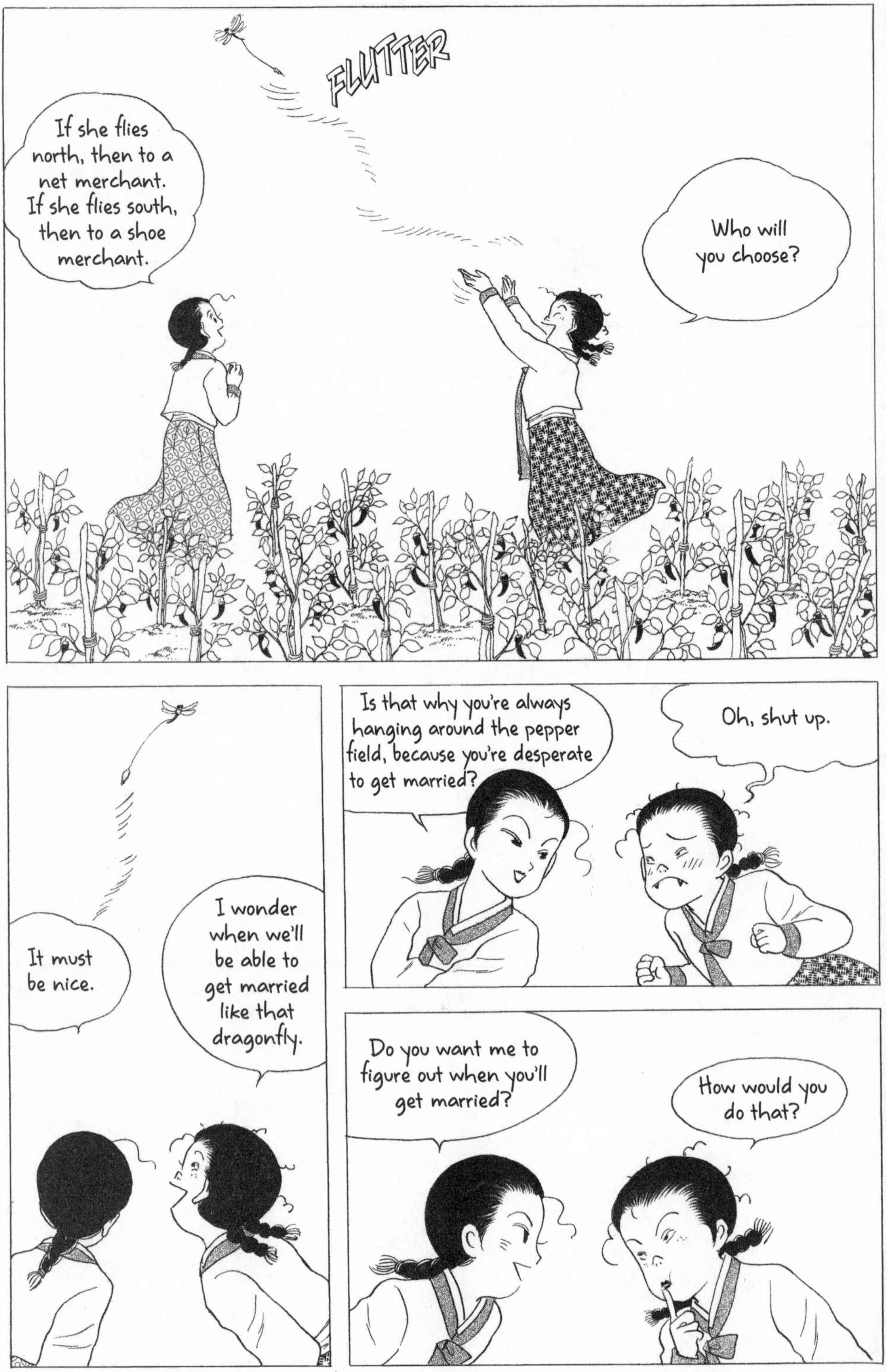
FLUTTER
If she flies north, then to a net merchant. If she flies south, then to a shoe merchant.
Who will you choose?
It must be nice.
I wonder when we'll be able to get married like that dragonfly.
Is that why you're always hanging around the pepper field, because you're desperate to get married?
Oh, shut up.
Do you want me to figure out when you'll get married?
How would you do that?

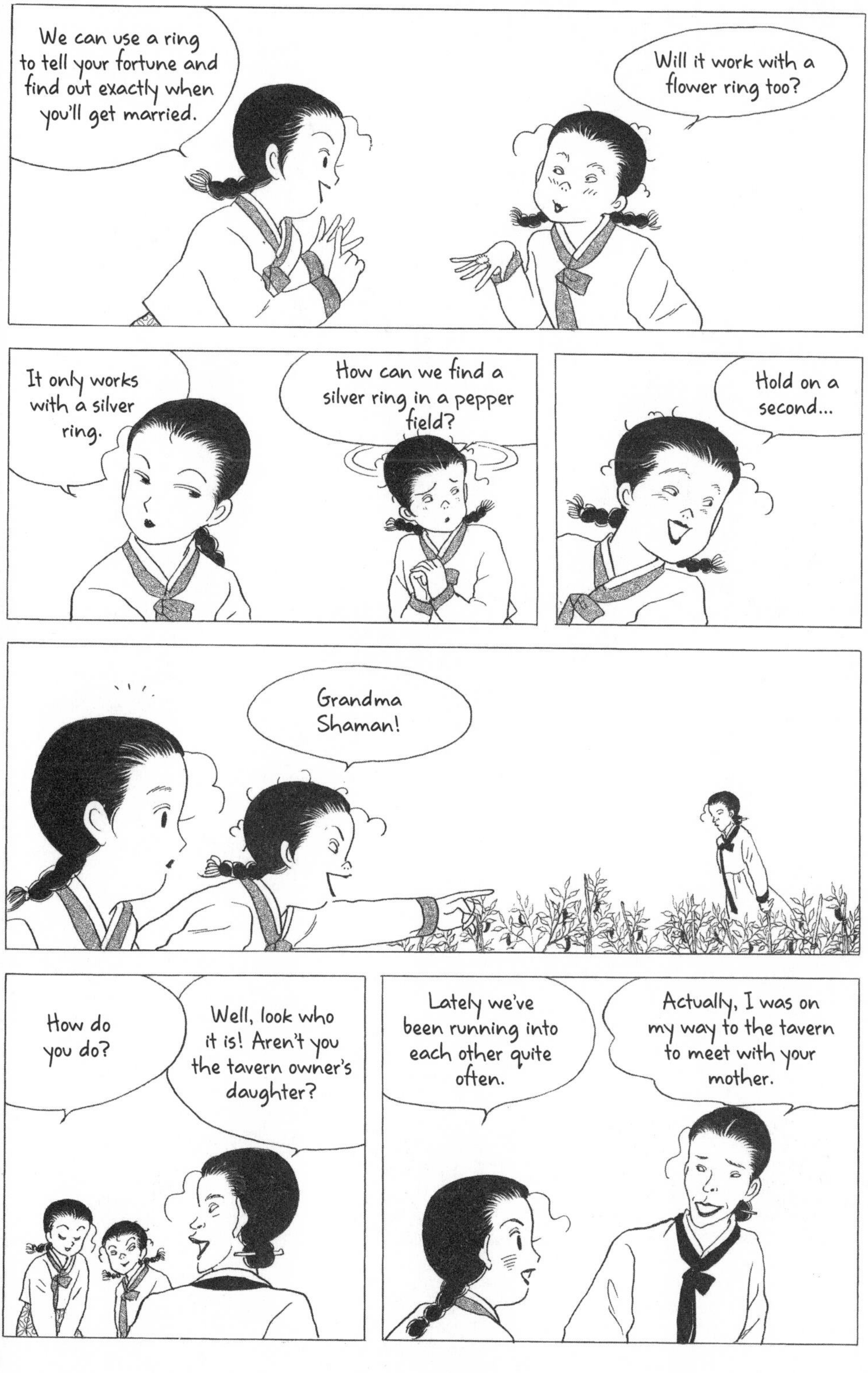
We can use a ring to tell your fortune and find out exactly when you'll get married.
Will it work with a flower ring too?
It only works with a silver ring.
How can we find a silver ring in a pepper field?
Hold on a second...
Grandma Shaman!
How do you do?
Well, look who it is! Aren't you the tavern owner's daughter?
Lately we've been running into each other quite often.
Actually, I was on my way to the tavern to meet with your mother.

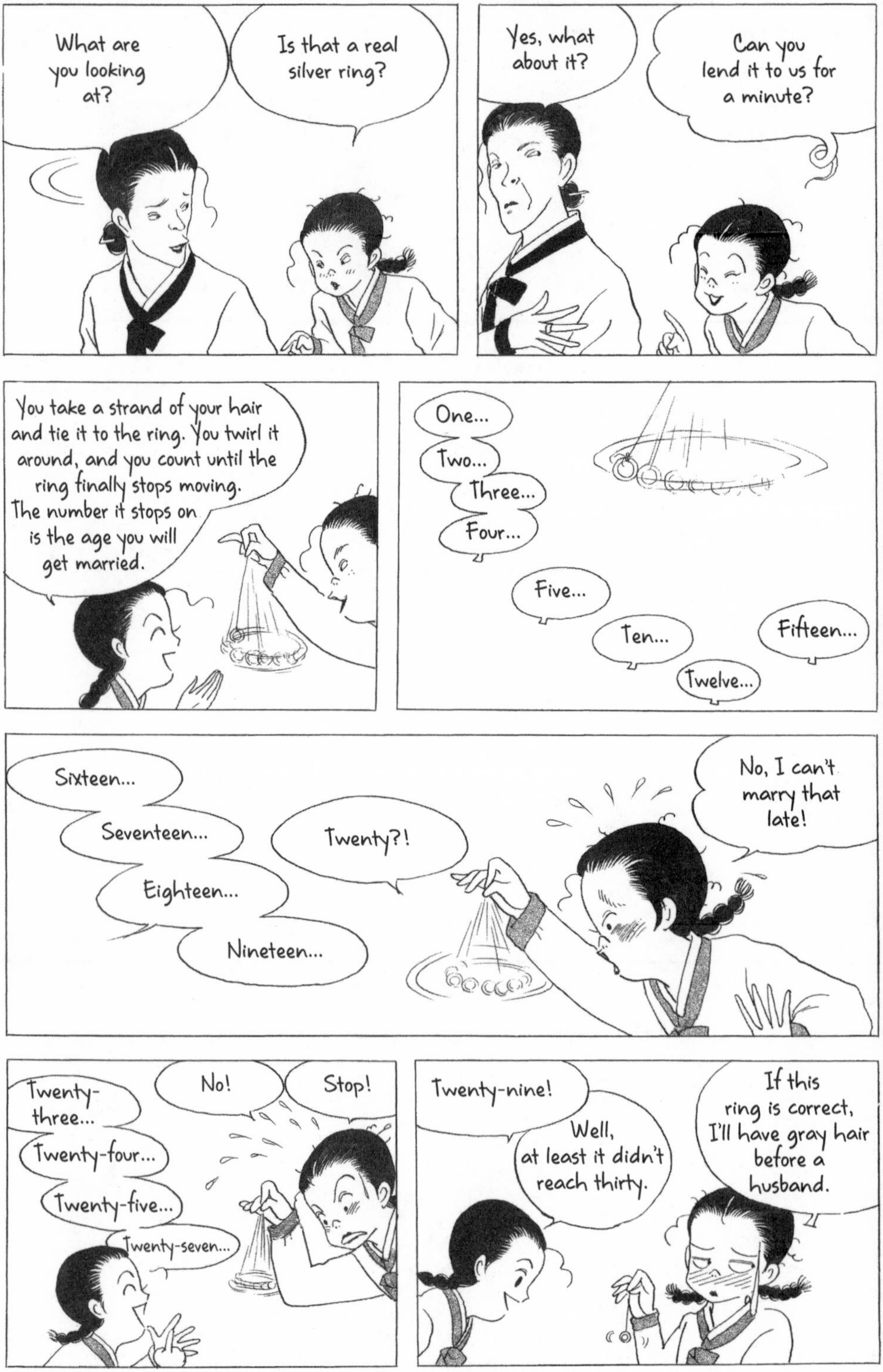
What are you looking at?
Is that a real silver ring?
Yes, what about it?
Can you lend it to us for a minute?
You take a strand of your hair and tie it to the ring. You twirl it around, and you count until the ring finally stops moving. The number it stops on is the age you will get married.
One...
Two...
Three...
Four...
Five...
Ten...
Twelve...
Fifteen...
Sixteen...
Seventeen...
Eighteen...
Nineteen...
Twenty?!
No, I can't marry that late!
Twenty-three...
No!
Stop!
Twenty-four...
Twenty-five...
Twenty-seven...
Twenty-nine!
Well, at least it didn't reach thirty.
If this ring is correct, I'll have gray hair before a husband.

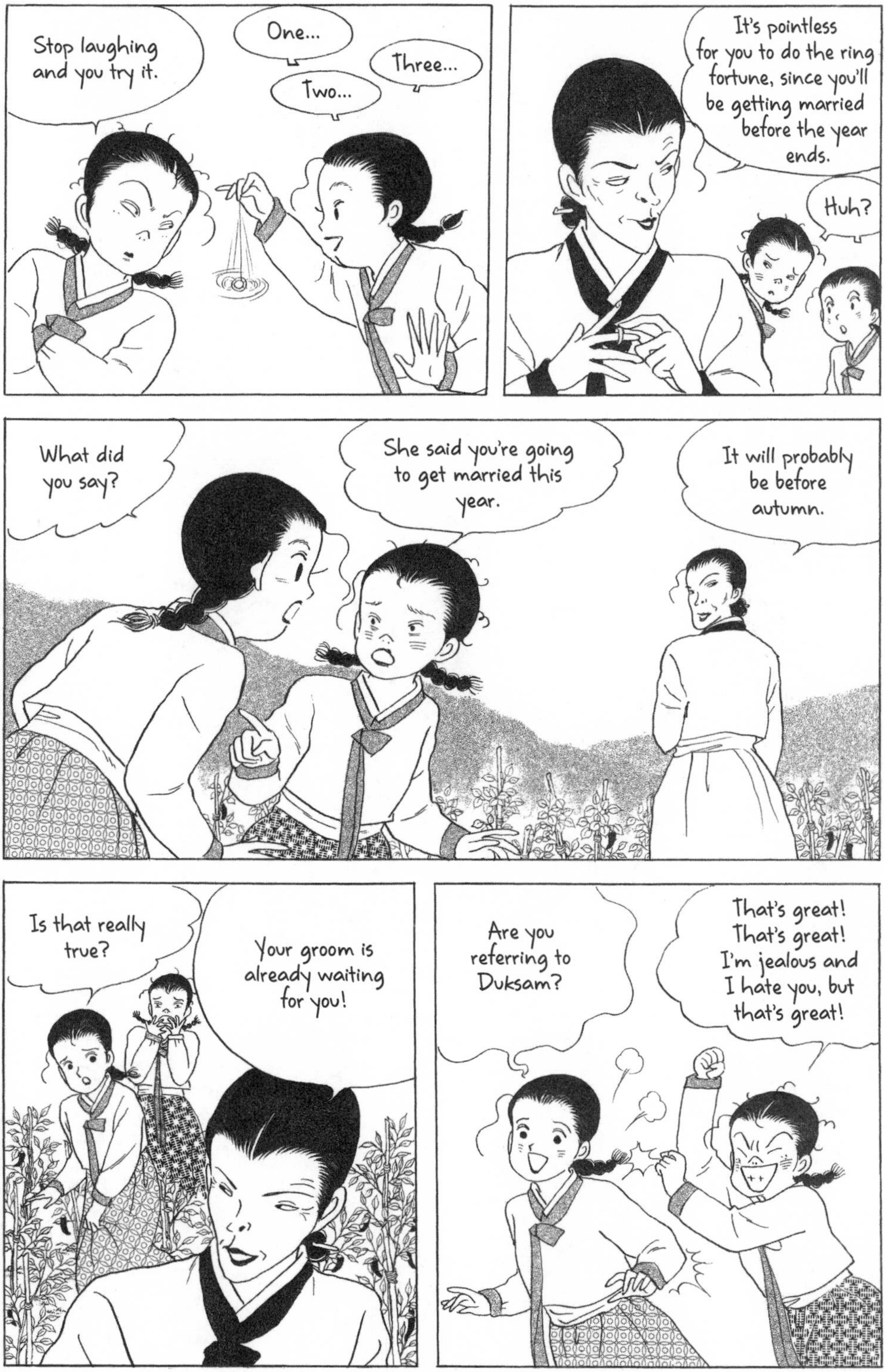
Stop laughing and you try it.
One...
Two...
Three...
It's pointless for you to do the ring fortune, since you'll be getting married before the year ends.
Huh?
What did you say?
She said you're going to get married this year.
It will probably be before autumn.
Is that really true?
Your groom is already waiting for you!
Are you referring to Duksam?
That's great! That's great! I'm jealous and I hate you, but that's great!

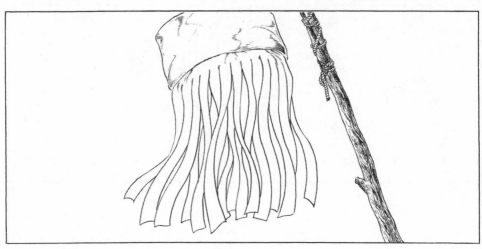

Why are you bringing that up again? I thought we already ended that discussion last time you were here.

I didn't come today to discuss things with you. I came today to complete a transaction.

I have nothing to transact with you, Grandma Shaman.

You work so hard trying to put food on the table for two. Imagine how much easier you'd have it if you had just one mouth to feed.

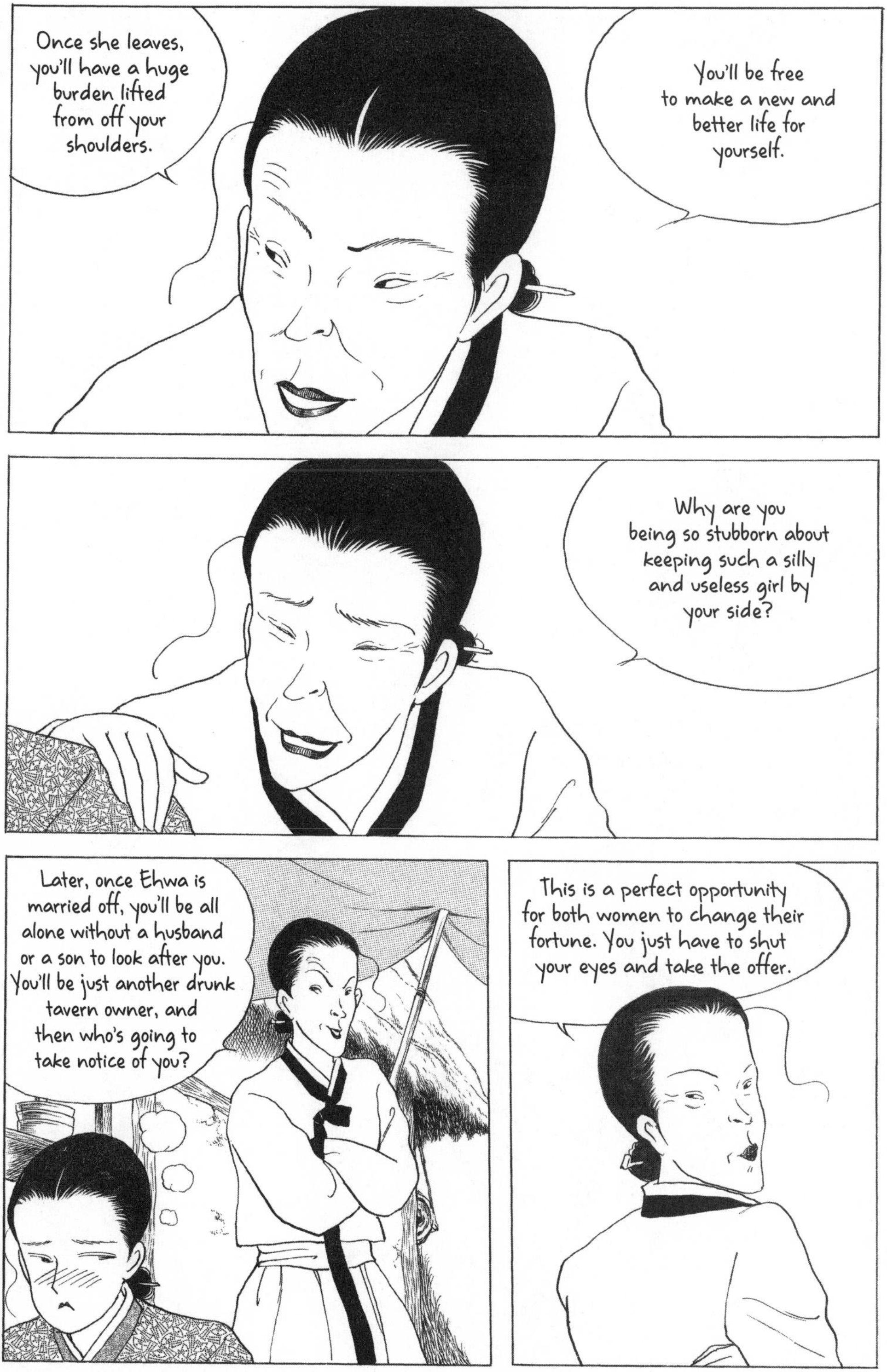
Once she leaves, you'll have a huge burden lifted from off your shoulders.
You'll be free to make a new and better life for yourself.
Why are you being so stubborn about keeping such a silly and useless girl by your side?
Later, once Ehwa is married off, you'll be all alone without a husband or a son to look after you. You'll be just another drunk tavern owner, and then who's going to take notice of you?
This is a perfect opportunity for both women to change their fortune. You just have to shut your eyes and take the offer.

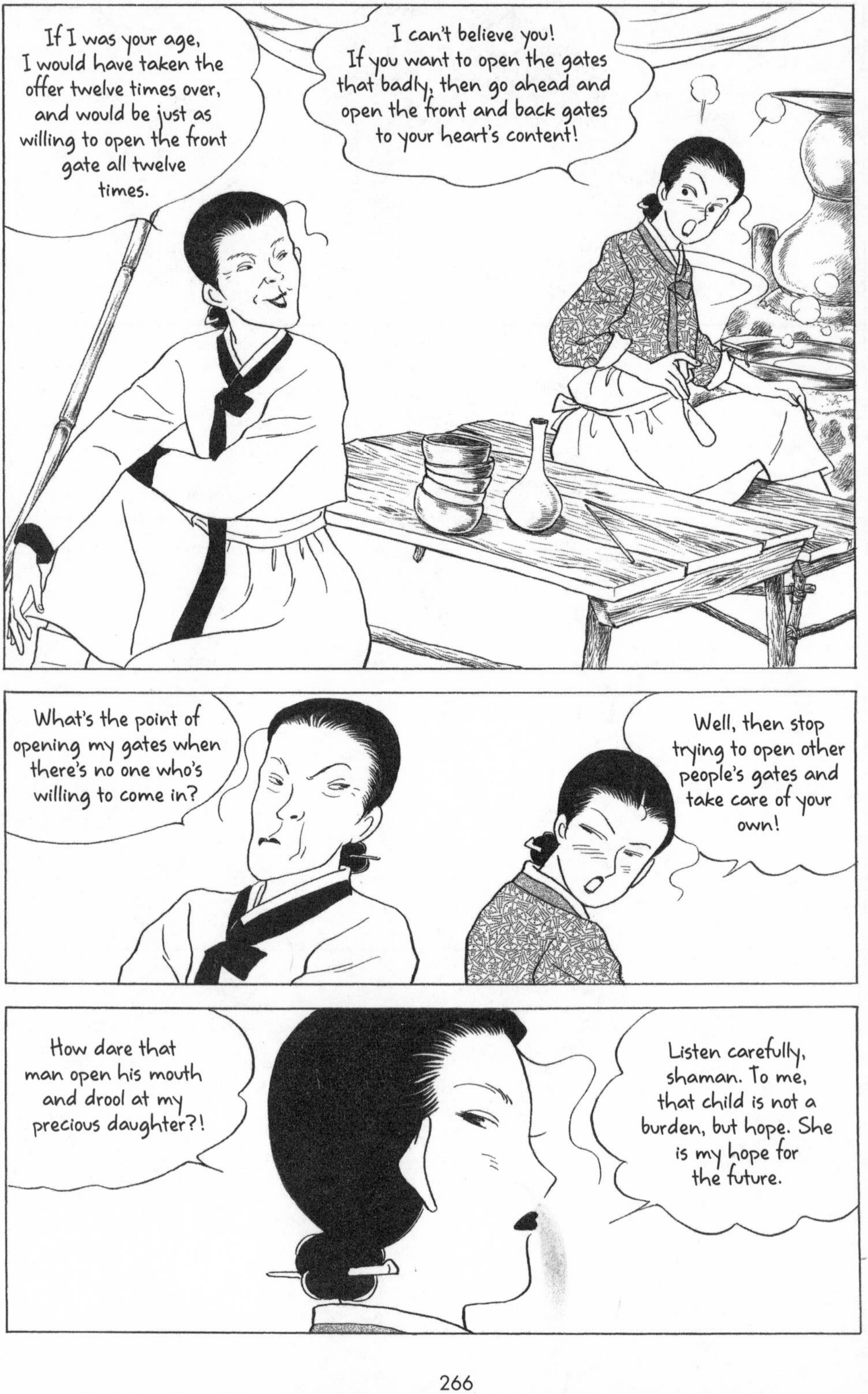
If I was your age, I would have taken the offer twelve times over, and would be just as willing to open the front gate all twelve times.
I can't believe you! If you want to open the gates that badly, then go ahead and open the front and back gates to your heart's content!
What's the point of opening my gates when there's no one who's willing to come in?
Well, then stop trying to open other people's gates and take care of your own!
How dare that man open his mouth and drool at my precious daughter?!
Listen carefully, shaman. To me, that child is not a burden, but hope. She is my hope for the future.

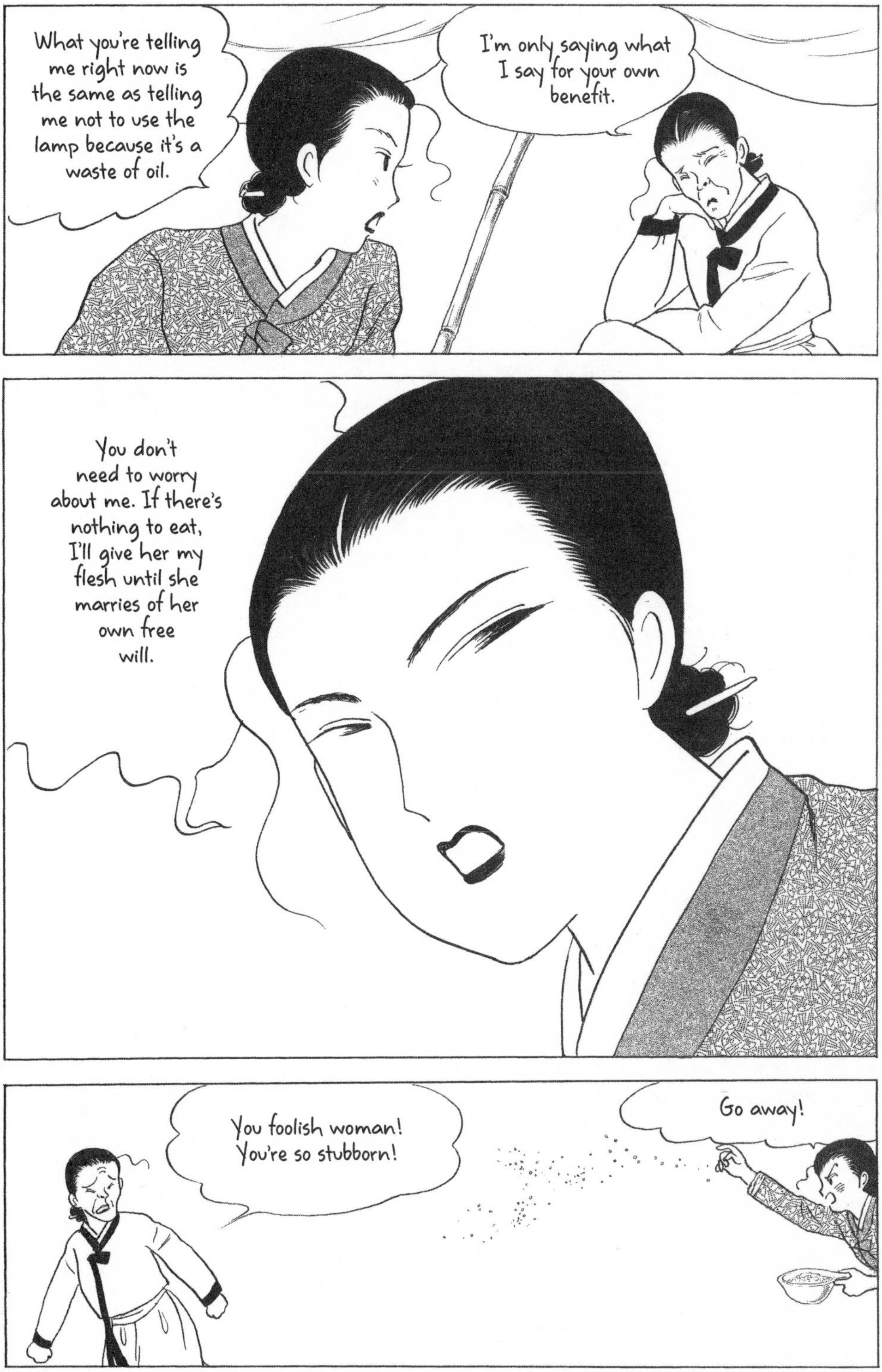
What you're telling me right now is the same as telling me not to use the lamp because it's a waste of oil.
I'm only saying what I say for your own benefit.
You don't need to worry about me. If there's nothing to eat, I'll give her my flesh until she marries of her own free will.
You foolish woman! You're so stubborn!
Go away!

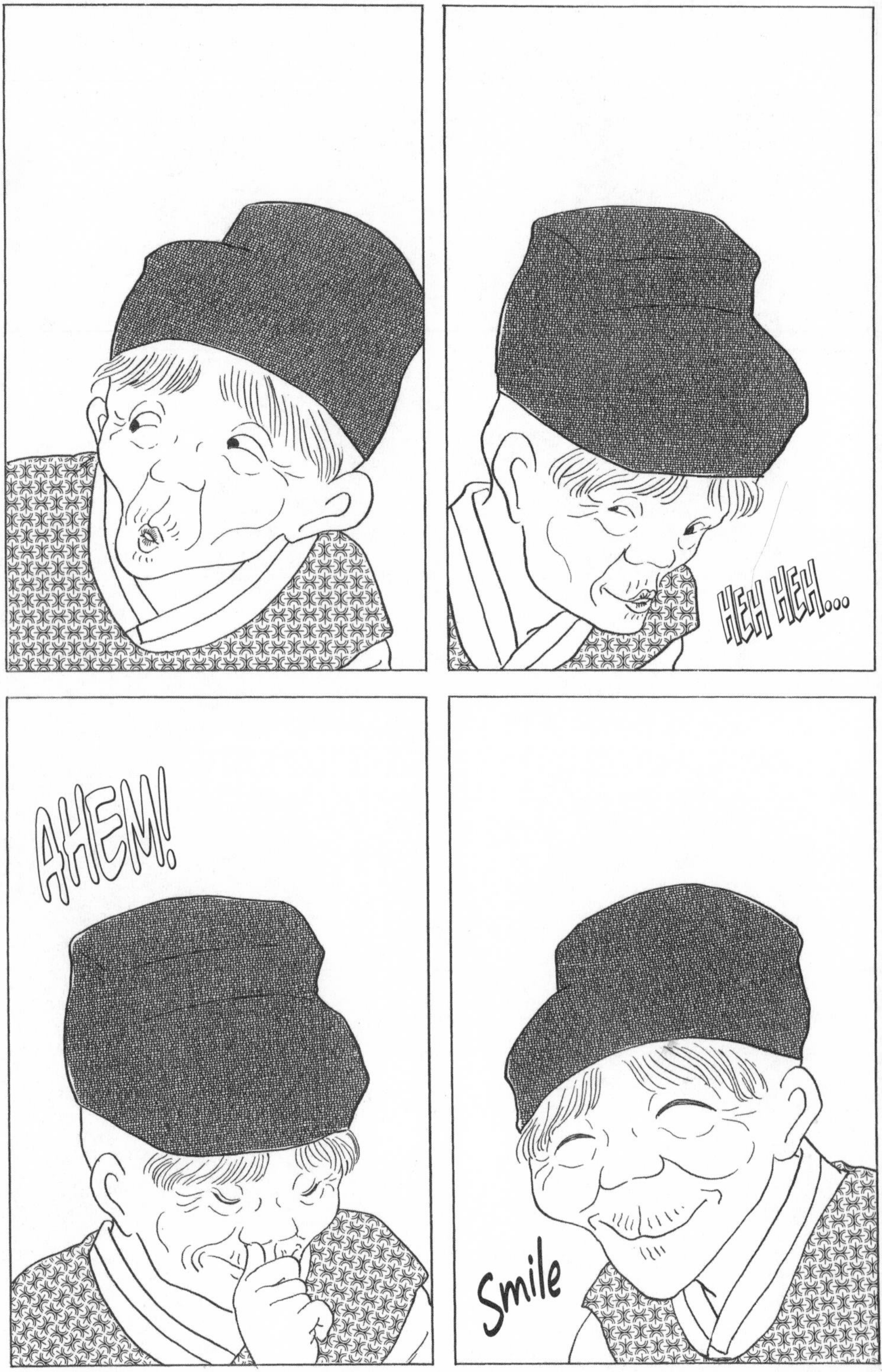
HEH HEH...
AHEM!
Smile

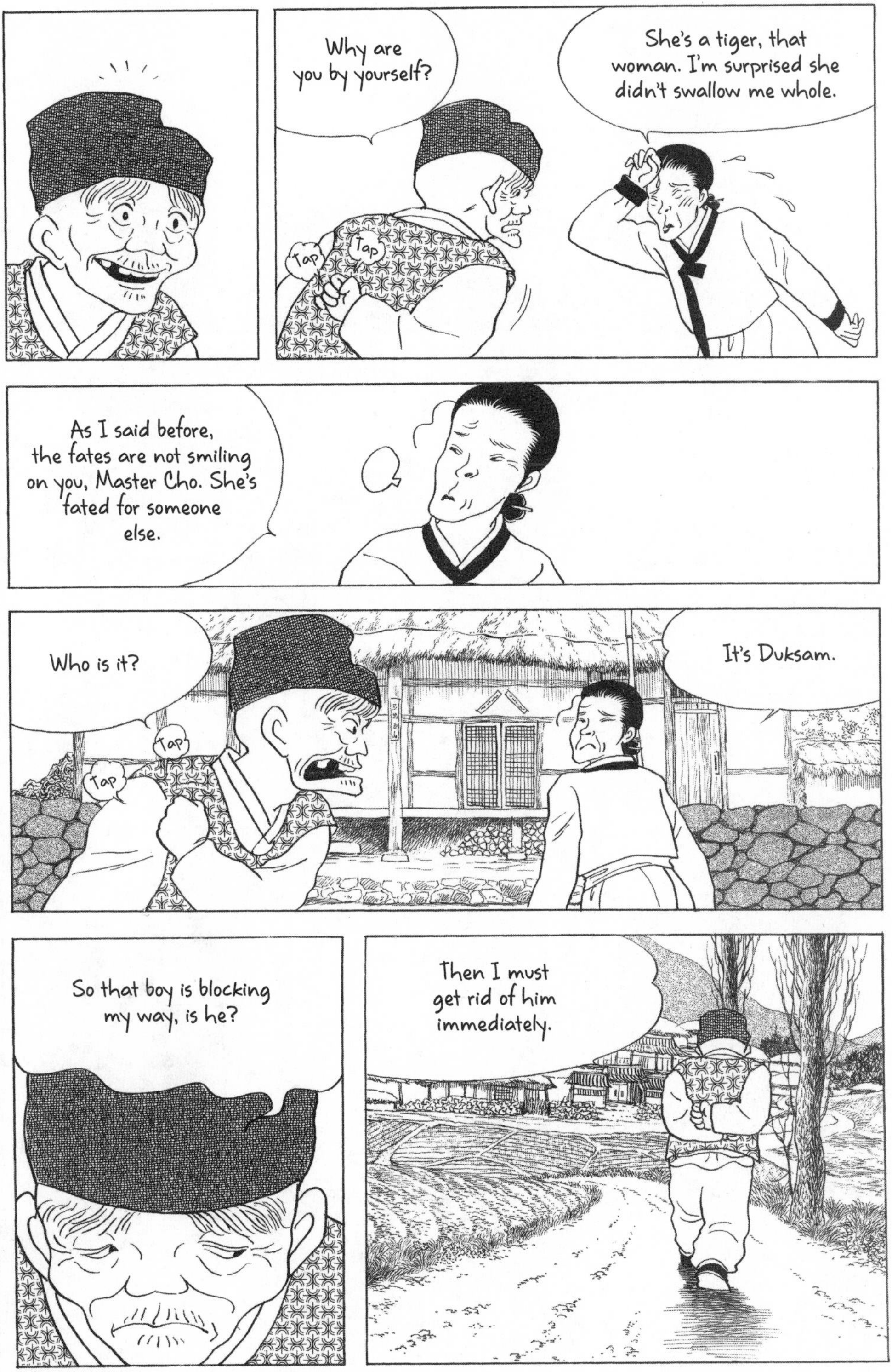
Why are you by yourself?
Tap
Tap
She's a tiger, that woman. I'm surprised she didn't swallow me whole.
As I said before, the fates are not smiling on you, Master Cho. She's fated for someone else.
Who is it?
Tap
Tap
It's Duksam.
So that boy is blocking my way, is he?
Then I must get rid of him immediately.

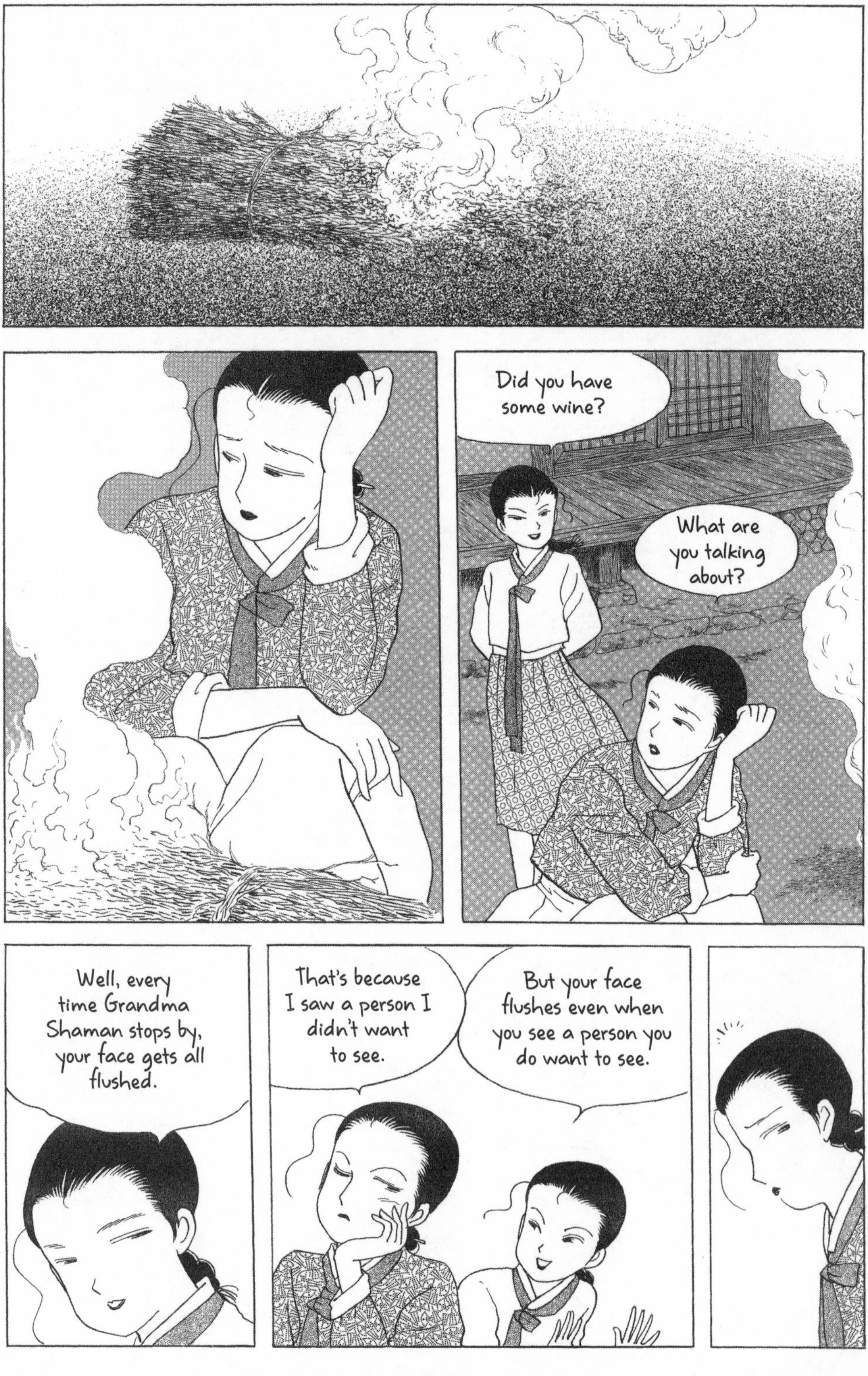

Did you have some wine?
What are you talking about?
Well, every time Grandma Shaman stops by, your face gets all flushed.
That's because I saw a person I didn't want to see.
But your face flushes even when you see a person you do want to see.

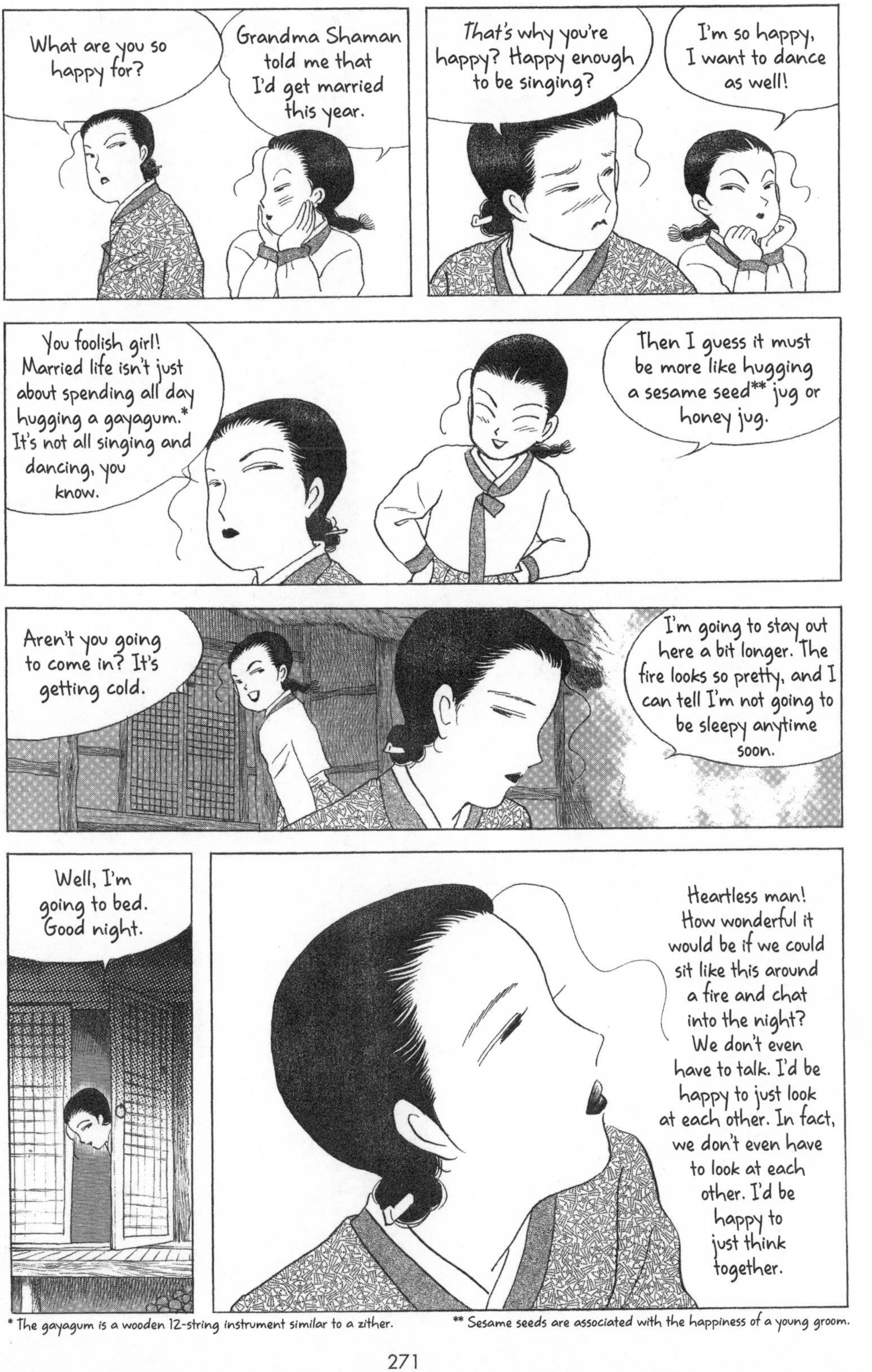
What are you so happy for?
Grandma Shaman told me that I'd get married this year.
That's why you're happy? Happy enough to be singing?
I'm so happy, I want to dance as well!
You foolish girl! Married life isn't just about spending all day hugging a gayagum.* It's not all singing and dancing, you know.
Then I guess it must be more like hugging a sesame seed** jug or honey jug.
Aren't you going to come in? It's getting cold.
I'm going to stay out here a bit longer. The fire looks so pretty, and I can tell I'm not going to be sleepy anytime soon.
Well, I'm going to bed. Good night.
Heartless man! How wonderful it would be if we could sit like this around a fire and chat into the night? We don't even have to talk. I'd be happy to just look at each other. In fact, we don't even have to look at each other. I'd be happy to just think together.

* The gayagum is a wooden 12-string instrument similar to a zither.

** Sesame seeds are associated with the happiness of a young groom.

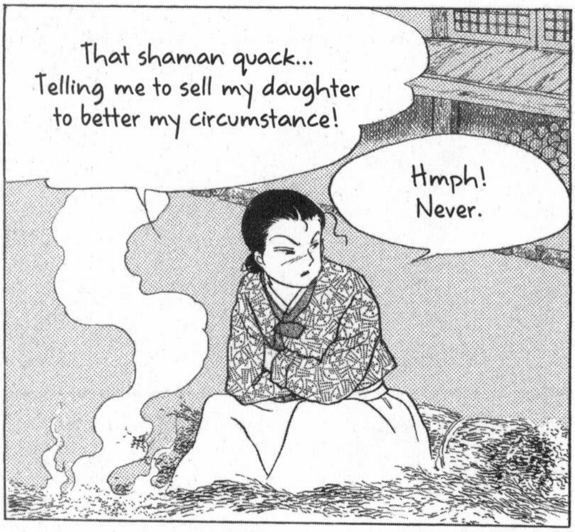
That shaman quack... Telling me to sell my daughter to better my circumstance!
Hmph! Never.

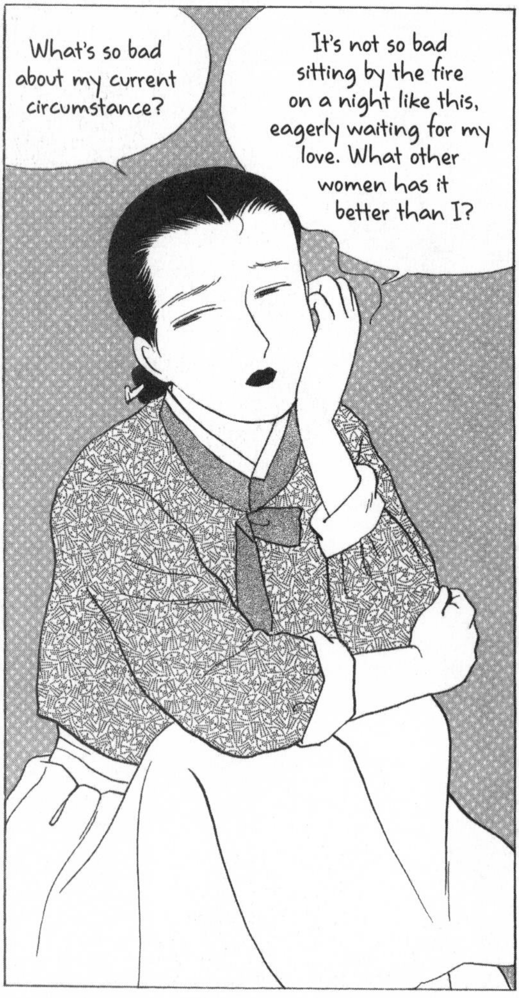
What's so bad about my current circumstance?
It's not so bad sitting by the fire on a night like this, eagerly waiting for my love. What other women has it better than I?

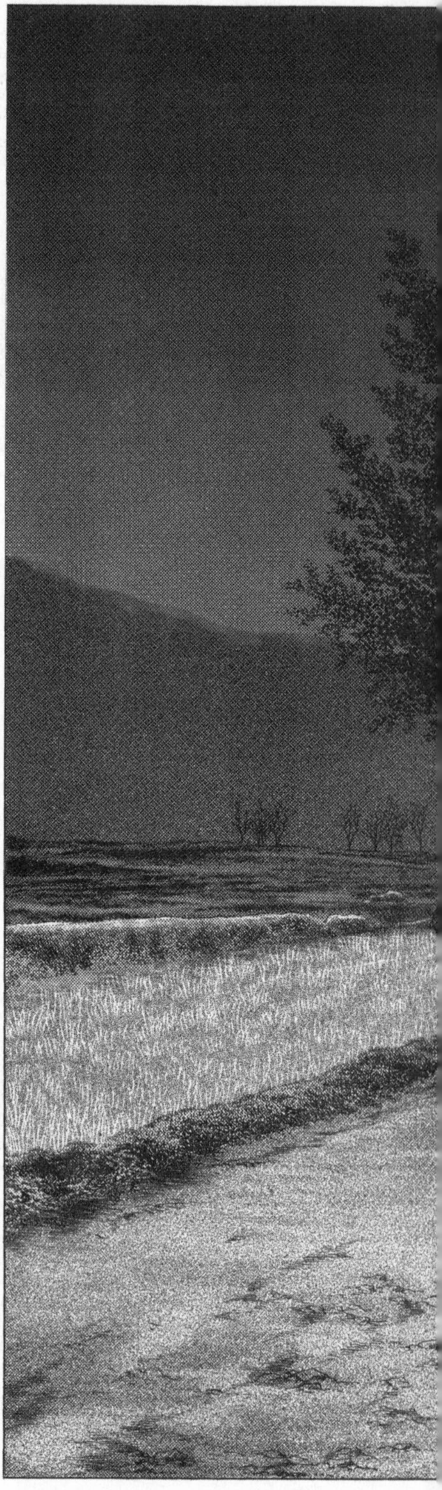

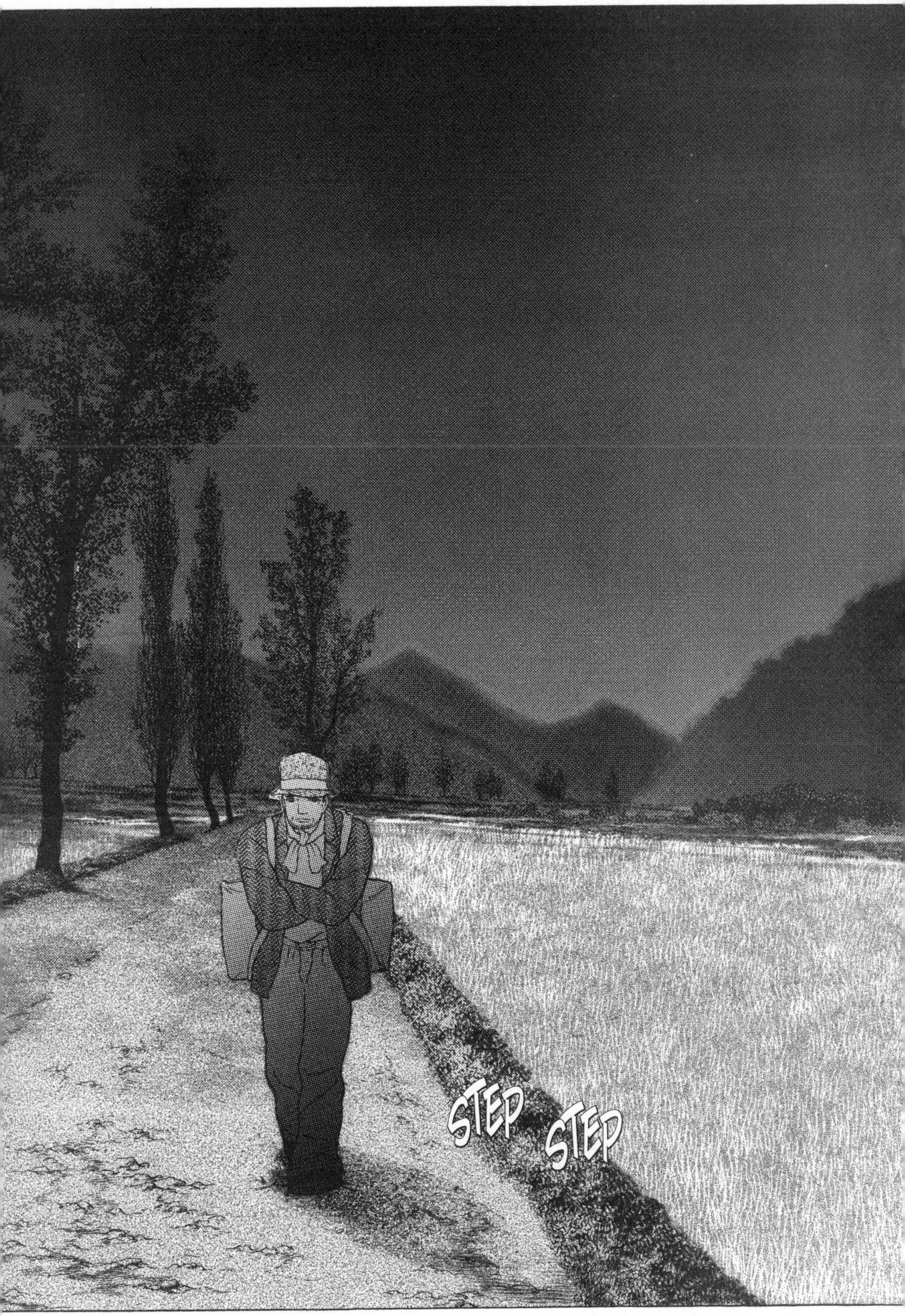
STEP STEP

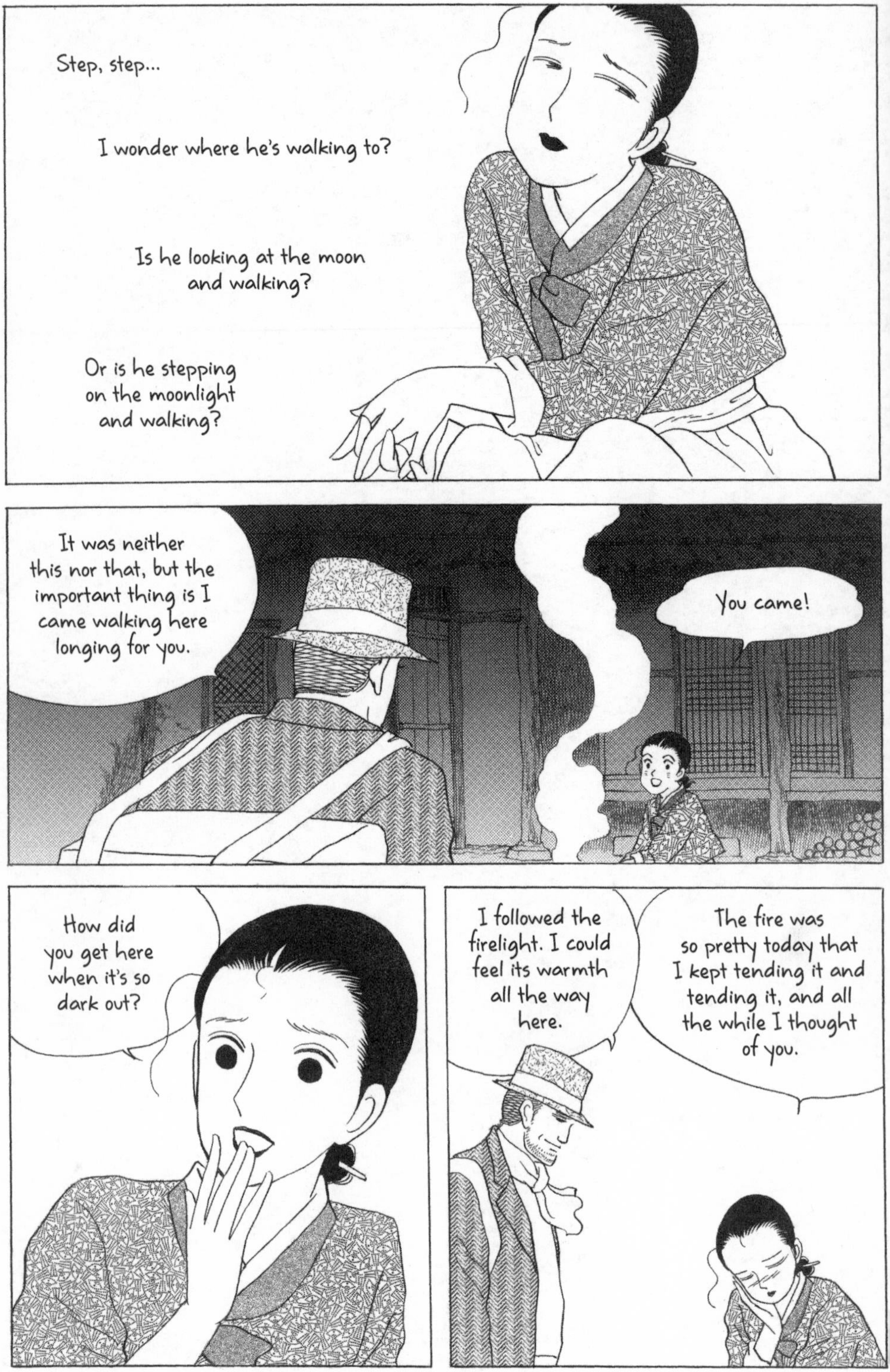
Step, step...
I wonder where he's walking to?
Is he looking at the moon and walking?
Or is he stepping on the moonlight and walking?
It was neither this nor that, but the important thing is I came walking here longing for you.
You came!
How did you get here when it's so dark out?
I followed the firelight. I could feel its warmth all the way here.
The fire was so pretty today that I kept tending it and tending it, and all the while I thought of you.

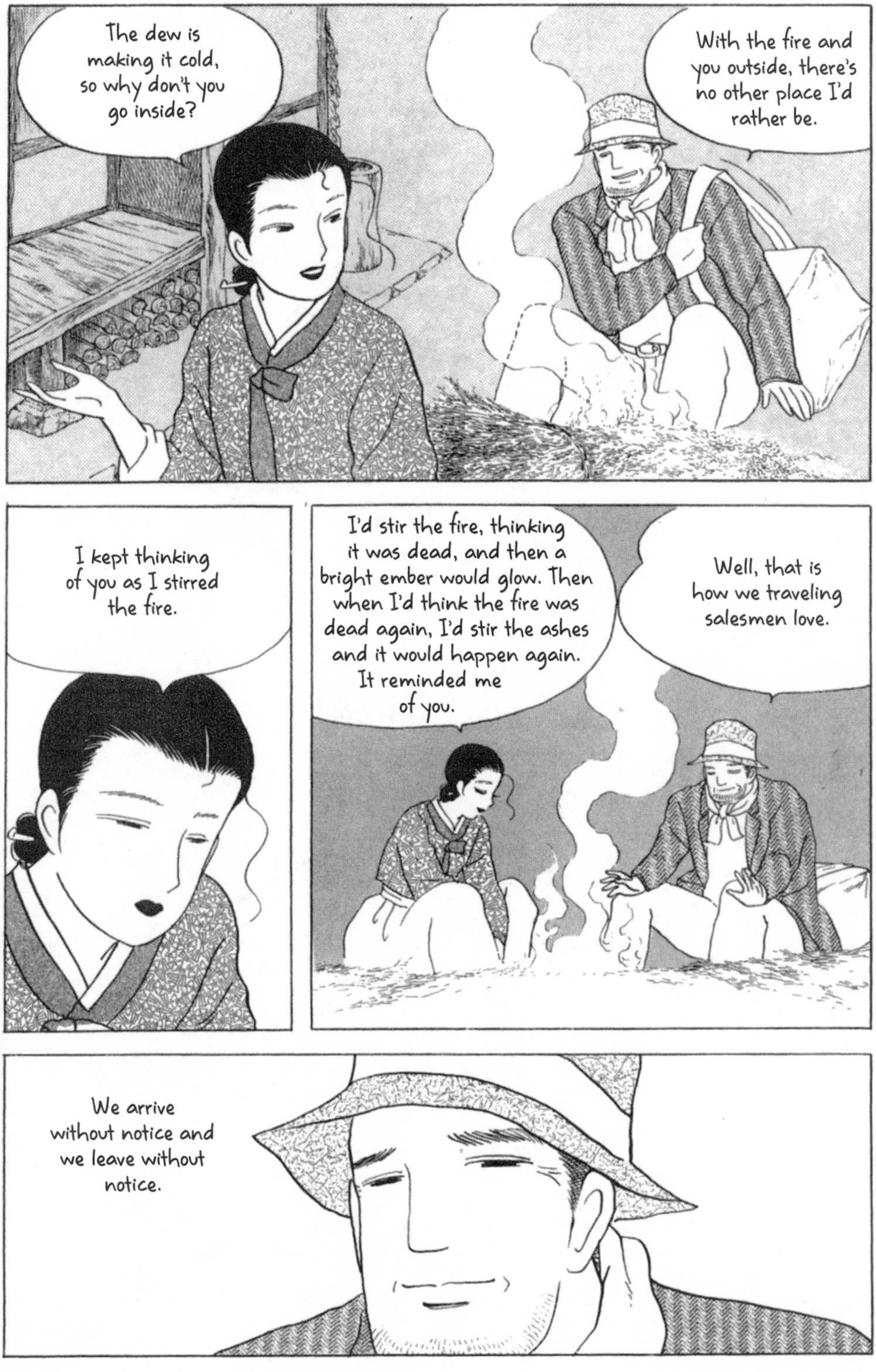
The dew is making it cold, so why don't you go inside?
With the fire and you outside, there's no other place I'd rather be.
I kept thinking of you as I stirred the fire.
I'd stir the fire, thinking it was dead, and then a bright ember would glow. Then when I'd think the fire was dead again, I'd stir the ashes and it would happen again. It reminded me of you.
Well, that is how we traveling salesmen love.
We arrive without notice and we leave without notice.

As I was searching for each ember, I thought of you and my heart felt like it was breaking, but now that you're here, I feel as if I'm the luckiest woman alive.

And why is that?

It's has to do with something that happened today.

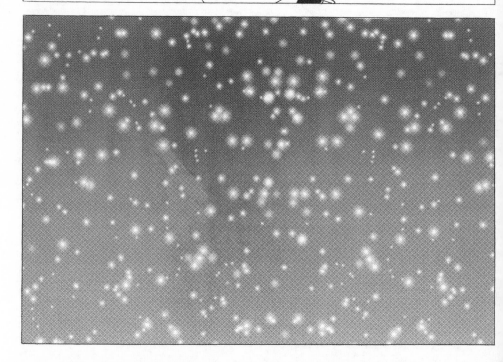

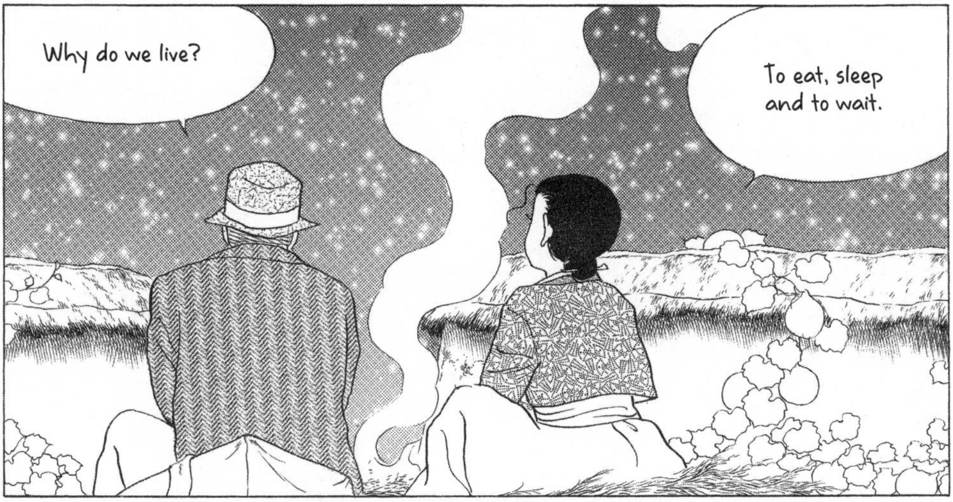
Why do we live?
To eat, sleep and to wait.
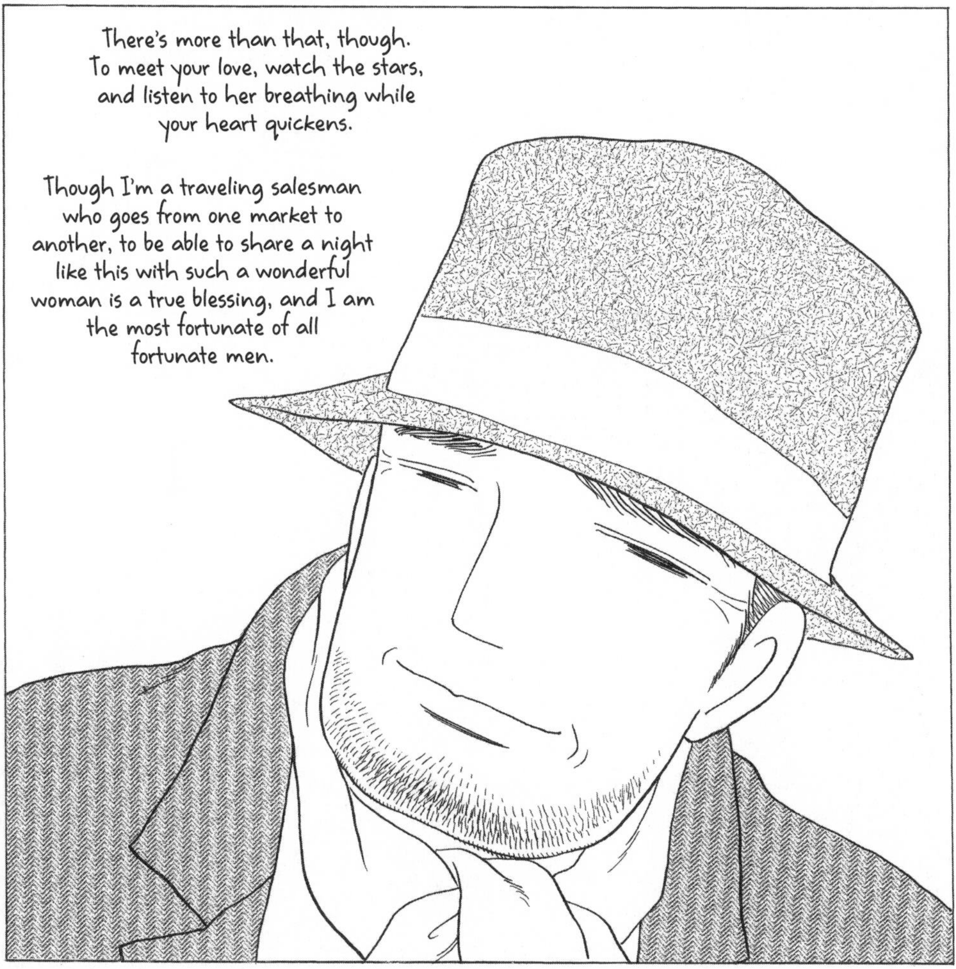
There's more than that, though. To meet your love, watch the stars, and listen to her breathing while your heart quickens.
Though I'm a traveling salesman who goes from one market to another, to be able to share a night like this with such a wonderful woman is a true blessing, and I am the most fortunate of all fortunate men.

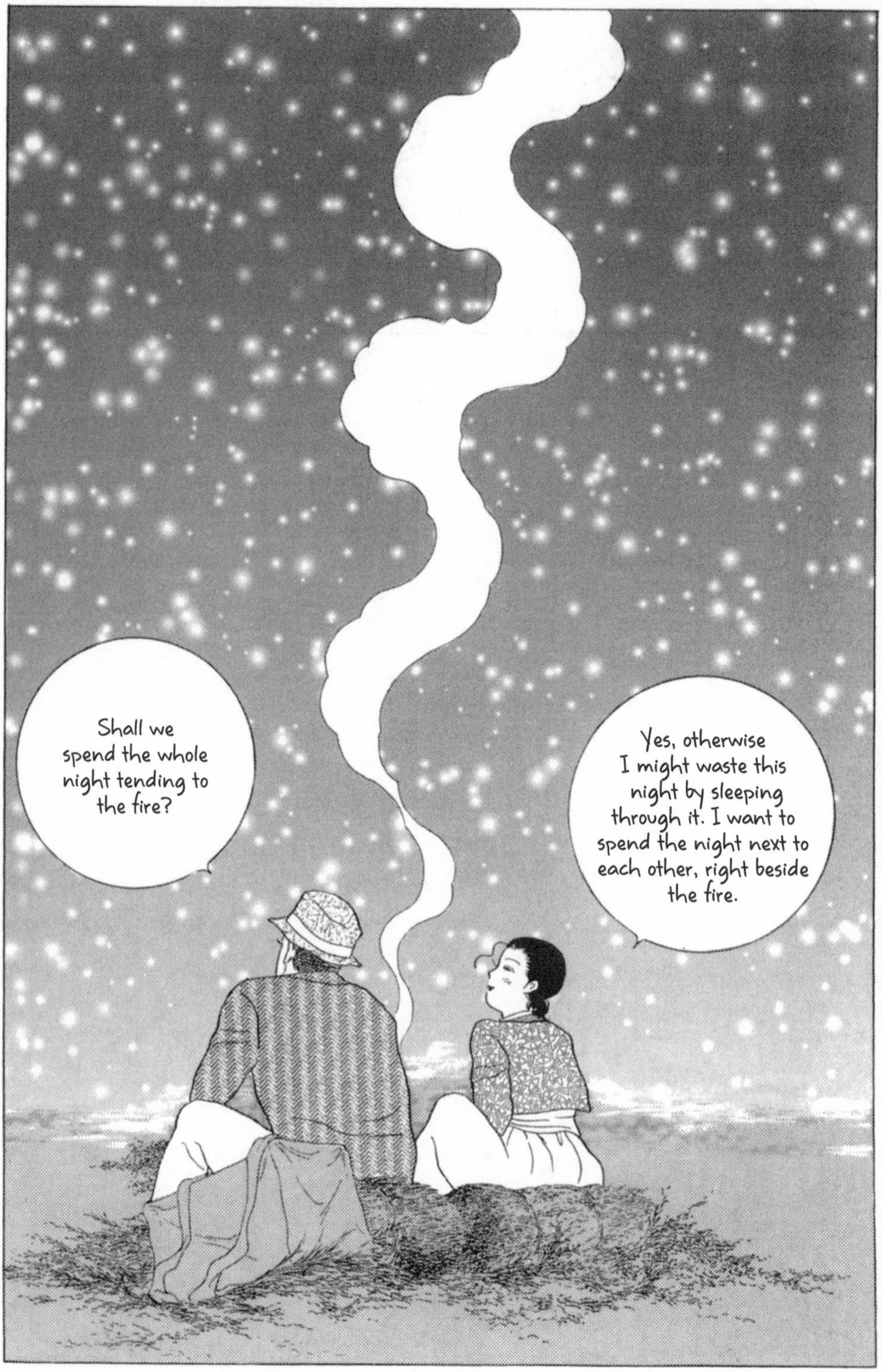
Shall we spend the whole night tending to the fire?
Yes, otherwise I might waste this night by sleeping through it. I want to spend the night next to each other, right beside the fire.

Chapter Ten

FIRE BUTTERFLY

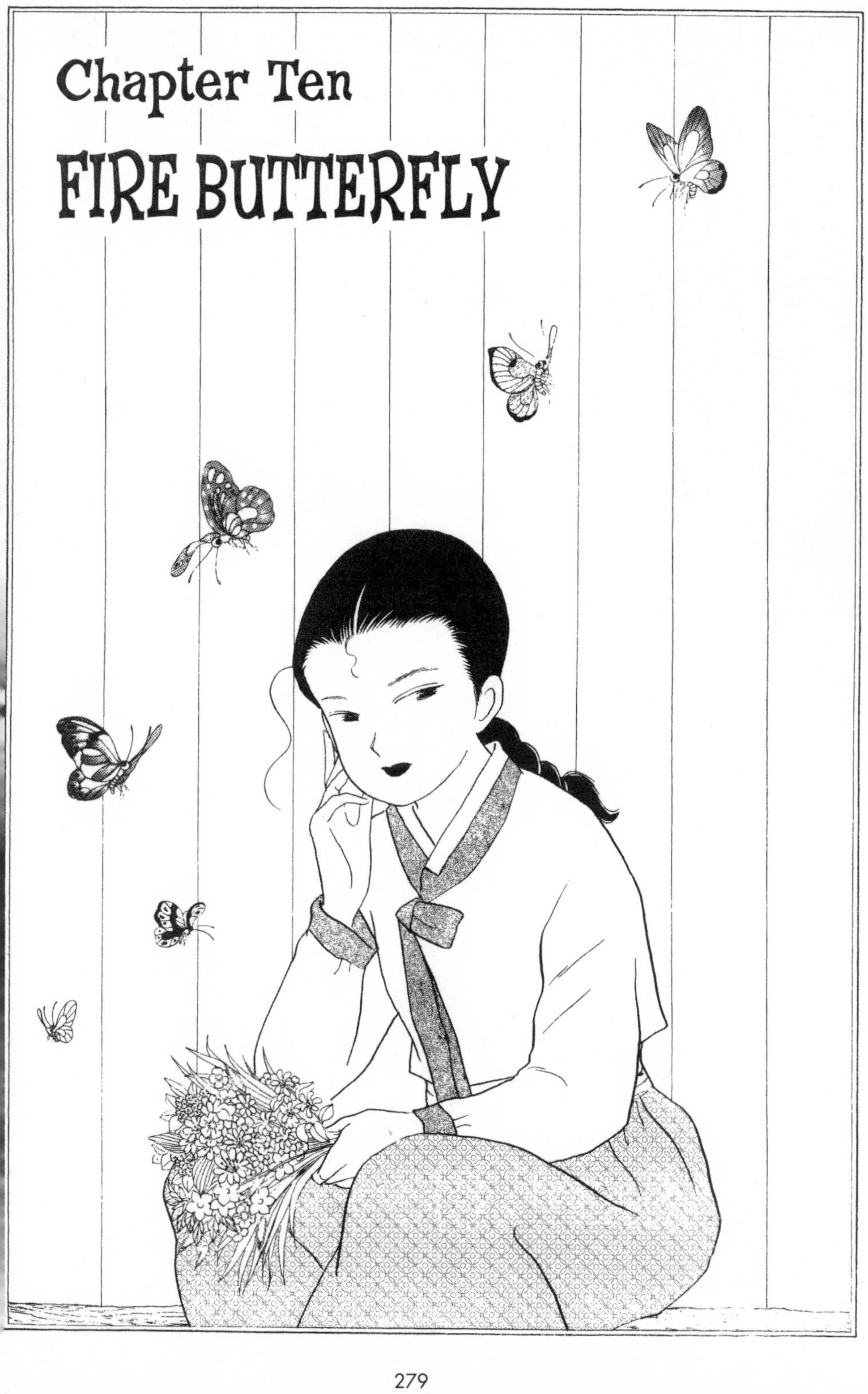

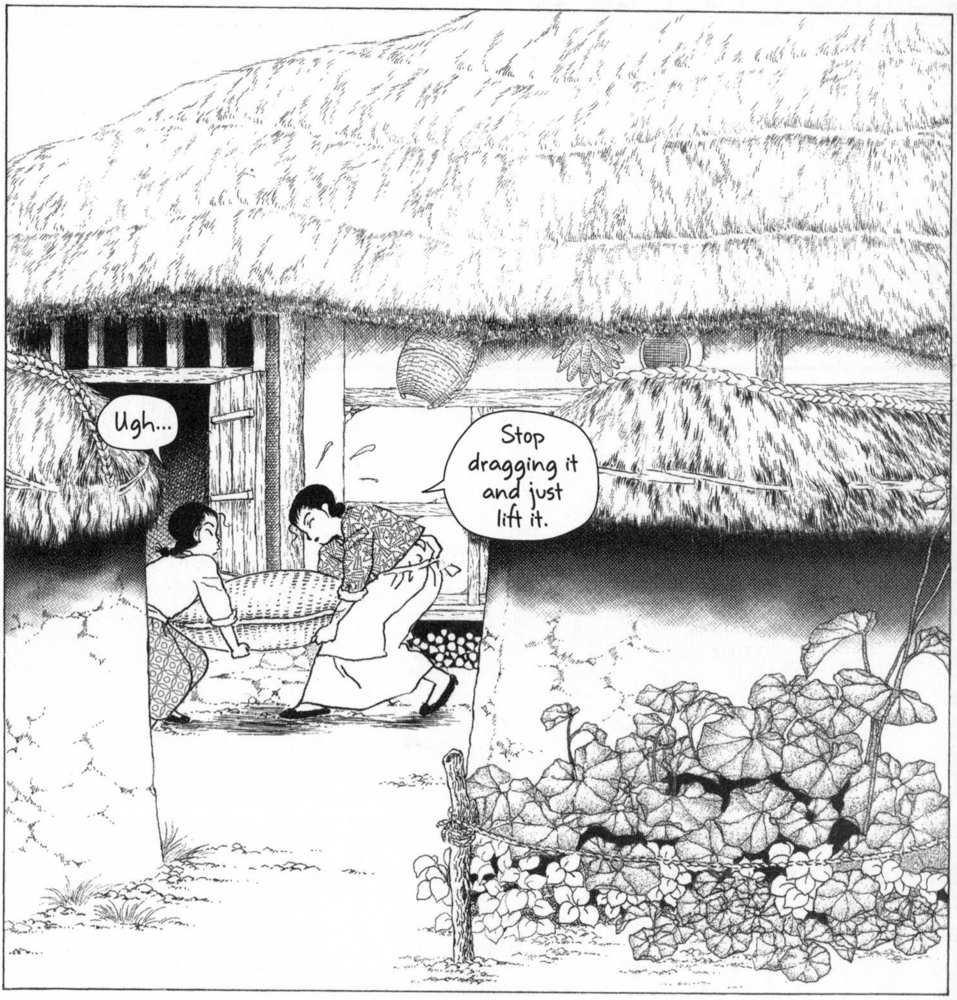
Ugh...
Stop dragging it and just lift it.

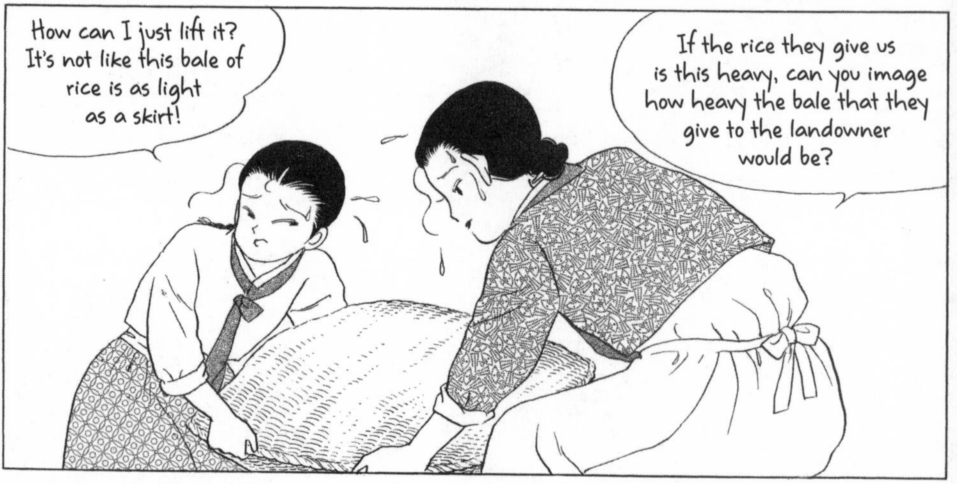
How can I just lift it? It's not like this bale of rice is as light as a skirt!
If the rice they give us is this heavy, can you image how heavy the bale that they give to the landowner would be?

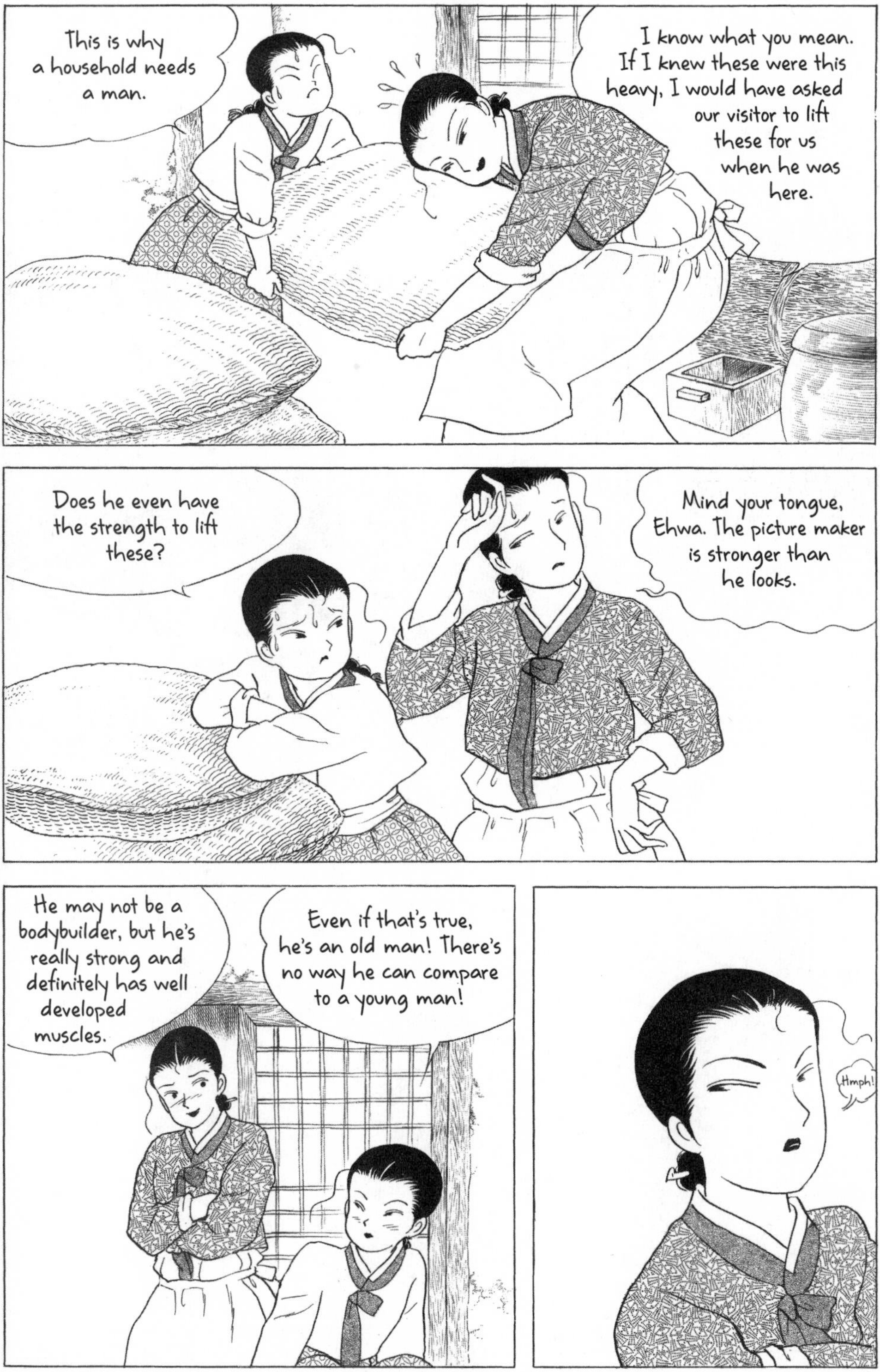
This is why a household needs a man.
I know what you mean. If I knew these were this heavy, I would have asked our visitor to lift these for us when he was here.
Does he even have the strength to lift these?
Mind your tongue, Ehwa. The picture maker is stronger than he looks.
He may not be a bodybuilder, but he's really strong and definitely has well developed muscles.
Even if that's true, he's an old man! There's no way he can compare to a young man!
Hmph!

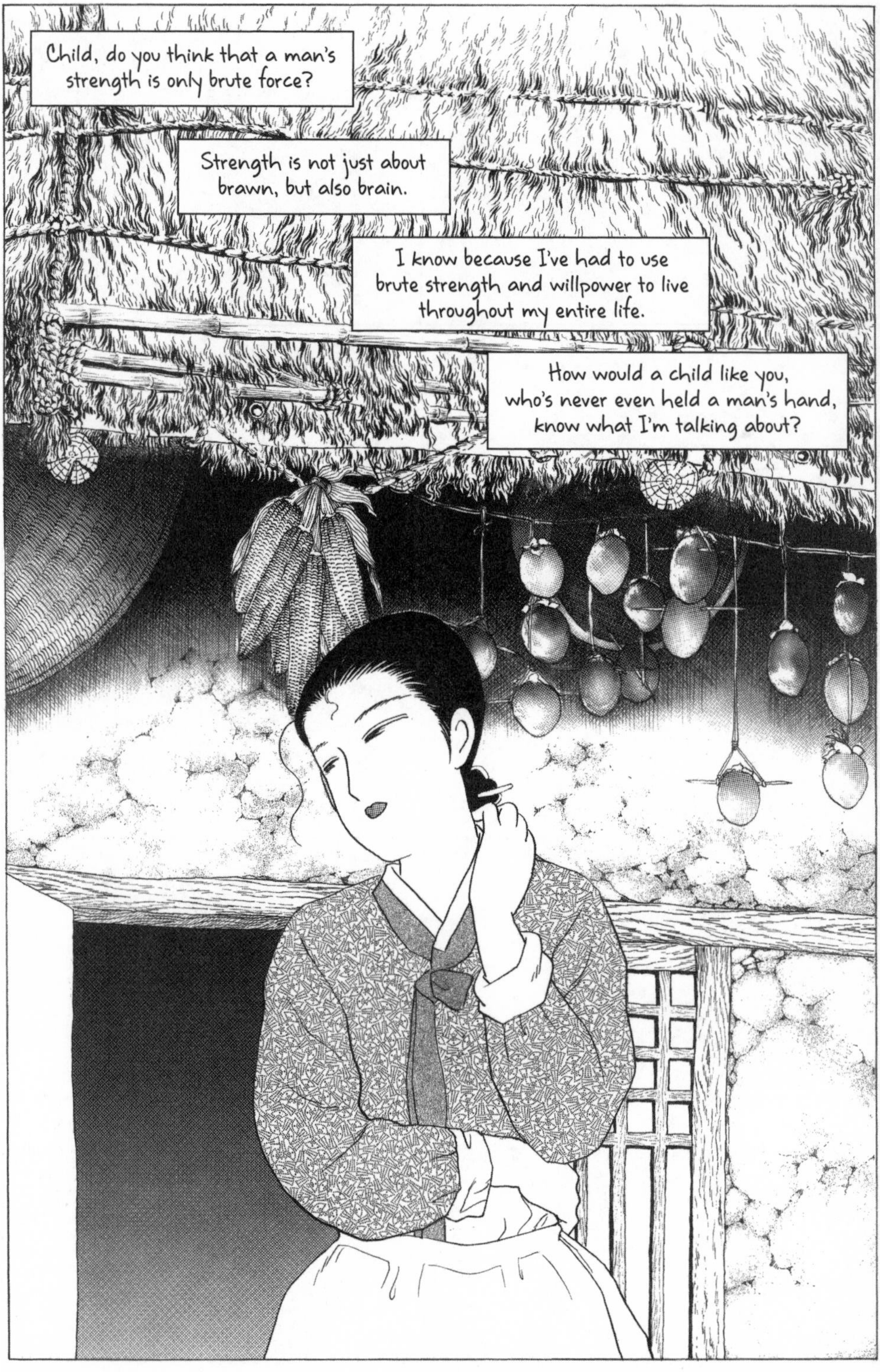
Child, do you think that a man's strength is only brute force?
Strength is not just about brawn, but also brain.
I know because I've had to use brute strength and willpower to live throughout my entire life.
How would a child like you, who's never even held a man's hand, know what I'm talking about?

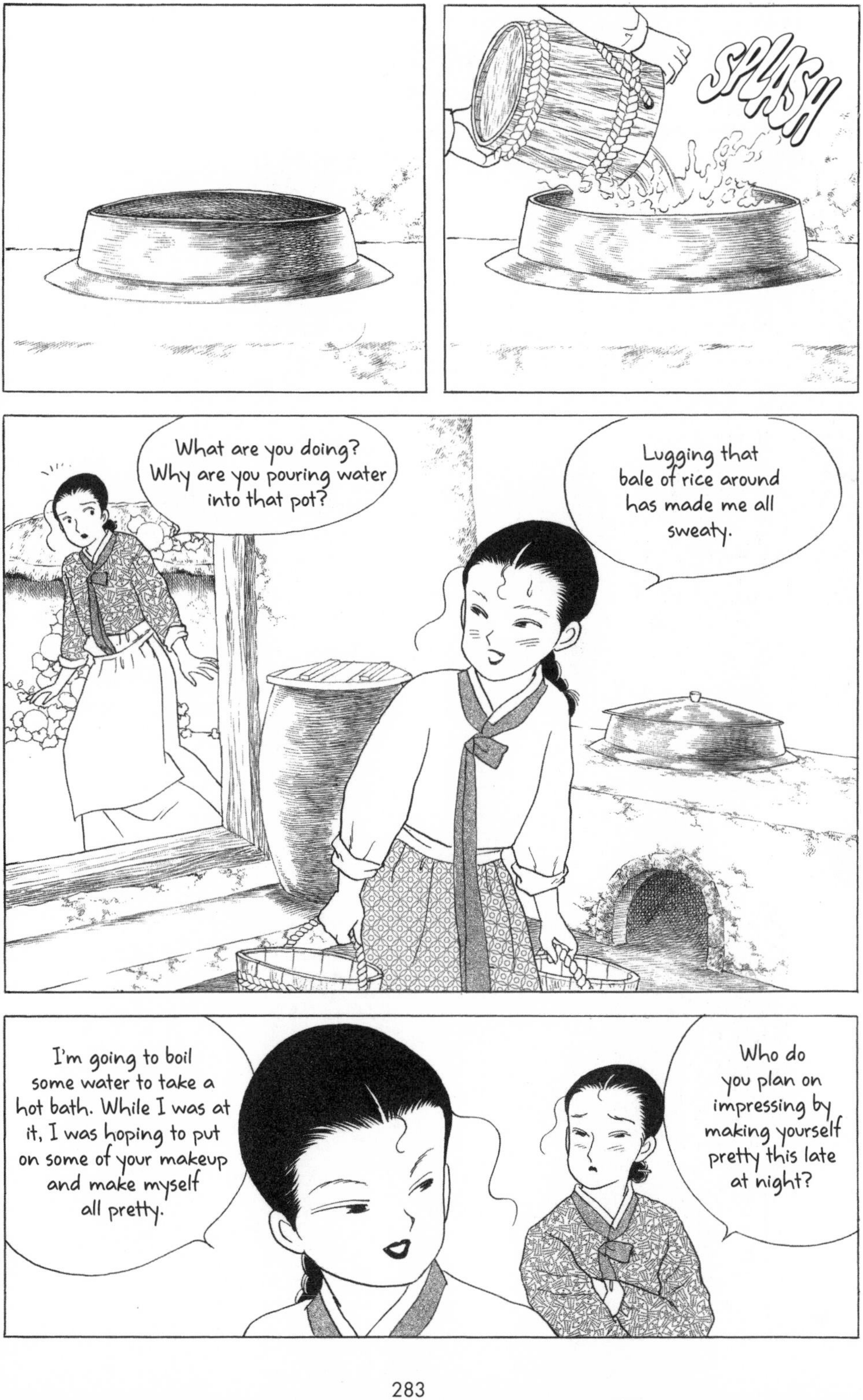
SPLASH
What are you doing? Why are you pouring water into that pot?
Lugging that bale of rice around has made me all sweaty.
I'm going to boil some water to take a hot bath. While I was at it, I was hoping to put on some of your makeup and make myself all pretty.
Who do you plan on impressing by making yourself pretty this late at night?

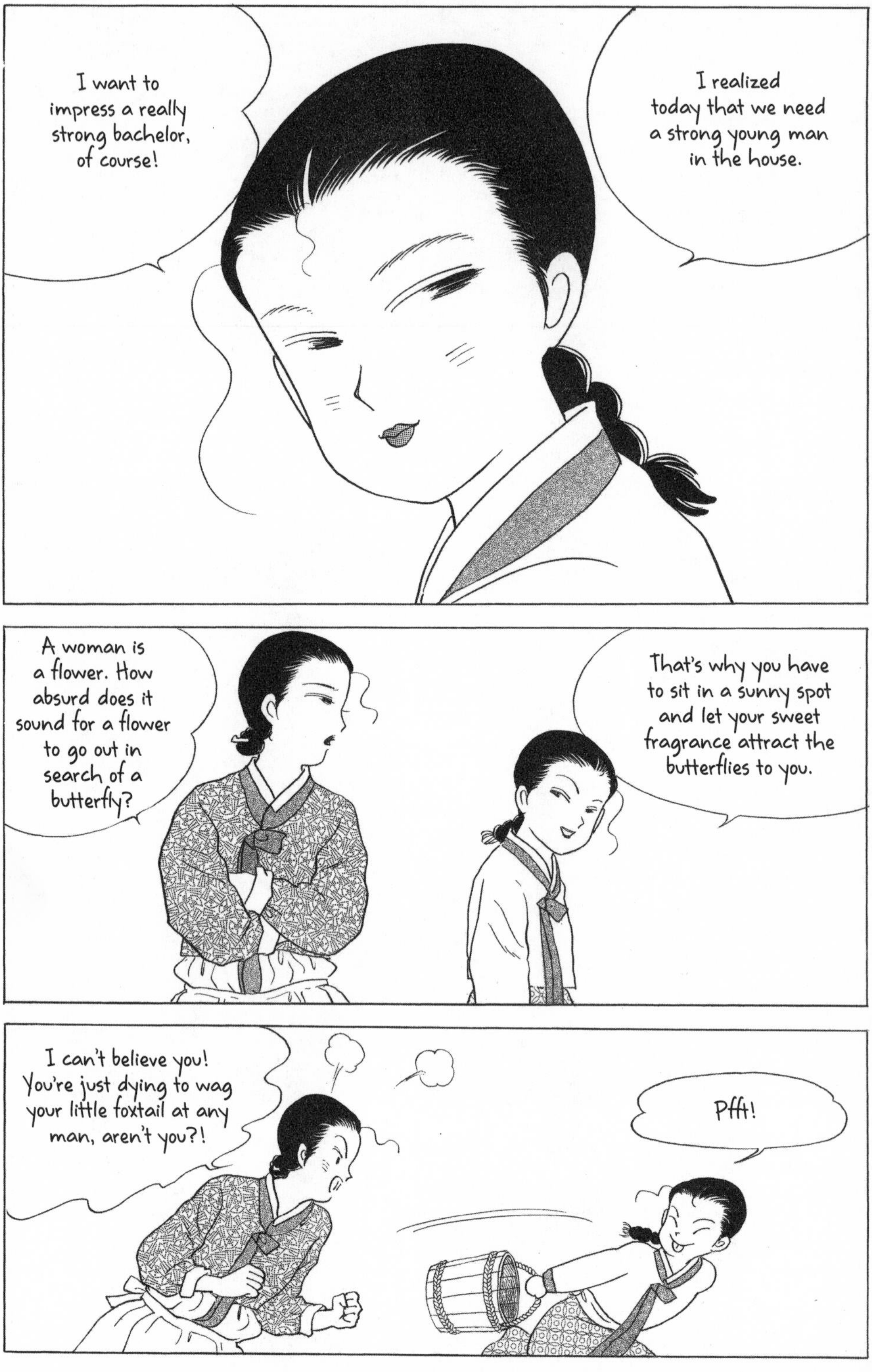

I want to impress a really strong bachelor, of course!
I realized today that we need a strong young man in the house.
A woman is a flower. How absurd does it sound for a flower to go out in search of a butterfly?
That's why you have to sit in a sunny spot and let your sweet fragrance attract the butterflies to you.
I can't believe you! You're just dying to wag your little foxtail at any man, aren't you?!
Pfft!

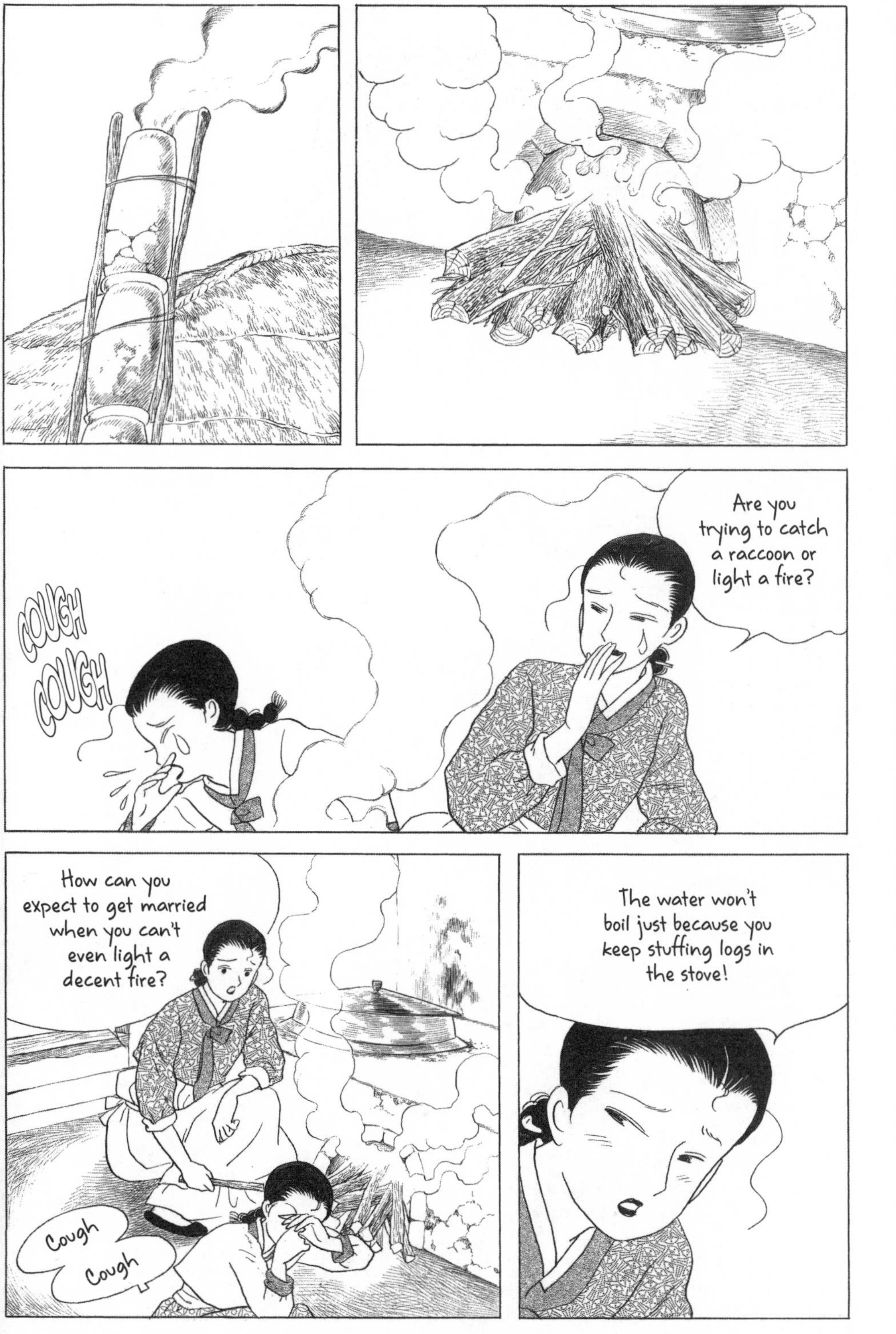
COUGH COUGH
Are you trying to catch a raccoon or light a fire?
How can you expect to get married when you can't even light a decent fire?
Cough Cough
The water won't boil just because you keep stuffing logs in the stove!

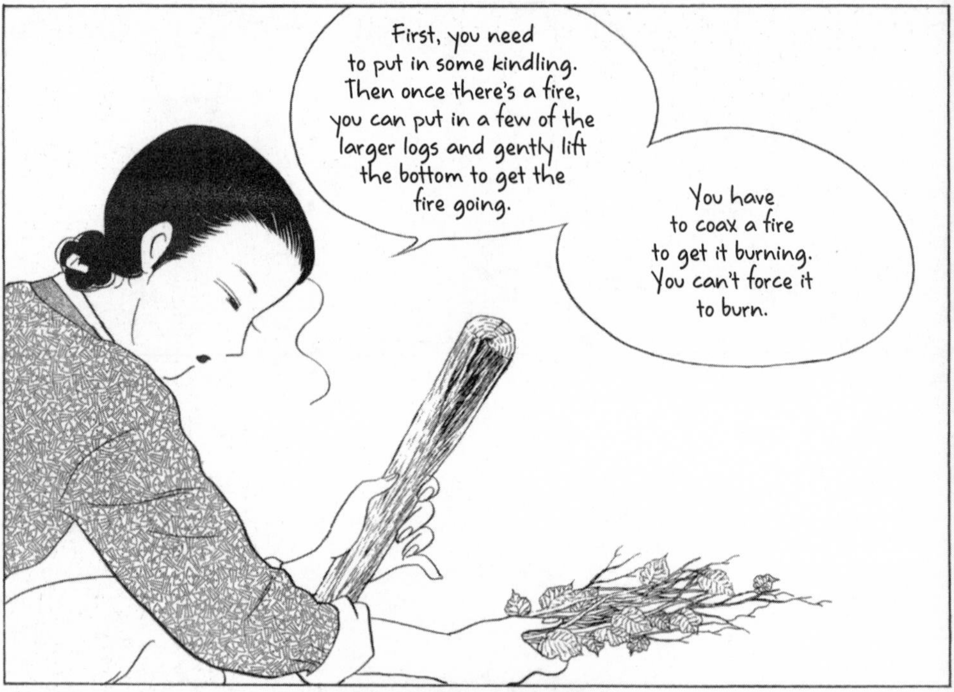
First, you need to put in some kindling. Then once there's a fire, you can put in a few of the larger logs and gently lift the bottom to get the fire going.
You have to coax a fire to get it burning. You can't force it to burn.

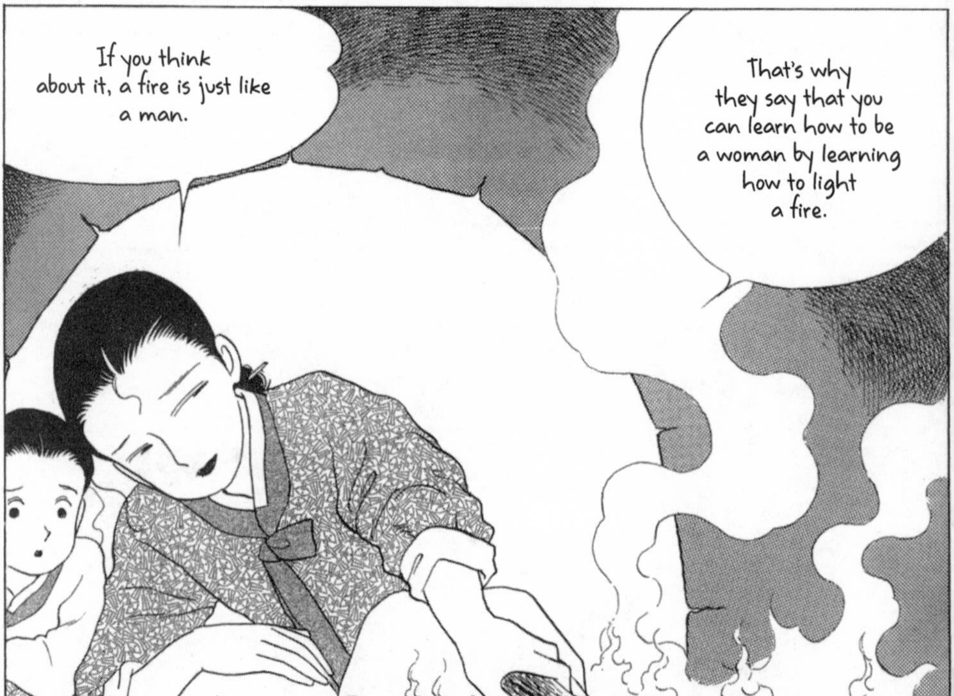
If you think about it, a fire is just like a man.
That's why they say that you can learn how to be a woman by learning how to light a fire.

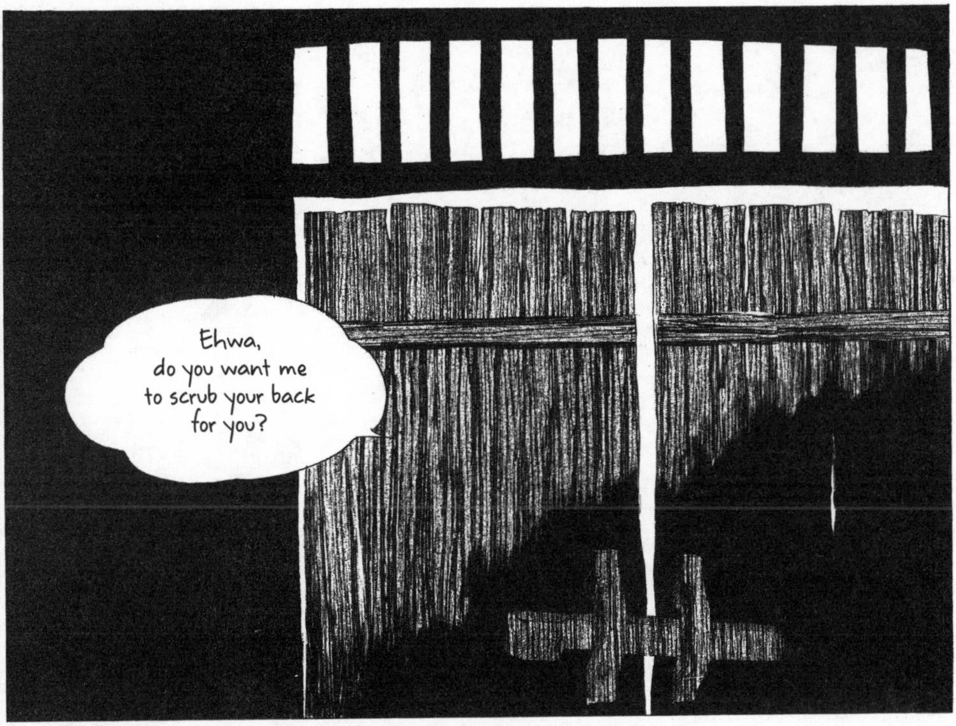
Ehwa, do you want me to scrub your back for you?

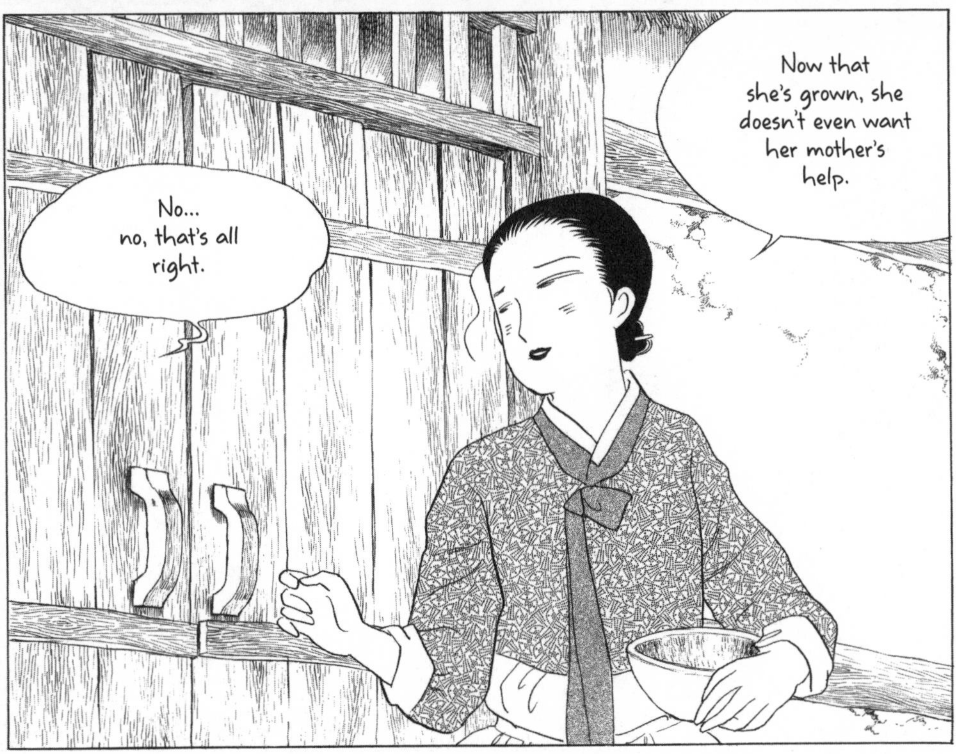
No... no, that's all right.
Now that she's grown, she doesn't even want her mother's help.

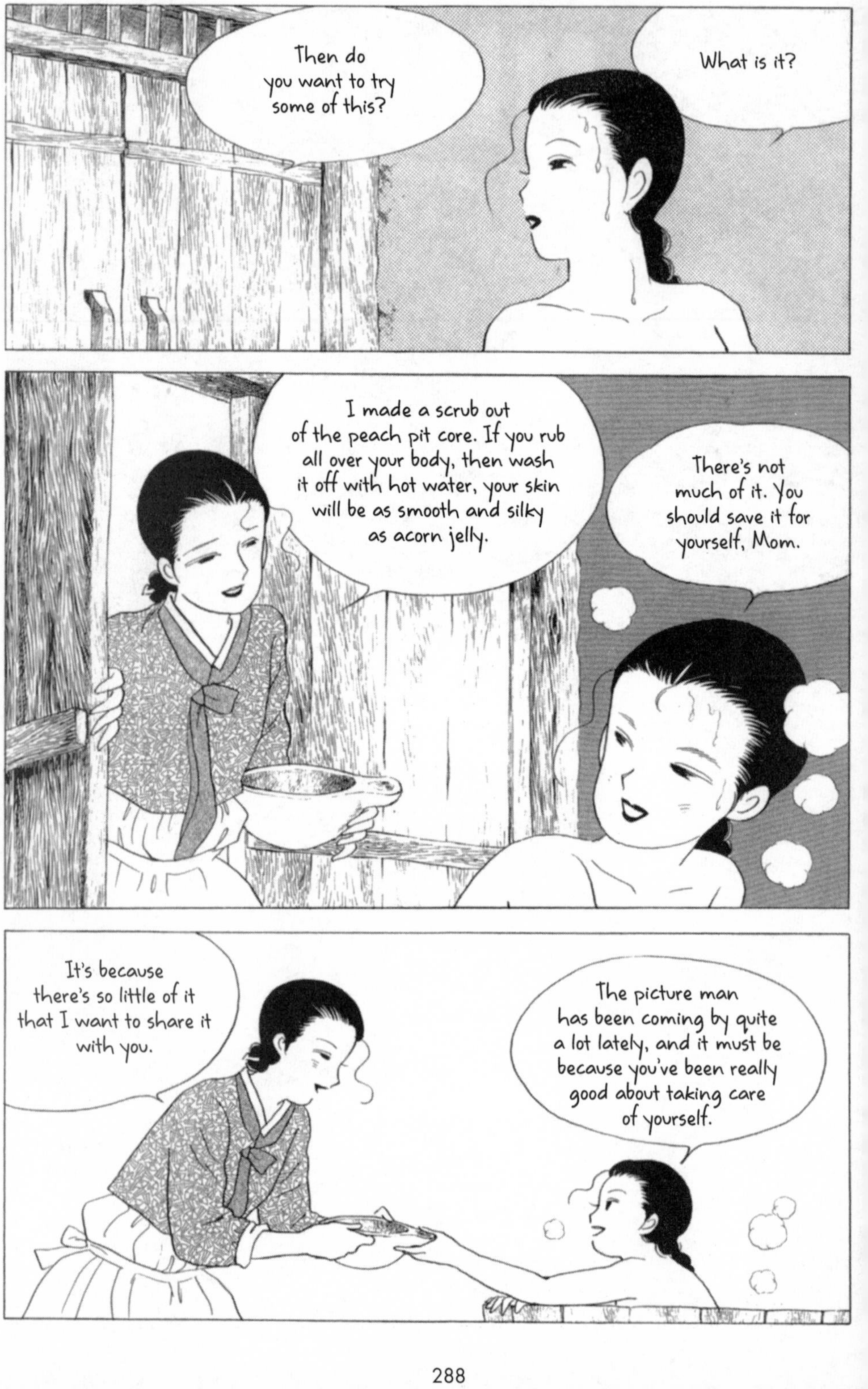
Then do you want to try some of this?
What is it?
I made a scrub out of the peach pit core. If you rub all over your body, then wash it off with hot water, your skin will be as smooth and silky as acorn jelly.
There's not much of it. You should save it for yourself, Mom.
It's because there's so little of it that I want to share it with you.
The picture man has been coming by quite a lot lately, and it must be because you've been really good about taking care of yourself.

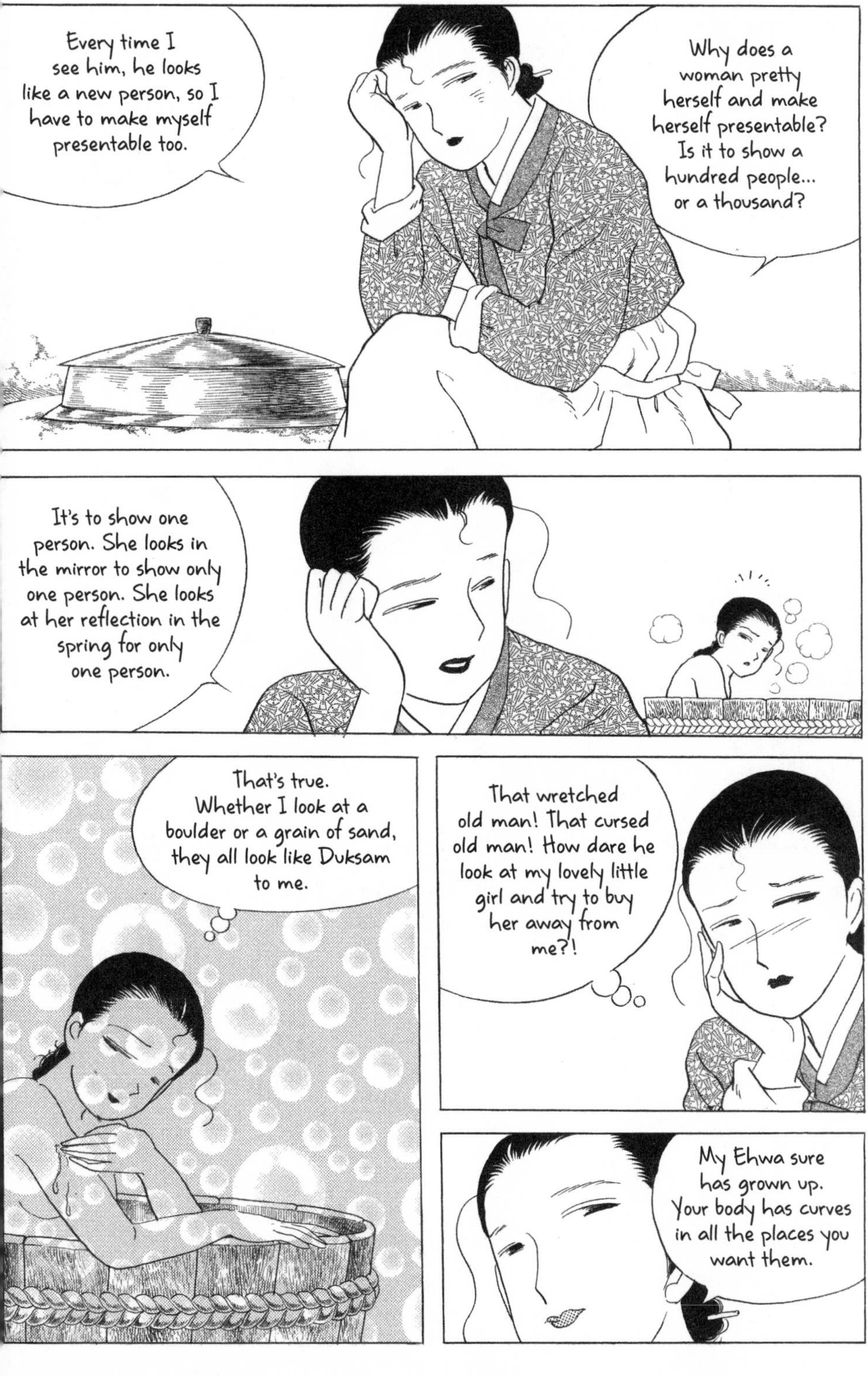
Every time I see him, he looks like a new person, so I have to make myself presentable too.
Why does a woman pretty herself and make herself presentable? Is it to show a hundred people... or a thousand?
It's to show one person. She looks in the mirror to show only one person. She looks at her reflection in the spring for only one person.
That's true. Whether I look at a boulder or a grain of sand, they all look like Duksam to me.
That wretched old man! That cursed old man! How dare he look at my lovely little girl and try to buy her away from me?!
My Ehwa sure has grown up. Your body has curves in all the places you want them.

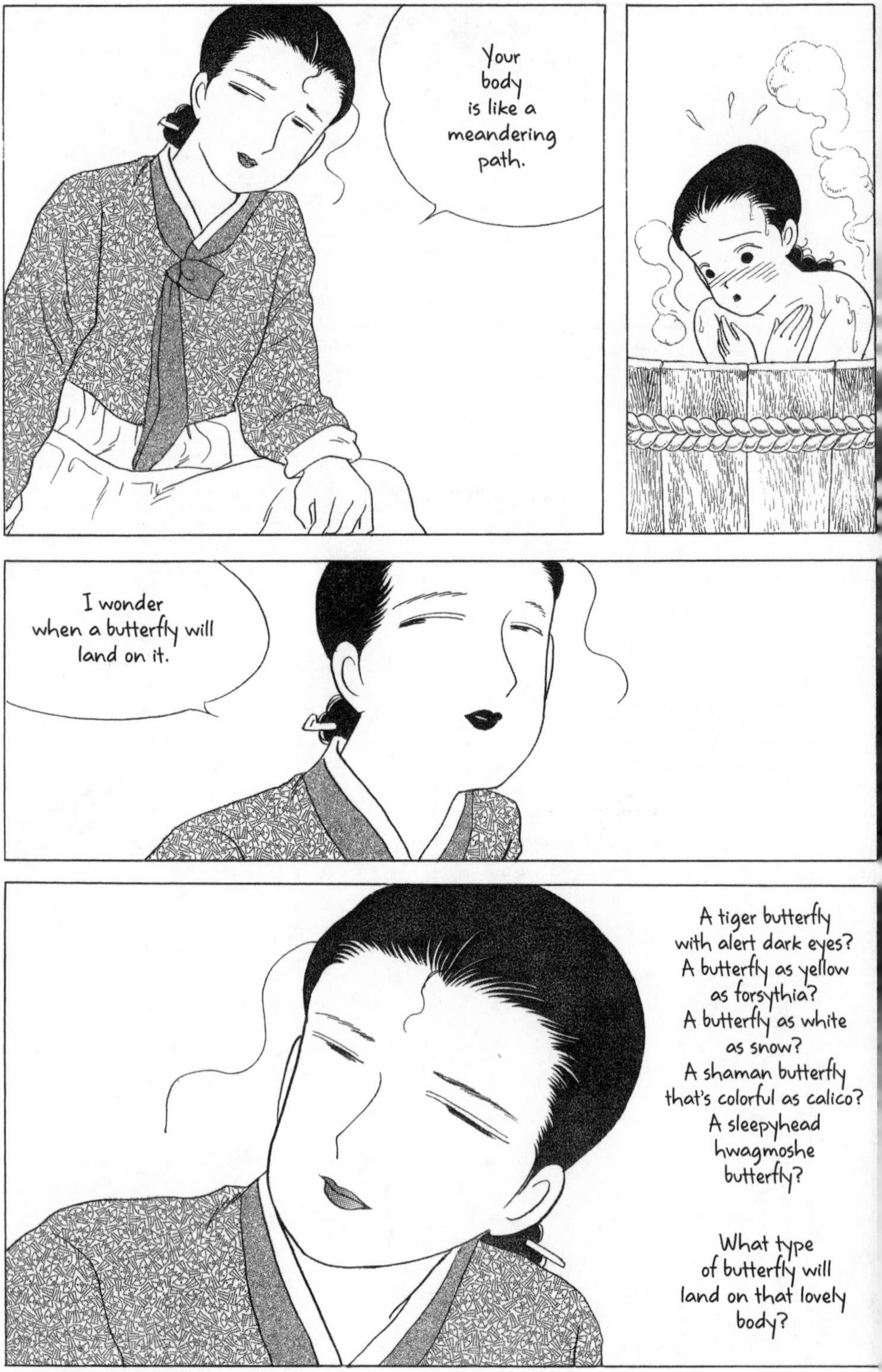
Your body is like a meandering path.
I wonder when a butterfly will land on it.
A tiger butterfly with alert dark eyes? A butterfly as yellow as forsythia? A butterfly as white as snow? A shaman butterfly that's colorful as calico? A sleepyhead hwagmoshe butterfly?
What type of butterfly will land on that lovely body?

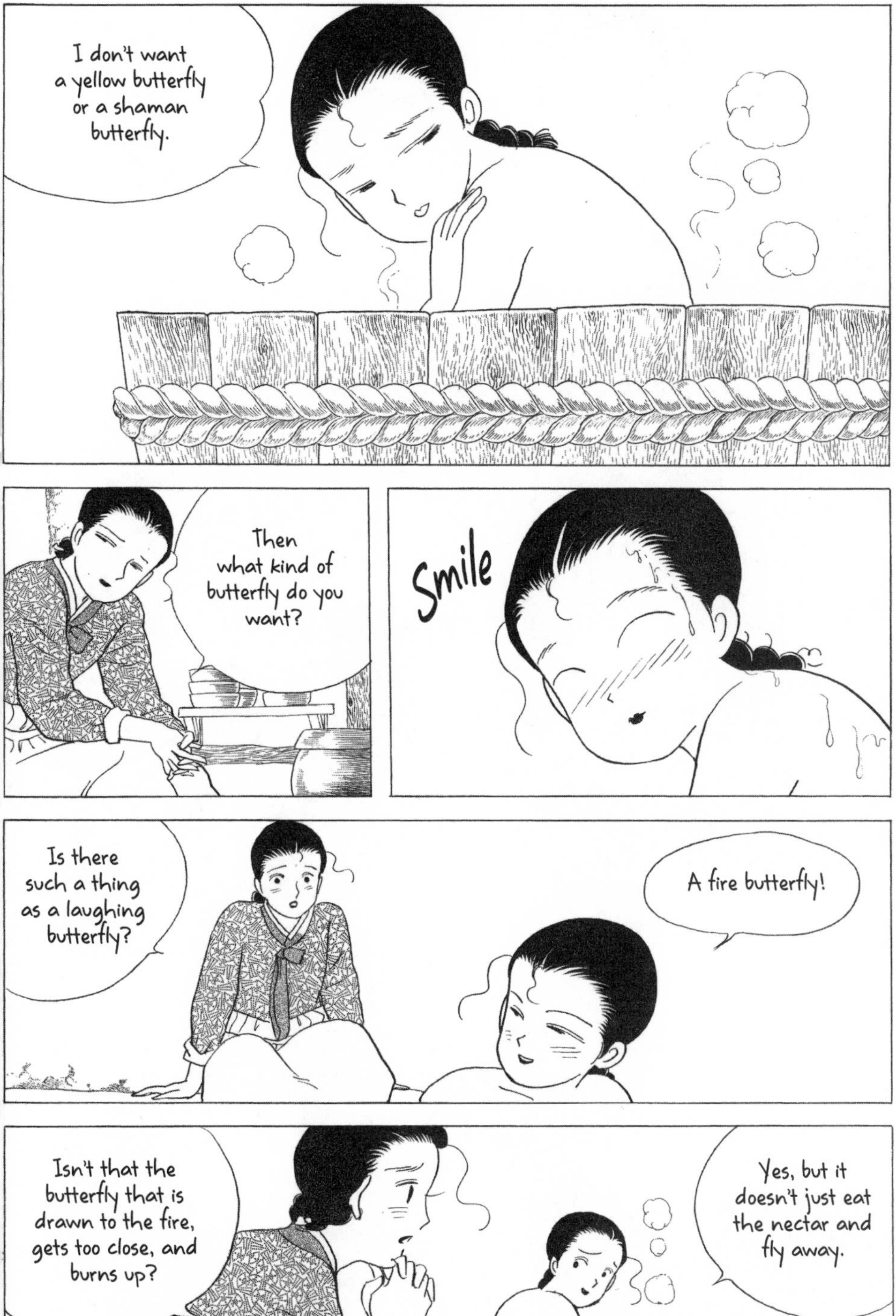
I don't want a yellow butterfly or a shaman butterfly.
Then what kind of butterfly do you want?
Smile
Is there such a thing as a laughing butterfly?
A fire butterfly!
Isn't that the butterfly that is drawn to the fire, gets too close, and burns up?
Yes, but it doesn't just eat the nectar and fly away.

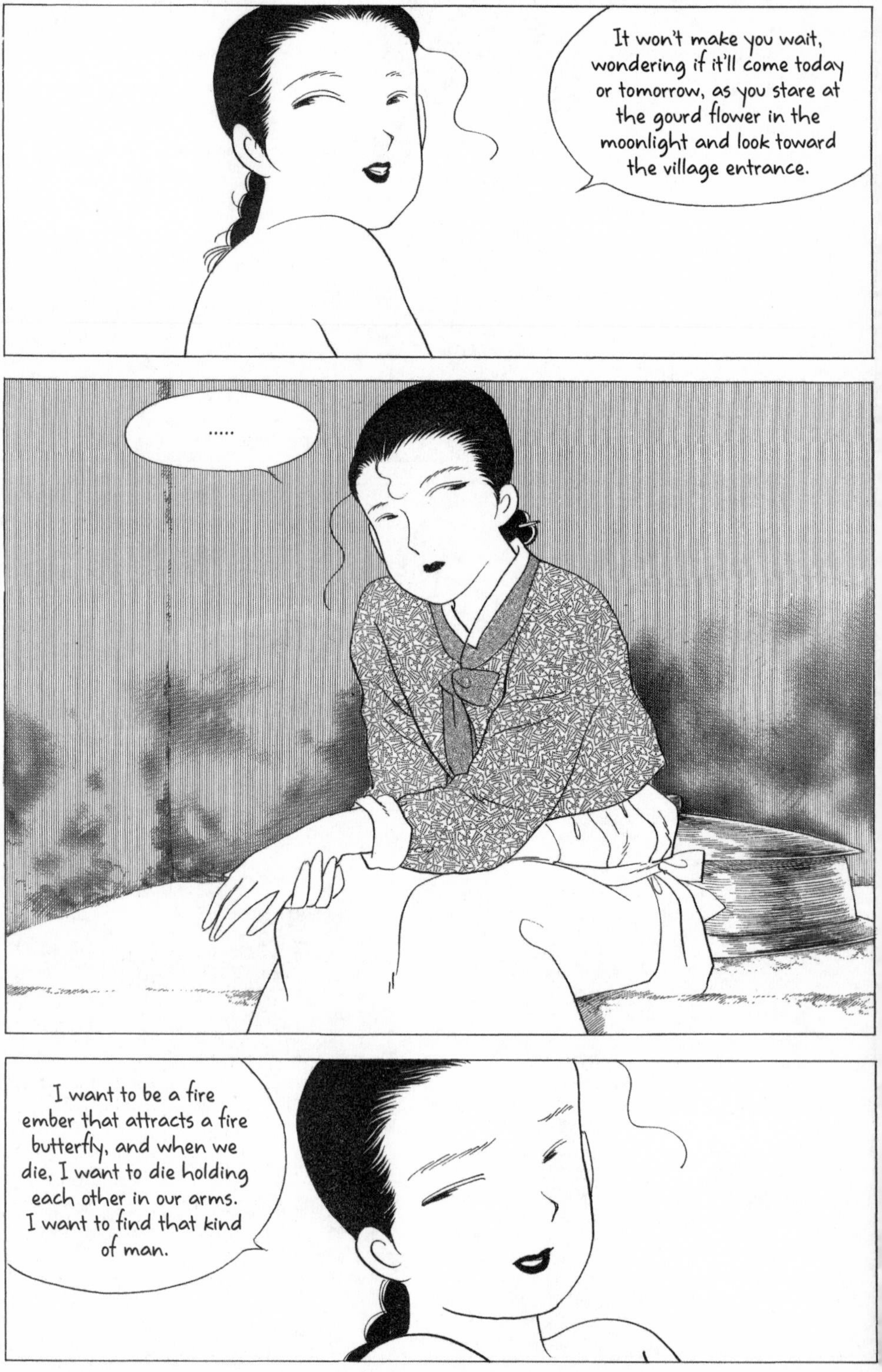
It won't make you wait, wondering if it'll come today or tomorrow, as you stare at the gourd flower in the moonlight and look toward the village entrance.
.....
I want to be a fire ember that attracts a fire butterfly, and when we die, I want to die holding each other in our arms. I want to find that kind of man.

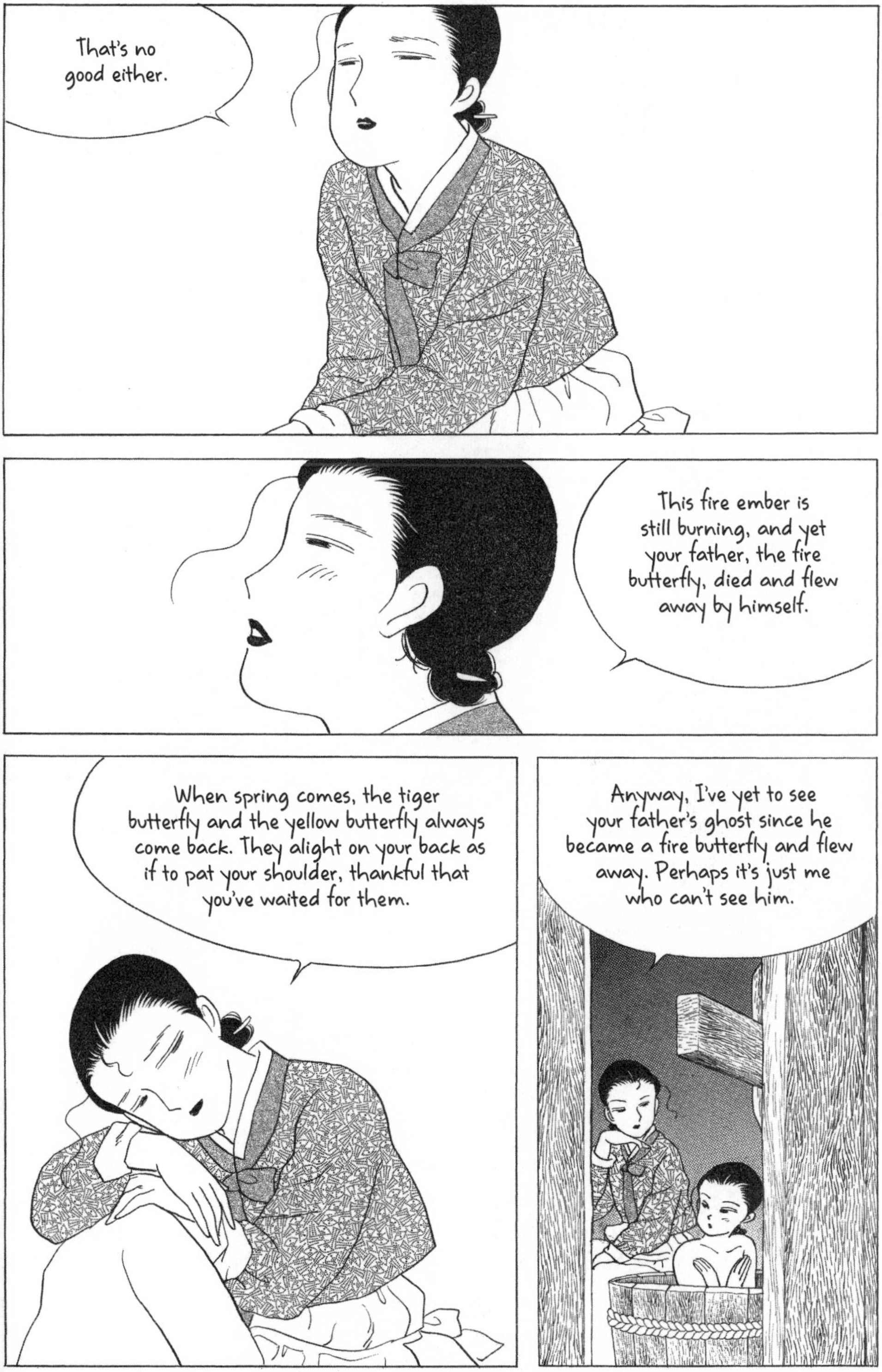
That's no good either.
This fire ember is still burning, and yet your father, the fire butterfly, died and flew away by himself.
When spring comes, the tiger butterfly and the yellow butterfly always come back. They alight on your back as if to pat your shoulder, thankful that you've waited for them.
Anyway, I've yet to see your father's ghost since he became a fire butterfly and flew away. Perhaps it's just me who can't see him.

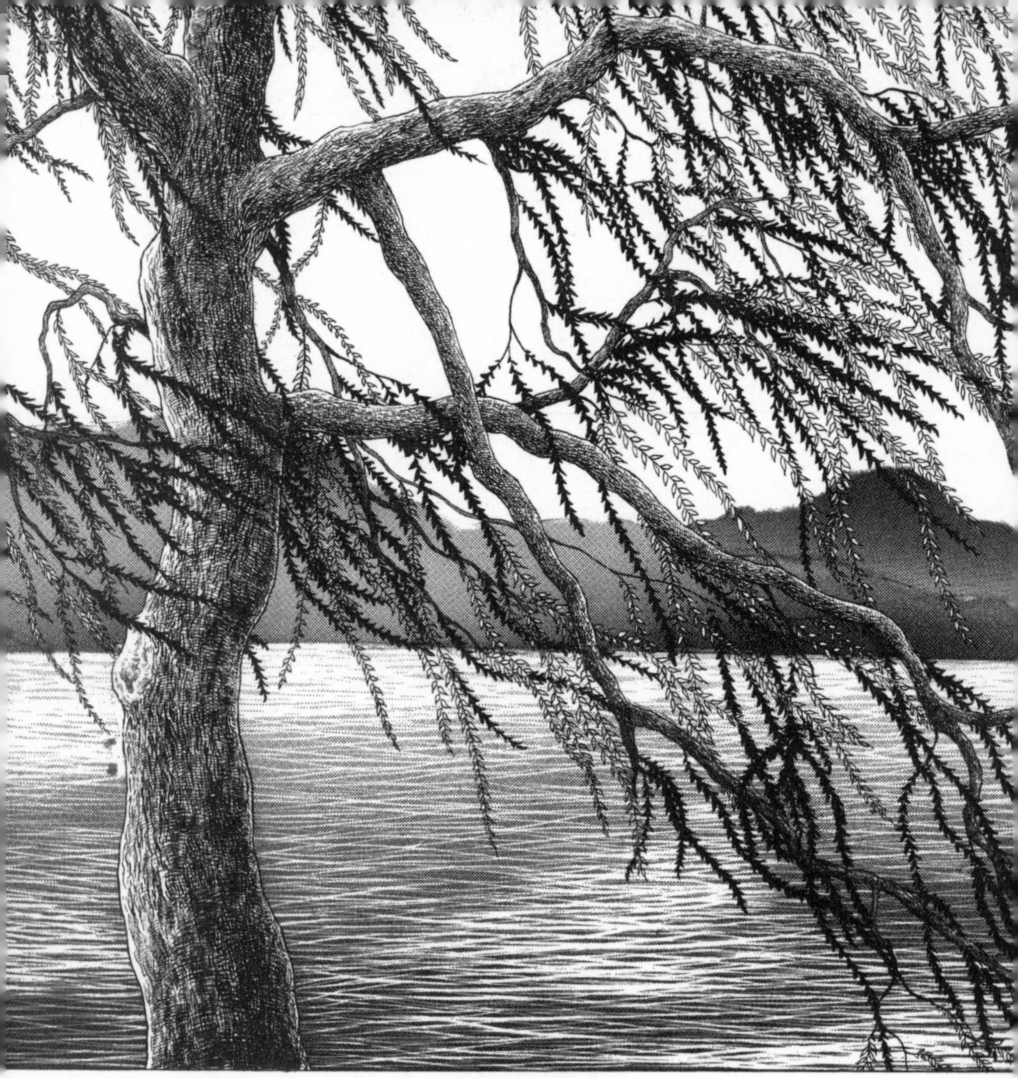

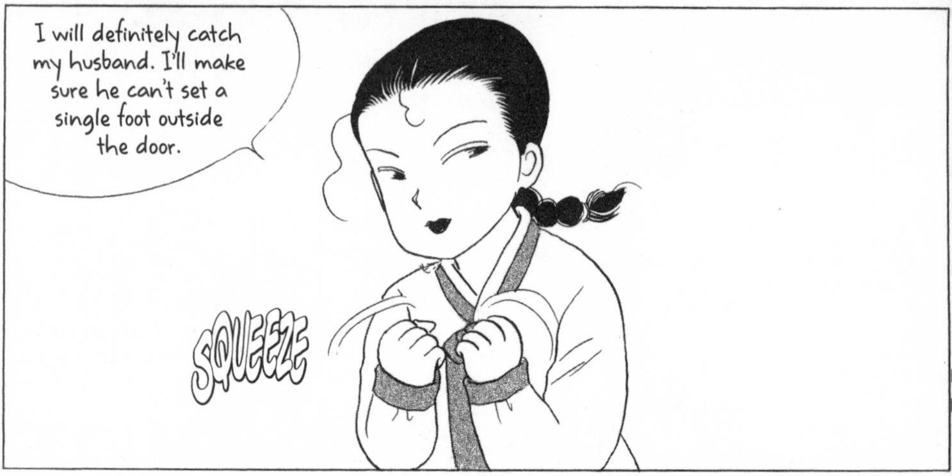
I will definitely catch my husband. I'll make sure he can't set a single foot outside the door.
SQUEEZE

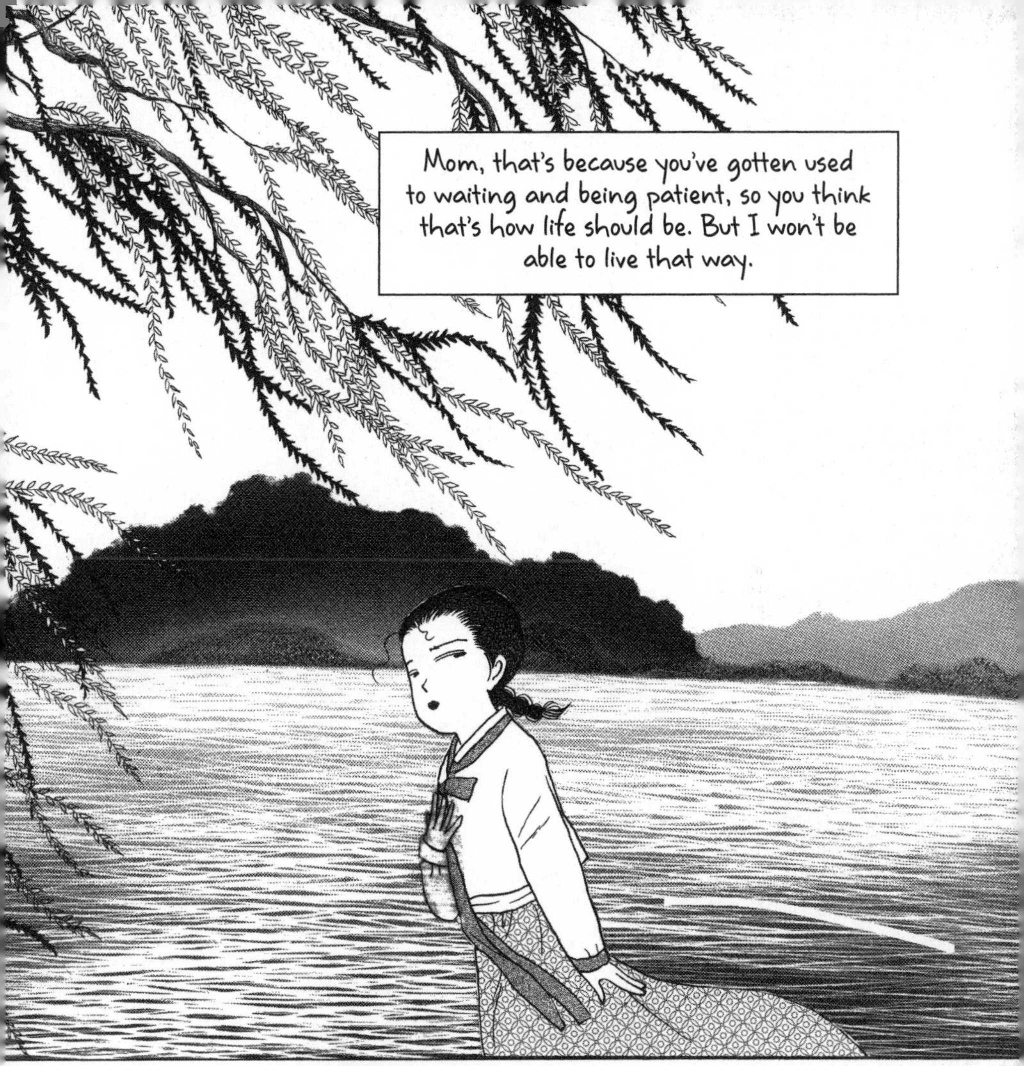
Mom, that's because you've gotten used to waiting and being patient, so you think that's how life should be. But I won't be able to live that way.

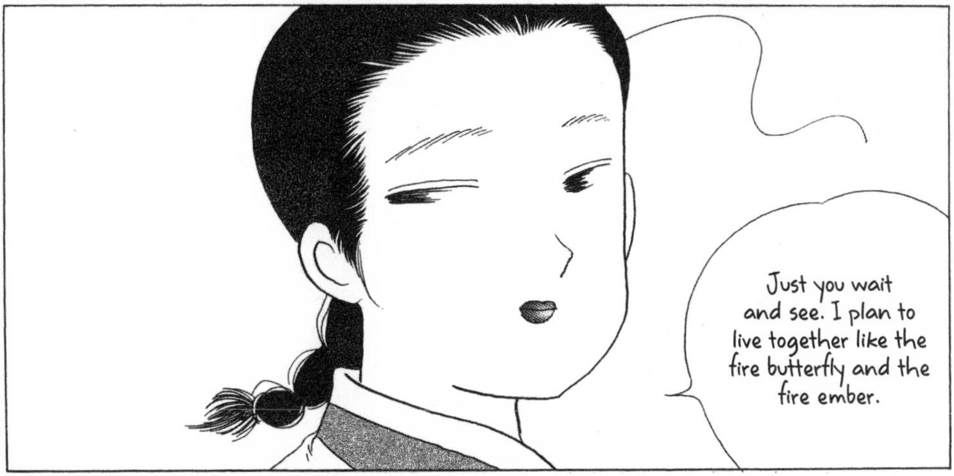
Just you wait and see. I plan to live together like the fire butterfly and the fire ember.

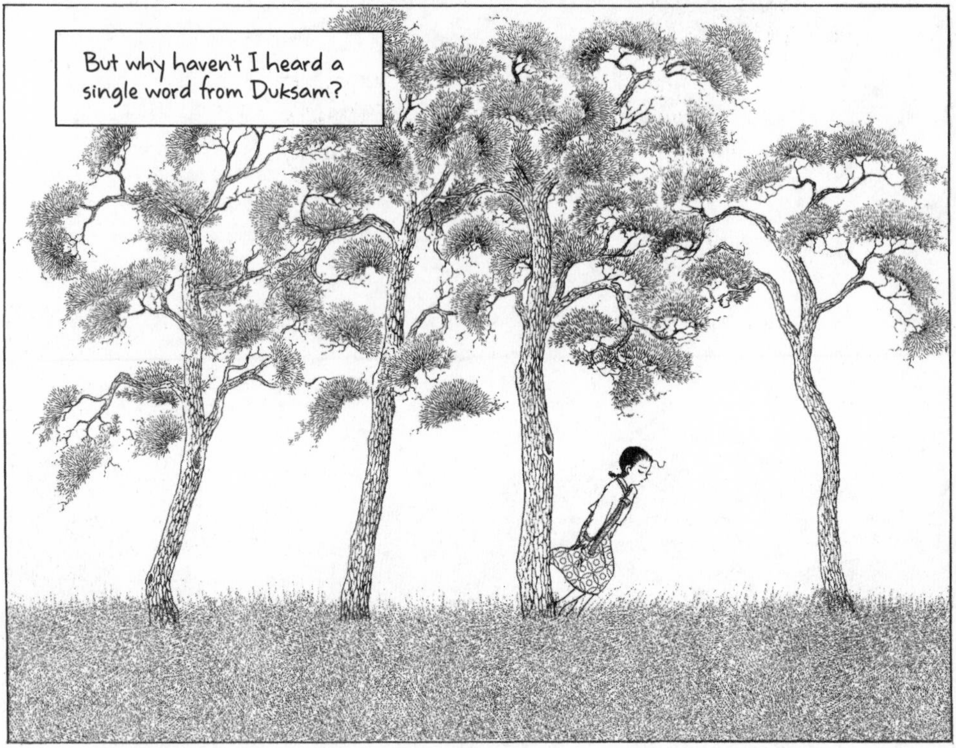
But why haven't I heard a single word from Duksam?

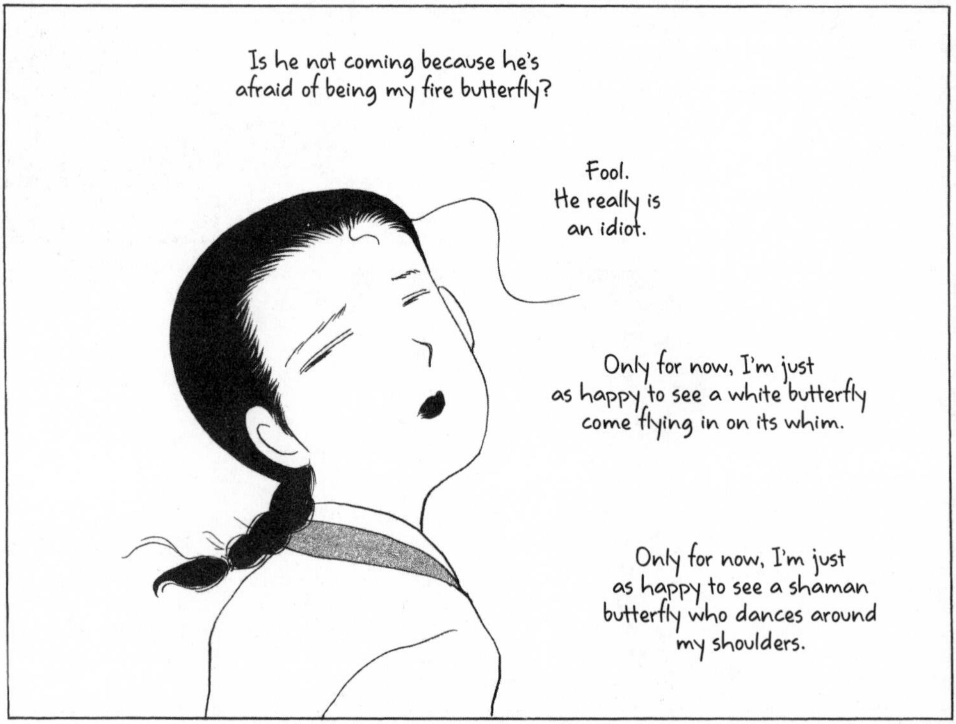
Is he not coming because he's afraid of being my fire butterfly?
Fool. He really is an idiot.
Only for now, I'm just as happy to see a white butterfly come flying in on its whim.
Only for now, I'm just as happy to see a shaman butterfly who dances around my shoulders.

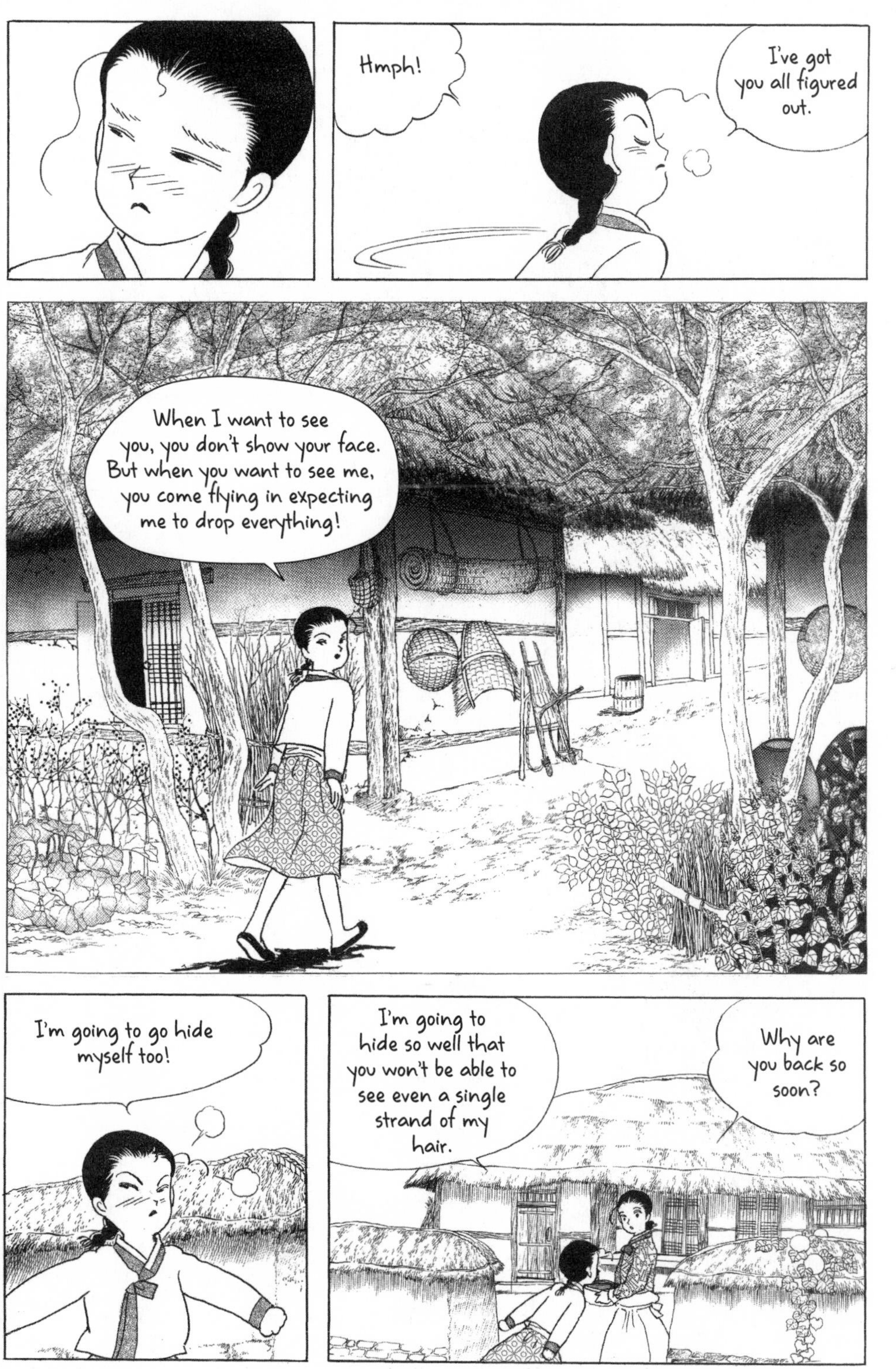
Hmph!
I've got you all figured out.
When I want to see you, you don't show your face. But when you want to see me, you come flying in expecting me to drop everything!
I'm going to go hide myself too!
I'm going to hide so well that you won't be able to see even a single strand of my hair.
Why are you back so soon?

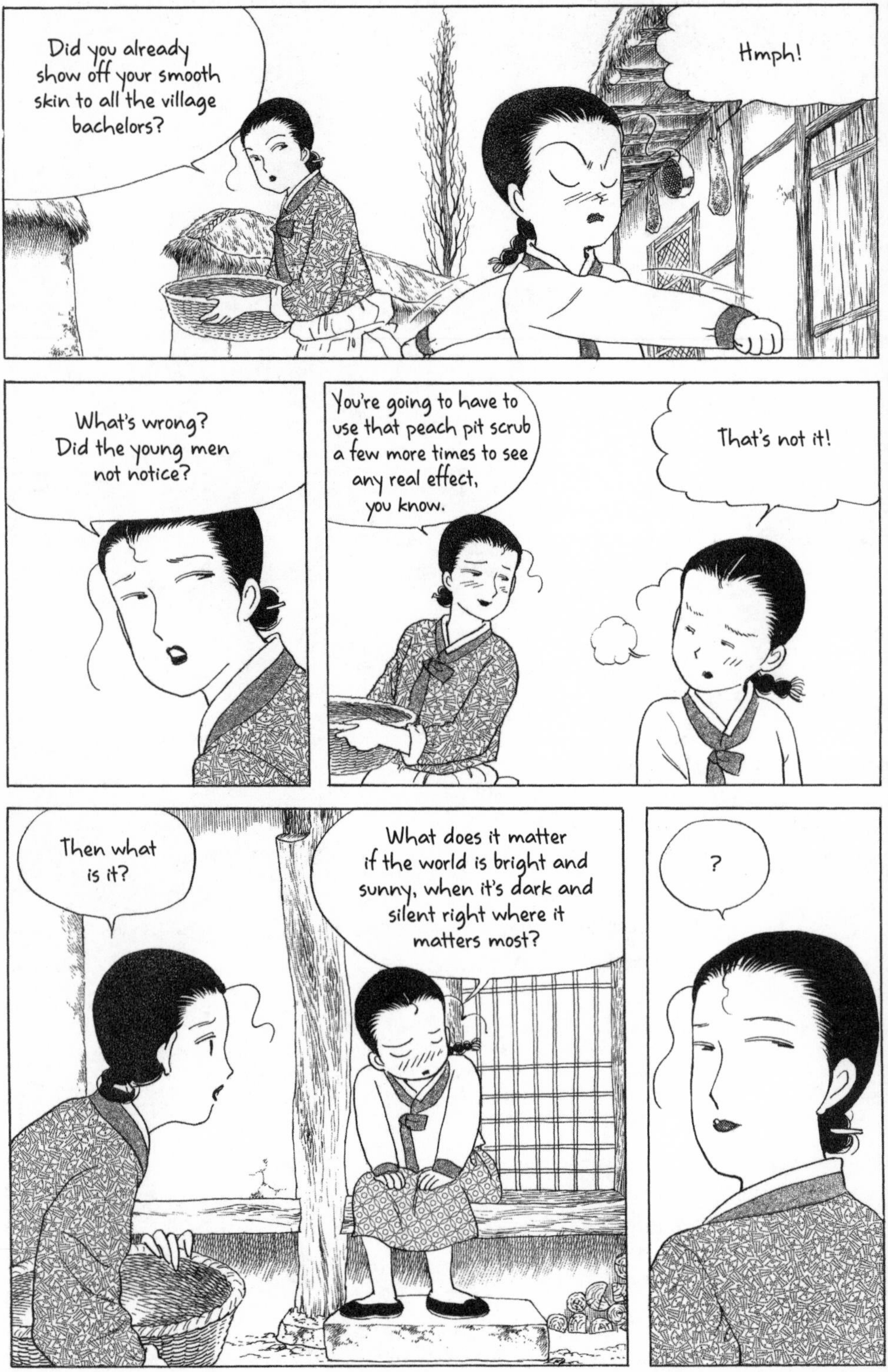

Did you already show off your smooth skin to all the village bachelors?
Hmph!
What's wrong? Did the young men not notice?
You're going to have to use that peach pit scrub a few more times to see any real effect, you know.
That's not it!
Then what is it?
What does it matter if the world is bright and sunny, when it's dark and silent right where it matters most?
?

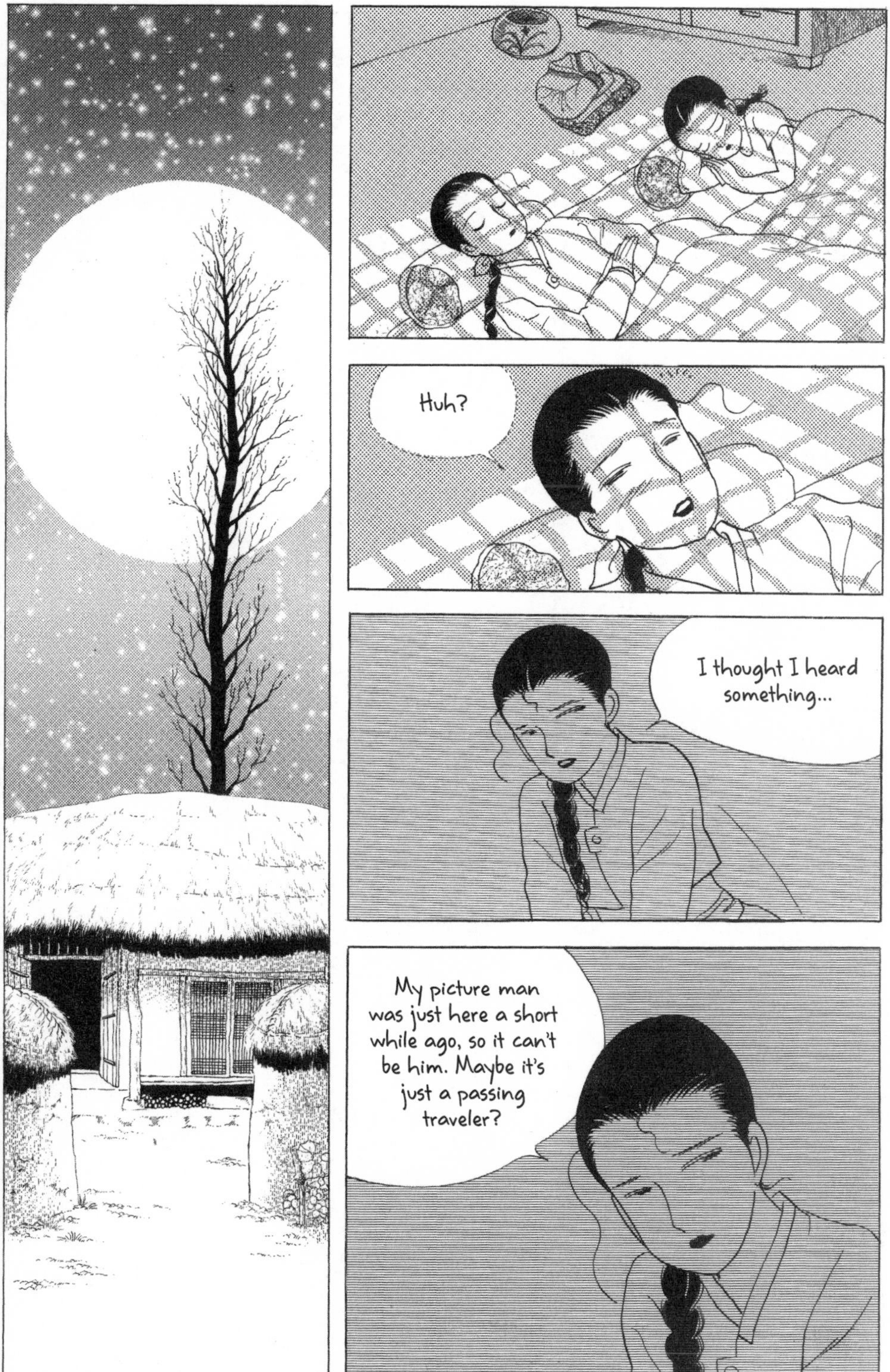
Huh?
I thought I heard something...
My picture man was just here a short while ago, so it can't be him. Maybe it's just a passing traveler?

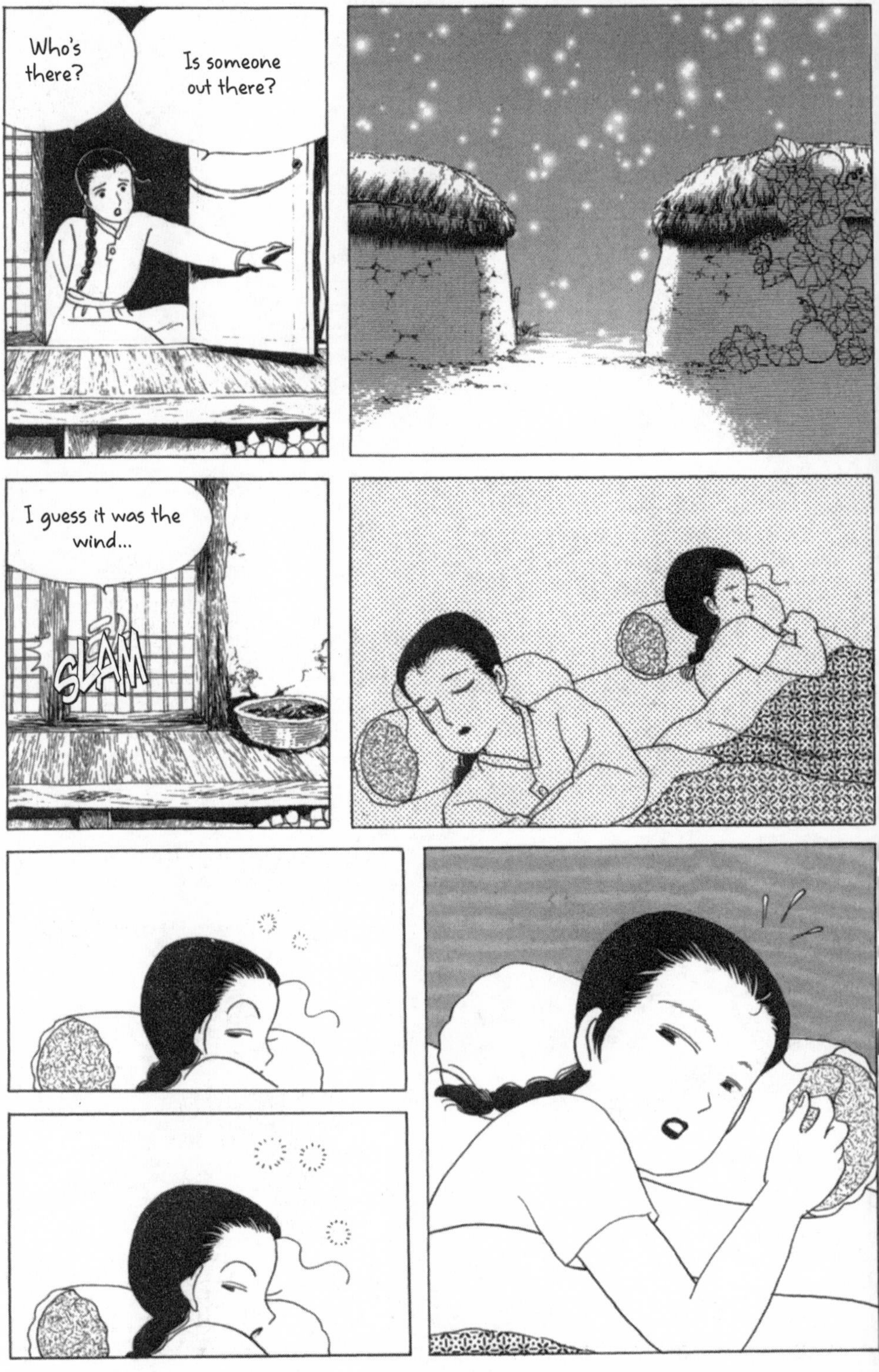
Who's there?
Is someone out there?
I guess it was the wind...
SLAM

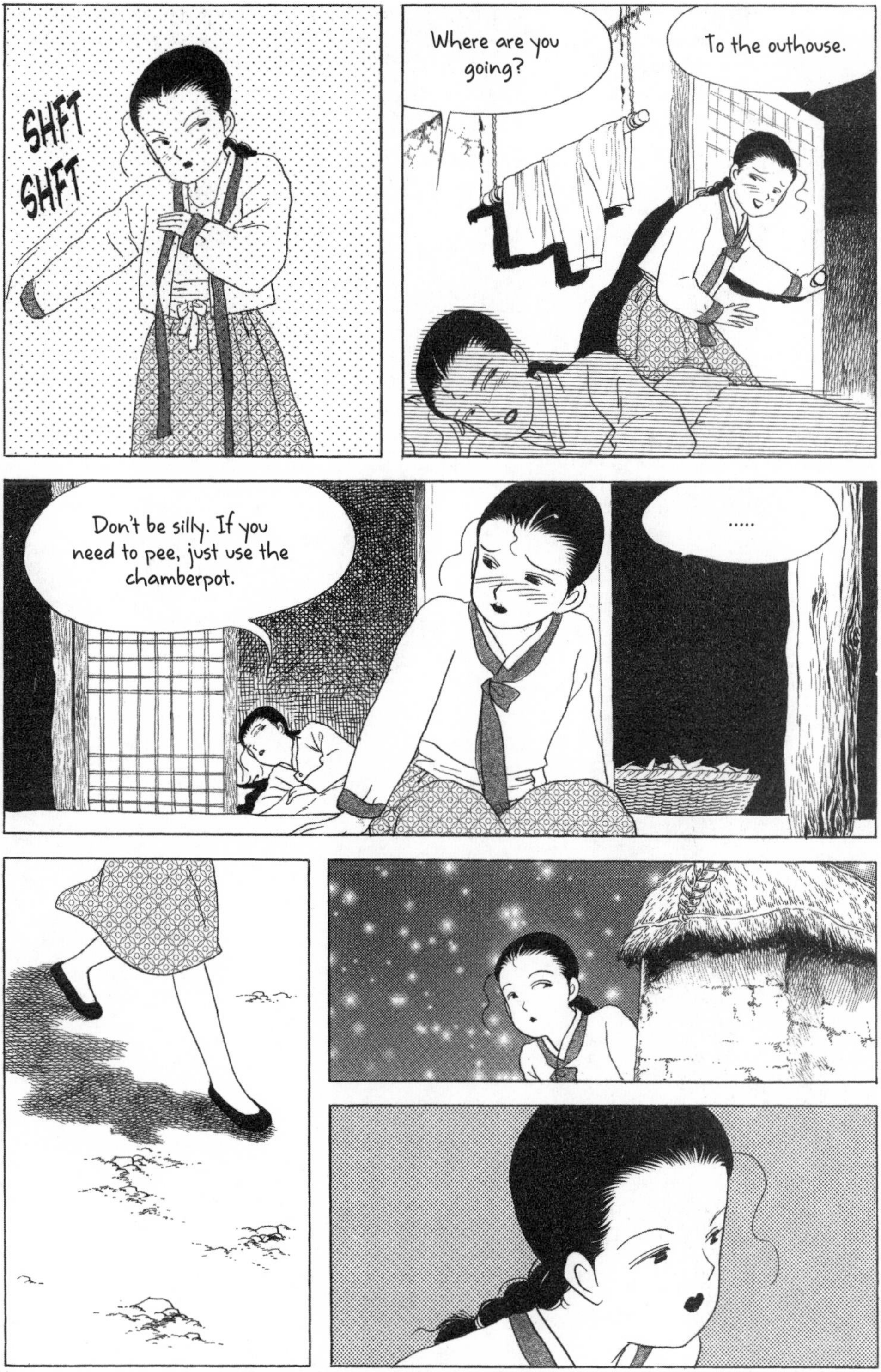
SHFT SHFT
Where are you going?
To the outhouse.
Don't be silly. If you need to pee, just use the chamberpot.
.....

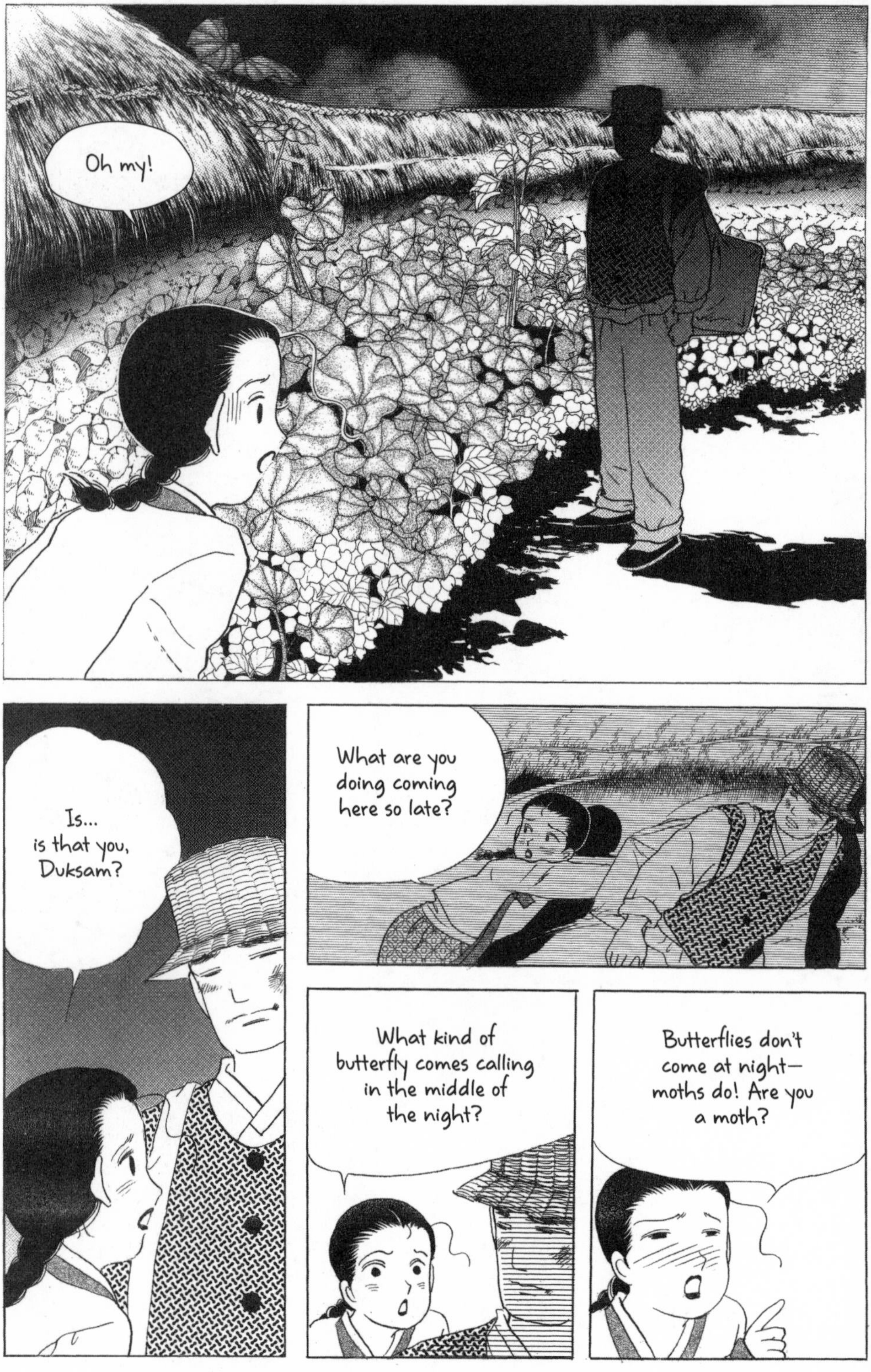
Oh my!
Is... is that you, Duksam?
What are you doing coming here so late?
What kind of butterfly comes calling in the middle of the night?
Butterflies don't come at night—moths do! Are you a moth?

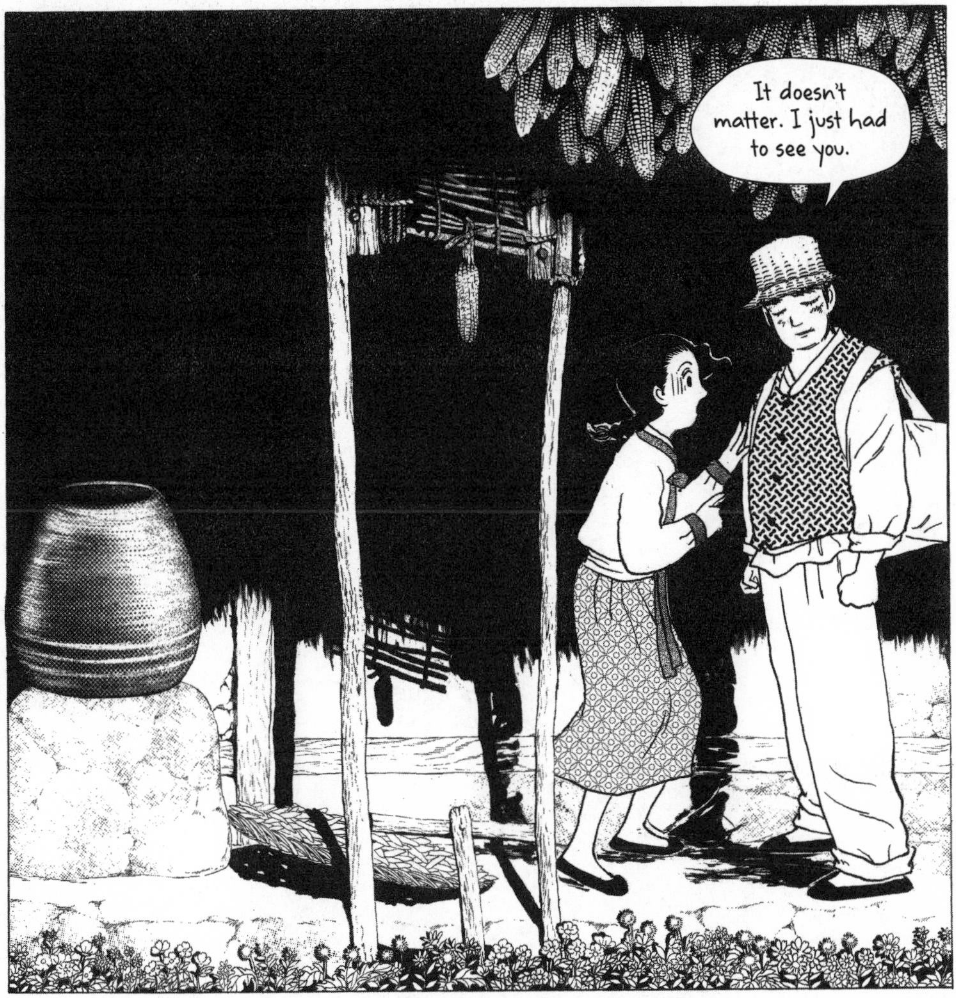
It doesn't matter. I just had to see you.
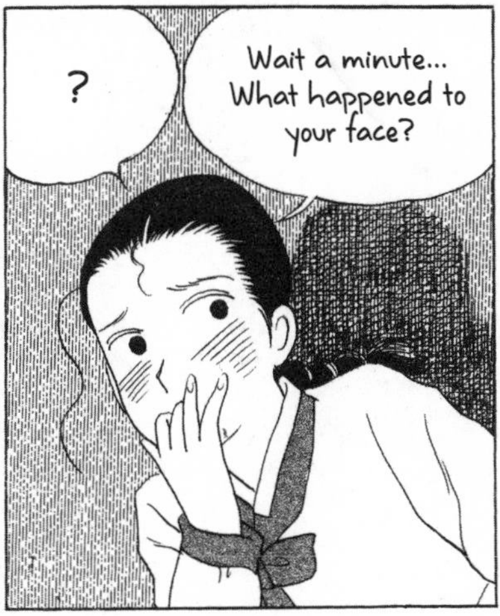
?
Wait a minute... What happened to your face?
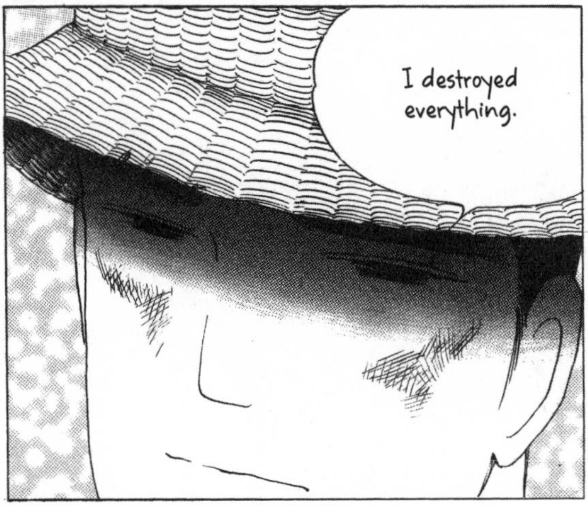
I destroyed everything.

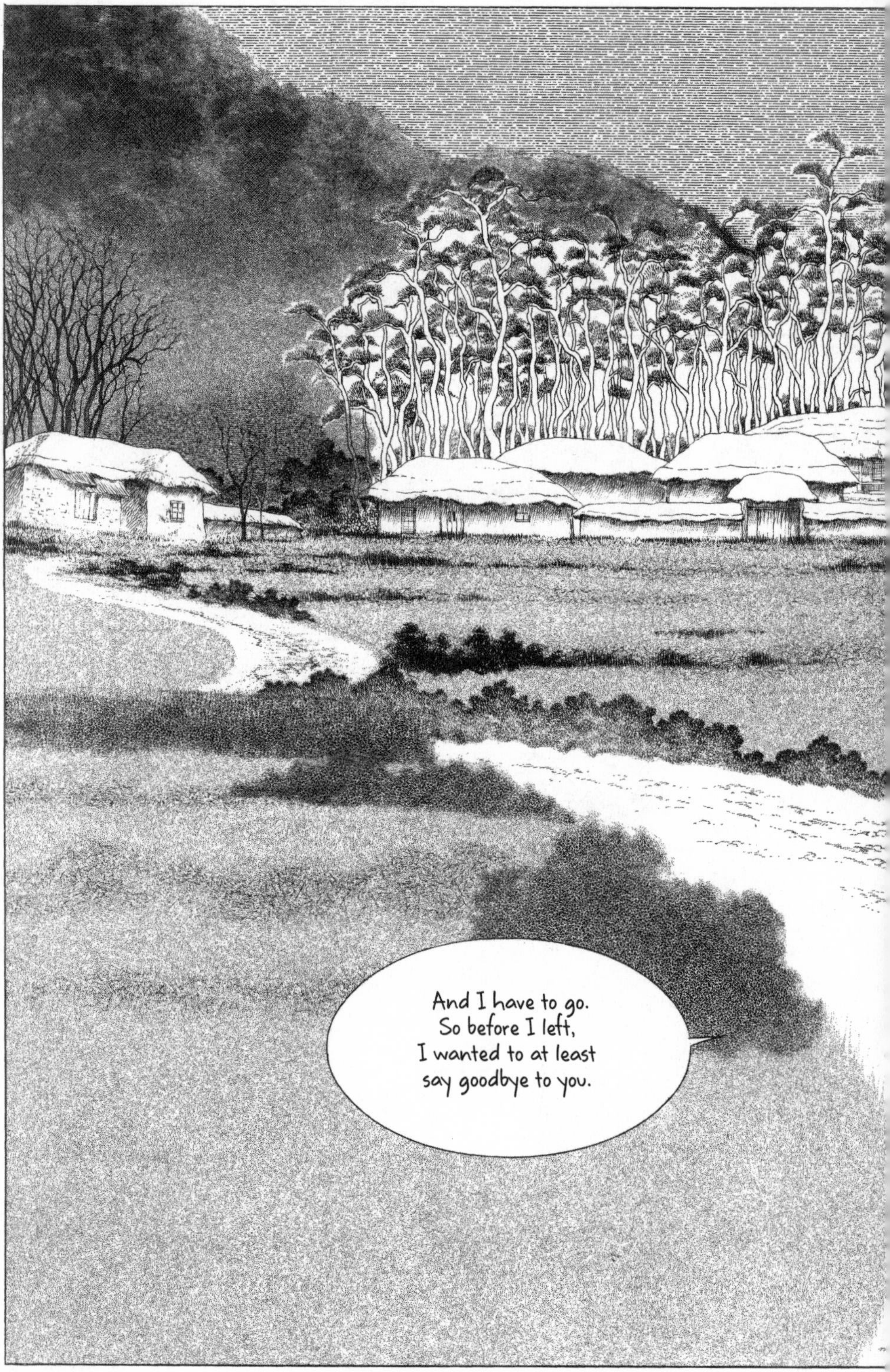
And I have to go. So before I left, I wanted to at least say goodbye to you.

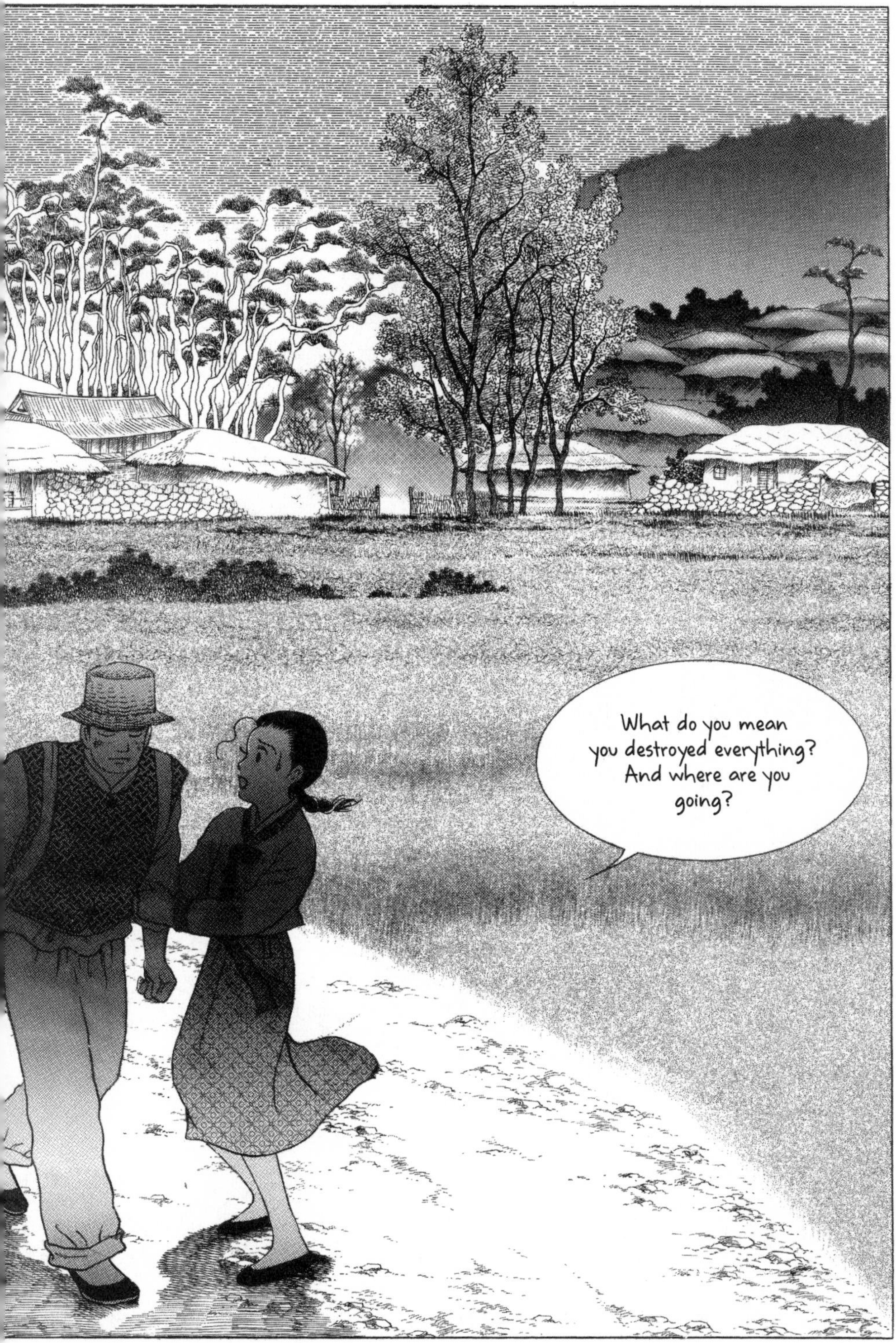
What do you mean you destroyed everything? And where are you going?

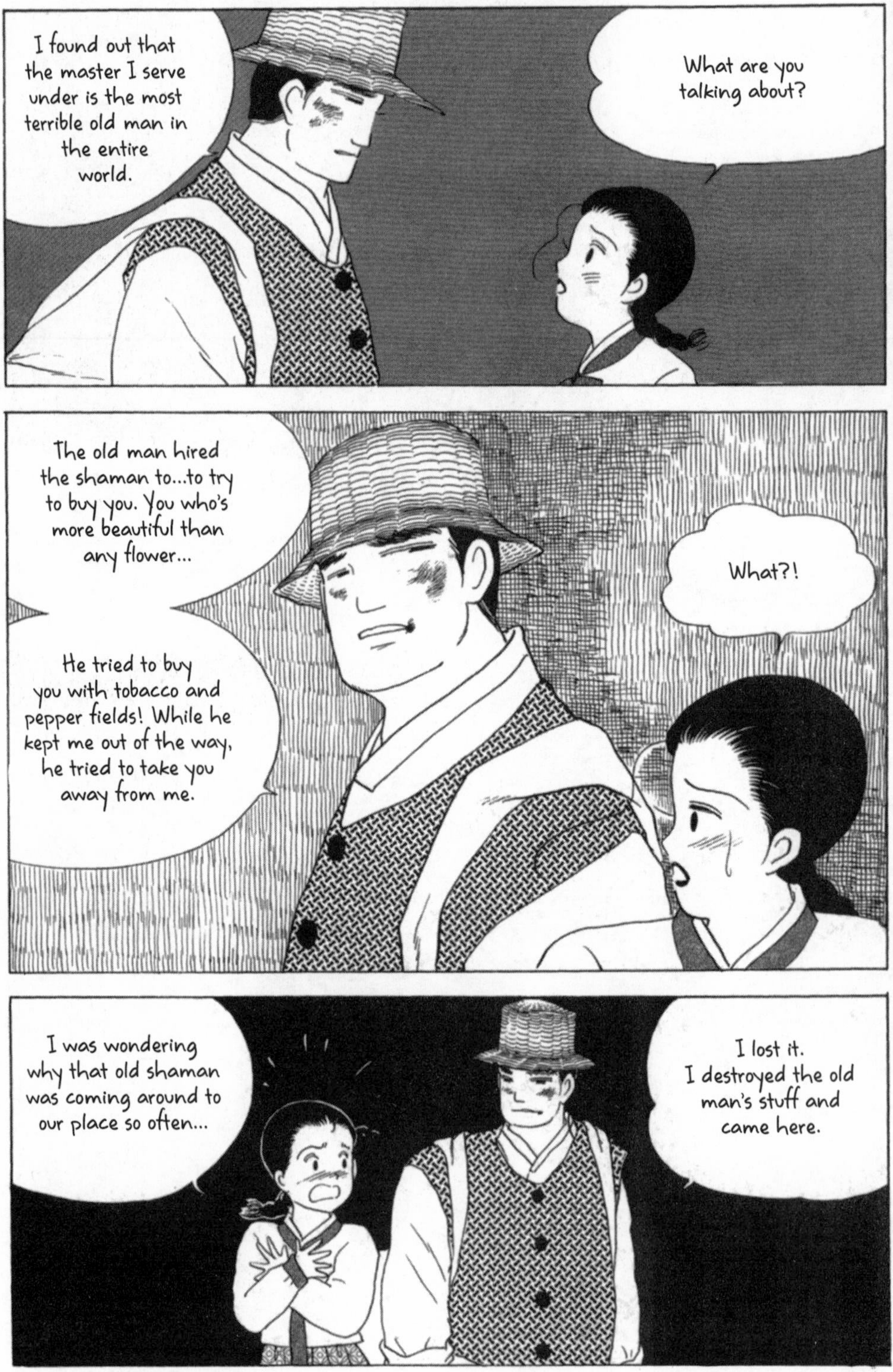
I found out that the master I serve under is the most terrible old man in the entire world.
What are you talking about?
The old man hired the shaman to...to try to buy you. You who's more beautiful than any flower...
He tried to buy you with tobacco and pepper fields! While he kept me out of the way, he tried to take you away from me.
What?!
I was wondering why that old shaman was coming around to our place so often...
I lost it. I destroyed the old man's stuff and came here.

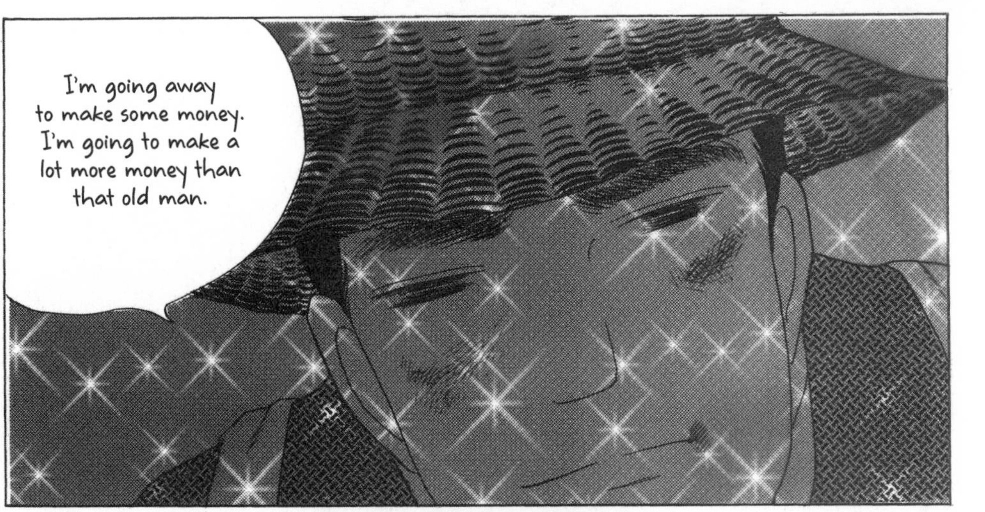
I'm going away to make some money. I'm going to make a lot more money than that old man.

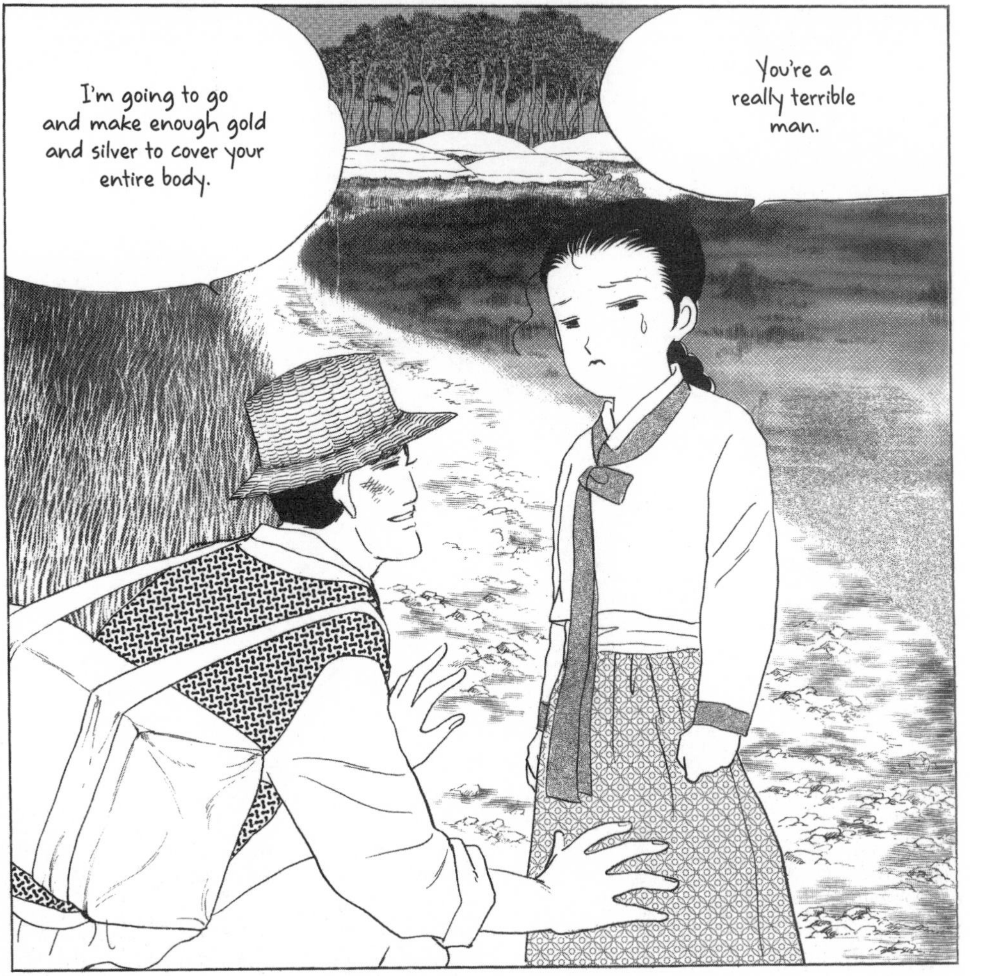
I'm going to go and make enough gold and silver to cover your entire body.
You're a really terrible man.

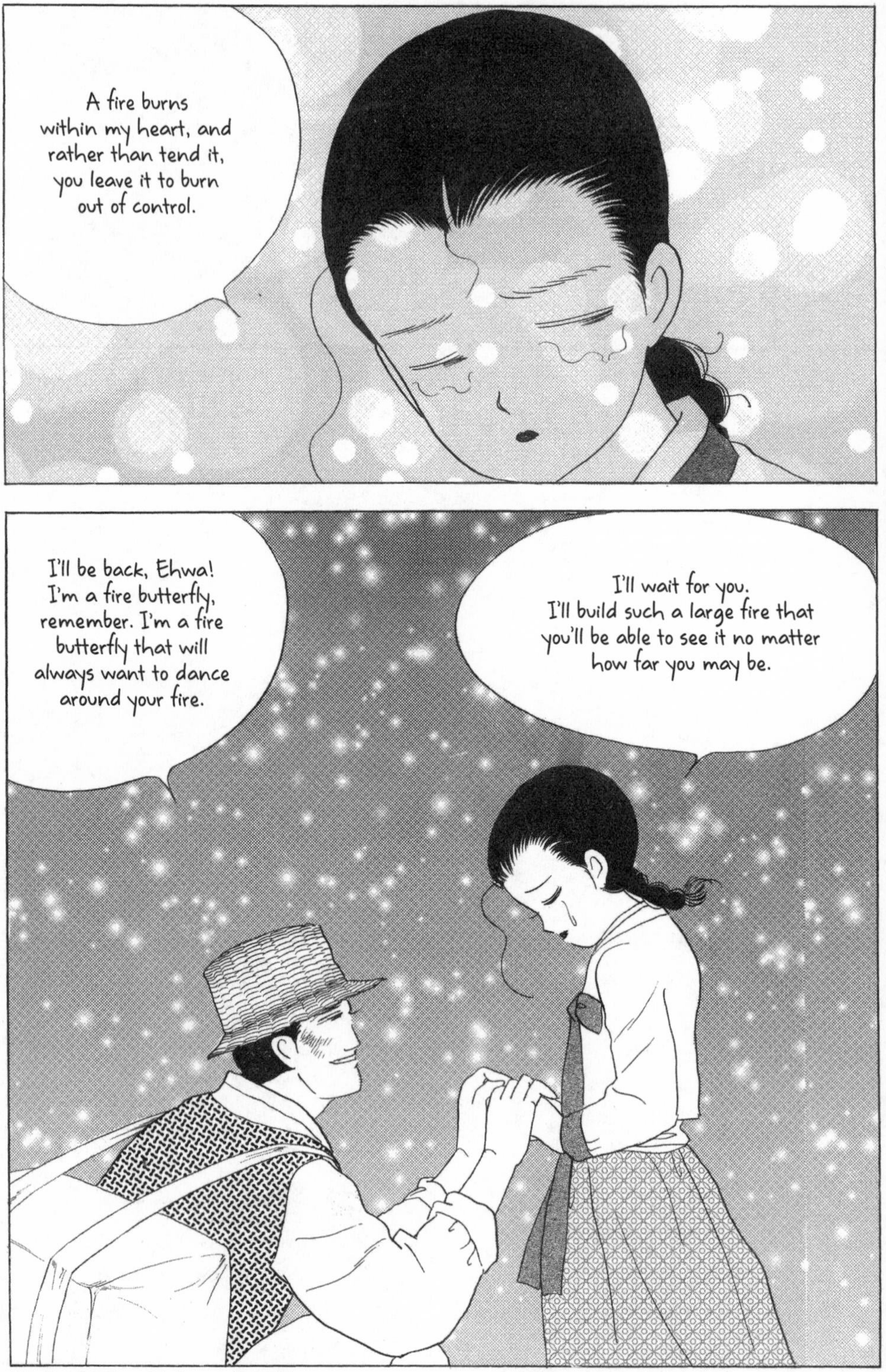
A fire burns within my heart, and rather than tend it, you leave it to burn out of control.
I'll be back, Ehwa! I'm a fire butterfly, remember. I'm a fire butterfly that will always want to dance around your fire.
I'll wait for you. I'll build such a large fire that you'll be able to see it no matter how far you may be.

End of The Color of Water

Continued in The Color of Heaven

THE COLOR TRILOGY
READING GROUP GUIDE

ABOUT THE COLOR TRILOGY

*In a turn-of-the-century rural village in southern Korea,
a girl falls in love for the first time as her widowed mother
falls in love again.*

THE COLOR OF EARTH:

Ehwa and her mother live alone in a tavern at the edge of their village. They have a quiet, wistful life together until Ehwa starts to notice boys, and her mother falls in love with a traveling pictographer who supports himself as a salesman. Over the next several years, Ehwa begins to learn about love as her mother cherishes the occasional visit from her "picture man."

THE COLOR OF WATER:

As Ehwa grows older, her feelings for the boys she meets change from crushes and vague longing to love. It is through her relationship with Duksam—and through having that relationship challenged by Master Cho—that Ehwa learns what it truly is to love. Meanwhile, Ehwa's mother contemplates what her life will be like, alone, once Ehwa marries.

THE COLOR OF HEAVEN:

The third and final volume of this series, *The Color of Heaven,* will see Ehwa rediscover love and embark upon marriage as her mother and the traveling pictographer decide to settle down together.

Kim Dong Hwa's delicate drawings and highly poetic language grace this three-volume epic with the light of a true master. An intimate portrait of the relationship between mother and daughter over the years, this trilogy is at once daring and sensitive in its portrayal of sexual awakening and reawakening.

ABOUT THE AUTHOR

Kim Dong Hwa is the author of many graphic novels—or manhwa, as they are called in Korea, where he lives. His books include the popular work *My Sky* and the literary piece *The Red Bicycle.*

ABOUT GRAPHIC NOVELS

A graphic novel is a long story told in the comics medium. You're familiar with comics; many of the best known are about superheroes or run in the Sunday papers, and many have recently been the basis for Hollywood films. But the medium goes far beyond that. Every topic that a work of fiction or non-fiction can explore, a graphic novel can explore, too.

In discussing graphic novels, there are a few basic terms that will be good to know.

PANEL

The images in graphic novels take place largely in sequential panels. A panel is a box that encloses the images. You can see in the three panels below that time is passing as Ehwa turns her head and sees the butterfly go by.

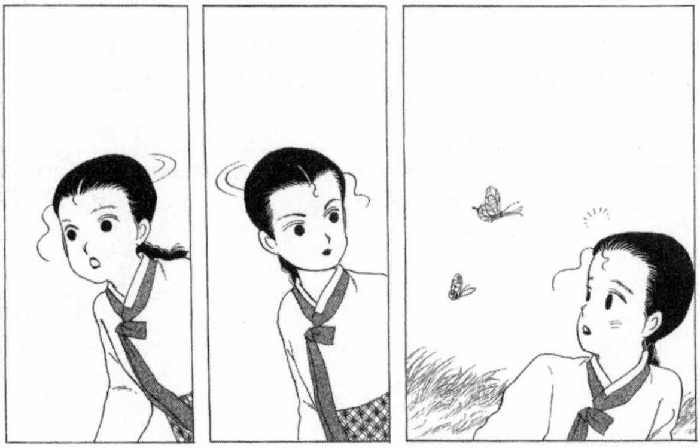

Speech Bubble

When characters in graphic novels speak, their words usually appear in bubbles near their heads. You can generally tell which bubbles belong to which character because the bubble will have a tail that points to an area around the speaker's head.

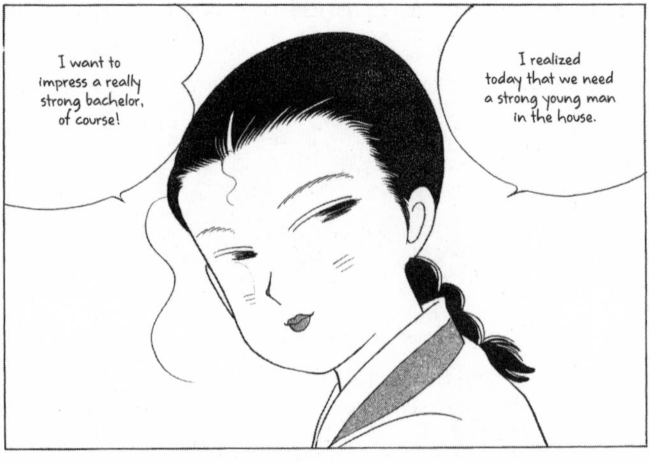
I want to impress a really strong bachelor, of course!
I realized today that we need a strong young man in the house.

Sound Effects

Sounds—dogs barking, water being wrung out of laundry, heavy breathing—are not conveyed in bubbles, but instead as dramatic lettering that is part of the background artwork, as you can see in the image below.

SPLASH
SPLASH
SKRITCH
DRIP

Text Box

Text that is not dialogue—either narration or thought—is typically conveyed in a box. Kim Dong Hwa does not use this technique very often in the Colors trilogy, instead mostly depicting thought and narration as a part of the panel without a box around it. (Occasionally, it is intentionally left ambiguous whether these words are thoughts, or spoken aloud. See for example Ehwa's mother's dialogue in the last panel of page 290.)

Acting like she knows everything! If she's pretty, it's because she got it from me.
She should be thankful I'm the one who brought her into this world. She's becoming so opinionated!

One of the most essential parts of reading graphic novels is reading the words and the pictures together: both, working simultaneously, tell the story. Look at the page below.

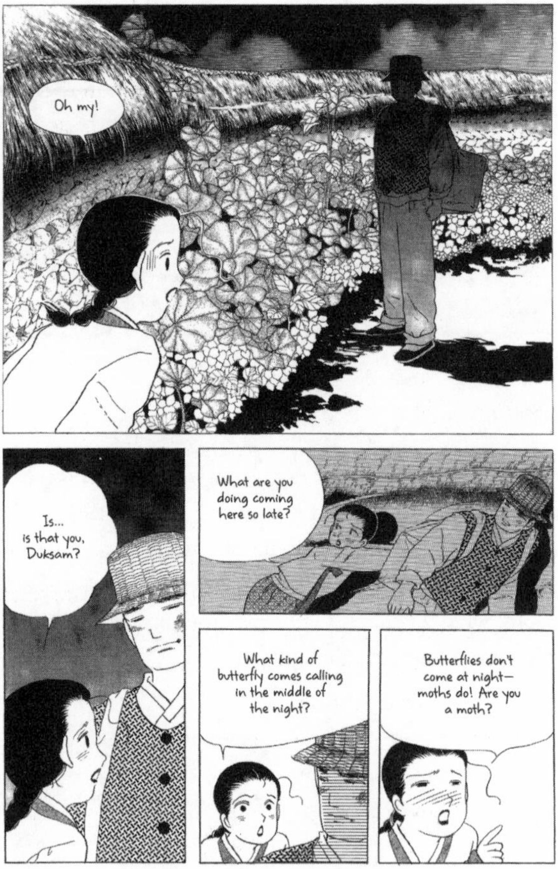
Oh my!
Is... is that you, Duksam?
What are you doing coming here so late?
What kind of butterfly comes calling in the middle of the night?
Butterflies don't come at night—moths do! Are you a moth?

Try reading just the words on this page–then just the artwork. Then read them together. How do the art and the text work together to tell the story? What is missing without the words? Without the art?

DISCUSSION QUESTIONS –
THE COLOR OF EARTH

- *The Color of Earth* opens with a scene in which men make derogatory remarks about Ehwa's mother, comparing her to a beetle. Throughout the story, this chauvinistic attitude continually comes up. What does this tell us about attitudes towards single women in the Korean society depicted in this book? What can you deduce about men's attitudes towards married women?

- The first boy that Ehwa falls in love with is a young Buddhist monk. Here are the ten precepts by which novice monks (called samaneras) are supposed to live:

    1. Refrain from killing living things.
    2. Refrain from stealing.
    3. Refrain from un-chastity (sensuality, sexuality, lust).
    4. Refrain from lying.
    5. Refrain from taking intoxicants.
    6. Refrain from taking food at inappropriate times (after noon).
    7. Refrain from singing, dancing, playing music or attending entertainment programs (performances).
    8. Refrain from wearing perfume, cosmetics and garland (decorative accessories).
    9. Refrain from sitting on high chairs and sleeping on luxurious, soft beds.
    10. Refrain from accepting money.

How does Chung-Myung resolve the gap between these precepts and his passion for Ehwa? What does this say about his faith?

- *The Color of Earth* explores puberty, detailing Chung-Myung's first wet dream and Ehwa's first menstruation. How are these two events treated in the book? What can we guess about the role of sexual development in becoming an adult member of society in Korea at the turn of the century?

- Ehwa's second crush, Master Sunoo, is studying away from home. He is the only person in this book who is mentioned as attending school. What does that say about the importance—and availability—of education in Korea at the turn of the century? What enables Master Sunoo to pursue an education when others do not?

- When Ehwa learns about pruning, she decides to treat her feelings the same way farmers treat flowering trees—pruning away small blossoms to give the larger blossoms the best chance to grow healthy and strong. Have you ever done this yourself, even if you thought of it in different terms? Do you think this technique works? How successfully does Ehwa use it?

- How does Ehwa deal with her mother's relationship with the picture man? How is her ability to understand her mother enhanced or made more difficult by her own blossoming awareness of love?

- "That's why you should be careful what you do," says Ehwa on page 242, when she reveals to Bongsoon that her sexually forward behavior is no longer a secret. In the close-knit village society in turn-of-the-century Korea, the court of public opinion was clearly a component of social and economic success. Is the same true in modern-day America?

- "What is wrong with kids these days?" says Ehwa's mother on page 264. What parts of Ehwa's life does Ehwa's mother think are wrong (or would think are wrong if she knew about them)? How are today's standards for "wrong" behavior similar to the standards of the old-fashioned Korea in the Colors trilogy? How are they different?

DISCUSSION QUESTIONS –
THE COLOR OF WATER

- Talk about the ways Ehwa's and her mother's perspectives on love are different. Which parts of their outlooks are the results of their experiences and which parts reflect the culture in which they live?

- How does Ehwa's experience growing up affect her mother's life and perspective? Are daughters generally aware of their effects on their mother's point of view and circumstances?

- Nature is used throughout *The Color of Water:* Ehwa's life is surrounded with fruit, flowers, and vegetables. How is the progress of her sexual awakening echoed in the art depicting the natural world around her?

- How does the pastoral setting of *The Color of Water* affect the tone of the book?

- Ehwa and her friend Bongsoon are often contrasted, with Ehwa portrayed as an unknowing innocent on the cusp of adulthood and Bongsoon as an irresponsible, precocious teenager whose judgment is often compromised by sexual desire. How does Kim Dong Hwa's visual depiction of Ehwa and Bongsoon lend weight to these characterizations?

- Teenagers often draw conclusions about the adult world from what they see around them. How do the men who frequent Ehwa's mother's tavern affect Ehwa's ideas about what adulthood is?

- A matchmaker (Grandma Shaman) plays a vital role in *The Color of Water* as a go-between for Master Cho and Ehwa. Matchmakers were an essential part of marriage arrangements in Korea during this time period. How do you think this affected—or exemplified—the societal conception of married life and love?

- At the end of the book, Duksam leaves Ehwa so he can earn enough money to return to their village and marry her. Do you think he's made the right decision? What do you think might have happened if he stayed?

- Ehwa lives in late nineteenth century Korea. How would the life of an American girl who lived during the same period be different?

- *The Color of Water* is an example of *manhwa*, the Korean version of a graphic novel. How does the medium affect the way Ehwa's story is told? Are there things the author did using this form that he would not have been able to do in prose? Are there things he couldn't do? Consider especially metaphor, narrative voice, a sense of place, symbolism, and whether these literary tropes can expand to a visual dimension.

OTHER READING

BLUE, BY KIRIKO NANANAN
A finely told story of first love, awkwardness, and the infinite horizons of being a teenager.

THE WALKING MAN, BY JIRO TANIGUCHI
A series of quiet vignettes about a newly married man exploring the rural beauty of his neighborhood in Japan.

First Second Books would love to hear about your reading group experience. Thoughts, discussions, and pictures are all welcome at mail@firstsecondbooks.com.